Healthy Heart Sourcebook for Women
Heart Diseases & Disorders Sourcebook, 2nd Edition
Household Safety Sourcebook
Immune System Disorders Sourcebook
Infant & Toddler Health Sourcebook
Infectious Diseases Sourcebook
Injury & Trauma Sourcebook
Kidney & Urinary Tract Diseases & Disorders Sourcebook
Learning Disabilities Sourcebook, 2nd Edition
Leukemia Sourcebook
Liver Disorders Sourcebook
Lung Disorders Sourcebook
Medical Tests Sourcebook, 2nd Edition
Men's Health Concerns Sourcebook, 2nd Edition
Mental Health Disorders Sourcebook, 2nd Edition
Mental Retardation Sourcebook
Movement Disorders Sourcebook
Obesity Sourcebook
Osteoporosis Sourcebook
Pain Sourcebook, 2nd Edition
Pediatric Cancer Sourcebook
Physical & Mental Issues in Aging Sourcebook
Podiatry Sourcebook
Pregnancy & Birth Sourcebook, 2nd Edition
Prostate Cancer
Public Health Sourcebook
Reconstructive & Cosmetic Surgery Sourcebook
Rehabilitation Sourcebook
Respiratory Diseases & Disorders Sourcebook
Sexually Transmitted Diseases Sourcebook, 2nd Edition
Skin Disorders Sourcebook
Sleep Disorders Sourcebook
Sports Injuries Sourcebook, 2nd Edition
Stress-Related Disorders Sourcebook
Stroke Sourcebook
Substance Abuse Sourcebook
Surgery Sourcebook
Transplantation Sourcebook
Traveler's Health Sourcebook
Vegetarian Sourcebook
Women's Health Concerns Sourcebook, 2nd Edition
Workplace Health & Safety Sourcebook
Worldwide Health Sourcebook

Teen Health Series

Cancer Information for Teens
Diet Information for Teens
Drug Information for Teens
Fitness Information for Teens
Mental Health Information for Teens
Sexual Health Information for Teens
Skin Health Information for Teens
Sports Injuries Information for Teens

Child abuse sourcebook

Child Abuse
SOURCEBOOK

Health Reference Series

First Edition

Child Abuse SOURCEBOOK

Basic Consumer Health Information about the Physical, Sexual, and Emotional Abuse of Children, with Additional Facts about Neglect, Munchausen Syndrome by Proxy (MSBP), Shaken Baby Syndrome, and Controversial Issues Related to Child Abuse, Such as Withholding Medical Care, Corporal Punishment, and Child Maltreatment in Youth Sports, and Featuring Facts about Child Protective Services, Foster Care, Adoption, Parenting Challenges, and Other Abuse Prevention Efforts

Along with a Glossary of Related Terms and Resources for Additional Help and Information

Edited by
Dawn D. Matthews

Omnigraphics

615 Griswold Street • Detroit, MI 48226

Edited by Dawn D. Matthews

Health Reference Series

Karen Bellenir, *Managing Editor*
David A. Cooke, MD, *Medical Consultant*
Elizabeth Barbour, *Permissions Associate*
Dawn Matthews, *Verification Assistant*
Carol Munson, *Permissions Assistant*
Laura Pleva Nielsen, *Index Editor*
EdIndex, Services for Publishers, *Indexers*

* * *

Omnigraphics, Inc.

Matthew P. Barbour, *Senior Vice President*
Kay Gill, *Vice President—Directories*
Kevin Hayes, *Operations Manager*
David P. Bianco, *Marketing Director*

* * *

Peter E. Ruffner, *President and Publisher*

Frederick G. Ruffner, Jr., *Chairman*

ISBN 0-7808-0705-7

Library of Congress Cataloging-in-Publication Data

Child abuse sourcebook : basic consumer health information about the physical, sexual, and emotional abuse of children, with additional facts about neglect, Munchausen syndrome by proxy (MSBP), shaken baby syndrome, and controversial issues related to child abuse, such as withholding medical care, corporal punishment, and child maltreatment in youth sports, and featuring facts about child protective services, foster care, adoption, parenting challenges, and other abuse prevention efforts ; along with a glossary of related terms and resources for additional help and information / edited by Dawn D. Matthews.-- 1st ed.
p. cm. -- (Health reference series)
Includes bibliographical references and index.
ISBN 0-7808-0705-7 (hardcover)
1. Child abuse--United States. 2. Child abuse--United States--Prevention. 3. Abused children--United States. I. Matthews, Dawn D. II. Health reference series (Unnumbered)
HV6626.52.C557 2004
362.76--dc22

2004006519

∞

This book is printed on acid-free paper meeting the ANSI Z39.48 Standard. The infinity symbol that appears above indicates that the paper in this book meets that standard.

Printed in the United States

Table of Contents

Part III: Intervention and Treatment for Child Abuse

Part IV: Child Abuse Research

Part V: Child Protective Services

Part VI: Parenting Challenges

Part VII: Additional Help and Information

Preface

About This Book

According to statistics compiled by the National Child Abuse and Neglect Data System, referrals concerning the safety and well-being of approximately five million children were made to child protective services agencies throughout the United States in 2001. Investigations of these referrals led to the identification of more than 900,000 children who were victims of various forms of mistreatment, including physical abuse, sexual abuse, neglect, medical neglect, and psychological maltreatment. Among their numbers were 1,300 child fatalities.

Child Abuse Sourcebook contains information about the various forms of child abuse, including physical abuse, sexual abuse, emotional abuse, and neglect. A discussion of the effects of child abuse provides facts about shaken baby syndrome, battered child syndrome, and the long-term consequences that continue into adulthood. Controversial issues related to child abuse, such as withholding medical care, corporal punishment, and child maltreatment in youth sports, are discussed. Sections on child protective services and parenting challenges describe various abuse prevention efforts, including foster care, adoption, and non-abusive disciplinary tactics. A glossary of related terms and directories of resources for further help and information are also provided.

Child abuse may occur within the context of other family violence issues. Readers seeking information about intimate partner violence, including physical violence, sexual assault, and emotional abuse may wish to consult *Domestic Violence Sourcebook*, a separate volume in the *Health Reference Series*.

How to Use This Book

This book is divided into parts and chapters. Parts focus on broad areas of interest. Chapters are devoted to single topics within a part.

Part I: Defining Child Abuse contains information about various forms of abuse, including physical, sexual, and emotional abuse. It discusses the most common relationships between children and those who abuse them and offers information about child abuse in community institutions, organizations, and youth sports.

Part II: Physical, Mental, and Emotional Effects of Child Abuse provides facts about the consequences of child abuse. A chapter addressing the link between adverse childhood events and adult health is included. Another chapter discusses issues related to the impact of domestic violence upon the children who witness it.

Part III: Intervention and Treatment for Child Abuse offers practical guidelines for those seeking to help an abused child. It includes information about reporting child maltreatment and also contains facts about the role medical and mental health communities can play in helping to treat child abuse victims.

Part IV: Child Abuse Research contains information about the ongoing efforts to identify and prevent the causes of child maltreatment. It discusses the relationship between substance abuse and child abuse and the impact of pre-natal exposure to alcohol and other drugs on child well-being. Parental abduction and the connection between animal cruelty and family violence are among the other topics addressed in this section.

Part V: Child Protective Services provides information about the legal issues involved in the effort to protect children and remove them from abusive situations when necessary. It explains various efforts undertaken by community and government agencies to prevent child abuse. Chapters about fostering and adopting abused children are also included.

Part VI: Parenting Challenges offers practical information about effective parenting, including suggestions for discussing the topic of sexual abuse with children. It contains chapters discussing controversial issues, such as spanking and withholding medical treatment for religious reasons. Information for parents of children with osteogenesis imperfecta (OI) who may be at risk for false accusations of child abuse is also provided.

Part VII: Additional Help and Information contains a glossary of important terms and directories of resources for further information about child abuse and neglect prevention, child welfare, and family violence. Information about reporting child abuse and child pornography is also included.

Bibliographic Note

This volume contains documents and excerpts from publications issued by the following U.S. government agencies: Administration for Children and Families (ACF); ARCH National Resource Center for the Respite and Crisis Care Services; Centers for Disease Control and Prevention (CDC); ERIC Clearinghouse on Elementary and Early Childhood Education; Federal Communications Commission; National Adoption Information Clearinghouse; National Clearinghouse on Child Abuse and Neglect Information; National Criminal Justice Reference Service; National Institute of Mental Health (NIMH); National Institute on Drug Abuse (NIDA); Substance and Mental Health Services Administration (SAMHSA); U.S. Department of Health and Human Services (HHS); U.S. Department of Justice (DOJ), Office of Juvenile Justice and Delinquency Prevention; and U.S. Office of Justice Programs, Office for Victims of Crime.

In addition, this volume contains copyrighted documents from the following organizations and individuals: American Academy of Family Physicians (AAFP); A.D.A.M., Inc.; American Humane Association; American Psychological Association; Brown University; Centre for Children and Families in the Justice System (London Family Court Clinic); Childhelp USA; Children's Healthcare Is a Legal Duty (CHILD), Inc.; Children's Defense Fund; Cincinnati Children's Hospital Medical Center/Mayerson Center for Safe and Healthy Children; Family Violence Prevention Fund; Dr. Istvan Hargitai; Humane Society of the United States; Kempe Children's Center and Kempe Children's Foundation; Minnesota Amateur Sports Commission; National Exchange Club Foundation, Nemours Center for Children's Health Media; Richard Niolon, PhD; Osteogenesis Imperfecta Foundation; Elizabeth Pantley; President and Fellows of Harvard College, Harvard Health

Publications/*Harvard Mental Health Letter*; Prevent Child Abuse America; Stepfamily Association of America; Regents of the University of Michigan; and University of Nebraska, Lincoln/Center on Children, Families, and the Law.

Acknowledgements

Special thanks go to the many organizations, agencies, and individuals who have contributed materials for this *Sourcebook* and to managing editor Karen Bellenir and permissions specialist Liz Barbour.

Note from the Editor

This book is part of Omnigraphics' *Health Reference Series*. The series provides basic information about a broad range of medical concerns. It is not intended to serve as a tool for diagnosing illness, in prescribing treatments, or as a substitute for the physician/patient relationship. All persons concerned about medical symptoms or the possibility of disease are encouraged to seek professional care from an appropriate health care provider.

Our Advisory Board

The *Health Reference Series* is reviewed by an Advisory Board comprised of librarians from public, academic, and medical libraries. We would like to thank the following board members for providing guidance to the development of this series:

Medical Consultant

Medical consultation services are provided to the *Health Reference Series* editors by David A. Cooke, M.D. Dr. Cooke is a graduate of Brandeis University, and he received his M.D. degree from the University of Michigan. He completed residency training at the University of Wisconsin Hospital and Clinics. He is board-certified in Internal Medicine. Dr. Cooke currently works as part of the University of Michigan Health System and practices in Brighton, MI. In his free time, he enjoys writing, science fiction, and spending time with his family.

Health Reference Series *Update Policy*

The inaugural book in the *Health Reference Series* was the first edition of *Cancer Sourcebook* published in 1989. Since then, the *Series* has been enthusiastically received by librarians and in the medical community. In order to maintain the standard of providing high-quality health information for the layperson the editorial staff at Omnigraphics felt it was necessary to implement a policy of updating volumes when warranted.

Medical researchers have been making tremendous strides, and it is the purpose of the *Health Reference Series* to stay current with the most recent advances. Each decision to update a volume will be made on an individual basis. Some of the considerations will include how much new information is available and the feedback we receive from people who use the books. If there is a topic you would like to see added to the update list, or an area of medical concern you feel has not been adequately addressed, please write to:

Editor
Health Reference Series
Omnigraphics, Inc.
615 Griswold Street
Detroit, MI 48226

The commitment to providing on-going coverage of important medical developments has also led to some format changes in the *Health Reference Series*. Each new volume on a topic is individually titled and called a "First Edition." Subsequent updates will carry sequential edition numbers. To help avoid confusion and to provide maximum flexibility in our ability to respond to informational needs, the practice of consecutively numbering each volume has been discontinued.

Part One

Defining Child Abuse

Chapter 1

What Is Child Abuse?

To prevent and respond to child abuse and neglect effectively, there needs to be a common understanding of the definitions of those actions and omissions that constitute child maltreatment. Unfortunately, there is no single, universally applied definition of child abuse and neglect. Over the past several decades, different stakeholders—including State and Federal legislative bodies, agency officials, and researchers—have developed definitions of maltreatment for different purposes. Definitions vary across these groups and within them. For example, legal definitions describing the different forms of child maltreatment for reporting and criminal prosecution purposes are found mainly in State statutes, and definitions vary from State to State. Similarly, agency guidelines for accepting reports, conducting investigations, and providing interventions vary from State to State and sometimes from county to county. In addition, researchers use varying methods to measure and define abuse and neglect, making it difficult to compare findings across studies. Despite the differences, there are commonalities across definitions. This chapter describes sources of definitions in Federal and State laws and summarizes those elements commonly recognized as child maltreatment.

"What Is Child Maltreatment," From: *A Coordinated Response to Child Abuse and Neglect: The Foundation for Practice*, National Clearinghouse on Child Abuse and Neglect Information, 2003. Available online at http://nccanch.acf.hhs.gov/pubs/usermanuals/foundation/chapthree.cfm.

Definitions in Federal Law

The Child Abuse Prevention and Treatment Act (CAPTA) provides minimum standards for defining physical child abuse, child neglect, and sexual abuse that States must incorporate in their statutory definitions to receive Federal funds. Under CAPTA, child abuse and neglect means:

- Any recent act or failure to act on the part of a parent or caretaker that results in death, serious physical or emotional harm, sexual abuse, or exploitation;
- An act or failure to act that presents an imminent risk of serious harm.

The definition of child abuse and neglect refers specifically to parents and other caregivers. A child under this definition generally means a person who is under the age of 18 or who is not an emancipated minor. In cases of child sexual abuse, a child is one who has not attained the age of 18 or the age specified by the child protection law of the State in which the child resides, whichever is younger.

While CAPTA provides definitions for sexual abuse and the special cases related to withholding or failing to provide medically indicated treatment, it does not provide specific definitions for other types of maltreatment—physical abuse, neglect, or psychological maltreatment.

CAPTA Definition of Sexual Abuse

CAPTA defines sexual abuse as:

- The employment, use, persuasion, inducement, enticement, or coercion of any child to engage in, or assist any other person to engage in, any sexually explicit conduct or simulation of such conduct for the purpose of producing a visual depiction of such conduct;
- The rape, and in cases of caretaker or inter-familial relationships, statutory rape, molestation, prostitution, or other form of sexual exploitation of children, or incest with children.

CAPTA Definition of Withholding of Medically Indicated Treatment

CAPTA defines the withholding of medically indicated treatment as:

- The failure to respond to the infant's life-threatening conditions by providing treatment...which, in the treating physician's reasonable medical judgment, will be most likely to be effective in ameliorating or correcting all such conditions.
- The term withholding of medically indicated treatment does not include the failure to provide treatment (other than appropriate nutrition, hydration, and medication) to an infant when, in the treating physician's reasonable medical judgment:
  - The infant is chronically and irreversibly comatose;
  - The provision of such treatment would merely prolong dying;
  - The provision of such treatment would not be effective in ameliorating or correcting all of the infant's life-threatening conditions;
  - The provision of such treatment would otherwise be futile in terms of the survival of the infant;
  - The provision of such treatment would be virtually futile in terms of the survival of the infant, and the treatment itself under such circumstances would be inhumane.

Sources of Definitions in State Law

While the Federal legislation sets minimum definitional standards, each State is responsible for providing its own definition of maltreatment within civil and criminal contexts. The problem of child maltreatment is generally subject to State laws (both statutes and case law) and administrative regulations. Definitions of child abuse and neglect are located primarily in three places within each State's statutory code:

Mandatory child maltreatment reporting statutes (civil laws) provide definitions of child maltreatment to guide those individuals mandated to identify and report suspected child abuse. These reports activate the child protection process.

Criminal statutes define those forms of child maltreatment that are criminally punish able. In most jurisdictions, child maltreatment is criminally punishable when one or more of the following statutory crimes have been committed: homicide, murder, manslaughter, false imprisonment, assault, battery, criminal neglect and abandonment, emotional and physical abuse, child pornography, child prostitution, computer crimes, rape, deviant sexual assault, indecent exposure, child endangerment, and reckless endangerment.

Juvenile court jurisdiction statutes provide definitions of the circumstances necessary for the court to have jurisdiction over a child alleged to have been abused or neglected. When the child's safety cannot be ensured in the home, these statutes allow the court to take custody of a child and to order specific treatment services for the parents and child.

Together, these legal definitions of child abuse and neglect determine the minimum standards of care and protection for children and serve as important guidelines for professionals regarding those acts and omissions that constitute child maltreatment.

Child protective services (CPS) workers use statutory definitions of child maltreatment to determine whether maltreatment has occurred and when intervention into family life is necessary. For particular localities within a State, local CPS policies and procedures, based on statutes and regulations, further define different types of maltreatment and the conditions under which intervention and services are warranted.

State Statutes

To review a summary of reporting laws, visit the State Statutes section of the National Clearinghouse on Child Abuse and Neglect's Web site at http://nccanch.acf.hhs.gov.

General Definitions by Type of Maltreatment

There are four commonly recognized forms of child abuse or maltreatment:

- Physical
- Sexual
- Neglect
- Psychological

There is great variation from State to State regarding the details and specificity of child abuse definitions, but it is still possible to identify commonalities among each different type of child maltreatment. These commonalities, in part, reflect societal views of parental actions that are seen as improper or unacceptable because they place children at a risk of physical and emotional harm.

Physical Abuse

Generally, physical abuse is characterized by physical injury, such as bruises and fractures that result from:

- Punching
- Beating
- Kicking
- Biting
- Shaking
- Throwing
- Stabbing
- Choking
- Burning
- Hitting with a hand, stick, strap, or other object

Although an injury resulting from physical abuse is not accidental, the parent or caregiver may not have intended to hurt the child. The injury may have resulted from severe discipline, including injurious spanking, or physical punishment that is inappropriate to the child's age or condition. The injury may be the result of a single episode or of repeated episodes and can range in severity from minor marks and bruising to death.

Some cultural practices are generally not defined as physical abuse, but may result in physically hurting children. For example:

- "Coining" or cao gio—a practice to treat illness by rubbing the body forcefully with a coin or other hard object.
- Moxabustion—an Asian folkloric remedy that burns the skin.

As Howard Dubowitz, a leading researcher in the field, explains: "While cultural practices are generally respected, if the injury or harm is significant, professionals typically work with parents to discourage harmful behavior and suggest preferable alternatives."

Sexual Abuse

Child sexual abuse generally refers to sexual acts, sexually motivated behaviors involving children, or sexual exploitation of children. Child sexual abuse includes a wide range of behaviors, such as:

- Oral, anal, or genital penile penetration;
- Anal or genital digital or other penetration;
- Genital contact with no intrusion;
- Fondling of a child's breasts or buttocks;

- Indecent exposure;
- Inadequate or inappropriate supervision of a child's voluntary sexual activities;
- Use of a child in prostitution, pornography, Internet crimes, or other sexually exploitative activities.

Sexual abuse includes both touching offenses (fondling or sexual intercourse) and nontouching offenses (exposing a child to pornographic materials) and can involve varying degrees of violence and emotional trauma. The most commonly reported cases involve incest—sexual abuse occurring among family members, including those in biological families, adoptive families, and step-families. Incest most often occurs within a father-daughter relationship; however, mother-son, father-son, and sibling-sibling incest also occurs. Sexual abuse is also sometimes committed by other relatives or caretakers, such as aunts, uncles, grandparents, cousins, or the boyfriend or girlfriend of a parent.

Child Neglect

Child neglect, the most common form of child maltreatment, is generally characterized by omissions in care resulting in significant harm or risk of significant harm. Neglect is frequently defined in terms of a failure to provide for the child's basic needs—deprivation of adequate food, clothing, shelter, supervision, or medical care. Neglect laws often exclude circumstances in which a child's needs are not met because of poverty or an inability to provide. In addition, many States establish religious exemptions for parents who choose not to seek medical care for their children due to religious beliefs that may prohibit medical intervention.

The Department of Health and Human Services' *Third National Incidence Study of Child Abuse and Neglect* (NIS-3) is the single most comprehensive source of information about the current incidence of child maltreatment in the United States. NIS-3 worked with researchers and practitioners to define physical, educational, and emotional neglect in a succinct and clear manner, as described in the following:

Physical Neglect

Refusal of health care—the failure to provide or allow needed care in accordance with recommendations of a competent health care professional for a physical injury, illness, medical condition, or impairment.

Delay in health care—the failure to seek timely and appropriate medical care for a serious health problem that any reasonable layman would have recognized as needing professional medical attention.

Abandonment—the desertion of a child without arranging for reasonable care and supervision.

Expulsion—other blatant refusals of custody, such as permanent or indefinite expulsion of a child from the home without adequate arrangement for care by others or refusal to accept custody of a returned runaway.

Inadequate supervision—leaving a child unsupervised or inadequately supervised for extended periods of time or allowing the child to remain away from home overnight without the parent or caretaker knowing or attempting to determine the child's whereabouts.

Other physical neglect—includes inadequate nutrition, clothing, or hygiene; conspicuous inattention to avoidable hazards in the home; and other forms of reckless disregard of the child's safety and welfare (e.g., driving with the child while intoxicated, leaving a young child in a car unattended).

Educational Neglect

Permitted chronic truancy—habitual absenteeism from school averaging at least 5 days a month if the parent or guardian is informed of the problem and does not attempt to intervene.

Failure to enroll or other truancy—failure to register or enroll a child of mandatory school age, causing the child to miss at least 1 month of school; or a pattern of keeping a school-aged child home without valid reasons.

Inattention to special education need—refusal to allow or failure to obtain recommended remedial education services or neglect in obtaining or following through with treatment for a child's diagnosed learning disorder or other special education need without reasonable cause.

Emotional Neglect

Inadequate nurturing or affection—marked inattention to the child's needs for affection, emotional support, or attention.

Chronic or extreme spouse abuse—exposure to chronic or extreme spouse abuse or other domestic violence in the child's presence.

Permitted drug or alcohol abuse—encouragement or permitting of drug or alcohol use by the child.

Permitted other maladaptive behavior—encouragement or permitting of other maladaptive behavior (e.g., chronic delinquency, severe assault) under circumstances where the parent or caregiver has reason to be aware of the existence and seriousness of the problem but does not intervene.

Refusal of psychological care—refusal to allow needed and available treatment for a child's emotional or behavioral impairment or problem in accordance with a competent professional recommendation.

Delay in psychological care—failure to seek or provide needed treatment for a child's emotional or behavioral impairment or problem that any reasonable layman would have recognized as needing professional, psychological attention (e.g., suicide attempt).

Spotlight on Chronic Neglect

One issue in defining child neglect involves consideration of incidents of neglect versus a pattern of behavior that indicates neglect. Susan J. Zuravin, from the University of Maryland at Baltimore School of Social Work, recommends that if some behaviors occur in a chronic pattern, they should be considered neglectful. Examples include lack of supervision, inadequate hygiene, and failure to meet a child's educational needs. This suggests that rather than focusing on individual incidents that may or may not be classified as neglectful, one should look at an accumulation of incidents that may together constitute neglect. If CPS focuses only on the immediate allegation before them and not the pattern reflected in multiple referrals, then many neglected children will continue to be inappropriately excluded from the CPS system. For example, a family exhibiting a pattern of behavior that may constitute neglect might include frequent reports of not having enough food in the home or keeping older children home from school to watch younger children. In most CPS systems, however, the criteria for identifying neglect focuses on recent, discrete, verifiable incidents.

One study found that many children who had been referred to CPS for neglect did not receive services because their cases did not meet the criteria for incidents of neglect. It also found, however, that all of these children had, in fact, suffered severe developmental consequences. In recognition of this issue, the Missouri Division of Family Services has assigned one of its CPS staff as a Chronic Neglect Specialist. This office defines chronic neglect as "...a persistent pattern of family functioning in which the caregiver has not sustained and/or met the basic needs of the children which results in harm to the child." The focus here is on the "accumulation of harm." CPS and community agencies across the country are recognizing the importance of early intervention and service provision to support families so that neglect does not become chronic or lead to other negative consequences.

Psychological Maltreatment

Psychological maltreatment—also known as emotional abuse and neglect—refers to a repeated pattern of caregiver behavior or extreme incident(s) that convey to children that they are worthless, flawed, unloved, unwanted, endangered, or only of value in meeting another's needs. Summarizing research and expert opinion, Stuart N. Hart, Ph.D., and Marla R. Brassard, Ph.D., present six categories of psychological maltreatment:

- Spurning (e.g., belittling, hostile rejecting, ridiculing);
- Terrorizing (e.g., threatening violence against a child, placing a child in a recognizably dangerous situation);
- Isolating (e.g., confining the child, placing unreasonable limitations on the child's freedom of movement, restricting the child from social interactions);
- Exploiting or corrupting (e.g., modeling antisocial behavior such as criminal activities, encouraging prostitution, permitting substance abuse);
- Denying emotional responsiveness (e.g., ignoring the child's attempts to interact, failing to express affection);
- Mental health, medical, and educational neglect (e.g., refusing to allow or failing to provide treatment for serious mental health or medical problems, ignoring the need for services for serious educational needs).

To warrant intervention, psychological maltreatment must be sustained and repetitive. For less severe acts, such as habitual scapegoating or belittling, demonstrable harm to the child is often required for CPS to intervene.

Psychological maltreatment is the most difficult form of child maltreatment to identify. In part, the difficulty in detection occurs because the effects of psychological maltreatment, such as lags in development, learning problems, and speech disorders, are often evident in both children who have experienced and those who have not experienced maltreatment. Additionally, the effects of psychological maltreatment may only become evident in later developmental stages of the child's life.

Although any of the forms of child maltreatment may be found alone, they often occur in combination. Psychological maltreatment is almost always present when other forms are identified.

Case Examples of Maltreatment

Physical Abuse

During a violent fight between her mother and her mother's boyfriend, 8-year-old Kerry called 911. She told the operator that her mother's boyfriend always hit her mommy when he came home drunk. In addition, Kerry said she was worried about her 5-year-old brother, Aaron, because he tried to help their mom and the boyfriend punched him in the face. As a result, Aaron fell, hit his head on the coffee table, and had not moved since. The operator heard yelling in the background and the mother screaming, "Get off the phone!" When the police and paramedics arrived, Aaron was unconscious and the mother had numerous bruises on her face.

Child Neglect

Robert and Carlotta are the parents of a 9-month-old son named Ruiz. Robert and Carlotta used various drugs together until Robert was arrested and sent to prison for distributing cocaine. Since Robert's arrest, Carlotta has been living with different relatives and friends. Recently, she left her son with her sister who also has a history of drug use. Her sister then went to a local bar and left Ruiz unattended. After hearing the baby boy cry for over an hour, the neighbors called the police. When Carlotta arrived to pick up Ruiz, the police and the CPS worker were also there. It appeared that she had been using drugs.

Sexual Abuse

Jody, age 11, said that she was asleep in her bedroom and that her father came in and took off his robe and underwear. She stated that he got into bed with her and pulled up her nightgown and put his private part on her private part. She stated that he pushed hard and it hurt. Jody said that the same thing had happened before while her mother was at work. Jody stated that she told her mother, but her father insisted that she was telling a lie.

Psychological Abuse

Jackie is a 7-year-old girl who lives with her mother. Jackie's mother often screams at her, calls her degrading names, and threatens to kill her when Jackie misbehaves. Jackie doesn't talk in class anymore, doesn't have any friends in her neighborhood, and has lost a lot of weight.

Chapter 2

Physical Abuse of Children

According to the National Child Abuse and Neglect Data System (NCANDS), three million children were reported in 2001 as victims of maltreatment. More than 903,000 of these children were substantiated or indicated abuse and neglect victims. And of these, 18% were determined to be victims of physical abuse. Further, an estimated 1,300 children died in 2001 as a result of child abuse and neglect. This figure is conservative due to the potential for misdiagnosis of cause of death.

What is child physical abuse?

Defined as non-accidental trauma or physical injury caused by punching, beating, kicking, biting, burning, or otherwise harming a child, physical abuse is the most visible form of child maltreatment.

Many times, physical abuse results from inappropriate or excessive physical discipline. A parent or caretaker in anger may be unaware of the magnitude of force with which he or she strikes the child.

Other factors that can contribute to child abuse include parents' immaturity, lack of parenting skills, poor childhood experiences, and social isolation, as well as situations of frequent crises, drug or alcohol problems, and domestic violence.

What should you look for if you suspect a child is being physically abused?

While injuries can occur accidentally when a child is at play, physical abuse should be suspected if the explanations do not fit the injury or if a pattern of frequency is apparent. The presence of many injuries in various stages of healing makes it obvious that the injuries did not all occur as a result of one accident.

Physical indicators of abuse include bruises; lacerations; swollen areas; and marks on the child's face, head, back, chest, genital area, buttocks, or thighs. Wounds like human bite marks, cigarette burns, broken bones, puncture marks, or missing hair may indicate abuse.

A child's behavior might also signal that something is wrong. Victims of physical abuse may display withdrawn or aggressive behavioral extremes, complain of soreness or uncomfortable movement, wear clothing that is inappropriate for the weather, express discomfort with physical contact, or become chronic runaways.

What You Can Do

Discipline effectively. Remember that kids will be kids. Children can be loud, unruly, and destructive. They will break things, interrupt telephone conversations, track mud through the house, not pick up their toys or clean their rooms, struggle over eating their vegetables, or pester routinely. Children will inevitably do things that may make their parents feel irritated, frustrated, disappointed, and mad. Changing a child's behavior is not easy. However, children should not be disciplined through violence.

It is better to deny children privileges when they do something unacceptable, as well as reward them when they do something good. This teaches children that there are consequences for their actions.

Regain control. Child abuse is a symptom of having difficulty coping with stressful situations. If you feel you are losing control, ask someone to relieve you for a few minutes. Then try these tips:

- Count to 10.
- Take deep breaths.
- Phone a friend.
- Look through a magazine or newspaper.
- Listen to music.

- Exercise.
- Take a walk (first make certain that children are not left without supervision).
- Take a bath.
- Write a letter.
- Sit down and relax.
- Lie down.

Get help. Support is available for families at risk of abuse through local child protection services agencies, community centers, churches, physicians, mental health facilities, and schools.

Report, report, report. If you suspect child abuse is occurring, first report it to the local child protective services agency (often called "social services" or "human services") in your county or state. Professionals who work with children are required by law to report reasonable suspicion of abuse or neglect. Furthermore, in 20 states, citizens who suspect abuse or neglect are required to report it. "Reasonable suspicion" based on objective evidence, which could be firsthand observation or statements made by a parent or child, is all that is needed to report.

What is NCANDS?

NCANDS is the primary source of national information on abused and neglected children known to public child protective services agencies. American Humane has provided technical assistance to this project since it's beginning in 1990. For a copy of this report, contact the National Clearinghouse on Child Abuse and Neglect Information at (800) 394-3366 or http://www.calib.com/nccanch. The publication is also available at http://www.acf.hhs.gov/programs/cb.

Chapter 3

Sexual Abuse of Children

What is child sexual abuse?

It is very difficult for most people to talk about sexual abuse and even more difficult for society as a whole to acknowledge that the sexual abuse of children of all ages—including infants—happens every day in this country. The sexual abuse of children has become the subject of great community concern and the focus of legislative and professional concern, as well. This is evidenced by steadily rising reports of sexual abuse, an expanding body of sexual abuse literature, public declarations from adult survivors, and increased media coverage of sexual abuse issues.

According to the National Child Abuse and Neglect Data System (NCANDS), in 1995, it is estimated that 12.6% of confirmed or substantiated cases of child abuse and neglect investigated by public child protective services agencies (CPS) were sexual abuse cases. This figure translates into nearly 2 child sexual abuse victims for every 1,000 children younger than age 18, or 126,095 victims in 1995. Other studies suggest that even more children suffer abuse and neglect than is ever reported to CPS. A 1995 Gallup Organization telephone survey indicates that as many as 19 per 1,000 children have suffered sexual abuse.

At the extreme end of the spectrum, sexual abuse includes sexual intercourse and/or its deviations. These behaviors may be the final

---

acts in a worsening pattern of sexual abuse. For that reason and because of their devastating effects, exhibitionism, fondling, and any other sexual contact with children are also considered sexually abusive.

Generally, nontouching sexual offenses include

- indecent exposure/exhibitionism,
- exposing children to pornographic material,
- deliberately exposing a child to the act of sexual intercourse, and
- masturbation in front of a child.

Touching sexual offenses include

- fondling,
- making a child touch an adult's sexual organs,
- any penetration of a child's vagina or anus—no matter how slight—by a penis or any object that doesn't have a valid medical purpose.

Sexual exploitation of a child is also an offense and can include

- engaging a child or soliciting a child for the purposes of prostitution and
- using a child to film, photograph, or model pornography.

These definitions are broad and general. In most states, the legal definition for the molestation of a child is an act of a person—adult or child—which forces, coerces, or threatens a child to have any form of sexual contact or to engage in any type of sexual activity at the perpetrator's direction.

What should I look for if I suspect a child is being sexually abused?

Child sexual abuse cases can be very difficult to prove largely because cases where definitive, objective evidence exists are the exception rather than the rule. The first indicators of sexual abuse may not be physical signs, but behavioral changes or abnormalities. Unfortunately, because it is usually so difficult to accept that sexual abuse may be occurring, the adult may misinterpret the signals and feel that the child is merely being disobedient or insolent. The reaction to the disclosure of abuse then becomes disbelief and rejection of the child's statements.

Sexual abuse is usually discovered in one of two ways: by direct disclosure (i.e., statements from the victim, victim's family member, or parent seeking help) or by nondirect methods (i.e., someone witnesses the abuse to the child, the child contracts a sexually transmitted disease, or the child becomes pregnant).

The child victim may be the only witness. In that case, the child's statements may also be the only evidence that sexual abuse has occurred. In such cases, the central issue sometimes becomes whether the child's statements can be trusted to be true. Some child welfare experts believe that children never lie about sexual abuse and that their statements must always be believed. But according to Douglas Besharov in his book, *Recognizing Child Abuse*, it is the job of the investigating child protective agency to make the determination as to whether sexual abuse has occurred. He writes, "As a general rule, all doubts should be resolved in favor of making a report (of sexual abuse). A child who describes being sexually abused should be reported unless there is clear reason to disbelieve the statement."

According to NCANDS statistics, only 4% of unsubstantiated reports of all forms of child abuse and neglect are intentionally false. Additional studies particular to false reports of child sexual abuse have found between 2% and 8% of reports to be deliberately false (May Quinn, 1991).

What are the effects of child sexual abuse?

Sometimes the child may be so traumatized by sexual abuse that years may pass before he or she is able to understand or talk about what happened. In these cases, adult survivors of sexual abuse may come forward for the first time at the age of 40 or 50 and divulge the horror of their experiences.

The sexual victimization of children is ethically and morally wrong. Its effects extend far beyond childhood occurrence. It robs children of their childhood and creates a loss of trust, feelings of guilt, and/or self-abusive behavior. It can lead to antisocial behavior, depression, identity confusion, loss of self-esteem, and other serious emotional problems.

How do I report child sexual abuse?

If you suspect sexual abuse and believe a child to be in imminent danger, call the police immediately. Remember that you may be the only person in a position to help a child who is being sexually abused, so you must contact the appropriate child protective agency any time sexual abuse is suspected.

What can parents do to protect their children?

Parents can help protect children against sexual abuse. They can teach their children about what appropriate sexual behavior is and when to say "no" if someone tries to touch sexual parts of their bodies or in any way that makes them feel uncomfortable. Parents can also observe their children when they interact with others to see if they are hesitant or particularly uncomfortable around a certain adult. Most importantly, children need to know that they can speak openly to a trusted adult and that they will be believed. Children who are victims of sexual abuse should always be reassured that they are not responsible for what has happened to them and they should not feel ashamed.

Sexual abuse is a problem that can affect all members of a community. You can do your part in your community to help combat this pervasive problem. You've taken the first step by educating yourself about sexual abuse. Make others aware of the problem also, by arranging for knowledgeable guest speakers to give presentations about sexual abuse to groups you belong to. Encourage your local school board to put programs in place that will educate both teachers and students about the problem. Offer encouragement for victims by supporting organizations that help victims of incest or by simply reassuring a victim of sexual abuse that they should not feel shame or guilt about what has happened to them. It is important to understand that troubled families can be helped and that everyone can play a part in the process.

The problem of child maltreatment will not go away on its own. If you suspect child abuse, report it to your local child protective agency or to the police if the child is in immediate danger. Help is available for families at risk of abuse.

Statistical Data

U.S. Department of Health and Human Services, National Center on Child Abuse and Neglect. (1997). *Child Maltreatment 1995: Reports from the States to the National Center on Child Abuse and Neglect.* (Washington, DC: U.S. Government Printing Office). A project of NCCAN, the National Child Abuse and Neglect Data System is the primary source of national information on abused and neglected children known to public child protective services agencies. American

Humane has provided technical assistance to this project since it's beginning in 1990. To obtain a copy of this report, contact the National Clearinghouse on Child Abuse and Neglect Information at (800) 394-3366 or in the metro Washington DC area at (703) 385-7565.

Other Resources

Besharov, D. J. (1990). *Recognizing Child Abuse: A Guide for the Concerned*. New York, NY: The Free Press.

The Gallup Organization. (1995). Disciplining children in America: A Gallup Poll report. Princeton, NJ: The Gallup Organization. Call 609-924-9600.

May Quinn, K. (1991). False and unsubstantiated sexual abuse allegations: Clinical issues. In M. Robin and J. Beker (Eds.), *Child and Youth Services: Assessing Child Maltreatment Reports,* 15(2), 145-157.

Chapter 4

Emotional Abuse of Children

What is emotional abuse?

Emotional abuse is commonly defined as a pattern of behavior that can seriously interfere with a child's positive emotional development. Those patterns of behavior can include

- constant rejection of the child;
- terrorizing;
- refusal to provide basic nurturance;
- refusal to get help for a child's psychological problems;
- failure to provide the physical or mental stimulation that a child needs to be able to grow; and
- exposing a child to corruption, including drug abuse and criminal behavior.

According to Douglas Besharov in his book, *Recognizing Child Abuse*, "emotional abuse is an assault on the child's psyche, just as physical abuse is an assault on the child's body." Children who are constantly shamed, terrorized, humiliated, or rejected suffer at least as much, if not more, than if they had been physically assaulted. In

---

fact, children who are physically abused also suffer psychologically, although it may be difficult to see the immediate effects.

An infant who is being severely deprived of basic emotional nurturance, even though physically well cared for, can fail to thrive and can eventually die. Less severe forms of early emotional deprivation may produce babies who grow into anxious and insecure children who are slow to develop or who might have low self-esteem.

Other types of abuse are usually identifiable because marks or other physical evidence is left, however, emotional abuse can be very hard to diagnose or even to define. In some instances, an emotionally abused child will show no signs of abuse. For this reason, emotional abuse is the most difficult form of child maltreatment to identify and stop, because often child protective services must have demonstrable evidence that harm to the child has been done before they can intervene.

Although the visible signs of emotional abuse can be hard to find, this type of abuse leaves hidden scars that manifest themselves in numerous behavioral ways. Insecurity, poor self-esteem, destructive behavior, angry acts (such as fire-setting, and/or cruelty to animals), withdrawal, poor development of basic skills, alcohol or drug abuse, suicide, difficulty forming relationships, and unstable job histories can all be possible results of emotional maltreatment.

Because of the difficulty in defining emotional abuse, we must be very careful not to lump all negative parental attitudes and/or actions under the category of emotional maltreatment. Even the best of parents have occasions when they have momentarily lost control and said hurtful things to their children, ignored them during a time when attention needs were critical, or unintentionally scared them. What is truly harmful, according to James Garbarino of the Family Life Development Center at Cornell University, and a national expert on emotional abuse, is "the chronic pattern that erodes and corrodes a child . . . that persistent, chronic pattern of behavior toward a child." It is important to understand that emotional abuse in not just an isolated incident. Dr. Arthur Green, Director of the Family Center at the Columbia Presbyterian Medical Center in New York City, says, "We're talking about the kind of things that a good mother may do 10% of the time, but a troubled mother does 80% or 90% of the time."

All children need acceptance, love, encouragement, discipline, consistency, and positive attention. Emotionally abused children often grow up thinking that they are deficient in some way and the ultimate tragedy of this kind of abuse is that when these children become parents, they may continue the cycle with their own children.

Emotional maltreatment can, and does, happen in all types of families, regardless of background. Most parents want the best for their children. However, due to stress, poor parenting skills, social isolation, lack of available resources, and inappropriate expectations of children, some parents harm their children.

What can you do when you feel that your behavior toward your child may be bordering on emotional abuse?

Here are some suggestions:

- Never be afraid to apologize to your child. If you lose your temper and say something in anger that wasn't meant to be said, apologize. Children need to know that adults can admit when they are wrong.
- Don't call your child names or attach labeling behavior to the child. Names such as "Stupid," "Lazy," or phrases like "Good for nothing," "You'll never amount to anything," "If you could only be more like your brother," and "You can never do anything right" tear at a child's self-esteem.
- Address the behaviors that need correcting and use time-out when the child misbehaves. Be sure to discuss the behavior that you are trying to change as the reason for the time-out and discuss your reasons with the child immediately after each time-out. Time-outs should be time-limited and never more than a few minutes.
- Compliment your child when you see good behavior.
- Learn to walk away from a situation when you feel that you are losing control. You can isolate yourself in another room for a few minutes (after first making sure that the child is safe), count to 10 before you say anything, ask for help from another adult, or take a few deep breaths before you start to yell at your child.

Source

Besharov, D. J. (1990). *Recognizing Child Abuse: A Guide for the Concerned.* New York, NY: The Free Press.

Chapter 5

Parental and Caregiver Neglect

Defining Neglect

Neglectful situations include:

- withholding of medically indicated treatment from newborn infants
- prenatal exposure to drugs
- failure to thrive/malnutrition

Differences in definitions of child neglect in State laws and in community standards reflect the significant variations in the judgments of professionals and nonprofessionals concerning what constitutes child neglect. Some State statutes emphasize the condition of the child without any mention of parental fault; others stress the condition of the child resulting from parental actions or fault. Some communities have determined that no child under age 10 should be left at home alone, while other communities "permit" working parents to leave their children unsupervised after school.

Defining neglect is complicated by the necessity of considering the following:

"Defining Neglect," from *Child Neglect: A Guide for Intervention,* 1993. National Clearinghouse on Child Abuse and Neglect Information (NCCANCH). Available online at http://nccanch.acf.hhs.gov/pubs/usermanuals/neglect/define.cfm. Despite the older date of this document the information and definitions are still relevant.

- What are the indispensable, minimally adequate types of care that children require?
- What actions or failures to act on the part of the parents or other caretaker constitute neglectful behavior?
- Must the parent's or caretaker's action or inaction be intentional, willful or not?
- What are the effects of the actions or inactions on the child's health, safety, and development?
- Is the family's situation a result of poverty, or a result of parental neglect?

Legal advocates have suggested that definitions of neglect which focus only on the behavior of the parent or caretaker are inadequate. They strongly advocate that the parents' behavior must result in some specific physical damage or impairment or some identifiable symptoms of emotional damage to a child resulting from the parents' behavior or failure to act. Some researchers have also included resultant damage to the physical, emotional, or intellectual development and well-being of the child in the definitions of neglect. Zuravin has concluded, on the contrary, that the focus should be on the actions of the parents, not on the consequences of their behavior, nor on their intent or culpability. Parents who leave preschool-aged children without adult supervision for an hour or more are neglectful, regardless of their intent, or whether the child suffers serious injury or not.

Conceptual definitions of neglect vary, in part, depending on the purpose for which the definition is used. Legal advocates insist on clear evidence of serious harm to a child before court intervention to remove a child from parents. On the other hand, for caseworkers intervening with a family to prevent placement and to protect the child from further harm, the definition of neglect must focus on parental omissions in care that are likely to increase the risk of harm to the child. For researchers interested in studying the long- and short-term consequences of neglect for the child, definitions of neglect would need to focus on parental behaviors that result in harm to the child.

Polansky's conceptual definition of child neglect is widely accepted:

> "A condition in which a caretaker responsible for the child, either deliberately or by extraordinary inattentiveness, permits the child to experience avoidable present suffering and/or fails to provide one or more of the ingredients generally deemed

essential for developing a person's physical, intellectual, and emotional capacities."

This definition meets the demand for inclusion of parental actions, which result in some negative consequences for the child, but fails to specify the required degree of harm to the child. The problem comes in defining what is "generally deemed essential" for a child's physical, intellectual, and emotional development. This definition is heavily dependent upon the ever-changing status of our knowledge about what is physically and psychologically essential for a child's healthy growth and development.

There is a lack of consensus among parents and even among child development researchers on what is essential for child development. Standards of what is essential continue to change as we learn more about child development and those things that impede or enhance children's physical, cognitive, emotional, and social development. For example, the legal requirement that children be restrained in car seats clearly defines a new standard for "minimally adequate care" of children while traveling in cars.

These operational definitions of neglect are highly dependent upon the standards of the local community and of the caseworker who investigates reports of neglect. However, infants and very young children left without adult supervision for hours, children who are not fed regularly, children who are not taken for necessary medical treatment when ill, chronically dirty, lice-infested children, or chronically truant children are consistently accepted as having experienced neglect.

Definitions of what is minimally adequate care or, conversely, inadequate care for children, must also take into account cultural variations in standards for adequate care of children. Significant differences in ratings of the severity of specific indicators of abuse and neglect among social workers, police, attorneys, and judges and among African-American, Hispanic, and white subjects were discovered in one study. African-American subjects rated indicators of physical neglect as significantly more severe instances of inadequate care than did whites or Hispanics. On the other hand, another study concluded that when presented with critical incidents descriptive of child neglect, there was substantial agreement among white, Hispanic, and African-American subjects on basic standards of care for children. Clearly, cultural variations require further consideration in practice and in research.

Poverty is a significant confounding factor in defining child neglect. Although most impoverished families manage to provide strong, nurturing care for their children, the association of child neglect with poverty is clearly supported by many studies. Families receiving Aid to Families with Dependent Children (AFDC) are often reported for neglect. Even among impoverished families, neglectful families are the "poorest of the poor," often lacking adequate housing, health care, and child care.

The difficulty comes in establishing the parents' accountability for providing minimally adequate necessities for their children, such as after school supervision and medical care, in the face of inadequate income, and the absence of accessible, affordable medical and supportive social services. Some State laws specifically exempt inadequate child care because of poverty from the definition of neglect by adding the clause "in spite of availability." Working parents without health insurance may find medical care for their children beyond their resources. Nevertheless, children who are deprived of medical treatment when they are ill are being neglected, regardless of the cause.

Types of Neglect

The Study of National Incidence and Prevalence of Child Abuse and Neglect sought to overcome the problem of nonuniform definitions of child neglect by utilizing a standard definition of neglect. The definitions of neglect included physical neglect, child abandonment and expulsion, medical neglect, inadequate supervision, emotional neglect and educational neglect by parents, parent substitutes, and other adult caretakers of children. The National Incidence Study (NIS) definitions are categorized as follows:

Physical Neglect

Refusal of Health Care: Failure to provide or allow needed care in accord with recommendations of a competent health care professional for a physical injury, illness, medical condition, or impairment.

Delay in Health Care: Failure to seek timely and appropriate medical care for a serious health problem which any reasonable layman would have recognized as needing professional medical attention.

Abandonment: Desertion of a child without arranging for reasonable care and supervision. This category included cases in which children were not claimed within 2 days, and when children were left by parents/substitutes who gave no (or false) information about their whereabouts.

Expulsion: Other blatant refusals of custody, such as permanent or indefinite expulsion of a child from the home without adequate arrangement for care by others, or refusal to accept custody of a returned runaway.

Other Custody Issues: Custody-related forms of inattention to the child's needs other than those covered by abandonment or expulsion. For example, repeated shuttling of a child from one household to another due to apparent unwillingness to maintain custody, or chronically and repeatedly leaving a child with others for days/weeks at a time.

Other Physical Neglect: Conspicuous inattention to avoidable hazards in the home; inadequate nutrition, clothing, or hygiene; and other forms of reckless disregard of the child's safety and welfare, such as driving with the child while intoxicated, leaving a young child unattended in a motor vehicle, and so forth.

Supervision

Inadequate Supervision: Child left unsupervised or inadequately supervised for extended periods of time or allowed to remain away from home overnight without the parent/substitute knowing (or attempting to determine) the child's whereabouts.

Emotional Neglect

Inadequate Nurturance/Affection: Marked inattention to the child's needs for affection, emotional support, attention, or competence.

Chronic/Extreme Abuse or Domestic Violence: Chronic or extreme spouse abuse or other domestic violence in the child's presence.

Permitted Drug/Alcohol Abuse: Encouraging or permitting drug or alcohol use by the child; cases of the child's drug/alcohol use were included here if it appeared that the parent/guardian had been informed of the problem and had not attempted to intervene.

Permitted Other Maladaptive Behavior: Encouragement or permitting of other maladaptive behavior (e.g., severe assaultiveness, chronic delinquency) in circumstances in which the parent/guardian had reason to be aware of the existence and seriousness of the problem but did not attempt to intervene.

Refusal of Psychological Care: Refusal to allow needed and available treatment for a child's emotional or behavioral impairment or problem in accord with competent professional recommendation.

Delay in Psychological Care: Failure to seek or provide needed treatment for a child's emotional or behavioral impairment or problem which any reasonable layman would have recognized as needing professional psychological attention (e.g., severe depression, suicide attempt).

Other Emotional Neglect: Other inattention to the child's developmental/emotional needs not classifiable under any of the above forms of emotional neglect (e.g., markedly overprotective restrictions which foster immaturity or emotional over dependence, chronically applying expectations clearly inappropriate in relation to the child's age or level of development, etc.)

Educational Neglect

Permitted Chronic Truancy: Habitual truancy averaging at least 5 days a month was classifiable under this form of maltreatment if the parent/guardian had been informed of the problem and had not attempted to intervene.

Failure to Enroll/Other Truancy: Failure to register or enroll a child of mandatory school age, causing the school-aged child to remain at home for nonlegitimate reasons (e.g., to work, to care for siblings, etc.) an average of at least 3 days a month.

Inattention to Special Education Need: Refusal to allow or failure to obtain recommended remedial educational services, or neglect in obtaining or following through with treatment for a child's diagnosed learning disorder or other special education need without reasonable cause.

According to the 1988 NIS-2 study, almost 43 percent of the identified neglect was physical neglect, which included children living in unsafe housing, not being fed nutritionally adequate meals, being consistently without adequate clothing, and receiving grossly inadequate care for personal hygiene. The second largest category of neglect was inadequate supervision of children (36.6 percent) and failure or delay in providing health care (20.8 percent).

Large numbers of very young children are left without supervision or left in the care of only slightly older children who lack the judgment and maturity to safely provide for the infants and very young children. One study indicated that 22 percent of all first-time reports to New York's central child abuse registry during 1982–1983 contained allegations of lack of supervision. Often, children are left in this dangerous situation while their parents work or attend to other business. This category of neglect is difficult to define. At what age may a child be left unattended, and for what period of time? At what age is a child competent to care for a younger sibling? Much depends upon the safety of the environment and the child's level of maturity and intelligence. These criteria are highly subjective and vary significantly among ethnic and subcultural groups. Young school-aged children in Oriental, Hispanic, and low-income African-American families are often expected to care for very young siblings in the absence of parents. Yet, studies have indicated a relatively high rate of injuries to children and child fatalities due to this type of neglect.

Thus, there are many types of child neglect and an array of contributing factors. Abandonment of the child may stem from parental alcoholism, drug abuse, or despair. Inattention to dangerous, avoidable hazards in the home, such as unprotected heaters or fireplaces, may stem from lack of knowledge, poverty, and/or apathy. A significant delay in obtaining medical treatment for serious, acute, or chronic illness or accidental injury may be the result of lack of knowledge, lack of transportation, prohibitive cost, or other barriers to seeking medical services. Sexual abuse may be the result of a parent's failure to provide adequate supervision of a young child. Alcohol and drug abuse is a factor in a rapidly increasing percentage of child neglect cases, with estimates now running as high as 70 percent in some urban areas. Some parents meet the minimal physical needs of their children, but ignore their need for critical emotional nurturance.

Withholding of Medically Indicated Treatment from Newborn Infants

The withholding of medically indicated treatment from newborn infants with serious birth defects that are life-threatening is a category of neglect that was defined in the amended Child Abuse Prevention and Treatment Act of 1984 (P.L. 984576). These situations have been referred to as "Baby Doe" cases, after a 1982 Indiana court case contesting the parents' rights to withhold medical treatment, food, and water from an infant who was born with a life-threatening but surgically correctable condition that prevented oral feeding.

The 1984 amendments to the Child Abuse Prevention and Treatment Act defined as neglectful: "The failure to provide treatment (including appropriate nutrition, hydration or medication) which, in the judgment of the physician would be most likely to be effective in ameliorating or correcting the life-threatening condition." The law and the regulations issued by the Department of Health and Human Services require that States receiving Federal funds for CPS programs regard the withholding of medically indicated treatment from these disabled infants with life-threatening conditions as a form of neglect and to actively investigate reported cases. Hospitals are likewise obligated to observe the provisions of the law and to post notices in newborn wards that failure to feed and provide care for disabled infants is a violation of Federal law.

The law does make exception for withholding treatment (other than nutrition, hydration, or medication) to an infant when, in the physician's reasonable medical judgment:

- The infant is chronically and irreversibly comatose.
- The provision of such treatment would merely prolong dying, be ineffective in correcting the life-threatening condition, or be futile in terms of the survival of the infant.
- The treatment would be virtually futile in terms of the survival of the infant and the treatment itself would in such a situation be inhumane. Food and water must always be provided regardless of the extent of disabilities, and "quality of life" cannot be used as a criterion for deciding upon appropriate medical treatment.

Decisions about minimally adequate care for these infants present difficult moral and ethical dilemmas for physicians, hospital personnel, and parents of infants born with severely disabling mental and physical handicaps.

Prenatal Exposure to Drugs

Considerable controversy surrounds the issue of prenatal exposure of infants to drugs and alcohol. Courts are still debating whether such exposure is neglectful behavior on the part of a pregnant woman. Pregnant women who abuse alcohol, however, have exposed their fetuses to the serious mental and physical disabilities known as fetal alcohol syndrome. An estimated 73 percent of pregnant women have used alcohol sometime during their pregnancy. The incidence of fetal alcohol syndrome is 1.9 births per 1,000. Prenatal exposure to cocaine and other drugs also results in negative developmental consequences for 30–40 percent of the estimated 500,000–740,000 drug-exposed infants in the United States.

Failure to Thrive/Malnutrition

Children whose physical development falls below the third percentile in height and or weight for no known medical reason have been designated "nonorganic failure to thrive." Recent thinking calls for categorizing all children whose development is thus significantly impeded by inadequate nutritional intake as "acutely malnourished." The parents' failure to provide necessary nutritional and/or emotional nurturing, often in spite of efforts to do so, presents a challenging problem which has proven difficult to remedy beyond immediate improvements with hospitalization. Failure to thrive children respond with improved weight gain and developmental progress to inpatient hospital treatment, which includes intensive enhancement of nutritional and emotional nurturing. Normal developmental progress frequently does not continue when the children are returned home to the care of parents, and follow-up studies indicate continuing developmental delays in about half of the children. Outcomes of intervention appear to bc related to the cause of failure to thrive and the parents' degree of awareness and cooperation with the treatment. The less chronic the developmental failure and the greater awareness and cooperation of parents, the more positive the outcomes.

Deficits in the critical bonding and attachment process between parent and child are thought to be at least partially responsible for the significant developmental delays among children. Depression and other personality problems in the parents, lack of knowledge about child care, poverty, and other sources of social stress have been identified as contributing causes of nonorganic failure to thrive.

Chronic vs. "New" Neglect

Recent studies have revealed significant differences in the characteristics and problems of chronically neglectful families and "new" neglectful families. Chronically neglecting families had more and older children, were poorer, had more problems, and less parenting knowledge than the newly neglecting families. Newly neglecting families had higher levels of stress, especially from recent serious illness or injury, and drugs were more likely to be a problem in their communities than for the chronically neglecting families.

The distinction between chronic and "new" cases of neglect may not hold up over time, however. "New" cases may actually represent the initial phase (stage) of chronic neglect. Whether this is so, requires further research on the outcomes of "new" neglectful families.

To summarize, the definition of child neglect is problematic because of the lack of consensus on what is considered minimally adequate care of children. Although there is general agreement among professionals and the general public on what is clearly inadequate care, there are differences among professionals and ethnic groups on minimally acceptable levels of physical, psychological, and educational care and nurturing for children of different ages. Conceptual definitions of neglect differ depending upon the purpose for which they are used. Clear evidence of specific harm to a child is needed in legal proceedings for removal of a child from a parent's custody. Protective services intervention to remedy parental omissions and prevent placements may use definitions of neglect that focus on parental skills deficits and the risk of harm to a child. There are newly debated areas of neglect that present difficult moral-ethical dilemmas, for example, prenatal exposure to drugs in utero. Research studies on neglect suggest that it is important for the child protection practitioner, policy maker, and the researcher to clearly differentiate among the specific types of neglect being considered.

Chapter 6

Munchausen Syndrome by Proxy (MSBP)

Background

Self-mutilation and fictitious diseases have been recorded in our written history since Biblical times and the middle ages. Baron Hieronymous Karl Friedrich von Munchausen was an eighteenth century German mercenary officer for the Russian cavalry. After his days in the military he entertained friends and told outlandish, overblown tales of his conquest.[1] In 1794, he married a seventeen-year-old maiden, Bernhardine Brun. Baron Munchausen was 74. A year later, they had a son and he died at age 1 under dubious circumstances.[2]

In 1877, Charcot described adults who exhibited a pattern of self-mutilation and falsifying medical records in order to gain hospital admission.[2] In 1951 Asher coined the term "Munchausen syndrome" to describe a pattern of factitious illness he observed in his patients.[3]

Discussion

Munchausen syndrome is a psychiatric disorder in which patients may inflict injuries upon themselves, fabricate symptoms, and attempt to deceive healthcare professionals in order to gain sympathy, attention, and hospitalization. The American Psychiatric Association's *Diagnostic and Statistical Manual of Disorders (DSM-IV)* defines it as the "intentional production of physical symptoms."[4]

"Munchausen Syndrome," by LCDR Steve Hargitai, DDS, MS, National Naval Medical Center, February 2001. Reprinted with permission of the author.

A variant form of, and more distressing, is a condition called Munchausen Syndrome by Proxy (MSBP). In these cases, the individual inflicts injuries on others for the same reasons, to gain attention. Unfortunately, it is usually a parent harming their child. This is a form of child abuse.

Epidemiology/Patient Profile

The prevalence of these syndromes is unknown.[5] There is no sex predilection in Munchausen's syndrome. However, in the case of MSBP, it is usually a mother inducing illness on her child. These people may have frontal temporal atrophy and other psychological defects.[6]

The typical patient is one who may have had extensive medical treatment as a child. They may have been abused. They tend to hold a grudge against the medical establishment, possibly for a previous bad experience in the healthcare setting. They may have a connection with the medical community. They may have been a professional or an employee in the healthcare system, or they may have had a parent who was a doctor or nurse. These people feel neglected, under-appreciated, and usually have trouble in their personal life.[4]

In the case of MSBP the parent, usually the mother, is very interested in the details of her child's illness. She seems friendly and very helpful. Fathers are usually unavailable.[7]

Recognition

A Munchausen patient is very skilled in faking injuries and illness. Differentiating factitious injuries from actual ones proves to be very difficult. It typically takes a long time and many visits before suspicion is raised among the medical staff. Often the medical team perpetuates the condition by performing a myriad of exams, tests, and surgeries. The signs and symptoms these patients present with are limited only by their imagination.

Munchausen patients are hospital hoppers. They roam from clinic to clinic as they exhaust the efforts of each. In one case a patient was hospitalized over 100 times in 18 months.[8]

Diagnosis can be made by careful history. Sometimes the injury does not coincide with the story. Do not underestimate their ability to deceive. Laboratory tests that seem irrational or unexplainable may be a clue. They may have extensive scarring from previous, unnecessary surgery.[9]

The MSBP parent can be identified by entirely different criteria. After physically injuring their child or inappropriately medicating them, they report to the clinic. The clues are as follows: an over-protective mother, the mother seems very medically knowledgeable, the parent does not leave the child's side, the parent is unusually calm in light of the child's situation, the child's symptoms improve when the mother is away, unstable relationship between parents, the child's condition is taking an unusual course and does not respond well to treatment or it responds only temporarily. The mother and child may return again in weeks or months after discharge with identical or new problems.

In MSBP, again the clinician should be cognizant of puzzling laboratory values and unusual physical signs. If permissible by law, a hidden camera may be employed to confirm suspicions. Often the mother is caught manipulating the machines, IV lines, altering dosages, and disconnecting vital equipment. When questioned, they become defensive and deny the accusations.

Cases

- A 30 year-old female mimicked a temporomandibular disorder, was treated surgically, and repeatedly re-opened her surgical site.[9]
- A 32 year-old woman with 10 previous TMJ surgeries underwent another TMJ surgery at UCLA dental school unbeknownst to the surgeon. She was caught repeatedly inserting her fingers into the wounds.[19]
- 57 year-old male claims he was assaulted with iron bar that broke his orbital rim. Indeed, he did have a step defect. On surgery, the bone was remodeled indicating this injury occurred long before.[1]
- A young male, substance abuser, and with ties to the healthcare community injected himself with insulin and applied atropine drops into his eye to gain hospitalization.[10]
- Female alleged being raped. She inserted wax crayons into her vagina.[11]
- A young woman complained of vaginal discharge. Testing revealed she was placing cigarette ashes into her underwear.[12]
- A 6-month-old girl was brought in with vaginal bleeding. Blood tests showed the blood was most likely that of the mother.[13]

- A mother poisons her two children with diphenhydramine.[7]
- A 73-year-old debilitated female had persistent hypoglycemia. The daughter was a surgical nurse who kept injecting her with insulin to keep her in the hospital. The daughter appeared very concerned whenever the staff was about to discharge her mother.[14]
- A 28-year-old male reports with a burning sensation of the left cheek periodically in the past year. He had peripheral scarring and hyperpigmentation. The man was an alcoholic and had a rocky relationship with his wife. Each time the man was inebriated and passed out, his wife would pour acid on his cheek in hopes of frightening him into abstaining from drinking.[15]
- A 34-year-old man sedated two female partners and injected them with gasoline. In prison, he did the same to his cellmate with turpentine.[16]
- A hospitalized patient with unexplained continued infection was found to be injecting his own feces into his IV line.

Consequences

People suffering from Munchausen syndrome or MSBP are pathologic liars and deny the diagnosis when confronted.[17] They can undergo many unnecessary hospitalizations and surgeries. In the case of MSBP, the child may be removed from the parents and placed in foster care. The child is indeed in danger of physical harm. This is a form of child abuse. These patients do not comply with the recommended psychiatric care. However, it can be treatable. The worst possible outcome is death from continued attempts at self-medicating, inducing injuries, and undergoing treatments and surgeries.

These patients represent a burden to the healthcare system. Wasted time and cost is extraordinary and is typically in the thousands per visit or higher.[18] Keeping blacklists and video monitoring may have legal consequences for the institution.

Conclusion

Healthcare professionals working in large institutions and even private practitioners need to be aware of this syndrome whenever there are continued patient visits with puzzling presentation and findings. The goal of the Munchausen syndrome sufferer is to gain emotional awards like attention and support. It is to be differentiated from malingering where they seek rewards such as convalescent leave or worker's compensation.

The opinions and assertions contained in this article are the private ones of the authors and are not to be construed as official or reflecting the views of the Department of the Navy.

References

1. Aghabeigi B, Manisali M, et al. Ocular Psychiatric disorders in maxillofacial injuries. *Int.l Journal of Oral and Maxillofacial Surgery,* 1998: 27: 195-198.
2. Asher Meadow. Website on MSP: www.bcpl.net/agravels/whatis.htm
3. Asher R. Munchausen's syndrome. *Lancet*, 1951: 1: 580-585.
4. American Psychiatric Association *DSM-IV. Diagnostic and Statistical Manual of Mental Disorders. Fourth edition.* Washington DC: American Psychiatric Association, 1994:445-471.
5. Edi-Osagie ECO, Hopkins RE, et al. Munchausen's Syndrome in Obstetrics and Gynecology: A Review. *Obstetrical and Gynecological Survey*, 1997: 53: 1: 45-49.
6. Babe KS, Peterson AM, et al. The pathogenesis of Munchausen's syndrome: A review and case report. *Gen Hosp Psychiatry*, 1992: 14: 273.
7. Arnold SA, Arnholz D, et al. Two Siblings Poisoned with Diphenhydramine: A case of Factitious Disorder by Proxy. *Annals of Emergency Medicine*, 1998: 32: 2: 256-259.
8. Goodlin RC. Pregnant Women with Munchausen's syndrome. *Am J Obstet Gynecol*, 1985: 153: 207.
9. Howard IA, Scrivani SJ. *The Interdisciplinary Approach to Oral, Facial, and Head Pain,* 2000: 131: 919-926.
10. Bretz SW, Richards JR. Munchausen syndrome presenting acutely in the emergency department. *J Emerg Med*, 2000: 18: 417-420.
11. Gibbon KL. Munchausen syndrome presenting as an acute Sexual assault. *Med Sci Law*, 1998: 38: 202-205.

12. Edi-Osagie ECO, Hopkins RE. Munchausen's syndrome: A bizarre case of refractory vaginal discharge. *Eur J Obstet Gynaeocol Reprod Biol*, 1997: 72: 105.

13. Hopkins RE, Ellis JE. Precocious menstruation: A warning. *Br J Sexual Med*, 1991: Spring: 12.

14. Ben-Chetrit E, Melmed RN. Recurrent hypoglycaemia in multiple myeloma: a case of Munchausen syndrome by proxy in an elderly patient. *Journal of Internal Medicine*, 1998: 244: 175-178.

15. Somani VK. Witchcraft's syndrome: Munchausen's syndrome by proxy. *Int J Dermatol*, 1998: 37: 229-230.

16. Sigal MD, Altmark D, et al. Munchausen syndrome by proxy: a perpetrator abusing two adults. *J Nerv Ment Dis*, 1985: 174: 696-698.

17. King BH, Ford CV. Pseudologia fantastica. *Acta Psychiatry Scand*, 1988: 77: 1.

18. Reich JD, Hanno PM. Factitious renal colic. *Urology*, 1997: 50: 858-862.

19. Stiles A., Mitrirattanakul S, et al. Munchausen syndrome presenting in a patient who has undergone temporomandibular joint surgery. *OOOOE*, 2001: 91(1): 20-22.

Chapter 7

Maltreatment of Children with Disabilities

The Risk and Prevention of Maltreatment of Children with Disabilities

Child maltreatment, also known as abuse and neglect, affects all types of children, but children with disabilities may be at even greater risk of being maltreated than children without disabilities. Why? And what can be done to prevent maltreatment of children with disabilities?

This chapter considers the scope and nature of the problem and ways to prevent it in light of current research. (This chapter will not address issues of reporting, assessing, investigating, or treating maltreatment of children with disabilities.)

This chapter contains information from "The Risk and Prevention of Maltreatment of Children with Disabilities," from *IN FOCUS: The Risk and Prevention of Maltreatment of Children with Disabilities.* National Clearinghouse for Child Abuse and Neglect Information, February 2001. Available online at http://nccanch.acf.hhs.gov/pubs/prevenres/focus.cfm. This chapter also contains text reprinted with permission from "Respite Care for Children with Developmental and/or Physical Disabilities: A Parent's Perspective," revised December 2003; "Respite Services for Families with Adolescents at Risk of Abuse or Neglect," revised December 2003; and "Respite for Foster Parents," revised 2003. These fact sheets are produced by the ARCH National Respite Network and Resource Center. Additional information is available on the ARCH website, http://www.archrespite.org

What is the scope of the problem?

Researchers have had difficulty estimating rates of maltreatment among children with disabilities. One reason is that States do not collect the same data about maltreated children in the same ways. Another reason is that researchers identify disabilities among maltreated children in different ways.

Maltreatment is generally defined using the Federal Child Abuse Prevention and Treatment Act (CAPTA) definition[1], but States vary in their guidelines used to substantiate, or identify, maltreatment. Disability is generally defined using the Federal Americans with Disabilities Act (ADA)[2], but only 19 States record pre-existing disabilities on their Child Protective Services (CPS) forms (Bonner, Crow and Hensley, 1997), so researchers must use other means to identify disabilities among children who have been maltreated. Given these difficulties, "The real extent of the problem . . . remains a frightening unknown" (Mitchell and Buchele-Ash, 2000, p. 227).

Nonetheless, available research has found that children with disabilities are more vulnerable to maltreatment than children without disabilities. The only national study conducted to date (Crosse, Kaye and Ratnofsky, n.d.), was completed in 1993. The study found that children with disabilities were 1.7 times more likely to be maltreated than children without disabilities. Crosse et al. used data from NIS-2, the second congressionally mandated National Incidence Study of child maltreatment. (NIS-1 was completed in 1980, NIS-2 in 1988, and NIS-3 in 1996.) The Crosse et al. study indicated that while 21.3 per 1,000 children without disabilities are maltreated each year, 35.5 per 1,000 children with disabilities are maltreated each year. Put another way, approximately 175,000 to 300,000 U.S. children with disabilities are maltreated each year, if it is estimated that between 9 percent and 15 percent of all children in the United States have a disability of some kind.

Crosse et al. acknowledge that their study may underestimate the incidence of maltreatment of children with disabilities. A study conducted in Omaha, Nebraska, in 1997 found that children with disabilities were 3.4 times more likely to be maltreated than were children without disabilities (Sullivan and Knutson, 2000). Although the Omaha study did not use a national sample, its findings underscore the need for more research on the scope of the problem.

These are the only two recent studies that have attempted to measure the scope of the problem. (Twenty-two studies were conducted in the United States between 1967 and 1992 [Sobsey, 1994], but this chapter addresses only the most current research.)

What are the characteristics of victims and perpetrators?

Some researchers have compared the characteristics of maltreated children with and without disabilities. Studies also have looked at characteristics of the adults who maltreat children with disabilities. Studies that compared the characteristics of maltreated children with and without disabilities reported different findings:

- Crosse et al. (n.d.) found that maltreated children with disabilities were generally older than maltreated children without disabilities.
- Sullivan and Knutson (2000) found they were generally the same age.
- Wolcott (1997) found they were generally younger.

In addition, Crosse et al. found that maltreated children with disabilities were disproportionately white as compared to maltreated children without disabilities, but Wolcott found the proportions of both groups who were white to be about the same. All three studies found that maltreated children with disabilities were more likely to be male than maltreated children without disabilities, although it should be noted that more males are diagnosed with disabilities.

Most studies of adult perpetrators indicate that the majority of perpetrators are family members; this is true for maltreated children with and without disabilities (Crosse et al., n.d.; Sullivan and Cork, 1996). Among all family members, mothers are most frequently the perpetrators of maltreatment (Crosse et al., n.d.; Sullivan and Knutson, 2000), although it should be noted that mothers are most often the primary caretakers of children (Sobsey, 1994). However, sexual abuse of children with disabilities is more often committed by males who are not relatives of the victims; this is also true for children without disabilities who are sexually abused (Sobsey, 1994; Sullivan and Knutson, 2000).

Non-family members who maltreat children with disabilities come in contact with their victims in many different ways. Perpetrators can include teachers, health care providers, residential care providers, transportation staff, volunteers, babysitters, and peers (Ammerman and Baladerian, 1993; Sobsey, 1994).

Is there a relationship between the type of maltreatment and type of disability?

Some studies have explored the relationship between the type of maltreatment and type of disability. Child welfare agencies generally group maltreatment into four categories: physical abuse, sexual abuse, neglect, and emotional maltreatment. Table 7.1 shows findings from two studies that explored the likelihood that children with disabilities will experience a particular type of maltreatment.

These studies both found that neglect was the most common form of maltreatment for children with disabilities as well as for children without disabilities. Sullivan and Knutson (2000) also found that "children with disabilities tended to be maltreated multiple times and in multiple ways" (p. 9).

Both of these studies (Crosse et al. and Sullivan and Knutson) also explored which types of disabilities place children at greatest risk of maltreatment. Disabilities examined in both studies include mental retardation, speech/language impairments, emotional disabilities, learning disabilities, and physical health impairments. Sullivan and Knutson also included hearing and visual impairments. Both studies found that of all types of disabilities, emotional and behavioral disorders showed the highest prevalence rate of abuse and neglect. Sullivan and Knutson (2000) found that children with behavioral disorders were at highest risk, followed by children with speech/language disorders, mental retardation, and health impairments. Crosse et al. (n.d.) found that serious emotional disturbance puts children at the highest risk, followed by learning disabilities, speech/language impairments, and physical health problems. (To fully understand these findings, it is helpful to understand each study's methodology. See References for a complete list of citations.)

Why are children with disabilities at higher risk for maltreatment than children without disabilities?

Researchers have identified a number of factors related to parents, children, families, service systems, and society at large that increase the

Table 7.1. Likelihood of Maltreatment of Children with Disabilities Compared to Children without Disabilities, by Type of Maltreatment

Type of Maltreatment	Crosse et al., not dated	Sullivan and Knutson, 2000
Neglect	1.6 times as likely	3.8 times as likely
Sexual Abuse	1.8 times as likely	3.1 times as likely
Physical Abuse	2.1 times as likely	3.8 times as likely
Emotional Maltreatment	2.8 times as likely	3.9 times as likely

potential for maltreatment of children with disabilities (Ammerman, 1997; Burrell, Thompson and Sexton, 1994; Mitchell and Buchele-Ash, 2000; Sobsey, 1994; Steinberg and Hylton, 1998). However, there is disagreement among researchers regarding the legitimacy of certain risk factors.

There is general acceptance that no single factor places any child at risk for abuse and neglect. Rather, it is the interaction of factors that seems to be important. Sobsey (1994) proposes the integrated ecological model of abuse to explain the interaction of factors that may lead to abuse or neglect. Sobsey's model (which is based on Bronfenbrenner's ecological model of child development) takes into account cultural and environmental factors as well as characteristics of the parent and child and their interactions. When using this model for abuse prevention, Sobsey focuses particularly on power inequities between the potential offender and potential victim.

Some of the factors that place children with disabilities at risk for abuse and neglect are the same factors that place all children at risk (Ammerman and Patz, 1996; Sobsey, 1994; Tomison, 1996). But many factors are more connected to disability-related issues (Tomison, 1996).

General Risk Factors for All Children

Certain factors related to parents are associated with increased risk of maltreatment for all children. Parental substance abuse is a risk factor identified by many researchers (Sobsey, 1994; Steinberg and Hylton, 1998; Wolcott, 1997). Other parent-related risk factors are poor coping skills, poor impulse control, and a history of violence (Ammerman and Baladerian, 1993; Sobsey, 1994). Parents with low self-esteem or who have been diagnosed with depression may be at greater risk for maltreating their children (Sobsey, 1994; Sullivan and Cork, 1996) as may be parents who were victims of child maltreatment themselves (Jones, Peterson, Goldberg, Goldberg, and Smith, 1995; Sobsey, 1994). Parents who are disabled may be at risk for maltreating their children, especially if they were raised in group care and lacked positive parenting models (Sobsey, 1994).

Factors Related to Disability

These include factors related to society, stress, families, the children, and non-familial caregivers.

Societal risk factors. Many researchers believe that societal attitudes and beliefs play a significant role in placing children with disabilities at risk for maltreatment. Steinberg and Hylton (1998) contend that some institutionalized beliefs, practices, and policies "devalue" children with disabilities. This may be manifested in ways that indicate children with disabilities are not as worthy of social, educational, or professional opportunities as children without disabilities. Children with disabilities may internalize societal attitudes and feel shame or feel less worthy of being treated respectfully (National Resource Center on Child Sexual Abuse, 1994). Sobsey (1994) adds that segregating children with disabilities tends to increase the perception of differences and suggests that ". . . group membership and social distance influence our attitudes about the acceptability of violence. Attitudes about individuals or groups that tend to depersonalize, dehumanize, or distance them appear to make violence against them more acceptable" (p. 307).

In addition, myths associated with children with disabilities can increase risk. Sobsey (1994) discusses the myth held by many that children with disabilities are not vulnerable to abuse; belief in this myth can result in a lack of awareness and attention to the problem. Steinberg and Hylton (1998), citing Baladerian (1994), discuss myths such as:

- Children with disabilities are asexual and therefore do not need sex education (denying them information that may help to prevent abuse)
- Some children with disabilities are unable to manage their own behavior (resulting in caretakers exerting unnecessary control)
- Some children with disabilities do not feel pain (resulting in aversive therapies being used)
- All caretakers are special and good (resulting in a lack of awareness and attention to signs of abuse or neglect).

Stress as a risk factor. Many researchers propose that stress is a critical factor in child maltreatment (Ammerman, 1997; Burrell, Thompson and Sexton, 1994; Rycus and Hughes, 1998; Tomison, 1996), while others say that little research supports this theory (Benedict, Wulff and White, 1992; Sobsey, 1994). And while stress may be a risk factor for some families, Sobsey states that most families that have children with disabilities do not, in fact, respond abusively to stress. Those supporting stress as a risk factor point to the increased demands of caring for children with disabilities, which may involve daily assistance with bathing, dressing, eating, transporting, and providing medical care (Ammerman and Baladerian, 1993; Rogow and Hass, 1999; Tomison, 1996). They also discuss the difficulties of coping with challenging behaviors such as temper tantrums, aggressiveness, and noncompliance (Ammerman, 1997; Jones, et al., 1995; Tomison, 1996). Some children with disabilities require much supervision and highly structured and consistent limit-setting (Ammerman and Patz, 1996; Kragthorpe, et al., 1997). In some cases, parents' lack of knowledge about caring for their children with disabilities can be a factor in their ability to cope with their children's needs. This lack of knowledge can result in unrealistic expectations for the children (Ammerman, 1993; Kragthorpe, et al., 1997).

A lack of resources can exacerbate a parent's stress. Most often discussed is a lack of social support, resulting in isolation of the family from their community. Sobsey (1994), citing Smith (1984), states that "A large body of research indicates that isolation from society increases risk and inclusion in society decreases it" (p. 160-1). Researchers have also explored the relationship between stress and a lack of financial resources and available services and their contribution to risk of maltreatment (Steinberg and Hylton, 1998). Poverty and/or inadequate supportive services can create stressful situations within a family. Ammerman and Patz (1996) and Rycus and Hughes (1998) specifically mention a lack of access to respite care as a risk factor. Without support for the family, parents may feel isolated, have little personal time for themselves, and become overwhelmed by their responsibilities (Ammerman, 1993; Tomison, 1996).

Familial risk factors. Many of the risk factors identified by researchers are specifically related to the family's reaction to the child with the disability. For example, the risk of maltreatment may be higher if the parents view the child as "different" and unlike any other child, if they "mourn" the loss of a "normal" child and become angry (Rycus and Hughes, 1998), or if they see the disability as an embarrassment or perceived punishment (Burrell, Thompson and Sexton, 1994).

Another potential risk factor involves unhealthy attachment or disruptions in the bonding and attachment between parent and child. Sobsey (1994) explains that healthy attachment is characterized by mutual pleasure and pain; if one individual suffers, the other suffers, and vice versa. Unhealthy attachment disrupts this mutuality. "Sadly, information given to parents by professionals at the time disability is diagnosed often implicitly or explicitly contains the message—'Don't get too attached to this child.'" (Sobsey, 1994, p.161-2). Disruptions in attachment can occur if there are frequent hospitalizations or if the child is unresponsive or unaffectionate (Ammerman and Patz, 1996; Sobsey, 1994; Tomison, 1996).

Some researchers have found that risk for maltreatment is higher for children with mild disabilities, and speculate that this could be because parents have expectations for them that cannot be fulfilled (Ammerman and Patz, 1996; Benedict, Wulff and White, 1992). Some researchers found a higher risk of neglect when parents could not, or did not, provide the level of care required by the child's disability (Ammerman and Baladerian, 1993; Jones, et al., 1995; Rycus and Hughes, 1998).

Child-related risk factors. Numerous risk factors related to the child with the disability have been identified. In actuality, many of the factors discussed here are considered "socially mediated effects of disability." This refers to people's response to the child with a disability, rather than to the child or the disability itself. Although some feel that viewing child-related characteristics as risk factors is "victim blaming" (Tomison, 1996), it is important to note these characteristics, especially in conjunction with the many other factors already discussed.

Because the care required by some children with disabilities is critical to their survival, many have been taught to obey those in authority and comply with their caretakers' requests or demands (National Resource Center on Child Sexual Abuse, 1994; Steinberg and Hylton, 1998). In fact, some children with disabilities may feel that their bodies don't belong to them (National Resource Center on Child Sexual Abuse, 1994; Steinberg and Hylton, 1998; Tobin, 1992). If a caretaker behaves inappropriately, a child may not complain or resist because he or she believes the caretaker knows what is best.

Many researchers have found that some children with disabilities lack the knowledge or understanding to know when behavior is wrong or inappropriate (Ammerman, 1992; Steinberg and Hylton, 1998; Wolcott, 1997). Even if they do recognize behaviors as wrong, some children with disabilities may not attempt to stop the abuse or neglect because they fear losing the relationship; they are emotionally dependent on their caretakers (National Resource Center on Child Sexual Abuse, 1994; Tobin, 1992). In some cases, their disability may prevent them from being able to defend themselves or escape (Ammerman, 1992; Steinberg and Hylton, 1998). Finally, children who have difficulty communicating may be at a higher risk for maltreatment because potential perpetrators may believe they can "get away with it," thinking that the child will not be able to report the behavior (Ammerman and Patz, 1993; Wolcott, 1997). "...[C]hildren with disabilities may be perceived as being relatively 'safe victims.'" (Dr. Frieda Meacham in National Symposium on Abuse and Neglect of Children with Disabilities, 1994).

Risk factors for institutional and non-familial abuse and neglect. Although maltreatment is most often perpetrated by family members, children with disabilities often are cared for by others, and the risk for maltreatment is present in these circumstances. Characteristics of institutional abuse include extreme power and control inequities, dehumanizing and detachment from the children, clustering of vulnerable children with those who might harm them, isolation of children, and an abusive subculture (Sobsey, 1994; Steinberg and Hylton, 1998). As with parents, issues of attachment can be factors in the risk for maltreatment by non-family caregivers. Sobsey (1994) states "Often paid caregivers are deliberately discouraged from becoming attached to clients by the ethic of professional detachment and the organizational needs of agencies.... The relatively weak bonds that formulate between staff and the people they serve cannot be expected to deter abuse..." (p. 162).

What can be done to prevent abuse and neglect of children with disabilities?

As Ammerman and Baladerian (1993) state, "The physical, emotional, and financial costs of abuse and neglect are so great as to make prevention the number one priority in the effort to eliminate maltreatment of children" (p. 9). If abuse or neglect does occur, it is important to report, investigate, and treat the problem. But it is equally important to address efforts to prevent abuse and neglect. Prevention may be aimed at the general public (known as primary prevention) or targeted specifically to families considered at risk of child maltreatment (known as secondary prevention). (A third form of prevention, not covered in this chapter, is known as tertiary prevention and is designed to prevent maltreatment from reoccurring.)

Because different, interrelated factors can contribute to child maltreatment, different, coordinated prevention strategies are needed. A multifaceted approach may be the most effective. Approaches may be parallel, in which separate programs are implemented for children with disabilities, or integrated, in which the needs of children with disabilities are accommodated in generic programs serving all children.

Prevention at the Societal Level

One of the first steps in prevention is raising awareness of the problem. Heightened awareness can lead to more funding for research and prevention programs and better programming to combat the problem. The National Symposium on Abuse and Neglect of Children with Disabilities (1995) recommended that 10 percent of Federal funds for child abuse awareness be devoted to disability issues.

Most experts in the field also recommend coordination among relevant parties to ensure that prevention efforts are comprehensive. Governments, services providers and local communities can work together to support families that have children with disabilities, and professionals from many fields can collaborate (Rogow and Hass, 1999). Educators and health care professionals, who are often in contact with children with disabilities, can be trained to understand the problem and their role in preventing it (Wolcott, 1997). One study found that 92 percent of special educators would attend specialized training if it were made available (Orelove, Hollahan and Myles, 2000).

At the societal level, prevention efforts often focus on changing societal attitudes about children with disabilities. The National Symposium on Abuse and Neglect of Children with Disabilities (1995) and Sobsey (1994) recommend promoting inclusion of children with disabilities into everyday life. Steinberg and Hylton (1998) add recommendations including the encouragement to value children with disabilities, see them as individuals and share responsibility for their well-being. Sobsey (1994) adds recommendations such as educating others specifically about people with disabilities, challenging negative attitudes and behaviors and personalizing interactions.

Mitchell and Buchele-Ash (2000) advocate enacting legislation that supports prevention and protection of children with disabilities. For example, the Federal Crime Victims with Disabilities Awareness Act of 1998 was enacted to increase awareness of crimes committed against people with disabilities (including child abuse and neglect), collect data, and develop strategies to address the needs of this population. Mitchell and Buchele-Ash also advocate for adoption of more prevention measures and provision of self-protection education for children with disabilities.

Family-Focused Prevention Efforts

Because much of the maltreatment of children with disabilities occurs within families, many prevention efforts focus on services to families. Goals of family-focused prevention efforts include increasing knowledge and understanding about the child's development; strengthening parenting skills; improving awareness of, and access to, resources; reducing isolation; and developing positive coping skills (Kragthorpe, et al., 1997; Rycus and Hughes, 1998; Steinberg and Hylton, 1998). Services can either be offered to all families that have children with disabilities or to families considered to be at risk of maltreating their children.

One service offered to all families that have children with disabilities is the Individualized Family Service Plan (IFSP). The IFSP is required by the Individuals with Disabilities Education Act (IDEA) for families and their young children with disabilities from birth to age 5. The IFSP includes a multidisciplinary assessment, goal setting and planning, linkage to services, and coordination and monitoring of services (Jones, et al., 1995). Parent involvement is critical to ensure that the plan addresses all of the family's identified needs.

The case management component of the IFSP is an important one. Case managers can advocate for and help coordinate a myriad of resources needed by families (National Symposium on Abuse and Neglect of Children with Disabilities, 1995; Rycus and Hughes, 1998). These services can include educational, medical, and recreational programs for the children; financial assistance for the families; respite care; counseling; and parenting programs. Parenting programs may provide information about the child's disability and realistic expectations for the child's development and may teach positive parenting skills (Ammerman, 1997; Rycus and Hughes, 1998; Sobsey, 1994).

One type of family-focused prevention program that is available to at-risk families that have children with disabilities involves home-visits by trained professionals or para-professionals (Jones, et al., 1995). (Home visitation programs are also widely available for many types of at-risk families.) Home visitation programs often start before or soon after the birth of a child to help build family strengths from the beginning, and may continue until the child is 5 years old. "Home-based services ... set the stage for services and support that are flexible, culturally competent, and responsive to family-identified needs...." (Sandall, 1997).

Another type of family-focused programming is called Parent-to-Parent support. Parents of children with disabilities can trade information on resources and problem-solve together when agency people are not available (i.e., after working hours). Parents who are at risk of maltreating their children with disabilities can benefit by talking with other parents in similar situations (Jones, et al., 1995). They may express vulnerabilities and explore painful options with other parents in ways they wouldn't feel comfortable doing with a professional. A survey conducted in 1996 found that "Parent to Parent support increases parents' sense of being able to cope [and] ... increases parents' acceptance of their situation" (Santelli, Turnbull, Marquis and Lerner, 1997, p. 78). In 1997, there were more than 500 local and 25 statewide Parent to Parent programs serving more than 35,000 parents nationally (Santelli, et al., 1997).

When targeting prevention programs to at-risk families, Sobsey (1994) states that it is important to identify the risk factors in families so programs can set priorities and tailor services to individual families. Many professionals discuss the need to focus on reducing the effects of stress on families that have children with disabilities (Burrell, Thompson and Sexton, 1994; Crosse et al., n.d.; Struck, 1999). For example, Rycus and Hughes (1998) state that services must address three factors in the stress equation:

- Reduce situational and psychological stress
- Strengthen the family's ability to cope and to access supportive resources
- Help the family achieve a realistic perception of their situation.

Family-focused prevention services are an important component in the overall effort to prevent abuse and neglect of children with disabilities. Tomison (1996) says that services should be available as long as a family needs them; once services are pulled out, the family that had been able to cope may fall apart. Public funding and medical insurance coverage are key factors in the availability, accessibility, and longevity of services delivered to families of children with disabilities.

Child-Focused Prevention Efforts

Child maltreatment prevention programs are rarely made available or accessible to children with disabilities (Baladerian, 1994), often due to a lack of funding or a mistaken belief that this population does not need prevention information. In actuality, "[w]ithholding knowledge from individuals with disabilities concerning self-protection increases their vulnerability to abuse and neglect" (Mitchell and Buchele-Ash, 2000, p. 235).

Ammerman and Baladerian (1993) say that child-focused prevention programs for children with disabilities should include sharing information about abuse (how to identify it, how to respond to it, how to tell others) and talking about feelings that may occur if abuse is attempted. In addition, Briggs (1995) states that parental involvement throughout the program is crucial to ensure all family members are aware of and support the program's teachings. A number of researchers talk about the need for more appropriate and accessible programming for children with disabilities (Baladerian, 1994; Kragthorpe, et al., 1997). Kragthorpe states that programs need to be inclusive and sensitive to ability levels, culture, and gender. Steinberg and Hylton (1998) recommend using developmentally appropriate concepts, concrete activities, and audiovisual aids. They also recommend, as does Baladerian in the National Symposium on Abuse and Neglect of Children with Disabilities (1995), that prevention programs for children with disabilities be ongoing rather than a one-shot effort; children with some disabilities may need lessons repeated frequently.

Many programs provide specific information about abuse—what it is, how to recognize it, and what rights children have (Ammerman and Baladerian, 1993; Sobsey, 1994; Tobin, 1992). In addition to education, teaching assertiveness skills is often mentioned as a component of prevention efforts (Baladerian, 1994; Sobsey, 1994; Tobin, 1992). However, Baladerian (1994) cautions that simply telling children with disabilities to say "no" to an adult is often not useful because they are taught to strongly respect and comply with adults in authority. Finally, many abuse prevention programs teach safety and self-defense skills (Baladerian, 1994; Sobsey, 1994; Wolcott, 1997). However, Sobsey (1994) states "... it is important to recognize that many abused people with disabilities, as with other victims of abuse, face extreme power inequities that no amount of individual training can overcome" (p. 178).

Prevention of Non-Familial Abuse and Neglect

Much of the literature examining prevention of non-familial abuse and neglect of children with disabilities focuses on the policies and procedures of agencies providing services to this population. These include careful screening of job applicants, training for staff in positive behavior management techniques, effective staff/client ratios, realistic staff expectations, strong supervision and support, and an explicit commitment to child protection (The Beach Center on Families and Disability, 1997; Kragthorpe et al., 1997; Sobsey, 1994; Steinberg and Hylton, 1998). The National Symposium on Abuse and Neglect of Children with Disabilities (1995) and Steinberg and Hylton (1998) also add that programs should have unannounced checks and investigations conducted by outside agencies. In addition, The Beach Center on Families and Disability (1997) adds that "An open environment that welcomes families has proven to be very effective in reducing abuse and neglect" (p. 2).

Families can play a role in preventing abuse and neglect by other caregivers. Ammerman and Baladerian (1993) say that a parent getting to know and being involved with a child's caretakers can be a deterrent to maltreatment. They add that parents should tell people who care for and interact with the child that the child has been trained in abuse prevention techniques and should discuss abuse awareness with their child.

Conclusion

Children with disabilities are more at risk of abuse and neglect than children without disabilities. The factors that place these children at higher risk include factors that place all children at risk of maltreatment in addition to other risk factors that are more directly related to disabilities. These include:

- Societal attitudes about disabilities
- Peoples' reactions to, and interactions with, children with disabilities (including family members and non-family caregivers)
- Factors that relate to the disability itself
- Program policies and procedures governing the care of children by others.

Primary prevention efforts can improve conditions for all families that have children with disabilities and secondary prevention programs can target children and families who are at high risk of maltreatment. Prevention strategies can attempt to improve:

- Societal attitudes
- Federal policies
- Family dynamics
- Children's knowledge and safety skills
- Programs' policies and procedures.

To justify more funding for prevention programs, including services for children and families and training for professionals, further research is needed to understand the scope and nature of the problem. Better documentation of disabilities in the Child Protective Services system would assist in this process. Current prevention programming should be evaluated to determine its effectiveness. Finally, as Sobsey (1994) states, "... before this problem can be successfully managed, society must adopt attitudes that allow all of its members to see the problem, recognize that it must be addressed, and believe that meaningful change is possible" (p. 304).

References

Ammerman, R.T. (1992). Sexually abused children with multiple disabilities: Each is unique, as are their needs. *NRCCSA News,* 1(4), 13-14.

Ammerman, R.T. (1997). Physical abuse and childhood disability: Risk and treatment factors. In R. Geffner, S.B. Sorenson, and P. K. Lundberg-Love (Eds.), *Violence and Sexual Abuse at Home: Current Issues in Spousal Battering and Child Maltreatment* (pp. 207-224). The Hawthorne Press, Inc.

Ammerman, R.T. and Baladerian, N.J. (1993). Maltreatment of children with disabilities. National Committee to Prevent Child Abuse.

Ammerman, R.T. and Patz, R. J. (1996). Determinants of child abuse potential: Contribution of parent and child factors. *Journal of Clinical Child Psychology,* 25(3), 300-307.

Baladerian, N.J. (1994). Abuse and neglect of children with disabilities. ARCH National Resource Center for Respite and Crisis Care Services.

The Beach Center on Families and Disability. (1997). How to reduce abuse and neglect of children with disabilities. University of Kansas.

The Beach Center on Families and Disability, the University of Kansas, and the Erikson Institute of Chicago. (1995). National symposium on abuse and neglect of children with disabilities. Abuse and neglect of children with disabilities: Report and recommendations. Lawrence, KS: Author.

Benedict, M.I., Wulff, L.M. and White, R.B. (1992). Current parental stress in maltreating and nonmaltreating families of children with multiple disabilities. *Child Abuse and Neglect,* 16(2), 155-163.

Bonner, B.L., Crow, S.M. and Hensley, L.D. (1997). State efforts to identify maltreated children with disabilities: A follow-up study. *Child Maltreatment,* 2(1), 52-60.

Briggs, F. (1995). Developing Personal Safety Skills in Children with Disabilities. Baltimore, MD: Paul H. Brookes Publishing Co.

Burrell, B., Thompson, B. and Sexton, D. (1994). Predicting child abuse potential across family types. *Child Abuse and Neglect,* 18(12), 1039-1049.

Crosse, S.B., Kaye, E. and Ratnofsky, A.C. (n.d.). A report on the maltreatment of children with disabilities. Washington, D.C.: National Center on Child Abuse and Neglect, DHHS.

Jones, D., Peterson, D.M., Goldberg, P.F., Goldberg, M. and Smith, J. (1995). Risky situations: Vulnerable children. Minneapolis, MN: PACER Center, Inc.

Kragthorpe, C., Schmalzer, S., Xiong, D., Villasenor, J., Smith, J., Goldberg, P. and Goldberg, M. (1997). Let's prevent abuse: A prevention handbook for people working with young families. Minneapolis, MN: PACER Center, Inc.

Mitchell, L.M. and Buchele-Ash, A. (2000). Abuse and neglect of individuals with disabilities: Building protective supports through public policy. *Journal of Disability Policy Studies,* 10(2), 225-243.

National Resource Center on Child Sexual Abuse, NCCAN. (1994). Responding to sexual abuse of children with disabilities: prevention, investigation, and treatment. In *National Symposium on Abuse and Neglect of Children with Disabilities: Advance Literature.* National Center on Child Abuse and Neglect.

Orelove, F.P., Hollahan, D.J. and Myles, K.T. (2000). Maltreatment of children with disabilities: training needs for a collaborative response. *Child Abuse and Neglect,* 24(2), 185-194.

Rogow, S. and Hass, J. (1999). The person within: Preventing abuse of children and young people with disabilities. Vancouver, BC: British Columbia Institute Against Family Violence.

Rycus, J.S. and Hughes, R.C. (1998). Field guide to child welfare, Volume III: Child development and child welfare. Washington, D.C.: Child Welfare League of America.

Sandall, S.R. (1997). Home-based services and supports. In *Infant Development and Risk,* Widerstrom, A.H., Mowder, B.A. and Sandall, S.R. Baltimore, MD: Paul H. Brookes Publishing Co.

Santelli, B., Turnbull, A., Marquis, J. and Lerner, E. (1997). Parent-to-parent programs: A resource for parents and professionals. *Journal of Early Intervention,* 21(1), 73-83.

Sobsey, D. (1994). *Violence and Abuse in the Lives of People with Disabilities: The End of Silent Acceptance?* Baltimore, MD: Paul H. Brookes Publishing Co.

Steinberg, M. A. and Hylton, J.R. (1998). Responding to maltreatment of children with disabilities: A trainer's guide. Wheeler, C.E., Ed. Portland, OR: Oregon Institute on Disability and Development, Child Development and Rehabilitation Center, Oregon Health Sciences University.

Struck, L.M. (1999). Assistance for special educators, law enforcement, and child protective services in recognizing and managing abuse and neglect of children with disabilities. Virginia Department of Social Services, Child Protective Services.

Sullivan, P.M. and Cork, P.M. (1996). Developmental disabilities training project manual. Omaha, NE: Boys Town National Research Hospital, Center for Abused Children with Disabilities.

Sullivan, P.M. and Knutson, J.F. (2000). Maltreatment and disabilities: A population-based epidemiological study. *Child Abuse and Neglect.*

Tobin, P. (1992). Addressing special vulnerabilities in prevention. *NRCCSA News,* 1(4), 5-14.

Tomison, A.M. (1996). Child maltreatment and disability. *Issues in Child Abuse Prevention,* 7, 1-11.

Wolcott, D. (1997). Children with disabilities: Risk factors for maltreatment. A dissertation presented to the College of Education, University of Denver.

Endnotes

1. The definition of "child abuse and neglect" from the Child Abuse Prevent ion and Maltreatment Act (CAPTA):

   "The term 'child abuse and neglect' means, at minimum, any recent act or failure to act on the part of a parent or caretaker, which results in death, serious physical or emotional harm, sexual abuse or exploitation, or an act or failure to act which presents an imminent risk of serious harm." 42 U.S.C.A. Section 5106g(2) (West Supp. 1998).

2. The definition of "disability" from the Americans with Disabilities Act (ADA):

   The term "disability" means, with respect to an individual—(A) a physical or mental impairment that substantially limits one or more of the major life activities of such individual; (B) a record of such an impairment; or (C) being regarded as having such an impairment. 42 U.S.C. Section 12102(2) (1999).

   The phrase physical or mental impairment includes, but is not limited to, such contagious and noncontagious diseases and conditions as orthopedic, visual, speech, and hearing impairments, cerebral palsy, epilepsy, muscular dystrophy, multiple sclerosis, cancer, heart disease, diabetes, mental retardation, emotional illness, specific learning disabilities, HIV disease (whether symptomatic or asymptomatic), tuberculosis, drug addiction, and alcoholism. ADA Title III Technical Assistance Manual Covering Public Accommodations and Commercial Facilities Section 36.104(1)(iii).

Respite Care for Children with Developmental and/or Physical Disabilities: A Parent's Perspective

Background: Over the past 25 years, parents have increasingly made the choice to keep their families together. Children with developmental or physical disabilities are no longer routinely placed in institutional care. As a result, the need for respite care (temporary child care) increased. Until recently, respite care has been either unavailable or unaffordable in many states. Numerous federal programs have the potential to fund limited respite opportunities for families of children with specific disabilities or income restrictions, but are not always used for this purpose. In many states Medicaid Home and Community Based Waivers for children with certain disabilities probably account for the largest federal source of funding, but long waiting lists persist. States and or agencies that administer respite projects have realized the need to provide other supports to families which are flexible and meet the needs of the whole family, not just the person with a disability. Respite care services form the basis for many state family support programs.

Purpose: For years families caring for a child with medical or physical involvements have been reluctant to allow others to provide care for their child in their own home. The two most common reasons stated by parents are: 1) concerns about the caregiver's training; and 2) feelings that no one can take care of their child as well as they can. Babysitters, in general, do not have the skills needed to provide the kind of support required to care for children with medical or physical disabilities. Respite care programs for families who have children with developmental and/or physical disabilities provide trained respite care providers for in-home or out-of-home "free" time (respite) for families.

Respite Programs: Highlighting the strengths and needs of the entire family, and not just the needs of the individual with a disability, has been a common thread in exemplary programs. Providing respite care for children with developmental or physical disabilities is not unlike providing respite for any other child. The respite provider needs to know the kinds of behaviors the child is likely to exhibit and be prepared to deal with any unusual needs of the child. This is true of any child. The behaviors and needs of children with disabilities may be more acute, but ascertaining them should be done in the same manner.

For the sake of those programs considering starting a respite program for families with children with developmental or physical disabilities, the following outline is designed to give an idea of the kinds of training and attitudes that are required to provide a quality program.

The Keys to a Successful Respite Program

- Help families feel comfortable and build trust. Spend enough time with the family to develop a level of trust that will allow a free flow of information.
- Provide a flexible structure. The agency should provide as many options as possible to meet the needs of the family, rather than fitting the family into the service available.
- Be family-focused. Empower families to make decisions for themselves. Discuss the strengths and needs of the whole family.
- Provide support. The administering agency and respite care providers must be available to field questions and concerns of parents that may be outside the realm of respite care. This might include linkage and referrals to other agencies or services.

- Allow families to train providers. Be sure to include families in the process of designing the child-specific portion of the provider's training.

Training

Because of the concern that families have about the specialized needs of their children, respite providers should be trained in first aid, CPR, disability awareness issues, specific medical conditions, behavior management, and individual "hands-on" training with the child for whom they will provide care. Many states and local programs have developed respite training manuals which are available to train local providers.

Building trust is probably the key ingredient in a successful respite program. Training respite workers is only one step in this process. Establishing close working relationships with the family and ensuring close supervision are other important parts of a successful program.

The Basics—These areas can be taught in a classroom setting using professional staff.

- CPR and First Aid
- Philosophy of family empowerment
- "How to speak DD"—introduction to developmental disability terminology
- "Don't Panic"—introduction to medical and environmental emergencies

The Details—These units should be presented in at least two different forums. The first, as a parent panel with discussion of some personal stories in each of the areas mentioned. The second, as a clinical approach to care, to include a speech therapist, an occupational therapist, and a physical therapist.

- Communication sensitivity—how to communicate with someone who does not talk very well, if at all.
- Eating etiquette—good table manners (skills) when working with someone who needs assistance.
- The comfort factor, or "how would you feel sitting in the same position all day?"

"Hands On"—This section should take place in the families' homes, and/or, the setting where the respite will actually occur.

- Meet the family and get to know the child
- Trainee asks parents about specific assistance he or she may need to provide
- Parents demonstrate how they assist their child to move, eat, and go to the bathroom
- Trainee works with the child on each of the specific skills parents request until parents are comfortable in how the trainee performs

Conclusion

Successful programs from around the country report that, once these key requirements are met, families will enthusiastically participate in respite services. Programs also report that this process takes some time. The trust that families need does not occur overnight. Allow a considerable amount of time for the program to be fully operational.

This can be one of the most rewarding programs to operate. Families and staff report many heartwarming tales of the benefits that respite has provided.

Respite Services for Families with Adolescents at Risk of Abuse or Neglect

Growing up in the United States today can be challenging for young people, who typically struggle with the desire for independence, physical changes, and questions about the future and the world around them. Societal issues facing adolescents include a significant increase in the breakdown of the family unit, an increase in violence toward and by adolescents, and the changing roles and attitudes of schools. Society also tends to judge adolescents' worthiness, motivation, and ability to be valuable contributors to their communities.

Even in the best of circumstances, adolescents and their families may struggle to meet these and other challenges. For a family at-risk because of poverty, inadequate parenting skills, or other factors, caring for an adolescent may be particularly stressful. Existing resources and coping mechanisms may be stretched to a breaking point.

Respite programs can make a dramatic impact on families with adolescents who are at risk of abuse and neglect by providing a safe haven in which family members can take a break from one another.

As with all respite programs designed to prevent child abuse and neglect, respite programs for adolescents offer support services to help strengthen families and enable them to remain together despite difficult times.

Program Design

Adolescents, like younger children, need a supportive environment and resource to turn to when their family lives become overwhelming and stressful. It is important that respite programs be designed in terms that are acceptable and inviting for adolescents. Services must be "age-appropriate," or resistance and rebellion may prohibit a young person's ability to accept and receive help.

Because adolescents are initiating and refining their interactions with those around them, the entire family must be considered when a respite program for adolescents is being developed. The program design should incorporate family-focused strategies that include parents, siblings, extended family and any other household members. Increasing the knowledge, cooperation, and support of all family members will ultimately strengthen the family as a unit and reduce the chance of abuse and neglect within the home. This family-centered approach to services will:

- focus on the needs of the family as a unit and how it functions
- view adolescents and their families in the context of their environment
- assess and deliver services in a comprehensive, coordinated manner
- provide a variety of services based on consumer needs
- facilitate accessibility of services after the thirty day time frame
- build upon family strengths and affirm cultural values
- tailor services to the needs of the community

In addition to respite, there are a variety of family support services that may be effective for adolescents who are at-risk and their families. These services may be individual or group-based and may be available in the adolescent's home, the school, or a community center. The combination of respite, family support services, and community services, such as recreational and academic enrichment activities, will help adolescents and their families experience positive growth and development.

Services to Parents

Developing positive parent-child interactions is critical to the success of any respite program for adolescents. Attention may need to be focused on poor communication, behavior management skills and unrealistic developmental expectations. Participation by both parent and child in affiliated family support services may enable parents to develop new skills in child rearing, build positive self esteem in themselves and their adolescents, and improve family-child relationships.

Communication Skills

Often adolescents do not believe their parents understand their needs, and parents do not feel their children understand them. Communication issues may be particularly challenging for families from other countries who speak their native language in the home. For example, often schools are unable to communicate directly with these parents due to language barriers, and students tell their parents what they want them to hear. This can lead to serious problems within the family and with the family's relationship to the community. The respite program can provide resources to help parents and adolescents develop better communication and interpersonal skills.

Parent Resources

Professional resources offer many education curricula specifically designed for parents of adolescents. These include such books as *Active Parenting of Teens* by Michael Popkin and Michele Cox; *Parenting Teenagers: Systematic Training for Effective Parenting of Teens* by Don Dinkmeyer and Gary Mckay; *Positive Discipline for Teenagers: Empowering Teens and Yourself Through Kind and Firm Parenting* by Jane Nelsen and Lynn Lott; and *Parents and Adolescents Living Together (Parts 1 and 2)* by Gerald Patterson and Marion Forgatch.

These resources provide information on improving communication skills, developing effective behavior management skills, and understanding developmental milestones. The knowledge gained in parent training programs will help parents develop confidence in their ability to guide their children through adolescence and into adulthood.

Support Groups

Many respite programs offer parent support groups as an effective strategy for providing parent education as well as support. A trained facilitator can assist the group in discussing issues of mutual concern.

Facilitators may be trained professionals or they may be volunteers who have come through the program themselves. Parents find it reassuring to hear from other parents who have "been there too." Developing a supportive peer group can also increase parents' confidence in their parenting skills.

Counseling

Therapeutic guidance for parents can be a link for bringing youth and parents closer together. By discussing issues such as self-esteem, divorce, substance abuse, and sexual abuse, adults may develop greater insight and understanding of themselves and their given situations, especially their role as parents.

Services to Adolescents

Respite programs for adolescents must carefully consider how respite will be offered and which types of support services will be most effective. Because of adolescents' developmental need to establish independence, challenging authority is a normal behavior that programs must be prepared to handle.

Center-Based Services

Center-based respite services for adolescents at risk of abuse and neglect may be provided in schools, churches, or community facilities and include activities such as camping trips, dances, sports leagues, theater, support groups, and remedial academic programs.

A center-based respite program can use incentives to promote leadership, cooperation, and peer-interaction skills such as team building and problem solving. Adolescents appreciate having a place they can call their own, where they can become involved in decorating walls, arranging rooms, helping with upkeep, caring for the center's pets or aquarium, and other activities that help build self-help skills.

Mentoring

Mentoring has proven to be effective in working with adolescents in respite programs. Through mentoring activities, adults offer friendship and provide positive role models to encourage adolescents to see life in a new way. It is important that mentors work in conjunction with parents to ensure that their relationship with adolescents will not contradict family values and traditions.

A mentor can help build an adolescent's self-esteem by giving positive feedback, by providing companionship that might not otherwise exist, by sharing concerns and discussing current issues, and by being someone to count on in a time of crisis.

Commonly, a male or female mentor will be matched to a young person of the same sex. They may help the teen academically by tutoring them or by attending class part of the school day. A mentor may advocate for a teen and calm a teen during an "acting out" period. Mentors may visit in the home or take walks to the park "just to talk." Often conversations may lead to topics the teen finds difficult to discuss with other people. While the teen receives support and encouragement, a true and valuable friendship—which is often a crucial missing piece in the life of an at-risk youth—may be formed.

Support Groups

Adolescent support groups, which offer peer support and mentoring in a safe and nonthreatening environment, may take place during school or after school. Sometimes it is assumed that adolescents already having difficulty in school should not miss class to attend an in-school support group. However, today's research supports opportunities for young people that will help them function better both in the classroom and outside the school setting. Divorce, peer pressure, alcohol and drugs, gangs, conflict resolution, friendships, sexuality and diseases, problem solving, or other topics suggested by adolescents are all issues that could be discussed through a teen support group.

Counseling

Respite programs may also offer adolescents individualized counseling. Individualized counseling provides a therapeutic relationship and helps guide and support a teen to tackle intimate areas of concern. The counselor and teen can develop an individualized plan with obtainable goals and objectives. For counseling to be effective, a true partnership that respects the adolescent's needs must be formed. "Stuffiness" on the part of the counselor could lead to resistance from young people seeking help. Counselors must maintain objectivity, advocating for both the adolescent and the family.

Summary

Adolescence, that time in life when individuals move from childhood to adulthood, is a major developmental milestone that can be challenging for families under the best of circumstances. For families that lack sufficient supports, the stress can lead to frustration and, at times, to violence. Respite programs can provide an important resource for such families. By having time apart from one another, the adolescent and family can create space to examine the sources of their conflicts and seek resolutions. Respite programs serving adolescents and their families will need to offer a variety of support services to help increase family stability. Effective respite programs can strengthen families and prevent abuse and/or neglect.

Respite for Foster Parents

Respite, once available only to immediate or extended family members, is now being offered to foster families across the country. Respite can enhance the treatment and care of children in foster care and prevent unnecessary placement disruptions due to foster parent exhaustion and burnout.

Foster families are expected to care for one or more children who have experienced abuse, neglect, abandonment, or drug or alcohol exposure. They also care for children who have disabilities, who are medically fragile or HIV positive. Many children in foster care demonstrate a significant amount of emotional disturbance as a result of abuse or neglect which can be very taxing for foster parents and their families. Even though foster parents care for children with numerous emotional and physical needs, these services are usually provided without relief from the caregiving routine. Until recently, foster parents have been precluded from using existing publicly funded respite resources or unable to pay private providers. These factors have sometimes made it difficult for states and counties to recruit and retain foster families at a time when they are in high demand.

Respite for foster parents was started as a way for human service agencies to support and recognize the outstanding care given by foster parents. In some programs, respite is a regular part of the family support package offered to foster families caring for children with multiple needs. Other agencies have offered respite to foster parents as an incentive to care for children who are medically fragile, or as an incentive to accept emergency placements. Although foster placements are generally temporary, many children in foster care are adopted by their foster parents. When this occurs, the respite care established as a support during foster placement should be continued.

Given the recent financial constraints at all levels of government, it has been difficult to increase foster parent reimbursement rates in any significant way. However, human service agencies recognize respite as a cost effective way to help ensure the quality of care in foster homes, to reduce multiple placements of children, and to minimize the high costs of recruiting, training, and licensing new foster homes. Promoting Safe and Stable Families, Title IV-B of the Social Security Act, legislation specifically targets foster and adoptive parents as eligible for respite care and should provide additional funding in this area.

Program Considerations

Organizations offering respite to foster families need to consider foster care regulations or other state-approved licensing authorities when developing their programs. For example, children in foster care may only receive care in settings approved by the foster care licensing authority (state, county, city) which acts as a guardian of the foster child. Therefore, the home of the respite provider would need to be licensed as a foster care home. Regulations may also define "temporary" care. After a certain number of consecutive days, care may no longer be considered respite, and transferring the child into a temporary foster home may be required.

In many states, foster care regulations also require that anyone caring for children in foster care settings be cleared through a state registry for child abuse allegations, undergo criminal background checks and have a current physical examination on file with the licensing agency. Organizations contemplating a respite program serving foster parents should first obtain copies of state foster care regulations, licensing guidelines and the foster parent handbook.

Although foster parents are reimbursed a certain amount each month for the care they provide, establishing an independent fund to pay all or part of respite services for foster parents will encourage them to use the services regularly and will reduce the financial stress on the foster parents.

A foster parent advisory board can help respite program designers understand the needs of foster parents and give the foster parents a sense of ownership and investment in the program Later, the advisory board may help promote the service to foster parents.

Since the needs of children in foster care are so diverse, it may be difficult to design a program which can serve a broad spectrum of needs. A community needs assessment which includes information about children placed by state child welfare agencies will help narrow the targeted population. In the beginning, trying to serve too many needs may decrease the quality of care and strain the program's financial and provider capabilities. For example, a program wishing to serve foster families with children who have chronic illnesses may initially need to decide to serve only children who are affected by HIV/AIDS. One of the reasons for this decision is largely a training issue. Both group and individual training can then be focused on the needs and condition of children affected by HIV/AIDS and their families to ensure a high quality of care. As the program becomes established, the target population can be broadened.

It is important for the respite program to pay particular attention to the match between the respite provider, the foster parent and the child(ren). The matching process should include face-to-face meetings with all three. Although there may be frequent changes in the foster family composition, providers with an appropriate skill level should be matched consistently with the same foster parents when possible. Consistent matching is helpful both for the foster parents and the child(ren), who may be in respite care for successive visits and will value the comfort and consistency of care providers.

The parents will begin to build trust in the respite provider by reviewing the general routine of the day, the child(ren)'s care needs, and the location of needed items in the foster home. When a respite provider is introduced to a foster family, an initial visit is desirable so the provider learns as accurately as possible the specific needs of the family. It is also important that the family understand what the respite provider can and cannot do. A supervisor should accompany the provider on this visit to act as a liaison between the family and the provider and between the family and the respite program.

Foster Parent Concerns

Foster parents may have some initial concerns about using respite services. They may feel that they should not need respite, since they knowingly and willingly took on the role of foster parent. Some foster parents may fear that if they use respite, it will be viewed as an admission that they are "stressed out" and unfit as foster parents. They may also worry about handling additional paperwork or other administrative tasks associated with using the respite service. Others may fear that if a problem occurs during a respite stay, their reputation as foster parents, or even their licensing, could be threatened.

Foster parents may be concerned that respite providers will not be able to care for the children adequately. For example, those who care for children affected by HIV/AIDS may fear that other providers will not offer the children the love and attention they need and have grown to expect. Foster parents of children with behavioral issues may worry if the children spend time in someone else's care, their hard work with the child on correcting behaviors and stabilizing the child's life will be undone.

To address the concerns of foster parents, the following strategies might be helpful:

- Arrange for respite program staff members and respite providers to attend foster parent groups or association meetings.
- Ask foster parents who have used and are satisfied with respite services to speak at the foster parent association meetings as a way to advertise the services.
- Offer joint training programs for respite providers and foster parents.
- Use existing foster parent and local agency newsletters to make program announcements and to highlight success stories.
- Believe in the importance of word of mouth advertising to spread the news that service is available.
- Educate case managers of foster and biological families about the need to provide respite and strategies to support its use.

Respite for foster parents is a preventive service. Foster families are often composed of single parents who are caring for a combination of their own children, children who have been adopted, children of family members and children in foster placement. It is not unusual for a foster parent to be caring for six or more children at a time, if licensing permits. The physical and emotional demands of caring for children with special needs create added stress. For example, in addition to the complex home care requirements of a child with special needs, there may be medical appointments, periodic hospitalizations, or any number of daily emergencies. Without a break, any parent can be taxed to the point of losing the ability to provide high quality care. This also places the children at risk. Providing respite enhances the quality of care for the child, gives foster parents a deserved and necessary break, and ensures healthy and stable placements for all children.

Respite Provider Recruitment, Screening, Training, and Retention

Provider recruitment strategies need to be tailored to the needs of children and families served. For example, if the program serves foster parents of infants and toddlers there will be a different pattern of usage from programs serving school-aged children which have a greater volume of weekday and daytime requests. To meet service needs, programs may need to hire individuals for whom being a respite provider is their primary occupation, rather than those for whom respite is a secondary job. This may require higher salaries and/or benefits.

Applicants for respite provider positions must be carefully screened about their motivations for providing respite. Some applicants may be interested in working with children in foster care because of their own personal experiences with foster care or with abusive or neglectful situations. While these experiences may sensitize the applicant to the trauma the children may be experiencing, they must be screened to ensure that they have processed any unresolved feelings. Potential providers need to understand that each child's experience is unique and cannot be compared to their own.

Care must also be taken to inform respite applicants that they are not expected to initiate or promote a therapeutic counseling relationship with the children. Foster parents are often trained to offer therapeutic care and would certainly want the respite offered to them to support any programs they have initiated with children in their care. Respite providers must be willing to bring serious concerns to the attention of the foster parents, who in turn can arrange for an ongoing relationship with a mental health professional.

Training for respite care providers should include the following topics:

- child development
- the types, indicators, effects and dynamics of child abuse and neglect and mandatory reporting requirements
- the concepts of attachment, bonding and the development of healthy relationships
- the phases of grief and its behavioral manifestations
- the rights of biological parents
- understanding feelings regarding the behavior of the biological parent toward the child
- first aid and CPR
- positive discipline techniques
- the impact of disabilities, chronic and terminal illnesses on a child's life

- working with assistive technology
- behavioral management techniques
- how to respond to children's questions about their foster home placement
- how to handle birth parent visits
- HIV/AIDS awareness and program protocols
- communication with foster parents
- the roles and responsibilities of respite providers
- confidentiality
- emergency procedures
- foster home regulations

The supervision of respite providers can be done in a group setting. Scheduling regular meetings as forums for support as well as feedback sessions, can increase the cohesiveness and commitment of the providers. Initially, a supervisor or trainer needs to help a provider learn the care requirements of each family for whom the provider works. Later, the supervisor may conduct periodic reviews of the provider's work. Regularly scheduled interviews between a supervisor and a provider can also offer opportunities for feedback and performance evaluation.

Retaining quality respite providers is a challenge to any program. Some incentives that can be offered to providers are: continued educational opportunities, a variety of care assignments for an individual provider, higher wages, benefit packages, frequent verbal and written praise and recognition, opportunities for rest and relaxation.

High provider retention serves a number of positive purposes for the respite program:

- Low turnover saves hiring and training many different providers
- Families want consistency in providers to build trust and confidence
- Providers increase their skills and experience the longer they work for the program

Unique Challenges in Serving Foster Parents

Foster parents experience frequent and dramatic changes in the number and needs of the children in their care, and even trained respite providers may be caught off guard by these situations. Providers may be unprepared to handle the numbers of children in a foster home at a particular time, or they may be unable to care for the needs of certain children. Respite providers need to know when and who to call for assistance.

Another challenge is that the foster parents who provide short term care for children may have little information to share with the respite provider about the child just placed in their home. Respite provider training should prepare them to enter each home for a respite visit knowing there may have been changes in the composition of the household. Providers must be flexible and prepared for unexpected emotional, medical and/or behavioral problems in the children, of which the foster parent may not yet be aware. When necessary, thorough telephone assessments of children newly placed in foster care may replace face-to-face meetings of the respite provider with the family.

Respite providers may also need to learn to handle the sometimes sudden departure of children. Providers may feel they did not have an opportunity for closure with a child or that a promised activity was left unfinished. Providers, like foster parents, may worry about a child's transition and future care. These issues can be addressed at staff support meetings, since most respite providers will experience similar situations. The respite program may also provide bereavement support groups to help providers understand and better handle the losses inherent in their work.

Summary

Foster parents and the children in their care benefit from the regular availability of respite. By providing a needed break from the responsibilities of caregiving, respite offers foster parents another incentive to continue doing the important work of caring for children. Respite providers working with foster families may become essential members of a needed support system for those families, but may require some additional training in topics such as loss, grief and attachment.

Chapter 8

Sibling Abuse

What is sibling abuse?

Sibling abuse is the physical, emotional or sexual abuse of one sibling by another. It can range from relatively mild forms of aggression occurring between siblings, such as pushing and shoving, to extremely violent behavior such as the use of weapons.

Typically, parents and society expect fights and other physical forms of aggression to occur among siblings. Because of this, sibling abuse often is not seen as a problem until serious injuries occur. Another problem is that in some cases, siblings may switch back and forth between the roles of abuser and victim.

Besides the immediate dangers of sibling abuse, the abuse can cause all kinds of problems on into adulthood. Being abused by a sibling can really mess up a person's life.

How common is sibling abuse?

Research shows that violence between siblings is quite common. In fact, it is probably even more common than child abuse (by parents) or

---

This chapter contains text from "Sibling Abuse," reprinted with permission from, Your Child: Development and Behavior Resources, http://www.med.umich.edu/1libr/yourchild/, a website of the University of Michigan Health System. Copyright © 2003 Regents of the University of Michigan; and "Sibling Sexual Abuse," by Richard Niolon, Ph.D., ©2000 updated 2002. Reprinted with permission. Dr. Niolon is an Associate Professor at the Chicago School of Professional Psychology, and also maintains a private practice in Chicago, IL. Additional information is available at www.psychpage.com.

spouse abuse. It has been estimated that three children in 100 are dangerously violent toward a brother or sister. Many researchers have estimated sibling incest to be much more common than parent-child incest.

How do I identify abuse? What is the difference between sibling abuse and sibling rivalry?

All siblings fight and call each other names, and some "play doctor." But there is a difference between typical behavior and abuse. Most importantly, if one child is always the victim and the other child is always the aggressor, it is an abusive situation.

Some possible signs of sibling abuse are:

- One child always avoids their sibling
- A child has changes in behavior, sleep patterns, eating habits, or has nightmares
- A child acts out abuse in play
- A child acts out sexually in inappropriate ways

What are some of the risk factors for sibling abuse?

Much more research needs to be done to find out how and why sibling abuse happens. Some risk factors are:

- Parents are not around much at home
- Parents are not very involved in their children's lives, or are emotionally unavailable to them
- Parents accept sibling rivalry as part of family life, rather than working to minimize it
- Parents do not stop children when they are violent (they may assume it was accidental or part of a two-way fight)
- Parents increase competition among children by:
    - playing favorites
    - comparing children
    - labeling children
- Children have inappropriate family roles, for example, they are burdened with too much care-taking responsibility for a younger sibling

- Children are exposed to violence:
  - in their family
  - in the media
  - among their peers
  - in their neighborhoods

How can I prevent abuse from taking place between my children?

- Minimize the rivalries between your children.
- Set ground rules to prevent emotional abuse, and stick to them. For example, make it clear you will not tolerate name-calling, teasing, belittling, intimidating, or provoking.
- Don't give your older children too much responsibility for your younger kids. For example, use after-school care programs, rather than leaving older children in charge of younger ones after school.
- Set aside time regularly to talk with your children individually, especially after they've been alone together.
- Model good conflict resolution skills for your children.
- Model non-violence for your children.
- Teach your children to own their own bodies.
- Teach them to say "no" to unwanted sexual touching.
- Create a family atmosphere where sexual issues and problems can be discussed.

What should I do if there's abuse going on between my kids?

When one sibling hits, bites, or physically tortures a brother or sister, the normal rivalry has become abuse. You can't let this dangerous behavior continue. Here's what to do:

- Whenever violence occurs between children, separate them.
- After a cooling off period, bring all the kids involved into a family meeting.
- Gather information on facts and feelings.

- State the problem as you understand it.
- Help the kids work together to set a positive goal. For example, they will separate themselves and take time to cool off when they start arguing.
- Brainstorm many possible solutions to the problem, and ways to reach the goal.
- Talk together about the list of solutions and pick the ones that are most acceptable to everyone.
- Write up a contract together that states the rights and responsibilities of each child. Include a list of expected behavior, and consequences for breaking the code of conduct.
- Make sure you don't ignore, blame, or punish the victim.
- Make your expectations and the family rules very clear.
- Continue to carefully monitor your kids' interactions in the future.
- Learn how to mediate conflicts and help your kids learn how to manage their anger.

If problems continue or violent behavior is extreme you should get professional help.

Can sibling relationships have lasting effects into adulthood?

In the last few years, more research has been done on the lasting effects of early experiences with sisters and brothers. Siblings can have strong, sometimes long lasting effects on one another's emotional development as adults.

Research indicates that long-term effects of sibling abuse can include:

- Depression, anxiety, and low self-esteem
- Inability to trust; relationship difficulties
- Alcohol and drug addiction
- Eating disorders

Even less extreme sibling rivalry during childhood can create insecurity and poor self-image in adulthood. Sibling conflict does not have to be physically violent to take a long-lasting emotional toll. Emotional abuse, which includes teasing, name-calling, and isolation can also do long term damage.

Sibling Sexual Abuse

Text under this heading is from "Sibling Sexual Abuse," by Richard Niolon, Ph.D., ©2000 updated 2002. Reprinted with permission. Dr. Niolon is an Associate Professor at the Chicago School of Professional Psychology, and also maintains a private practice in Chicago, IL. Additional information is available at www.psychpage.com.

Child sexual abuse is a difficult thing to define. While an adult having contact with a child is easily defined as abuse, especially if that adult is related to the child, more difficult issues come into play when the perpetrator is another child in the family, especially when the child is 10 years old or younger. Cantwell (1988) reported several cases investigated in Denver in which children under the age of 10 years were molesting younger peers, sometimes siblings or cousins and sometimes unrelated children, in a variety of settings including multi-family households, school busses, and neighborhood children's homes. Parents may interpret this behavior at times as normal child sexual curiosity, or may spank the children to halt this behavior. Often in these cases, the child perpetrators were abused themselves at a young age, but, due to the shock experienced on discovery of the abuse and the focus on the victim, they did not receive services and their own history of abuse was not discovered until later.

Frequency

Typically sibling or cousin sexual contact is defined as abuse when it is marked by a five year difference; when the children are less than five years apart in age, the interaction is not deemed abusive unless force, coercion, injury, or penetration occurs. The criteria of force and/or coercion may be the most highly associated with negative outcomes, regardless of the specific sexual behavior (e.g., kissing, fondling, simulated intercourse, or exhibition) experienced (Haugaard and Tilly, 1988). Incidence of sibling or cousin sexual abuse varies greatly among studies, ranging from 10% to 40% among those reporting sexual abuse, although sibling and cousin sexual abuse are about equal in such samples (De Jong, 1988). Typically, the abuse begins when the victim is around six to seven years of age.

It is unclear whether non abuse contacts always result in psychological harm or maladjustment. It may be that normal sexual curiosity between siblings and cousins that happens only once is not harmful. As to repeated sexual contact between the children, two models have typically been proposed. In the first model of contact, often called nurturance-oriented, the children consensually seek sexual contact with each other over time, in part to provide nurturing and affection that is missing elsewhere in the family. It may begin with elements of loyalty, mutual satisfaction, and support, and may or may not turn coercive or lead to abuse outside the home as the child grows older. Some argue, however, that sibling sexual contact during preteen and teen years, even if consensual, interferes with the development of social skills and support systems beyond the family. This may prevent appropriate separation and differentiation from the family (Cicirelli, 1995).

The second model of contact entails a clear attempt by the abuser to experience some power, either for it's own sake or to possibly re-enact and master their own experiences of abuse. Research has attempted to study this type of abuse and isolate its effects. However, such abuse is often associated with sexual abuse and promiscuity, as well as additional family dysfunction, and it is difficult to determine the effects of sibling abuse as separated from other forms of abuse (Cicirelli, 1995).

Consequences

Some of the research (Meiselman, 1978) comparing incest victims and non-abused women indicates that incest victims have more problems in romantic and family relationships, and more sexual problems. They appear to show no significant differences in regards to presence of depression, suicide risk, substance abuse, or anxiety, although they are likely to have more severe depression when it is present. Other studies (Herman, 1981) show that incest victims are more likely to suffer physical abuse in the family along with the sexual abuse, to experience teen pregnancy, to run away, and to make suicide attempts when compared to the average teen. Those attempting suicide are more likely to do so without obvious signs of depression, to attempt while using substances, and to attempt during the adolescent years between the ages of 14 and 16 (Goodwin, 1982). Finkelhor (1979, 1984) found college students reporting childhood sexual abuse had lower self-esteem, and others have found that incest victims were more likely to suffer more victimizing incidents over a longer period of time, and to wait longer for treatment after disclosure.

Edwall and Hoffman studied teens admitting and denying incest, as previous research (Russell, 1986) found that 23% of adolescent girls entering treatment reported some intrafamilial abuse. They found incest victims:

- were more likely to have experienced physical abuse, and their siblings were more likely to have experienced physical and sexual abuse
- were more likely to abuse substances in general, but alcohol and stimulants were typically their drugs of choice, and they often started abusing alcohol by the age of 9 years
- were more likely to have had a psychiatric hospitalization, to experience clinical levels of depression, and be at risk for suicide
- were more likely to believe that their parents were ashamed of them and did not love them
- were more likely to have required police involvement and to have been picked up by police for running away
- non-significant trend for an increased risk of abuse outside of the family, increased substance abuse by either or both parents, and increased history of divorce and remarriage in the family

Higgs and colleagues (Higgs et al, 1992) found offered that children who experienced more frequent incidents of incest, who had a close relationship with the abuser, who experienced violence during some of the abuse and consent during other sexual experiences, and who engaged in more serious sexual behavior (i.e., intercourse) were more likely to become abusers themselves. Further, failing to internalize aspects of a nurturing and psychologically aware parent can lead to a failure to develop the kind of empathy that would inhibit abuse of others.

Causes

De Jong (1988) and Daie et al. (1989) present several factors in families that can lead to sibling or cousin abuse. Abuse can arise in an environment that:

- fails to protect the child, though poor supervision/monitoring and poor choices regarding babysitters and surrogate caretakers; examples include allowing children to remain in the care known siblings abusers, or a general lack of supervision of the children and knowledge about their activities in and out of the home.

- fails to set appropriate boundaries though inappropriate sleeping arrangements and clear parent-child hierarchies for child care; examples include allowing older opposite-sex children to sleep with parents in the absence of the same-sex parent, or flagrant nudity or lack of privacy in the family. Inappropriate parental interests in children's sexual development and experiences, or extremely relaxed views of sex, can both lead to greater freedom to explore sexual relations with peers and siblings.

Others (Smith and Israel, 1987) argue that open parental sexual activity, especially in cases where one parent is having an affair, is an especially significant indicator. Parents who turn outside the family for their needs, marking a disintegration of family structure and an increase in anxiety in siblings, may promote a sexual relationship between siblings in an attempt to nurture each other.

Lack of supervision and care by two parents; the absence of a parent can arise through physical absence from the home (e.g., divorce, death, abandonment, or work), or emotional absence due to physical or psychological illness (e.g., hospitalization due to depression, alcoholism, or dependent personality disorder). Some (Smith and Israel, 1987) have argued that this dynamic is one of the most salient of sibling incest families.

A multi-familial home were older children have caretaking responsibility for younger children; combined with poor boundaries, can allow older children to pressure younger children into meeting their sexual interests and needs.

Daie cites a case in which a physically abused boy in turn abused his sister, with sexual abuse being a minor part at first, but becoming the predominant form of the abuse over time.

A rigid family structure; discouraging open communication between children and parents, children and outsiders, and even between parents, often shows devaluing attitudes toward women, and enforce parental authority (often the father's power) unquestioningly over the family. This often leads to isolation, secretiveness, and enmeshment.

Others (Smith and Israel, 1987) argue that extreme repressive attitudes toward sex may lead to increased interest on the part of the children in exploring sex. A history of child sexual abuse in one parent may lead to the kind of denial and repression that prevents one parent from noticing the signs of sibling sexual activity. In either case, this rigid and repressing environment may be more likely to lead to parent-child abuse rather than sibling-sibling abuse. However, brother-sister abuse can result, modeling father-daughter abuse, as if the father's actions tacitly gave permission to the brother to abuse.

Cicirelli (1995) notes that the stereotypes of incest occurring primarily in poor, less educated, ethnic minority families has not been supported by literature. Sibling abuse happens in families at all levels of income and education, and across ethnicities.

Further, Smith and Israel (1987) note that there is no type of sibling who is likely to abuse, and personality characteristics are highly varied across abusers. Rather, sibling sexual abuse is the result of fragmenting and dysfunctional family processes, and not a cause of the family dysfunction. In response to the inadequacies of the family, a stronger and inappropriately close sibling bond may develop to compensate for the parents' dysfunction, or an abusive bond may develop and replicate the parents' dysfunction.

In families where abuse occurs, the dysfunction that led to the abuse may also lead to a poor response once the abuse is discovered. Wiehe (1990) noted that poorly responding families typically:

- denied the allegations of abuse
- ignored or minimized the abuse, explaining it as normal child behavior
- acknowledged the abuse, but blamed or otherwise punished the abused child
- acknowledged the abuse, but failed to protect the child and halt it
- acknowledged the abuse, but their own dysfunction prevented them from responding to alter the environment

Poorly responding families may be perpetuating the abuse in two ways. First, they fail to halt the abuse in the home. Second, by failing in this, they create a sense that the child can not be protected, and that the perpetrator was chosen over the victim. Such actions and the feelings of helplessness and rejection that result may prompt the abused child to become an abuser as well, seeking power and revenge (Johnson, 1989).

References

Cantwell, H., (1988). Child Sexual Abuse: Very Young Perpetrators. *Child Abuse and Neglect,* 12, 579-582.

Cicirelli, V. C. (1995). *Sibling Relationships Across the Life Span.* New York: Plenum Press.

Daie, N., Witztum, E., and Eleff, M. (1989). Long-term effects of sibling abuse. *Journal of Clinical Psychiatry,* 50(11), 428-431.

De Jong, A. (1988). Sexual Interactions Among Siblings and Cousins: Experimentation or Exploitation? *Child Abuse and Neglect,* 12(2), 271-279.

Edwall, G., and Hoffman, N. (1988). Correlates of incest reported by adolescent girls in treatment for substance abuse. In L. Walker (Ed.), *Handbook on Sexual Abuse of Children: Assessment and Treatment Issues.* New York: Springer Publishing Company.

Finkelhor, D. (1979). *Sexually Victimized Children.* New York: Free Press.

Finkelhor, D. (1984). *Child Sexual Abuse: Theory and Research.* New York: Free Press.

Goodwin, J. (1982). Suicide Attempts: A preventable Complication of Incest. In J. Goodwin, (Ed.), *Sexual Abuse: Incest Victims and Their Families.* Boston: John Wright.

Haugaard, J., and Tilly, C., (1988). Characteristics predicting children's responses to sexual encounters with other children. *Child Abuse and Neglect,* 12, 209-218.

Herman, J. (1981). Father-daughter incest. Cambridge, MA: *Harvard University Press.*

Higgs, D. C., Canavan, M. M., and Meyer, W. J. (1992). Moving from defense to offense: The development of an adolescent female sex offender. *Journal of Sex Research,* 29(1), 131-139.

Johnson, T. C. (1989). Female child perpetrators: Children who molest other children. *Child Abuse and Neglect,* 13(4), 571-585.

Meiselman, K. (1978). *Incest.* San Francisco: Jossey-Bass.

Russell, D. (1986). *The Secret Trauma: Incest in the Lives of Girls and Women.* New York: Basic Books.

Smith, H., and Israel, E. (1987). Sibling incest: A study of the dynamics of 25 cases. *Child Abuse and Neglect,* 11(1), 101-108.

Weihe, V. R. (1990). *Sibling Abuse: Hidden Physical Emotional, and Sexual Trauma.* Lexington, MA: D. C. Heath.

Chapter 9

Abuse at the Hands of Other Children: Bullying

Every day in our schools and communities, children are teased, threatened, or tormented by bullies. Bullying is a problem that creates a climate of fear, that affects the whole school, and in some cases, the entire community. When we fail to recognize and stop bullying behavior as it occurs, we actually promote violence. We are saying to the bully, "You have the right to hurt people," and to the victim, "You are not worth protecting." Safe schools are everyone's responsibility and everyone can help keep our schools safe.

What Is Bullying?

Bullying involves repeated acts of physical, emotional, or social behavior that are intentional, controlling, and hurtful. Bullying is a learned behavior, evident as early as two years of age. Bullying can be either direct or indirect. Direct bullying usually is seen and felt readily. Indirect bullying (deliberate exclusion, name calling, etc.) is much more difficult to identify, often is more difficult to remedy, and should be clearly seen as different from direct bullying. Boys are more typically engaged in direct bullying and girls in indirect bullying, but that is not always the case. Just be alert and consider the following:

"Take Action against Bullying," Doc. No. SVP-0056, National Mental Health Information Center, Substance Abuse and Mental Health Services Administration, 2003.

- Bullying is defined by a power imbalance between the bully and the target.
- A bully's power can be derived from physical size, strength, verbal skill, popularity, or gender.
- A bully's target feels tormented, helpless, and defenseless.
- Bullying can include hitting, name-calling, threatening, intimidating, kicking, spreading rumors, teasing, pushing, tripping, excluding someone from a group, or destroying someone's things.

Why Stop Bullying?

- Bullying interferes with learning in school and may lead to increased absenteeism and dropout rates.
- Students feel less safe and less satisfied in school when there are high levels of bullying in the school.
- Bullying children may become bullying adults and are more likely to become child and spouse abusers.
- The longer bullying lasts, the harder it is to change. Bullies identified by age 8 are six times more likely to have a criminal conviction by age 24.
- Bullying may be linked to other delinquent, criminal and gang activities, such as shoplifting, drug abuse, and vandalism.
- The targets of bullies grow socially insecure and anxious with decreased self-esteem and increased depression rates, even into adulthood.

Is Your Child Being Bullied?

If your child exhibits one or more of these warning signs, he/she may be a victim of bullying. Talk with your child to explore further whether or not he/she is being bullied.

A child being bullied often:

- Withdraws socially; has few or no friends.
- Feels isolated, alone, and sad.
- Feels picked on or persecuted.
- Feels rejected and not liked.
- Frequently complains of illness.

- Doesn't want to go to school; avoids some classes or skips school.
- Brings home damaged possessions or reports them "lost."
- Cries easily; displays mood swings and talks about hopelessness.
- Has poor social skills.
- Talks about running away; talks of suicide.
- Threatens violence to self and others.
- Changes in eating or sleeping patterns.
- Takes, or attempts to take, "protection" to school (a stick, knife, gun, etc.).
- Displays "victim" body language—hangs head, hunches shoulders, avoids eye contact.

Children being bullied may show some of these signs, or may show few.

If you suspect your child is being bullied:

Do

- Make sure your child knows being bullied is not his or her fault.
- Let your child know that he or she does not have to face being bullied alone.
- Discuss ways of responding to bullies.
- Teach your child to be assertive.
- Tell your child not to react, but to walk away and get help if pursued.
- Tell your child to report bullying immediately to a trusted adult.
- Contact the school/teacher.

Don't

- Ask children to solve a bullying problem between themselves—because of the differences in power, the child who has been bullied will suffer further. Bullying problems require adult intervention.
- Advise the bullied child to fight the bully—fighting is in violation of the school conduct code and the child might be seriously injured.

- Try to mediate a bullying situation. Bringing together children who are bullied and those who do the bullying, to "work out" the problems between them, generally is not a good idea. It may further victimize a child who is being bullied and it sends the wrong message to both parties.
- Blame either the victim or the bully. Instead, gather as much information as possible. Look at your own child's behavior and style of interaction and consider how you might help him/her to handle these types of situations in the future. Contact the school for assistance.

Warning Signs Indicating a Bully

A bully often:

- Seeks to dominate and/or manipulate others.
- Enjoys feeling powerful and in control (whether real or not).
- Is both a poor winner (boastful and arrogant) and a poor loser.
- Seems to derive satisfaction from other's fears, discomfort, or pain.
- Is good at hiding behaviors or doing them where adults can't notice.
- Is excited by conflicts between others.
- Blames others for his/her problems.
- Displays uncontrolled anger.
- Has a history of discipline problems.
- Displays a pattern of impulsive and chronic hitting, intimidating, and aggressive behaviors.
- Has a history of violent and aggressive behaviors.
- Displays intolerance and prejudice towards others.
- May use drugs, alcohol, or be a member of a gang.
- Lacks empathy towards others.

If You Think Your Child Is a Bully

- Be sure that your child knows that bullying is NOT acceptable behavior.

- Tell your child the penalties for bullying and be sure that you enforce them fairly and consistently.
- Help your child learn alternative ways to deal with anger and frustration.
- Teach and reward more appropriate behavior.
- Work out a way for your child to make amends for the bullying.
- Help your child develop an understanding of the impact of their bullying on the target.
- Seek help or counseling if the behavior continues.
- If contacted by the school, stay calm; try not to become angry and defensive. Make yourself really listen. Remember this is ultimately about the well-being of your child.

Bullying Prevention Programs

When developing and implementing bullying prevention programs, be sure to include the following steps:

- Increase the awareness of everyone at school (students, staff and parents) toward bullying problems.
- Assess the scope of the problem.
- Identify both the children who are bullying and the children who are being bullied.
- Intervene in a timely manner with clear and consistent consequences for the child who is bullying and with support and protection for the child who is being bullied.
- Encourage by-standers to intervene appropriately to help stop the bullying.
- Reward pro-social behavior of all students.

Bullying: No Way

Prevent your child from becoming a victim:

- Instill self-confidence in your child.
- Help your child establish good social skills.
- Teach your child to speak out for him or herself.

- Teach your child to seek help, if harassed, from you and other caring adults.

Prevent your child from becoming a bully:

- Present yourself as a model of non-violent behavior.
- Clearly state that violence is not acceptable.
- Assist your child in finding non-violent strategies for anger management and conflict resolution.
- Seek help from mental health/school counselors to help stop bullying and aggressive behavior.

What More Can You Do?

Research has found that remarkable things can happen if parents and caregivers spent at least 15 minutes of undivided time a day listening and talking with their children? Research also tells us that children really do look to their parents and caregivers for advice and help about difficult choices and decisions.

The information in your hands right now and other companion materials about bullying are part of "15+ Make Time to Listen... Take Time to Talk," an initiative developed by the Substance Abuse and Mental Health Services Administration, part of the U.S. Department of Health and Human Services, to promote healthy child development and to prevent youth and school-based violence.

The initiative builds on both the value children place on the advice they get from important adults in their lives and the benefits of those special 15 minutes each day. The listening and talking theme, however, also can be adapted by teachers, counselors, and other adults who are involved in the lives and futures of children.

Whether focused on bullying—as is this text—or on general principles of healthy development and behavior, the messages exchanged between children and their parents and caregivers in just these 15 minutes or more a day, can be instrumental in building a healthier and safer future for children as individuals, as family members, and as active and engaged participants in the life of their communities.

For more information contact the Substance Abuse and Mental Health Services Administration by calling toll-free 800-789-2647 or visiting the website at http://www.mentalhealth.samhsa.gov.

Chapter 10

Child Abuse by Babysitters and Caregivers

Introduction

The Office of Juvenile Justice and Delinquency Prevention (OJJDP) is committed to improving the justice system's response to crimes against children. OJJDP recognizes that children are at increased risk for crime victimization. Not only are children the victims of many of the same crimes that victimize adults, they are subject to other crimes, like child abuse and neglect, that are specific to childhood. The impact of these crimes on young victims can be devastating, and the violent or sexual victimization of children can often lead to an intergenerational cycle of violence and abuse.

In recent years, parents and policymakers have become increasingly concerned with ensuring the safety of children when they are in the custody of childcare workers. Such concerns have sparked extensive debates about how childcare providers should be hired and screened and whether routine criminal background checks should be used to uncover potential offenders. These safety concerns have even prompted the use of surveillance devices to monitor workers who care for children (Wen, 2000).

Unfortunately, information that might clarify these issues is limited. For example, public data on juvenile abuse and crime victimization do not routinely present the identity of perpetrators in a way that

"Crimes Against Children by Babysitters," from the Office of Juvenile Justice and Delinquency Prevention, U.S. Department of Justice. *Juvenile Justice Bulletin,* September 2001. NCJ 189102. Available online at http://www.ncjrs.org/html/ojjdp/jjbul2001_9_4/contents.html.

allows identification of specific groups of offenders, such as teachers or daycare operators. Instead, perpetrators are grouped more generally, either as undifferentiated childcare providers or simply as acquaintances of the victim.

Parents are particularly concerned about babysitters, whose recruitment and screening are often informal. Nonfamilial paid babysitters have generated anxiety ever since they became a nearly universal social phenomenon in the post-World War II childrearing environment (Kourany, Gwinn, and Martin, 1980). As mothers entered the workforce and fewer families lived with other relatives, more and more parents relied on babysitters to care for their children. Concerns about babysitters may have increased in recent years, especially in the wake of cases like that of Louise Woodward, the Boston-area au pair convicted of killing 8-month-old Matthew Eappen, who was in her full-time care (Doherty, 1997; Kahn, 1997).

Despite such publicity, the literature on the offenses of babysitters is scant (Margolin, 1990; Margolin and Craft, 1990; Martin and Kourany, 1980). However, this lack of information is beginning to change. Babysitters are one of the new categories of offenders for whom specific information is now being collected within the Federal Bureau of Investigation's (FBI's) growing National Incident-Based Reporting System (NIBRS). The availability of these data for the first time, combined with public and policy interest, makes babysitter offenses worthy of analysis.

Analysis of NIBRS data on crimes against juveniles (ages 0 to 17) reveals the following information:

- Babysitters are responsible for a relatively small portion of the reported criminal offenses against children: 4.2 percent of all offenses for children under age 6—less than the percentage accounted for by family members or strangers.
- Among the reported offenses that babysitters commit, sex crimes outnumber physical assaults nearly two to one.
- Children most at risk of physical assaults by babysitters are younger (ages 1–3) than those at risk of sex crimes (ages 3–5).
- Males constitute the majority of sex-offending babysitters reported to the police (77 percent); females make up the majority of physical assaulters (64 percent).
- Juvenile offenders are responsible for nearly half the babysitter sex crimes known to police (48 percent) but only 15 percent of the physical assaults.

- Babysitter offenses rarely result in death, but victims of babysitter crimes known to police are more likely than other child crime victims to suffer an injury (75 percent versus 53 percent for victims under age 6).

The Data

NIBRS, which compiled the data that are the basis of this analysis, was created to eventually supplant the existing Uniform Crime Reports (UCR) program as the national statistical database of crimes reported to the police. NIBRS can collect considerably more detailed information about crime incidents than UCR, including the range of offenses committed, victim characteristics (including age), offender characteristics, and incident circumstances. While NIBRS is not yet national in scope and only encompasses jurisdictions in 17 States, the combined reports for 1995, 1996, 1997, and 1998 yielded 1,427 babysitter victimizations for analysis. Given the general absence of data on this group of offenders, this large number of cases merits investigation—even though the cases are not nationally representative and the findings drawn from them are preliminary.

"Babysitter" is a term with some ambiguity. Children are cared for by a variety of people, including close and extended family, friends, family daycare operators, professional daycare centers, and schools; some of these providers may be paid while others are not. The term "babysitter" may be loosely applied to any of these providers, with the exception of schools and, possibly, daycare centers. Fortunately, the NIBRS system uses the more common meaning of the term, following the usage typical of many State child protective agencies (Margolin, 1990; U.S. Department of Health and Human Services, 2001). NIBRS considers babysitters to be those persons who temporarily care for children for pay, usually in the child's or babysitter's home. This usage excludes preschool and commercial daycare center staff members but includes both licensed and unlicensed home-based daycare providers. NIBRS protocols, like those of many State child protective services, also exclude family offenders from the babysitter category. Offenders who commit crimes against family members are identified in NIBRS by their family relationship to the victim, and not as babysitters, because NIBRS only categorizes offenders in a single relationship category. As a result, babysitters identified by NIBRS reporting agencies are not members of the victim's family. Thus, the majority of babysitter offenders identified in NIBRS are paid nonfamily juveniles or adults caring for children in a home setting.

However, NIBRS relies on local law enforcement agencies to collect data, and specification practices may vary somewhat from agency to agency.

An accurate number of children in the United States cared for by babysitters (as defined in NIBRS) is difficult to estimate. The National Child Care Survey (NCCS) estimated that, in 1990, 14 percent of the 18.5 million children under age 5 had a nonrelative in-home provider or family daycare as their primary childcare arrangement (Hofferth et al., 1991). However, NCCS and other childcare surveys tally only children's primary arrangements. Large numbers of children whose primary arrangements involve care by their own mother, another relative, or a daycare center are also occasionally cared for by babysitters. Therefore, it seems likely that a majority of all young children are exposed to paid babysitters at some time.

Findings

Reporting

Babysitters were only a small portion of the offenders in NIBRS jurisdictions who committed violent crimes against children. They accounted for 0.5 percent of offenders who committed crimes against juveniles (youth under age 18) and 4.2 percent of those who committed crimes against young children (those under age 6).[1] In contrast, family members (including nonparental offenders) accounted for 21.4 percent of offenders who committed crimes against all juveniles and 53.5 percent of those who committed crimes against young children. (Parental family offenders alone are 12 percent and 36 percent, respectively.) Complete strangers accounted for 11.0 percent of offenders against juveniles and 5.6 percent of offenders against young children. In assessing these figures, it would be useful to compare babysitters with other categories of professional childcare providers, such as teachers or youth workers, but such comparisons are not possible because these categories are not separately identified in NIBRS.

Victim Characteristics

Children under age 6, the group most likely to be cared for by babysitters, are also those most likely to be victimized by them. Children in this age group made up 60 percent of the victims of babysitter crimes in the NIBRS jurisdictions, although youth 12 and older were sometimes victimized. (The victims in the older age group may have included disabled youth who still require some professional childcare.) In terms of racial distribution, juvenile victims of babysitter offenses known to police were more likely to be white (92 percent) than juvenile crime victims in general (75 percent). This racial disparity may exist because nonwhite children are less likely to be cared for by paid nonfamily babysitters due to cost factors and the greater availability of care by relatives (Casper, 1997).

Among babysitter offenses that were reported to the police, sex offenses outnumbered physical assaults 65 percent to 34 percent. Most of the sex offenses involved fondling rather than the more serious crimes of rape or sodomy (41 percent, 9 percent, and 11 percent of all babysitter offenses, respectively). Simple assaults made up 25 percent of all reported babysitter offenses, whereas aggravated assaults accounted for 9 percent. A very small fraction of the offenses entailed a kidnapping (0.5 percent) or homicide (0.6 percent).

The age distribution of victims in NIBRS reports varies, depending on the type of offense. Children ages 1 to 3 faced the greatest risk of physical assault, whereas children ages 3 to 5 were most vulnerable to sex offenses. Victim gender also varied by type of offense. More boys than girls were victims of physical assault by babysitters (54 percent versus 46 percent), whereas girls made up 65 percent of the sex offense victims.

Offender Characteristics

Overall, among babysitters, male offenders outnumbered female offenders (63 to 37 percent) in police reports.[2] However, this percentage masks the true disproportion in the risk of male offending, in that most children are exposed to more female than male babysitters, both in terms of numbers and the amount of time spent in their care. No reliable information is available about the overall gender ratio of babysitters, but one teen survey found that females were twice as likely as males to have had babysitting experience (Kourany, Martin, and LaBarbera, 1980). Among adult babysitters, the ratio is considerably higher (U.S. Bureau of the Census, 2001). Therefore, the true risk of a male babysitter offending is likely much greater than the two-to-one ratio of male to female offenders found in the data.

Males were disproportionately involved in sex offenses (77 percent of offenders known to police). Females committed the majority of the physical assaults (64 percent of offenders). Of babysitters who committed sex offenses, males were more likely than females to target female victims and victims ages 6 and older. They were also more likely to be adults (58 percent), whereas female sex offenders were predominantly juveniles (67 percent), mostly ages 13 to 15.

In addition to gender of the offenders, one of the most dramatic differences between sex offenses and physical assaults reported in NIBRS jurisdictions was the offender age profile. Nearly half (48 percent) of the babysitter sex offenders were themselves juveniles. On the other hand, only 15 percent of the physically assaultive babysitters were under age 18. This age pattern—teens over represented in the commission of sex offenses and adults in the commission of physical offenses—held true for both male and female offenders. One possible explanation for this pattern may be that adult babysitters are more likely to be given responsibility for young children for longer periods (e.g., a whole day or several days a week) than teenage babysitters, and this continuous exposure creates the kind of stress and control-related conflicts that tend to trigger physical assaults on young children. Sex offenses, by contrast, are often crimes of opportunity that occur during the more occasional exposures that children have with teen babysitters.

Injury

Death was a relatively uncommon outcome for victims of babysitter crimes in NIBRS jurisdictions (0.6 percent). However, babysitter victims were more likely to sustain injuries than juvenile victims of other offenders. Among juvenile victims of physical assault, 67 percent of those assaulted by babysitters incurred a major or minor injury, compared with 52 percent of victims of other offenders. For assault victims under age 6, the injury discrepancy was even larger (75 percent of babysitter victims injured versus 53 percent of victims of other offenders). Sexual assault injury rates are fairly low and similar for babysitters and nonsitters alike.

Implications

Police data reveal that babysitters do indeed commit serious crimes against children in their care. While NIBRS data cannot be used to estimate national crime statistics, the numbers extrapolated from NIBRS jurisdictions (which represent about 6 percent of the Nation's crimes for 1997 and 1998) suggest that roughly 7,000 to 8,000 babysitter offenses—the majority of which are sex crimes—are reported to police over the course of a year. This estimate is certainly large enough to justify that precautions be taken by parents in screening and hiring care providers.

However, the threat posed by babysitters, especially when compared with other childhood threats, should not be overemphasized. Babysitters were responsible for only 4.2 percent of the reported crimes against children under 6 years—fewer than crimes committed by family members, other acquaintances, or even strangers. Given the large number of children exposed to babysitters, this is a relatively small percentage. The data reinforce other studies that suggest primary efforts should seek to shield young children from crimes committed by family perpetrators, not childcare providers (Finkelhor and Ormrod, 2001). It is important to keep in mind, however, that the numbers in NIBRS represent only the most serious criminal acts, the ones reported to the police; therefore, they do not fully reflect the scope of babysitter misconduct. Although sexual acts toward children are usually considered very serious and reported to police, many acts of physical assault by babysitters, even those resulting in injury, are unlikely to be reported. In addition, episodes of babysitter neglect and emotional abuse are rarely reported to police. Data from child protection agencies might document more instances of physical abuse, neglect, and emotional abuse, but parents are probably more inclined to simply terminate a babysitter's services than bother with official police or child protection reports. In addition, babysitter crimes may be disproportionately obscured because younger victims are often unable to communicate this abuse to their parents.

In short, crime reports on babysitters are only a crude guide to the perils children face in the company of babysitters. For example, the finding of NIBRS data that sex offenses by babysitters outnumber physical assaults may only reflect the kind of crime considered serious enough to be reported to police. In reality, physical assaults may be more common than sex offenses but less reported. Similarly, to the extent that physical assaults are underreported compared with sex offenses, the offenses of female babysitters may be underreported compared with those of males. Other NIBRS findings may not be so tainted by reporting biases. Children under 6 are likely the main targets of babysitter offenses because they spend the most time with babysitters. Teenagers likely commit more of the sex offenses against children because the sexual pressures and conflicts of their adolescence may motivate them to take advantage of the children in their care. Male babysitters probably outnumber female babysitters among offenders because males outnumber females in virtually all categories of crime, including family offenses and offenses against children.

Also, despite their limitations, NIBRS data highlight the diversity of offenders and victims. It is now clear that both female and male babysitters commit sexual offenses. Sexual assaults do occur against some very young children, and some older children also are being criminally victimized by babysitters.

These data are neither comprehensive nor detailed enough to offer strong guidance about preventive efforts. However, the young age of sexual abuse victims does confirm the potential value of providing preschool children with age-appropriate awareness about inappropriate touching (Wurtele et al., 1989). The frequent appearance of adolescent sexual abusers in NIBRS babysitter data suggests that parents may need to carefully screen and train young babysitters with this in mind. The preponderance of male offenders, given the relatively small number of males in the childcare workforce, certainly contributes to the already evident dilemma of those who would increase children's exposure to nurturant males. Unfortunately, the implications of all these findings have policy complexities that require better data than NIBRS can currently provide about the particular features of offenders, victims, their families, and the process by which potential babysitters are screened and chosen.

NIBRS is still in its formative stage, and its data may prompt more questions rather than provide firm answers. However, to the extent that its data remind the public and policymakers of the diverse perils that confront children, including threats from babysitters and other care providers, NIBRS may eventually improve the entire effort of crime prevention and detection for this vulnerable population.

Notes

1. Counts of offenders by relationship to victim are based only on victimizations where perpetrators can be identified as family members, strangers, babysitters, or other acquaintances, thus excluding the "unknown" category. Furthermore, comparisons of babysitter-perpetrated offenses with those committed by nonbabysitters are limited to only incidents involving crimes against persons (homicide, sexual assault, assault, kidnapping, and nonforcible sex offenses) because these are the only crimes linked in NIBRS data to babysitter offenders.

2. Some babysitter victimizations are perpetrated by multiple sitters, or by one sitter and other offender(s), yielding mixed offender patterns and offender-victim associations. In cases with multiple offenders, nonbabysitter offenders are identified by their relationship to the victim, not to the babysitter. To

avoid ambiguity, only incidents containing a single babysitter acting alone are used when specifying offender characteristics and describing offender-victim links. Single babysitters acting alone accounted for 93 percent of all babysitter victimizations reported in 1995, 1996, 1997, and 1998 NIBRS data.

References

Casper, L.M. 1997. Who's minding our preschoolers? Fall 1994 (Update). *Current Population Reports* (P70-62). Washington, DC: U.S. Department of Commerce, Bureau of the Census, pp. 1-89.

Doherty, W.F. 1997. Manslaughter and she walks. *Boston Globe* (November 11). Retrieved August 8, 2000, from the Web: www.bostonglobe.com.

Federal Bureau of Investigation. 1995-98. National Incident-Based Reporting System (NIBRS). Master computer files of final data for each year. Washington, DC: U.S. Department of Justice, Federal Bureau of Investigation.

Finkelhor, D., and Ormrod, R.K. 2001. Child Abuse Reported to the Police. *Bulletin.* Washington, DC: U.S. Department of Justice, Office of Justice Programs, Office of Juvenile Justice and Delinquency Prevention.

Hofferth, S.L., Brayfield, A., Deich, S., and Holcomb, P. 1991. National Child Care Survey, 1990. Washington, DC: *The Urban Institute Press.*

Kahn, R. 1997. Prosecutors detail case against au pair. *Boston Globe* (March 8). Retrieved August 8, 2000, from the Web: www.bostonglobe .com.

Kourany, R.F.C., Gwinn, M., and Martin, J.E. 1980. Adolescent babysitting: A 30-year-old phenomenon. *Adolescence* 15(60):939-945.

Kourany, R.F.C., Martin, J.E., and LaBarbera, J.E. 1980. Adolescents as babysitters. *Adolescence* 15(57):155-158.

Margolin, L. 1990. Child abuse by babysitters: An ecological-interactional interpretation. *Journal of Family Violence* 5(2):95-105.

Margolin, L., and Craft, J.L. 1990. Child abuse by adolescent caregivers. *Child Abuse and Neglect* 14:365-373.

Martin, J.E., and Kourany, R.F.C. 1980. Child abuse by adolescent babysitters. *Child Abuse and Neglect* 4:15-22.

U.S. Bureau of the Census. 2001. Tables of Detailed Occupation, 1990. Retrieved June 21, 2001, from the Web: www.census.gov/hhes/www/occupation.html.

U.S. Department of Health and Human Services, Administration on Children, Youth and Families. 2001. *Child Maltreatment* 1999. Washington, DC: U.S. Government Printing Office.

Wen, P. 2000. Wary parents using cameras, criminal checks on caregivers. *Boston Globe* (July 17). Retrieved August 8, 2000, from the Web: www.bostonglobe.com.

Wurtele, S.K., Kast, L.C., Miller-Perrin, C.L., and Kondrick, P.A. 1989. Comparison of programs for teaching personal safety skills to preschoolers. *Journal of Consulting and Clinical Psychology* 57(4):505-511.

Chapter 11

Child Abuse in Community Institutions and Organizations

A Closer Look at Specific Community Institutions and Organizations

Within our communities, there are many types of institutions and organizations that have become part of our everyday lives. Prominent among these are educational and vocational institutions, religious and spiritual institutions, sporting, cultural, and recreational organizations, and special needs facilities. Our five critical dimensions are discussed in relation to the dynamics of abuse in the previously noted groups of community institutions and organizations. We approached this task by combining the literature on familial and institutional abuse with knowledge derived from popular media reports, public lawsuits, and clinical involvement with survivors of such experiences. We consider the significance of these institutions and organizations by examining their mission and purpose, the influence and power of offenders in each setting, the extent of child involvement,

---

Excerpted with permission from "Child Abuse in Community Institutions and Organizations: Improving Public and Professional Understanding" (September 2001), by David Wolfe. The University of Western Ontario, and Peter G. Jaffe, Jennifer L. Jetté, and Samantha E. Poisson, of the Centre for Children and Families in the Justice System of the London Family Court Clinic. The complete text of this paper is available at http://www.lfcc.on.ca/institutional.pdf. A subsequent version of this paper was published in *Clinical Psychology: Science and Practice,* volume 10, Number 2, Summer 2003.

and the numerous abuse and post-abuse events that affect children's disclosure and recovery.

Educational and Vocational Institutions

Parents, governments, and society almost universally accept the importance of education in the normal development of children and adolescents. Children begin school at the tender age of four or five and in most jurisdictions must continue to attend until they are at least sixteen.

The mission of educational and vocational institutions is to enable individuals to acquire knowledge and interpersonal skills to prepare them for lifelong learning so that they may realize their potential and contribute positively to their community. The importance of having an education is becoming ever more salient, and therefore the negative effects of not being able to obtain an education are even more serious. Advances in technology have created a plethora of jobs that require extensive training, and the minimum level of education required to do many pre-existing jobs has been rising steadily. This may partially explain the increase in the number of individuals receiving their high school diploma. In 1966, only 30 per cent of 18 year-olds completed high school, by 1996 this figure had risen to 77.2 per cent.

If one were to examine educational and vocational institutions in terms of potential risk for institutional abuse and subsequent psychological harm, a number of features stand out. Perhaps most striking is the non-voluntary nature of school and the large amount of time children spend in school. Between the ages of five and sixteen, children spend the majority of their time at school, which poses a risk for some forms of maltreatment in this setting. The fact that children may be at the same school with the same teacher(s) or other school personnel for many years creates the potential for ongoing abuse.

The high esteem in which most educational institutions and those that work within these institutions are held can also be risk factors. As alluded to previously, most cultures consider school a normal part of a child's development. Every day, parents send their children off to school and essentially transfer their parental authority to teachers, principals, and other school personnel. We trust these individuals with our children's lives, and most often that trust is well deserved. Our children also come to trust and admire their teachers, and other adults they come into contact with at school. Without this trust, our schools could not function properly. Children need to feel as though they are in a safe and caring environment in order to express their full potential.

Teachers and administrators need the authority to make decisions and care for the children when their parents are not present.

In addition, teachers are powerful figures in children's lives. Many children consider their teachers to be mentors and role models, particularly when the relationship extends outside of the classroom (e.g., coaching, tutoring). Teachers have a great deal of control over whether a child's classroom experiences are positive or negative. Teachers also have control over the child's marks. When a teacher abuses a child, the child may be reluctant to disclose for a number of reasons. Knowing that teachers are generally well respected, children may fear that they will not be believed. They also may fear that if they tell of the abuse they will lose their teacher's favor, their marks may suffer, or their teacher will make school life difficult for them.

Many educational districts also face difficulties responding to allegations of abuse by a teacher, due in part to well-meaning safeguards that protect teachers from complaints lodged by students and parents. To by-pass such obstacles and minimize accountability, some school boards silently transferred teachers who were alleged to abuse students from school to school, resulting in further allegations. This practice further traumatizes victims by creating self-doubt and minimizing their experiences. Recently, increased awareness of incidents in which school boards failed to respond appropriately to repeat offenders has led to changes in policy and practice. Nonetheless, the professional and scientific literature on abuse by teachers is disproportionately focused on false allegations rather than the prevention and treatment of actual incidents of abuse.

When abuse does occur in an educational or vocational setting, the effects can be devastating. Children are left with feelings of shame, worthlessness, confusion, and guilt. Children may also experience Post-Traumatic Stress Disorder or similar symptoms, including avoidance of school and fear associated with educators; loss of trust in or fear of adults, especially educators; loss of interest in school; denial of or refusal to discuss the traumatic event; nightmares; and excessive crying. As parents, survivors may be re-traumatized when they send their children to school, fearing that they, too, will be victimized.

As a consequence of these institutions' failure to act in cases of child abuse, the importance of an education and associated interest in learning and achievement may be compromised. Survivors are left feeling disillusioned with the system, either as a result of the abuse itself or how the abuse was handled (or mishandled), and as a result they avoid any reminders of school and school-related activities. These feelings may continue into adulthood and prevent victims and survivors from obtaining the same level of education or employment they might have otherwise obtained.

Religious and Spiritual Organizations and Institutions

For thousands of years, religion has been a driving force in human culture. Religious beliefs have laid the foundation for traditions, laws, and even guided the development of entire civilizations. Many religious and spiritual organizations are powerful institutions based on complex belief systems and age-old doctrine; others are more loosely formed and are passed from generation to generation through folklore and tradition.

Religious and spiritual organizations and institutions serve an important function for many individuals, communities and cultures. They provide moral, ethical and spiritual guidance for both adults and children. Religious teachings provide individuals with a context for their creation, as well as an explanation for what will happen to their soul after they die. Perhaps most significant, religions are generally organized around the worship of a divine power, or God, who is believed to be all-powerful and all forgiving.

Within these organizations, religious leaders (e.g., priests, ministers, and rabbis) and other representatives of the institution wield a great deal of power. These leaders are often thought of as representatives of God, and are treated with a great deal of respect and authority. From a very young age, parents teach their children by both direct instruction and modeling to respect and obey their religious leaders. Other individuals, such as Sunday school teachers, youth leaders, and choirmasters, are also considered trustworthy by virtue of their strong affiliation with the religious organization. Parents take pride in their children's involvement in religious activities and generally encourage participation, considering these activities the safest and most wholesome activities for their children to be partaking in.

The prominence of religious and spiritual organizations and institutions in modern societies varies greatly. In some parts of the world, religion and culture are almost synonymous. In other regions, there is much more diversity. The degree to which a child is involved with religious institutions may depend on a number of factors, including their family or ethnic background, as well as the neighborhood, community or geographic region in which they live. If a child's family is quite devout, that child may have daily contact with the religious organization. He or she may attend a religious school, go to daily or weekly religious ceremonies, or participate in special activities within the organization (e.g., youth group, reading at mass). If a child's family is less involved with the religious organization, his or her contact may be limited to a weekly celebration in which the child is accompanied by his or her parents.

The influence and power of religious and spiritual organizations as well as the absolute trust that is often imparted to individuals within these organizations can have devastating consequences for children abused by religious leaders and other individuals affiliated with the organization. The perpetrator of the abuse may use his or her position within the church or the organization to obtain compliance from the child. Perpetrators may coerce victims by telling them that what they are doing is the will of God or that God will punish them if they do not do what they are told. Often explicit threats are not even necessary, as the child has been raised to never question the authority of his or her religious leader.

Once the abuse has occurred, the decision to disclose can be very difficult for a child. The perpetrator may have used the child's religious beliefs to frighten him or her into silence (e.g., "you will go to hell if you tell anyone"). The child may also be aware that his or her acts were in some way sinful or against their religious beliefs, with or without threats from the perpetrator. For example, a number of Christian religions consider premarital sex and homosexual acts to be sinful. A child may not disclose abuse because he or she fears religious condemnation for participating in these forbidden, sinful acts, even when they were not consensual.

Children who disclose abuse within religious and spiritual organizations and institutions may face a number of obstacles. When children make allegations of abuse against religious leaders and other well-respected individuals associated with these organizations, they may not be believed. The perpetrators tend to be well liked and personable, and their followers will often believe them, rather than the victim, in the face of such accusations. When multiple victims come forward, they are sometimes accused of colluding against the perpetrator or the institution. The victims and their families are often rejected by their religious community or totally excommunicated. This leaves them feeling alienated, humiliated and stigmatized. The loss of community support during such a stressful time may make it difficult for the family to cope and to help their child deal with the trauma associated with both the abuse and the disclosure (presuming family members believe and support the victim).

The institution's response to allegations of abuse by individuals within their organization can also add to the trauma experienced by victims and survivors. Priests, ministers and other religious leaders are often transferred to other communities to continue their ministry. Often victims are not given any type of apology, formal or informal. This may increase their feelings of self-blame and injustice and prevent them from obtaining closure.

Abuse by a trusted religious figure may destroy a child's belief that the world is a safe place. Having been raised to believe that God is good, and belief in God provides protection from evil, children have difficulty reconciling how a trusted religious figure could commit such evil deeds. What once made sense no longer makes sense. What was once safe is no longer safe. This disruption of safety may cause the world to seem chaotic or unstructured. Children may try to compensate for this by reorganizing their world. This might include blaming themselves for the abuse, engaging in self-destructive or age-inappropriate behaviors to survive the abuse, or in some cases acting out their anger and rage by abusing others.

When a religious leader or a member of the clergy or religious order perpetrates child abuse, it is often found that the victim or survivor's belief in or perception of God, spiritual practices, attendance at religious services, and trust in religious representatives is severely negatively affected. Victims, particularly children, have difficulty separating the offending clergy from the religious organization or God. In some religions, religious leaders are called father and are a representative of God. To be violated by a priest, for example, is to be violated by God, Christ, and the church. Victims or survivors may feel that God failed to protect them, and may fear further abuse if they return to the church. This sense of betrayal can cause a crisis of faith that may destroy a victim's comfort with and belief in important religious rituals, symbols or icons or even worse, a complete abandonment of their faith.

Sporting, Cultural, and Recreational Organizations

An area that is often overlooked when considering child abuse in institutions and organizations is abuse that occurs in sporting, recreational and cultural organizations. The reason for this may be that these organizations are rarely thought of as institutions despite the fact that they have existed for a long time and are an important part of many cultures. Included in this category are a wide range of teams, clubs, groups, and organizations, serving a wide range of children. They may be community-based, such as a neighborhood hockey league, or they may be part of a larger institution, for example a school volleyball team or a church choir. These clubs or groups may themselves form a large organization, or they may be local and independent.

This category also takes into account activities and organizations that are increasingly becoming a part of children's lives that for various reasons previously have not been considered under the rubric of institutional abuse. Technology has created a new means of accessing vulnerable children, through devices such as the Internet. Predators who once had to stalk playgrounds, schoolyards and neighborhoods and try to entice their victims under the watchful eye of their parents now can sit at their computer and visit children's chat rooms and cyber-clubs. They can befriend children, or even pretend to be a child, while the victim's parents are in the very same room. Although the child may never find out that their online friend is really a pedophile, if their cyber-club ever did decide to meet, the results could be disastrous. Other activities that are not traditionally thought of as institutions, but which harbor the potential for child abuse include the fashion industry, modeling, and the visual arts, among others.

The mission and purpose of these organizations and institutions vary greatly. However, all seem to be focused on extracurricular, recreational or leisure activities that develop children's knowledge, abilities, social skills and/or life skills through being part of a team, club or group. Even when an organization has a well-established mission, it may serve a different function in different children's lives. For a less fortunate child, the support offered by an organization's leader or the opportunities available through the local youth club may help compensate for a troubled life. For a more privileged child the same experiences may be more leisurely or recreational in nature. Similarly, for most children and youths, playing on sports teams is an enjoyable past time or extracurricular activity. However, some children aspire to participate in college or professional athletics, and sporting organizations can take on an even more powerful role in their lives.

The extent of a child's involvement with an organization as well as the influence and power of the adults within the organization both must be considered when evaluating the vulnerability of a child within that organization. Some children's participation in the activities associated with an organization may be minimal. They may only attend weekly meetings, games or practices. Other children may be highly involved with an organization. A child aspiring to be a professional swimmer may be involved in a number of swimming-related activities: school swim team, community swimming league, and swimming lessons. He or she may also be involved in activities geared at raising funds to travel to various tournaments and swim meets. Although ostensibly the child's participation in these activities may be voluntary, there may be pressure from both internal and external sources (i.e., parents and coaches) to be successful.

The coaches and leaders of sporting, cultural and recreational organizations are often in a position of trust and authority. When organizations are part of a larger institution (e.g., a school or a religious organization) their leaders are often considered trustworthy by virtue of their affiliation with the institution. Principal care and responsibility for children is sometimes handed over to coaches, chaperones and leaders for extended periods of time, particularly when the activity takes place away from home, as is the case in many tournaments or traveling leagues. Children's vulnerability may be further increased by their desire for special attention or rewards (e.g., scholarships, special privileges) or their fear of punishment or exclusion should they disobey.

When abuse does occur, the very qualities that make these types of organizations so valuable to a child's development can be one of the major obstacles to disclosure. In many cases, the coach or leader who perpetrated the abuse is well liked by the victim's fellow group members or teammates. This is particularly true if the group or team has been successful. Children may fear that if they disclose the abuse they will not be believed or they will lose the respect and friendship of their peers. They may also fear that if they report the abuse they will jeopardize their dreams, either because they feel they need the special treatment or training they have been receiving, or because they fear the consequences of disclosure. This may cause children to remain silent and tolerate the abuse much longer than they would in other situations, in a sense accommodating the abuse.

When a child does decide to report abuse that occurred in these types of organizations, the outcome may not be favorable. Victims may find themselves ostracized by fellow teammates or group members, thus losing their sense of team identity at an already difficult time. If the perpetrator was an important figure in the community or if the organization was significant to the community, the victim may be shocked by the rallying of support for the perpetrator. The victim may be labeled a whistle blower or a liar and as a result be further victimized. Even when the victim is acknowledged, the organizational response may be one of minimization, with the perpetrator simply being transferred or given a mere slap on the wrist.

Sporting, cultural and recreational organizations are meant to be enjoyable activities. Besides school, they are one of the major means by which children can broaden their horizons and develop a sense of self-esteem. When abuse occurs within these organizations, a child's confidence, self-esteem and ability to trust is eroded. The trauma of the abuse may lead to a decline in the child's performance (both within and outside of the organization), which subsequently may interfere with his or her ability to achieve his or her future goals. The child may also experience a loss of interest in and pleasure from activities that were once very important in his or her life. Even children who were not abused but who witnessed the abuse may be adversely affected. They may be frightened into compliance or they may come to resent the special attention that the victim receives.

Special Needs Services and Facilities (Correctional, Mental Health, Health, Social Services, Foster Care, and Residential Schools)

In every community there are organizations that address special needs of children and youth. The types of services offered by these organizations are quite diverse and depend on the needs of the children being helped. Some try to compensate for disadvantages, lack of opportunity, family problems, or missing elements in a child's life (e.g., providing role models and support for children with a variety of special needs). State and provincial child protective and social service organizations provide assistance for children in need of care and protection. Other special needs organizations address specific problems or disabilities. Mental health services assist children with emotional, psychological, psychiatric, or behavioral problems. Correctional services provide programs for children who have become involved with the legal system. There are also organizations and institutions, often residential, which help children with physical and developmental disabilities.

Considering the dynamics of child abuse within special needs organization presents a unique challenge because of the wide range of services offered by each of these institutions. Many of these organizations provide everything from emergency care, crisis intervention, or short-term care, all the way up to long-term residential placements. Each of these types or levels of care is associated with unique risk factors for abuse. For example, the risk factors for a child receiving outpatient treatment at a mental health clinic will be very different from a child who is in a group home for children with behavior problems. Similarly, a youth who is in a secure custody detention center may be much more vulnerable to abuse than a youth who is on probation, although both are involved with correctional services.

Children's involvement with special needs organizations frequently is non-voluntary and sometimes even their parents have little control over their well being. Children often come to the attention of social services because of some type of family breakdown. Parental rights may be temporarily or even permanently terminated. The child then becomes the responsibility of social services. Although it may be in the best interest of the child to be removed from his or her family, in the event that abuse occurs within the social services organization, without the support of his or her family the child may not know where to turn.

In other cases, the very reason that children come to the attention of special needs organizations (i.e., their special needs) may make them more vulnerable to abuse, make it more difficult for them to report abuse that has occurred, or damage their credibility when they do disclose abuse. For example, research has shown that children who are deaf or hard of hearing are at an increased risk of sexual abuse, even more so than children with other disabilities, likely as a result of their difficulty understanding or verbalizing episodes of abuse. Other disadvantages which bring children to the attention of special needs organizations, such as family problems or past abuse, may make children more vulnerable to abuse, and may also make it difficult for them to report abuse. Children with behavior problems or mental health problems may be reluctant to disclose abuse for fear that they will not be believed. Staff within correctional facilities or mental health facilities may feel that children within these settings are safer targets because if they do disclose they are less likely to be believed because of their past behavior. The very behavior problems that led to their institutional care may end up undermining their credibility when they disclose abuse.

As we have seen in the other non-familial institutions and organizations discussed previously, adults often have considerable control over children by virtue of their position within special needs organizations. Many of them are professionals or paraprofessionals, such as doctors, psychologists, social workers, childcare workers and counselors, who are trusted by parents, children, and the community in general. When abuse does occur within a special needs organization, victims face similar obstacles to disclosure, such as fear that they will not be taken seriously or believed, particularly for those with a history of mental health or behavior problems. If they report the abuse but are not believed, they may face repercussions from both the perpetrator and other staff within the institution. Children may also choose not to disclose the abuse for fear that the consequences of disclosing will be worse than enduring the abuse. For example, a child who has been placed in multiple foster homes may fear that if he or she discloses abuse, the next placement will be a group home or residential facility. As was the case with other types of non-familial abuse, the effects of abuse occurring in special needs facilities can be institution specific, such as a sense of isolation and general mistrust of helping institutions and organizations. This problem compounds the difficulty in accessing therapy and support, as all counselors may be seen as untrustworthy and potentially abusive.

Chapter 12

Child Maltreatment in Youth Sports

What Is Child Maltreatment in Youth Sports?

Sports are an excellent way for boys and girls to improve their physical abilities, social skills, self-esteem, confidence, understanding of competition and cooperation and leadership abilities. When the people who should be guiding young athletes are instead emotionally, physically or sexually abusive, it becomes a hostile, destructive environment that erodes self-esteem, confidence and trust. The child is not only assaulted by the immediate behaviors, but is also often robbed of the potential benefits of sports and recreation.

The most common form of maltreatment in youth sports is emotional abuse. Physical abuse, sexual abuse and sexual harassment are other types of maltreatment/abuse. There are legal definitions of maltreatment/abuse and there are gray areas where there is debate about whether a behavior is appropriate or maltreatment.

While we have little factual data on how often abuse occurs in youth sports, some are beginning to study the issue. The Minnesota Amateur Sports Commission (MASC) conducted a survey in 1993 and found the following incidences of abuse in sports in Minnesota:

From "Keeping Youth Sports Safe and Fun," by Cordelia Anderson, M.A., 1994. Reprinted with permission of the Minnesota Amateur Sports Commission, http://www.masc.state.mn.us. © Minnesota Amateur Sports Commission. Despite the older date of this document, the information addresses issues of current concern. Resources verified January 2004.

- 45.3% of males and females surveyed said they have been called names, yelled at or insulted while participating in sports.
- 17.5% of people surveyed said they have been hit, kicked or slapped while participating in sports.
- 21% said they have been pressured to play with an injury; while 8.2% said they have been pressured to intentionally harm others while playing sports.
- 3.4% said they have been pressured into sex or sexual touching, while 8% of all surveyed said they have been called names with sexual connotations while participating in sports.

The following are not legal definitions, but are brief descriptions to help you begin thinking about what might constitute maltreatment/abuse:

Emotional abuse. It's not unusual for people to minimize the damaging effects of physical or sexual abuse. It's even more difficult for some to see the damage, or potential damage, from emotional abuse. This is especially true when behavior that is emotionally abusive is thought of as discipline, or when people insist the language they use is simply how I've always talked, or are emphatic that no harm was meant, so none was done. It's easier for people to understand the damage done from physical assault, than from what is viewed as just words. But consider the impact of yelling at children:

- "you're stupid"
- "you're a klutz"
- "you're an embarrassment"
- "you're not worth the uniform you play in."

These statements can make young athletes feel like their very being is wrong—like they are worthless. Statements such as these can be very painful, and for some children, damaging. Statements can be particularly damaging if they are made because of a child's gender or race.

Children take the negative things that important adults say, like parents and coaches, very seriously. Statements such as these may not seem serious to the adults and not all children are deeply affected by such statements. However, from a child's point of view, being yelled at or hearing put downs can be humiliating, degrading and shaming. When a pattern of this type of communication becomes common, it can be highly destructive to a child's spirit, motivation and self-esteem. Especially when coming from someone the child looks up to, like a parent or a coach.

Over time a young athlete may believe what is said to them and their behavior and attitude is likely to get worse instead of better. It is far more helpful to:

- in a clear and non-threatening manner, explain the specific behaviors the child did or did not do
- offer alternatives
- create a constructive environment, (an environment that is child-friendly and supportive) for the child to learn in
- catch children doing something right and give them praise and support

Philosophical abuse. Philosophical abuse describes extreme reactions to statements like, "No pain, no gain." "No pain, no gain" refers to effort versus output or productivity. The slogan is not meant to pressure an injured player to continue playing or to deliberately encourage injuring an opposing player to gain advantage.

Philosophical abuse also refers to the winning at all cost mentality like, "There's no place other than first place," or "Winning isn't everything, it's the only thing." When winning and minimizing serious injuries overrides the rights of a child for safe participation in sports, it's abusive and it sets the stage for other forms of abuse.

Physical abuse. There is a lot of rough and physical contact inherent in many sports. However, hitting children on the back of the head, kicking them, throwing equipment at them or shaking them are indications the person is out of control of both their behavior and feelings. These behaviors are not disciplinary. They are abusive. A one-time incident may be serious enough to warrant an intervention. A pattern of physically abusive behavior on the part of a coach or parent requires intervention.

Sexual abuse. All touch is not sexually abusive. The kind of touch that many of us need and appreciate is:

- respectful of a person's personal boundaries and comfort level
- public (done in front of others), not secret
- nurturing, not sexualized

Touch may be especially appropriate and appreciated when a young athlete needs comfort, reassurance, and support. What does it mean to sexualize touch?

- fondling instead of a hug
- a long kiss on the lips
- seductive stroking of various body parts from a coach or a parent

When a person misuses physical or emotional power over another person, and uses sexual touch, instead of being respectful and nurturing, this is abusive use of touch. In some cases the appropriateness of the touch may be confusing, while in other cases the contact is clearly sexual abuse, such as when a coach or parent has sex with a child.

For a consensual relationship to take place both people need to have equal power and equal knowledge. Even when the coach and the athlete are both adults or are close to each other in age, the coach is in a position of power over the athlete. Therefore, a sexual relationship can be abusive. The role of the coach should be more similar to that of a teacher than to an intimate friend.

Sexual harassment is commonly referred to as sexual comments, contact or behaviors that are offensive, uninvited or unwelcome. A one-time incident may constitute sexual harassment but often harassment is a pattern of behavior over a period of time.

Sexual harassment. Sexual harassment may be initiated by teammates, other athletes, coaches, officials or the spectators. Sexual harassment can occur independent of the intent of the person doing it. What's critical is how the person it's happening to perceives it—it's defined by the eye of the beholder.

What may seem like just a joke, just having fun, or a compliment to one person may make someone else feel threatened or unsafe. It is sexual harassment when the behaviors create a hostile or intimidating environment. Young athletes need encouragement and feedback regarding their athletic skills, not intimidating comments regarding their body parts, sexual development or perceived sexual behaviors.

Steps in Avoiding Abuse

There are numerous steps that we each can take to keep child maltreatment out of youth sports.

Coaches

Volunteering your time as a coach is already both a contribution and a sacrifice. Asking volunteer coaches for any more of their time to receive training is not something people are anxious to do. Most coaches want to do a good job. They want to be positive role models for children and they want children under their guidance to be safe. Remember that as a coach:

Treat all children with equal respect. Your job is to help all children develop their skills, not just the ones who are already obviously the talented athletes. Some children could become better athletes if they had the opportunity for more skill development, and/or time to mature physically and emotionally.

Keep the reason for the game in perspective. Winning is not everything. Your job is to help each child play his or her best. You may feel great pressure from parents, more accomplished athletes on your team, organizations, sponsors and within yourself to win, win, win. Keep in mind girls and boys want to do well, they want to win, but most of all they want to have fun and they all want to be able to play.

Use appropriate discipline. Make sure that your methods of discipline are for the purpose of developing appropriate behavior, motivation and self discipline in the athlete, rather than to humiliate or harm the athlete. Rigorous training activities as punishment for negative behaviors are more likely to decrease child's interest in physical fitness and training, than to improve negative behaviors.

Take injuries seriously. Injuries need to be attended to and taken seriously. Winning is not worth compounding injuries or risking long term damage to a child's body or ability to play. Further, encouraging young athletes to injure opposing players is not what the game is about.

Replace put downs with instruction. Put downs from you or allowing them from other team members are likely to make children who make a mistake feel worse about themselves and feel more insecure. We all make mistakes. It's not fair to expect a child athlete to have a perfect game. Most of us don't learn by being yelled at. We learn by getting good instructions about what we could do better.

Motivate with praise, not name calling. Telling a boy he plays like a girl or like a sissy is often used as shaming put downs. These types of comments are used to hurt, not help. When using such phrases to insult boys, there is also a negative message about all girls. When such comments are said to girls, they can feed a sense that girls are inferior to boys.

Do not accept abusive behavior. Teammates, parents or other coaches may behave in ways you identify as abusive. Let it be known that you do not condone such behaviors on your team or in your crowds. Behaviors like name calling, including berating the other team, can lead to a negative and hostile atmosphere.

The more you learn about maltreatment and abuse, the more you may be in a position to intervene and/or report it. Remember, you are in a leadership position, you're a role model and you can make a difference.

Parents

Prepare young children to be athletes. A girl's abilities or interests in sports are as important as a boy's. Studies indicate that despite the fact girls are equally physically capable as boys, by age six girls are behind boys in basic skill development (throwing, catching, running, etc.). Parents tend to not spend as much time doing things like playing catch with their daughters as they do with their sons. Such games are great ways to spend time with all children and help them to develop basic physical skills and confidence. The benefits and possibilities of children in sports and recreation are so exciting that it's easy to become overzealous. As important as it is to spend time with children so they can develop athletic skills, it is also important to remember, children are children. They aren't only interested in sports. They're learning about who they are and what interests them. Be realistic about expectations. Encourage them to try a variety of activities, not just activities that are typically expected because of their gender, ethnicity or race.

Help your child find the coach and team that works for her/him. Different coaches, leagues and associations have different styles and values. Check out the coach's style and how s/he treats the children. Ask whatever questions you need to make sure the environment and experience will be positive for your child.

Encourage instead of yell. If you find yourself yelling at a child for their mistakes, keep in mind that everyone makes mistakes. Your child is probably painfully aware of hers/his. Your understanding can help your child improve their skills and cope with mistakes by providing the support needed to keep taking risks.

Remember the purpose of the game. Winning is not everything. Supporting a child to try their hardest and to deal with failure and loss is what you can do best.

Coaching from the sidelines. You may have a good deal of expertise about the game being played. You may also have a lot of passion about what's going on when your son or daughter is on the team. Try to avoid being a sidelines coach. If you have feedback for the coach, give it to her/him in a calm and respectful manner after, not during, the game.

Be a positive role model for your child. Yelling at the coach, referees or your child's teammates is not positive role modeling for your children. You want to be proud of your daughter/son for their efforts as an athlete and they want to be proud of having you on the sidelines. It's helpful to take a deep breath when we're angry or frustrated so we have time to think about what values our behavior is teaching our children.

Put your child's needs first. If you're wondering if you have your children's best interest in mind, or if you've become hooked in projecting your own needs on to them, take a moment and ask yourself, "Who is getting whose needs met here?" Your child's need may be to be with their friends and to learn some new skills. While it's easy to understand how a parent's need can slip into wanting a child to be the star on the team, that goal may not be the same as the child's.

Evaluate yourself. Are you an equal opportunity parent? Do you give the same perks for daughters as sons? Are you an askable parent? Do your children really think you'll listen to their concerns? Are you supportive of your child's interest as well as your own? Do your children want to be involved in a different sport or activity than what you want them to be? How do you respond when other fans in the stands are behaving in inappropriate or abusive ways? Are you a parent whose children are proud to have you in the stands or coaching their teams?

Examine your expectations. Are you expecting to see your money's worth out of your investment in equipment, camps and training costs at the expense of your child's emotional and physical well being? Success is not just making the varsity team or getting a scholarship. Success is improving skills, learning how to be a good sport and trying your best.

Youth Athletes

It's important for coaches to help you figure out how to play a better game. Coaches need to encourage you to try harder, improve your skills and play your best. Coaches should try to be fair to everyone, but no one is perfect. If your coach is:

- saying things that hurt your feelings
- behaving in ways that scare you
- touching you in a way that mixes you up, doesn't feel safe or feels more like a sexual touch than a caring touch, tell your coach how you feel. S/he may appreciate hearing that their behavior hurts you in some way.

You may like the coach. You may be afraid of the coach. You may want to protect the coach. If you don't feel safe, or are uncomfortable talking to your coach, talk to someone else. Let your parents know what's bothering you so they can help you. If your parent(s) are behaving in ways that are embarrassing to you at games (yelling at the other fans, officials, coaches, athletes), talk to them about how you feel about their behavior. If your parent(s) say things to you that make you feel bad about yourself (put downs, insults, name calling), let them know how that feels. If you don't feel like you can talk to your parent(s) about the behaviors that bother you, talk to someone else. Try talking to your coach or another adult. Maybe they can talk to them for you. If your coach allows behaviors to take place that you're uncomfortable with, talk to your coach or your parents or another adult. As a player, you have rights and responsibilities:

- to be able to play the game
- to learn new skills to improve your ability
- to learn what you need to do to improve, without being put down or getting called names
- to be treated with respect whether or not you're the best athlete on the team, whether or not your parents are watching, whatever race or culture you are, whether you're male or female
- to be able to play without fearing your coach's or your parents' behavior

- to treat other athletes with respect
- to try your hardest without purposely injuring another athlete
- to have fun
- to learn that winning isn't everything and to know that part of being a good sport is learning how to lose
- to know that trying your hardest is first priority when playing

As a player, your responsibilities are to practice, take risks to improve, try your best, support your team and be a fair loser, as well as a good winner. Early involvement in sports and recreation can ensure the following benefits:

- the desire to stay physically fit and active throughout life
- learning that the true spirit of competition involves trying your best against an opponent who is at their physical and mental best
- understanding that sports and recreation are not about hurting other people, but instead about healthy competition, fitness and fun.

Further Information

American Sport Education Program (ASEP)
Box 5076
Champaign, IL 61825-5076
Phone: 217-351-5076; Fax: 217-351-2674
Website: http://www.asep.com
E-Mail: asep@hkusa.com

Sells training books and videos for coaches and parents.

Children's Trust Fund
P.O. Box 1641
Jefferson City, MO 65102-1614
Phone: 573-751-5147; Fax: 573-751-0254
Toll Free TDD: 800-735-2966
Website: http://www.ctf4kids.org
E-Mail: ctf@mail.oa.state.mo.us

Materials dealing specifically with prevention of abuse in youth sports. Works with Child Abuse Prevention Councils in Missouri to implement abuse prevention in sports programs.

Institute for the Study of Youth Sports
Michigan State University
213 I.M. Sports Circle
East Lansing, MI 48824-1049
Phone: 517-353-6689
Fax: 517-353-5363
Website: http://ed-web3.educ.msu.edu/ysi
E-Mail: ythsprts@msu.edu

Collects and analyze research on youth and sports activity.

Minnesota Amateur Sports Commission
1700 105th Ave. NE
Blaine, MN 55449-4500
Phone: 612-785-5630
Fax: 763-785-5699
Website: http://www.masc.state.mn.us
E-Mail: masc@mnsports.org

Information, research and publications relating to amateur sports in Minnesota, including Breaking Barriers Girls' and Women's Sports Initiative resources and sports ethics information.

National Alliance for Youth Sports
2050 Vista Parkway
West Palm Beach, FL 33411
Toll Free: 800-688-KIDS (2057)
Phone: 561-684-1141
Fax: 561-684-2546
Website: http://www.nays.org
E-Mail: nays@nays.org

Chapter 13

Crimes against Children on the Internet

New computer technology presents complex challenges for law enforcement agencies and victim service providers. These professionals must protect Internet users as they conduct investigations, secure evidence, identify and apprehend offenders, and help child victims and their families. Based on the knowledge and experience of those working with child victims, this chapter focuses attention on child victims of Internet-based crimes, highlighting the challenges for law enforcement personnel and victim service providers, examining who the child victims are, and determining how best to respond to these victims' needs and the needs of their families.

The growth of technology has changed our lives dramatically. Computers were viewed as a luxury or even an extravagance 30 years ago. We relied on television, newspapers, and radio as primary sources of news and information. Cables, modems, and online services were virtually nonexistent.

Today, computers are prevalent in businesses, homes, schools, libraries, and even airports. The World Wide Web provides instant access to news, reference information, shopping, banking, stock trading, auctions, and travel information and reservations. People routinely use the Internet to take college courses, play games, listen to music, and view videos. Chat rooms and e-mails are now replacing telephones as our favorite means of long-distance communication.

"Internet Crimes against Children," from Office for Victims of Crime, Office of Justice Programs, *OVC Bulletin,* December 2001. Available online at http://www.ojp.usdoj.gov/ovc/publications/bulletins/internet_2_2001/NCJ184931.pdf.

The proliferation of computer technology obviously has enhanced our lives in many ways, such as enabling improved productivity and efficiency at work, school, and home. Anyone with access to a computer and modem now has unparalleled recreational and educational opportunities. Unfortunately, criminals are also using modern technology—to prey on innocent victims. Computers and the Internet have made the predator's job easier. Historically, child predators found their victims in public places where children tend to gather—schoolyards, playgrounds, and shopping malls. Today, with so many children online, the Internet provides predators a new place—cyberspace—to target children for criminal acts. This approach eliminates many of the risks predators face when making contact in person.

Scope of the Problem

The sheer number of young people using computers today makes our concern for them well founded. Recent years have seen a great increase in access to and use of the Internet. By the end of 1998, more than 40 percent of all American homes had computers, and 25 percent had Internet access.[1] This trend is expected to continue. Children and teenagers are one of the fastest growing groups of Internet users. An estimated 10 million kids are online today. By the year 2005, this figure is expected to increase to 77 million.[2] With so many youth online and vulnerable to predators, it is extremely important for parents, law enforcement officials, prosecutors, and victim service providers to know as much as possible about Internet crimes against children so they can prevent victimization and prosecute offenders.

Children as Targets of Internet Crimes—Who Is Vulnerable?

Traditionally, both intrafamilial offenders and strangers have found that young children and teenagers are perfect targets for criminal acts because they are often trusting, naive, curious, adventuresome, and eager for attention and affection. However, the most attractive factor to predators is that children and teenagers historically have not been viewed as credible witnesses. Today, the danger to children is even greater because the Internet provides predators anonymity. Whether the victimization occurs in person or over the Internet, the process is the same—the perpetrator uses information to target a child victim. For example, the predator may initiate an online friendship with a young person, sharing hobbies and interests. This may lead to the exchange of gifts and pictures. Just like the traditional predator who targets children in person, the online predator usually is willing to spend considerable time befriending and grooming a child. The predator wants to build the child's trust, which will allow the predator to get what he or she ultimately wants from the child.

Although no family is immune to the possibility that their child may be exploited and harassed on the Internet, a few factors make some children more vulnerable than others. Older children tend to be at greater risk because they often use the computer unsupervised and are more likely to engage in online discussions of a personal nature. Some victims become unwitting participants as they actively participate in chat rooms, trade e-mail messages, and send pictures online. Troubled or rebellious teens who are seeking emancipation from parental authority can be susceptible to Internet predators. The risk of victimization is greater for emotionally vulnerable youth who may be dealing with issues of sexual identity. These young people may be willing to engage in conversation that is both titillating and exciting but appears innocent and harmless. Unfortunately, Internet interactions that initially appear innocent can gradually lead to sexually explicit conduct.[3]

Types of Internet Victimization

Internet crimes are often thought of as victimless. Nothing could be further from the truth. Children and teenagers can and do become victims of Internet crimes. Predators contact teenagers and children over the Internet and victimize them by:

- Enticing them through online contact for the purpose of engaging them in sexual acts.
- Using the Internet for the production, manufacture, and distribution of child pornography.
- Using the Internet to expose youth to child pornography and encourage them to exchange pornography.
- Enticing and exploiting children for the purpose of sexual tourism (travel with the intent to engage in sexual behavior) for commercial gain and/or personal gratification.

Unique Characteristics of Cyber Crimes

Several characteristics distinguish Internet crimes from other crimes committed against children.

Physical contact between the child and the perpetrator does not need to occur for a child to become a victim or for a crime to be committed. Innocent pictures or images of children can be digitally transformed into pornographic material and distributed across the Internet without the victims' knowledge.

The Internet provides a source for repeated, long-term victimization of a child that can last for years, often without the victim's knowledge. Once a child's picture is displayed on the Internet, it can remain there forever. Images can stay on the Internet indefinitely without damage to the quality of the image.

These crimes transcend jurisdictional boundaries, often involving multiple victims from different communities, states, and countries. The geographic location of a child is not a primary concern for perpetrators who target victims over the Internet. Often, perpetrators travel hundreds of miles to different states and countries to engage in sexual acts with children they met over the Internet. Many of these cases involve local, state, federal, and international law enforcement entities in multiple jurisdictions.

Many victims of Internet crimes do not disclose their victimization or even realize that they have been victims of a crime. Whereas children who experience physical or sexual abuse may disclose the abuse to a friend, teacher, or parent, many victims of Internet crimes remain anonymous until pictures or images are discovered by law enforcement during an investigation. The presumed anonymity of Internet activities often provides a false sense of security and secrecy for both the perpetrator and the victim.

Youth Internet Safety Survey

Although it was clear that young people are using the Internet in ever-increasing numbers, no research existed on how many youth encounter unwanted sexual solicitations and exposure to sexual material and harassment online. To obtain a clearer picture of the scope of the problem, the National Center for Missing and Exploited Children (NCMEC) provided funding to Dr. David Finkelhor, Director of the Crimes Against Children Research Center at the University of New Hampshire, to conduct a research survey in 1999 on Internet victimization of youth. His research provides the best profile of this problem to date.

Crimes Against Children Research Center staff interviewed a nationally representative sample of 1,501 youth, aged 10 to 17, who used the Internet regularly. Regular use was defined as using the Internet at least once a month for the past 6 months on a computer at home, at school, in a library, at someone else's home, or in some other place.

Survey Areas

The survey looked at four types of online victimization of youth, which Finkelhor[4] defined as:

- Sexual solicitation and approaches: Requests to engage in sexual activities or sexual talk or to give personal sexual information that were unwanted or, whether wanted or not, made by an adult.
- Aggressive sexual solicitation: Sexual solicitations involving offline contact with the perpetrator through mail, by telephone, or in person, or attempts or requests for offline contact.
- Unwanted exposure to sexual material: When online, opening e-mail, or opening e-mail links, and not seeking or expecting sexual material, being exposed to pictures of naked people or people having sex.
- Harassment: Threats or other offensive content (not sexual solicitation) sent online to the youth or posted online for others to see.

The survey also explored Internet safety practices used by youth and their families, what factors may put some youth more at risk for victimization than others, and the families' knowledge of how to report online solicitations and harassment.

Statistical Findings

The survey results offered the following statistical highlights:[5]

- One in 5 youth received a sexual approach or solicitation over the Internet in the past year.
- One in 33 youth received an aggressive sexual solicitation in the past year. This means a predator asked a young person to meet somewhere, called a young person on the phone, and/or sent the young person correspondence, money, or gifts through the U.S. Postal Service.
- One in 4 youth had an unwanted exposure in the past year to pictures of naked people or people having sex.

- One in 17 youth was threatened or harassed in the past year.
- Most young people who reported these incidents were not very disturbed about them, but a few found them distressing.
- Only a fraction of all episodes was reported to authorities such as the police, an Internet service provider, or a hotline.
- About 25 percent of the youth who encountered a sexual approach or solicitation told a parent. Almost 40 percent of those reporting an unwanted exposure to sexual material told a parent.
- Only 17 percent of youth and 11 percent of parents could name a specific authority, such as the Federal Bureau of Investigation (FBI), CyberTipline, or an Internet service provider, to which they could report an Internet crime, although more indicated they were vaguely aware of such authorities.
- In households with home Internet access, one-third of parents said they had filtering or blocking software on their computers.

Other Findings

The survey results confirm what is already known: although the Internet is a wonderfully fun and educational tool, it can also be very dangerous. According to the survey, one in five youth who regularly use the Internet received sexual solicitations or approaches during a 1-year period. The survey also found that offenses and offenders are more diverse than previously thought. In addition to pedophiles, other predators use the Internet. Nearly half (48 percent) of the offenders were other youth, and one-fourth of the aggressive episodes were initiated by females. Further, 77 percent of targeted youth were age 14 or older—not an age characteristically targeted by pedophiles. Although the youth stopped most solicitations by leaving the website, logging off, or blocking the sender, the survey confirmed current thinking that some youth are particularly vulnerable to online advances.

Most youth reported not being distressed by sexual exposures online. However, a significant 23 percent reported being very or extremely upset, 20 percent reported being very or extremely embarrassed, and 20 percent reported at least one symptom of stress. These findings point to the need for more research on the effects on youth of unwanted exposure to sexual materials and the indicators of potentially exploitative adult-youth relationships.

The large number of solicitations that went unreported by youth and families was of particular interest. This underreporting is attributed to feelings of embarrassment or guilt, ignorance that the incident was a reportable act, ignorance of how to report it, and perhaps resignation to a certain level of inappropriate behavior in the world.

Possibly due to the nature and small sample size of the survey, there were no reported incidences of traveler cases.[6] The survey also revealed no incidences of completed Internet seduction or sexual exploitation, including trafficking of child pornography. Despite the findings of this survey, law enforcement agencies report increasing incidents of Internet crimes against children.

Recommendations

Among the many findings of Finkelhor's survey, the most significant is that we are only beginning to realize the extent of the complex and increasingly prevalent phenomenon of Internet-based crimes against children. We have much to learn about the magnitude of the problem, the characteristics of its victims and perpetrators, its impact on children, and strategies for prevention and intervention.

Information and Intervention Resources

National Center for Missing and Exploited Children

The National Center for Missing and Exploited Children is a comprehensive resource for families, victim service practitioners, and law enforcement personnel. NCMEC is supported by the U.S. Department of Justice's Office of Juvenile Justice and Delinquency Prevention (OJJDP) and functions as a clearinghouse and resource center for collecting and distributing information about missing, runaway, and sexually exploited children, including exploitation resulting from Internet solicitations. In partnership with the U.S. Postal Inspection Service, U.S. Customs Service, and FBI, NCMEC operates the CyberTipline, an online form for reporting suspected child sexual exploitation (www.missingkids.com/cybertip), and the Child Pornography Tipline (1-800-843-5678). Through the CyberTipline and the telephone hotline, NCMEC

- Receives reports 24 hours a day, 7 days a week, of child sexual exploitation and the production and distribution of pornography on the Internet. Calls to the toll-free Child Pornography Tipline can be received from the United States, Canada, Mexico, and the United Kingdom.
- Receives reports of offenses such as child pornography, child sex tourism, online enticement of children for sexual acts, and child

sexual molestation (outside the family). Analysts review each report and provide information to investigating law enforcement agencies.

- Provides leads on child exploitation cases to appropriate law enforcement authorities and agencies.

NCMEC case managers work directly with law enforcement personnel, offering technical assistance, resources, information, and advice on child sexual exploitation. NCMEC also has developed specialized training programs, materials, and curricula designed for law enforcement personnel. Training is available at little or no cost to local jurisdictions through OJJDP. For more information on current programs, call 1-800-843-5678.

Internet Crimes Against Children Task Force Program

In 1998, the Missing Children's Program of OJJDP initiated its Internet Crimes Against Children (ICAC) task force program, a national effort to combat the threat of offenders who use the Internet to sexually exploit children. Through this program, state and local law enforcement agencies can acquire the skills, equipment, and personnel resources to respond effectively to ICAC offenses. The program encourages law enforcement agencies to develop specialized multijurisdictional, multi-agency responses to prevent, interdict, investigate, and prosecute Internet crimes against children. As of mid-2000, 30 ICAC task forces were participating in the ICAC task force program. Each task force is composed of federal, state, and local law enforcement personnel; federal and local prosecution officials; local educators; and service providers such as mental health professionals. These task forces serve as valuable regional resources for assistance to parents, educators, prosecutors, law enforcement personnel, and others who work on child victimization issues. You can obtain more information on this and other law enforcement programs from the OJJDP website at http://ojjdp.ncjrs.org/programs/programs.html.

Federal Bureau of Investigation

The FBI has established the Innocent Images program to focus specifically on computer-facilitated child sexual exploitation. Each FBI Field Division has designated two Crimes Against Children Coordinators to work with state and local law enforcement officials to investigate and prosecute cases that cross jurisdictional boundaries.

OVC has placed a victim witness coordinator in the Innocent Images program to focus greater attention on the needs of child victims.

U.S. Postal Inspection Service

The U.S. Postal Inspection Service protects children online by monitoring the transmission of child pornography through the mail. Increased amounts of pornography are being sent through U.S. mail as more illicit websites emerge advertising child pornographic material for sale. In response, the U.S. Postal Inspection Service is tracking down these materials. In addition, the U.S. Customs Service Cyber Smuggling Center monitors the illegal generation, importation, and proliferation of child pornography.

The Future

The future holds many challenges for those fighting Internet crimes against young people. Cases involving Internet crimes against children are complex and labor intensive for both the police and prosecutors. The time between victimization and arrest can be lengthy. These cases are usually multi-jurisdictional, which presents challenges in the investigation and prosecution of a case and can present problems for the criminal justice system, the child victim, and the family in terms of resources, travel, and court appearances.

Challenges

Child victimization on the Internet is a complex matter. The full impact of such victimization on children is not completely understood. Family dynamics often play a significant role in children's denial of a crime and their willingness to participate in the investigation and prosecution. A child's ability to acknowledge and accept the crime can be linked to family values, peer pressure, and feelings of guilt, shame, and embarrassment. Denial and recantation can be common among children who unwittingly participated in the crime. Because of these issues, the greatest challenges facing law enforcement and victim service professionals are to identify the victims, protect their privacy, and serve them without further victimization.

Until more knowledge is gathered about Internet crime and its effects on victims, law enforcement and victim service professionals will continue working on Internet child exploitation using the tactics and standard approaches that have proved effective for working with other types of child victims.

For Children

- Ensure that the interview is conducted with developmentally appropriate language. A child's ability to relate to concepts and receive messages varies depending on his or her stage of development. The interviewer must assess the child's developmental level and adapt the interview accordingly.
- Ensure that the interview is conducted in a culturally sensitive manner with culturally appropriate language. Determine which words the child is comfortable with. Is an interpreter needed? If so, use a professional interpreter and not a family member. Family members inadvertently may interject their interpretations into the translation and may prejudice the child's account.
- Be patient with victims. At first, many victims will deny their involvement. However, with continued support and encouragement, the child victim usually will divulge and discuss the victimization.
- Avoid duplicative interviews when possible. Multiple interviewers and interviews tend to confuse and intimidate children, especially younger ones, and may re-victimize the child and produce inconsistent victim statements. Joint or taped interviews minimize the number of interviews required and maintain consistent phrasing of questions.
- If the victim is from another jurisdiction, work with victim witness staff in that community to ensure that victim services are provided.
- Do not show surprise or shock. Remember, the youth is probably already feeling guilt, shame, or embarrassment about what occurred.
- Be honest with the child about what he or she can expect from the investigation and prosecution of the case and about any future contact he or she may have with the perpetrator.
- Talk to the child victim about a victim impact statement and restitution if the case will be prosecuted and if it is developmentally appropriate. Regardless of the child's age, find ways to give him or her a sense of control over the situation—provide choices, no matter how small, and help him or her prepare for the court process. Consider requesting a guardian ad litem to represent and support the child throughout the legal process.

Make the child familiar with the courtroom environment. A properly prepared child may find active involvement in the case empowering.

For the Family

- Internet crimes against children impact the entire family. Family members may feel guilty for not protecting their child more effectively. They also may feel anger or shame about their child's involvement in the crime. Family members are secondary victims and need to be offered support and information to help them understand the nature of these crimes and know how to better handle their often conflicting feelings.
- Assist families victimized by Internet crime who require travel and lodging arrangements related to the legal proceedings, such as depositions and hearings.
- Prepare the family for media and press coverage. Be sensitive to the privacy needs of the victim and family. Will the victim's name appear in any public documents? If so, can these documents be sealed if the family so desires?
- Help the family understand what their child is experiencing so they can help the child and feel some sense of control over the situation.[7]

Notes

1. Falling Through the Net: Defining the Digital Divide, July 8, 1999, National Telecommunications and Information Administration, U.S. Department of Commerce.
2. Statistics, ProtectKids.org, www.protectkids.org/statistics.htm.
3. Magid, Lawrence, 1992, *Child Safety on the Information Highway* (pamphlet), National Center for Missing and Exploited Children.
4. Finkelhor, David, Kimberly J. Mitchell, and Janis Wolak, 2000, Online Victimization: A Report on the Nation's Youth, National Center for Missing and Exploited Children: Arlington, VA.
5. Ibid.

6. A traveler case is when an adult travels to meet and have sex with a youth he or she met on the Internet.

7. Turman, K.M., and K.L. Poyer, 1998, *Child Victims and Witnesses: A Handbook for Criminal Justice Professionals,* Office for Victims of Crime, U.S. Department of Justice: Washington, DC.

Part Two

Physical, Mental, and Emotional Effects of Child Abuse

Chapter 14

The Consequences of Child Abuse and Neglect

What Are the Consequences of Child Abuse and Neglect?

The consequences of child maltreatment can be profound and may endure long after the abuse or neglect occurs. The effects can appear in childhood, adolescence, or adulthood, and may affect various aspects of an individual's development (e.g., physical, cognitive, psychological, and behavioral). These effects range in consequence from minor physical injuries, low self-esteem, attention disorders, and poor peer relations to severe brain damage, extremely violent behavior, and death.

While substantial evidence exists for the negative consequences of maltreatment, practitioners should be aware of the limitations of current research. First, many research efforts have studied the effects of child maltreatment among individuals from lower socio-economic backgrounds, prison populations, mental health patients, or other clinical populations who may exhibit the most serious behavior problems

---

Text under the heading "Age Specific Short- and Long-Term Consequences of Neglect," is excerpted from "Short- and Long-Term Consequences of Neglect," from *Child Neglect: A Guide for Intervention,* National Clearinghouse on Child Abuse and Neglect, 1993, available online at http://nccanch.acf.hhs.gov/pubs/usermanuals/neglect/conseq.cfm. Despite its date, this document introduces issues of current concern. Also included is updated text from "What are the Consequences of Child Abuse and Neglect?" from *A Coordinated Response to Child Abuse and Neglect: The Foundation for Practice,* National Clearinghouse on Child Abuse and Neglect, 2003, available online at http://nccanch.acf.hhs.gov/pubs/usermanuals/foundation/chapsix.cfm.

and whose families often have had many other problems (e.g., poverty, parental substance abuse, domestic violence). Further, many early studies examining consequences did not compare outcomes among maltreated individuals with outcomes among individuals who had not experienced maltreatment. In addition, studies often rely on official records or self-reporting of current or past child maltreatment, both of which may undercount the true prevalence of maltreatment. Finally, the nature and extent of maltreatment are different for each child and family, and these differences may influence the consequences.

Despite these challenges, it is still possible to identify effects that have been more commonly associated with individuals who have experienced abuse and neglect. These effects are discussed as they relate to three overlapping areas:

- Health and physical effects
- Intellectual and cognitive development
- Emotional, psychological, and behavioral consequences

While maltreated children have a higher risk of certain problems, it cannot be concluded that any given consequence will always occur. Not all children who have been maltreated will suffer severe consequences. A number of factors may influence the effects of maltreatment, including the child's age and developmental status at the time of the maltreatment, as well as the type, the frequency, the duration, and the severity of the maltreatment and co-occurring problems. In addition, research has identified certain protective factors that mediate the effects of maltreatment.

Health and Physical Effects

Health and physical effects can include the immediate effects of bruises, burns, lacerations, and broken bones and also longer-term effects of brain damage, hemorrhages, and permanent disabilities. Negative effects on physical development can result from physical trauma (e.g., blows to the head or body, violent shaking, scalding with hot water, or asphyxiation) and from neglect (e.g., inadequate nutrition, lack of adequate motor stimulation, or withholding medical treatments).

Physical Effects on Infants

Infants and young children are particularly vulnerable to the physical effects of maltreatment. Shaking an infant may result in bruising, bleeding, and swelling in the brain. The health consequences of shaken baby syndrome can range from vomiting or irritability to more severe effects, such as concussions, respiratory distress, seizures, and death. Other possible consequences include partial loss of vision or blindness, learning disabilities, mental retardation, cerebral palsy, or paralysis.

Infants who have been neglected and malnourished may experience a condition known as nonorganic failure to thrive. With this condition, the child's weight, height, and motor development fall significantly below age-appropriate ranges with no medical or organic cause. The death of the child is the end result in extreme cases. Nonorganic failure to thrive can result in continued growth retardation as well as cognitive and psychological problems. Even with treatment, the long-term consequences can include continued growth problems, diminished cognitive abilities, retardation, and socio-emotional deficits such as poor impulse control.

Effects on Brain Development

Over the last decade, researchers have enhanced the field's understanding of the adverse effects of maltreatment on early brain development. Recent brain research has established a foundation for the neurobiological explanations for many of the physical, cognitive, social, and emotional difficulties exhibited by children who experienced maltreatment in their early years. One explanation begins with the link between chronic physical abuse, sexual abuse, or neglect and the chronic stress it typically causes in a young child. In reaction to this persistent stress associated with ongoing maltreatment, the child's brain may strengthen the pathways among neurons that are involved in the fear response. As a result, the brain may become wired to experience the world as hostile and uncaring. This negative perspective may influence the child's later interactions, prompting the child to become anxious and overly aggressive or withdrawn.

Research shows that maltreatment also may inhibit the appropriate development of certain regions of the brain. A neglected infant or young child, for example, may not be exposed to stimuli that would activate important regions of the brain and strengthen cognitive pathways. Consequently, the connections among neurons in these inactivated regions can literally whither away, hampering the individual's later functioning. If the regions responsible for emotional regulation are not activated, the child may have trouble controlling his or her emotions and behaving or interacting appropriately (e.g., impulsive behavior, difficulties in social interactions, or a lack of empathy).

Other Health-Related Problems

Maltreatment may affect an individual's health in a number of direct and indirect ways. Victims of sexual abuse, for example, may become infected with sexually transmitted diseases including syphilis and human immunodeficiency virus (HIV). Studies have found that women who had experienced sexual abuse were more likely to experience ongoing health problems such as chronic pelvic pain and other gynecologic problems, gastrointestinal problems, headaches, and obesity. Recent research suggests that adults who were maltreated as children show higher levels of many health problems not typically associated with abuse and neglect—heart disease, cancer, chronic lung disease, and liver disease. The link between maltreatment and these diseases may be depression, which can influence the immune system and may lead to higher risk behaviors such as smoking, alcohol and drug use, and overeating.

Cognitive Development and Academic Achievement

Current research differs on findings related to the consequences of maltreatment on cognitive development, verbal abilities, and problem-solving skills. Some studies find evidence of lowered intellectual and cognitive functioning in abused children as compared to children who had not been abused, and other studies find no differences.

Research has consistently found that maltreatment increases the risk of lower academic achievement and problematic school performance. Abused and neglected children in these studies received lower grades and test scores than did nonmaltreated children.

Emotional, Psychosocial, and Behavioral Development

All types of maltreatment—physical abuse, sexual abuse, neglect, and psychological or emotional maltreatment—can affect a child's emotional and psychological well-being and lead to behavioral problems. These consequences may appear immediately after the maltreatment or years later.

Emotional and Psychological Consequences

While there is no single set of behaviors that is characteristic of all children who have been abused and neglected, the presence of emotional and psychological problems among many maltreated children is well documented. Clinicians and researchers report behaviors that range from passive and withdrawn to active and aggressive. Physically and sexually abused children often exhibit both internalizing and externalizing problems. Emotional and psychosocial problems identified among individuals who were maltreated as children include:

- Low self-esteem
- Depression and anxiety
- Post-traumatic stress disorder (PTSD)
- Attachment difficulties
- Eating disorders
- Poor peer relations
- Self-injurious behavior (e.g., suicide attempts)

Maltreated children who developed insecure attachments to caregivers may become more mistrustful of others and less ready to learn from adults. They also may experience difficulties in understanding the emotions of others, regulating their own emotions, and in forming and maintaining relationships with peers.

Violence, Substance Abuse, and Other Problem Behaviors

Individuals victimized by child maltreatment are more likely than people who were not maltreated to engage in juvenile delinquency, adult criminality, and violent behavior. A study sponsored by the National Institute of Justice followed cases from childhood through adulthood and compared arrest records of a group of substantiated cases of maltreatment with a comparison group composed of individuals who were not officially recorded as maltreated. While most members of both groups had no juvenile or adult criminal records, being abused or neglected as a child increased the likelihood of arrest as a juvenile by 53 percent and as a young adult by 38 percent. Physically abused children were the most likely of maltreated children to be arrested later for violent crime, followed closely by neglected children.

Other studies also have found maltreated children to be at increased risk (at least 25 percent more likely) for a variety of adolescent problem behaviors, including delinquency, teen pregnancy, drug use, low academic achievement, and mental health problems. It must be underscored, however, that while the risk is higher, most abused and neglected children will not become delinquent, experience adolescent problem behaviors, or become involved in violent crime. Research also suggests a relationship between child maltreatment and later substance abuse. In addition to being a risk factor, child maltreatment, particularly sexual abuse, may be a precursor of substance abuse.

Resilience

Not every child who is maltreated will experience the negative consequences discussed previously. Protective factors that appear to mediate or serve as a buffer against the effects of the negative experiences may include:

- Personal characteristics, such as optimism, high self-esteem, high intelligence, or a sense of hopefulness.
- Social support and relationships with a supportive adult(s).

The finding that the seriousness of negative effects experienced by victims can be influenced by the availability of support from parents, relatives, professionals, and others has important implications for prevention and early intervention.

Studies have documented the link between abuse and neglect of children and a range of physical, emotional, psychological, and behavioral problems. In addition to the tragic consequences endured by the children who have been maltreated, society pays a high monetary cost for child maltreatment. The costs for child maltreatment include both direct costs (i.e., those associated with the immediate needs of abused and neglected children) and indirect costs (i.e., those associated with the longer term and secondary effects of child maltreatment). Since some maltreatment goes unrecognized and it is difficult to link costs to specific incidents, it is not possible to determine the actual cost of child abuse and neglect. As estimated by Prevent Child Abuse America, the total annual cost of child abuse and neglect in the United States may be as high as $94 billion, as shown in Table 14.1.

Age Specific Short- and Long-Term Consequences of Neglect

Infants and Toddlers

Limited research evidence from studies of small samples of neglected infants and toddlers reveals that children who are victims of physical and emotional neglect suffer severe and continuing problems in functioning. These studies suggest that the failure to develop secure attachments with primary caregivers results in further developmental problems. Egeland and colleagues' longitudinal Mother-Child Interaction Study revealed significant developmental deficits in neglected preschool children. Behavior that indicates infants' lack of secure psychological attachment to their mothers began to manifest itself at 12 months of age and got progressively more prevalent through the preschool years. Two-year-olds demonstrated significant deficits in coping skills, more frustration, anger, and noncompliance when compared to nonneglected children in control groups. Neglected preschool children also manifested lower self-esteem, poorer control over impulses, and expressed less positive and more negative affect than the nonmaltreated children. When placed in an experimental Barrier Box situation, where desirable toys were placed in a locked Plexiglas box that prevented access to the toys, the neglected children were the least creative in seeking solutions to the dilemma. They were distractible and hyperactive, reluctant to seek help, and showed the most negative and least positive affect of the children. They were also the least persistent in problem solving.

Table 14.1. The Estimated Costs of Child Maltreatment

Source of Costs	**Estimated Annual Cost**
Direct Costs	
Hospitalization	$6,205,395,000
Chronic health problems	$2,987,957,400
Mental health care system	$425,110,400
Child welfare system	$14,400,000,000
Law enforcement	$24,709,800
Judicial system	$341,174,702
Total direct costs	$24,384,347,302
Indirect Costs	
Special education	$223,607,803
Mental health and health care	$4,627,636,025
Juvenile delinquency	$8,805,291,372
Lost productivity to society (due to unemployment)	$656,000,000
Adult criminality	$55,380,000,000
Total indirect costs	$69,692,535,227
Total Cost	$94,076,882,529

At 42 months of age, the physically neglected children lacked persistence and enthusiasm and were negative and noncompliant in response to their mothers' efforts to teach them simple tasks. In a preschool classroom, these children were seen as more dependent and less able to control impulses than the nonmaltreated children. Children whose parents were emotionally neglectful manifested sharp declines on appropriate indicators of development from infancy through the toddler period.

Observations of peer interactions among a group of 14- to 61-month-old children that included a very small sample of four neglected children, suggest that neglected children, when compared with nonmaltreated children, exhibit less positive and less negative affect, initiate fewer interactions and fewer positive behaviors toward others, and engage in less complex play with peers. Group interventions to improve peer interactions were effective with abused but not with the neglected children.

Kindergarten and Early School Years

As neglected children grow older, developmental deficits are still apparent. They are less well-prepared for learning. One study indicated that maltreated (mostly neglected) preschool and early school-aged children, when compared to nonmaltreated children from AFDC-recipient families, were less secure in their readiness to learn. The conclusion was that maltreated preschool and early school-aged children are less securely ready to learn in the company of novel adults.

Teachers have rated neglected children as "extremely inattentive, uninvolved, reliant, lacking in creative initiative, and as having much difficulty in comprehending day-to-day schoolwork." They were described as lacking "persistence, initiative and confidence to work on their own... They were dependent on the teacher—somewhat helpless, passive and withdrawn, and at times angry." Egeland et al.'s study concluded that physically neglected children suffered the most severe developmental consequences of the four maltreated groups of children studied—neglected, physically abused, sexually abused children, and children whose parents were psychologically unavailable.

Older School-Aged Children

School-aged children with histories of neglect have serious learning deficits. They score significantly lower on measures of school performance than physically abused or nonmaltreated children, particularly in the areas of reading and math. Lack of intellectual stimulation in the neglectful home environment appears to result in significant language deficits. Teachers report that neglected children work at below average levels and learn at below average levels. They also rate neglected children as having more behavioral problems in school than nonmaltreated children. Neglected children are absent from school significantly more often and have a higher percentage of grade repeats than nonmaltreated children.

One study of maltreated children revealed that the maltreated 6 to 9-year-old children but not 4 to 5-year-olds were rated by their mothers as having significantly more behavioral problems, especially symptoms of depression and social withdrawal than nonmaltreated children from lower income families. However, neglected children were not differentiated from abused children. Further research is needed to specify developmental effects for children by type of maltreatment and by age.

Adolescents

Juvenile delinquency is frequently associated with child abuse and neglect. Research findings are complicated because of weak research designs and inconsistencies in the definitions of delinquent acts and child abuse and neglect. Yet, there is evidence of a high incidence of abuse and neglect among delinquent populations and a high incidence of delinquency among maltreated adolescents.

Retrospective studies of delinquents have reported rates of abuse and neglect that vary from 9 to over 60 percent, depending on the source of the information. Self-reports of prior abuse and neglect among delinquents run as high as 51 percent. A study of 5,136 children in 1,423 families reported for child maltreatment in New York revealed that 42 percent of the families subsequently had at least 1 child taken to court for delinquent or ungovernable behavior. This rate was five times greater than the rate in the general population of families in the counties studied. A recent prospective study by Widom did not differentiate neglected from abused children, but revealed that 29 percent of the subjects who were abused and neglected as children had an adult criminal record, compared to 21 percent of the nonmaltreated controls.

Most often in research, neglect is not distinguished from abuse, and the causal sequence between child maltreatment and delinquent behavior is not clear. There are also significant variables that mediate the relationship between maltreatment and delinquency. Widom's recent study would indicate that race, age, sex, identified behavior problems in mother's employment, and father's alcoholism all can increase or reduce the chances of criminal arrest for a maltreated child.

Mediating Effects

Negative developmental consequences for neglected children are not inevitable. Other factors have been identified, which either buffer or add to the effects of neglect on children. Stability of the children's living environment has been identified as modifying the negative effects of maltreatment, whereas multiple out-of-home placements, multiple life stresses, and parental depression contribute to more negative developmental effects of neglect and abuse on children. Children with higher IQs also appear to suffer less serious developmental effects.

Neglect-Related Child Fatalities

Studies of child fatalities related to child maltreatment indicate that children die from neglect almost as often as from physical abuse. A review of 556 child fatality cases reported to Child Protective Services (CPS) agencies in 1986 indicated that 44.3 percent were related to physical neglect.

Margolin's study of 82 fatalities over an 8-year period revealed that 34 (40 percent) were from neglect. The typical neglect fatality was a male child (male children were twice as likely as females to die) under age 3, living with a single mother and two or three siblings. The child typically died because a caregiver was not there at a critical moment. The fatal neglect was most often a preventable accident associated with a single, life-threatening incident. In 39 percent of the cases, the neglectful families were previously known to CPS agencies. Margolin discovered that several items from Polanksy's Childhood Level of Living Scale were significantly correlated with fatal child neglect. These items concerned exercise of judgment about leaving children alone.

Alfaro's review of nine child fatality studies also concluded that fatalities from neglect were almost as frequent as from abuse. Neglect was identified as contributing to the child's death in from 25 percent to 70 percent of the cases. Although many of Alfaro's findings were consistent with those of Margolin, the neglect-related fatalities were most often from two-parent homes. The victims were most often males, under age 2, and often the youngest or only child in the family. Alfaro concluded that fatal child neglect is difficult to predict and prevent. Reliable predictors do not exist, and in 70 percent of the cases, the families had not been previously reported for child abuse or neglect.

To summarize, the indications from limited research are that child victims of neglect fail to develop secure psychological attachments as infants, and this seriously handicaps their subsequent development. Neglected preschool children demonstrate lack of readiness for learning, behavior problems, and less active interaction with peers. School-aged neglected children do poorly in school, but the connection between delinquency and abuse is less clear. Neglected children under age 3 are at high risk for child fatalities. However, children who have higher IQs and/or who live in less stressful, stable home environments suffer less serious effects of neglect.

Additional Information

For those who would like to follow-up on this information the full text of this document, including links to the notes, is available online at http://nccanch.acf.hhs.gov/pubs/usermanuals/neglect/conseq.cfm.

Chapter 15

Recognizing Signs of Child Abuse

Unthinkable as it is to imagine someone intentionally hurting a child, about 1 million children are abused every year in the United States. And these are only the reported incidents—many more are unreported and undetected, often because children are afraid to tell.

When mistreatment becomes abuse, children are injured, neglected, and emotionally damaged. Approximately 1,000 to 1,300 U.S. children are known to die as a result of physical abuse, and those who survive suffer emotional trauma that lasts long after the bruises have healed.

Some studies report that in the United States, as many as one out of every eight boys and one out of every four girls is sexually abused before turning 18 years old. In 90% of these cases, sexual abuse occurs in the home, particularly when younger children are involved. A child who knows the abuser (about 90% of cases involve an abuser who was previously known to the child) usually senses that the abuse is wrong, but he may feel trapped by the affection he feels for the person or fearful of the power the abuser has over him, so he doesn't tell. Whatever the statistics, one thing we know is that child abuse is too frequent and too often hidden.

This information was provided by KidsHealth, one of the largest resources online for medically reviewed health information written for parents, kids, and teens. For more articles like this one, visit www.KidsHealth.org or www.TeensHealth.org.

Emotional abuse can be just as damaging. The effects can last a lifetime, stripping a child of self-esteem and affecting his relationships, happiness, and success.

Four Types of Abuse

Abuse of a child can mean physical abuse, physical neglect, sexual abuse, or emotional abuse. Physical abuse can include the following actions when they are continuous, pervasive, and extreme, and if they are done intentionally to harm a child:

- hitting
- throwing
- kicking
- choking
- biting
- shaking
- beating with an object
- burning with a match, cigar, or cigarette
- scalding with hot water
- pushing and holding a child underwater
- tying up a child
- starving or failing to provide food for a child

The following actions can be considered physical neglect if they interfere with a child's growth and development:

- not providing adequate housing or warm clothing in cold weather
- locking a child in a closet or room
- leaving a child alone for extended periods of time
- not providing medical care when a child is sick or injured
- placing a child in a physically dangerous situation

These actions can be considered sexual abuse:

- fondling, touching, or kissing a child's sex organs
- making a child touch someone else's sex organs

- having sex with a child
- showing a child pornographic material
- showing sex organs to a child
- forcing a child to undress
- forcing a child to have sex with someone
- making a child pose or perform for pornographic pictures or videos
- telling a child "dirty" stories

Emotional abuse occurs when a parent ignores, terrorizes, blames, belittles, or otherwise makes a child feel that he's worthless and incompetent.

Shaken baby/shaken impact syndrome is a specific form of child abuse. It's the leading cause of death in child abuse cases in the United States. Most incidents last just 5 to 20 seconds, but that's enough time to cause sufficient brain damage to kill the baby. In some cases, a blow to the head accompanies the shaking.

Signs of Abuse

Of course, all children get scratches, bruises, and cuts from time to time. That's the nature of childhood—a time that's full of tumbling, climbing, and adventures. That makes it difficult to tell what's normal and what may be a sign of abuse. Unfortunately, there's no one telltale sign that a child is being abused. Bruises, black eyes, and broken bones are certainly clues, but other signs are less obvious. Children who have been abused may behave differently. They may have nightmares or trouble sleeping. Their school performance may suddenly decline. In addition, they may:

- have a poor self-image
- be unable to love or trust others
- be aggressive or disruptive (become bullies)
- display intense anger or rage
- act out in the classroom
- act out sexually
- be self-destructive, self-abusive, or suicidal
- feel sad, passive, withdrawn, or depressed

- have difficulty forming new relationships
- use drugs or alcohol
- avoid going home after school
- show a fear of certain adults

Children who witness abuse but are not victims themselves may also display some or all of the above signs. It's important to note that these symptoms are all nonspecific, meaning they could result from a number of causes—not just child abuse. Children who are under stress from a variety of sources—including parental separation, divorce, and visitation and custody arrangements—may show similar symptoms.

Those who abuse children may show certain nonspecific signs as well. For example, parents who abuse their children may avoid other parents in the neighborhood, may not participate in school activities, and may be uncomfortable talking about their children's injuries or behavioral problems.

What to Do if You Suspect Abuse

Abuse is not a private family matter, although it most often occurs within families and often every attempt is made to keep it secret. Once you suspect child abuse, you need to act to protect the child from further possible harm. It doesn't matter if you're wrong: it's better to be wrong than sorry. Here's what to do:

- If you suspect that a child is being abused, it's your responsibility to contact your local child protective services agency, police, hospital, or emergency hotline. If necessary, you may remain anonymous. The child's safety is the immediate issue: you could save his life.
- If you have abused your own child or think that you might, talk with a friend, relative, or your child's doctor, or other trusted adult immediately. These people can refer you to a mental health professional who can help.
- If you suspect that someone you know is abusing a child, such as a babysitter or child care provider, there are specific steps to take. "If parents have a reasonable suspicion that a caregiver is abusing their child, they should protect the child by limiting or supervising contact with that person. They should then talk

to the child in a way that's not alarmist, at the child's developmental level," advises Paul Robins, Ph.D., a behavioral health specialist.

Your child should know about the different kinds of abuse and how to spot it. "The issue is helping kids identify what adults can and can't do, what's OK and not OK, and helping kids know who they can talk with once something happens," Dr. Robins says. They should be told that they don't have to do everything adults (such as teachers or babysitters) tell them to do, especially when they think it's wrong.

Dr. Robins continues, "Parents must educate their children at home, when children are cognitively able to understand, because this is when they begin to be on their own more. It's not too early to talk to a preschooler, in a very basic way. Pick up a book about the subject and read it with your child."

Adults who sexually abuse children often tell them that their relationship is a "secret" or that, if they tell anyone about what's happening, they will be hurt or get in trouble or that the person they tell will get hurt. Be sure your child knows that he can always come to you if he thinks someone is being abusive, even if that person has told him to keep it a secret.

A parent who learns that their spouse or close relative is committing child abuse may be in shock; it would be natural not to want to believe someone you love could be abusive of your child—and the reality can rock your world. Sometimes the facts may seem to horrible to face and the consequences to great, which can leave a parent confused and paralyzed. In some cases, a parent may choose to ignore or deny suspicions or even disbelieve a child sharing such information. While not all suspicions and accusations turn out to be true, all deserve serious attention and immediate action with the help of professionals. And your child always deserves to be heard, protected, and helped no matter what.

Helping Your Child Heal

If your child tells you about an abusive experience, remain calm and let him know that you believe him. Your reaction can either help him begin to recover or further traumatize him. Here are some tips:

- Listen carefully and calmly, no matter how upset you are. You'll need to remember what your child tells you, so pay attention. And let your child know that he's being heard.

- Assure your child that you're glad that he told you of the abuse, that it was in no way his fault, and that you will make sure it doesn't happen again. Encourage him to tell you everything, but avoid asking too many specific questions. Specific questions may mislead or confuse your child, or they may be asked in a way that prompts a particular answer. Later, this may seriously affect the ability of investigators to find out exactly what did or did not happen. If investigators can't determine that abuse has occurred, they can't protect your child.
- Don't say anything bad about the perpetrator. He or she may be someone the child truly cares for. If you make threats, your child may feel the need to protect the person and not be as forthcoming with details.
- If you think that your child wants to say more but is afraid, encourage him to tell his story to a favorite stuffed animal or doll while you listen. Or provide a tape recorder or telephone for the child to talk into. It may be easier for the child to talk to an inanimate object than to you or another person.

Your child will need medical care if he has been sexually molested or physically injured. Even if signs of abuse are not evident, it's best to err on the side of caution and take him to the doctor anyway. Above all, keep your child in safe environments and assume the allegation is true until proven otherwise.

The American Academy of Pediatrics' Committee on Hospital Care recommends that children who are suspected abuse victims be brought to a hospital, where the initial diagnosis can be made and treatment can be given. Hospitals are havens for abused children, especially battered children who may need imaging studies (X-rays) or cultures for a diagnosis to be made. Imaging can indicate broken bones, which are often the only sign that infants and young children have been abused, as they can't or won't speak of the abuse themselves.

Psychological help is also strongly recommended. Without it, children who have been abused tend to repeat the pattern of abuse with their own children. As adults, they have trouble establishing and maintaining close relationships and they are at greater risk for anxiety, depression, substance abuse, medical illness, and problems at work.

Chapter 16

Shaken Baby Syndrome

Shaken Baby/Shaken Impact Syndrome

Several years ago, when a young au pair from Great Britain was charged in the death of the 8-month-old Massachusetts boy in her care, the case received phenomenal media coverage both in the United States and abroad. Lawyers for the prosecution and the defense waged a charged battle throughout the trial, trying to assign the blame for Matthew Eappen's death. But when it was all over, the only thing that was clear was that Matthew's case had become one of the most publicized cases of shaken baby/shaken impact syndrome (SBS).

What Is SBS?

SBS is the leading cause of death in child abuse cases in the United States. The syndrome results from injuries caused by someone vigorously shaking an infant, usually for 5 to 20 seconds, which causes brain damage. In some cases, the shaking is accompanied by a final impact to the baby's head against a bed, chair, or other surface.

Although SBS is occasionally seen in children up to 4 years old, the vast majority of incidents occur in infants who are younger than 1 year old; the average age of victims is between 3 and 8 months.

This information was provided by KidsHealth, one of the largest resources online for medically reviewed health information written for parents, kids, and teens. For more articles like this one, visit www.KidsHealth.org or www.TeensHealth.org. © 2001 The Nemours Center for Children's Health Media, a division of The Nemours Foundation.

Approximately 60% of shaken babies are male, and children of families who live at or below the poverty level are at an increased risk for SBS (and any type of child abuse).

How It Happens

When someone forcefully shakes a baby, the child's head rotates about uncontrollably because infants' neck muscles are not well developed and provide little support for the head. The violent movement pitches the infant's brain back and forth within the skull, rupturing blood vessels and nerves throughout the brain and tearing the brain tissue. The brain strikes the inside of the skull, causing bruising and bleeding to the brain. The damage is even greater when the shaking ends with an impact (hitting a wall or a crib mattress, for example), because the forces of acceleration and deceleration associated with an impact are so strong. After the shaking, swelling in the brain can cause enormous pressure within the skull, compressing blood vessels and increasing overall injury to its delicate structure.

Normal interaction with a child, like bouncing the baby on a knee, will not cause SBS, although it is important never to shake a baby under any circumstances because gentle shaking can rapidly escalate. Pediatrician Allan DeJong, MD, says, "When you shake your baby hard enough to give them these injuries, you know you've crossed the line. This is something violent."

Diagnosing SBS

To diagnose SBS, doctors look for hemorrhages in the retinas of the eyes (which are extremely rare in any accidental injuries, such as falls), skull fractures, swelling of the brain, subdural hematomas (blood collections pressing on the surface of the brain), rib and long bone (bones in the arms and legs) fractures, and bruises around the head, neck, or chest.

SBS often has irreparable consequences. In the worst cases, the death rate is almost half of all babies involved. Children who survive may suffer partial or total blindness, hearing loss, seizures, developmental delays, impaired intellect, speech and learning difficulties, problems with memory and attention, or paralysis (some particularly traumatic episodes leave children in a coma). Severe mental retardation may also result.

Even in milder cases, where the baby looks normal immediately after the shaking, he may eventually develop one or more of these problems. Sometimes the first sign of a problem isn't noticed until the child enters the school system and exhibits behavioral problems or learning difficulties. By that time, however, it is more difficult to link these problems to a shaking incident from several years before.

Effects of SBS

In any SBS case, the duration and force of the shaking, the number of episodes, and whether impact is involved all affect the severity of the infant's injuries. In the most violent cases, children may arrive at the emergency room unconscious, suffering seizures, or in shock. But in many cases, where the infants don't exhibit such severe symptoms, they may never be brought to medical attention.

In milder cases, the infant may seem lethargic or irritable or perhaps will not be feeding well. Unfortunately, unless a doctor has reason to suspect SBS, these cases are often misdiagnosed as a viral illness or colic. "Their brain may have been scrambled [by the shaking], but not to the point of significant brain injury, yet they could have been a shaken baby," Dr. DeJong notes. Lacking a diagnosis of SBS and subsequent intervention, these children may be shaken again, worsening any brain injury or damage.

Besides lethargy, a baby who has been shaken may experience vomiting, poor sucking or swallowing, decreased appetite, lack of smiling or vocalizing, rigidity, seizures, difficulty breathing, altered consciousness, unequal pupil size, an inability to lift his head, or an inability to focus his eyes or track movement.

What makes SBS so devastating is that it usually involves a total brain injury. Because the infant's brain has little stored information and few developed capacities to make up for the deficit, the brain's adaptive abilities are substantially impaired, says Jane Crowley, PsyD, a pediatric rehabilitation psychologist. For example, a child whose vision is severely impaired will not be able to learn through observation, which decreases his overall ability to learn. The development of language, vision, balance, and motor coordination, all of which occur to varying degrees after birth, are particularly likely to be affected in any child who was a victim of SBS.

Such impairment can require rigorous physical and occupational therapy to help the child acquire skills that would have developed on their own had the brain injury not occurred. Therapists do this by providing a sensory-rich environment, which forces the child to be attentive. Therapists often work one on one with a child, concentrating on building his ability to pay attention. Therapists use sound and other stimuli to increase the child's interest in objects, such as repeatedly squeaking a toy near his ear. As he gets older, a child who was shaken as a baby may require special education and continued therapy to help with language development and daily living skills, such as dressing himself.

Your Child's Development and Education

After your child turns 3, it is your school district's responsibility to provide additional special educational services. Before age 3, your child can receive speech or physical therapy through the Department of Public Health. Federal law requires that each state provide these services for children who have developmental disabilities as a result of being shaken as babies.

Can SBS Be Prevented?

While the consequences of SBS are terrible, it is important to remember that the syndrome is 100% preventable. The perpetrators in SBS cases are almost always parents or caregivers, who shake the baby out of frustration when he is crying inconsolably. It is estimated that males, often in their early 20s, usually either the baby's father or the mother's boyfriend, are the perpetrators in 65% to 90% of cases. Caregivers who shake babies usually do so out of the stress of dealing with a fussy baby. Sadly, the shaking has the desired effect: although at first the baby cries more out of fear, he eventually stops crying as his brain is damaged.

Finding ways to alleviate the caregiver's stress at these critical moments will significantly reduce the risk to the child. If a baby in your care won't stop crying, try the following:

- make sure the baby's basic needs are met (for example, he isn't hungry and doesn't need to be changed)
- check for signs of illness, like fever or swollen gums
- rock or walk with the baby
- sing or talk to him
- offer the baby a pacifier or a noisy toy
- take him for a ride in his stroller or in his car seat in the car
- swaddle the baby snugly in a blanket

- turn on the stereo, run the vacuum cleaner or the clothes dryer, or run water in the tub (babies like rhythmic noise)
- hold the baby close against your body and breathe calmly and slowly
- call a friend or relative for support or to take care of the baby while you take a break
- if nothing else works, put the baby on his back in his crib, close the door, and check on him in 10 minutes

Chapter 17

Battered Child Syndrome

Definition

Battered child syndrome refers to children who have undergone physical abuse that has left them with both physical and psychological trauma.

Causes, Incidence, and Risk Factors

Physical abuse of children occurs in every socioeconomic class, though it is most common amongst the poor due to increased stress and greater lack of control over stressful circumstances. Abuse tends to occur at moments of greatest stress, when the perpetrator strikes out in anger at the child. Many perpetrators were themselves abused as children and they often don't realize that abuse is not appropriate discipline. Abusers also frequently have poor impulse control, which prevents them from thinking through the consequences of their actions.

Because of the relative size and strength difference between adults and children, the abused child can be severely injured or killed unintentionally. Shaking an infant, for example, can cause bleeding over the brain (subdural hematoma) which can cause permanent brain damage or death (shaken baby syndrome).

The incidence of child abuse is remarkably high. The total abuse rate is 25.2 per 1,000 children with physical abuse counting for 5.7

per 1000, sexual abuse 2.5 per 1,000, emotional abuse 3.4 per 1000 and neglect accounting for the vast majority, 15.9 per 1,000 children. Of course, these categories often overlap, with sexual and physical abuse often occurring together and with sexual abuse, physical abuse or neglect seldom occurring without emotional abuse.

These numbers may also be underestimates due to failure to diagnose or report this problem. Risk factors include poverty, lack of education, single parenthood, alcoholism or other drug addictions and a host of other factors.

Symptoms

- Appearance at an emergency room with an injured child and one or both of the following:
  - An improbable explanation of the cause of the injury
  - An injury that is not recent
- Bruise marks shaped like hands, fingers, or objects (such as a belt)
- Specific patterns of scalding (seen when a conscious child is immersed in hot water)
- Burns from an electric stove, radiator, heater or other hot objects on the child's hands or buttocks
- Cigarette burns on exposed areas or the genitals
- Black eyes in an infant
- Human bite marks
- Lash marks
- Choke marks around neck
- Circular marks around wrists or ankles (twisting)
- Separated sutures
- Bulging fontanelle
- Unexplained unconsciousness in infant

Signs and Tests

Physical examination may show other injuries, such as:

- Multiple retinal hemorrhages (bleeding in the back of the eye)

- Internal damage such as bleeding or rupture of an organ from blunt trauma
- Any fracture in an infant that is too young to walk or crawl
- Evidence of epiphyseal fractures (often multiple) of long bones or spiral type fractures that result from twisting
- Fractured ribs
- Evidence of skull fracture (multiple fractures of different ages may be present)
- Subdural hematoma (collection of blood in the brain) without plausible explanation

Tests that reveal physical injuries include:

- Bone x-ray
- Skull x-ray and/or MRI or CT scan

Treatment

Physical injuries are treated as appropriate for the specific injury. Counseling or intervention of some type for the parent(s) is mandatory. Life-threatening abuse or abuse resulting in permanent damage to the infant or child may result in incarceration for the perpetrator. In some cases, the child may be temporarily or permanently removed from further danger.

Many states require that known or suspected child abuse be reported to the police, and reporting is automatic. Child protection services are also notified. The disposition of the child will be determined by the severity of the abuse, the likelihood of recurrence, and other factors. Decisions regarding placing the child with an outside caregiver or returning the child to the home usually are made by the appropriate government agency through the court system. The structure of these agencies varies from state to state.

Support Groups: Support groups are available for survivors of abuse and for abusive parents who want to get help.

Expectations (Prognosis): The child's recovery depends on the severity of the injuries, and the outcome of the family or abuser rests with the authorities. Child protection agencies generally make every effort to reunite families when possible.

Complications: Physical abuse of a child can lead to severe brain damage, disfigurement, blindness, crippling, and death. Abused individuals may carry emotional scars for a lifetime. Children can be removed permanently from the parents' custody if the parents are the perpetrators and the cause is sufficient to warrant termination of parental rights.

Calling Your Health Care Provider: Call your health care provider or protective services if you suspect or know that someone is being abused.

Prevention

Recognition of pending abuse can help prevent actual abuse. Warning signs include the following:

- Abuse history (such as previous abuse of the child or the child's siblings)
- Lack of apparent parental love or concern
- Failure to maintain the child's proper hygiene or care
- Parental alcohol or drug problems
- Parental emotional problems or mental illness
- History of abuse in the parent's childhood
- High stress factors in the family life

Intervention with counseling may prevent abuse when any of these factors are present. Watchful guidance and support from the extended family, friends, clergy, or other supportive persons or groups may prevent abuse or may allow early intervention in cases of abuse.

Chapter 18

The Effects of Abuse on Children's Brain Development

How the Brain Develops

What we have learned about the process of brain development has helped us understand more about the influence of genetics and environment on our total development—the "nature versus nurture" debate. It appears that genetics predispose us to develop in certain ways. But our interactions with our environment have a significant impact on how our predispositions will be expressed; these interactions organize our brain's development and, therefore, shape the person we become.

Sensitive Periods

> "It is now clear that what a child experiences in the first few years of life largely determines how his brain will develop and how he will interact with the world throughout his life."
>
> —*Ounce of Prevention Fund, 1996*

Researchers believe that during these years there may be sensitive periods for development of certain capabilities. Because synapses

---

Excerpted from "Understanding the Effects of Maltreatment on Early Brain Development," from "IN FOCUS: Understanding the Effects of Maltreatment on Early Brain Development," October, 2001. National Clearinghouse on Child Abuse and Neglect Information. The entire text of this document, including references, is available online at http://nccanch.acf.hhs.gov/pubs/focus/earlybrain.cfm.

are being formed at such an intense pace during this time, the opportunities for learning are almost limitless. But as the process of pruning synapses starts to increase, especially after age 3, these opportunities begin to decrease. If certain synapses and neuronal pathways are not repeatedly activated, they may be discarded, and the capabilities they promised may be diminished. For example, all infants have the capacity, indeed the genetic predisposition, to form strong attachments to their primary caregivers. But if a child's caregivers are unresponsive or threatening, and the attachment process is disrupted, the child's ability to form any healthy relationships during his or her life may be impaired.

Although the first few years may be the prime time for learning, children and adults can learn later in life, but it is more difficult. This is especially true if a young child was deprived of certain stimulation, which resulted in the pruning of synapses and the loss of neuronal pathways. An analogy has by offered that of a country that has a dense network of branching streets; a traveler can go anywhere he wants, even unfamiliar places, by following the roads. If there are few roads, the traveler can still go places, but he has to travel cross-country and break new ground. It is doable, but much harder. As children progress through each developmental stage, they will learn and master each step more easily if their brains have built an efficient network of pathways.

While research has shown that the brain is more malleable in the first few years than at any other time in life, researchers disagree on how flexible or rigid the sensitive periods are. But they do agree that the experiences of the first few years form the foundation for children's future functioning.

Malnutrition

Malnutrition, both before and during the first few years after birth, has been shown to result in stunted brain growth and slower passage of electrical signals in the brain. These effects on the brain are linked to cognitive, social, and behavioral deficits with possible long-term consequences. For example, iron deficiency (the most common form of malnutrition in the United States) can result in cognitive and motor delays, anxiety, depression, social problems, and problems with attention. Protein deficiency can result in motor and cognitive delays and impulsive behavior. The social and behavioral impairments may be more difficult to repair than the cognitive impairments, even if the nutritional problems are corrected.

Memories

The organizing framework for children's development is based on the creation of memories. When repeated experiences strengthen a neuronal pathway, the pathway becomes sensitized, and, at some point, it becomes a memory. Memories are an indelible impression of the world; they are the way in which the brain stores information for easy retrieval.

There are different types of memories, such as motor, cognitive, and emotional memories. Memories help us to navigate our world without having to really think about it. Children learn to put one foot in front of the other to walk. They learn words to express themselves. And they learn that a smile usually brings a smile in return. At some point, they no longer have to think much about these processes—their brains manage these experiences with little effort because the memories that have been created allow for a smooth, efficient flow of information.

The creation of memories is part of our adaptation to our environment. Our brains attempt to understand the world around us and fashion our interactions with that world in a way that promotes our survival and, hopefully, our growth. But if the early environment is abusive or neglectful, our brains will create memories of these experiences that may adversely color our view of the world throughout our life.

Effects of Maltreatment on Brain Development

Babies' brains grow and develop as they interact with their environment and learn how to function within that environment. When babies' cries bring food or comfort, they are strengthening the neuronal pathways that help them learn how to get their needs met, both physically and emotionally. But babies who do not get responses to their cries, and babies whose cries are met with abuse, learn different lessons. The neuronal pathways that are developed and strengthened under negative conditions prepare children to cope in that negative environment, and their ability to respond to nurturing and kindness may be impaired.

Stress

Brief periods of moderate, predictable stress are not problematic; in fact, they prepare the child to cope with the general world. The body's survival actually depends upon the ability to mount a response to stress. But prolonged, severe, or unpredictable stress—including abuse and neglect—during a child's early years is problematic. The brain's development can literally be altered by these experiences, resulting in negative impacts on the child's physical, cognitive, emotional, and social growth.

Chronic stress sensitizes neural pathways and over-develops certain regions of the brain involved in anxiety and fear responses, and often results in the under-development of other neural pathways and other regions of the brain. Children who experience the stress of physical or sexual abuse will focus their brains' resources on survival and responding to threats in their environment. Children who experience the chronic stress of neglect—e.g., remaining hungry, cold, scared, or in pain—will also focus their brains' resources on survival. This chronic stimulation of the brain's fear response means that the regions of the brain involved in this response are frequently activated. When they are, other regions of the brain, such as those involved in complex thought, can not also be activated and are therefore not available to the child for learning.

Because the brain ultimately controls all bodily functions, experiences that alter brain development also alter our bodies' responses. Studies have shown that the overwhelming stress of maltreatment experiences in childhood is associated with alterations of biological stress systems and with adverse influences on brain development. One example of the effects of early maltreatment on brain and body functions involves the chemical cortisol. Cortisol is a hormone that helps the body prepare to cope with stress through its effects on metabolism and the immune system. Studies have shown that many infants and children who have been maltreated have abnormal secretions of cortisol, indicating that their bodies' responses to stress have been impaired. More research is needed to understand why this occurs and what effects this may have on the children's emotional and social development, but this information provides some evidence of altered brain activity in maltreated children.

A key issue in understanding altered brain development in children who have been maltreated is that the way in which their brains develop is often a very adaptive response to their negative environment, but it is maladaptive in other environments. If a child lives in a threatening, chaotic world, his brain will be hyper-alert for danger; his survival may depend on it. But if this environment persists, and the child's brain is focused on developing and strengthening its strategies for survival, other strategies may not develop as fully. If a child lives in a world that ignores him, if he is not provided with appropriate stimulation for growth, his brain will focus on survival from day to day and may not fully develop healthy cognitive and social skills. The result may be a child who has great difficulty functioning when presented with a world of kindness, nurturing, and stimulation. It is an unfamiliar world to him; his brain has not developed the pathways and the memories to adapt to this new world.

Persistent Fear Response

Fear is necessary to our basic survival. We must be able to detect threats and respond. Indeed, the brain is uniquely designed to sense, process, and store threatening information and to mobilize the body in response to threats. All parts of the brain and body are used in this response.

Early experiences of trauma can also result in extreme anxiety, depression, and difficulty forming attachments to other people. As well as creating permanent memories which shape the child's perception of and response to his environment. While this adaptation may be necessary for survival in a hostile world, it can become a way of life that is difficult to change, even if the environment improves.

Dissociative and Hyper-Arousal Responses

Dr. Bruce Perry, former head of the Child Trauma Academy at Baylor College of Medicine in Houston, Texas, offers this example of dissociative and hyper-arousal responses in the same child for different events.

> "T is a twelve year old girl. From birth until age five she lived in a household characterized by domestic violence. During this time, she was noted to be quiet, compliant, tuned out, daydreamed and generally a good little girl. She reports little memory of the fighting but her mother describes finding her in her bed, rocking, with covers over her head after some of the fights in the home . At age 12, her mother re-married but unfortunately, episodes of domestic violence resumed in this household. This time, however, T was loud, combative, angry and would run away from the home each time these events took place. She was noted to have attention problems at school that turned out to be hypervigilance. Rather than tuning out and withdrawing into a dissociative shell, this child was sensitized to fighting and had dramatic and pronounced hyperarousal during conflict."

Hyper-Arousal

When a child is exposed to chronic, traumatic stress, his brain sensitizes the pathways for the fear response and literally creates memories such that his fear response becomes almost automatic; he doesn't really think about it. This is called a state of hyper-arousal. His brain has adapted to a world that is unpredictable and dangerous; it is hyper-vigilant, focused on non-verbal cues that may be threatening. The regions of the brain involved in the hyper-arousal response are always on, and because of this, the child may frequently experience hyperactivity, anxiety, impulsivity, and sleep problems. Hyper-arousal is most common in older children and in males.

In the state of hyper-arousal, similar to Post Traumatic Stress Disorder (PTSD), the brain's alarm system becomes particularly sensitive to threatening environmental cues, and the child may respond anxiously or aggressively. The regions of the brain involved in the hyper-arousal response become re-activated when the child is exposed to a reminder of the earlier trauma (such as thinking or dreaming about it), to perceived threats (which may not seem threatening to others), and sometimes to generalized reminders (signals). An example of an 8-year-old boy who became extremely agitated—sobbing and hysterical—when the staff at his group home refused to cut up his hot dog before he ate it. The child had been sexually abused by his father and other men. Foods such as hot dogs, bananas, and Popsicles evoked his brain's fear response, and until the signal was removed or altered, his brain experienced it as a threat. Another example is that of a child who had committed an impulsive, violent act and explained it by saying "I could tell he was going to jump me—he looked me in the eyes." In his mind, his brain, the simple act of looking him in the eye was perceived as a threat that required a defensive response.

Not only may children in a state of hyper-arousal react anxiously or aggressively to perceived threats, they may actually provoke threatening behavior from others in order to have some control over it. Predictability of threat is important. Children who have been victims of unpredictable physical or sexual abuse learn (consciously or unconsciously) that if abuse is going to happen, it is better to control when it happens. They may engage in aggressive, provocative behavior to elicit a predictable response. For example, a girl who has suffered repeated sexual abuse from her father may attempt to seduce a male teacher. She may believe that men will invariably try to have sex with her, so she tries to control when and with whom.

Dissociation

While hyper-arousal is more common in older children and males, dissociation is more common in younger children and in females—children who often feel or are immobile or powerless. Dissociation is characterized by first attempting to bring caretakers to help, and if this is unsuccessful, becoming motionless (freezing) and compliant and eventually dissociating; this is often called the "surrender" response. People describe children in a dissociative state as numb, non-reactive, or acting like they aren't there.

Just as children in a state of hyper-arousal have sensitized neural pathways controlling their response to a threatening environment, children in a state of dissociation have sensitized neural pathways that elicit a different response. A child in a dissociative state, when presented with a threat, may freeze, both physically and cognitively. When an adult asks or tells them to do something, they don't respond. If the adult becomes angry and more threatening, the child becomes even more anxious and moves further into full dissociation.

Disrupted Attachment Process

At the foundation of much of our development is the concept of attachment which refers to the emotional relationships we have with other people. One of the first priorities of an infant is to form an attachment to his primary caregiver. This relationship not only provides the foundation for future emotional relationships, it also provides the base for other learning, because babies and children learn best when they feel safe, calm, protected, and nurtured by their caregivers. If the attachment process is disrupted, as can occur with abusive and neglectful caretakers, the child's brain will be more focused on meeting his day-to-day needs for survival rather than building the foundation for future growth.

Much of a child's emotional development is rooted in his relationships with his early primary caregivers. For example, it appears that aggressive, submissive, and frustration behaviors may be genetically encoded. If relationships with the caregivers are positive, the child's cognitive structures learn to regulate these emotions and behaviors. If the relationships are negative or weak, the lower-brain responses become dominant and the cognitive regulating structures do not develop to their full capacity—the young child may not fully develop the cognitive ability to control his emotions, nor develop an awareness of others' emotions.

One example of a potential effect of poor early attachments is impaired social cognition. Social cognition involves an awareness of oneself in relation to others and an awareness of the emotions of others. If these abilities are poorly developed, many types of social interactions may be experienced as stressful/unfamiliar, strange situations that are difficult for the child to incorporate because he does not have a strong internal representation (memory) of what is happening and how to respond. Children who have been abused and neglected often lack empathy and truly do not understand what others feel like when they do something hurtful.

Neglect—Lack of Stimulation

While chronic abuse or neglect can result in sensitized fear response patterns, neglect alone also can result in other problems. Although neglect often is thought of as a failure to meet a child's physical needs for food, shelter, and safety, neglect also can be a failure to meet a child's cognitive, emotional, or social needs. For children to master developmental tasks in these areas, they need opportunities, encouragement, and acknowledgment from their caregivers. If this stimulation is lacking during children's early years, the weak neuronal pathways that had been developed in expectation of these experiences may wither and die—the children may not achieve the usual developmental milestones.

For example, babies need to experience face-to-face baby talk and hear countless repetitions of sounds in order to build the brain circuitry that will enable them to start making sounds and eventually say words and form sentences. If babies are ignored, if their caregivers do not provide this type of intense verbal interaction, their language development may be delayed. If a child does not receive kindness as an infant, he may not know how to show kindness as an adult. If a child's cries for attention are ignored as a toddler, he may not know how to interact positively with others later. These capacities may not fully develop because the required neuronal pathways were not activated enough to form the memories needed for future learning.

Global Neglect

The term "global neglect" is used when a child has experienced deprivations in more than one domain, i.e., language, touch, and social interaction. Children who were adopted from Romanian orphanages in the early 1990s are often considered to be globally neglected;

they had little contact with caregivers and little to no stimulation from their environment—little of anything required for healthy development. One study found that these children had significantly smaller brains than the norm, suggesting decreased brain growth.

This type of severe, global neglect can have devastating consequences. The extreme lack of stimulation may result in fewer neuronal pathways available for learning; genetically normal children may be at a permanent intellectual disadvantage. The lack of opportunity to form an attachment with a nurturing caregiver during infancy may mean that some of these children will always have difficulties forming meaningful relationships with others. But these studies also found that time played a factor—children who were adopted as young infants have shown more recovery than children who were adopted as toddlers.

Pervasive and Long-Term Effects

Maltreatment during infancy and early childhood has been shown to negatively affect early brain development and can have enduring repercussions into adolescence and adulthood. As mentioned earlier, the experiences of infancy and early childhood literally provide the organizing framework for the expression of children's intelligence, emotions, and personalities. When those experiences are primarily negative, children may develop emotional, behavioral, and learning problems that persist throughout their lifetime, especially in the absence of targeted interventions.

While some children seem unaffected or minimally affected by their traumatic experiences, in reality, it is often the adults around them who are misreading their cues. These children are communicating non-verbally with us, and we need to learn the language and educate others who work with children who have been maltreated about this language. Children do not just get over it. As they attempt to cope, as their brains adapt to the negative environments, their true emotional, behavioral, cognitive, and social potential may be diminished.

Children who have experienced chronic abuse and neglect during their first few years may live in a persistent state of hyper-arousal or dissociation, anticipating threats around every corner, and their ability to benefit from social, emotional, and cognitive experiences may be impaired. The various regions of the brain can not grow without being activated, and certain regions can not be activated when others are. To learn and incorporate new information, whether it be a lesson in the classroom or a new social experience, the child's brain must be in a state of attentive calm, a state the traumatized child rarely achieves. It is not uncommon for teachers who work with traumatized children to observe that the children are really smart, but they do not learn easily; they are often diagnosed with learning disabilities. Children who have not been able to develop healthy attachments with their caregivers, and whose early emotional experiences have not laid the necessary groundwork for healthy emotional development, may have a limited capacity for empathy. The ability to feel remorse and empathy are built on experience. In the extreme, if a child feels no emotional attachment to any human being, he can not be expected to feel remorse for hurting or even killing someone. One example is of a 15-year-old boy who felt no remorse for having committed murder. The boy had been neglected and humiliated by his primary caretakers as a child. He is literally emotionally retarded. The part of his brain which would have allowed him to feel connected to other human beings—empathy—simply did not develop.

The effects of abuse and neglect on the developing brain during children's first few years can result in various mental health problems. For example:

- Diminished growth in the left hemisphere may increase the risk for depression.
- Irritability in the limbic system can set the stage for the emergence of panic disorder and post-traumatic stress disorder (PTSD).
- Smaller growth in the hippocampus and limbic abnormalities can increase the risk for dissociative disorders and memory impairments.
- Impairment in the connection between the two brain hemispheres has been linked to symptoms of attention-deficit/hyperactivity disorder (ADHD).
- Severely neglected children who have been deprived of sensory stimulation—including touch, movement, and sound—may be at risk for Sensory Integration Disorder (SID).
- Children who have been raised in environments that totally disregarded their needs for comfort, stimulation, and affection may be at risk for Reactive Attachment Disorder.

We are learning more about the serious, long-term consequences of abuse and neglect on brain development, and subsequent physical, cognitive, emotional, and social growth. What do we do with this information? What does it mean for biological parents, foster and adoptive parents, professionals, the child welfare system, and for society? How can we use this knowledge to improve our interventions with children who have been abused and neglected, and, most importantly, to prevent abuse and neglect from occurring? While these questions may be challenging, this growing body of knowledge compels us to work towards finding the answers.

Implications for Practice and Policy

The knowledge we have gained from research examining the effects of maltreatment on brain development can be helpful in many ways. With this information, we are better able to understand what is happening within the brains of children who have been abused and neglected. In fact, much of this research is providing further, solid evidence for what professionals and caregivers have been describing in behavioral, emotional, and psychological terms. We can use this information to improve our systems of care, and to strengthen our prevention efforts.

There has been some encouraging progress in States' recognition of early brain development research and how this information can be used to improve services. In a survey conducted by the Child Welfare League of America in 2000, 31 States reported that they had reviewed relevant research findings. Many also reported that they had engaged in efforts to increase awareness about early brain development, and that both legislative and policy changes had occurred to enhance prevention, early intervention, and healthy child development programs.

The Child Welfare System

While the goal of the child welfare system is to protect children, many child welfare interventions—such as investigation, appearance in court, removal from home, placement in a foster home, etc.—may actually reinforce the child's view that the world is unknown, uncontrollable, and frightening. These experiences can actually contribute to the traumatized child's catalog of fearful situations. In addition, many child welfare systems in the United States do not provide comprehensive assessments to all children in their care, and therefore the treatments provided may not be the most effective—they may not accurately target each child's unique experience.

As much as possible, the child welfare system needs to address these deficits and reform practice to provide consistency, repetition, nurturance, predictability, and control (returned to the child) to diminish the fearful nature of the interventions. In addition, child welfare systems should provide comprehensive assessments for all children as soon as possible to examine their physical, cognitive, emotional, and social development. Accomplishing these objectives will require the participation of all stakeholders including policymakers; family court judges; managers; child welfare workers; medical, mental health, and education professionals; kinship, foster, and adoptive parents; and the parents and children themselves. Every group must examine its contribution to the development of the children served by the child welfare system, and strive to provide that contribution in a manner that will promote healthy development for each child.

The Role of Professionals

One of the first tasks for professionals who work with children who have been maltreated is to educate themselves about the effects of maltreatment on early brain development, as well as interventions likely to be effective. For example, talk therapy must do more than talk if the child is in a persistent hyper-arousal state; the child's brain may well be unresponsive to verbal interactions. Professionals who are knowledgeable about this issue need to educate others who work with and care for the children. Information can be provided to foster parents and other caregivers to help them understand the effects of maltreatment on children's brain development, how those early experiences may influence current behavior and functioning, and what can be done to help the children recover their lost potential. CPS workers, judges, and teachers also may not be knowledgeable about these issues; they can benefit from opportunities to understand the importance of their contributions to the child's environment. By working in a coordinated manner, professionals and caregivers can help to minimize unpredictable, unknown, and frightening experiences and assist the child's movement along a path of healthy development.

Human service professionals are increasingly receptive to new knowledge about human brain development. Professionals across disciplines are engaged in exciting new efforts to rethink the brain and apply the knowledge and ideas to support the healthy development and well-being of children. As these efforts begin to offer meaningful information, it must be translated into policies and practices for the front-line workers and caregivers in order to have the most impact on improving child well-being in child welfare systems.

The Role of Caregivers

Many children who have suffered abuse and neglect are removed from their homes by the child welfare system for their safety. These children may be temporarily cared for by extended family, foster parents, or group home staff, and some will be adopted. While many caregivers have an innate sense about how to raise children, familiarity with the effects of maltreatment on brain development and the possible manifestations of those effects are not likely to be common knowledge.

It is important for caregivers to have realistic expectations for the children in their care. Children who have been abused or neglected may not be functioning at their chronological age in terms of their physical, social, emotional, and cognitive skills. They may also be displaying unusual and/or difficult coping behaviors. For example, abused or neglected children may:

- Be unable to control their emotions and have frequent outbursts
- Be quiet and submissive
- Have difficulties learning in school
- Have difficulties getting along with siblings or classmates
- Have unusual eating or sleeping behaviors
- Attempt to provoke fights or solicit sexual experiences
- Be socially or emotionally inappropriate for their age
- Be unresponsive to affection.

It is easy for foster parents to become confused, frustrated, and sometimes devastated from the lack of response and reciprocity to the love, affection, attention, and care they offer. Even caregivers with the best of intentions can misunderstand a child's behavior, fashion their response based on that misunderstanding, and then wonder why their response was not effective.

To be more effective in their roles, caregivers who serve abused and neglected children could benefit from training and support related to the effects of maltreatment on early brain development. Understanding some basic information about the neurobiology underlying many challenging behaviors may help caregivers shape their responses more effectively. But while a general understanding is helpful, foster parents and other caregivers need to know the history of their particular foster children's experiences in order to tailor their approaches. They may need to develop some special skills to cope with the children's special needs.

In general, children who have been abused or neglected need nurturance, stability, predictability, understanding, and support. They may need frequent, repeated experiences of these kinds to begin altering their view of the world from one that is uncaring or hostile to one that is caring and supportive. Until that view begins to take hold in the child's mind, the child may not be able to truly engage in a positive relationship. And the longer the child lived in the abusive or neglectful environment, the harder it will be to convince his brain that his world can change. But one thing we have learned from research is that environment does make a difference. Consistent nurturing from caregivers who receive training and support may offer the best hope for the children who need it most.

Intensive, Early Intervention

Intensive, early interventions are key to minimizing the long-term effects of early trauma on children's brain development. Two studies that have shown this impact include the following:

- Craig Ramey of the University of Alabama at Birmingham reported that vulnerable children who received services from 4 months to 5 years old showed better cognitive development than those receiving services from age 5 to age 8; the difference was even more pronounced at age 12 than at age 8.
- From a study of the development of children adopted from Romanian orphanages, when each child was 6 years old, the researchers assessed what proportion of the adopted children were functioning normally. They found that 69 percent of the children adopted before the age of 6 months were functioning normally, 43 percent of the children adopted between the ages of 7 months and 2 years, and 22 percent of the children adopted between the ages of 2 years and 3½ years.

Indeed, many studies have shown the effectiveness of early intervention, but we now have a better understanding of why early intervention makes a difference. In order to heal a damaged or altered brain, interventions must activate those portions of the brain that have been altered. Because brain functioning is altered by repeated experiences that strengthen and sensitize neuronal pathways, interventions can not be constrained to weekly therapy appointments. Interventions must address the totality of the child's life, providing frequent, consistent replacement experiences so that the child's brain can begin to incorporate a new environment—one that is safe, predictable and nurturing.

Although early interventions show the most promise for significant recovery from abuse and neglect, later interventions are not futile. However, as children get older, recovery from lost or altered brain functioning may be slower and less complete than recovery attempted earlier in the children's lives. But some recovery is certainly possible; while a negative environment may contribute to deficits, a positive environment can contribute to growth.

Prevention

While early intervention with maltreated children can minimize the effects of abuse and neglect, it is equally or even more important to prevent problems before they start. Prevention efforts can target the general population (primary or universal prevention), educating the public and changing policies to promote healthy brain development. For example, one prevention strategy might involve expanding education efforts that target women who may become pregnant about the effects of alcohol on the developing brain of the fetus. An example of a policy change might involve expanding family leave to allow more parents time off from work to care for and build an attachment to a newborn or adopted child.

Prevention efforts also can target children and families considered to be at-risk of developing problems before problems develop (secondary or selected prevention). By the time a child who has been abused or neglected comes to the attention of professionals, it is likely that some damage already has been done. Secondary prevention efforts must reach out to at-risk families before this point. There are many home visitation programs that provide services to at-risk families before and after the birth of a child—services that support children's healthy development—that have proven to be successful in preventing future problems.

Many researchers examining the effects of maltreatment on early brain development agree that this knowledge should be used to expand and strengthen prevention efforts. Without expanded prevention, our society will continue to fight an uphill battle to repair the damage that has been done to thousands of children who have been abused and neglected. Society can not continue to ignore the laws of biology; the more we learn about early brain development, the more responsibility we have to act on that knowledge.

Chapter 19

The Relationship between Adverse Childhood Events and Adult Health

The Adverse Childhood Experiences (ACE) Study

The Adverse Childhood Experiences Study is a major piece of medical research that compares current adult health to childhood experiences decades earlier. The findings are important medically, socially, and economically. They provide a remarkable insight into how we become what we are as individuals and as a nation. The ACE Study reveals a powerful relationship between our emotional experiences as children and our adult emotional health, physical health, and mortality. Moreover, the time factors in the Study make it clear that time does not heal some of the adverse experiences we found so common in the childhoods of a population of middle-aged, middle class Americans. One doesn't "just get over" some things.

How does one perform reverse alchemy, going from a normal newborn with almost unlimited potential to a diseased, depressed adult? How does one turn gold into lead? The ACE Study was triggered by observations we made in the mid 1980s in an obesity program at Kaiser Permanente's San Diego Department of Preventive Medicine. This program had a high dropout rate, and the first of many counterintuitive findings was that the great majority of these dropouts actually

---

"Reverse Alchemy in Childhood: Turning Gold Into Lead" by Vincent J. Felitti, M.D., is reprinted with permission from the Family Violence Prevention Fund. This articles originally appeared in the *Family Violence Prevention Fund Health Alert,* Volume 8, Number1, Summer 2001. For additional information, visit www.endabuse.org

were successfully losing weight. Detailed life interviews of almost 200 such individuals revealed that childhood abuse was remarkably common and antedated the onset of their obesity. Many patients spoke openly of an association between the two. The counterintuitive aspect was that for many people obesity was not their problem; it was their protective solution to problems that previously had never been discussed with anyone. An early insight was the memorable remark of a woman who was raped at twenty-three and gained 105 pounds in the year subsequent: "Overweight is overlooked and that's the way I need to be." The contrast was striking between this statement and her desire to lose weight.

Similarly, two men who were guards at the State Penitentiary became anxious after each losing over one hundred pounds. They made it clear that they felt much safer going to work looking big as a refrigerator rather than normal size. Overall, we found the simultaneous presence of opposing forces to be common; many of our weight program patients were driving with one foot on the brakes and one on the gas, wanting to lose weight but fearful of change.

In 1990 in Atlanta, I presented information about the frequent relationship of obesity and abusive childhood experiences to a largely skeptical audience at the North American Association for the Study of Obesity. Unexpectedly, this led to contacts with researchers at the Centers for Disease Control and Prevention who recognized the importance of what had been reported. They proposed a large epidemiological study to provide definitive evidence of our clinical observations. This was the beginning of the Adverse Childhood Experiences Study that was carried out in the Department of Preventive Medicine where we had been carrying out detailed biomedical, psychological, and social (biopsychosocial) evaluations of over 50,000 adult Kaiser Health Plan members each year. It was relatively easy to ask 30,000 adults coming through the Department if they would be interested in helping us understand how childhood events might affect adult health status. Seventy-one percent agreed to, understanding the information they provided about their childhoods would never be in their medical records.

The ACE Study compared the current adult health status of these many thousands of participants to seven categories of adverse childhood experience that we frequently identified in the weight program. Three categories were of personal abuse: recurrent physical abuse, recurrent emotional abuse, and sexual abuse. Four were categories of household dysfunction: growing up in a household with an alcoholic or a drug user; where someone was imprisoned; where someone was chronically depressed, mentally ill, or suicidal; and where the mother was treated violently. In addition, we decided to follow this large cohort for at least five years into the future to compare childhood experiences against adult pharmacy utilization, doctor office visits, Emergency Department use, hospitalization, and death. For purposes of analyzing the huge mass of information we gathered, an ACE Score was constructed. An individual exposed to none of these categories had an ACE Score of zero; an individual exposed to any four had an ACE Score of four, etc.

Because the average participant was 57 years old, we actually measured the effect of these childhood experiences on adult health status a half-century later. The retrospective and prospective components of the Study were designed with great skill by Robert Anda M.D., my co-principal investigator at CDC. Here I will only touch upon some highlights of our findings; details may be sought in the anchor article of a series of publications deriving from the ACE Study. The initial article was published in May 1998 in the *American Journal of Preventive Medicine,* Vol.14:245-258; full text can be accessed from the journal's website at www.ajpm-online.net.

Adverse Childhood Experiences are Common and Dramatically Affect Adult Health

Our first finding was that adverse childhood experiences are vastly more common than acknowledged. Of equal importance was our observation that they had a powerful correlation to adult health a half century later. It is this combination that makes them so important. Slightly more than half of our middle class American population experienced one or more of the categories we studied. One in four were exposed to two categories of abusive experience, one in sixteen to four categories. Given an exposure to one category, there is 80% chance likelihood of exposure to another. All this, of course, is well shielded by social taboos against obtaining this information. Furthermore, one may miss the forest for the trees if one studies these issues individually. They do not occur in isolation; for instance, a child does not grow up with an alcoholic or domestic violence in an otherwise ideal household. How will these childhood experiences play out decades later in a doctor's office?

Smoking is a useful starting example to illustrate what we found; more over, it provides us with a minimally threatening topic. In California there are now profound social pressures against smoking; persisting in the face of these is often attributed to addiction. Did you know that current smoking has a high degree of association with what happened decades ago in childhood?

Lest one doubt the significance of this, we found that chronic obstructive pulmonary disease (COPD, emphysema) has a strong relationship to the ACE Score. A person with a mid-range ACE Score of four is 390% more likely to have COPD than is a person with an ACE Score of zero. What does this do to the conventional concept of smoking that attributes addiction to characteristics that are intrinsic within nicotine? We instead found addiction attributable to characteristics that are intrinsic in early life experiences. If early emotional stresses predict COPD, is COPD properly understood as a psychosomatic condition? Are certain common chronic diseases the result of attempts at self treatment of concealed problems?

When we looked at self-defined current depression, we found that an individual with an ACE Score of four or more was 460% more likely to be suffering from depression than an individual with an ACE Score of zero. Should one doubt the reliability of this, we found that there was a 1,220% increase in the history of attempted suicide between these two groups. At higher ACE Scores, the prevalence of attempted suicide increases twenty–thirty fold. Using the analytic technique of population attributable risk, we found that about 80% of attempted suicides could be attributed to adverse childhood experiences.

Intravenous (IV) drug use is a major public health problem. In spite of massive efforts to curtail it, little progress has been made. We saw that intravenous drug use may properly be viewed as a personal solution to problems that are well concealed by social niceties and convention. For instance, a male child with an ACE Score of six has a 4,600% increase in the likelihood of later becoming an IV drug user. This relationship to adverse childhood experiences is powerful and graded at every step; it provides an exemplary dose-response curve. Since no one shoots heroin to get endocarditis or AIDS, might it be used for relief of profound anguish dating back to childhood experiences; might it be the best coping device an individual can find? If so, is this a public health problem or a personal solution? How often are public health problems personal solutions? Is drug abuse self-destructive or is it a desperate attempt at self-healing, albeit at a significant future cost? This is an important point because primary prevention is far more difficult than anticipated. Is this because incomplete understanding of the benefits of so-called health risk behaviors leads them to be viewed as irrational and having solely negative consequences? Does this leave us mouthing cautionary platitudes instead of understanding the cause of our intractable public health problems?

Beyond these three examples, we found many other measures of adult health to have a strong, graded relationship to what happened in childhood: hepatitis, heart disease, fractures, diabetes, obesity, alcoholism, occupational health, and job performance. These are detailed in the original and subsequent articles and will further be reported in publications of the yet-to-be-analyzed prospective arm of the ACE Study.

Early Intervention and Prevention Must Be Engaged

What do these findings mean for medical practice and for society? Clearly, we have shown that adverse childhood experiences are both common and destructive. This combination makes them one of the most important, if not the most important, determinants of the health and well being of the nation. Unfortunately, these problems are painful to recognize and difficult to deal with. Most physicians would far rather deal with traditional organic disease. Certainly, it is easier to do so, but that approach also leads to treatment failures and the frustration of expensive diagnostic quandaries where everything is ruled out but nothing is ruled in.

Our approach to many common adult chronic diseases reminds us of the relationship of smoke to fire. It is tempting initially to treat the smoke because that is the most visible aspect of the problem. What we have learned in the ACE Study represents the underlying fire. Fortunately, fire departments learned to distinguish cause from effect long ago; else, they would carry fans rather than water hoses to their work.

If the treatment implications of what we found in the ACE Study are far-reaching, the prevention aspects are positively daunting. The very nature of the material is such as to make one uncomfortable. Why would one want to leave the relative comfort of traditional organic disease and enter this area of threatening uncertainty that none of us have been trained to deal with? And yet, literally as I am writing these words, I am interrupted to consult on a 70 year old woman who is diabetic and hypertensive. The initial description given to me left out the fact that she is morbidly obese. Review of her chart shows her to be chronically depressed, never married, and, because we ask the question of 57,000 adults a year, to have been raped by her older brother six decades ago when she was ten. He also molested her sister who is said also to be leading a troubled life. We found that 22% of our Kaiser members were sexually abused as children. How does that affect a person later in life? That simple question is useful to ask patients, "How did that affect you later in life?"

What is this woman's diagnosis? Is she just another hypertensive, diabetic old woman or is there more to the practice of medicine? Here is the way we conceptualized her problems:

- Childhood sexual abuse
- Chronic depression
- Morbid obesity
- Diabetes mellitus
- Hypertension
- Hyperlipidemia
- Coronary artery disease
- Macular degeneration
- Psoriasis

This is not a comfortable diagnostic formulation because it points out that our attention is focused on tertiary consequences, far downstream. It reveals that the primary issues are well protected by social convention and taboo. It points out that we have limited ourselves to the smallest part of the problem, that part where we are comfortable as mere prescribers of medication. Which diagnostic choice shall we make? Who shall make it? And, if not now, when?

Selected articles published from the ACE study include:

Relationship of childhood abuse and household dysfunction to many of the leading causes of death in adults: The Adverse Childhood Experiences (ACE) study. Felitti, VJ, Anda, RF, Nordenberg, D, et al. *American Journal of Preventive Medicine,* 1998 May; Vol 14 (4): 245-258.

Adverse childhood experiences and smoking during adolescence and adulthood. Anda RF; Croft JB; Felitti VJ; et al. *JAMA,* 1999 Nov 3; Vol 282 (17): 1652-1658.

Unintended pregnancy among adult women exposed to abuse or household dysfunction during their childhood. Dietz PM; Spitz AM; Anda RF; et al. *JAMA,* 1999 Oct 13; Vol 282 (14): 1359-1364.

Adverse childhood experiences and sexually transmitted diseases in men and women: a retrospective study. Hillis SD; Anda RF; Felitti VJ; Nordenberg D; Marchbanks PA, *Pediatrics,* 2000 Jul; Vol 106 (1): E11.

Chapter 20

Witnessing Domestic Violence: The Impact on Children

Estimates of the number of women nationwide who experience domestic violence vary widely. The latest information from the U.S. Department of Justice indicates that:

- Approximately one million violent crimes are committed by former spouses, boyfriends, or girlfriends each year, and about 85 percent of their victims are women.[1]
- In 1998, about 7.7 per 1,000 women, and 1.5 per 1,000 men age 12 or older experienced a violent victimization by a current or former spouse, girlfriend, or boyfriend.[2]
- Nearly 75 percent of all one-on-one violence against women was inflicted by offenders whom the victims knew. In 29 percent of all one-on-one violence against women, the perpetrator was a husband, ex-husband, boyfriend, or ex-boyfriend.[3] Thirty percent of all female murder victims were killed by an intimate, compared to 2 percent of all male murder victims.[4]
- For three out of four women who have experienced domestic violence, the offense occurred in or near their own home. Sixty percent report it occurred between 6 p.m. and 6 a.m.[5]

Children's Defense Fund, "Domestic Violence and Its Impact on Children," Washington, D.C. 2000.

Children Witnessing Domestic Violence

The emotional toll on children who witness threats or violence against others can be substantial, especially when those involved are familiar to the child and the violence takes place in the home—a place where victims should feel safe. Children, who do not get help, can be harmed when they witness domestic violence, regardless of whether or not they are directly abused themselves.

- It is estimated that between 3.36 and 107 million children witness domestic violence each year.
- Studies have found that 80 to 90 percent of children living in homes with domestic violence are aware of the violence.[8] Often, parents tend to underreport the extent to which children are aware of the violence, mistakenly reporting that the children were asleep or otherwise preoccupied when the violence occurred.[9]
- Forty-five percent of female victims of domestic violence between 1993 and 1998 lived in households with children under the age of 12.[10]
- About four in 10 violent offenders in state prison for domestic violence were residing with their children under age 18 prior to entering prison.[11]

Co-Occurrence of Child Abuse and Domestic Violence

Often, children who witness domestic violence also are physically, sexually, or emotionally abused themselves.

Both child maltreatment and domestic violence occur in an estimated 30 to 60 percent of families where there is some form of family violence.[12]

Some experts argue that domestic violence is the single major precursor to child abuse and neglect fatalities in this country, of which five are estimated to occur every day.[13]

In a national survey of over 6,000 families, 50 percent of the men who frequently assaulted their wives also frequently abused their children and the more frequent the violence against the woman, the more likely it is that the children are also abused.[14]

The Impact on Children from Witnessing Domestic Violence

Research in this area is still in its infancy and much of the following data are based upon small studies examining survey questions or case-record reviews. In lieu of more in-depth studies, Doctors Peled, Jaffee, and Edleson, in Ending the Cycle of Domestic Violence, summarize the past two decades of research surrounding the impact of domestic violence on children and present a picture of its adverse effects, which are described below. These effects may be intensified when the child feels that he has lost the support of his parents or other caregivers and also struggles with feelings of guilt and blame. It is important to note that the impact of witnessing violence can be moderated by a number of factors, including effective treatment and support from caring adults.

Psychological and Behavioral Problems

Children who witness violence at home are at risk of suffering from numerous emotional and behavioral disturbances as diverse as withdrawal, hypervigilance, nightmares, self-blame, developmental regression, and post traumatic stress disorder.[15]

Children who witness domestic violence also experience symptoms such as anxiety, aggression, temperamental problems, depression, less empathy, and low self-esteem. Lower verbal, cognitive, and motor abilities are also documented as symptoms in children who witness domestic violence.[16]

Physical Symptoms

Children who witness domestic violence may display the following symptoms: sleep disorders, headaches, stomach aches, diarrhea, ulcers, asthma, enuresis, and depression. Such complaints are often identified as reactions to stress.[17]

Academic Problems

Children of women who are battered have been found to have high rates of poor school performance, truancy, absenteeism, and difficulty concentrating.[18]

Increased Likelihood of Aggressive Behavior and Delinquency

A comparison of delinquent and non-delinquent youths found that a history of family violence or abuse is the single most significant difference between the two groups as to whether they are delinquent.[19]

Numerous studies have shown that children exposed to domestic violence are more likely to be violent. Studies also suggest that children's exposure to adult domestic violence may generate attitudes justifying their own use of violence.[20]

Male children who witness violence are at an increased risk of becoming perpetrators. Growing up in a violent home is the strongest predictor of becoming a batterer in the teen and adult years.[21]

Longer-Term Problems

Retrospective studies indicate that there may also be negative effects in adulthood from witnessing domestic violence, including depression, trauma-related symptoms, low self-esteem for women, and trauma-related symptoms among men. These findings were independent of other factors such as parental substance abuse and divorce.[22]

Among women who had witnessed domestic violence as a child, greater distress and lower social adjustment existed when compared to non-witnesses.[23]

Resiliency of Children Who Witness Domestic Violence

While the research is clear that children exposed to domestic violence are at risk of suffering negative consequences, it is important to keep in mind that not all children are effected the same way. Dr. Jeffrey Edleson, a well-known researcher in the field of domestic violence and its impact on children, urges caution in interpreting the data.

> "While it is true that on average children exposed to adult domestic violence show greater problems than other children, it is also true that large numbers of individual children who were exposed to domestic violence did not show measurably greater problems than comparison children in these studies. These findings suggest that we must pay careful attention to the frequency and severity of violence in each home, the degree to which each child is exposed to this violence, and the protective factors operating in a child's environment."

> "The degree to which a child is affected by exposure to violence will depend on how all these factors vary. Protective factors may include a protecting but battered mother, extended family members and siblings, teachers or others. Protective factors may also include the child's own internal capacities to cope with stress. At this point in time, there is minimal information on how these factors all interact to moderate the degree of harm a

child experiences as a result of exposure to violence. These research findings do raise the possibility that some children may not be directly harmed by exposure to violence under certain conditions. We need to be very careful to assess each child's situation and determine the level of harm a child experiences."

—Dr. Jeffrey Edleson

Similarly, a new report from the "Future of Children" series by the David and Lucile Packard Foundation confirms the good news about resiliency. "Not all children exposed to violence suffer significant harmful effects. Based on research...concerning children's resilience in the face of community violence and war, it is likely that the most critical protective factor for a child is the existence of a strong, positive relationship between the child and a competent and caring adult. Children exposed to violence need to be able to speak openly with a sympathetic adult about their fears and concerns, and also, ideally, have someone intervene to improve the situation. Most children rely on one or both parents to provide nurturing support in the face of crises and emotionally challenging situations, but ongoing exposure to violence can sometimes hamper the parents' abilities to meet these needs. Parents living with chronic violence may feel emotionally numb, depressed, irritable, or uncommunicative, and thus may be less emotionally available to their children."[24]

Endnotes

1. C.M. Rennison and S. Welchans, Intimate Partner Violence, Bureau of Justice Statistics Special Report, (Washington, DC: U.S. Department of Justice, 2000).

2. Supra note 1.

3. Bureau of Justice Statistics, Violence Against Women: Estimates from the Redesigned Survey (Washington, DC: U.S. Department of Justice, 1995).

4. Ibid.

5. Supra note 1.

6. B.E. Carlson, "Children's Observations of Interparental Violence," in A.R. Roberts (Ed.), *Battered Women and Their Families* (New York: Springer, 1984): 147-167.

7. M.A. Straus and R. Gelles, *Behind Closed Doors: Violence in the American Family* (Garden City, NY: Doubleday, 1980); M.A. Straus, "Children as Witnesses to Marital Violence: A Risk Factor for Lifelong Problems Among a Nationally Representative Sample of American Men and Women," in D.F. Schwartz (Ed.) *Children and Violence: Report of Twenty-Third Ross Roundtable on Critical Approaches to Common Pediatric Problems* (Columbus, OH: Ross Laboratories, 1992): 98-109.

8. Supra note 7.

9. M. O'Brien, et al, "Reliability and Diagnostic Efficacy of Parent's Reports Regarding Children's Exposure to Marital Aggression," *Violence and Victims,* 9, (1994): 45-62; P.G. Jaffe, et al, *Children of Battered Women,* (Newberry Park, CA: Sage, 1990).

10. Supra note 1.

11. Supra note 1.

12. J. L. Edleson, "The Overlap Between Child Maltreatment and Woman Battering," *Violence Against Women,* 5, no. 2 (February 1999): 134-154.

13. U.S. Advisory Board on Child Abuse and Neglect, A Nation's Shame: Fatal Child Abuse and Neglect in the United States: Fifth Report (Washington, DC: U.S. Department of Health and Human Services, April 1995): 124.

14. M.A. Straus and R. Gelles, *Physical Violence in American Families,* (New Brunswick, NJ: Transaction Publishers, 1996).

15. E. Peled, P. G. Jaffe and J. L. Edleson, Editors, *Ending the Cycle of Domestic Violence: Community Responses to Children of Battered Women* (Thousand Oaks, CA: Sage Publications, 1995).

16. Ibid.

17. Ibid.

18. Ibid.

19. Ibid.

20. Ibid.

21. Ibid.

22. L. Silvern, et al, "Retrospective Reports of Parental Partner Abuse: Relationships to Depression, Trauma Symptoms and Self-Esteem Among College Students," *Journal of Family Violence,* 10, 177-202 (1995).

23. K. Henning, et al, "Long-term Psychological and Social Impact of Witnessing Physical Conflict Between Parents," *Journal of Interpersonal Violence,* 11, 35-51 (1996).

24. Center for the Future of Children, The David and Lucile Packard Foundation, Domestic Violence and Children, *The Future of Children,* 9 (3) (Winter 1999).

Part Three

Intervention and Treatment for Child Abuse

Chapter 21

What to Do When a Child Tells You He or She Is Being Abused

Reaction to Revelation of Sexual Abuse Plays Important Role in Healing, Prosecution

According to Childhelp USA®, hundreds of thousands of child sexual abuse reports are made each year throughout the country. It is suspected that the majority of incidents of sexual abuse are never reported to the authorities.

If a child were to reveal his or her painful secret to you, would you know how to react? According to professionals who work with abused children, your immediate response plays an important role in how well the child rebounds from the emotional wounds. In addition, what you say—or don't say—may determine whether a strong case can be built against the person responsible for the abuse.

Childhelp USA is asking everyone to learn the following information so they are prepared to help a child victim, if the situation arises.

Be open and understanding. Try to stay calm. If you react strongly, the child may stop talking, take back information or internalize this as another reason to feel bad about him or herself. Reassure the child that you are glad that he/she told someone.

 Additional information about the treatment and prevention of child abuse and neglect is available at www.childhelpusa.org. Referral and crisis intervention is available 24 hours a day by calling the Childhelp USA National Child Abuse hotline at 1-800-4-A-CHILD (1-800-422-4453).

Don't try to conduct an investigation, yourself. Let the professionals ask questions regarding what happened, when, and with whom. Defense attorneys often attempt to discredit information provided by the child, if the child has been asked leading questions about the abuse. If the child tells you of the sexual abuse immediately after it occurred, DO NOT bathe the child, or wash or change his or her clothes. You may destroy valuable evidence.

Let the child talk as much as he or she wishes. Often, they have been carrying this secret for a long time and need to let it out to lessen their burden. Find a quiet place to talk. Encourage the child to express his or her feelings, but don't interrogate them.

Understand that the child is probably having mixed feelings. Frequently, the perpetrator of sexual abuse is someone close to the child. Although the child may have strong negative feelings about the person's abusive behavior, he or she also may love them for other behaviors.

Believe the child. Children rarely make up stories about sexual abuse. Also, they tend to keep the abuse a secret for a long time because they have been threatened by the perpetrator and repeatedly told the abuse is their own fault. Reassure the child that they are not to blame for what happened.

Explain what you will do next to help them. Suspected abuse is sufficient reason to make a report. Immediately call your local police and child protective services offices. Abuse must be reported within the state in which it occurred. When you call, be prepared to provide (if possible): the child's name, age, address, gender, school attended, and the names of the parents. If you aren't sure of the local reporting number, call the Childhelp USA® National Child Abuse Hotline, 1-800-4-A-CHILD (1-800-422-4453) to obtain it.

Chapter 22

Questions about Reporting Child Abuse and Neglect

Taking the First Step

Deciding whether to report suspected child abuse can be a difficult and confusing process, yet it is the important first step toward protecting a child who might be in danger. Professionals who work with children are required by law to report suspected neglect or abuse. About 20 states require that every citizen who suspects a child is being abused or neglected must report. However, regardless of whether you are among those mandated to report, accurate reporting of the suspected maltreatment of any child is a moral obligation. Reasonable suspicion based on objective evidence is all that is needed to report. That evidence might be your firsthand observation or statements made by a parent or a child.

Unfamiliarity with state reporting laws and ignorance of the dynamics of abuse and neglect are two of the most frequent reasons people give for nonreporting. Frustration with lack of response by child welfare professionals to a complaint and an unwillingness to get involved are other reasons given for failure to report. Others include not wanting to make things worse for the child, an unwillingness to provide the time-consuming court testimony that might be necessary, or a reluctance to risk angering the family. All of these reasons are understandable yet any one of them could lead to the death of a child

---

that might otherwise have been prevented if the person with the information had only reported it.

What happens after I make the decision to report suspected child abuse and/or neglect?

Several events might take place before and after the initial complaint is filed. First, depending on where you live, you might report suspected abuse and/or neglect to your local child protective agency. These agencies are sometimes called Social Services, Human Rehabilitative Services, Human Welfare, or Children and Family Services. If you feel that a child is in an emergency situation, you should call your local law enforcement agency immediately.

The person responding to your call may ask you several questions about what you are reporting. This is done to ensure that enough information is available for the investigative team to make decisions concerning whether abuse and/or neglect has occurred. You might be asked to give names of the family and child; your reasons for suspecting abuse; the names, addresses, and telephone numbers of other witnesses; your relationship to the alleged victim; previous suspicious injury to the child; or your name, address, and telephone number. Anonymous reports can be made in every state, however, child welfare agencies generally try to discourage anonymity for many reasons. Not knowing the identity of the reporter denies the child welfare worker the opportunity to get more information during the investigative process or to call the reporter as a crucial evidentiary witness if the case goes to trial.

Unfortunately, over the last several years, many child welfare agencies have been severely under funded and understaffed. Sometimes the investigation of abuse and neglect complaints will be prioritized according to the immediate risk to the child. Be patient. You may have to call more than once.

Who investigates complaints of child abuse and neglect?

The state or county agency that provides child protective services has the legal authority to provide services when needed and to explore, study and evaluate the facts. Child welfare workers base their decision on whether to remove a child from the family on two issues:

1. What is the immediate danger or risk to child?
2. What is the motivation, capacity, and intent of the alleged perpetrator?

During the investigative process, the child welfare worker may call on a variety of supportive assistance from individuals and organizations in the community. It then becomes the responsibility of the child welfare worker to organize or provide any needed services for the child and the family.

What happens to the child and family?

With the enactment of PL 96-272, it is legally mandated that child welfare workers make all reasonable efforts to reunite the family whenever possible. If, after a thorough investigation, it is determined that the child is in need of substitute care, the child is placed in temporary foster care or in another safe alternative until the immediate danger has passed and services can be provided for the child and family. Sometimes criminal child abuse charges have to be filed depending on the nature and severity of the abuse or neglect. There is a range of legal penalties for child maltreatment from mandatory therapy to incarceration.

Will I be able to find out what happens to the child?

Individuals who report suspected child maltreatment should be allowed to know whether their suspicions were founded and what steps the investigation agency took to protect the child. However, there is a great deal of confusion about whether information from child welfare cases should be shared.

Legally, there is no impediment to providing general feedback to the child abuse or neglect reporter. Some states even require that child welfare agencies report back to reporters. Many times, child welfare agencies, overburdened with high caseloads and time demands, will not report back, and other agencies will wrongly claim that they cannot release the results of their investigations because the information is confidential.

If the agency does not voluntarily provide such information to you, you will have to request it. Mandated reporters of child abuse need to know the circumstances of an investigation so that they can keep track of any conditions that might further endanger the child. Professionals who work with child victims may have to know information to treat the victims in their care. The most difficult confidentiality issue to resolve concerns the reporting individual's need to know versus the family's right to privacy. So, the distinction is usually made to provide less specific information to individuals outside the child welfare professional community. This means that if the reporter is a family friend, neighbor, or relative, the information won't be provided in detail. The child welfare agency may give feedback that indicates that the reporter was right in making a referral and that the agency will be working with the family.

What happens if I report abuse and the case is unsubstantiated?

All states have laws that protect the reporter of suspected abuse or neglect from legal liability as long as the report was made in good faith and not maliciously. Only a small percentage of reports are deliberately false. Another percentage of reports may be classified as unsubstantiated. This means that there might not have been sufficient information regarding the allegation or the identity of the family, or that the state law contained narrow criteria for substantiating a case. All reports regardless of whether they are substantiated are kept on file at the agency. Criteria for substantiation varies from state to state because definitions of child abuse and neglect vary from state to state.

If you are unsure of the legal definitions of abuse or neglect in your community, contact your local CPS agency for information. In addition, you can contact us for more information on what you can do—and what we are doing—to assure that children's interests and well-being are fully, effectively, and humanely guaranteed. Knowing how, when, and what to report about child abuse and neglect may make a life or death difference for a child.

The problem of child maltreatment will not go away on its own. If you suspect child abuse is occurring, report the abuse to your local child protective agency or to the police if the child is in immediate danger. Help is available for families at risk of abuse.

Chapter 23

Reporting Child Maltreatment Involving Substance Abuse

Determining if and when parental substance abuse should be reported to a Child Protective Services (CPS) agency is a difficult but important issue. To make such a determination, it is necessary to understand the requirements related to mandatory reporting of child abuse and neglect. Although it is a matter of serious debate whether these reporting laws apply to the unborn, there is no doubt that they do apply to infants and children who receive neglectful or abusive care from their chemically involved parents or who are in imminent danger of receiving such care.

Reporting Obligations

State laws, policies, guidelines, and definitions govern the reporting of child maltreatment, including cases involving parental substance abuse. Readers are advised to check the reporting mandates

---

"Reporting Child Maltreatment in Cases Involving Parental Substance Abuse," from *Protecting Children in Substance-Abusing Families*, National Clearinghouse on Child Abuse and Neglect Information (NCCANCH), 1994. Despite the date of this document, it still provides an overview of these issues. A copy of the entire manual is available online at the new NCCANCH website at http://nccanch.acf.hhs.gov/pubs/usermanuals/subabuse/report.cfm. More recent information specifically related risks associated with parental operation of methamphetamine laboratories is excerpted from "Information Bulletin: Children at Risk," National Drug Intelligence Center, U.S. Department of Justice, July 2002.

and procedures specific to their States in each of the areas included in the following discussion.

Reporting Parental Substance Abuse

We are all aware that all reasonable suspicions of child maltreatment must be reported. However, without specific State legislation, parental substance abuse (in and of itself) is not reportable as a form of child maltreatment. Only when there is reason to believe that the parent's alcohol or other drug abuse is so severe that the child has been or is likely to be harmed due to such substance abuse, should a report to CPS be filed.

Reporting Substance Abuse during Pregnancy

Problems arise in determining whether fetal exposure to harmful substances during pregnancy should be reported under child abuse and neglect reporting laws. The mother's right to privacy must be balanced against the fetus' right to a safe, healthy environment. In many States, a fetus is not defined as a minor child or juvenile (any child from birth to 18), thus precluding any child abuse or neglect action within the child welfare and juvenile court system.

However, there are a number of States that weigh the rights of the fetus more heavily than the mother's right to privacy. CPS agencies in these States accept reports of prenatal substance abuse so that they may offer services for the pregnant mother and the unborn. One State has a provision that specifically allows applications by a relative or an agency for the care or custody of an unborn when the unborn's welfare is in danger and the pregnant mother is in the State at the time of application for services.

Until explicit laws are created to deal with the question of reporting substance abuse during pregnancy, professionals will need to continue to infer the answer on the basis of existing State child abuse and neglect reporting laws.

Reporting Drug and Alcohol-Affected Infants

An increasing number of States have dealt with the issue of prenatal alcohol and other drug abuse by mandating that substance-affected infants be reported at the time of birth. Some States specifically mention prenatal drug exposure in their statutes defining child abuse and neglect. However, these States often limit the definition of drug exposure to illegal substances. Although prenatal exposure to alcohol is a leading cause of mental retardation, only four States currently require that Fetal Alcohol Syndrome (FAS) be reported.

The condition of the infant that triggers mandatory reporting laws varies from State to State. Some States require only a positive toxicology screen at birth. Other States require physical signs of addiction or dependence. Still others require reporting of drug and alcohol-affected infants based on a more general assessment of the newborn's imminent risk of harm or need for protection.

Most States, however, have no explicit laws requiring the reporting of prenatal substance exposure. In these States, the determination of whether professionals should report such cases requires a legal analysis of existing child abuse and neglect reporting laws.

Variations in Reporting

Professionals mandated to report reasonable suspicions of substance abuse that may cause risk to a child sometimes choose not to report. Private physicians, for instance, may not want to risk the loss of paying clients or the control that they maintain over their patients' care. On the other hand, physicians in public clinics, emergency rooms, or hospitals tend to report a much higher proportion of their patients. While their reports seem to indicate a higher use of substances among poor clients, the settings themselves may in fact be at cause, and clients' help-seeking is often what is measured rather than incidence of abuse.

Additional factors also may come into play. In a study of reporting practices of mandated reporter professionals, it was found that those who believed that reporting would do more harm than good failed to report. Reporting may also be influenced by statutes that require hospital staff to conduct a thorough medical and social assessment of each infant prenatally exposed to drugs to determine whether the newborn's condition should be reported. In California, for example, the assessment of risk factors includes not only the toxicology screen, but also the child's physical condition as well as parental and environmental factors in the home that may place the infant at risk (See California Penal Code, Sec. 11165.13). Other States that require reporting of every newborn with a positive toxicology screen conceivably could have more reports made as a rule, particularly if these additional factors can constitute the basis of a report.

The National Clearinghouse on Child Abuse and Neglect Information is developing a State statute database that will provide information on a number of elements in State reporting laws, including substance abuse. This resource will be helpful if individuals need to know about specific State laws or wish to make comparisons of reporting requirements among States.

Confidentiality

The Child Abuse Prevention and Treatment Act requires confidentiality of child abuse records to protect the rights of the parents and the child in civil but not in criminal proceedings. Federal funding statutes require States to make unauthorized disclosure of these records a criminal offense. However, States are permitted to except disclosures when requested by the following:

- agencies or organizations, including a designated multidisciplinary case consultation team, that are legally mandated to receive and investigate reports of known and suspected child abuse and neglect;
- courts (which may subpoena records in some restricted cases);
- grand juries;
- a properly constituted authority investigating a report of known or suspected child abuse or neglect or providing services to a child or family which is the subject of a report;
- a physician who has before him/her a child for whom the physician has reasonable suspicion of abuse or neglect;
- anyone legally authorized to place a child in protective custody and who needs the information to determine whether to place the child;
- agencies with authority to diagnose or treat a reported child;
- anyone who is the subject of a report (the identity of the reported cannot be revealed if to disclose would endanger the life or safety of the reported; most States protect this confidential disclosure);
- the child, attorney, or guardian ad litem for the child;
- State or local officials responsible for administration of the CPS caseworker or for oversight of the enabling or appropriating legislation;

- individuals, agencies, or organizations conducting bona fide research, with no identifying information made available;
- the original reporter, who may be provided with feedback or a summary of the outcome of the report;
- agencies or persons conducting background screening for child-related employment; and
- the U.S. Department of Health and Human Services and the Comptroller of the United States or any of their representatives (45 CFR 1340.14).

Confidentiality normally protects the patient or client from any unauthorized disclosure of information. However, all States now have mandatory child abuse reporting laws that abrogate the professional/patient or client privilege. Mandated reporters are protected from civil or criminal liability for any report made in good faith. In many States this immunity extends to participation in judicial proceedings arising from the reports. It is also important to note that individuals providing treatment services under programs funded through the Federal Alcohol and Drug Rehabilitation Act are required to report suspicions of child abuse pursuant to State child abuse reporting laws.

Furthermore, many States have statutory exceptions that allow discriminant sharing of multidisciplinary agency information about children who are alleged or found to be abused or neglected. Information from normally confidential sources should be shared in order to coordinate service delivery and provide effective support to the family. Sharing medical, mental health, social welfare, substance abuse treatment, criminal, probation, and educational information is crucial to providing protection for a child, especially when the child is living in the home or when a return to the parents is anticipated.

Methamphetamine Laboratories: Special Concerns Regarding Exposed Children

An increasing number of children in the United States are exposed to toxic chemicals because methamphetamine laboratories are being operated in or near their homes. In addition, these children often are abused or neglected by the parents, guardians, or others who operate these laboratories. The number of children found at seized methamphetamine laboratory sites in the United States more than doubled from 1999 through 2001.

Methamphetamine laboratory sites typically contain toxic chemicals and waste as well as finished product and drug paraphernalia. Children who inhabit homes where laboratories are present often inhale dangerous chemical fumes or gases or ingest toxic chemicals or illicit drugs. Exposure to these substances can cause serious short- and long-term health problems including damage to the brain, liver, kidneys, lungs, eyes, and skin. Children whose parents or guardians produce or abuse methamphetamine also are likely to develop emotional and behavioral problems stemming from abuse or neglect. In addition, inhaling or ingesting toxic substances such as those present at methamphetamine laboratories may cause cancer or death.

Few areas of the country have programs in place to coordinate the social and legal aspects of cases involving children at methamphetamine laboratories; however, implementation of an effective program is possible, as illustrated by the Drug Endangered Children (DEC) program in California.

Strategies to Assist Children at Risk

Law enforcement authorities, prosecutors, social workers, medical professionals, and hazardous materials cleanup crews are increasingly aware of the serious risks faced by children who are present at methamphetamine laboratories. However, many communities have not yet implemented strategies that allow legal, social, and medical professionals to combine their resources effectively and break the cycle of child endangerment.

Butte County, California, developed a collaborative effort to improve the safety and health of children endangered by drug production, distribution, and abuse in 1993 when it initiated the Drug Endangered Children (DEC) program. DEC brings together law enforcement officers, social workers, public health nurses, and district attorneys in a cooperative effort to remove children from homes where methamphetamine is produced and to safeguard the children from further abuse and neglect.

A key component of the DEC program is a response team that is on call 24 hours a day. The DEC Response Team—which includes social workers, trained fire department personnel (members of the hazardous materials unit, in particular), public health nurses, and law enforcement personnel—is called upon frequently to treat and care for children found at laboratory sites and assist with the criminal investigation. The entire DEC Response Team receives specialized training regarding methamphetamine production and the circumstances specific to drug endangered children, and all personnel have experience or receive training in criminal investigations related to evidence collection in child endangerment cases.

In Butte County, California, where the DEC program was informally developed in 1993, the team has removed 80 to 100 children from drug-related endangerment situations each year since its inception and has successfully prosecuted hundreds of cases of child endangerment. Other counties in California have had similar success, and nine other states (Washington, Oregon, Idaho, Nevada, Utah, Arizona, Oklahoma, Missouri, and Illinois) have begun to replicate DEC Response Teams in their local communities.

Chapter 24

Questions and Answers about Examining and Treating Victims of Child Abuse

Frequent Questions: Examining and Treating Victims

Does counseling help child abuse victims?

Yes—and they need it immediately.

First, the child has to be in a safe environment. After that, counseling should begin. Abused children need help expressing their fears and other emotions and coming to grips with the abuse. Besides the victim, every family member should receive counseling. Forgetting is not the answer. The best way to break the cycle of abuse and prevent an abuse victim from becoming an abuser is to intervene early. This is the best time to make a positive impact on the victim's life.

Even children age 2 and younger need counseling. Abused toddlers are likely to act the abuse out in their play with other children. So counseling may take the form of play therapy combined with counseling parents or caregivers on how to set limits on behavior.

Especially in cases of sexual abuse, counseling "booster shots" can be valuable. Revisiting issues of abuse at various stages of development can help the victim learn to come to terms with it in different ways as he or she matures emotionally and mentally.

This chapter contains information from "Frequent Questions: Examining and Treating Victims" and "Frequent Questions: Detecting Child Abuse." Reprinted with permission from the Cincinnati Children's Hospital Medical Center website, http://www.cincinnatichildrens.org.

Why do doctors order x-rays when testing for physical abuse? Should I let them take the x-rays? Isn't all that radiation bad?

Doctors order x-rays to look for fractures. Specialized imaging, such as CAT scans and MRIs, may be ordered to look for bleeding in the brain, which can result from child abuse. Such imaging is the only real way to find these problems.

The amount of radiation from x-rays and other more advanced forms of imaging is actually fairly small. Even a full skeletal survey, the most extensive form of ordinary x-rays that obtains an image of every bone in the body, is only equivalent to a year's worth of everyday background radiation that your child would encounter by just walking around. A CAT scan is the equivalent of two years of background radiation. An x-ray of the hand amounts to only a day's worth of background radiation. And x-ray of an arm is equivalent to about a week. The increased risk of cancer from even the most extensive of these procedures is fairly small.

Will my child ever get over the abuse?

With proper support from parents and caregivers and professional counseling, it is possible for children to get over sexual or physical abuse and live normal, healthy lives. Children who have the best prognosis are those who have good relationships with parents and receive professional counseling. It also helps for children to receive counseling "booster shots" after the abuse occurs. This can help children deal mentally and emotionally with the abuse at various stages of development.

Can my child get AIDS (HIV) from sexual abuse?

It depends on what happened. If the child has been fondled or penetrated with a finger, there is virtually no risk. If the abuse involved oral sex, infection is possible but very unlikely. If the abuse involved genital-to-genital contact, the risk is greater but still rare. The risk is greater in parts of the country, such as major metropolitan areas, where HIV infection is widespread. Likewise, a child is at increased risk for other sexually transmitted disease from genital-to-genital or oral-genital contact.

Can a doctor make a determination of sexual abuse after a physical examination?

Sometimes. In most cases, even when a perpetrator confesses, the physical examination of the child reveals no physical evidence of abuse.

If vaginal penetration occurred, great force was used or the abuse was repetitive, it is more likely that physical evidence will be present.

I don't want my daughter upset by the examination. Can she be sedated?

Sedation may be offered if the examination must be completed and your daughter is overly upset. Before sedation is considered, the physician, nurse or social worker will explain the examination to your daughter and attempt to reassure her. If the examination can be deferred, her examination be rescheduled for a time when she may be more emotionally able to consent to the examination.

How painful is the physical examination for sexual abuse? Is it like an adult pelvic examination?

The examination is not physically painful. It mainly involves visual examination with minimal physical contact. Unlike adult pelvic examinations, an internal examination is usually not required in young children.

What types of sexual abuse are consistent with normal examinations?

Oral contact, digital fondling, genital rubbing, vaginal penetration after puberty, rectal penetration, partial or attempted vaginal penetration, and penetration that has had time to heal.

Can the number of abuse episodes and when they occurred be determined by exam?

The examiner usually cannot determine the number of episodes that occurred. If evidence of chronic anal abuse is present, multiple episodes of abuse occurred. Vaginal injuries do not reliably differentiate between single episodes of abuse and multiple episodes.

If the injuries are acute (redness, swelling, tenderness, fresh abrasions or tears), the examiner may reliably identify the injury as relatively recent, most likely having occurred within a few days of the examination. Dating injuries within hours or to specific days is usually not possible.

Why does one examiner's report differ from another's?

Examination findings may differ when:

- Acute injuries heal between examinations
- One of the examinations was not optimal because the child was uncooperative
- The skill levels of the examiners differ (Examiners with expert training will provide a more accurate and informative examination.)

Frequent Questions: Detecting Child Abuse

My child bruises easily. Will I be accused of child abuse?

All children who are physically active get bumps and bruises, which in themselves are not evidence of child abuse.

Physicians look for a plausible history to explain bruises and a pattern of bruises consistent with a child's normal activity. Infants, because they don't walk and are not very active are not prone to bruising. Toddlers, however, typically have bruises on their shins and foreheads from running and falling into things—but they don't normally have bruises in protected areas like the inside their thigh. The severity and the number of bruises are other factors physicians observe.

If a child truly does bruise more easily than normal, that could be a sign of a serious problem that requires medical attention. Clotting disorders and some connective tissue diseases are among the conditions that may actually cause a child to bruise easily.

When I bring my child to the emergency room for an injury, I'm afraid I'll be accused of child abuse. What should I say to the doctors and nurses when I bring my child in with an injury?

This is a concern often in the back of parents' minds, because they've heard stories of how child abuse is frequently seen in the emergency room. When doctors and nurses start asking parents about the specifics of how an injury occurred, parents sometimes feel they're being interrogated. Parents should keep in mind that physicians and nurses need to be looking for child abuse, because they'll miss opportunities to protect children if they don't. They also need to have a thorough understanding of how injuries occur in order to provide the best care. Parents who bring their children in for accidental injuries should not hesitate to answer questions and shouldn't feel they're being singled out.

My daughter (or son) has genital (or rectal) warts (or herpes). Does this mean he/she was sexually abused?

Genital warts and herpes are conditions that are frequently sexually transmitted, but sexual contact is only one of the ways children can get these infections. Both conditions also can be spread through non-sexual touching. Your child may have a wart or herpes infection elsewhere on her/his body and spread the infection to the genitalia or rectum.

When children are diagnosed with an infection that can be transmitted sexually, a parent and physician should investigate for possible sexual abuse. A physician or social worker will likely interview your child to see if he/she provides a history of abuse and perform an examination and tests to see if he/she has any other physical indications of sexual abuse, such as presence of other sexually transmitted diseases or physical injuries.

My child's doctor says her vaginal examination was normal, but she says she was penetrated. How can this be so?

In some cases, even when vaginal penetration has occurred, a medical examination will not detect it. Other times, the examination may suggest penetration when in fact none has occurred. The idea that a girl's hymen is always broken if penetration occurs is a myth. Prior to puberty, a girl's vaginal opening is quite small. Her hymen is tissue that partially covers the vaginal opening. Often—but not always—penetration beyond the hymen and into the vagina will cause damage that a physician will observe. Contact around and to the hymen, however, may cause pain to the child without producing noticeable injury. The child may describe this degree of contact as penetration, and in some states it constitutes legal penetration. After the onset of puberty, the opening of the vagina becomes enlarged. Penetration beyond the hymen then may occur more often without any tearing or signs of injury to the hymen.

Can bicycle injuries or other straddle-type injuries break my daughter's hymen?

Most straddle injuries do not result in injury to the hymen.

Chapter 25

Medical Exams for Suspected Sexual Abuse

Indications of Sexual Abuse

Any severe changes in a child's behavior should be regarded carefully as potential signs of abuse or other trauma. Caregivers and healthcare professionals should specifically look for:

- Injury/trauma to genital area
- Torn, stained or bloodied underclothing
- Itching in genital area
- Sexually transmitted disease
- New fears of persons or places
- Withdrawn behavior
- Sexual play beyond what is considered normal
- Sleep problems or nightmares
- Unusual aggressiveness
- Fear that something is wrong with the genital area

This chapter contains information from "Sexual Abuse: Child Anatomy," "Sexual Abuse: Description of the Medical Examination," "Sexual Abuse: Indications of Sexual Abuse," "Sexual Abuse: Physical Conditions that Mimic Sexual Abuse," "Sexual Abuse: Preparation for the Medical Exam," and "Sexual Abuse: Timing of the Medical Examination." Reprinted with permission from the Cincinnati Children's Hospital Medical Center website, http://www.cincinnatichildrens.org.

Disclosure of abuse may be a process that occurs over time. Be conscious not to shut the door when a child begins to tell you about abuse. Instead, ask questions such as "Can you tell me more about that?" Stress that the abuse is not the child's fault.

Description of the Medical Examination

Knowing what to expect in the examination can help alleviate anxiety over the process. To avoid unnecessary and potentially detrimental repetitive questioning of the child, a detailed history should be provided to the examiner prior to the evaluation.

Each examiner will have an individualized approach, which may include:

- Introductory dialog with the child and caregiver
- Questions about the child's medical history and the alleged abuse
- A brief physical examination
- External inspection of the anogenital area
- Vaginal speculum and digital exam (adolescent girls only)
- Photographs or video recordings of the examination
- Collection of specimens for testing
- Discussion of exam findings with the child and the caregiver

The child, the parent, or both will be asked questions about the child's current health, past medical history, medications, recent behavior changes and about any current complaints or symptoms, information about possible earlier trauma or abuse involving the anogenital area, other problems in this area, and possible sexual activity.

Questions about the alleged abuse may also be asked if a forensic interview of the child has not been done, or if the examiner was not given the history of the alleged abuse. In some cases, the examiner may need to ask the child specific questions about the abuse when the information is needed to determine the need for medical testing and treatment.

Timing of the Medical Examination

The medical exam should be conducted according to the following criteria:

- *Same-Day Evaluation*
  - The child should be seen as soon as possible if the abuse occurred within the past 72 hours. The likelihood of recovering forensic material decreases with passing time. The child should not bathe or change clothing prior to the examination.
  - The child is in pain, is bleeding, or is having other serious physical symptoms.
  - The child is suicidal or threatening to harm him/herself.
  - The child was assaulted/abused within the last 72 hours by a perpetrator with HIV or hepatitis.
- *Evaluation within a Few Days*
  - The child is having less serious symptoms such as discharge, pain with urination, or itching.
  - The child or family is unwilling to wait because of anxiety, stress or other reasons.
  - The child could be pregnant as a result of the abuse.
- *Evaluation within a Few Weeks*
  - Exclusion of the above indications.

Preparing for the Medical Exam

It is important that both caretaker and child are prepared for the exam.

First, seek an examiner with sex abuse evaluation training and then explain the evaluation process to the child. In most situations, an examiner who has specific training in sexual abuse will provide a more complete and accurate evaluation than an examiner without such training. Clinics or other practices that specialize in child abuse evaluations are preferable to emergency departments or general practitioners. Urgent evaluations for forensic evidence collection or serious symptoms may require the use of the emergency department.

Explain the evaluation process to the child and reassure him/her that the evaluation should not be painful. The evaluation for most children will include a medical history, a short general physical examination and external inspection.

It is highly unusual for a pre-adolescent child to require an internal vaginal or rectal examination, making the examination is different and less invasive than an adult pelvic examination. This preparation should reduce the child's and caretaker's anxiety and will contribute to a more comfortable and informative examination.

Child Anatomy

The following information on anatomical structures will help with interpreting reports of medical exams. Familiarity with these terms and structures also helps dispel certain myths about anatomy.

The hymen is the source of many myths about female anatomy. The facts are:

- Every girl is born with a hymen.
- Hymens vary in shape and in size among individual females.
- The hymen changes significantly during puberty.
- After puberty, bleeding from hymenal injury may or may not occur during first-time intercourse.

The following information describes the commonly encountered terminology for male and female anatomy:

Anal verge: the area between the external and internal anal skins.

Anus: the opening of the rectum between the buttocks.

Fossa navicularis: the area of mucosal skin between the posterior fourchette and the hymen in females.

Glans: the tip of the penis surrounding the urethral opening.

Hymen: a membrane that partially covers the opening of the vagina. The hymen may be thin or thick, may cover most of the vaginal opening or very little of it, and varies in shape. Terms used to describe the appearance of a normal hymen include crescentic (crescent-shaped), annular (round), redundant (folded), estrogenized (thickened) and septate (two openings).

Introitus (hymenal opening): the opening in the middle of the hymen. Objects entering the vagina first pass through the introitus. Hymenal injury from vaginal penetration often occurs at the introitus.

Labia: the lips surrounding the vaginal opening. There are two sets of labia; one is the labia major (outer set), and the other is the labia minor (inner set). After puberty, the labia enlarge and more completely cover the opening of the vagina.

Phimosis: adhesion of the prepuce (foreskin) to the glans in males.

Posterior fourchette: the area of mucosal skin where the labia minora meet (opposite end to the clitoris).

Prepuce (foreskin): tissue that covers the glans in uncircumcised males. The prepuce is removed during circumcision.

Rugae: folds of skin which radiate outward from the anus.

Sphincter: the muscles that surround the anus.

Urethral meatus: the opening of the urethra from the bladder to the exterior through which urine passes.

Vagina: a tubular structure inside the body, bordered by the hymen at the outer end and by the cervix internally.

Physical Conditions that Mimic Sexual Abuse

Many conditions cause symptoms that may be mistaken by parents and caretakers as symptoms of sexual abuse. Following are physical conditions identified as those, which mimic sexual abuse. These conditions can be caused by a number of factors:

Non-specific vaginitis: many causes, including poor hygiene, bubble bath, antibiotics, nylon underwear, and bed wetting.

Vaginitis: many causes, including pinworms, streptococcal infection, and fungus infection.

Vaginal foreign bodies: may cause bloody, foul smelling discharge. This is often caused by residual toilet paper in the vagina.

Peri-anal strep infection: presents with anal bleeding and redness.

Lichen sclerosus: hourglass-shaped area of hypo-pigmented skin surrounding the anus and genitalia, often with blood blister and other skin changes. Bleeding is common.

Straddle injuries (accidental trauma): abrasions, bruising, swelling of the labia. Occasionally may involve the introitus.

Urethral prolapse: the urethra protrudes past the urethral opening and presents with a bloody, or blood-tinged, swollen lesion around the top of the introitus. Often, the urethral origin of this mass cannot be easily recognized and it may be mistaken for trauma.

Chapter 26

Cognitive Behavioral Therapy for Child and Adolescent Traumatic Stress

Trauma Focused Cognitive Behavior Therapy (TF-CBT) is a treatment intervention designed to help children, youth, and their parents overcome the negative effects of traumatic life events such as child sexual or physical abuse; traumatic loss of a loved one; domestic, school, or community violence; or exposure to disasters, terrorist attacks, or war trauma. It was developed by integrating cognitive and behavioral interventions with traditional child abuse therapies, in order to focus on enhancing children's interpersonal trust and re-empowerment.

TF-CBT can be provided to children 3 to 18 years old, and their parents, by trained mental health professionals in individual, family, and group sessions in outpatient settings. TF-CBT targets symptoms of Posttraumatic Stress Disorder (PTSD), which often co-occur with depression and acting-out behaviors. PTSD includes an array of anxiety symptoms as well as:

- Intrusive thoughts of the traumatic event
- Avoidance of reminders of the trauma
- Emotional numbing
- Excessive physical arousal/activity

"Trauma Focused Cognitive Behavior Therapy (TF-CBT)," SAMSHA Model Programs. U.S. Department of Health and Human Services, Substance Abuse and Mental Health Services Administration, Center for Substance Abuse Prevention, 2003. Available online at http://modelprograms.samhsa.gov/print.cfm?pkProgramid=90.

- Irritability
- Trouble sleeping or concentrating

The intervention also addresses issues commonly experienced by traumatized children, such as poor self-esteem, difficulty trusting others, mood instability, and self-injurious behavior, including substance use.

Program Background

TF-CBT was originally developed and tested for sexually abused boys and girls, ages 3 to 14, and for their non-abusive parents. Many of these children had sexualized behaviors as well as other behavioral problems, anxiety, depression, and problematic attributions about the abuse. Although these children were from diverse socioeconomic backgrounds, most were from poor or working class urban or rural families and primarily White and African American. TF-CBT was developed and tested at the Allegheny General Hospital Center for Traumatic Stress in Children and Adolescents, in Pittsburgh, PA, with grants from the U.S. Department of Health and Human Services' National Institute of Mental Health and National Center for Child Abuse and Neglect, and the Department of Justice Office for Victims of Crime, the Allegheny-Singer Research Institute, and the Jewish Healthcare Foundation of Pittsburgh.

TF-CBT is currently being modified and disseminated for use in broader community settings through the National Child Traumatic Stress Initiative network, which is funded by the Center for Mental Health Services of the Substance Abuse and Mental Health Services Administration. Numerous therapy and treatment elements have been incorporated into the design of the TF-CBT model, in hopes of avoiding some of the long-term negative effects of child traumatic stress such as increased risk of substance abuse, suicide attempts, relationship difficulties, smaller brains, and lower IQs.

Protective Factors

Protective Factors to Increase:

- *Individual*
    - Stress management skills
    - Affective regulation
    - Problem-solving and safety skills
    - Communication skills

    - Self-esteem
    - Interpersonal trust

- *Family*
    - Effective parenting skills
    - Parental support of the child
    - Stress management skills

Risk Factors

Risk Factors to Decrease:

- *Individual*
    - Poor self-esteem
    - Impaired interpersonal trust
    - Self-injury
    - Aggression towards others
- *Family*
    - Inappropriate parenting practices
    - Parental trauma-related emotional distress
    - Inadequate parental support of the child
    - Lack of safety in the home setting

Target Population

TF-CBT was designed for children 3 to 18 years old who have developed significant emotional or behavioral difficulties following exposure to a traumatic life event. It has been adapted for use in children exposed to events such as traumatic loss of a loved one, physical abuse, domestic and community violence, motor vehicle accidents, fires, tornadoes and hurricanes, industrial accidents, and terrorist attacks. The boys and girls tested came from all socioeconomic backgrounds, have lived in a variety of settings (with parents, other relatives, foster placements, group homes, residential treatment facilities), and from diverse ethnic groups. TF-CBT has been adapted for Hispanic/Latino children and some of its assessment instruments are available in Spanish.

Benefits

- Develops adaptive skills for dealing with stress

- Decreases children's anxiety about thinking or talking about the event
- Enhances accurate and helpful cognitions
- Enhances children's personal safety skills
- Resolves parental distress about the child's experience
- Enhances parental support for their children
- Prepares children to anticipate and cope with traumatic and loss reminders

How It Works

Traumatized children may develop extreme fear of anything that reminds them of the traumatic event. This can lead to avoidance of traumatic reminders and extreme emotional and physiological guardedness. Whether or not children have PTSD, these symptoms can significantly interfere with their ability to function and develop optimally. TF-CBT helps children talk directly about their traumatic experiences in a supportive environment where they can become less fearful, less avoidant, and more able to tolerate trauma-related thoughts and feelings. This treatment model also teaches children how to examine their thoughts, feelings and behaviors, and how to change these in order to feel better. It also provides children with tools such as relaxation and deep breathing techniques, problem solving, and safety education to help them manage stressful situations in the future.

A parental treatment component is an important element of TF-CBT. With it, parents are assisted in:

- Exploring their own thoughts and feelings about the child's experience and resolving their personal trauma-related distress
- Learning effective parenting skills
- Providing optimal support to their children

Several child-parent sessions are included in the TF-CBT intervention, during which the child is encouraged to discuss the traumatic experience directly with the parent, and both parent and child learn to communicate questions, concerns, and feelings more openly. This intervention is typically provided in outpatient mental health facilities but has been used in hospital, group home, school, community, and in-home settings.

Chapter 27

Cognitive Behavioral Therapy for Child Sexual Abuse

Cognitive Behavioral Therapy for Child Sexual Abuse (CBT-CSA) is a treatment approach designed to help children and adolescents who have suffered sexual abuse overcome posttraumatic stress disorder (PTSD), depression, and other behavioral and emotional difficulties. The program helps children to:

- Learn about child sexual abuse as well as healthy sexuality
- Therapeutically process traumatic memories
- Overcome problematic thoughts, feelings, and behaviors
- Develop effective coping and body safety skills

The program emphasizes the support and involvement of non-offending parents or primary caretakers and encourages effective parent-child communication. Cognitive behavioral methods are used to help parents learn to cope with their own distress and respond effectively to their children's behavioral difficulties. This CBT approach is suitable for all clinical and community-based mental health settings and its effectiveness has been documented for both individual and group therapy formats.

Excerpted from "Cognitive Behavioral Therapy for Child Sexual Abuse (CBT-CSA)," SAMSHA Model Programs, U.S. Department of Health and Human Services, Substance Abuse and Mental Health Services Administration, Center for Substance Abuse Prevention, 2003. Available online at http://modelprograms.samhsa.gov/print.cfm?pkProgramid=90.

Target Population

CBT-CSA is designed for children and adolescents 3 through 18 years old who have experienced sexual abuse and are exhibiting post-traumatic stress, depression, and other abuse-related difficulties (e.g., age-inappropriate sexual behaviors, problematic fears, social isolation). Children are generally referred for treatment following an investigation conducted by child protection or law enforcement personnel in which allegations of sexual abuse are found to be credible. Whenever possible, a nonoffending caregiver or parent is encouraged to participate along with the child. The program may be utilized in private and/or public clinics and has demonstrated success with Black/African American, Hispanic/Latino, and White children from all socioeconomic backgrounds. The research participants were primarily seen at a public clinic on a medical school campus, but therapists in community settings, including child protection offices in urban, suburban, and rural settings, have also delivered the treatment program.

Benefits

In the aftermath of child sexual abuse, CBT-CSA:

- Helps children talk about their experiences and cope with their feelings and concerns
- Assists parents in coping with abuse-specific distress and responding effectively to their children's emotional and behavioral problems
- Improves parent-child communication and interactions

Following are some proven results of CBT-CSA:

- 63% reduction in children's PTSD symptoms
- 41% reduction in children's levels of depression
- 23% reduction in children's acting-out difficulties
- Reductions in children's levels of PTSD, depression, and acting-out behaviors were maintained for 2 years

Participation in group CBT-CSA led to:

- 26% reduction in parents' emotional distress related to the abuse

- 45% reduction in parents' intrusive thoughts about the abuse
- 45% improvement in body safety skills in young children

How It Works

The treatment program consists of parallel sessions with the child and his or her nonoffending parent(s), as well as joint parent-child sessions in the later stages of therapy. The treatment approach can be effectively implemented in 12 sessions and has been applied to both individual and group therapy formats.

The specific components of treatment for both the child and parent include:

- Education about child sexual abuse and healthy sexuality
- Coping skills training, including relaxation, emotional expression, and cognitive coping
- Gradual exposure and processing of traumatic memories and reminders
- Personal body safety skills training

Parents are also provided with behavioral management training to strengthen children's positive behaviors while minimizing behavioral difficulties. Joint parent-child sessions are designed to help parents and children practice and utilize the skills learned, while also fostering more effective parent-child communication about the abuse and related issues.

Implementation Essentials

Therapists seeking training in this treatment approach should have experience working with children and families and prior training in and knowledge of child sexual abuse dynamics, child abuse reporting laws, child protection systems, and community victim advocacy resources.

Training and Technical Assistance

Several levels of training are available:

- Half- and/or full-day introductory workshops can be offered to introduce skilled mental health professionals to the program's overall approach

- Two- to four-day seminars, offering more intensive training to direct service providers and/or supervisors
- Intensive training with ongoing professional consultation including weekly or biweekly review of audiotaped sessions and feedback

Program Background

CBT-CSA was developed following a series of assessment studies that documented the wide array of emotional and behavioral difficulties exhibited by children who have experienced sexual abuse. These studies indicated that while some children suffer minimal difficulties following sexual abuse, others experience serious psychiatric disorders, with one of the most common disorders being PTSD. In addition, assessment research has clearly revealed the important role nonoffending parents play in the recovery process. Thus, a treatment program was developed for abused children and their nonoffending parents specifically designed to improve PTSD and other abuse-related difficulties (e.g., age-inappropriate sexual behaviors, depression, acting-out behaviors, etc.). To date, seven treatment outcome studies (two pre- and post-test designs and five randomized control trials) have documented the efficacy of this treatment approach.

Dr. Deblinger and her colleagues, Dr. Judith Cohen, and Anthony Mannarino, Ph.D., from Allegheny General Hospital, are currently completing a multisite treatment outcome investigation for children who have suffered sexual abuse and collaborating on a manual for children exposed to other forms of traumatic stress. Melissa Runyon, Ph.D., and Felicia Neubauer, L.C.S.W., from the University of Medicine and Dentistry of New Jersey-School of Osteopathic Medicine, are also collaborating with Dr. Deblinger on the development of modified treatment programs for children who have suffered physical abuse and/or domestic violence.

Evaluation Design

In a series of randomized control trials, this CBT approach led to significant reductions in parental emotional distress, as well as significant improvements with respect to PTSD, depression, behavior problems, and personal safety skills in children. Research examining the impact of the parent and child components of this treatment demonstrated the significant value of parental participation in treating children's acting-out behaviors and depression. The findings also suggested the critical importance of the CBT child interventions in effectively treating PTSD in the population. A recent follow-up study has documented the maintenance of children's improvements with respect to PTSD, depression, and behavior problems over a 2-year period. The results of a recent study comparing group CBT-CSA to a support group approach suggest that cognitive behavioral strategies are significantly more effective in enhancing children's personal safety skills and reducing parents' abuse-specific distress. Program results have been reported in journal articles published in the *Journal of the Academy of Child and Adolescent Psychiatry, Child Maltreatment,* and *Child Abuse and Neglect: The International Journal.*

Research funding that has contributed to the development and evaluation of this treatment program has been provided by the Foundation of the University of Medicine and Dentistry of New Jersey and the U.S. Department of Health and Human Services' National Center on Child Abuse and Neglect and National Institute of Mental Health. Victims of Crime Act grants, grants and contracts administered by the New Jersey Division of Youth and Family Services, and private and corporate donations have also funded individual and group therapy services provided at the center.

Target Areas

Protective Factors to Increase

- Individual
    - Emotional expression skills
    - Relaxation skills
    - Cognitive coping skills
    - Personal safety skills
    - Self-esteem
- Peer
    - Positive peer relations
    - Assertiveness skills
- Family
    - Parent emotional stability and support
    - Sharing of praise and positive feedback
    - Effective discipline and limit setting
    - Parent-child communication skills
    - Cohesive family interactions

- Society
    - Public education about child sexual abuse
    - Multidisciplinary team approach

Risk Factors to Decrease

- Individual
    - Emotional and behavioral difficulties
    - Avoidance and social isolation
    - Shame and self-blame regarding abuse
- Family
    - Lack of parental support
    - Parental emotional difficulties
    - Ineffective parenting skills
    - Problematic family interactions
- Society
    - Lack of access to specialized treatment services
    - Ineffective system response to allegations

Chapter 28

Questions and Answers about Recovered Memories of Childhood Abuse

Following are some questions and answers that reflect the best current knowledge about reported memories of childhood abuse. They will help you better understand how repressed, recovered, or suggested memories may occur and what you can do if you or a family member is concerned about a childhood memory.

Can a memory be forgotten and then remembered? Can a "memory" be suggested and then remembered as true?

These questions lie at the heart of the memory of childhood abuse issue. Experts in the field of memory and trauma can provide some answers, but clearly more study and research are needed. What we do know is that both memory researchers and clinicians who work with trauma victims agree that both phenomena occur. However, experienced clinical psychologists state that the phenomenon of a recovered memory is rare (e.g., one experienced practitioner reported having a recovered memory arise only once in 20 years of practice). Also, although laboratory studies have shown that memory is often inaccurate and can be influenced by outside factors, memory research usually takes place either in a laboratory or some everyday setting.

"Questions and Answers about Recovered Memories of Childhood Abuse," produced by the American Psychological Association's Office of Public Affairs, available online at http://www.apa.org/pubinfo/mem.html. Reviewed by David Cooke, MD, March 2004.

For ethical and humanitarian reasons, memory researchers do not subject people to a traumatic event in order to test their memory of it. Because the issue has not been directly studied, we cannot know whether a memory of a traumatic event is encoded and stored differently from a memory of a nontraumatic event.

Some clinicians theorize that children understand and respond to trauma differently from adults. Some furthermore believe that childhood trauma may lead to problems in memory storage and retrieval. These clinicians believe that dissociation is a likely explanation for a memory that was forgotten and later recalled. Dissociation means that a memory is not actually lost, but is for some time unavailable for retrieval. That is, it's in memory storage, but cannot for some period of time actually be recalled. Some clinicians believe that severe forms of child sexual abuse are especially conducive to negative disturbances of memory such as dissociation or delayed memory. Many clinicians who work with trauma victims believe that this dissociation is a person's way of sheltering himself or herself from the pain of the memory. Many researchers argue, however, that there is little or no empirical support for such a theory.

What's the bottom line?

First, it's important to state that there is a consensus among memory researchers and clinicians that most people who were sexually abused as children remember all or part of what happened to them although they may not fully understand or disclose it. Concerning the issue of a recovered versus a pseudomemory, like many questions in science, the final answer is yet to be known. But most leaders in the field agree that although it is a rare occurrence, a memory of early childhood abuse that has been forgotten can be remembered later. However, these leaders also agree that it is possible to construct convincing pseudomemories for events that never occurred.

The mechanism(s) by which both of these phenomena happen are not well understood and, at this point it is impossible, without other corroborative evidence, to distinguish a true memory from a false one.

What further research is needed?

The controversy over the validity of memories of childhood abuse has raised many critical issues for the psychological community. Many questions are at this point unanswered. This controversy has demonstrated that there are areas of research which should be pursued; among them are the following:

- Research to provide a better understanding of the mechanism by which accurate or inaccurate recollections of events may be created;
- Research to ascertain which clinical techniques are most likely to lead to the creation of pseudomemories and which techniques are most effective in creating the conditions under which actual events of childhood abuse can be remembered with accuracy;
- Research to ascertain how trauma and traumatic response impact the memory process;
- Research to ascertain if some people are more susceptible than others to memory suggestion and alteration and if so, why.

Much of this research will profit from collaborative efforts among psychologists who specialize in memory research and those clinicians who specialize in working with trauma and abuse victims.

If there is so much controversy about childhood memories of abuse, should I still seek help from a mental health provider if I believe I have such a memory?

Yes. The issue of repressed or suggested memories has been overreported and sensationalized by the news media. Media and entertainment portrayals of the memory issue have succeeded in presenting the least likely scenario (that of a total amnesia of a childhood event) as the most likely occurrence. The reality is that most people who are victims of childhood sexual abuse remember all or part of what happened to them. Also true is the fact that thousands of people see a psychologist every day and are helped to deal with such things as issues of personal adjustment, depression, substance abuse and problems in relationships. The issues of childhood abuse or questionable memory retrieval techniques never enter into the equation in the great majority of therapy relationships.

What should I know about choosing a psychotherapist to help me deal with a childhood memory or any other issue?

The American Psychological Association has released to the public the following advice to consider when seeking psychotherapy services.

First, know that there is no single set of symptoms which automatically indicates that a person was a victim of childhood abuse. There have been media reports of therapists who state that people (particularly women) with a particular set of problems or symptoms must have been victims of childhood sexual abuse. There is no scientific evidence that supports this conclusion.

Second, all questions concerning possible recovered memories of childhood abuse should be considered from an unbiased position. A therapist should not approach recovered memories with the preconceived notion that abuse must have happened or that abuse could not possibly have happened.

Third, when considering current problems, be wary of those therapists who offer an instant childhood abuse explanation, and those who dismiss claims or reports of sexual abuse without any exploration.

Fourth, when seeking psychotherapy, you are advised to see a licensed practitioner with training and experience in the issue for which you seek treatment. Ask the therapist about the kinds of treatment techniques he or she uses and how they could help you.

How can I expect a competent psychotherapist to react to a recovered memory?

- A competent psychotherapist will attempt to stick to the facts as you report them. He or she will be careful to let the information evolve as your memory does and not to steer you toward a particular conclusion or interpretation.
- A competent psychotherapist is likely to acknowledge that current knowledge does not allow the definite conclusion that a memory is real or false without other corroborating evidence.

What credentials should I look for when selecting a mental health provider?

You should choose a mental health professional as carefully as you would choose a physical health provider. For example, licensed psychologists have earned an undergraduate degree and have completed 5–7 years of graduate study culminating in a doctoral degree and including a one-year, full-time internship. All psychologists are required to be licensed or certified by the state in which they practice and many states require that they keep their training current by completing continuing education classes every year. Members of the American Psychological Association are also bound by a strict code of ethical standards.

Once the provider's competency has been established, his or her experience dealing with the issues you want help with is important.

Also important is your level of comfort with the provider. Psychotherapy is a cooperative effort between therapist and patient, so a high level of personal trust and comfort is necessary. However, you should be concerned if your therapist reports to you that a large number of his or her patients recover memories of childhood abuse while in treatment.

There are a number of good ways to get a referral to a mental health professional. Your state psychological association will be able to provide you with referrals to psychologists in your community. Many state associations are located in their state capital. Also, because so many physical ailments have psychological components, most family physicians have a working relationship with a psychologist. Ask your doctor about a referral. Your church or synagogue and school guidance program or university counseling centers also usually maintain lists of providers in the community.

APA also has published a brochure of advice about the selection of a mental health provider entitled "How to Choose a Psychologist".

Editor's note [in original document]: This document is being released at the direction of the APA Board of Directors. It is based on numerous reports and documents, including, but not limited to, the work of the APA Working Group on the Investigation of Memories of Childhood Abuse.

Part Four

Child Abuse Research

Chapter 29

Why Do People Abuse Children?

What Factors Contribute to Child Abuse and Neglect?

There is no single known cause of child maltreatment. Nor is there any single description that captures all families in which children are victims of abuse and neglect. Child maltreatment occurs across socio-economic, religious, cultural, racial, and ethnic groups. While no specific causes definitively have been identified that lead a parent or other caregiver to abuse or neglect a child, research has recognized a number of risk factors or attributes commonly associated with maltreatment.

Children within families and environments in which these factors exist have a higher probability of experiencing maltreatment. It must be emphasized, however, that while certain factors often are present among families where maltreatment occurs, this does not mean that the presence of these factors will always result in child abuse and neglect. The factors result in child abuse and neglect. The factors that may contribute to maltreatment in one family may not result in child abuse and neglect in another family. For example, several researchers note the relation between poverty and maltreatment, yet it must be noted that most people living in poverty do not harm their children. Professionals who intervene in cases of child maltreatment must

---

From "What Factors Contribute to Child Abuse and Neglect," in *A Coordinated Response to Child Abuse and Neglect: The Foundation for Practice,* 2003. National Clearinghouse on Child Abuse and Neglect. Available online at http://nccanch.acf.hhs.gov/pubs/usermanuals/foundation/chapfive.cfm.

recognize the multiple, complex causes of the problem and must tailor their assessment and treatment of children and families to meet the specific needs and circumstances of the family.

Risk factors associated with child maltreatment can be grouped in four domains:

- Parent or caregiver factors
- Family factors
- Child factors
- Environmental factors

It is increasingly recognized that child maltreatment arises from the interaction of multiple factors across these four domains. The sections that follow examine risk factors in each category. Available research suggests that different factors may play varying roles in accounting for different forms of child maltreatment (physical abuse, sexual abuse, neglect, and psychological or emotional abuse). Some of these differences are highlighted throughout the chapter.

A greater understanding of risk factors can help professionals working with children and families both to identify maltreatment and high-risk situations and to intervene appropriately. Assessment of the specific risk factors that affect a family may influence the prioritization of intervention services for that family (e.g., substance abuse treatment). Moreover, addressing risk and protective factors can help to prevent child abuse and neglect. For example, prevention programs may focus on increasing social supports for families (thereby reducing the risk of social isolation) or providing parent education to improve parent's age-appropriate expectations for their children.

Parent or Caregiver Factors

Parent or caregiver factors potentially contributing to maltreatment relate to:

- Personality characteristics and psychological well-being
- History of maltreatment
- Substance abuse
- Attitudes and knowledge
- Age

Personality Characteristics and Psychological Well-Being

No consistent set of characteristics or personality traits has been associated with maltreating parents or caregivers. Some characteristics frequently identified in those who are physically abusive or neglectful include low self-esteem, an external locus of control (i.e., belief that events are determined by chance or outside forces beyond one's personal control), poor impulse control, depression, anxiety, and antisocial behavior. While some maltreating parents or caregivers experience behavioral and emotional difficulties, severe mental disorders are not common.

Parental Histories and the Cycle of Abuse

A parent's childhood history plays a large part in how he or she may behave as a parent. Individuals with poor parental role models or those who did not have their own needs met may find it very difficult to meet the needs of their children.

While the estimated number varies, child maltreatment literature commonly supports the finding that some maltreating parents or caregivers were victims of abuse and neglect themselves as children. One review of the relevant research suggested that about one-third of all individuals who were maltreated will subject their children to maltreatment. Children who either experienced maltreatment or witnessed violence between their parents or caregivers may learn violent behavior and may also learn to justify violent behavior as appropriate.

An incorrect conclusion from this finding, however, is that a maltreated child will always grow up to become a maltreating parent. There are individuals who have not been abused as children who become abusive, as well as individuals who have been abused as children and do not subsequently abuse their own children. In the research review noted previously, approximately two-thirds of all individuals who were maltreated did not subject their children to abuse or neglect.

It is not known why some parents or caregivers who were maltreated as children abuse or neglect their own children and others with a similar history do not. While every individual is responsible for his or her actions, research suggests the presence of emotionally supportive relationships may help lessen the risk of the intergenerational cycle of abuse.

Substance Abuse

Parental substance abuse is reported to be a contributing factor for between one- and two-thirds of maltreated children in the child welfare system. Research supports the association between substance abuse and child maltreatment. For example:

- A retrospective study of maltreatment experience in Chicago found children whose parents abused alcohol and other drugs were almost three times likelier to be abused and more than four times likelier to be neglected than children of parents who were not substance abusers.
- A Department of Health and Human Services study found all types of maltreatment, and particularly neglect, to be more likely in alcohol-abusing families than in nonalcohol-abusing families.

Substance abuse can interfere with a parent's mental functioning, judgment, inhibitions, and protective capacity. Parents significantly affected by the use of drugs and alcohol may neglect the needs of their children, spend money on drugs instead of household expenses, or get involved in criminal activities that jeopardize their children's health or safety. Also, studies suggest that substance abuse can influence parental discipline choices and childrearing styles.

Over the past decade, prenatal exposure of children to drugs and alcohol during their mother's pregnancy and its potentially negative, developmental consequences has been an issue of particular concern. The number of children born each year exposed to drugs or alcohol is estimated to be between 550,000 and 750,000. While this issue has received much attention, children who are exposed prenatally represent only a small proportion of children negatively affected by parental substance abuse.

The number and complexity of co-occurring family problems often makes it difficult to understand the full impact of substance abuse on child maltreatment. Substance abuse and child maltreatment often co-occur with other problems, including mental illness, HIV/AIDS or other health problems, domestic violence, poverty, and prior child maltreatment. These co-occurring problems produce extremely complex situations that can be difficult to resolve. Because many of the problems may be important and urgent, it can be difficult to prioritize what services to provide. Additionally, identifying and obtaining appropriate resources to address these needs is a challenge in many communities.

Attitudes and Knowledge

Negative attitudes and attributions about a child's behavior and inaccurate knowledge about child development may play a contributing role in child maltreatment. For example, some studies have found that mothers who physically abuse their children have both more negative and higher than normal expectations of their children, as well as less understanding of appropriate developmental norms. Not all research, however, has found differences in parental expectations.

A parent's lack of knowledge about normal child development may result in unrealistic expectations. Unmet expectations can culminate in inappropriate punishment (e.g., a parent hitting a one-year-old for soiling his pants). Other parents may become frustrated with not knowing how to manage a child's behavior and may lash out at the child. Still others may have attitudes that devalue children or view them as property.

Age

Caretaker age may be a risk factor for some forms of maltreatment, although research findings are inconsistent. Some studies of physical abuse, in particular, have found that mothers who were younger at the birth of their child exhibited higher rates of child abuse than did older mothers. Other contributing factors, such as lower economic status, lack of social support, and high stress levels may influence the link between younger childbirth—particularly teenage parenthood—and child abuse.

Family Factors

Specific life situations of some families—such as marital conflict, domestic violence, single parenthood, unemployment, financial stress, and social isolation—may increase the likelihood of maltreatment. While these factors by themselves may not cause maltreatment, they frequently contribute to negative patterns of family functioning.

Family Structure

Children living with single parents may be at higher risk of experiencing physical and sexual abuse and neglect than children living with two biological parents. Single parent households are substantially more likely to have incomes below the poverty line. Lower income, the increased stress associated with the sole burden of family responsibilities, and fewer supports are thought to contribute to the risk of single parents maltreating their children. In 1998, 23 percent of children lived in households with a single mother, and 4 percent lived in households with a single father. A strong, positive relationship between the child and the father, whether he resides in the home or not, contributes to the child's development and may lessen the risk of abuse.

In addition, studies have found that compared to similar non-neglecting families, neglectful families tend to have more children or greater numbers of people living in the household. Chronically neglecting families often are characterized by a chaotic household with changing constellations of adult and child figures (e.g., a mother and her children who live on and off with various others, such as the mother's mother, the mother's sister, or a boyfriend).

The Child Abuse and Father Absence Connection

The rate of child abuse in single parent households is 27.3 children per 1,000, which is nearly twice the rate of child abuse in two parent households (15.5 children per 1,000).

An analysis of child abuse cases in a nationally representative sample of 42 counties found that children from single parent families are more likely to be victims of physical and sexual abuse than children who live with both biological parents. Compared to their peers living with both parents, children in single parent homes had:

- 77 percent greater risk of being physically abused;
- 87 percent greater risk of being harmed by physical neglect;
- 165 percent greater risk of experiencing notable physical neglect;
- 74 percent greater risk of suffering from emotional neglect;
- 80 percent greater risk of suffering serious injury as a result of abuse;
- 120 percent greater risk of experiencing some type of maltreatment overall.

A national survey of nearly 1,000 parents found that 7.4 percent of children who lived with one parent had been sexually abused, compared to only 4.2 percent of children who lived with both biological parents.

Using data from 1,000 students tracked from seventh or eighth grade in 1988 through high school in 1992, researchers determined that only 3.2 percent of the boys and girls who were raised with both biological parents had a history of maltreatment. However, a full 18.6 percent of those in other family situations had been maltreated.

A study of 156 victims of child sexual abuse found that the majority of the children came from disrupted or single-parent homes; only 31 percent of the children lived with both biological parents. Although stepfamilies make up only about 10 percent of all families, 27 percent of the abused children in this study lived with either a stepfather or the mother's boyfriend.

Marital Conflict and Domestic Violence

According to published studies, in 30 to 60 percent of families where spouse abuse takes place, child maltreatment also occurs. Children in violent homes may witness parental violence, may be victims of physical abuse themselves, and may be neglected by parents who are focused on their partners or unresponsive to their children due to their own fears. A child who witnesses parental violence is at risk for also being maltreated, but, even if the child is not maltreated, he or she may experience harmful emotional consequences from witnessing the parental violence.

Stress

Stress is also thought to play a significant role in family functioning, although its exact relationship with maltreatment is not fully understood. Physical abuse has been associated with stressful life events, parenting stress, and emotional distress in various studies. Similarly, some studies have found that neglectful families report more day-to-day stress than non-neglectful families. It is not clear, however, whether maltreating parents actually experience more life stress or, rather, perceive more events and life more events and life experiences as being stressful. In addition, specific stressful situations (e.g., losing a job, physical illness, marital problems, or the death of a family member) may exacerbate certain characteristics of the family members affected, such as hostility, anxiety, or depression, and that may also aggravate the level of family conflict and maltreatment.

Parent-Child Interaction

Families involved in child maltreatment seldom recognize or reward their child's positive behaviors, while having strong responses to their child's negative behaviors. Maltreating parents have been found to be less supportive, affectionate, playful, and responsive with their children than parents who do not abuse their children. Research on maltreating parents, particularly physically abusive mothers, found that these parents were more likely to use harsh discipline strategies (e.g., hitting, prolonged isolation) and verbal aggression and less likely to use positive parenting strategies (e.g., using time outs, reasoning, and recognizing and encouraging the child's successes).

Child Factors

Children are not responsible for being victims of maltreatment. Certain factors, however, can make some children more vulnerable to maltreating behavior. The child's age and development—physical, mental, emotional, and social—may increase the child's vulnerability to maltreatment, depending on the interactions of these characteristics with the parental factors previously discussed.

Age

The relationship between a child's age and maltreatment is not clear cut and may differ by type of maltreatment. In 2000, for example, the rate of documented maltreatment was highest for children between birth and 3 years of age (15.7 victims per 1,000 children of this age in the population) and declined as age increased. The inverse relationship between age and maltreatment is particularly strong for neglect, but not as evident for other types of maltreatment (physical, emotional, or sexual abuse).

Infants and young children, due to their small physical size, early developmental status, and need for constant care, can be particularly vulnerable to child maltreatment. Very young children are more likely to experience certain forms of maltreatment, such as shaken baby syndrome and nonorganic failure to thrive. Teenagers, on the other hand, are at greater risk for sexual abuse.

Disabilities

Children with physical, cognitive, and emotional disabilities appear to experience higher rates of maltreatment than do other children. A national study, completed in 1993, found that children with disabilities were 1.7 times more likely to be maltreated than children without disabilities. To date, the full degree to which disabilities precede or are a result of maltreatment is unclear.

In general, children who are perceived by their parents as different or who have special needs—including children with disabilities, as well as children with chronic illnesses or children with difficult temperaments—may be at greater risk of maltreatment. The demands of caring for these children may overwhelm their parents. Disruptions may occur in the bonding or attachment processes, particularly if children are unresponsive to affection or if children are separated by frequent hospitalizations. Children with disabilities also may be vulnerable to repeated maltreatment because they may not understand that the abusive behaviors are inappropriate, and they may be unable to escape or defend themselves in abusive situations. Some researchers and advocates have suggested that some societal attitudes, practices, and beliefs that devalue and depersonalize children with disabilities sanction abusive behavior and contribute to their higher risk of maltreatment. For instance, there may be greater tolerance of a caregiver verbally berating or physically responding to a disabled child's inability to accomplish a task or act in an expected way than there would be if similar behavior was directed at a normally abled child.

Other Child Characteristics

While some studies suggest that infants born prematurely or with low birth-weight may be at increased risk for maltreatment, other studies do not. The relationship between low birth-weight and maltreatment may be attributable to higher maternal stress heightened by high caregiver demands, but it also may be related to poor parental education about low birth-weight, lack of accessible prenatal care, and other factors, such as substance abuse or domestic violence.

Child factors such as aggression, attention deficits, difficult temperaments, and behavior problems—or the parental perceptions of such problems—have been associated with increased risk for all types of child maltreatment. These factors may contribute indirectly to child maltreatment when interacting with certain parental characteristics, such as poor coping skills, poor ability to empathize with the child, or difficulty controlling emotions. In addition, these same child characteristics may be reinforced by the maltreatment (e.g., a physically abused child may develop aggressive behaviors that elicit harsh reactions from others) and create conditions that can lead to recurring maltreatment.

Environmental Factors

Environmental factors are often found in combination with parent, family, and child factors, as highlighted in previously. Environmental factors include poverty and unemployment, social isolation, and community characteristics. It is important to reiterate that most parents or caregivers who live in these types of environments are not abusive.

Poverty and Unemployment

Poverty and unemployment show strong associations with child maltreatment, particularly neglect. The NIS-3 study, for example, found that children from families with annual incomes below $15,000 in 1993 were more than 22 times more likely to be harmed by child abuse and neglect as compared to children from families with annual incomes above $30,000. It is important to underscore that most poor people do not maltreat their children. However, poverty—particularly when interacting with other risk factors such as depression, substance abuse, and social isolation—can increase the likelihood of maltreatment. In 1999, 85 percent of States identified poverty and substance abuse as the top two problems challenging families reported to child protective service (CPS) agencies.

Rod Plotnik, emeritus professor, Department of Psychology, San Diego State University, describes several theories related to the association between poverty and maltreatment, all of which may hold some truth. One theory is that low income creates greater family stress, which, in turn, leads to higher chances of maltreatment. A second theory is that parents with low incomes, despite good intentions, may be unable to provide adequate care while raising children in high-risk neighborhoods with unsafe or crowded housing and inadequate daycare. A third theory is that some other characteristics may make parents more likely to be both poor and abusive. For example, a parent may have a substance abuse problem that impedes the parent's ability to obtain and maintain a job, which also may contribute to abusive behavior. A final theory is that poor families may experience maltreatment at rates similar to other families, but that maltreatment in poor families is reported to CPS more frequently, in part because they have more contact with and are under greater scrutiny from individuals who are legally mandated to report suspected child maltreatment.

Social Isolation and Social Support

Some studies indicate that compared to other parents, parents who maltreat their children report experiencing greater isolation, more loneliness, and less social support. Social isolation may contribute to maltreatment because parents have less material and emotional support, do not have positive parenting role models, and feel less pressure to conform to conventional standards of parenting behaviors. It is not clear, however, whether social isolation in some cases precedes and serves as a contributing factor to maltreatment or whether it is a consequence of the behavioral dynamics of maltreatment.

Violent Communities

Children living in dangerous neighborhoods have been found to be at higher risk than children from safer neighborhoods for severe neglect and physical abuse, as well as child sexual victimization. Some risk may be associated with the poverty found in dangerous neighborhoods, however, concerns remain that violence may seem an acceptable response or behavior to individuals who witness it more frequently.

Societal attitudes and the promotion of violence in cultural norms and the media have been suggested as risk factors for physical abuse. In addition, while the research is controversial, some studies show a positive relationship between televised violence and aggressive behaviors, particularly for individuals who watch substantial amounts of television.

Protective Factors

Just as there are factors that place families at risk for maltreating their children, there are other factors that may protect them from vulnerabilities—factors that promote resilience. In general, research has found that supportive, emotionally satisfying relationships with a network of relatives or friends can help minimize the risk of parents maltreating children, especially during stressful life events. For example, parents who were abused as children are less likely to abuse their own children if they have resolved internal conflicts and pain related to their history of abuse and if they have an intact, stable, supportive, and nonabusive relationship with their partner. Additionally, programs on marriage education and enhancement may provide a roadmap of expected challenges such as the birth of the first child, parenting adolescents, and common gender differences which may act as a protective factor by strengthening families.

Chapter 30

Understanding the Causes of Child Neglect

Effective intervention to prevent or remedy child neglect requires an understanding of the causes. However, specification of the causes of neglect is hampered by the limited research on child neglect. Most studies of child maltreatment include both neglectful and abusive families and fail to differentiate between the groups, thus making it impossible to identify results specifically related to neglect. The numbers of studies that focus specifically on child neglect are few in comparison to studies on other types of maltreatment. Studies are most often based on small, selected samples of reported and verified neglect, composed almost exclusively of very low-income families. For these reasons, the information about causes of neglect is limited and must be considered as only suggested by the existing research.

Nevertheless, it is clear from existing studies and from the experience of practitioners that there is no single cause of the inadequate parenting we term child neglect. Thus, understanding the causality of child neglect requires that it be viewed from a broad ecological-systems perspective. Building on the previous work of child development experts,

---

"Understanding the Causes of Neglect," from *Child Neglect: A Guide for Intervention,* National Clearinghouse on Child Abuse and Neglect, 1993. Available online at the new NCCANCH website http://nccanch.acf.hhs.gov/pubs/usermanuals/neglect/causes.cfm. Despite the older date of this document, the information is still pertinent to those seeking to understand the causes of child neglect. Additional information regarding child neglect research is from "Research on Child Neglect RFA [Request for Applications]: The Federal Child Neglect Research Consortium," National Institute of Mental Health, updated January 2003.

Urie Bronfenbrenner, James Garbarino, and others, Belsksy has proposed that the causes of child maltreatment be considered in such an ecological framework.[1] Belsky and Vondra[2] have proposed that the determinants of adequate parenting arise from three sources:

- parents' own developmental history and resultant personal psychological resources,
- characteristics of the family and child, and
- contextual sources of stress and support.

Belsky and Vondra suggest that these factors interact to influence parenting. The sources of influence on parenting are interactive and often reciprocal. The developmental experiences of parents influence their personality and psychological resources, which directly influence both their parenting attitudes and behavior and their ability to develop supportive relationships with others. Parenting behavior influences the child's personality and behavior, which reciprocally influences parents' response to the child. The social context of the parent-child relationship, which includes the marital relationship, social network supports, and work-related factors, is highly influential on parenting.

Parents' Developmental History and Personality Factors

The ability of a parent to provide adequate care for a child depends partly on his/her emotional maturity, coping skills, knowledge about children, mental capacity, and parenting skills.

Belsky and Vondra review evidence from numerous studies that provide support for the conclusion that "at least under certain stressful conditions, developmental history influences psychological well-being, which in turn affects parental functioning and, as a result, child development."[3]

These authors cite, among others, the Berkeley Growth Study, which provided data to support the linkages between personality, parenting, and then to child development. Growing up in unstable, hostile, nonnurturing homes led to unstable personalities when the children became adults, which led to stressful marriages and abusive parenting practices with their own children. Belsky and Vondra conclude from their review of relevant research that parental personality is the most influential factor on parenting because the personal psychological resources of the individual are also influential in determining the marital partner, the quality of the marital relationship, and the amount of social support one receives.

Child development researchers have used attachment theory to shed light on the personality development of abusive and neglectful mothers. Egeland and colleagues have concluded from their longitudinal study of high-risk mothers and children that the mothers' lack of secure psychological attachment and psychological immaturity result from inadequate care received as children. They found that regardless of level of stress or the availability of emotional supports for parenting, the emotional stability of the mother was the most significant predictor of maltreatment. Mothers who were no longer maltreating their children at a 6-year follow-up were "more outgoing, more mature and less reactive to their feelings, more realistic in problem solving" than those who continued to neglect and abuse.[4] Others have also concluded that anxious or insecure emotional attachment between children and their parents results from interactions with parents who are physically or emotionally inaccessible, unresponsive, or inappropriately responsive to their children.[5] The conclusion of these studies is that it is not so much the inadequate or abusive nurturing experienced as children, but the unacknowledged deprivations and unresolved feelings around these early experiences that leave the parents unable to offer their children the consistent nurturing needed for the development of secure psychological attachments.

A cycle of neglect is suggested in numerous studies.[6] In Egeland et al.'s longitudinal study of maltreatment, only two out of the eight mothers who had been physically neglected as children were providing adequate care for their children. For the 35 mothers who had grown up in emotionally supportive homes, 20 were providing adequate care for their children; only 1 was maltreating her child.[7] Results of a study by Main and Goldwyn of 30 middle class women, not known to be abusive or neglectful, indicated that a mother's rejection by her own parents in childhood was strongly related to her own infant's avoidance of her following brief separations.[8] Over 56 percent of the 46 neglectful mothers in Polansky's study felt unwanted as children, and 41 percent had experienced some long-term out-of-home care as a child.[9] Nevertheless, the direct cause-effect relationship between parental history of neglect and subsequent neglect of children is not clearly established by the research. Most of the studies cited above are based on high risk or clinical samples or retrospective studies of identified neglectful parents who are not representative of the population of neglect victims.

Indeed, the indication is that there are important mediating factors in the transmission of neglect from one generation to the next. Victims of neglect who do not repeat the cycle have fewer stressful life events; stronger, more stable and supportive relationships with husbands or boyfriends; physically healthier babies; and fewer ambivalent feelings about their child's birth. They are also less likely to have been maltreated by both parents and more apt to have reported a supportive relationship with one parent or with another adult.[10] These mediating factors provide critical indicators for interventions to improve parenting potential.

Polansky and colleagues identified distinguishing psychological characteristics of neglectful mothers, first among poor whites in rural areas of the South, then among poor whites in Philadelphia.[11] From the research with rural, Appalachian mothers, Polansky et al. identified five distinct types of neglectful mothers:

- impulse-ridden mothers,
- apathetic-futile mothers,
- mothers suffering from reactive depression,
- mentally retarded mothers, and
- psychotic mothers.[12]

The subsequent study in Philadelphia confirmed the first two classifications of neglectful mothers and identified character disorders, rather than neuroses or psychoses, as the predominant psychiatric diagnosis of neglectful mothers. Polansky and colleagues described the characteristic modal personality for neglectful mothers as:

> "Less able to love, less capable of working productively, less open about feelings, more prone to living planlessly and impulsively, but also susceptible to psychological symptoms and to phases of passive inactivity and numb fatalism."[13]

Polansky et al. referred to the personalities of neglectful parents as "infantile or narcissistic" to reflect their markedly immature personality development resulting from early emotional deprivation. Many neglectful mothers are indeed psychologically immature and childlike in their inabilities to consider the needs of others, postpone gratification of basic impulses, and to invest themselves emotionally in another person. Polansky and colleagues found impulsivity to be the personality characteristic that was most highly correlated with neglect among the low-income white mothers studied.[14]

This characteristic of neglectful mothers is corroborated by Friedrich, Tyler, and Clark's study of the personality characteristics of low-income, abusive, neglectful, and nonmaltreating control mothers.[15] The authors found that the neglectful mothers, when compared with the other two groups on standard psychological measures, were the most pathological of the three groups and were characterized as "the most hostile, most impulsive, under most stress, and the least socialized."[16] The neglectful mothers as a group were judged to be "more dysfunctional than the abusive mothers, less socialized, more angry, more impulsive, more easily aroused (by infant cries) and have greater difficulty habituating to stressful and nonstressful stimuli."[17]

Neglecting parents also score significantly higher on the rigidity, loneliness, unhappiness, and the negative concept of self and child dimensions of Milner's Child Abuse Potential Inventory.[18]

Depression

Although not consistently supported by research, clinical depression has also been associated with mothers who neglect. Studies of depressed women by psychiatric researchers have consistently found that depressed mothers are more likely than nondepressed mothers to be hostile, rejecting, and indifferent toward their children and to be neglectful especially with respect to feeding and supervision.[19]

Evidence for the association of depression and neglect from studies of neglect is mixed. Polansky's descriptions of neglectful mothers in Appalachia paint a picture of depressed women.[20] But only two controlled studies of neglectful mothers have specifically examined the relationship between depression and neglect. One study did not find a significant difference between small samples of neglectful, abusive, and normal mothers on a measure of psychopathology that included depression.[21]

Zuravin's more recent study of neglecting and nonneglecting, Aid to Families with Dependent Children (AFDC) mothers did find a significant relationship between depression and neglect.[22] Results of a controlled study of neglectful families currently in progress adds further support for the relationship between depression and neglect. Scores on a standardized measure of depression indicated that 60 percent of neglectful mothers versus only 33 percent of a comparison group of low-income nonneglecting mothers had a "clinically significant" problem with depression.[23] Further research is needed to firmly establish the relationship of clinical depression and neglect, but such a diagnosis should be considered when assessing child neglect and appropriate clinical treatment offered if indicated.

Poor Social Skills

As Polansky et al. suggest, neglectful parents are typically not only deficient in their parenting skills, but have pervasive deficiencies in coping skills in many areas of living.[24] The researchers' initial studies of neglectful mothers in Appalachia revealed that deficiencies in social skills and poor self-esteem resulted in neglectful mothers selecting equally ineffectual, unsuccessful male partners, who only served to confirm and compound their deficiencies.[25] A subsequent study, which included neglectful fathers, revealed deficiencies in social participation and in their abilities to invest themselves emotionally in another person and in productive work.[26]

In Egeland et al.'s longitudinal mother-child study, the existence of an intact, long-term, stable relationship with a husband or boyfriend was found to be the critical factor distinguishing mothers who discontinued maltreating their children from those who continued to maltreat.[27] Belsky has suggested that the relationship between mother and spouse or boyfriend is the most critical supportive linkage for parents.[28] The majority of neglectful mothers lack this critical support. Neglectful mothers also have significant deficiencies in their social-communication and problem-solving skills.[29] Polansky has characterized neglectful mothers as "verbally inaccessible." They lack the ability to express their own feelings in words, and therefore are not good candidates for traditional psychotherapy. He explains that they are psychologically detached or "split off" from their own feelings, and thus, are unable to recognize feelings and put them into words.[30]

Neglectful parents have also been found to lack knowledge of and empathy for children's age-appropriate needs.[31] They have more unrealistic and more negative expectations of their children than non-neglecting parents.[32]

Substance Abuse

Abuse of alcohol or drugs is often present in cases of child neglect. Recent reports from urban Child Protective Services (CPS) agencies indicate that substance abuse is a factor in a growing percentage of child neglect cases. Estimates range from a low of less than 24 percent[33] to 80 to 90 percent of all child maltreatment reports.[34] An earlier study found that 52 percent of the children removed from their homes for severe child abuse or neglect had at least one parent with a history of alcoholism.[35] A study of women served in a Chicago alcoholism treatment program reported that 65 to 75 percent of the women were neglectful toward their children.[36] The epidemic of cocaine addiction in urban inner-city areas has resulted in large increases in the numbers of neglect reports. The alarming increase of cocaine-affected infants has placed large burdens on the already overtaxed child welfare system.[37] In spite of these associations, there is yet insufficient data to conclude that substance abuse causes neglect, but it is an increasingly significant contributing factor.

Characteristics of Children and Family System Factors

Research suggests that certain factors in family composition, size, and patterns of interaction contribute to child neglect. Even some characteristics of children may contribute to neglectful parenting.

Child Characteristics

Studies have not identified unique characteristics of neglected children that contribute to neglect. However, Crittenden's studies of parent-child interactions in abusive and neglectful families suggest that the children in neglectful families develop behavior patterns as a result of the interactions that make them more likely to experience further neglect.[38] As a result of the mother's inattention, the neglected child often develops patterns of either extremely passive, withdrawing behavior or random, undisciplined activity. Both of these patterns are likely to result in further inattention and distancing on the part of the child's neglectful parent. Studies have not clearly established the relationship between handicapped children and neglect. However, Belsky and Vondra cite numerous studies that support the association of prematurity, "difficult" temperament, and mentally handicapped children with tendencies of their parents to be less responsive, less attentive to their needs.[39] Younger children are more vulnerable to serious injury from neglect, but when educational neglect is included, older children are more often neglected.[40]

Family Composition

Most neglectful families are single-parent families. The absence of the father in the majority of neglectful families means lower income and less tangible resources to provide for children's needs. Polansky, Chalmers, Buttenweiser, and Williams found that neglectful families with fathers present in the household had significantly higher income and provided better physical care than the single-parent families, but not better emotional/cognitive care.[41] The physical absence or emotional disengagement of the father has been identified as contributing to deprived parenting in families of failure to thrive infants.[42] Beyond these studies, little research attention has been focused on fathers or adult males in neglectful families.

Family Size

Chronic neglectful families tend to be large families with fewer resources to meet basic needs than other families. Numerous studies have discovered that neglectful families on the average have more children than nonneglecting families. Studies of neglectful families by Polansky in Philadelphia and in Georgia found that neglectful families averaged 3.5 or more children, compared to significantly fewer children in similarly situated (low socioeconomic status [SES]) nonneglecting control families.[43] Similar patterns of larger than average number of children in neglectful families were discovered by Giovannoni and Billingsley and by Wolock and Horowitz.[44] *The Study of National Incidence and Prevalence of Child Abuse and Neglect* reported that the estimated rate of neglect among families with four or more children was almost double the rate among families with three or fewer children.[45]

Family Interaction Patterns

Patterns of verbal and nonverbal communication between neglectful parents and children have been characterized as infrequent and predominantly negative. Burgess and Conger found that there were significantly fewer positive interactions and more negative interactions between neglectful parents and their children than in either abusive or in nonmaltreating families studied.[46] These researchers found that, compared with abusive mothers and nonmaltreating controls, the neglectful mothers stood out as the most negative and least positive in their relationships with other family members.

Crittenden similarly concluded that "neglecting mothers offered so little stimulation and responded to so few infant signals that they left their infants socially powerless and largely responsible for their own stimulation. Their infants showed correspondingly depressed levels of activity which reduced both the stimulations and feedback available to the already unresponsive mother. Mutual passivity was easily maintained."[47] This low level of positive interaction and stimulation between neglectful mothers and their children was confirmed by a series of studies by Crittenden and others.[48]

Crittenden describes distinctive patterns of interaction in neglecting, abusing and neglecting, and in marginally maltreating families observed in a small sample of these families.[49] The neglecting families in this study were largely young families with few children, with more than one adult caretaker, usually the maternal grandmother or mother's boyfriend. Parental coping strategies were withdrawal, deference to others whenever possible, or leaving tasks undone. Discipline was rarely used with the children. The parents' informal support networks were characterized by almost daily contact with relatives, who offered some tangible, but not emotional, support.

The neglecting parents are characterized by Crittenden as unresponsive and withdrawn: "They responded to few of their children's overtures when interacting with them and initiated almost no activity... Their children responded with a reduction in communicative activity."[50] Toddlers in the neglectful homes, as soon as they were able to walk, sought out their own stimulation through uncontrolled exploratory activity. Neglectful mothers largely ignored these toddlers on the loose, only infrequently and ineffectively attempted to exercise some control by yelling at them, often without bothering to observe the results. The children merely imitated the parent's disregard.

Neglecting families who were also abusive were typically large, very unstable, and disorganized, with children sired by several different fathers. The mother had often lived with a series of men, been alone, and lived with her own mother for periods of time. "The only certainty was that the present structure, too, would change."[51] The parent-child interactions in these families vacillated from the extremes of nonsystematic, unpredictable, violent episodes of physical punishment in an effort to control the children's behavior to sullen withdrawal. The goal was momentary peace and quiet relief from the chaos in the family. Children react to their highly unpredictable environment by being always on guard and chronically anxious. The need to be ever vigilant to unpredictable violent adult reactions resulted in the children experiencing significant developmental delays.

The marginally maltreating families were typically two-parent families, but with different fathers for the children. The mother-partner relationships were unstable and often physically abusive. These families were disorganized and chaotic, constantly reacting to a series of day-to-day crises with frantic, ineffectual activity. There were no consistent rules or expectations of the children, and discipline was an expression of parents' frustration. The marginally maltreating parents were not able to engage in systematic problem solving, but instead stumbled from crisis to crisis trying to cope with whatever limited methods and help they could muster. These mothers were not always angry and could respond empathetically to their children's distress when it was expressed dramatically through tears or tantrums. Consequently, tears and tantrums were frequent, but the solace that resulted was short-lived and not secure.

These distinctively different patterns of interaction in contrasting types of neglecting families reinforce the need to assess each neglectful family independently. Individualized family patterns suggest the need for individualized interventions to remedy the neglect.

Contextual Sources of Stress and Support

Neglectful families do not exist in a vacuum. The availability of formal and informal supports for parenting from outside the family system are critical determinants of the adequacy of parenting. Schools, churches, work settings, neighborhoods, and communities can supplement parents' resources for providing adequate care for children. On the other hand, these systems can produce additional demands and stressors, which make parenting more difficult.

Unemployment, which causes psychological and economic stress, is frequent in neglectful families.[52] Neglectful families are less likely to be involved in church or other formal organizations that might be sources of tangible or psychological support. Neglectful families tend to live in impoverished neighborhoods and view their neighborhoods as less helpful and less supportive than do nonneglectful parents. Chronically neglecting families are viewed as deviant, even by their similarly impoverished neighbors, who avoid social contacts with them.[53] Families of color, who are over represented in child neglect statistics, must also cope with the stress of racial prejudice in many communities.

Informal Support Systems

Most parents must rely at times on supportive relationships with spouses, other relatives, neighbors, and friends to cope with demanding parenting tasks, especially in times of illness, loss of income, or other life crises. Supportive linkages are particularly critical when the parent or child is handicapped by physical or emotional disabilities, or when there are many children to care for and few economic resources. Neglectful parents typically lack strong informal helping resources.[54] The social networks of neglectful mothers tend to be dominated by relatives who are critical, rather than supportive. Interactions with relatives may be frequent, but not very helpful. Because neglectful parents often lack the necessary social skills to maintain relationships, already weak linkages tend to break down, leaving the parents isolated and lonely.[55]

Stress

The coping abilities of neglectful families are severely taxed by stressful life circumstances. As indicated previously, the majority of neglectful families are poor, and not only poor, but usually the poorest of the poor. A high proportion of reported neglectful families are dependent upon public assistance for income, and they have the lowest income and the fewest material resources even among AFDC recipient families.[56]

Although chronic neglectful families are poorer and have more problems, the new neglectful families are under greater stress. For example, Nelson et al. found that 75 percent had experienced a serious illness or injury within the previous 3 years.[57]

People of color are over represented in neglectful families.[58] However, because of the higher incidence of poverty among Native Americans, Hispanics, and African-Americans, this overrepresentation seems to disappear when Socioeconomic Status (SES) is held constant.[59] The ethnic and cultural differences in child maltreatment are small or nonexistent when families have adequate economic and social resources, but the combination of racial discrimination and poverty places unusual stresses on families of color that frequently overwhelm their coping resources.[60]

In summary, the causes of child neglect are multiple and complex. Most often neglect is the result of a combination of personal deficits in parents, conflictual, nonsupportive family systems and informal support networks, highly stressful life circumstances, and absence of environmental supports for parenting.

Notes

1. U. Bronfenbrenner, The Experimental Ecology of Human Development (Cambridge, MA: *Harvard University Press,* 1979); J. Garbarino, "The Human Ecology of Child Maltreatment: A Conceptual Model for Research," *Journal of Marriage and the Family* 39(1977):72217235; and J. Belsky, "Child Maltreatment: An Ecological Integration," *American Psychologist* 4(1980):320335.

2. J. Belsky and J. Vondra, "Lessons from Child Abuse: The Determinants of Parenting," in D. Cicchetti and V. Carlson, *Child Maltreatment* (Cambridge: Cambridge University Press, 1989), 153202.

3. Ibid., 168.

4. R. Pianta, B. Egeland, and M. F. Erickson, "The Antecedents of Maltreatment: Results of the Mother-Child Interaction Project," in D. Cicchetti and V. Carlson, *Child Maltreatment* (Cambridge: Cambridge University Press, 1989), 241.

5. P. M. Crittenden and M. D. S. Ainsworth, "Child Maltreatment and Attachment Theory," in D. Cicchetti and V. Carlson, *Child Maltreatment* (Cambridge: Cambridge University Press, 1989), 432464.

6. Polansky et al., Damaged Parents; P. M. Crittenden, "Sibling Interaction: Evidence of a Generational Effect in Maltreating Families," *Child Abuse and Neglect* 8(1984):433438; Pianta, Egeland, and Erickson, "The Antecedents of Maltreatment: Results of the Mother-Child Interaction Research Project," 203253; and B. Egeland and M. Erickson, "Rising Above the Past: Strategies for Helping New Mothers Break the Cycle of Abuse and Neglect," *Zero to Three* 11(1990):2935.

7. B. Egeland, "The Consequences of Physical and Emotional Neglect on the Development of Young Children," Research Symposium on Child Neglect (Washington, DC: National Center on Child Abuse and Neglect, 1988).

8. M. Main and R. Goldwyn, "Predicting Rejection of her Infant from Mother's Representation of Her Own Experience: Implications for the Abused-Abusing Intergenerational Cycle," *Child Abuse and Neglect* 8(1984):32033217.

9. Polansky et al., Damaged Parents, 151.

10. Egeland and Erickson, "Rising Above the Past: Strategies for Helping New Mothers Break the Cycle of Abuse and Neglect," 2935; and J. Kaufman and E. Zigler, "Do Abused Children Become Abusive Parents?," *American Journal of Orthopsychiatry* 56(1987):186192.

11. N. Polansky, R. Borgman, and C. DeSaix, *Roots of Futility* (San Francisco: Jossey Bass, 1972).

12. Ibid.

13. Polansky et al., Damaged Parents, 109.

14. Ibid., 51.

15. W. N. Friedrich, J. D. Tyler, and J. A. Clark, "Personality and Psychophysiological Variables in Abusive, Neglectful and

Low-Income Control Mothers," *Journal of Nervous and Mental Disease* 173(1985):449460.

16. Ibid., 457.

17. Ibid., 459.

18. J. S. Milner and K. R. Robertson, "Comparison of Physical Child Abusers, Intrafamilial Sexual Child Abusers, and Child Neglecters," *Journal of Interpersonal Violence* 5(1990):3748.

19. M. M. Weissman, E. S. Paykel, and G. L. Klerman, "The Depressed Woman as Mother," *Social Psychiatry* 7(1972):98108; and C. Longfellow, P. Zelkowitz, and E. Saunders, "The Quality of Mother-Child Relationships," in D. Belle, ed., *Lives in Stress: Women and Depression* (Beverly Hills, CA: Sage, 1981), 163176.

20. Polansky, Borgman, and DeSaix, Roots of Futility.

21. A. H. Green et al., "Psychological Assessment of Child-Abusing, Neglecting, and Normal Mothers," *The Journal of Nervous and Mental Diseases* 168(1980):356360.

22. S. J. Zuravin, "Child Abuse, Child Neglect and Maternal Depression: Is there a connection?," in Research Symposium on Child Neglect (Washington, DC: U.S. Department of Health and Human Services, National Center on Child Abuse and Neglect, 1988), 34.

23. J. M. Gaudin et al., "Relationships Among Loneliness, Depression and Social Supports In Neglcctful Families," *American Journal of Orthopsychiatry* (In Press).

24. Polansky et al., Damaged Parents, 39.

25. Polansky, Borgman, and DeSaix, Roots of Futility.

26. Polansky et al., Damaged Parents, 115.

27. B. Egeland, "Breaking the Cycle of Abuse: Implications for Prediction and Intervention," in K. Browne, C. Davies, and P. Stratton, eds., *Early Prediction and Prevention of Child Abuse* (Chichester, England: John Wiley, 1988), 92.

28. J. Belsky, "Child Maltreatment: An Ecological Integration," *American Psychologist* 4(1980):320335.

29. S. T. Azar et al., "Unrealistic Expectations and Problem-Solving Ability in Maltreating and Comparison Mothers," *Journal of Consulting and Clinical Psychology* 52(1984):687690.

30. Polansky et al., Damaged Parents.

31. J. M. Jones and R. L. McNeely, "Mothers Who Neglect and Those Who Do Not: A Comparative Study," *Journal of Contemporary Social Work* (1980):559567; and R. C. Herrenkohl, E. C. Herrenkohl, and B. P. Egolf, "Circumstances Surrounding the Occurrence of Child Maltreatment," *Journal of Consulting and Clinical Psychology* 51(1983):424431.

32. Azar et al., "Unrealistic Expectations and Problem-Solving Ability in Maltreating and Comparison Mothers," 687690; and D. T. Larrance and C. T. Twentyman, "Maternal Attributions and Child Abuse," *Journal of Abnormal Psychology* 92(1983): 449457.

33. M. J. Martin and J. Walters, "Familial Correlates of Selected Types of Child Abuse and Neglect," *Journal of Marriage and the Family* (1982):267276.

34. National Committee for the Prevention of Child Abuse (NCPCA), "Substance Abuse and Child Abuse," NCPCA Fact Sheet (Chicago: NCPCA, 1989), 14.

35. R. Famularo, "Alcoholism and Severe Child Maltreatment," *American Journal of Orthopsychiatry* 53(1986):481485.

36. Alcoholism and Child Neglect (Springfield, IL: Illinois Department of Children and Family Services, 1987), 4.

37. D. Priddy, "A Social Worker's Agony: Working With Children Affected by Crack/Cocaine," *Journal of the National Association of Social Workers* 35(1990):193288; and C. Johnston, "The Children of Cocaine Addicts: A Study of Twenty-five Inner City Families," *The Social Worker* 58(1990):5356.

38. Crittenden and Ainsworth, "Child Maltreatment and Attachment Theory"; P. M. Crittenden, "Abusing, Neglectful, Problematic, and Adequate Dyads: Differentiating by Patterns of Interaction," *Merrill-Palmer Quarterly* 27:118; and P. M. Crittenden, "Family and Dyadic Patterns of Functioning in Maltreating Families," in K. Browne, C. Davies, and P. Stratton, eds., *Early Prediction and Prevention of Child Abuse* (Chichester, England: John Wiley, 1988), 161189.

39. Belsky and Vondra, "Lessons from Child Abuse: The Determinants of Parenting," 153202.

40. U.S. Department of Health and Human Services, Study of National Incidence and Prevalence of Child Abuse and Neglect.

41. N. A. Polansky et al., "The Absent Father in Child Neglect," *Social Service Review* (1979):6374.

42. R. J. Gagan, J. M. Cupoli, and A. H. Watkins, "The Families of Children Who Fail to Thrive: Preliminary Investigations of Parental Deprivation Among Organic and Non-Organic Cases," *Child Abuse and Neglect* 8(1984):93103; and Kempe and Goldbloom, "Malnutrition and Growth Retardation (Failure to Thrive) in the Context of Child Abuse and Neglect."

43. Polansky et al., Damaged Parents; and N. A. Polansky et al., "The Psychological Ecology of the Neglectful Mother," *Child Abuse and Neglect* (1985):265275.

44. J. M. Giovannoni and A. Billingsley, "Child Neglect Among the Poor: Study of Parental Adequacy in Families of Three Ethnic Groups," *Child Welfare* 19(1970):196204; and Wolock and Horowitz, "Child Maltreatment and Material Deprivation Among AFDC-Recipient Families," 175194.

45. U.S. Department of Health and Human Services, Study of National Incidence and Prevalence of Child Abuse and Neglect.

46. R. L. Burgess and R. D. Conger, "Family Interaction in Abusive, Neglectful, and Normal Families," *Child Development* 49(1978):11631173.

47. Crittenden, "Abusing, Neglecting, Problematic, and Adequate Dyads: Differentiating by Patterns of Interaction," 210.

48 P. Crittenden and J. D. Bonvillian, "The Relationship Between Maternal Risk Status and Maternal Sensitivity," *American Journal of Orthopsychiatry* 54(1984):25062; J. A. Aragona and S. M. Eyeberg, "Neglected Children: Mothers' Report of Child Behavior Problems and Observed Verbal Behavior," *Child Development* 52(1981):596602; D. M. Bousha and C. T. Twentyman, "Mother-Child Interaction Style in Abuse, Neglect, and Control Groups," *Journal of Abnormal Psychology* 93(1984):106114; and Azar et al., "Unrealistic Expectations and Problem-Solving Ability in Maltreating and Comparison Mothers," 687690.

49. Crittenden, "Family and Dyadic Patterns of Functioning in Maltreating Families," 161189.

50. Ibid., 173.

51. Ibid., 175.

52. American Humane Association, Highlights of Official Child Neglect and Child Abuse Reporting: 1986 (Denver: American Humane Association, 1988), 2633; and Nelson, Saunders, and Landsman, Chronic Neglect in Perspective: A Study of Chronically Neglecting Families in a Large Metropolitan County, Final Report.

53. Polansky et al., "The Psychological Ecology of the Neglectful Mother," 265275; Wolock and Horowitz, "Child Maltreatment and Maternal Deprivation Among AFDC-Recipient Families," 175194; J. Garbarino and D. Chairman, "Identifying High Risk Neighborhoods," in J. Garbarino and S. H. Stocking, eds., *Protecting Children from Abuse and Neglect* (San Francisco: Jossey-Bass, 1980), 94108; and American Humane Association, Highlights of Official Child Neglect and Child Abuse Reporting: 1986.

54. Polansky et al., Damaged Parents; Polansky et al., "The Psychological Ecology of the Neglectful Mother," 265275; and Wolock and Horowitz, "Child Maltreatment and Maternal Deprivation Among AFDC-Recipient Families," 175194.

55. J. M. Gaudin et al., "Remedying Child Neglect: Effectiveness of Social Network Interventions," *Journal of Applied Social Sciences* 15(19901991):97123; Giovannoni and Billingsley, "Child Neglect Among the Poor: A Study of Parental Adequacy in Families of Three Ethnic Groups," 196204; and Polansky et al., "The Psychological Ecology of the Neglectful Mother," 265275.

56. L. H. Pelton, The Social Context of Child Abuse and Neglect (New York: Human Science Press, 1981); Polansky et al., "The Psychological Ecology of the Neglectful Mother," 265275; and Wolock and Horowitz, "Child Maltreatment and Maternal Deprivation Among AFDC-Recipient Families," 175194.

57. Nelson et al., Chronic Neglect in Perspective: A Study of Chronically Neglecting Families in a Large Metropolitan County.

58. American Humane Association, Highlights of Official Child Neglect and Child Abuse Reporting: 1986, 33.

59. A. Kadushin, "Neglect in Families," in E. Nunnally, C. Chilman, and F. Cox, eds., *Mental Illness, Delinquency, Addictions and Neglect: Families in Trouble Series, Vol. 4,* (Newbury Park, CA: Sage, 1988), 156.

60. J. Garbarino and E. Aaron, "The Significance of Ethnic and Cultural Differences in Child Maltreatment," *Journal of Marriage and the Family* 15(1983):773783.

Research on Child Neglect

The National Institutes of Health (NIH) announced a special trans-NIH, interdepartmental Request for Applications (RFA) focusing on "Research on Child Neglect" for fiscal year 2000. This initiative encouraged research on the etiology, extent, services, treatment, management, and prevention of child neglect. This Request for Applications (RFA) was intended to stimulate the development of programs of child neglect research at institutions that currently have strong research programs in related areas (for example, child development, injury prevention, developmental neurobiology, child abuse, substance abuse, population research, craniofacial and dental public health, health services) but are not engaged in extensive research focusing on child neglect. A second goal of this RFA was to bring the expertise of researchers from the child health, education, and juvenile justice fields into the child neglect research field and to promote their collaborations with each other and with child neglect and child abuse researchers.

This RFA, coordinated under the auspices of the NIH Child Abuse and Neglect Working Group, was a joint effort of several components of the NIH, including the Office of Behavioral and Social Sciences Research, the National Institute on Alcohol Abuse and Alcoholism, the National Institute of Child Health and Human Development, the National Institute of Dental and Craniofacial Research, the National Institute on Drug Abuse, the National Institute of Mental Health, and the National Institute of Neurological Disorders and Stroke. Joining with NIH in this groundbreaking endeavor are the Children's Bureau of the Administration on Children, Youth and Families; the National Institute of Justice, and the Office of Juvenile Justice and Delinquency Prevention, both within the Office of Justice Programs, Department of Justice; and the Office of Special Education Programs, within the Department of Education.

Child neglect is a serious public health, justice, social services, and education problem, not only compromising the immediate health of our nation's children, but also threatening their growth and intellectual development, their long-term physical and mental health outcomes, their propensity for pro-social behavior, their future parenting practices, and their economic productivity as eventual wage earners. The sponsoring organizations are jointly issuing this RFA because neglect is a multi-faceted problem involving many agencies in its consequences, prevention, and control. The RFA is intended to go beyond what any single organization would be likely to accomplish individually, since child neglect requires multi-disciplinary solutions which cross-cut the missions of NIH and these partner agencies.

Over $3 million dollars (annual total cost) was pledged by the co-sponsors, for grants begun in fiscal year 2000, and fifteen grants were awarded at September/October 2000 NIH council meetings to form the core research site participants in the Federal Child Neglect Research Consortium. Grants were awarded for up to 5 years, on issues such as: the antecedents and consequences of neglect; instrument development; treatment, preventive intervention, and service delivery (including legal processes, protective services, mental health services and court-ordered interventions) for child neglect; and mediating factors such as foster care, domestic violence, welfare reform, and disabilities or other special characteristics of neglected populations and their caretakers.

For More Information

For information about NIMH and its programs, please e-mail, write or phone:

National Institute of Mental Health (NIMH)
Office of Communications
6001 Executive Boulevard, Room 8184, MSC 9663
Bethesda, MD 20892-9663
Toll-Free: 866-615-NIMH (6464)
Phone: 301-443-4513
Website: http://www.nimh.nih.gov
E-mail: nimhinfo@nih.gov

For abstracts of funded career development awards in child abuse and neglect visit http://www.nimh.nih.gov/canwg/canabscardev.cfm.

Chapter 31

National Statistics on Child Abuse and Neglect

An estimated 903,000 children across the country were victims of abuse or neglect in 2001, according to national data released by the Department of Health and Human Services (HHS). The statistics indicate that about 12.4 out of every 1,000 children were victims of abuse or neglect, a rate comparable to the previous year's victimization rate of 12.2 out of 1,000 children.

"A nation as compassionate as ours should ensure that no child is a victim of abuse or neglect. The number of children that are being abused and neglected this country is an unacceptable daily tragedy," HHS Secretary Tommy G. Thompson said. "We must do more to protect our most vulnerable children. That's why President Bush has proposed an important new approach to give states the tools and resources they need to prevent abuse and care for these young victims."

As part of HHS' fiscal year 2004 budget request, the Bush Administration is proposing a new approach to protecting children in the child welfare system. Under the plan, states and tribes would have the option of using some money now designated solely for foster care to support a range of abuse-preventive services and programs. The

---

This chapter begins with "National Statistics on Child Abuse and Neglect," from U.S. Department of Health and Human Services, 2003. Available online at http://www.hhs.gov/news/press/2003pres/20030401.html. It also includes "Chapter 3: Victims" from *Child Maltreatment 2001*. U.S. Department of Health and Human Services. Administration on Children, Youth, and Families, 2001. Available online at http://www.acf.hhs.gov/programs/cb/publications/cm01/chapterthree.htm.

proposal provides the flexibility and sustained financial support necessary to build innovative programs for children and families aimed at preventing maltreatment and removal from home.

"Every time a child is abused or neglected, the whole human race suffers," said Wade F. Horn, Ph.D., assistant secretary for children and families. "President Bush's plan to prevent this terrible problem will point the way to happier lives for many children."

The data are based on information collected through the National Child Abuse and Neglect Data System (NCANDS). The data show that child protective service agencies received about 2,672,000 reports of possible maltreatment in 2001. There were 903,000 substantiated cases of maltreatment of children—the majority of which involved cases of neglect. About 1,300 children died of abuse or neglect, a rate of 1.81 children per 100,000 children in the population.

The rate of child neglect and abuse in 2001 was about 19 percent less than the rate in 1993, when maltreatment peaked at an estimated 15.3 out of every 1,000 children. As recently as 1998, the rate was 12.9 per 1,000 children. The rate dropped to 11.8 per 1,000 children in 1999—considered a statistical "outlier" that was unduly influenced by census population estimates—and then returned to 12.2 per 1,000 children in 2000.

The 2001 data were released by HHS' Administration for Children and Families at a joint press conference with Prevent Child Abuse America marking April as Child Abuse and Neglect Prevention Month. The St. Louis event also highlighted the public and private partnerships for prevention that are crucial to addressing maltreatment successfully.

Victims: Child Maltreatment 2001

The role of the child protective services (CPS) agency is to respond to the needs of children who are alleged to have been maltreated and to ensure that they remain safe. In 2001, three million children were the subjects of a CPS investigation or assessment. Approximately 30 percent were found to have experienced or to have been at risk of experiencing abuse or neglect. These children are considered victims of child maltreatment.

Victimization Rates

Approximately 903,000 children were victims of abuse and neglect during 2001. This national estimate is based on data from 51 States. In these States, 12.4 children for every 1,000 children in the population were victims of abuse or neglect. A child was counted each time he or she was found to be a victim of maltreatment. The 2001 victimization rate of 12.4 is comparable to the 2000 rate of 12.2 per 1,000 children in the population, especially given that the child population base numbers were estimated. Both the 2000 and 2001 rates are lower that the 1998 rate. The 1999 rate is considered an outlier that was unduly influenced by the census population estimates.

Types of Maltreatment

During 2001, 59.2 percent of victims suffered neglect (including medical neglect); 18.6 percent were physically abused; 9.6 percent were sexually abused; and 6.8 percent were emotionally or psychologically maltreated. In addition, 19.5 percent of victims were associated with other type of maltreatment, which was not coded as one of the main types of maltreatment. For example, some States included "abandonment," "threats of harm to the child," and "congenital drug addiction" as "Other." The percentages total more than 100 percent of victims because children may have been victims of more than one type of maltreatment.

The rates of victimization by type of maltreatment have fluctuated slightly from year to year. Five-year trends of the rates of physical abuse and sexual abuse per 1,000 children in the population show a decrease. Five-year trends of the rates of medical neglect and psychological maltreatment per 1,000 children in the population depict slightly fluctuating rates. For the same timeframe, the rate of neglect per 1,000 children in the population had shown a decrease from 7.5 in 1997 to 6.5 in 1999. For 2001, the rate was 7.1.

Sex and Age of Victims

For 2001, 48.0 percent of child victims were male, and 51.5 percent of the victims were female. The sex for 0.5 percent of child victims was unknown or not reported.

Children in the age group of birth to 3 years accounted for 27.7 percent of victims. Overall, the rate of victimization is inversely related to the age of the child. These proportions have remained constant during the past 5 years.

Race and Ethnicity of Victims

Half of all victims were White (50.2%); a quarter (25.0%) were African American; and a sixth (14.5%) were Hispanic. American Indians and Alaska Natives accounted for 2.0 percent of victims, and Asian-Pacific Islanders accounted for 1.3 percent of victims. These percentages have remained stable for the past several years.

Child Maltreatment Recurrence (Child File)

For most children who experience maltreatment recurrence, the efforts of the CPS system have not been successful in preventing subsequent victimization. However, recurrence may also be influenced by an increased exposure to reporting sources, including service providers. Thus, analyses of short-term recurrence, as in this report, reflect observed recurrence and should be supplemented by analyses of recurrence across longer periods.

Recurrence within 6 months of the initial substantiated or indicated maltreatment occurred with 8.9 percent of abuse or neglect victims. Twelve States—Arizona, Arkansas, Delaware, Maine, Michigan, Minnesota, Nebraska, Pennsylvania, South Carolina, Texas, West Virginia, and Wyoming—had a recurrence rate equal to or less than 6.1 percent, which is the national child safety standard used in evaluating State outcome performance by the Child and Family Services Reviews (CFSR).[1]

Twenty-one States provided sufficient data to support an analysis of the factors that influence the likelihood of recurrence. In this analysis, recurrence is defined as a second substantiated or indicated maltreatment occurring within a 6-month period. The major results of the analysis are summarized in the following:

- Children who had been victimized prior to a first report in 2001 were more than twice as likely to experience recurrence compared to children without a prior history of victimization.
- In comparison to children who experienced physical abuse, children who were neglected were 44 percent more likely to experience recurrence. Children who experienced additional types of maltreatment were 17 percent more likely to experience recurrence, and children who had experienced multiple forms of maltreatment were 14 percent more likely to experience recurrence than physically maltreated children were.
- Children who received post-investigation services were 50 percent more likely to be maltreated again; children placed in foster care were 23 percent more likely to experience abuse and neglect than children who were not placed.

- The youngest children (from birth through age 3) were most likely to experience a recurrence of maltreatment.
- Compared to White children, African American children were 17 percent less likely to experience recurrence. Children of Hispanic ethnicity were 20 percent less likely and Asian Pacific Islanders were 27 percent less likely to experience recurrence than White children.
- Children reported by "Other" or "Unknown Sources," which for the most part are nonprofessionals, were 34 percent more likely to experience recurrence than children reported by Social Services or Mental Health Services Personnel. Children reported by law enforcement were 19 percent less likely to experience recurrence than children reported by Social Services or Mental Health Services Personnel.
- Children for whom the perpetrator was the father or a nonparent were less likely to experience recurrence than children who were abused by just their mother.

The regression analysis results support a general conclusion that younger children, those neglected or who experience multiple maltreatment forms, those maltreated by their mothers, and those who have been reported before are the most vulnerable to continued maltreatment. Children and their families who have received services, including placement, and those reported by nonprofessionals or educators also are more likely to experience recurrence. These findings are consistent with those reported in the analysis of recurrence for the 1999 data, the first year this analysis was prepared.

Note

1. The CFSR was mandated by the Adoption and Safe Families Act of 1997 (P.L. 105-89). The national standards were defined in an Information Memorandum issued by the Administration for Children and Families on August 16, 2001.

Chapter 32

Child Fatalities Due to Maltreatment

Children are one of the most vulnerable groups in our society. Child fatalities due to maltreatment represent the worst case scenario in attempts to protect children. Despite the efforts of the child protection system, child fatalities remain a serious problem. Although the untimely deaths of children due to illness and accidents have been closely monitored, the same cannot be said of children who have died as the result of physical assault or severe neglect. Intervention strategies targeted at resolving this problem face complex challenges.

Child Fatalities Due to Maltreatment Are Increasing

Although child deaths caused by abuse and/or neglect are relatively infrequent, the rate of child maltreatment fatalities, confirmed by Child Protective Services (CPS) to have been the result of child maltreatment, has steadily increased over the last decade. The National Child Abuse and Neglect Data System (NCANDS) reported that in 1997 there were an estimated 1,196 child fatalities, or 1.7 children per 100,000 in the general population. (This estimate was based on reports from 41 States that reported a total of 967 fatalities.) The U.S. Advisory Board on Child Abuse and Neglect in *A Nation's Shame:*

Text in this chapter is from "Child Fatalities Fact Sheet," produced by the Centers for Disease Control and Prevention (CDC), August 2003. Available online at http://nccanch.acf.hhs/gov/pubs/factsheets/fatality.pdf; And "Fact Sheet: Homicide Risk Among Infants," produced by the Centers for Disease Control and Prevention, March 2002. Available online at http://www.cdc.gov/od/oc/media/pressrel/fs020308.htm.

Fatal Child Abuse and Neglect in the United States, reported that a more realistic estimate of annual child deaths as a result of abuse and neglect, both known and unknown to CPS agencies, is about 2,000, or approximately five children per day. Experts such as Ryan Rainey from the National Center for Prosecution of Child Abuse believe that the number of child deaths from maltreatment per year may be as high as 5,000.

The Actual Number of Child Fatalities May Be Underreported

Determining the actual numbers of children who die annually from abuse is complex. Many researchers and practitioners believe that child fatalities are underreported because some deaths labeled as accidents, child homicides, and/or Sudden Infant Death Syndrome (SIDS) might be attributed to child maltreatment if more comprehensive investigations were conducted. It is difficult to distinguish a child who has been suffocated from a child who has died as a result of SIDS, or a child who was dropped, pushed, or thrown from a child who dies from a legitimate fall. Some researchers and practitioners have gone so far as to estimate that there may be twice the number of deaths as a result of abuse and/or neglect as are reported by NCANDS if cases unknown to CPS agencies are included.

There is a Lack of Standard Terminology for Child Fatalities

To further complicate the issue, different terminology is used to discuss child fatalities, sometimes interchangeably. NCANDS defines child fatality as a child dying from abuse or neglect, because either (a) the injury from the abuse or neglect was the cause of death, or (b) the abuse and/or neglect was a contributing factor to the cause of death. Researchers such as Finkelhor and Christoffel use the term child abuse homicide to define a childhood death resulting from maltreatment (either assault or neglect) by a responsible caretaker. Law enforcement and criminal justice agencies also use the term child abuse homicide, but their definition, while including the caretaker as perpetrator, also includes the criminal act of homicide by non-caretakers (death at the hands of another, felony child endangerment, and criminal neglect). More specifically, the term infanticide is increasingly used to define the murdering of children younger than 6 or 12 months by their parents.

Young Children are the Most Vulnerable

Research supports that very young children (age 5 and younger) are the most frequent victims of child fatalities. NCANDS data for 1997 from a subset of States demonstrated that children 3 or younger accounted for 77 percent of fatalities. This population is the most vulnerable for many reasons including their small size and inability to defend themselves. The fatal abuse usually occurs in one of two ways: repeated abuse and/or neglect over a period of time (battered child syndrome) or in a single, impulsive incident of assault (drowning, suffocating, or shaking the baby, for example).

Primary Caretakers are the Most Frequent Perpetrators

No matter how the fatal abuse occurs, one fact of great concern is that most of the perpetrators are, by definition, primary caretakers such as parents and other relatives.

Though there is no single profile for the perpetrator of fatal child abuse, there are consistent characteristics that reappear in studies. Frequently the perpetrator is a young adult in his/her mid-20s without a high school diploma, living at or below the poverty level, depressed, and who may have difficulty coping with stressful situations. In many instances, the perpetrator has experienced violence first-hand.

The Response to Fatal Child Abuse or Neglect Is Complex

The response to the problem is often hampered by inconsistencies:

- The inaccurate reporting of the number of children who die each year as a result of abuse and neglect
- The lack of national standards for child autopsies or death investigations
- The different roles that CPS agencies play in the investigation process
- The use in many States of an elected coroner who is not required to have any medical or child abuse and neglect training rather than a medical examiner.

Child Fatality Review Teams

To address some of these inconsistencies, multidisciplinary/multiagency Child Fatality Review Teams have emerged in many

States to provide a coordinated approach to the investigation of child deaths. These teams are comprised of prosecutors, coroners or medical examiners, law enforcement personnel, CPS workers, public health care providers, and others.

The teams review cases of child deaths and facilitate appropriate follow-up. The follow-up may include assuring that services are provided for surviving family members, providing information to assist in the prosecution of perpetrators, and developing recommendations to improve child protection and community support systems. In addition, teams can assist in determining avenues for prevention efforts and improving training for front-line workers. Well-designed, properly organized Child Fatality Review Teams appear to offer the greatest hope for defining the underlying nature and scope of fatalities due to child abuse and neglect and for offering solutions.

Prevention Services Are Key

When addressing the issue of child maltreatment, and especially child fatalities, prevention is a recurring theme. In 1995, the U.S. Advisory Board on Child Abuse and Neglect recommended a universal approach to the prevention of child fatalities that would reach out to all families through the implementation of several key strategies. These efforts would begin by providing services such as home visitation by trained professionals or paraprofessionals, hospital-linked outreach to parents of infants and toddlers, community-based programs designed for the specific needs of neighborhoods, and effective public education campaigns.

Homicide Risk among Infants

- Homicide is the 15th leading cause of infant death in the United States. The risk of homicide is greater in infancy than in any other year of childhood before age 17.
- Infants are at greatest risk for homicide during the first week of infancy and the first day of life.
- Among homicides during the first week of life, 82.6% occurred on the day of birth.
- The homicide rate on the first day of life was more than ten times greater than the rate during any other time of life.
- Among homicides on the first day of life, previous work has shown that 95% of victims are not born in a hospital.

- The second highest peak in risk for infant homicide occurs during the eighth week of life and may be due to a caregiver's reaction to an infant's persistent crying. Infant crying duration peaks at six to eight weeks of age.
- Among homicides during the first week of life, 89% of perpetrators are female, usually the mother. Mothers who kill their infants are more likely to be adolescents and have a history of mental illness.

References

Christoffel, K.K. (1992). Child abuse fatalities. In S. Ludwig, and A.E. Kornberg. (Eds.), *Child Abuse. A Medical Reference (2nd ed.).* New York: Churchill Livingstone, Inc.

Department of Justice. Office of Juvenile Justice and Delinquency Programs. (1994, February 16-17). Child fatality review teams: A multi-agency approach. (Participant Guide). National Training Teleconference.

Finkelhor, D. (1997). In G. Kaufman Kantor, and J. Jasinski (Eds.), *Out of the Darkness: Contemporary Perspectives on Family Violence.* Thousand Oaks, CA: Sage Publications.

Kaplan S.R. (1996). Child fatalities and child fatality review teams. Washington, DC: ABA Center on Children and the Law.

Lewit, E.M. (1994). Reported child abuse and neglect. In *The Future of Children (Sexual Abuse of Children),* (4)2.

National Center on Child Abuse and Neglect. (1992). National child abuse and neglect data system: 1990 summary data component, Working Paper 1. Washington, DC: U.S. Department of Health and Human Services.

U.S. Advisory Board on Child Abuse and Neglect. (1995). A nation's shame: Fatal child abuse and neglect in the United States. Washington, DC: U.S. Department of Health and Human Services.

U.S. Department of Health and Human Services, Children's Bureau. (1999). Child maltreatment 1997: Reports from the states to the national child abuse and neglect data system. Washington, DC: U.S. Government Printing Office.

Walsh, B. (1994). Section II: Criminal Investigation of Physical Abuse and Neglect. In J. Briere, L. Berliner, J.A. Bulkley, C. Jenny, and T. Reid

(Eds.), *The APSAC Handbook on Child Maltreatment.* Chicago, IL: American Professional Society on the Abuse of Children (APSAC).

Wang, C.T., and Daro, D. (1998). Current trends in child abuse reporting and fatalities: The results of the 1997 Annual Fifty State Survey. Chicago, IL: National Committee to Prevent Child Abuse.

Chapter 33

The Relationship between Parental Alcoholism or Other Drug Problems and Child Maltreatment

The relationship between parental alcohol or other drug problems and child maltreatment is becoming increasingly evident. And the risk to the child increases in a single parent household where there is no supporting adult to diffuse parental stress and protect the child from the effects of the parent's problem. The following is a summary of what we know.

What is the scope of the problem?

Both alcohol and drug problems are widespread in this country. Almost 14 million adult Americans abuse alcohol.[1] The number of illicit drug users exceeds 12 million.[2] Illicit drugs include marijuana, cocaine,

---

Text in this chapter includes "Fact Sheet: The Relationship Between Parental Alcohol or Other Drug Problems and Child Maltreatment," © 1996 Prevent Child Abuse America, http://www.preventchildabuse.org. Reprinted with permission. Available online at http://preventchildabuse.org/learn_more/research_docs/parental_alcohol.pdf; and "Characteristics of Parents at Risk," from *Protecting Children in Substance-Abusing Families*, National Clearinghouse on Child Abuse and Neglect Information, 1994. A copy of the complete document is available online at the new NCCANCH website at http://nccanch.acf.hhs.gov/pubs/usermanuals/subabuse/atrisk.cfm. Despite the older dates of these documents, they provide background information and descriptions that are still pertinent. This chapter also includes additional text with current statistics from "Children Living with Substance-Abusing or Substance-Dependent Parents," *The NHSDA Report*, National Household Survey on Drug Abuse, Office of Applied Studies, Substance Abuse and Mental Health Services Administration, (SAMHSA), June 2, 2003. Additional copies of this report or other reports from the Office of Applied Studies are available online at http://www.drugabusestatistics.samhsa.gov.

inhalants, hallucinogens, heroin, and non-medical use of psychotherapeutics.[2] With more than 6.6 million children under the age of 18 living in alcoholic households[3], and an additional number of children living in households where parents have problems with illicit drugs, a significant number of children in this country are being raised by addicted parents.

Child maltreatment has become a national epidemic. More than one million children are confirmed each year as victims of child abuse and neglect by state child protective service agencies.[4] Every day at least three children die as a result of abuse and neglect.[4] State child welfare records indicate that substance abuse is one of the top two problems exhibited by families in 81% of the reported cases.[4]

Do parental alcohol or other drug problems cause child maltreatment?

Recent research on the connection between these problems and child maltreatment clearly indicates a connection between the two behaviors. Among confirmed cases of child maltreatment, 40% involve the use of alcohol or other drugs.[5] This suggests that of the 1.2 million confirmed victims of child maltreatment, an estimated 480,000 children are mistreated each year by a caretaker with alcohol or other drug problems.[5] Additionally, research suggests that alcohol and other drug problems are factors in a majority of cases of emotional abuse and neglect. In fact, neglect is the major reason that children are removed from a home in which parents have alcohol or other drug problems. Children in these homes suffer from a variety of physical, mental, and emotional health problems at a greater rate than do children in the general population. Children of alcoholics suffer more injuries and poisonings than do children in the general population.[6] Alcohol and other substances may act as disinhibitors, lessening impulse control and allowing parents to behave abusively. Children in this environment often demonstrate behavioral problems and are diagnosed as having conduct disorders.[7] This may result in provocative behavior. Increased stress resulting from preoccupation with drugs on the part of the parent combined with behavioral problems exhibited by the child adds to the likelihood of maltreatment.

What characteristics do parents with alcohol and other drug problems and parents involved in child maltreatment share?

Histories of these parents reveal that typically both were reared with a lack of parental nurturing and appropriate modeling and often grew up in disruptive homes.[8] Family life in these households also has similarities. The children in often lack guidance, positive role modeling, and live in isolation. Frequently, they suffer from depression, anxiety, and low self-esteem. They live in an atmosphere of stress and family conflict. Children raised in both households are themselves more likely to have problems with alcohol and other drugs.[9]

Does the use of alcohol or other drugs by pregnant women affect their infants?

Pregnant women who use alcohol may bear children suffering from fetal alcohol syndrome (FAS). FAS is the leading known environmental cause of mental retardation in the western world.[10] Each year 4,000 to 12,000 babies are born with the physical signs and intellectual disabilities associated with FAS, and thousands more experience the somewhat lesser disabilities of fetal alcohol effects.[11]

How does a parent's alcohol or other drug problem affect children?

Children of alcoholics are more likely than children in the general population to suffer a variety of physical, mental, and emotional health problems.[12] Similar to maltreatment victims who believe that the abuse is their fault, children of alcoholics feel guilty and responsible for their parent's drinking problem.[13] Both groups of children often have feelings of low self-esteem and failure and suffer from depression and anxiety. It is thought that exposure to violence in both alcohol abusing and child maltreating households increases the likelihood that the children will commit and be recipients of acts of violence. Additionally, the effects of child maltreatment and parental alcohol abuse don't end when the children reach adulthood. Both groups of children are likely to have difficulty with coping and establishing healthy relationships as adults. In addition to suffering from all the effects of living in a household where alcohol or child maltreatment problems exist, children whose parents abuse illicit drugs live with the knowledge that their parents' actions are illegal. While research is in its infancy, clinical evidence shows that children of parents who have problems with illicit drug use may suffer from an inability to trust legitimate authority because of fear of discovery of a parent's illegal habits.

Are these patterns passed on from one generation to the next?

Some individuals can and do break the cycle of abuse. These resilient children share some characteristics that lead to their successful coping skills such as ability to obtain positive attention from other people, adequate communication skills, average intelligence, a caring attitude, a desire to achieve, a belief in self-help.[14] Additionally, the involvement of a caring adult can help children develop resiliency and break the cycle of abuse. However, a significant number of individuals fall victim to the same patterns exhibited by their parents. Those who have been severely physically abused often have symptoms of post-traumatic disorder and dissociation.[15] Individuals suffering from mental health disorders may use alcohol and illicit drugs to decrease or mitigate their psychological distress.[16] Research suggests that adults who were abused as children may be more likely to abuse their own children than adults who were not abused as children.[17]

Why are these patterns so hard to break?

One explanation for the continuing cycle is the secrecy, denial, and stigma involved in both problems. Many child maltreatment cases do not get reported and many children of alcoholics go unidentified. Within both populations, victims often are afraid to speak up because they do not think anyone will believe them. Often they do not realize that what seems to be normal behavior is indeed maltreatment, and learn to repeat these behaviors unconsciously. The lack of positive parental role modeling and lack of development of coping skills increases the difficulty of establishing healthy relationships as an adult. It may not be until they seek help as disturbed adults that they are made cognizant of the root of their emotional problems.

Can we treat child maltreatment when alcohol or other drugs are a problem?

Research has shown that when families exhibit both of these behaviors, the problems must be treated simultaneously in order to insure a child's safety. Although ending the drug dependency does not automatically end child maltreatment, very little can be done to improve parenting skills until this step is taken. It should be noted that the withdrawal experienced by parents who cease using alcohol or other drugs presents specific risks. The effects of withdrawal often cause a parent to experience intense emotions, which may increase the likelihood of child maltreatment.[18] During this time, lasting as long as two years, it is especially important that resources be available to the family.

How can we prevent these problems?

Aside from promoting awareness of the link between parental alcohol or other drug problem and child maltreatment and cross-training professionals in the recognition and treatment of both problems, prevention services need to be available for all. Among the preventive efforts Prevent Child Abuse America believes to be most effective are:

- Prevention education for all children, adolescents, and young adults.
- Direct access to supportive services for all children of parents with alcohol or other drug problems before child maltreatment occurs, with an emphasis on validation of feelings, supporting self-esteem, and intensive parenting and prevention education and support for all new parents.
- Access to self-help groups and other supportive services for all parents under stress and all victims and survivors of abuse.
- Education of all who work with children and families, including teachers, service providers, obstetricians, pediatricians, and emergency room personnel, regarding the interplay between a parent's alcohol or other drug problems and child maltreatment.

Characteristics of Parents at Risk

Parents who abuse alcohol and/or other drugs come from all walks of life, all ethnic backgrounds, and all socioeconomic levels. Further, alcohol and other drugs are not discriminatory in their effects on individuals who abuse them. This chapter describes the most common behavioral patterns associated with substance abuse that can be observed across the entire societal spectrum.

By the time they are identified by professionals, substance-abusing parents generally have progressed to the final stage of chemical dependency, and their long-term alcohol and/or other drug use is deeply entrenched and seriously disabling. If they do not have substantial financial and family supports to provide for them, these parents/caregivers often have limited ability to meet their own survival needs, let alone those of their dependent or, particularly, medically fragile children. However, even when substance-abusing parents do have financial and family supports, and therefore may be invisible to child welfare systems, their alcohol and/or drug abuse problem still has a devastating impact on family functioning and their children's healthy development.

Thus, a basic knowledge of the dynamics and effects of alcohol and other drug abuse is fundamental for professionals working with substance-abusing families. Many chemically involved parents are sincere in their desire to meet their children's needs, but they are limited in their physical, financial, social, and/or emotional abilities to do so. Substance abuse has a profound impact on a parent's capacity to provide the consistent nurturing and hands-on care that children require in order to thrive. Unless professionals are aware of the nature of substance abuse; the chronic, often relapsing nature of this disorder; and the unique characteristics and problems of chemically involved parents; services provided for parents and children may prove inappropriate or inadequate.

Substance abuse is a problem that affects all aspects of an individual's personal and family life. Strategies for intervention, therefore, generally acknowledge the following three basic assumptions:

- A true chemical dependency becomes the central organizing force around which the life of the substance abuser revolves, and that dependency affects every significant aspect of that person's functioning.
- The abuse of alcohol or other drugs on the part of even one family member, particularly if that person happens to be a parent, has a profound impact on the lives of all members of that family.
- The chemically involved parent has a range of serious medical and/or psychiatric problems, some of which may predate his/her alcohol and/or drug use and some of which may be the consequence of the dependency. All of these problems need to be addressed if intervention is to succeed.

The Nature of Substance Abuse

The impact of alcohol and other drug abuse varies widely from individual to individual. The following characteristics seem fairly universal, however, regardless of the substance or substances of choice, and can help us to understand the nature of most chemical dependencies. By building upon this understanding, professionals will be better equipped to design realistic service plans that are more likely to be effective.

Alcohol and other drug abuse is progressive. People do not set out to become alcoholics or addicts. First-time users universally resist the notion that they could ever become dependent on any chemical. It is with an accumulation of time and experience that the casual user becomes a substance abuser and that life can no longer be endured clean and sober.

Experimental use. Early use is described as experimental. The user generally is motivated by curiosity or social pressure to try substances reputed to alter ways of thinking and feeling. Use during this phase is occasional, frequently unplanned, and involves little, if any, reorganization of lifestyle to accommodate it. Similarly, there may be no detectable deterioration in health, relationships, or ability to function as expected.

Intensified use. Progressively more regular use begins to impact the user's life in more significant ways. Because it is both planned and more frequent than experimental use, increased amounts of time, thought, energy, and money go into the acts of scoring and using. At this stage, one's social life may revolve around getting high, and peer relationships often change accordingly. The economic and personal costs escalate as the ability to function at school or work declines, and mood swings become more prominent.

Habitual use. Habitual use marks the onset of chemical dependency. Tolerance to the original drug of choice has developed, a problem remedied either by using larger amounts of the same drug or recourse to drugs that will produce a more intense experience. Solitary use increases; now the emphasis is on simply getting high, rather than on the social experience of partying with one's peers. The user is increasingly preoccupied with drug use and may turn to dealing or other criminal activity to support a growing dependency on more potent and more expensive drugs. Deterioration in all significant areas of functioning is present.

Dependency. Dependency, or addiction, is said to exist when the user can no longer manage life without getting high. Use may occur continuously or in binges, but now the substance plays such a central role in the individual's life that everything else tends to revolve around it. The effects of the alcohol and/or other drug use on health, finances, relationships, and emotional stability are profound as the user finds it increasingly difficult to perform even ordinary tasks. Judgment at this stage can be severely impaired.

The onset of chemical dependency is insidious. Chemical dependency sneaks up on the individual who is, in any case, often not the best judge of his/her own addiction. In actuality, the lines drawn by professionals to note phases of drug and alcohol use (experimental, regular, habitual, and so on) are blurred, and precisely when the user moves from one phase to the next depends on many factors, including:

- physiological and psychological makeup,
- drug of choice,
- means of ingestion, and
- prior history.

A dependency can evolve over a long period of time (months or even years) or, as many crack addicts report, it can occur over the course of a weekend.

The earlier the person starts to use, the more likely that person is to become chemically dependent. Although there are exceptions to this rule, generally, children who are introduced to drugs while still very young are more susceptible to heavier use and abuse than individuals whose experimentation occurs at a later age.

Anyone can become an addict. Chemical dependency cuts across all racial, social, and economic lines. No one is immune. Although some individuals seem to have a higher threshold of addiction than others, exposure to the right substance of abuse under the right circumstances (times of stress, loss, pain, or boredom) has the potential to seduce anyone into a true chemical dependency.

Substance abuse is a family problem. Substance abuse is a family problem in both a biological and a psychological sense. There is a growing body of evidence that certain people (some children of alcoholics, for instance) are biologically at highest risk of becoming chemically dependent. It is a family problem, also, insofar as coping behaviors are learned within the context of the family. Children of substance-abusing parents may learn to cope with unpleasantness in their lives as their parents have done before them, by taking substances into the body to effect a change in mental status. Finally, it is a family problem because everyone in the family is profoundly affected by the alcohol and/or drug abuse of even one of its members.

Denial is intrinsic to the problem of alcohol and other drug abuse. It is well known that the substance abuser generally denies that there is a problem or minimizes its extent. It is less well known that the entire family, to protect its integrity and tenuous ability to function, also often denies the existence and impact of the problem.

Alcohol and other drug abuse is a systemic problem. Substance abuse impacts every aspect of the user's physical, emotional, work, and social life. Health, jobs, school, and relationships are affected. With chronic abuse, no significant area of functioning remains untouched.

Substance abuse often afflicts those individuals who are already the most vulnerable, the least equipped to cope. Frequently, persons most severely impacted by substance abuse come from families with multiple stresses, including alcohol and/or other drug abuse problems, mental health disorders, failures in school and/or employment, and/or a history of physical and/or sexual abuse. These individuals, already struggling to cope, are then further impaired by their drug use. Thus, they tend to come to treatment in very serious condition and typically need a wide range of services.

The Chemically Involved Parent

The preceding description of the nature of substance abuse provides a background against which to better understand the characteristics and needs of substance-abusing parents. Because chemical dependencies have certain characteristics in common, it follows that victims also have much in common with one another. There is no typical substance abuser; however, the following summary of characteristics is intended to sensitize professionals to the issues with which many chemically involved parents struggle.

Childhood Deprivation

Many substance-abusing parents report histories of significant childhood deprivation. Often, this history includes an early home life marked by family violence, parental substance abuse, or parental psychiatric disorders. Parents who grew up in such environments often report deprivation in many areas of their lives—economic, physical, social, and emotional.

In families with inadequate early caregiving, oftentimes parents were poorly nourished, they may not have been provided with necessary health care, and their educational needs may have been neglected. Thus, as adults and parents, such individuals have numerous and chronic medical, dental, and educational problems that require attention. Developmental assessments, educational testing, and speech and other therapies that were overlooked during childhood can result in serious deficits that last a lifetime.

Many substance-abusing parents also recount histories of growing up in households in which there was a blurring of boundaries between parental and child roles. As young children, such parents often assumed primary responsibility for taking care of household and family needs. Although it may have filled a void or a need within the family, this role reversal may have also seriously interfered with the parent's timely acquisition of age-appropriate life skills and experiences. Thus, as adults, such individuals often have an impaired ability to form truly mutual adult relationships and a healthy self-concept that are prerequisites to successful parenting.

Frequently, the emotional and protective needs of parents who experienced early deprivation also were neglected. Adults who grew up in such homes may have difficulty remembering occasions when warmth and affection were freely and consistently expressed. Parents often report feeling that their needs for protection, comfort, reassurance, and support were met infrequently, if at all. During early childhood, their fears were often disregarded. When they were teenagers, their parents were often inattentive or incapable of maintaining the delicate balance between structure and freedom that adolescents need as they negotiate their way from childhood to responsible adulthood.

Finally, significant numbers of substance-abusing parents report histories of severe neglect, physical abuse, and/or sexual abuse during their childhood and teenage years. As adults, such parents are more likely to become involved in unhealthy and abusive relationships. As one might predict, spousal abuse and domestic violence are, in fact, common occurrences in the lives of adults who seek treatment for alcohol and other drug abuse. Moreover, having grown up in homes in which parenting was unpredictable and discipline often abusive, chemically involved parents frequently are ill equipped to provide effective parenting for their own children. The risk that they will perpetuate the cycle of abuse or neglect with their offspring is considerable.

Survival Needs

Regardless of socioeconomic status, substance-abusing parents commonly have a range of basic unmet survival needs. Substance abuse among low-income parents often quickly leads to impoverishment, but even successfully employed individuals may eventually find themselves homeless or facing homelessness. As a result of their alcohol and/or other drug use, many substance-abusing parents lack stable housing, food, clothing, and basic personal necessities for themselves and their children. They may live on the street, in temporary shelters, in substandard housing, or be on the brink of eviction. Furthermore, as noted above, chemically involved parents may have extensive and chronic medical and/or psychiatric problems that require immediate care and often long-term intervention. Often, such parents have little knowledge of how to locate and mobilize needed resources on their own behalf.

Psychiatric Disorders

A significant percentage of chemically dependent adults suffer from a psychiatric disorder of sufficient severity to require intervention. Post-traumatic stress disorder is not uncommon, particularly in substance abusers with histories of child sexual abuse or alcoholic parents. Alcohol and other drugs may be used to medicate the intrusive symptoms associated with the disorder (panic attacks, obsessive ruminations, flashbacks, nightmares). For some individuals, another underlying condition such as a depression, personality disorder, or psychotic illness preexisted the chemical dependency, and the drug and/or alcohol use was essentially an ill-advised attempt to self-medicate. For other chemically involved adults, the psychiatric disorder may be the consequence of long-term addiction or alcoholism. In any case, a psychiatric disorder may profoundly impact the sufferer's ability to function as well as to benefit from services offered to the family.

As children, many chemically involved parents experienced periods of parental absenteeism or even parental death. Many of these parents recall having been moved frequently from caregiver to caregiver. Such experiences of loss, inconsistency, and perceived abandonment can create feelings of anger, mistrust, low self-esteem, and confusion that complicate relationships well into adulthood.

Denial

It is virtually a given in the field of substance abuse treatment that most clients, particularly those who are involuntary, will deny the extent of their abuse of alcohol and/or other drugs. Thus, the chemically involved parent more often than not minimizes the problem, denies its impact on the family, and is resistant to treatment.

Often, parents will emphatically deny any drug or alcohol use whatsoever. In cases of prenatal substance abuse, parents may explain that positive toxicology reports are lab errors or reflect a one-time lapse that occurred, unfortunately, just prior to delivery. At the time of assessment and sometimes well into the course of treatment, it is commonplace for both clients and families to deny the reality of a parent's devastating, long-term, polydrug abuse.

Frequently, this denial is tenaciously held and will not readily be relinquished, particularly in a setting that is felt to be adversarial. For example, substance-abusing parents who have reasonable fears about losing custody of their children may not admit to any alcohol and/or drug abuse. Given the stressful circumstances that surround allegations of child abuse and the power agencies have to disrupt parents' and children's lives in profound and painful ways, professionals should neither be surprised nor take it personally when they are met with a wall of denial and resistance.

Denial and resistance, however, are not necessarily insurmountable obstacles to treatment. Professionals need to understand the function and importance that these defenses have played in the lives of parents. By building meaningful relationships with parents and taking the time necessary to work through denial and resistance, it is often possible for professionals to form a supportive and mutually respectful treatment alliance with the parent and the family.

In summary, chemical dependency has a profound impact on virtually every area of individual and family functioning. Personal drug and alcohol use can seriously impair judgment and limit the users' abilities to take care of themselves and their children. The history of deprivation, inconsistency, loss, and abuse that many chemically dependent parents experienced during their childhood years bodes poorly for their own ability to parent and, without intervention, predisposes these individuals to repeat similar patterns with their own children.

The Needs of Children and Parenting Tasks

Different types of families (e.g., two-parent families, grandparent/grandchild families, single-parent families, stepfamilies, adoptive families, and foster care families) are capable of assisting children to become competent and self-assured adults, as long as the caregivers assume primary responsibility for both the life support and socialization needs of family members. This goal can be accomplished in a variety of ways, depending on family configuration, resources, and cultural background. However, when one or both caregivers abuse alcohol and/or other drugs, basic parental responsibilities can be profoundly affected.

Children need to live in a home with sufficient and well-managed income so that the family's basic economic needs are met. Chemically involved parents may spend money on alcohol and/or other drugs and fail to provide for their children's basic needs. Thus, these parents may not meet their children's nutritional, housing, and medical requirements. Chemically involved parents may care deeply about their children, but the special relationship they have with their drug(s) of choice can dominate family finances in a way that is detrimental to all family members.

Children must receive appropriate and consistent discipline so that they understand and internalize the rules of the family and of the culture. Again, this objective can be accomplished in various ways, but it must be done in a manner that builds trust, cooperation, and self-assurance. Caregivers, who themselves grew up in dysfunctional homes, often have no model of appropriate discipline and may unconsciously emulate their own inadequate parents. Consequently, these parents may use means of controlling and instructing their children that inspire fear, anger, and rebellion.

A learned pattern of inappropriate discipline may be further compounded by the effects of a parent's own drug or alcohol use. In chemically involved families, parental decisions about what is or is not acceptable behavior and judgment about what constitutes an appropriate parental response to that behavior may vary from one moment to the next. The dramatic mood swings that accompany drug use and withdrawal as well as the profound, often chronic psychiatric disorders that result from or coexist with long-term substance abuse can make it very difficult for chemically involved caregivers to exercise good judgment and respond appropriately and consistently to their children's behaviors.

Children need parents who are responsible for dealing with community agencies and major social systems, and who are capable of making the decisions that affect the well-being of all family members. Children lack the experience and the legal authority to interact successfully with school systems, housing authorities, health care providers, and other community agencies. It is the parents' responsibility to interact with these systems, deciding when and how they need to be accessed in order for family needs to be met. However, chemically involved parents often may be physically or psychologically absent when such needs arise. Consequently, many chemically involved parents do not obtain medical care or needed educational services for their children. These parents may forfeit eligibility for low-cost housing, public health services, public assistance, vocational rehabilitation, and a range of other opportunities that, if accessed, could greatly enhance the quality of life for all family members. When parents are unable to accomplish these tasks for their children, tasks that children cannot accomplish for themselves, basic family needs are not met.

Children need parents who accept the primary responsibility for home maintenance and housekeeping. Although this responsibility can and should be shared among family members, it ultimately falls to the parents to ensure that the home environment is both safe and clean. Chemically involved parents often find it difficult to accomplish the tasks associated with running a household, and basic maintenance and housekeeping tasks are either neglected or left to young children, who may lack the skills or motivation needed to accomplish them successfully. When bottles and dishes aren't washed, soiled diapers and garbage aren't disposed of properly, and plumbing isn't operable, unsafe and unhealthy conditions exist for all family members.

Children need to be free of the primary responsibility for child care. Child care is a task that can be shared, particularly within large families, but the ultimate responsibility for seeing that children's needs are met resides with the parents. Although the parentified child in a chemically involved family often does care for younger children, this child almost certainly lacks the judgment, experience, and maturity to care safely and properly for other siblings over time. It is destructive for older children as well as for younger siblings if the locus of child care is placed in children's hands.

Children need nurturing families. Loving and caring within families can and should flow freely in both directions between older and younger members. It is the responsibility of parents to make sure that this nurturing is available. Sober and emotionally stable parents are usually able to defer their own emotional needs or surmount obstacles such as fatigue and ill health when their children need care and attention. However, chemically involved parents may become so caught up in the cycle of alcohol and other drug abuse that they remain largely unaware of their children's need for nurturing. Children in such families often experience the pain, uncertainty, and loneliness that result from feeling a lack of caring and love.

Children need to experience appropriate roles and boundaries within the family. In healthy families, it is clear to all members precisely who are the adults and who are the children, and who is in charge of whom. Unfortunately, in families in which one or both caregivers is a substance abuser, roles and boundaries are often ill-defined. It is not unusual in chemically involved families to see a toddler ruling the roost with a heavy and tyrannical hand. Nor, with boundaries so blurred and roles confused, is it at all unusual for children to become victims of sexual abuse.

Summary

To begin to establish an effective treatment alliance with a substance-abusing family, it is important for professionals to acknowledge the following basic principles regarding alcohol and other drug abuse:

- To work effectively with a substance-involved family, professionals must explore their own attitudes, feelings, and experiences related to alcohol and/or other drug abuse. Substance abuse is a complex problem, and objectivity can only be maintained if service providers are able to distance themselves from their own personal experiences, prejudices, and preconceptions. A basic understanding of addiction and its impact on individuals and families, therefore, is also critical. Further, an informed team approach is essential in effectively serving substance-abusing families.
- An individual may become involved in the abuse of alcohol and/or other drugs for a wide variety of reasons. These issues can be ferreted out over time by professionals working with the family, and this information can help professionals and family members determine the most appropriate treatment and intervention strategies.
- It is essential to recognize that parents may not be ready to engage in treatment when the professional first becomes involved with them. However, this does not mean that service providers cannot help parents become ready to consider treatment. This process is often time-consuming, but it can lead to successful intervention.
- Although relapse is an inherent part of substance abuse, a failure in treatment may not necessarily be due to the disease. Rather, some treatment failures occur because the treatment program is not well suited to the individual substance abuser. Thus, professionals need to explore with the parent the possible causes of any unsuccessful treatment effort.

- Professionals also need to be aware of the range and variety of treatment services that are available within their individual communities. Unfortunately, some communities offer only a limited array of substance abuse treatment services that may not address many clients' needs. (For instance, many programs will not enroll women who have children.) In such cases, professionals can become advocates to inform their communities about the need for new and expanded services.

In summary, in order to provide effective services, professionals should understand the power and tenacity of substance abuse, including its chronic and relapsing nature, the central role that it plays in the chemically involved parent's life, and the parent's attachment to the substance(s) used. Professionals also need to remember that the substance-abusing parent often has multiple, long-standing problems, some of which may not even surface until the parent has entered treatment and attained sobriety. Further, the abuse of alcohol and/or other drugs is not merely a disease of the individual, but, rather, a problem that affects the whole family. Chemically involved parents are often the victims of intergenerational substance abuse. Involving them as well as their children in treatment can be a beginning step in breaking a cycle of substance abuse, ineffective parenting, family violence, and child abuse and neglect.

Sources

1. National Institute of Alcohol Abuse and Alcoholism. 1994. *Alcohol Health and Research World* 18(3):243.
2. Substance Abuse and Mental Health Services Administration, U. S. Department of Health and Human Services. 1995. *National household survey on drug abuse: Population estimates 1994*. Research Triangle Park, NC: Research Triangle Institute.
3. Russell, M., C. Henderson, and S. B. Blume. 1984. *Children of alcoholics: A review of the literature*. New York: Children of Alcoholics Foundation, Inc.
4. Lung, C. T. and D. Daro. 1996. *Current trends in child abuse reporting and fatalities: The results of the 1995 annual fifty state survey*. Chicago, Illinois: National Committee to Prevent Child Abuse.

5. Children of Alcoholics Foundation, Inc. 1996. *Collaboration, coordination and cooperation: helping children affected by parental addiction and family violence*. New York: Children of Alcoholics Foundation.

6. Bijur, P.E., M. Kurzon, M.D. Overpeck, and P.C. Scheidt. 1992. Parental alcohol use, problem drinking and child injuries. *Journal of the American Medical Association* 23:3166-3171.

7. West, M., and R Prinz. 1987. Parental alcoholism and childhood psychopathology. *Psychological Bulletin* 102(2):204-218.

8. Behling, D.W. 1979. Alcohol abuse as encountered in 51 instances of reported child abuse. *Clinical Pediatrics* 18(2):87-91.

9. Children of Alcoholics Foundation, Inc. 1992. *Help for inner-city children of addicted parents*. New York: Children of Alcoholics Foundation, Inc.

10. National Institute of Alcohol Abuse and Alcoholism.1993. *Eighth special report to U.S. Congress on alcohol and health*. (March):221.

11. SAMHSA, Center for Substance Abuse Prevention. 1993. *Toward preventing perinatal abuse of alcohol, tobacco and other drugs*. USDHHS, Technical Report, No. 9 p. 1.

12. Children of Alcoholics Foundation, Inc.1990. *Children of alcoholics in the medical system: Hidden problems, hidden costs*. New York: Children of Alcoholics Foundation, Inc.

13. Russell, M., C. Henderson, and S. Blume. 1985. *Children of alcoholics: A review of the literature*. New York: Children of Alcoholics Foundation, Inc.

14. Werner, E.E. 1986. Resilient offspring of alcoholics: A longitudinal study from birth to age 18. *Journal of Studies on Alcohol* 47(1):34-40.

15. Briere, J. 1996. A self-trauma model for treating adult survivors of severe child abuse. In *The APSAC Handbook on Child Maltreatment* (pp. 140-157) edited by J. Briere, L. Berliner, J.A. Bulkley, C. Jenny, and T. Reid. Newbury Park, CA: Sage.

16. Kelley, S.J. 1996. Do substance abusing mothers experience increased parenting stress? Paper presented at the International

Congress of the International Society on the Prevention of Child Abuse and Neglect. Dublin, Ireland.

17. Ziegler, E., and J. Kaufman. 1987. Do abused children become abusive parents? *American Journal of Orthopsychiatry* 57(20):187-192.

18. Zuskin, R., and D. DePanfilis. 1987. Working with CPS families with alcohol or other drug (AOD) problems. *The APSAC Advisor* 8(1): 7-11.

Children Living with Substance-Abusing or Substance-Dependent Parents

- In 2001, more than 6 million children lived with at least one parent who abused or was dependent on alcohol or an illicit drug during the past year.
- Past year substance abuse or dependence by parents involved approximately 10 percent of children aged 5 or younger.
- Among parents who lived with one or more children, fathers were more likely than mothers to abuse or be dependent on alcohol or an illicit drug.

The National Household Survey on Drug Abuse (NHSDA) asks respondents aged 12 or older to report on their alcohol or illicit drug use, as well as their symptoms of substance abuse or dependence during the past year. Illicit drugs include marijuana/hashish, cocaine (including crack), inhalants, hallucinogens, heroin, or prescription-type drugs used nonmedically. The NHSDA defines abuse and dependence using criteria in the American Psychiatric Association's *Diagnostic and Statistical Manual of Mental Disorders (DSM-IV)*, which includes such symptoms as physical danger, trouble with the law due to substance use, increased tolerance, and interference in everyday life during the past year.

The NHSDA sample includes representative subsamples of mothers and fathers, as well as mother-father pairs who live in the same household. The survey obtains information about children living in the household, including age and relationship to the respondent. This report focuses on biological, step, adoptive, and foster children younger than 18 years of age who were living with one or both parents at the time of the survey interview. (The 2000 Current Population Survey estimated that 96 percent of children younger than 18 years of age lived with at least one parent).[2]

Numbers of Children

The 2001 NHSDA estimated that almost 70 million children younger than 18 years of age lived with at least one parent. Over 6 million (9 percent) lived with at least one parent who abused or was dependent on alcohol or an illicit drug during the past year.[3] Of these children, more than 4 million lived with a parent who abused or was dependent on alcohol only, almost 1 million lived with a parent who abused or was dependent only on an illicit drug, and more than 0.5 million lived with a parent who abused or was dependent on both alcohol and an illicit drug.

Children's Ages

Table 33.1 shows the percentages of children who lived with at least one substance-abusing or substance-dependent parent, by children's

Table 33.1. Estimated Numbers (in Thousands) and Percentages of Children* Aged 17 or Younger Living with One or More Parents ** with Past Year Substance Abuse or Dependence, 2001

Ages of Children (Years)	Estimated Numbers (in Thousands)	Percentage	Standard Error
Younger than 3	1,078	9.8	0.81
3 to 5	1,115	9.8	1.10
6 to 11	1,816	7.5	1.28
12 to 17	2,100	9.2	0.81

*Children include biological, step, adoptive, or foster.

**Children aged 17 or younger who were not living with one or more parents for most of the quarter of the NHSDA interview are excluded from the present analysis. According to the 2000 Current Population Survey, this amounts to approximately 3 million or 4 percent of children aged 17 or younger.

Source: SAMHSA 2001 NHSDA

age. Past year substance abuse or dependence by parents involved approximately 10 percent of children aged 5 or younger compared with 8 percent of children aged 6 to 11 and 9 percent of youths aged 12 to 17.

Substance-Abusing or Substance-Dependent Fathers and Mothers

Among parents living with their children, fathers (8 percent) were more likely than mothers (4 percent) to abuse or be dependent on alcohol or an illicit drug during the past year. Compared with other adults of the same general age range, parents were less likely to have abused or been dependent on substances. For example, overall rates of substance abuse or dependence among persons aged 18 to 50 in 2001 were 14 percent for males and 6 percent for females.[4]

Notes

1. American Psychiatric Association. (1994). *Diagnostic and statistical manual of mental disorders (4th ed.).* Washington, DC: Author
2. U.S. Bureau of the Census, Fertility and Family Statistics Branch. (2001, June 29). Living arrangements of children under 18 years old: 1960 to present. Retrieved April 7, 2003, at http://www.census.gov/population/socdemo/hh-fam/tabCH-1.xls
3. To calculate an unduplicated estimate of children living with at least one parent who met the criteria for substance abuse or dependence, the estimated number of children living with two substance-abusing or substance-dependent parents (mother-father pairs) was subtracted from the sum of the estimated number of children living with a substance-abusing or substance-dependent father and the estimated number of children living with a substance-abusing or substance-dependent mother. To correct problems with analysis weights for the mother-father pair sample, a special adjustment was applied to ensure the age distribution of children in two-parent households and the total number of children in these households were consistent with those obtained from the standard person level analytic weights.

4. In 2001, 96 percent of parents living with a child were aged 18 to 50.

The National Household Survey on Drug Abuse (NHSDA) is an annual survey sponsored by the Substance Abuse and Mental Health Services Administration (SAMHSA). The 2001 data are based on information obtained from 68,929 persons aged 12 or older, including 9,646 mothers living with a child younger than 18 years of age, 5,524 fathers living with a child younger than 18 years of age, and 1,088 mother-father pairs living in the same household with a child younger than 18 years of age. The survey collects data by administering questionnaires to a representative sample of the population through face-to-face interviews at their place of residence.

The *NHSDA Report* is prepared by the Office of Applied Studies (OAS), SAMHSA, and by RTI in Research Triangle Park, North Carolina. Information and data for this text are based on the following publication and statistics:

Office of Applied Studies. (2002). *Results from the 2001 National Household Survey on Drug Abuse: Volume I. Summary of national findings* (DHHS Publication No. SMA 02-3758, NHSDA Series H-17). Rockville, MD: Substance Abuse and Mental Health Services Administration.

Chapter 34

Childhood Sex Abuse Increases Risk for Drug Dependence in Adult Women

Women who are sexually abused during childhood are at increased risk for drug abuse as adults, according to NIDA-supported research conducted at the Medical College of Virginia Commonwealth University in Richmond. Using data gathered from interviews of 1,411 adult twins, Dr. Kenneth Kendler and his colleagues assessed the association between three levels of childhood sex abuse (nongenital, genital, and intercourse) and six adult disorders—major depression, generalized anxiety disorder, panic disorder, bulimia nervosa, alcohol dependence, and drug dependence. Women who experienced any type of sexual abuse in childhood were roughly three times more likely than nonabused girls to report drug dependence as adults.

"Overall, childhood sexual abuse was more strongly associated with drug or alcohol dependence than with any of the psychiatric disorders," Dr. Kendler says. "Only drug and alcohol dependence were significantly associated with all levels of abuse."

Among more than 1,400 adult females, childhood sexual abuse was associated with increased likelihood of drug dependence, alcohol dependence, and psychiatric disorders. The associations are expressed as odds ratios: for example, women who experienced nongenital sexual

---

"Childhood Sex Abuse Increases Risk for Drug Dependence in Adult Women," by Pat Zickler. From *NIDA Notes,* Volume 17, Number 1, April 2002. National Institute on Drug Abuse (NIDA), 2002. Available online at http://www.nida.nih.gov/NIDA_Notes/NNVol17N1/Childhood.html.

abuse in childhood were 2.93 times more likely to suffer drug dependence as adults than were women who were not abused.

In this study, 1,411 women born between 1934 and 1974 responded to written questionnaires that asked them if, before they reached age 16, any adult or person older than they had ever ("never," "once," or "more than once"):

- involved them in an incident that included an invitation or request to do something sexual,
- kissed or hugged them in a sexual way,
- subjected them to genital display or exposure,
- touched or fondled them in a sexual way,
- made them touch the older person or adult in a sexual way, or
- attempted intercourse.

In addition, the researchers conducted written interviews with 90 percent of the twins' parents to assess family environment and parental psychopathology. The parental interviews did not mention possible sexual abuse of the children, but did provide data on family financial status; parents' disciplinary practices, including spanking, slapping, or hitting; church attendance; and measures of harmony, discord, authoritarianism, and protectiveness.

"Controlling for family factors and parental psychopathology produced a small change in some of the associations, but the increased odds of reporting drug or alcohol dependence in adulthood after suffering sexual abuse as a child can't be explained by these background factors," Dr. Kendler says.

The women who participated in the research are part of an ongoing research investigation of female twins included in the Virginia Twin Registry, which represents a large cross-section of the population and includes data on a broad range of research topics, including psychiatric and substance abuse disorders.

"This study has particular significance because it is based on data from women in the general population," says Dr. Cora Lee Wetherington of NIDA's Division of Neuroscience and Behavioral Research. "Numerous clinical studies have documented high rates of childhood sexual abuse among women in treatment.

This study, the first to document it in a nonclinical population, is particularly important in addressing questions concerning the relationship between sexual abuse and patterns of drug abuse and addiction."

Source

Kendler, K.S., et al. Childhood sexual abuse and adult psychiatric and substance use disorders in women: An epidemiological and co-twin control analysis. *Archives of General Psychiatry* 57(10):953-959, 2000.

Chapter 35

The Lasting Impact of Pre-Natal Exposure to Alcohol and Other Drugs

This chapter describes the health and development of children exposed prenatally to alcohol and/or other drugs. The neurodevelopmental consequences of such exposure, particularly in the long term, are not all known. Research is currently being conducted to help us better understand these consequences. In discussing the common health concerns and developmental patterns that have been observed in this population, it is important for professionals to consider the following issues:

Polysubstance abuse. Most substance abusers use multiple drugs or drugs, alcohol, and nicotine in combination. In some cases, this polysubstance abuse may occur without the user's knowledge because it is common practice among street dealers to substitute drugs and to cut the purity of illicit substances with a variety of adulterants.

Text in this chapter is excerpted from "Children of Chemically Involved Parents: Special Risks," from *Protecting Children in Substance-Abusing Families*, National Clearinghouse on Child Abuse and Neglect Information, 1994. Available online at http://nccanch.acf.hhs.gov/pubs/usermanuals/subabuse/specrisk.cfm. Despite the older date of this document, it still provides pertinent background information and descriptions. Additional facts from newer research is excerpted from the following documents from the National Institute on Drug Abuse (NIDA) "Prenatal Exposure to Alcohol," *Alcohol Research and Health*, Vol. 24, No. 1, 2000, "Prenatal Drug Exposure and Drug-Abusing Environments," Child and Adolescent Workgroup (CWAG), 2001, and "The Neurobehavioral Legacy of Prenatal Tobacco Exposure," by Jill Schlabig Williams, *NIDA Notes*, February 2004.

Furthermore, although parents may report use of only alcohol, nicotine, or a single drug, such statements regarding drug and alcohol use during pregnancy are often unreliable, in part because of parental inaccuracy in recalling their actual drinking or drug use during periods of intoxication.

Range of outcomes. Any alcohol or other drug use during pregnancy potentially can affect fetal health and well-being. There are no known safe levels of prenatal drug, alcohol, or nicotine use. However, among infants who have been prenatally exposed to these substances, a wide range of health and developmental patterns have been observed. The medical and developmental complications associated with prenatal substance abuse will be discussed later in this chapter. Because there is a broad continuum of effects of prenatal drug, alcohol, or nicotine exposure (varying from severe to mild to no apparent effect), outcomes for individual children cannot be predicted.

Multiple etiologies. There clearly are adverse immediate and long-term effects of alcohol and other abuse during pregnancy, but there are also a number of other maternal health, nutritional, and lifestyle factors that greatly impact fetal growth and development. These factors also significantly contribute to the increased risk of developmental difficulties throughout childhood. Substance-abusing mothers often have compromised health, no matter what their socioeconomic status. Smoking, poor nutrition due to excessive dieting or inappropriate selection of food, poverty, or other lifestyle influences may complicate the effects of substances on the fetus.

Environmental impact. Children in substance-abusing families are at double jeopardy—they are both biologically and environmentally at risk. Moreover, the interplay between biological and environmental factors is extremely significant because biological problems can be exacerbated or mitigated by environmental influences. For example, a home environment that is responsive and nurturing can help reduce the negative developmental effects of low birth weight. On the other hand, an environment that does not provide adequate nurturing can increase the risk of negative developmental outcomes associated with low birth weight.

Limitations of research. Obtaining accurate self-reports about alcohol or other use is difficult and limits epidemiological and clinical research on causality. Most documentation about the serious side effects of prenatal alcohol and other drug exposure in infants and children has been noted in cases of alcoholic and drug-dependent mothers. Little is known regarding the effects of experimental or sporadic drug and alcohol use during pregnancy, in part because the identification of occasional users is much more difficult. Even less is known about the effects of paternal substance abuse. Furthermore, the standardized measures currently used to evaluate infants and young children of chemically involved parents are not sufficiently sensitive to subtle behavioral and cognitive deficits.

Keeping these issues in mind, and the fact that many important questions regarding the effects of maternal drug and alcohol abuse remain unanswered, the following sections will discuss the common neonatal and infant complications that have been described in some substance-exposed infants and young children as well as the developmental patterns that have been observed in this high-risk population. It is important to note that the descriptions contained in this chapter are intended to provide general information and follow-up guidelines. Concerns about individual children need to be discussed with the child's pediatrician, a child psychiatrist, other health care providers, family members, and any other professionals who are involved in providing care.

Neonatal and Infant Complications

There are a number of pediatric medical complications associated with prenatal substance abuse. These include neurological disturbances, prematurity, infectious diseases, Fetal Alcohol Syndrome (FAS), Sudden Infant Death Syndrome (SIDS), failure to thrive (FTT), intrauterine growth retardation (IUGR), and central nervous system (CNS) disorders.

Neurological Symptoms

Various neurological disturbances have been noted in newborns who have been exposed prenatally to drugs and alcohol. The following symptoms are most commonly observed:

- irritability,
- tremors or jitteriness,
- prolonged or high-pitched crying,
- increased or decreased muscle tone,

- alternating periods of lethargy and irritability,
- frantic sucking of hands,
- uncoordinated sucking,
- seizures,
- fever,
- sweating,
- diarrhea,
- excessive vomiting,
- unusual or rapid (nystagmus) eye movements, and
- disturbances in sleep patterns.

Infants born to mothers who abuse stimulants such as cocaine and methamphetamine may appear lethargic and unresponsive during the first few days following birth. When such infants are alert, however, they are often easily overstimulated and may progress from being asleep to a state of loud crying within seconds. As they become older, infants who were lethargic during the immediate postnatal period often become more irritable and difficult to console. However, these behaviors often are self-limiting and may subside by age 2.

The majority of infants born to mothers who have used narcotics such as heroin or methadone during pregnancy become symptomatic within 72 hours after birth. Although irritability and tremulousness often decline over the first month of life, some narcotic-exposed infants remain symptomatic for many months. Initially, infants may have red, dry skin on their knees, elbows, and cheeks as a result of their excessive body movements. Frequently, these infants have diarrhea and episodes of vomiting that interfere with weight gain. These newborns may require medication in order to calm them, help them suck and swallow more successfully, and also limit their bouts of diarrhea.

Medication for symptomatic infants is warranted when the infant's vomiting or diarrhea causes weight loss or dehydration. The Neonatal Narcotic Abstinence Scale is used to determine which infants require medication. Commonly used medications include paregoric and phenobarbital. Infants who have seizure activity require immediate treatment with anticonvulsants.

Prematurity

Prematurity is defined as birth at less than 37 weeks of gestational age. Usually, premature infants weigh less than 2,500 grams. However, low birth weight also may occur in full-term infants of substance-abusing women. Prematurity in and of itself poses a distinct set of biological risks that can result in chronic illness for the infant and interfere with normal growth and development. In general, preterm delivery occurs in less than 10 percent of the newborn population. However, the risk of prematurity among substance-exposed infants is higher.

The problems commonly observed in preterm infants, including those who were prenatally exposed to drugs, are intracranial hemorrhages, bronchopulmonary dysplasia (BPD), retinopathy of prematurity (ROP), respiratory distress syndrome (RDS), and disorders that interfere with normal feeding ability. Infants who display these conditions are often termed medically fragile.

Intracranial Hemorrhages

Intracranial hemorrhages refer to bleeding into the brain tissue. Such an occurrence is known to be a risk factor for later physical and/or intellectual problems. Cerebral palsy, or impaired motor movements, for instance, can occur when there has been an intracranial bleed or an interference with the blood flow to specific areas of the brain.

Because a hemorrhage can obstruct the normal flow of cerebral spinal fluid that circulates around the nervous system, some preterm infants who experience intracranial bleeding require treatment for hydrocephalus, an accumulation of serous fluid within the cranium that can interfere with physical and/or intellectual development. Treatment for hydrocephalus involves the surgical insertion of a ventricular peritoneal (VP) shunt, or tube, that provides drainage of the fluid from the brain into the abdominal cavity.

One of the most well-recognized complications of prematurity is BPD, a condition that affects lung tissue and interferes with normal breathing functions. Following their discharge from the neonatal intensive care unit (NICU), children with this condition may continue to require oxygen, have complex medication regimens, and need special home-monitoring of their heart and respiratory rates. Children with BPD are at increased risk for poor weight gain, serious respiratory tract infections, multiple hospitalizations, and delayed development.

Preterm infants are at risk for developing a disease involving the vessels in the eye called ROP. Multiple causes of this disorder have been suggested; however, no specific cause has been identified to date, and no fully adequate treatment modalities have been developed. All preterm infants should receive a thorough eye evaluation by an ophthalmologist before they are discharged from the nursery. In some cases, ROP improves over time, but in other cases, children may be left with varying degrees of a visual handicap.

Diseases that Interfere with Normal Feeding Ability

There are several medical problems that may interfere with an infant's ability to take all of its daily nutrition by mouth. Infants with certain neurologic conditions may not be able to suck and swallow normally. Infants with BPD may expend too many calories working to breathe or may become short of breath while feeding. In such cases, supplemental gavage/forced feeding (formula given through a small tube that passes through the mouth or nose into the stomach) may be required. In more severe cases, a gastrostomy tube (feeding tube) is surgically placed into the stomach to augment caloric intake or to bypass oral feeding when an infant is unable to suck or swallow effectively.

Another, less common medical complication that may interfere with feeding is necrotizing enterocolitis (NEC). The cause of this disease is not known; however, it sometimes results in damage to the gastrointestinal tract making it impossible for the child's intestines to absorb food. In such cases, some type of total parenteral nutrition (TPN), for example, intravenous (IV) feeding, may be required.

Infectious Diseases

Infants with prenatal substance exposure are frequently exposed to infectious diseases of the mother, either prenatally or at the time of delivery. A mother who has multiple sexual partners, a history of prostitution, or a history of injection drug use is at increased risk of acquiring a variety of infectious diseases that can be passed to the child. Because many infectious agents cross the placenta, infants born to infected mothers are at increased risk of acquiring their mothers' infections during pregnancy. The infectious diseases most commonly seen in infants of substance abusers with multiple sexual partners are gonorrhea, syphilis, herpes, chlamydia, hepatitis B, and human immunodeficiency virus (HIV) and/or acquired immunodeficiency syndrome (AIDS). Multi-drug-resistant tuberculosis (TB) is yet another infectious disease experienced by some infants.

Fetal Alcohol Syndrome (FAS)

Alcohol consumption during pregnancy may result in a pattern of birth defects known as FAS. The diagnosis of FAS is based on three factors: prenatal and postnatal growth retardation, including low birth weight and microcephaly (abnormally small head); CNS abnormalities, including intellectual impairment, developmental delays, behavior dysfunction, and neurological abnormalities; and abnormalities of the face. Children with a confirmed history of prenatal alcohol exposure, who display some of the symptoms associated with FAS but who do not meet all of the diagnostic criteria, are diagnosed with Fetal Alcohol Effect (FAE). As the child matures, problems with learning, attention, memory, and problem solving are common, along with incoordination, impulsiveness, and hyperactivity.

Facial characteristics associated with FAS include small eyes, short eye openings, epicanthic folds, flat upturned nose, indistinct philtrum (groove in the midline of the upper lip), thin upper lip, crossed eyes, droopy eyelids, and malformation of the external ear.

Sudden Infant Death Syndrome (SIDS)

Children who have been prenatally exposed to drugs may have an increased risk of dying from SIDS. SIDS, sometimes called crib death, is defined as the sudden death of an infant under 1 year of age that remains unexplained after autopsy, investigation of the death scene, and review of the case history. In the United States, SIDS is the leading cause of death in infants between 1 and 12 months of age. SIDS may have multiple causes, and it is almost impossible to predict when it will occur. Children who die from SIDS commonly exhibit no other sign of illness immediately prior to their death.

Failure to Thrive (FTT)

FTT is a syndrome of disordered growth and development characterized by a marked deceleration in weight gain and a slowing in acquisition of developmental milestones. There are many reasons why an infant may not gain weight. Medical reasons resulting from biological causes include vomiting, excessive diarrhea, poor swallowing, cystic fibrosis, and congenital heart disease. Of course, infants also will fail to gain weight if they are given insufficient protein and calories. This may occur if the caregiver mixes formula improperly, does not feed frequently enough, or fails to respond to the infant's signals when he/she is hungry. FTT can also result from psychosocial deficits in the caregiver-infant relationship, such as failure to provide adequate physical nurturing in the form of contact comfort (holding, cuddling, or touching).

In infants who were prenatally exposed to drugs and alcohol, FTT may be due to both medical and environmental factors. A pattern of poor sucking, swallowing difficulties, and distractibility has been observed in many of these infants. In addition, children who live in dysfunctional, chemically involved families are at increased risk for parental neglect and for receiving inadequate nutrition on a consistent basis. Furthermore, some infants prenatally exposed to drugs are born very small for gestational age and, in spite of adequate caloric intake, may never attain average growth parameters.

Accurate diagnosis of FTT often entails hospitalization in order to determine the exact causes. In cases of environmental FTT, once adequate calories and/or appropriate nurturing care are offered, weight gain usually occurs immediately. Unfortunately, this simple medical treatment cannot be effective on a long-term basis unless a thorough evaluation is made to determine the reasons for the child's poor weight gain.

Intrauterine Growth Retardation (IUGR)

The term IUGR is used interchangeably with small for gestational age (SGA) to describe fetuses with suboptimal growth (generally with birth weight below the 3rd percentile for age). Causes for IUGR vary. It often is associated with congenital infections (that is, infections that are present during pregnancy and passed on to the fetus) such as rubella, cytomegalic virus (CMV), or HIV. Genetic abnormalities, such as those seen in rather rare chromosomal disorders (trisomy 13 and 18), also may result in IUGR. However, the most common causes of IUGR are related to conditions that result in reduced transport of nutrients from mother to fetus via the placenta during pregnancy. Hypertension (high blood pressure), for instance, frequently causes constriction of the blood vessels, including those that lead from the placenta to the fetus, thus restricting the transport of nutrients that are important for growth. Although many individuals suffer from hypertension because of a genetic predisposition, obesity, and/or stress, drugs such as cocaine, methamphetamine, and PCP also may bring about this condition. Further, IUGR may be seen in cases of insufficient maternal caloric intake. Depending on the cause, interference with fetal growth may begin during the first trimester, or its onset can occur later, during the second or third trimester of pregnancy.

Central Nervous System (CNS) Disorders

A CNS disorder is any condition or malformation that affects the brain. These disorders may originate in utero, or they may be caused by postnatal factors. Prenatal CNS disorders include viral infections [e.g., HIV, rubella, CMV, or toxoplasmosis] or congenital malformations of the brain (e.g., hydrocephalus, microcephaly, or porencephalic cysts). During delivery, certain conditions, including severe perinatal asphyxia, in some cases may lead to CNS impairment that results in physical disabilities such as cerebral palsy or vision and hearing deficits. Postnatal events may also lead to CNS disorders. These include bacterial or viral infections (e.g., meningitis or encephalitis), tumors (malignant or benign), and intracranial bleeds (usually seen in preterm infants).

Specific to children who have been exposed prenatally to alcohol and/or other drugs, reports have shown an increased incidence of decreased brain growth in utero in newborns, in some cases leading to microcephaly. Some infants who were exposed to cocaine and methamphetamine have been reported to have experienced three separate CNS lesions prenatally—hemorrhage into the ventricles, areas of necrosis in the brain matter, and cavitary lesions. In a few cocaine-exposed newborns, there have been reports of infarctions, or severe constrictions of major blood vessels, that have resulted in damage to certain areas of the brain.

A very important CNS condition that is seen in children under 2 years of age is inflicted trauma to the head, sometimes including skull fractures. In infants younger than 4 months of age, when children have only minimal head control, cases of Shaken Baby Syndrome are sometimes observed. This syndrome has been noted to occur when a caregiver is under stress, becomes frustrated with an irritable baby, and holds the infant by the shoulders or arms, shaking or forcibly slamming the child against a surface, such as a crib mattress. Only rarely are there obvious physical signs of abuse. However, resulting injuries may include intracranial bleeding, retinal hemorrhages, or occasional skull fractures, with long-term consequences that may include cerebral palsy, blindness, seizure disorders, or even death.

Developmental Concerns

Prenatally drug-exposed infants and young children are at increased risk for developmental problems. Regardless of their health status, all such children need to be evaluated from a developmental standpoint at least once during the first 6 months of life, again at 1 year, and at least every year thereafter until they are school age. Children with recognized developmental problems will need more frequent assessments.

Developmental screening in drug- and alcohol-exposed children is critical because early intervention and early identification of developmental problems are key to optimizing the children's social, language, cognitive, and motor development. As has been demonstrated in other high-risk groups of children (e.g., preterm children, children born small for gestational age, and children with diagnosed physical and/or mental disabilities), infants who experience responsive caregiving environments and young children who are in center-based programs generally show better developmental outcomes than children who do not have these experiences. Through home-, center-, and school-based programs, children affected by parental alcohol and/or other drug abuse can be exposed to enriched environments and given opportunities that will foster their developmental potential.

Developmental Patterns of Prenatally Drug-Exposed Children

Infants and young children exposed prenatally to drugs or alcohol display a wide array of developmental patterns that range from normal to deviant. It bears repeating that these patterns are the result of complex interactions among biologic and environmental factors. It is important to keep in mind that children of substance abusers, whether they reside in poor, middle-class, or wealthy households, are at high-risk for environmental deprivation, a critical factor in determining a child's long-term emotional, social, and intellectual development. We can do little to alter biological influences, but we can often mitigate biological risks by promoting healthy environments.

Infancy (0 to 15 Months)

Unpredictable sleeping patterns. Most infants develop predictable sleeping patterns by 4 to 6 months of age. Although newborns generally have short periods of sleep throughout the 24-hour cycle, the typical infant is able to sustain a 6- to 7-hour nighttime sleep sometime between 4 and 6 months of age. Some infants who have been prenatally exposed to drugs or alcohol continue to demonstrate sleeping patterns more typical of a newborn throughout the first year.

Feeding difficulties. By the time they are 2 weeks old, most infants have established a somewhat regular pattern of feeding and are able to suck effectively enough to have regained their birth weight. However, infants prenatally exposed to drugs or alcohol may have a variety of feeding difficulties.

Feeding problems commonly reported by caregivers of prenatally drug and alcohol-exposed infants include prolonged feeding time due to uncoordinated and ineffective sucking movements or lethargy, infant distractibility during feeding, frequent spitting up of formula, and increased need to suck (hyperphagia).

Irritability. A range of temperaments is seen in all neonates. Some infants tend to be easygoing and are readily soothed when fussy, but others tend to be more irritable and are harder to calm. Caring for these infants is more difficult. Infants who have been prenatally exposed to drugs and alcohol often display such irritability. They can be easily overstimulated and, once aroused, have great difficulty calming themselves.

Atypical Social Interactions. Social interactions begin at birth. When awake, the newborn infant will respond by turning toward a voice and will visually connect and look at the caregiver. These are brief behaviors, but they are especially rewarding to parents as they begin the attachment process. By 4 months of age, the typical infant is cooing in response to social exchanges, makes direct eye contact, and has a social smile for persons in the immediate environment. At 6 months of age, this highly social child becomes more discriminating and smiles less at strangers.

Infants who have been prenatally exposed to drugs and/or alcohol may have a number of atypical social responses, including indirect gaze, gaze aversion, and less marked stranger discrimination during the second half of the first year.

Delayed language development. Language development during early infancy involves cooing, smiling, chuckling, squealing, and crying. Infants who have had prenatal exposure to drugs and alcohol may demonstrate fewer vocalizations and less babbling.

Increased muscle tone and poor fine motor development. Motor development follows a similar pattern in all healthy infants. However, there is some variation in the age at which individual milestones are normally achieved. Young infants exposed prenatally to heroin and methadone generally reach gross motor milestones at appropriate ages. However, these infants frequently exhibit increased muscle tone (stiffness). In contrast, young infants exposed to stimulants such as cocaine may have decreased muscle tone and variable motor development, though most demonstrate attainment of milestones at an appropriate age. Furthermore, among older infants who were prenatally substance-exposed, there may be problems with fine motor coordination, unsteadiness in the movement of extremities, and mild problems with balance.

Toddlerhood (15 to 36 Months)

Atypical Social Interactions. Toddlers see themselves as the center of the universe, around which all activities focus. The pronoun "mine" epitomizes this particular age. The building of trust in one's own social relationships is an important behavior learned during this period.

An important factor that determines later successful social interaction relates to the kinds of early experiences children have with their parents/caregivers. If a child has a secure attachment relationship with his/her primary caregiver, there is increased likelihood that the child will later have effective social interactions. Because children who are raised in chaotic home situations are at high-risk for later problems with appropriate social behaviors, one of the important tasks professionals face is to ensure that children have opportunities to acquire the trust needed for later healthy interpersonal relationships.

Toddlers who have had prenatal drug or alcohol exposure, or who live in environments in which there is unpredictability in caregiving may demonstrate atypical social behaviors, including overfriendliness, withdrawal, and impulsive behaviors.

Delayed language development. Toddlers have a growing vocabulary but understand (receptive language) more words than they are capable of speaking (expressive language). Toddlers who were prenatally substance-exposed or who live in substance-abusing households tend to have decreased vocalizations and immature pronunciation of single words.

Minimal play strategies. Play is central to the young child's early cognitive development. A toddler's pretend play with dolls, baby bottles, cooking utensils, and trucks becomes more elaborate. Children's interactions with toys and other objects within their environment become more purposeful and organized, and their activities are sequenced, with a beginning, middle, and end. For instance, most toddlers will hold a baby doll, feed it, and then put it to bed. In testing situations, some substance-affected children appear less able to independently organize a meaningful sequence of play with such common toys.

Preschool Years (3 to 5 Years)

Preschoolers are more socially independent and are able to learn to share and take turns. Their language skills are more sophisticated, and their attention spans are sufficient to allow them to learn within a group setting that provides less individualized attention.

Many children who live in chaotic environments and/or who have suffered prenatal substance exposure show increased activity levels, short attention spans, impulsivity (e.g., they lose control easily), mood swings, and problems with moving from one activity to another.

Some substance-affected preschoolers also may continue to demonstrate difficulties in the auditory processing of spoken words as well as visual processing of material presented to them in the form of pictures. Furthermore, some demonstrate sporadic mastery of tasks, in which the skills they demonstrate one day are absent another. Concern about the social development of substance-affected preschoolers also has led to ongoing research into the patterns of attachment and social interaction within this high-risk population of children.

School and Teenage Years

Little is known about the long-term biological effects of prenatal exposure to drugs; longitudinal prospective studies are needed to build a solid base of knowledge. However, children who exhibit language delays, distractibility, and/or problems with fine motor coordination during the preschool period are at increased risk for learning problems during their school and teenage years. For children who were prenatally exposed to alcohol, there is growing information about the cognitive development of school-aged children with FAS. By the time such children reach elementary school age, many demonstrate cognitive skills that fall within the mentally retarded range. Other less severely affected children display attention deficit disorder and specific learning problems related to difficulties with visual and auditory processing.

In the absence of research data describing the long-term effects of prenatal substance exposure, there are still a number of ways in which professionals can provide services for children and adolescents from substance-abusing families. Sometimes, older children may come to professionals' attention because of the birth of a younger substance-exposed sibling in the family. Other children may demonstrate problem behaviors in school (e.g., depression, learning difficulties, repeated absences) that can alert professionals to a possible problem with alcohol and/or other drug abuse within the family. Additionally, children may come to the attention of professionals through the child welfare system. The children also may begin experimenting with or abusing drugs and/or alcohol themselves. Further, law enforcement professionals also may be in a position to identify family substance abuse problems when adolescents engage in acting-out behaviors.

Whatever behavioral symptoms a child may demonstrate (and whatever their cause), as he/she passes from preschool into elementary school and beyond, available testing measures become increasingly more sensitive in identifying learning strengths as well as problems. A team of teachers, psychologists, speech and language therapists, hearing and vision specialists, nurses, and other professionals can be called in to assess difficulties with learning that may be related to short attention span, speech and language problems, impulsivity, difficulties with short-term memory, auditory and visual processing, etc. Based on such an evaluation, school personnel can more readily develop effective educational programs to help the child or adolescent compensate for identified problems.

However, more often than not, this educational intervention alone is not sufficient to support ongoing success in learning for children who live in substance-involved households. Unlike many children who have learning difficulties but who have grown up in stable family environments, the majority of drug-affected children have experienced environmental instability that may have included multiple placements, child abuse and neglect, inconsistent parenting (possibly including extended parental absences), domestic violence, and other stressors related to alcohol and/or other drug abuse. Thus, social workers, other mental health professionals, and members of the clergy may also need to provide services to help identify, treat, and prevent mental health disorders in such children.

For children who experience problems in school and who also are growing up in dysfunctional homes, the cumulative effects of both academic failure and environmental instability may greatly impair their functioning in a variety of other areas. Poor peer social relationships and low self-esteem place such children and adolescents at high-risk for depression, suicide, substance abuse, teenage pregnancy, and school dropout.

Summary

The point at which a substance-affected child becomes visible to professionals usually depends on the child's age, and it is important to remember that the child welfare system may not always be the primary identifier. A prenatally substance-exposed newborn is most likely to be identified within the health care system on the basis of maternal or infant signs and symptoms, as is a toddler, who may have problems with infections, FTT, etc. A preschooler, on the other hand, may be more visible within programs such as Head Start or early intervention programs for special-needs children, in which the child or his/her parents may demonstrate behaviors that are suggestive of a substance abuse problem within the family. Teachers and other educational professionals may identify school-aged children from alcohol- and/or other drug-abusing families on the basis of child or parental behavior or the content of the children's conversations with staff and peers. Adolescents from substance-abusing families also may demonstrate problem behaviors at school, or within the community, thus coming to the attention of law enforcement professionals.

At any one of these points of visibility, professionals can garner their resources and provide intervention. An interdisciplinary approach that encompasses the children's problems as well as those of other family members is most likely to be effective in helping families with problems related to alcohol and/or other drug abuse. Further, it is important to remember that child development is an ongoing process. Just as early intervention has been shown to have a positive impact, comprehensive, coordinated efforts can be helpful at whatever stage they are begun.

Prenatal Exposure to Alcohol

At birth, children with fetal alcohol syndrome (FAS) are recognizable by their apparent growth deficiency and characteristic minor facial anomalies that tend to become less noticeable and adopt a more normal appearance as the child matures. Less evident at birth—but far more devastating to FAS children and their families—are the lifelong effects of alcohol-induced damage to the developing brain. In addition to deficits in general intellectual functioning, persons with

FAS often demonstrate difficulties with learning, memory, problem-solving and attention as well as difficulties with mental health and social interactions.

However, the diagnosis of FAS identifies only a relatively small proportion of children affected by alcohol exposure before birth. Many children with significant prenatal alcohol exposure lack the characteristic facial defects and growth deficiency of FAS but still have serious alcohol-induced mental impairments. This condition is referred to as "alcohol-related neurodevelopmental disorder" (ARND). In addition, some prenatally exposed children without FAS facial features exhibit other alcohol-related physical abnormalities of the skeleton and certain organ systems; these anomalies are referred to as alcohol-related birth defects (ARBD).

Effects of Prenatal Alcohol Exposure on Brain Structure and Function

Although not as obvious at birth as the characteristic facial features associated with FAS, the effects of alcohol-induced damage to the developing brain and spinal cord, or central nervous system (CNS), are just as deleterious. The problems that result from this damage become apparent during childhood and adolescence. They include reductions in general intellectual functioning and academic skills as well as deficits in verbal learning, spatial memory and reasoning, reaction time, balance, and other cognitive and motor skills. These deficits are particularly serious, because they are pervasive and persist throughout the person's life. In fact, some deficits, such as problems with social functioning, appear to worsen as the sufferer reaches adolescence and adulthood, possibly leading to an increased rate of mental health disorders.

Effects on Cognitive and Motor Functions

Researchers have also investigated more specific aspects of brain functioning and behavior, rather than overall intellectual functioning, in exploring the effects of prenatal alcohol exposure. Two studies in both preschool and school-age children found that children with FAS, as well as alcohol-exposed children who did not meet all the FAS criteria, experienced deficits in numerous areas. The most prominent of these deficits were in integrating visual information with coordinated movements, controlling precise movements (for example, speed and coordination of finger movements), language, and general intellectual functioning.

Although research has well established that heavy prenatal alcohol exposure leads to neurobehavioral impairment, the effects of lower levels of alcohol exposure are not as clear. Many of the problems linked to FAS also seem to exist in children whose mothers drank moderate amounts of alcohol when pregnant. These problems include deficits in general intellectual functioning, visual-spatial reasoning, attention, and academic achievement, including:

- Learning and memory
- Visual-spatial functioning (the ability to see objects and understand their spatial relationships
- Executive functioning (activities that require complex thought processes and behaviors, such as planning, organizing, sequencing, and other forms of abstract thinking)
- Attention
- Motor control

Effects on Mental Health and Psychosocial Behavior

Both the psychosocial and psychiatric effects of prenatal alcohol exposure also profoundly influence the lives of alcohol-exposed children and their families. Impaired social functioning, disturbed behaviors, and psychiatric disorders are common in people with FAS. These problems, which can occur with or without mental retardation and persist into adulthood, often disrupt daily life and magnify other FAS-related problems.

Mental Health: In a large study of secondary disabilities in persons of various ages with FAS or FAE, 94 percent of the participants had a history of mental health problems. Attention deficits were the most frequent problems in children and adolescents and occurred in 61 percent of the subjects. Among adults, depression was the most frequently reported problem (52 percent). Other studies found that preschool and school-aged children prenatally exposed to alcohol showed behaviors characteristic of people with autism, such as impairments in social interaction and communication.

Psychosocial Behavior: Other studies have indicated additional impairments in social abilities and psychological functioning in alcohol-exposed children. For example, compared with control children, children prenatally exposed to alcohol had greater problems with respect to anxiety, social skills, and academic achievement; significantly higher scores on scales measuring behavioral problems, such as anxiety, depression, and attention problems; and more deficits in social skills, such as manners and interactions with others. The differences in social skills were greater at older ages, indicating that social skills developed more slowly in the FAS children.

Prenatal Drug Exposure and Drug-Abusing Environments

Prenatal Exposure to Methamphetamine Increases the Male Offspring's Vulnerability, When Adults, to Methamphetamine's Neurotoxicity, in Mice

The use of club drugs, such as methamphetamine, by women of childbearing age has become a public health concern. Dr. Alfred Heller and his colleagues at the University of Chicago and Illinois Institute of Technology, modeled this situation in mice. They administered a neurotoxic dose of methamphetamine to pregnant mice during gestational days 7 to 18. Fetal exposure alone did not produce neurotoxicity. The researchers also gave methamphetamine to the offspring after they had become young adults (11 weeks of age), at minimally neurotoxic doses. They observed an enhanced neurotoxicity in the male offspring when they were injected with methamphetamine as adults. The neurotoxicity was evidenced by greater methamphetamine-induced lasting reductions of dopamine and its metabolites in the striatum and of dopamine in the ventral brainstem. Some effects of prenatal methamphetamine exposure were observed in female offspring, but these were much less than those seen in males. The ability of methamphetamine to induce neurotoxicity is associated, in part, with its ability to raise body temperature (hyperthermia). These doses of methamphetamine did not raise the body temperature of the adult female offspring, while the methamphetamine injections did raise the body temperature of the adult males. However, the hyperthermic response to methamphetamine was the same in the adult males whether or not they had been exposed to methamphetamine in utero. These findings raise the concern that male methamphetamine abusers may have an enhanced risk for the neurotoxic effects of the drug if they were previously exposed to it in utero. Furthermore, the mother's methamphetamine abuse may predispose her male offspring to other neuropathological disorders, such as Parkinson's disease.

Heller, A., Bubula, N., Lew, R., Heller, B., and Won, L. Gender-Dependent Enhanced Adult Neurotoxic Response to Methamphetamine Following Fetal Exposure to the Drug. *J. Pharmacol. Exp. Ther.*, 298 (2), pp. 1-11,

Developing Language Skills of Cocaine-Exposed Infants

In a prospective, longitudinal, quasi-experimental, matched cohort design, Singer et al. assessed the association between level of fetal cocaine exposure and auditory comprehension skills underlying speech-language skills at 1 year corrected age. Maternal self-report and meconium assay were used to define 3 cocaine exposure groups, including nonexposure (n = 131), heavy exposure (n = 66), and light exposure (n = 68). After controlling for drug, medical, and environmental factors, several differences among the exposure groups emerged indicating an association between amount of cocaine exposure and poor infant outcomes. Infants in the heavy exposure group received lower total language scores than infants in the light exposure and nonexposure groups. And, in comparison to infants in the nonexposure group, infants in the heavy exposure group received lower auditory comprehension scores and were more likely to be classified as mildly delayed by total language scores. These findings document significant behavioral teratogenic effects of heavy prenatal exposure to cocaine on developmental precursors of speech-language development.

Singer, L.T., Arendt, R., Minnes, S, Salvator, A., Siegel, A.C., and Lewis, B.A. Developing Language Skills of Cocaine-Exposed Infants. *Pediatrics*, 107, pp. 1057-1064, 2001.

The Neurobehavioral Legacy of Prenatal Tobacco Exposure

More than 17 percent of pregnant women between the ages of 15 and 44 smoke, according to the 2002 National Survey on Drug Use and Health. Much is known about the adverse effects of smoking during pregnancy: Cigarette smoke reduces blood flow through the placenta by as much as 38 percent, and pregnant smokers are more than twice as likely as nonsmokers to have an infant with low birthweight. New research by NIDA [National Institute on Drug Abuse]-funded investigators now provides the first evidence of toxic effects of prenatal exposure to tobacco smoke on newborn neurobehavior. This finding begins to fill in our picture of how the adverse neurological effects of prenatal exposure manifest from the earliest days of life to later observed effects, including lower IQ and increased risk of developing attention-deficit/hyperactivity disorder.

Drs. Barry M. Lester and Karen L. Law and their colleagues at Brown Medical School in Providence, Rhode Island, used the Neonatal Intensive Care Unit Network Neurobehavioral Scale (NNNS) to document the effects of maternal smoking on 1- to 2-day-old infants. The researchers found significant differences in short-term neurobehavioral status in tobacco-exposed newborns compared with unexposed newborns and noted that neurobehavioral impact worsened as the mothers' smoking levels rose.

"This study offers the first solid evidence of a dose-response relationship between maternal smoking during pregnancy and newborn neurobehavior," says Dr. Lester. "Babies born to mothers who smoked while pregnant are stressed, which could affect their development."

"Focusing on newborn neurobehavioral outcomes is important," comments Dr. Vincent Smeriglio, Chair of NIDA's Child and Adolescent Work Group. "It invites us to think about the continuity of consequences, as we see these very early behavioral differences in prenatally exposed children and consider them in light of effects in older children" (see below, "Cognitive Deficits Persist Into Early Adolescence for Children of Smoking Mothers"). "This research is providing an important piece of the puzzle linking prenatal exposure to cigarette smoke and long-term behavioral outcomes," Dr. Smeriglio says.

"Infants exposed to tobacco in the womb showed statistically significant differences that suggest toxic effects of prenatal tobacco exposure on the newborn neurological system," says Dr. Lester. The tobacco-exposed infants were highly aroused and reactive as indicated by the higher excitability and handling scores, and their muscles were more rigid. They also showed signs of stress and drug withdrawal consistent with what has been reported in infants exposed to other drugs. When the total stress/abstinence scores were broken down into subscales, exposed infants showed significant CNS, gastrointestinal, and visual effects. Further, infants prenatally exposed to tobacco required more handling to keep them in a quiet and alert state.

"These infants' higher scores in such areas as excitability and arousal reflect that nicotine is a stimulant," says Dr. Lester. The researchers also found consistent dose-response relationships for both the cotinine bioassay results and the self-reports of number of cigarettes smoked per day. "These results indicate that greater exposure to tobacco smoke is related to increasingly negative neurobehavioral effects," he adds, "and that these children may be at increased risk for future neurobehavioral problems."

Dr. Lester is currently designing a larger, multisite study focusing on the neurobehavioral effects of prenatal exposure to cigarette smoke. Future research will attempt to pinpoint which components of tobacco are responsible for the known neuro-behavioral effects; determine whether those effects are long-term; clarify whether newborns experience nicotine withdrawal; and separate the effects of prenatal exposure from those of postnatal exposure through second-hand smoke or breastfeeding.

With valid information on the potential neurobehavioral effects of prenatal tobacco exposure, more pregnant women may be swayed to quit smoking, notes Dr. Lester. "The smoking effects observed in our study underscore the importance of smoking cessation programs, particularly for women of childbearing age," he says.

Cognitive Deficits Persist Into Early Adolescence for Children of Smoking Mothers

Teenage children of mothers who smoked during pregnancy perform more poorly on tests of general intelligence and on tasks requiring auditory memory than do children who were not exposed to cigarette smoke before birth, according to NIDA-supported researchers at Carleton University in Ottawa, Canada. Dr. Peter Fried and his colleagues, who have followed the development of children born to smoking mothers as part of the Ottawa Prenatal Prospective Study, previously reported poorer cognitive abilities in children of smokers when the children were ages 5 to 6 and 9 to 12. "The results we see now that the children are 13- to 16-year-olds continue to suggest that exposure to cigarettes before birth has negative impact on general IQ and on auditory memory. And the effects are dose-related: The deficits are more severe in children of heavy smokers," Dr. Fried says.

In some areas of cognitive function, the gap in test results between exposed and unexposed children has narrowed as the children have grown, observes Dr. Fried. This improvement is most notable in tests that measure achievement rather than innate ability. For instance, although measured IQ remains lower for exposed children, their scores on reading and language skills are equivalent to those of unexposed children. "This comparative improvement in achievement is associated most strongly with the educational level of the parents. Achievement tests are in many ways a measure of formal learning acquired at home and in school. It appears that family and environmental factors that support learning can help moderate the negative effects seen in measures of ability," Dr. Fried explains.

"The improvements found in this most recent evaluation of these children are encouraging," says Dr. Vincent Smeriglio, chair of NIDA's Child and Adolescent Work Group. "Nonetheless, the continued finding of poorer performance as the exposed children enter adolescence underscores the damage that appears to be done by smoking during pregnancy. These kids may be catching up in some ways, but they started out with a serious disadvantage."

Sources

Fried, P.A.; Watkinson, B.; Gray, R. Differential effects on cognitive functioning in 13- to 16-year-olds prenatally exposed to cigarettes and marihuana. *Neurotoxicology and Teratolgy* 25(4):427-436, 2003.

Law, K.L.; Stroud, L.R.; LaGasse, L.L.; Niaura, R.; Liu, J.; Lester, B. Smoking during pregnancy and newborn neurobehavior. *Pediatrics* 111(6):1318-1323, 2003.

Chapter 36

Risk Factors for Parental Abduction

"You'll never see your child again!" When are these words an idle threat spoken in anger and frustration and when are they a warning that a parent intends to abduct his or her child, depriving the child and the other parent of future contact?

Although custody laws vary from State to State, abducting one's own child is a crime in every State. If a parent or other family member takes, hides, or keeps a child away from a parent with custody or visitation rights, then he or she may have committed a crime. More important, a child often is harmed by life on the run and by being deprived of his or her other parent. Prior to abduction, many of these children have been exposed to neglectful and abusive behaviors in their homes and have witnessed high levels of conflict between their parents. These children are at risk for psychological harm.

The U.S. Department of Justice, Office of Juvenile Justice and Delinquency Prevention, funded a research study on prevention of family abduction through early identification of risk factors to answer the following questions:

- What type of parent abducts his or her child?

Excerpted from "Early Identification of Risk Factors for Parental Abduction," by Janet R. Johnston, Inger Sagatun-Edwards, Marth-Elin Blomquist, and Linda K. Girdner. From *OJJDP Juvenile Justice Bulletin,* March 2001. U.S. Department of Justice, 2001. Available online at http://www.ncjrs.org/pdffiles1/ojjdp/185026.pdf; And "The Amber Plan," from *FCC Consumer Advisory*, Federal Communications Commission, 2003. Available online at http://www.fcc.gov/cgb/consumerfacts/AMBERPlan.html.

- What role does family violence play in increasing the likelihood of abduction?
- How can one identify which child is at risk of being abducted by a parent or other family members?
- What can be done to prevent family abductions and protect the child?

This chapter describes the findings of these multiple discrete research projects. The authors also recommend steps that communities can take to help protect children from family abduction.

Profiles of Parents at Risk for Abducting Their Children

Profile 1: When There Has Been a Prior Threat of or Actual Abduction

When a parent has made credible threats to abduct a child or has a history of hiding the child, withholding visitation, or snatching the child from the other parent, there is great distrust between the parents and a heightened risk of further custody violation. This risk profile is usually combined with one or more of the other profiles. In these cases, the underlying psychological and social dynamics that motivate the abduction need to be understood and addressed. When other risk factors are present, one or more of the following are general indicators of an imminent threat of flight with the child:

- The parent is unemployed, homeless, and without emotional or financial ties to the area.
- The parent has divulged plans to abduct the child and has the resources or the support of extended family and/or friends and underground dissident networks needed to survive in hiding.
- The parent has liquidated assets, made maximum withdrawals of funds against credit cards, or borrowed money from other sources.

Profile 2: When a Parent Suspects or Believes Abuse Has Occurred and Friends and Family Members Support These Concerns

Many parents abduct their child because they believe that the other parent is abusing, molesting, or neglecting the child. These abducting parents feel that the authorities have not taken them seriously or properly investigated the allegations. Repeated allegations increase the hostility and distrust between the parents. Parents who have the fixed belief that abuse has occurred—and will continue to occur—then rescue the child, often with the help of supporters who concur with their beliefs, justify their actions, and often help with the abduction and concealment. Supporters might include family members, friends, or underground networks (usually women) that help protective parents (usually women) obtain new identities and find safe locations.

In a large number of cases, the child has been previously exposed to neglectful, endangering, or violent environments (e.g., domestic violence or substance abuse). In these cases, the courts and child protective services may have failed to protect the child and the concerned parent or family member. They may have trivialized the allegations, dismissing them as invalid or the product of a contentious divorce. Often, however, the allegation of sexual abuse by a father or stepfather that motivates a mother to abduct her child is unsubstantiated. In these cases, the abduction can psychologically harm the child and the other parent, possibly leaving their relationship in serious need of repair.

Profile 3: When a Parent Is Paranoid Delusional

Although only a small percentage of parents fit this profile, these parents present the greatest risk of physical harm or death to the child, regardless of whether an abduction occurs. Parents who fit the paranoid profile hold markedly irrational or psychotic delusions that the other parent will definitely harm them and/or the child. Believing themselves to be betrayed and exploited by their former partner, these parents urgently take what they consider to be necessary measures to protect themselves and the child.

Psychotic parents do not perceive the child as a separate person. Rather, they perceive the child as part of themselves—that is, as a victim (in which case they take unilateral measures to rescue the child)—or they perceive the child as part of the hated other parent (in which case they may precipitously abandon or even kill the child). Marital separation and/or the instigation of the custody dispute generally triggers an acute phase of danger for these psychotic individuals. The result can be not only parental abduction, but also murder and suicide.

Profile 4: When a Parent Is Severely Sociopathic

Sociopathic parents are characterized by a long history of flagrant violations of the law and contempt for any authority—including that of the legal system. Their relationships with other people are self-serving, exploitive, and highly manipulative. These people are also likely to hold exaggerated beliefs about their own superiority and entitlement and are highly gratified by their ability to exert power and control over others. As with paranoid and delusional parents, sociopathic parents are unable to perceive their children as having separate needs or rights. Consequently, they often use their children as instruments of revenge or punishment or as trophies in their fight with the former partner. Sociopathic parents have no qualms about continuing coercive, controlling, and abusive behavior or abducting their child, nor do they believe that they should be punished for their actions. Like paranoia, a diagnosis of severe sociopathy is rare.

Profile 5: When a Parent Who Is a Citizen of Another Country Ends a Mixed-Culture Marriage

Parents who are citizens of another country (or who have dual citizenship with the United States) and have strong ties to their extended family in their country of origin have long been recognized as potential abductors. The risk of abduction is especially acute at the time of parental separation and divorce, when these parents may feel cast adrift from their mixed-culture marriage and may need to return to their ethnic or religious roots to find emotional support and reconstitute a shaken self-identity. Often in reaction to being rendered helpless or feeling rejected and discarded by the former spouse, such parents may try to take unilateral action by returning with the child to their family of origin. This is a way of insisting that the abducting parent's cultural identity be given preeminent status in the child's upbringing.

Profile 6: When Parents Feel Alienated From the Legal System and Have Family / Social Support in Another Community

Many subgroups of potential abductors feel alienated from the judicial system. Following is a list of five such subgroups.

Subgroup 1. Parents who are indigent and poorly educated lack knowledge about custody and abduction laws and cannot afford the legal representation or psychological counseling that would help them resolve their disputes. Those parents who have extended family or other social, emotional, and economic support in another geographical community may be at risk for abducting their children.

Subgroup 2. Many parents cannot afford and are unaware of the need to access the court system. In addition, those who have had prior negative experiences with civil or criminal courts do not expect family courts to be responsive to their values or their plight.

Subgroup 3. Parents who belong to certain ethnic, religious, or cultural groups may hold views about childrearing that are contrary to the prevailing custody laws that emphasize gender neutrality and the rights of both parents. These parents instead turn to their own social networks for support and use informal self-help measures rather than the courts in disputes over the children.

Subgroup 4. A mother who has a transient, unmarried relationship with her child's father often views the child as her property, and her extended family supports this belief. Many of the women in this subgroup assume they have sole custody of their child and are genuinely surprised when they are informed that the father—by law in California and most other States—has joint rights to the child.

Subgroup 5. Parents who are victims of domestic violence are at risk of abducting their child, especially when the courts and community have failed to take the necessary steps to protect them from abuse or to hold the abuser accountable. Joint custody, mediated agreements, and visitation orders often leave victims vulnerable to ongoing violence, despite separation from the abuser. When such victims abduct their child, the violent partners may successfully obscure the facts about the abuse and activate the abduction laws to regain control of their victims.

Study Findings

According to studies, children abducted by their parents or other family members were usually preschoolers. In the majority of cases, one child was abducted.

Mothers and fathers were equally likely to abduct. The abducted child's parent, usually in his or her mid-twenties or mid-thirties, almost always carried out the abduction, although the child's grandparent or stepparent occasionally was the abductor.

Almost two-thirds of the abductions were post-custodial offenses; that is, the abduction occurred after the issuance of a court order dictating the custody of the child. In the Statewide Study, however, abductions were more evenly divided between pre- and post-custodial offenses.

Mothers were more likely to abduct when a custody order existed, whereas fathers were more likely to abduct when no custody order existed. The Statewide Study found that fathers were twice as likely as mothers to abduct in the absence of a custody order.

Fathers were much more likely to use force to abduct their children or to retain them by not returning them from a visitation, whereas mothers rarely used force to abduct their children. Instead, mothers were more likely to flee with the children or to deny the fathers visitation. These patterns of behavior reflect that mothers usually have physical possession of their children.

Divorced parents were the largest category of abductors, followed by unwed and separated parents. When compared with custody-litigating parents, abducting parents were far more likely to be unwed. This group of unwed abducting parents also included a subgroup of unwed parents who had cohabited or had brief transitory relationships.

Studies found that more than one-half of the abducting parents were poor, unemployed, unskilled or semiskilled, and poorly educated. Consequently, the poor were over-represented in the population of abductors and their families.

Compared with custody-litigating mothers, mothers in abducting families were more likely to be unemployed, depend on public assistance, and receive no child support from the fathers. Many mothers had few, if any, economic incentives to remain in the geographical area.

According to all three studies, rates of reported abductions and abduction arrests varied by race and ethnic background. The proportions of Caucasian and Hispanic abductors were similar to the percentages of these racial groups in the general population: Caucasians were the largest group of abductors, followed by Hispanics. In cases reported to the justice system, African Americans who abduct were over-represented and Asians who abduct were underrepresented relative to their percentage in the population. With the exception of the Caucasian group, fathers were more likely than mothers to abduct.

Abductors were disproportionately unwed, low-income parents. Specifically, many of these young parents had brief relationships with one another and never developed a pattern of working together as parents. The mothers and their extended family felt that the child belonged to them and that the fathers had few, if any, custodial or visitation rights. Rather than looking to the legal system to assign physical possession and visitation rights to specific individuals, the mothers relied on their extended family and friends to help raise the child and make informal custody decisions. These parents did not use family courts to resolve custody disputes because they could not afford legal representation and because the legal system was largely foreign to them. Instead, they abducted their children without regard to legal ramifications.

Records showed that about one-fourth of the abductors did not operate alone in the act of abducting. Many abductors relied on a network of family and social support to carry out and maintain the abduction. A significant proportion of abductors (almost three-fifths of women and two-fifths of men) received moral support for their actions and practical help in planning the abduction. The network of supporters provided money, food, and lodging and was willing to conceal the whereabouts of the child. This widespread support for their actions may be one reason why many abductors do not recognize that their actions are illegal.

Parents in abducting families—especially mothers—were significantly less likely than parents in high-conflict, custody-litigating families to have legal representation. The custody-litigating families were somewhat more likely than the abducting families to have detailed custody and visitation orders, to include provisions for therapy, and to have been granted restraining (stay away) orders. While abducting families were significantly less likely than custody-litigating families to go to family court (on custody, visitation, child support, spousal support, property, or restraining orders), they were more likely to have come into contact with the juvenile court.

The numbers of substantiated allegations of neglect and unsubstantiated allegations of sexual abuse were higher among abducting families than among custody-litigating families. Abducting parents frequently alleged that child protective services and family courts did not take their complaints seriously or failed to conduct a thorough investigation. Rates of allegations of parental substance abuse were similar in abducting and custody-litigating families.

Family violence and/or child abuse was a dynamic in many abducting families. Mothers—whether they were abductors or left behind parents—more often claimed that child and/or spousal abuse had occurred. Women abductors were more likely to see the abduction as an attempt to protect their children from abusive fathers or spouses, whereas male abductors were more likely to claim that they were attempting to protect their children from neglectful mothers. Men—whether they were left behind or abducting parents—were more likely to be accused of domestic violence and sexual abuse. Little evidence was shown that formal criminal charges of domestic violence offenses had occurred either prior to or around the time of the abduction.

Both the custody-litigating parents and the sample of abductors and left behind parents reported similarly high incident rates of domestic violence, including severe physical aggression. Despite California's affirmative defense for parents who take their children to flee violence, not all cases involving domestic violence were identified and provided protection under this defense. For a small number of parents, attempts to escape the violence by fleeing with the children backfired. For example, some women with few resources who were caught abducting their children had no place to stay after recovery and therefore resorted to returning to their abusive partners. Other mothers fitting this profile remained separated but were subject to court-ordered visitation arrangements that put them and their children at ongoing risk of being physically harmed and terrorized by their violent and controlling ex-partner.

Compared with the general adult population, the high-conflict, litigating families and abducting families demonstrated similarly higher levels of anger, lower levels of cooperation, a pervasive distrust of the ex-partner's parenting, greater emotional distress, and behaviors indicative of character disorders. This signaled that anger and spite, which are more often attributed to separation and divorce, were not sufficient in themselves to motivate abduction.

About one-half of the abductors and two-fifths of the left behind parents had criminal arrest records. More than one-half of those who were arrested for criminal custodial interference had a previous arrest record. Of these, one-third had been incarcerated. Far more men than women had arrest records prior to the abduction, and ethnic and racial minorities were more likely than nonminorities to have been arrested for more serious offenses. Those with criminal arrest records were more likely to have been arrested for pre-custodial offenses, indicating that most had not attempted to resolve the custody dispute through the court system. Abductors had high levels of narcissistic and sociopathic character disorders. People with these character disorders often have contempt for the law and feel that laws do not apply to them and, therefore, they can easily run afoul of the criminal justice system.

Only about 10 percent of those arrested for criminal custodial interference were rearrested for a subsequent abduction. Higher recidivism rates were shown, with self-reports of reabductions at 30 percent. This difference is likely due to the fact that parents do not always report abductions—particularly short-term snatchings—to law enforcement or the district attorney. Also, the district attorneys' criteria for defining a complaint as an abduction case may differ from the parents' criteria. For example, a district attorney is more likely to perceive a violation as an abduction when a noncustodial parent does not return the child and is less likely to perceive a violation as an abduction when a custodial parent chronically withholds visitation.

Together, these findings suggest a number of interrelated family risk factors that predict child abduction by a parent, especially when children are very young. Parents and family members at risk are those who make persistent allegations of child abuse/neglect and family violence, have narcissistic/sociopathic personality traits, and have a history of trouble with the law. Others who are at risk include those who are unmarried, less educated, poor, and of ethnic minority status (especially those whose extended family live in another geographical area or another country). All of these factors make parents less likely to resolve custody disputes by using the formal, legal system. Instead they turn to their own families and social networks for emotional support and practical help, which may include abduction. Six profiles of separating/divorced parents at risk for abducting their children are proposed on the basis of these findings. To the extent that families meet the criteria for more than one profile, the risk for abduction is probably increased.

What Children at Risk for Abduction Deserve from Their Communities

What can be done to help parents at risk for abducting their children make better choices? What can the courts, public agencies, and private and nonprofit organizations do to help families resolve their disputes amicably while addressing their legitimate concerns about protecting their children to reduce the risk of abduction and the possibility of the children being harmed?

Increased Parental Access to Legal Information and Representation

Problem 1: Parents generally lack knowledge of or access to legal information. Most parents are not familiar with custody and visitation laws. Many of them do not know that moving to a new location without going to court to obtain a custody order or to modify an existing order can be a crime when it violates the rights of the other parent. Unwed parents often do not know they should have a custody order. Grandparents, stepparents, and others who support parents in abducting their children generally do not know that they may be committing a felony by aiding and abetting the abductor.

Recommendation: Develop public education programs that discuss relevant laws for parents. Communities or organizations should develop public education campaigns, including public service announcements, to educate the public about custody and visitation laws and the crime of parental abduction. These campaigns should provide information—via radio, television, the Internet, and printed materials—that will increase public awareness. For example, programs or organizations that target at-risk populations can provide informational brochures to parents in these programs. Examples of such programs or organizations include public welfare offices, child support enforcement offices, programs for unwed parents, organizations serving immigrant and ethnic communities, mental health agencies, the courts, and missing children's organizations and clearinghouses.

Problem 2: Parents and children are unable to obtain affordable legal representation. Educating parents about the need for custody orders and ways to prevent abductions does little good if they are unable to access the legal system. Most low-income parents are unable to find affordable representation in custody and visitation cases. Many middle-class parents in the midst of a divorce cannot afford to hire attorneys for the period of time needed to resolve contested custody cases. Legal services offices often do not represent parents in custody cases, unless the case fits under a separate priority set by the office, such as the prevention of domestic violence. Unwed mothers who seek public assistance are required to cooperate with welfare agencies in determining paternity and child support, yet neither the mothers nor the fathers receive help in obtaining a court order that specifies their custody and visitation rights.

Recommendation: Develop community-based programs that increase the parents' access to legal representation. The courts should appoint custody evaluators, guardians ad litem (legal representatives), or attorneys who represent children to provide the parents with information and recommendations. More programs that provide legal representation on a pro bono or sliding scale basis should be developed. Parents who do not have legal representation should still be able to obtain legal information and advice. Barriers that prevent attorneys from offering partial services should be removed to enable parents to get the help they most need from attorneys. Courts should also be more user-friendly by allowing the offices of the clerks of the court to assist the expanding population of pro se parents (i.e., parents who do not retain a lawyer and represent themselves in court).

In addition, jurisdictions should streamline procedures for obtaining custody and visitation orders to make them available to low-income, unwed parents. Programs for parents, starting with the birth of the child, should clarify custody rights and responsibilities. Parents should be able to obtain readily enforceable custody orders and acquire legal assistance to obtain child custody and visitation orders when courts determine paternity and child support.

Problem 3: Enforcing custody orders is time-consuming and costly. When a child is abducted after a custody order is obtained, the left behind parent often questions the usefulness of the custody order. The left behind parent faces the prospect of hiring two attorneys (one attorney in each State if the abducting parent traveled to another State), filing enforcement proceedings with the court, and waiting for a court date. Meanwhile, the abducting parent may flee again with the child. Many left behind parents know where their child is, but they are unable to recover him or her.

Recommendation: Pass State laws that mandate district attorneys to enforce custody orders. California is the only State that currently has an expedited enforcement measure for child custody orders. The measure mandates that the district attorney take whatever civil and criminal remedies are necessary to locate and recover children abducted by family members and to enforce child custody orders. In July 1997, the National Council of Commissioners of Uniform State Laws approved the Uniform Child-Custody Jurisdiction and Enforcement Act (UCCJEA), which contains a similar provision. As of February 2001, 21 States and the District of Columbia had enacted the UCCJEA, and it had been introduced in the legislatures of 10 other States.

Protection of Children's Interests and Needs

Problem 1: Under current Federal and State law, abduction is not a crime against the child. Under current law, the parent whose custody or visitation rights have been interfered with by the abduction of his or her child is the victim of family abduction. The law casts abducted children as possessions that parents have rights in, not as victims of a crime.

Recommendation: Modify laws so that family abductions are crimes against the child. In lieu of, or in addition to, criminal custodial interference laws that recognize the rights of the left behind parent, laws should recognize that family abduction is a type of abuse against the child. Child victims of abduction should be eligible for services under the Victims of Crime Act, 42 U.S.C. Section 10601.

Problem 2: Children can be harmed by recoveries, post-abduction placements, and custody orders that abruptly disrupt their relationship with their primary parent. Although society increasingly recognizes that the child is harmed when his or her relationship with a caring left behind parent is disrupted, society may not fully understand the problems that arise when the bond between the child and his or her abducting parent is disrupted. The child should not inadvertently be punished for the parent's actions, particularly if the child's primary bond is with that parent. In some instances, the child is more traumatized by these disruptions than by the actual abduction. In cases of long-term abduction, the child may be returned to a parent who is virtually a stranger and be cut off from the only known parent.

Recommendation: Involve social services at each phase of decision making that affects the child and minimize the disruption to the child's relationship with a primary parent. Law enforcement officers and social services should coordinate their efforts when the officers plan to recover the child or arrest the abductor. These two groups should know enough about the case to assess whether the child would experience harm if unaccompanied by the abducting parent during the recovery and return or to determine whether the abducting parent presents a potential physical or flight risk to the child. A mental health or social services professional should also be present when the child is reunited with the left behind parent or soon after. This professional can help facilitate the child's transition and ease the feelings of anger, guilt, and fear that often accompany it.

If the left behind parent obtained an ex parte (without notice to the other party) custody order after the abduction, then there was no full hearing on the best interests of the child. In these cases, a hearing should be scheduled promptly after the child is recovered to determine custody and visitation, as ex parte orders are meant to be temporary. As appropriate, judges should consider alternatives to abrupt shifts in the child's caretaking arrangements, so that the child can gradually enter into new arrangements, building the parent-child relationship over time.

The AMBER Plan

A recently enacted component of the Emergency Alert System (EAS) has been credited with aiding in the rescue of several missing children who were kidnapped by strangers. It's called the AMBER Plan.

Background

The AMBER Plan is named for a 9-year-old girl who was kidnapped by a stranger and later found dead in 1996. In response to that tragedy, the radio stations in that area agreed to repeat news bulletins about abducted children, hoping the bulletins might help save the life of a child. The name now stands for America's Missing: Broadcast Emergency Response.

It Works Like This

Once police officials have confirmed a missing child report, an alert is sent to radio stations, television stations, and cable companies. Broadcasters interrupt programming to relay the information using the EAS to voluntarily deliver the information to the community—the same concept used during severe weather or national emergencies. A description of the abducted child, suspected abductor and details of the abduction are broadcast to millions of listeners and viewers. (The alert is read after a distinctive sound tone and the statement: "This is an AMBER Alert.") The alert also provides information about how members of the public who have information relating to the abduction may contact the police or other appropriate law enforcement agency.

The goal of the AMBER Plan is to galvanize an entire community, adding millions of extra eyes and ears to watch, listen, and help in the safe return of the child and apprehension of the suspect.

The EAS is used to notify the public about severe weather and other national emergencies. In order to prevent the over use of the EAS system, two criteria must usually be met to enact the AMBER Plan:

- A child must be 15 years of age or younger, or have a proven mental or physical disability; and
- Police must believe the child is in danger of serious bodily harm or death.

What You Can Do

If you see a child, adult, or vehicle fitting the AMBER Alert description, immediately call the telephone number given in the AMBER Alert and provide authorities with as much information as possible.

Remember: The AMBER Alerts are only used for the most serious child abduction cases, where the police believe the child is in danger of serious bodily harm or death, not for runaways or most parental abductions.

For additional information on the AMBER Plan, visit the National Center for Missing and Exploited Children's (NCMEC) Website, www.missingkids.com.

Chapter 37

Animal Cruelty and Family Violence: Making the Connection

Pets are part of the family in the majority of American households, where nearly three-quarters of families with school-age children have at least one companion animal. These animals are often treated like members of the family, but if the family is experiencing violence they can become targets as well. Pets are often an important source of comfort and stability to the victims of abuse, particularly children. But abusive family members may threaten, injure, or kill pets, often as a way of threatening or controlling others in the family.

A 1997 survey of 50 of the largest shelters for battered women in the United States found that 85% of women and 63% of children entering shelters discussed incidents of pet abuse in the family. Children who have witnessed domestic violence or who have been the victims of physical or sexual abuse may also become animal abusers themselves, imitating the violence they have seen or experienced. A study conducted in 1995 noted that 32% of the pet-owning victims of domestic abuse reported that one or more of their children had hurt or killed a pet. Similarly, a 1983 study noted that children were reported to be abusive to animals in more than a third of a sample of

---

This chapter contains text from "Animal Cruelty and Family Violence: Making the Connection," "Frequently Asked Questions about Animal Cruelty," "Children and Animal Cruelty: What Parents Should Know," and "10 Things Teens Can Do to Help Stop Animal Cruelty." Reprinted with permission from The Humane Society of the United States. For additional information, visit The Humane Society of the United States website at www.hsus.org.

pet-owning families referred to New Jersey's Division of Youth and Family Services for suspected child abuse.

It is essential for those who respond to family violence to be alert to this connection. Professionals in domestic violence intervention, law enforcement, child protection, human and veterinary medicine, education, and animal care and control should get to know their counterparts in other professions and work together to establish strategies for a coordinated response to these needs.

In fact, professionals who help families in crisis are increasingly recognizing the role that animals play in the dynamics of family violence. Many law enforcement agencies are training officers who respond to domestic violence calls to be alert for signs that a situation is life-threatening. These include situations where the batterer has threatened suicide, is displaying a firearm, or has hurt or killed a family pet.

In addition, local domestic violence shelters and animal protection organizations have begun partnering to develop safe havens for the pets of domestic violence victims because many victims delay leaving the abusive batterer out of fear for their pets' safety. All too often, batterers punish victims for leaving by abusing or killing the pets. Yet, with the help of over 100 safe haven programs currently operating around the United States, many domestic violence victims no longer have to choose between their safety and their pets.

The First Strike® campaign can help in the process of bringing professionals together from a variety of agencies. We facilitate workshops and provide educational materials specifically for various professionals working to prevent family violence. For more information, please call our First Strike toll free line at 1-888-213-0956.

Frequently Asked Questions about Animal Cruelty

What is animal cruelty?

Animal cruelty encompasses a range of behaviors harmful to animals, from neglect to malicious killing. Most cruelty investigated by humane officers is unintentional neglect that can be resolved through education. Intentional cruelty, or abuse, is knowingly depriving an animal of food, water, shelter, socialization, or veterinary care or maliciously torturing, maiming, mutilating, or killing an animal.

Why is it a concern?

All animal cruelty is a concern because it is wrong to inflict suffering on any living creature. Intentional cruelty is a particular concern because it is a sign of psychological distress and often indicates that an individual either has already experienced violence or may be predisposed to committing acts of violence.

Is there any evidence of a connection between animal cruelty and human violence?

Absolutely. Many studies in psychology, sociology, and criminology during the last 25 years have demonstrated that violent offenders frequently have childhood and adolescent histories of serious and repeated animal cruelty. The FBI has recognized the connection since the 1970s, when its analysis of the lives of serial killers suggested that most had killed or tortured animals as children. Other research has shown consistent patterns of animal cruelty among perpetrators of more common forms of violence, including child abuse, spouse abuse, and elder abuse. In fact, the American Psychiatric Association considers animal cruelty one of the diagnostic criteria of conduct disorder.

Why would anyone be cruel to animals?

There can be many reasons. Animal cruelty, like any other form of violence, is often committed by a person who feels powerless, unnoticed, and under the control of others. The motive may be to shock, threaten, intimidate, or offend others or to demonstrate rejection of society's rules. Some who are cruel to animals copy things they have seen or that have been done to them. Others see harming an animal as a safe way to get revenge on someone who cares about that animal.

What happens when authorities prosecute an animal cruelty case?

Depending on the severity of the case, individuals found guilty may be imprisoned. Appropriate sentencing can also include individual or family counseling, community service, or diversion programs. It is rarely the goal of the authorities to imprison a child for cruelty to animals. Law enforcement officers and judges recognize that cruelty to animals is one part of a complex problem. Sometimes the official response to animal cruelty provides a family its first opportunity to get help.

Can reports be made anonymously?

While many jurisdictions will respond to an anonymous complaint, successful prosecutions often depend on an identifiable witness who can authenticate evidence.

Will I be required to testify?

If a case goes to trial and you have identified yourself as the complainant in either a written or an oral report, you may be called to testify.

Children and Animal Cruelty: What Parents Should Know

As natural explorers, don't all children sometimes harm animals?

Absolutely not. While some children kill insects, few torture pets or other small creatures. If allowed to harm animals, children are more likely to be violent later in life. Animal cruelty, like any other violence, should never be attributed to a stage of development.

What kind of children are cruel to animals?

Serious or repeated animal cruelty is seen more often in boys than in girls. Children as young as four may harm animals, but such behavior is most common during adolescence. Cruelty is often associated with children who do poorly in school and have low self-esteem and few friends. Children who are cruel to animals are often characterized as bullies and may have a history of truancy, vandalism, and other antisocial behaviors.

What does animal cruelty indicate about family dynamics?

Researchers say that a child's violence against animals often represents displaced hostility and aggression stemming from neglect or abuse of the child or of another family member. Animal cruelty committed by any member of a family, whether parent or child, often means child abuse occurs in that family.

What should I do if my child or a neighbor's child has harmed an animal?

If you suspect your child has deliberately harmed an animal, talk to your child. Try to discover what caused the cruelty. Communicate with your child, your child's teachers, and your child's friends. The more you know about your child's activities, the better able you will be to guide your child in making compassionate and humane choices.

Something as serious as animal cruelty, however, should not be handled alone. Seek help from a family counselor, school counselor, pediatrician, or clergy member. If you know another child who has harmed an animal, report what you know immediately to your local animal-welfare organization or police department. Alert the child's school principal or guidance counselor.

What should I tell my child about the other child's behavior?

Explain that animal abuse is often a sign of other serious problems and should be addressed by the proper authorities. Knowing that a friend has serious problems can be quite troubling for a child, as can witnessing animal cruelty. Your child may need to sort out the feelings the incident raises.

What should I do if an otherwise good child harms an animal one time?

Though innocent exploration may be corrected simply by talking with the child, any time a child causes an animal pain or suffering you should be concerned.

What is the difference between innocent exploration and calculated animal cruelty?

Innocent exploration may come of simple curiosity, but calculated animal cruelty is motivated by a desire to harm. While even innocent acts of cruelty should be addressed, it is particularly important to intervene when a child is insensitive to the obvious distress of an animal, repeats a harmful behavior, or derives pleasure from causing an animal pain.

How can I teach my child to respect animals?

Teach by example; use real-life situations to instill a sense of respect for all life. Invite your child to help you feed the birds or rescue a bug. With older children, discuss animal-cruelty cases publicized in the news. Encourage children to speak up for animals.

How can my child's school incorporate humane education?

Humane education should be part of every school curriculum. The Youth Education Division of the Humane Society of the United States

(HSUS) publishes materials that help teachers establish a classroom theme of kindness, respect, and tolerance. For subscription information, contact the HSUS's Youth Education Division, P.O. Box 362, East Haddam, CT 06423-0362.

10 Things Teens Can Do to Help Stop Animal Cruelty

Whether it's a case of neglect or a malicious act of cruelty, you can help protect animals. Why should you care? Because it's the right thing to do. Because cruelty to animals is illegal in all 50 states. And because people who harm animals may also harm people. Stopping cruelty to animals helps everyone.

What Can You Do?

1. Get help for the animal. If you see someone hurting an animal or if you know of someone whose animal looks sick, injured, or deprived of adequate food, water, or shelter, get help. Call the police, your local animal shelter, or a trusted adult. Do not try to help the animal yourself—that could put you in danger.

2. Get the facts. Write everything down. As a witness, you'll need to provide the date, time, location, and any other details you can remember, including descriptions of the animal, the type of cruelty, and the person who may be responsible for it.

3. Get the word out. Educate your friends, family, and teachers about animal cruelty and its connection to human violence by sharing information and materials from The Humane Society of the United States' First Strike campaign. For more information, call 1-888-213-0956, or write to us at First Strike, The HSUS, 2100 L St., NW, Washington, DC 20037.

4. Be a role model. Let your actions be a guide. Be kind to animals and let others know that hurting animals is wrong. Speak up for animals and urge others to do the same.

5. Be a responsible pet owner. Don't let your cats and dogs roam. Cats are safest indoors. When outdoors, dogs should be walked on a leash or supervised in a fenced yard. It's up to you to keep your pets safe.

6. Keep a lookout. If you see a stray or injured animal, contact your local animal care and control agency or the police. Provide a description of the animal and the location.

7. Make the Internet work. If you find an Internet site that promotes animal abuse, urge the service provider that hosts the web site to remove it immediately. You can find the address of the web site's provider at networksolutions.org.

8. Stop cruelty before it begins. Teach elementary schoolchildren in your community to be kind to animals via *KIND News,* a nine-times-a-year newspaper published expressly for kids. The prize-winning publication is produced by The National Association for Humane and Environmental Education (NAHEE), the youth service division of The HSUS. NAHEE also produces other publications and has programs like Adopt-a-Classroom.

9. Start a club. Start an animal protection club at your school. Visit the HumaneTeen web site and click on "Start a Club" for tips and activity suggestions.

10. Join the HumaneTeen Network. The HumaneTeen Network is a free online service that provides members with e-mail updates on the latest animal and environmental issues. To join, visit their web site and click on "Join the Network." For more information about animal cruelty, click on "Understanding Animal Cruelty."

References

Ascione, F. R. 1995. Domestic violence and cruelty to animals. Paper presented at the 4th International Conference on Family Violence, Durham, NH, July 24, 1995.

Ascione, F. R. 1997. The abuse of animals and domestic violence: a national survey of shelters for women who are battered. *Society and Animals,* 5(3): 205-218.

DeViney, L., J. Dickert and R. Lockwood. 1983. The care of pets within child abusing families. *International Journal for the Study of Animal Problems,* 4(4): 321-336.

Part Five

Child Protective Services

Chapter 38

Questions Parents Ask about Legal Issues Related to Child Abuse

Why can't I raise my child the way I want without interference?

People in our society, including child care professionals, legislators, and judges believe that a parent is in the best position to provide for the well-being and growth of a child. Although the child's interests are usually met by the parent(s), the state and society have a compelling concern for the welfare of a child. The parental role is defined not only by duties but obligations. Written into the Colorado statutes is the idea of a mutually beneficial relationship between a parent and child:

> As used in this chapter, parent and child relationship means the legal relationship existing between a child and his natural or adoptive parents incident to which the law confers or imposes rights, privileges, duties, and obligations.
>
> If the relationship fails to provide the necessities of life for the child, the state has the authority to intervene. The Children's Code defines the behaviors and actions of a parent which would cause the state to take action.

Reprinted with permission from the Kempe Children's Center and Kempe Children's Foundation, Denver, Colorado. For additional information, visit www.kempe.org. This material was written as a public service to assist lay people in understanding issues raised when a child is being abused and is not intended to provide legal, medical, psychological, or other professional advice.

NOTE: This chapter is prepared as a public services to assist people in Colorado in understanding the concerns raised and decisions which might be made if children might be being abused. It is not intended to provide legal, medical, psychological, or other professional advice in any way. If issues are raised for you personally, it is necessary that you seek appropriate professional advice for your situation and relative to your state laws.

What does the law say my rights and responsibilities are to my child when I become a parent?

Parental rights include the idea of duties and obligations to the child and his/her welfare. While many consider the rights of a parent to be fundamental, they are not absolute. It is unacceptable conduct for a parent to purposely endanger the life or health of a child through physical, sexual, or psychological abuse.

The legal system further reflects the basic societal belief that children should receive at least a minimum standard of care. Following is a list of factors which one court considered relevant to the question of whether a particular child was minimally well cared for. Does the parent:

1. Express love and affection for the child
2. Express personal concern over the health of the child
3. Supply necessary food, clothing, and medical care
4. Provide an adequate home
5. Give social and religious guidance

Failure to provide this care at least minimally is considered neglect. Parents are also required by law to protect their children from any sort of harm whenever possible. Insufficient action on the part of the parent to protect or seek medical care for his/her child can be considered neglect.

What is the difference between discipline and abuse?

No reasonable adult will deny the need for disciplinary action when raising a child. The form of discipline imposed, however, must be reasonable for the situation and understandable to the child. Colorado statutes recognize and "take into account accepted child-rearing practices of the culture in which the child participates." Physical punishment should be restricted to those parts of the body that will not put a child's health in danger. Even then, the punishment must not exceed certain limits. Examples of excessive punishment would be bruising or leaving cuts. The intent is to make the child understand a wrong behavior, not instill unreasonable fear. A child's misbehavior, no matter how egregious, never justifies conduct whose reasonably foreseeable consequence was or could have been the child's serious physical injury.

In what ways do our laws respond to possible parental abuse or neglect of a child?

If investigation, conducted by a law enforcement officer, protective service worker, or other persons assigned by the court, provides enough information that a child has been abused and/or neglected, a treatment or punishment approach can be taken. Depending on the fact of the case, two different agencies can be involved: protective services and county attorneys work on civil child protection cases. Law enforcement and district attorneys prosecute child abuse as a crime.

While criminal cases, which are directed at punishing the perpetrator, are more likely to attract public concern, they are much less likely to occur than a civil child protection hearing. An adjudicatory hearing is held in a civil, juvenile, or family court to determine if a child is dependent or neglected. The terms dependent and neglected are used interchangeably and stand for a single concept which includes child abuse. This child protective services hearing is completely separate from the criminal system but may occur before, during or after any criminal case deemed necessary by the district attorney. At the civil adjudicatory hearing, the judge must first determine is a child is abused or neglected. Then lager, if there is enough evidence of abuse or neglect, the court may order a treatment plan for the parents who must follow and complete it with some amount of success. The situation is reevaluated until a final decision is made as to the child's best interests.

What should I do if my child is mistreated or abused by a friend, spouse, or babysitter?

Parents have an obligation to keep their children safe and protect them whenever possible. If you find out that a third party has been abusing your child, it is your responsibility to seek immediate medical attention. Make sure the child is out of danger both physically and emotionally. A report of the abuse should be made either to the Department of Social Services or law enforcement. A parent who knows his/her child is being abused but fails to respond can be held accountable under child protection laws for unacceptable failure to protect a child.

Who can take my child out of the home?

Only a few public authorities can order removal of a child, and then only in limited, necessary circumstances. A court order to remove a child to foster care can be sought by protective services workers, law enforcement officers, hospital administrators, and physicians if they reasonably believe the child has been abused or neglected by a caretaker. Judges in each district are available around the clock to grant the court order.

If a child is in immediate danger, a law enforcement officer may take the child into protective custody without a court order when police officers removed children from what appeared to be harmful situations involving family members. The officer must then notify the parents as soon as possible of the child's placement. A hearing must be held within forty-eight hours to determine whether further detention of the child is justified.

If a law enforcement office or child protection worker comes to see my child, what would I do?

Law enforcement officers and child protection workers are required to respond immediately to reports of child abuse and neglect. An initial visit is usually necessary to assess the welfare of the child and the condition of the home environment to determine whether or not the child is safe. A parent is under no obligation to speak to either the law enforcement officer or child protective worker. Refusing to answer questions, however, can lead the investigator to think the parent is hiding something. If the child appears to be in immediate danger, a law enforcement office can place the child in protective custody. A child protective worker however, must receive a court order to remove a child or, alternatively, must gain the assistance of law enforcement.

Investigators should open a case with an open mind and no prejudicial feelings toward a parent, so many recommend that the best course of action for a parent is to cooperate. Unfortunately, a parent's cooperation in an investigation does not necessarily make the process any easier on them. Investigators may be forced to ask very personal questions not only of the parent, but friends, relatives, and professionals involved with the family. By refusing the initial offer of help, the parent(s) force the child protection worker to file a motion with the courts in order to gain access to the child. If needed to require cooperation, a civil adjudication hearing is held to determine if the child is dependent or neglected. At the hearing, parents are entitled to defend themselves and to have an attorney present throughout the court proceedings. If they cannot afford an attorney, the court will appoint one for them.

What happens if my child is taken into protective custody by a law enforcement officer or child protection worker?

After a child has been placed in protective custody, the child protection worker or law enforcement officer involved in the case must notify the parents of the child's placement and inform them of their right to a court hearing within forty-eight to seventy-two hours. A judge will then determine whether to detain the child further or return him/her home.

Once my child is removed, will I get him/her back?

Upon completion of an investigation, a child protection worker must decide whether the report of the child abuse is founded. If abuse is determined, the case worker can recommend a treatment plan to the parents. Upon successful completion, the caseworker must decide if the behavior of the parents and the condition which created the abuse has been rectified.

When parents disagree with a case worker's recommendations the matter can be taken to court for an adjudicatory hearing. This is a civil hearing for a judge to determine if a child is dependent or neglected. If the child is deemed dependent or neglected, the judge can then order the parents to comply with a treatment plan. The parent(s) must convince the judge that the treatment is successful and the child will be safe at home.

Cooperation with a treatment plan, however, does not necessarily end intervention. If completion of the treatment does not assure the child's safety, a more drastic outcome may be sought. If substantial compliance with the treatment plan is not successful in correcting the conduct or condition which initially led to state intervention, termination of the parent-child relationship is proper.

How is it determined if my child is dependent, neglected, or abused?

The child protective worker plays a key role in child abuse cases. Upon deciding a case is founded, a case worker will recommend a treatment plan for the parents and child to rectify the abusive or dangerous situation. Parents are under no obligation to cooperate with this plan, but it is often in their best interest to do so. If parents refuse to accept treatment, the case worker can file a motion requesting a finding of dependency and neglect with a court.

The result is an adjudicatory hearing in which a judge may declare the child dependent or neglected based on evidence given by the case worker, as well as the parents. The judge can then order the parent(s) to comply with a treatment plan, if appropriate.

A case worker has the power to close a case, thus ending intervention, if the parent(s) voluntarily sought successful treatment and the child is out of danger, and thus a court was not involved. If treatment was ordered by the court, a case worker can influence a judge's decision as to the success of the treatment and future safety of the child. In the cases where treatment is unsuccessful, a case worker can suggest the termination of the parent-child relationship as a last resort. The final decision on forced relinquishment of parental rights is up to the judge.

If the court find that my child is dependent, neglected, or abused, what can it do?

If a judge finds a child to be dependent or neglected, he/she may order a treatment plan for the parents. The court has a number of options in placing the child during the period of treatment. One or both of the parents may take legal custody with supervision by child protective services. If the child is in danger at home, the court can place him/her in foster care with relatives or an agency placement. A visitation schedule may be drawn up for the parents whose child is placed out of the home.

Once the treatment plan has been completed, the judge must evaluate its success. If further treatment is needed, the judge can order a continuation for six months. Successful completion of the treatment plan, and the assurance of the judge that the child will remain safe, ends intervention from child protective services. When it is apparent that no treatment will be successful, the judge may need to take a more drastic step.

How can I avoid having my child taken away permanently?

Only in extreme circumstances will the courts terminate a parent-child relationship. Termination is a result of the failure to correct behavior conditions which jeopardize the health and welfare of a child. A motion for termination is filed only after an adjudication hearing has been attempted.

Cooperation with the system is the best advice for those who do not want to forfeit parental rights. Child protective workers and the courts are looking for some indication in the parent(s) that they want the child and are willing to do what is best for the child to get him/her back. Parents should make a point to attend every scheduled visit with their child. Failure to attend without a legitimate excuse leads case workers and the courts to believe a parent is not interested in the child. Intervention in domestic affairs are to ensure the safety of the child. The ultimate goal of a child protective action is to help the parents care adequately for their children.

Chapter 39

The Community's Role in Child Abuse Prevention

Building Gateways to Prevention in Your Community

We all have a role to play in building strong communities in which families and children are valued and supported. It is in these kinds of communities that children are safest from abuse and neglect. Here are some things you can do as a concerned individual.

The Five R's

Prevent Child Abuse America has developed the following "Five R's," which can help individuals better understand the role they can play in child abuse prevention.

Raise the issue. Call or write your candidates and elected officials to educate them about issues in your community and the need for child abuse prevention, intervention, and treatment programs. Contact your local school district and faith community to encourage them to sponsor classes and support programs for new parents. Reach out to kids and parents in your community. Anything you do to support kids and parents in your family and extended community helps to reduce the likelihood of child abuse and neglect.

Text in this chapter is excerpted from "What Individuals Can Do: Building Gateways to Prevention in Your Community," and "What Organizations Can Do: How to Start a Child Abuse Prevention Program in Your Community," both from *Gateways to Prevention: What Everyone Can Do to Prevent Child Abuse*. Child Abuse Prevention Community Resource Packet, National Clearinghouse on Child Abuse and Neglect Information, 2003.

Be a good neighbor. Offer to baby-sit. Donate your children's used clothing, furniture, and toys for use by another family. Be kind and supportive, particularly to new parents and children.

Remember the risk factors. Child abuse and neglect occur in all segments of our society, but the risk factors are greater in families where parents:

- Abuse alcohol or drugs
- Are isolated from their families or communities
- Have difficulty controlling their anger or stress
- Appear uninterested in the care, nourishment, or safety of their children
- Seem to be having serious economic, housing, or personal problems

Recognize the warning signs. Some of the warning signs that a child might be abused or neglected include:

- Nervousness around adults
- Aggression toward adults or other children
- Inability to stay awake or to concentrate for extended periods
- Sudden, dramatic changes in personality or activities
- Acting out sexually or showing interest in sex that is not appropriate for his or her age
- Frequent or unexplained bruises or injuries
- Low self-esteem
- Poor hygiene

Report suspected abuse or neglect. If you suspect abuse or neglect is occurring, report it—and keep reporting it—until something is done. Contact child protective services (in your local phone book) or your local police department.

Other Ways You Can Help

Build a support network by getting involved in your neighborhood. Develop friendly relationships with your neighbors and their children. Problems often seem less overwhelming when you have support nearby. Get involved in your child's school. Join the parent-teacher organization and attend school events. Talk to your friends and neighbors about child abuse and how to prevent it.

Learn how your community supports children and families. The following programs may be offered through schools, healthcare clinics, social service agencies, or community- or faith-based organizations:

- Parent education programs teach parents about child development and parenting skills.
- Home-visiting programs provide social support, education, and crisis intervention to families at risk for abuse.
- Substance abuse treatment programs can help parents overcome problems with alcohol or other drugs.
- Well-baby programs provide health and education services to new parents.
- Childcare programs offer affordable childcare services. This may allow parents to maintain full-time jobs or stay in school while keeping their children safe.
- Respite care provides relief to families with a child or other family member who is ill or has a disability.
- Parent mentor programs match experienced, stable parents with parents at risk for abuse. Mentors provide support and model positive parenting skills.
- Family support centers offer an array of preventive support services, including many of those listed previously, as well as referral to other community services.
- Parent support groups offer a place for parents to meet and discuss parenting issues, exchange ideas, and offer support.

Take part in community prevention efforts.

- Help local organizations distribute educational materials on parenting and child abuse prevention.
- Encourage local schools or other community organizations to provide parenting education.

- Request a speaker or in-service training through the child protective services hotline.
- Offer to speak to the media and other groups about your own experiences as a parent. Parents Anonymous Inc. has a resource guide, *Media Guide for Parent Leaders,* that may be helpful.
- Organize a fundraiser or a food drive to support an organization that helps families in your community.
- Help the public library develop resources for parents. Work with the librarian to develop a collection of resources on child development and parenting skills.
- Provide friendship and guidance to parents and children who need your help by volunteering for programs such as Befriend-a-Child or Court Appointed Special Advocates (CASA).
- Contact your elected officials and ask them to support funding for prevention efforts and policies that support children and families.
- Make a donation to an organization that works to prevent child abuse. You can donate money, or give clothing, food, or toys to a social service agency that helps families in your community.
- Start or join a community coalition to prevent child abuse and neglect.

How to Start a Child Abuse Prevention Program in Your Community

This information provides a starting point for community members who want to establish a child abuse and neglect prevention program. The steps described here are common to most prevention initiatives. Because each community is unique, the process will unfold differently in each. The three main phases of launching a prevention program are, planning, implementation, and continuation.

Phase One: Planning

During the planning phase, community members need to take steps to mobilize support, assess needs, secure funding, and plan for evaluation.

Mobilizing community support. In some communities, a well-publicized and tragic incident catalyzes community efforts to prevent child abuse and neglect. In other communities, an individual or group might build on a general community awareness and concern to create a formal prevention program aimed at keeping children safe and families strong. Potential stakeholders in prevention efforts include educators, law enforcement officers, health and human services staff, community leaders (such as presidents of neighborhood associations), clergy and spiritual leaders, parents, local government personnel, and business leaders.

Assessing community resources. A community resource assessment gathers information about community assets as well as gaps in services. Identified stakeholders help assess the scope and quality of services by pooling information from their own organizations and agencies as well as gathering demographic data. Many colleges and universities provide technical assistance to communities conducting resource assessments.

Selecting the prevention program design. Prevention programs take many forms including family resource centers, home visiting programs, parenting education programs, and public awareness campaigns.

Planners will use the information gathered through the assessment to design a program appropriate for their community. Whatever design they select, planners need to ensure that the prevention program reflects an understanding of, and respect for, cultural norms that influence child rearing. Onc way that prevention programs can bridge cultural gaps is by delivering services and materials in languages other than English. Draw on a particular cultural community's strengths by involving members in planning the program. Involve parents in developing and delivering services as board members, task force members, and volunteers.

Securing funding. Some communities might have sufficient resources to launch a prevention program, but many communities will need to secure funding, possibly from more than one source. The four main sources of funds for prevention programs are the Federal government, State governments, foundations, and corporations. Along with start-up funds, planners must consider how they will fund the program over the long haul.

Evaluating the program. Planners should build evaluation into the prevention program and budget. An evaluator should participate in program planning and be viewed by the community as an integral part of the program. Emphasizing evaluation right from the start can help persuade funding sources to commit financial resources to the program. Again, many colleges and universities can provide technical assistance in designing and implementing program evaluations.

Phase Two: Implementation

During phase two, the group recruits and trains staff, starts delivering services, and begins to use feedback to improve service delivery.

Recruiting and training staff. When recruiting staff, consider an individual's ability to understand and meet the community's expectations and to deliver services with cultural sensitivity and competence. The composition of the staff should mirror the community being served. Recruiting neighborhood residents as staff will bring credibility to program efforts. Consider serving as a training ground for neighborhood residents re-entering the workforce or a field placement for graduate students in social work and early childhood education. Remember that an important part of staff training is to treat community members with respect and dignity.

Ensuring access. Make sure that the program's target audiences have easy access to services. Locate programs in the community to be served. Ensuring access to public transportation, providing child care, and linking the program to established community programs and institutions increase the likelihood that residents will take part in the program. Get the word out about the program using materials and channels familiar to community members—notices in grocery stores, brochures in medical clinics, and advertisements in church bulletins and free community papers.

Using feedback to improve services. Build frequent opportunities for information updates and feedback into the program. Ask for feedback from community members who come back for services and from those who don't. Schedule staff retreats to review progress and update strategic plans. Look at both tangible and intangible results. Celebrate even the smallest success with the community as a whole.

Phase Three: Continuation

For programs to succeed in the long-term in preventing child abuse and neglect, they must become a permanent part of the community's public landscape and secure long-term funding. The keys to securing continuation funding are:

- Start early
- Establish a team that includes program personnel and community supporters
- Develop a plan that targets sources and has a step-by-step timeline
- Generate data showing the effectiveness of the program
- Work at continuation every day.

Program framers must solidify relationships with funding sources and develop a team of supporters that are knowledgeable about, and feel a sense of ownership of, the prevention program. Program staff, board members, volunteers, consumers, referral sources, and community leaders are all part of the team that will help embed the program in the community.

Utilization data (e.g., number of participants served, amount of services offered) are helpful, but outcome data are critical. What difference does the program make? If this program is not continued, what will the community lose? What costs, economic and human, will be incurred? Programs that last are able to show that they work.

Resources

The Asset-Based Community Development Institute
Institute for Policy Research
Northwestern University
2040 Sheridan Road
Evanston, IL 60208-4100
Phone: 847-491-8712
Fax: 847-491-9916
Website: http://www.nwu.edu/IPR/abcd.html
E-Mail: achambers@northwestern.edu

The National Clearinghouse on Child Abuse and Neglect Information
330 C Street, SW
Washington, DC 20447
Phone: 800-FYI-3366 or 703-385-7565
Fax: 703-385-3206
Website: http://www.calib.com/nccanch
E-Mail: nccanch@calib.com

The Department of Health and Human Services
Children's Bureau
330 C Street, SW
Washington, DC 20447
Phone: 202-205-8618
Website: http://www.acf.hhs.gov/programs/cb

The Foundation Center
79 Fifth Avenue
New York, NY 10003-3076
Toll Free: 800-424-9836
Phone: 212-620-4230
Fax: 212-807-3677
Website: http://www.fdncenter.org

Chapter 40

Types and Effectiveness of Existing Child Abuse Prevention Programs

What Kinds of Prevention Programs Currently Exist?

Child maltreatment prevention services operating in communities today generally fall within a typology that includes several major approaches or methodologies: public awareness activities, skill-based curricula for children, parent education programs and support groups, home visitation programs, respite and crisis care programs, and family resource centers. In recent years, programs have been developed and implemented in a wider array of settings including prisons, places of worship, hospitals, and schools.

Public Awareness Activities

Public awareness activities are an important part of an overall approach to address child abuse and neglect. Such activities have the

---

Text in this chapter is from "What Kinds of Prevention Programs Currently Exist?" available online at http://nccanch.acf.hhs.gov/topics/prevention/emerging/kinds.cfm, and "What Do We Know about the Effectiveness of Prevention?" available online at http://nccanch.acf.hhs.gov/topics/prevention/emerging/effective.cfm. Both excerpted from "Emerging Practices in the Prevention of Child Abuse and Neglect," 2003. National Clearinghouse on Child Abuse and Neglect Information. The full report on the Emerging Practices project, "Emerging Practices in the Prevention of Child Abuse and Neglect, can be found on the National Clearinghouse on Child Abuse and Neglect Information Website: http://www.calib.com/nccanch/prevention/emerging/report/index.cfm.

potential to reach diverse community audiences, including parents and prospective parents, children, and community members. In designing prevention education and public information activities, national, State, and local organizations use a variety of media to promote these activities, including:

- Public service announcements
- Press releases
- Posters
- Information kits and brochures
- Television or video documentaries and dramas

Through these media, communities are able to promote healthy parenting practices, child safety skills, and protocols for reporting suspected maltreatment.

One of the largest child maltreatment public awareness initiatives is focused on the prevention of Shaken Baby Syndrome. A national network of State contacts for Don't Shake the Baby was established to ensure that all professionals involved in the care of children (e.g., teachers, physicians, nurses, home visitors, parent educators) became aware of the dangers associated with shaking infants. In addition to professionals, this campaign targeted parents to alert them to the dangers of shaking their babies and to provide information on positive coping skills when caring for a crying infant. Another initiative designed to capture attention and raise public awareness is STOP IT NOW!, which is a primary prevention media campaign that targets male and female sexual abuse perpetrators and other adults, calling on abusers and potential abusers to stop and seek help. STOP IT NOW! also increases public awareness about the trauma of sexual abuse. People are encouraged to call a toll-free help line for information and referrals regarding child sexual abuse.

Prevent Child Abuse America, formerly the National Committee to Prevent Child Abuse, also directs efforts to increase public awareness of the dangers and signs of child maltreatment. In collaboration with *Marvel Comics,* Prevent Child Abuse America developed Spider-Man comic books to address child sexual abuse and other child safety issues. In addition, Prevent Child Abuse America distributes an information packet each year to assist community groups in planning Child Abuse Prevention Month activities. Chapters in 37 States and one in the District of Columbia provide ongoing public awareness and other activities to prevent child maltreatment.

State Children's Trust Funds (CTFs) exist in all 50 States and the District of Columbia with the specific goal of preventing child maltreatment. CTFs and their local councils and affiliates coordinate prevention activities throughout each State by promoting and funding a variety of community-based programs, including public awareness campaigns, home visitation programs, skills-based curricula for children, and parent education and support activities. In addition, many CTFs develop and distribute public awareness materials for community groups, schools, and many other professionals working with children. These materials may include posters, bookmarks, magnets, and scripts for public service announcements. Many of the Children's Trust Funds also have been designated as the State lead agencies for the Community-Based Family Resource and Support (CBFRS) program.

Skills-Based Curricula for Children

Many schools and social service organizations in local communities offer skills-based curricula to teach children safety and protection skills. Most of these programs focus efforts on preventing child sexual abuse and teaching children to distinguish appropriate touching from inappropriate touching. Other programs focus on preparing young people to function successfully in society, while still others teach or enhance protective behaviors in children. Curricula may have a parent education component as well to give parents and other caregivers the knowledge and skills necessary to recognize and discuss sexual abuse with their children. Curricula may use various methods to teach children skills, including:

- Workshops and school lessons
- Puppet shows and role-playing activities
- Films and videos
- Workbooks, storybooks, and comics

Examples of skill-based curricula include programs such as Talk About Touching, Safe Child, Good Touch/Bad Touch, Kids on the Block, and Illusion Theater.

Parent Education Programs and Parent Support Groups

Perhaps the most prominent prevention activity is parent education. Typically, these programs focus on decreasing parenting practices and behaviors associated with child abuse and neglect. Though parent education programs may serve the general community, many are directed at populations determined to be at risk for child maltreatment. These programs address issues such as:

- Developing and practicing positive discipline techniques
- Learning age-appropriate child development skills and milestones
- Promoting positive play and interaction between parents and children
- Locating and accessing community services and supports

Parent education programs are designed and structured differently, usually depending on the curriculum used and the target audience. Programs may be short-term, offering classes once weekly for 6–12 weeks, or programs may be more intensive, offering services more than once weekly for up to a year. Well-known parent education programs include Parents as Teachers, National Parent Aide Network, Meld, Effective Parenting Information for Children (EPIC), Parents and Children Together (P.A.C.T.), and the Nurturing Program.

The Parents as Teachers program targets parents with children from birth to 5 years old and focuses on child development; recommends activities that encourage language development, intellectual growth, and social and motor skills; and strengthens the parent-child relationship. This program has 4 components, including personal home visits, group meetings, developmental screenings, and connection to community resources.

The National Parent Aide Network, a component of the National Exchange Club Foundation, is a national network of professionally trained individuals who become friends and role models to parents and teach them how to be responsible and bond with their children. Parent aides provide support, encouragement, and genuine and caring friendships; focus on the good qualities of the parents; serve as an outside social control to stop abuse immediately; and address special needs of the family by referring them to community agencies when necessary.

Meld offers educational and support services for parents to help them set goals and make decisions for their education, work, and family life that increase their self-confidence, self-sufficiency, and ability to manage a family successfully, and to reduce family isolation that can lead to abuse and neglect.

Effective Parenting Information for Children (EPIC) provides a series of workshops to train parents and teachers to assist children in developing life skills and civic values leading to responsible adulthood and parenting.

Parents and Children Together (P.A.C.T.) is a program in which parents and children participate in playtime, build family skills, and connect emotionally. P.A.C.T. also encourages parents to focus on child development and communication.

The Nurturing Program is a family-based program that involves both parents and children in activities, focusing on building a positive regard for self and others. There are 15 Nurturing Programs that are focused on specific populations (e.g., Parents and Children Birth to 5 Years, Parents and Children 4 to 12 Years, Hispanic Parents and Children Birth to 5 Years, and Families in Substance Abuse Recovery). Programs are home based or group based and range from 1½ to 3 hours per week for 9–45 weeks.

In addition to parent education programs, parent support groups also work to strengthen families and prevent child maltreatment. Two well-known programs include:

Parents Anonymous Inc., founded in 1969, leads an international network of accredited organizations that implement community-based, weekly, free-of-charge Parents Anonymous Groups for parents and other caregivers. In Parents Anonymous Groups, co-led by parent group leaders and group facilitators, parents find a caring, mutually supportive environment where they can learn new parenting strategies and create long-lasting, positive changes in their families. Their children participate in complementary Parents Anonymous Children's Programs that promote positive social and emotional development.

Circle of Parents, a collaboration of Prevent Child Abuse America and the National Family Support Roundtable, provides parent self-help support groups to anyone in a parenting role. These groups offer parents a place to discuss the challenges of raising kids and to exchange ideas. Funded through a grant from the Children's Bureau, Office on Child Abuse and Neglect, this is an effort to expand and enhance parent self-help support groups across the country. Most established groups have a free program for children as well. The groups provide a place where anyone in a parenting role can discuss the successes and challenges of raising children, find and share support, and learn new parenting skills.

Home Visitation Programs

Home visitation programs have existed in the United States since the late 19th century. As a strategy for preventing child maltreatment, home visitation came to the forefront of the national agenda in 1991 when the U.S. Advisory Board on Child Abuse and Neglect recommended universal implementation of home visitation programs. Rather than a specific program or activity, home visitation is a strategy for service delivery. Many organizations and agencies in fields as varied as education, maternal and child health, and health and human services use home visitation programs to strengthen and support families.

Home visitation programs offer a variety of family-focused services to pregnant mothers and families with new babies and young children. Activities offered through home visitation programs may include structured visits in the family's home, informal visits, and telephone calls that focus on topics such as:

- Positive parenting practices and nonviolent discipline techniques
- Child development
- Availability and accessibility of social services
- Establishment of social supports and networks
- Advocacy for the parent, child, and family
- Maternal and child health issues
- Prevention of accidental childhood injuries through the development of safe home environments

As the popularity of home visitation programs has increased, so too has the number and diversity of organizations offering these services. Both large and small organizations are establishing programs and providing community-based services to a wide-ranging population. For example:

Nurse Family Partnership, originally established as the Prenatal/Early Infancy Project at experimental sites in Elmira, New York, and Memphis, Tennessee, provides services to first-time mothers from the early stages of pregnancy through the child's first two years of life. Nurses provide home visits in accordance with a structured schedule, focusing on maternal health, parental role and life course, family and friends, and community services. The program, which is now available in numerous states, targets critical pregnancy outcomes, the prevention of child abuse and neglect, and subsequent unintended pregnancies.

Healthy Families America (HFA), a national initiative launched in 1992 by Prevent Child Abuse America and modeled after Hawaii's Healthy Start, links expectant and new mothers to trained staff who provide home visits and referrals to community services. HFA currently has home visitation programs in over 420 communities in the United States and Canada.

Early Head Start, an outgrowth of Head Start established in 1994 specifically for low-income families with infants and toddlers and pregnant women, promotes healthy prenatal outcomes, enhances the development of very young children, and promotes healthy family functioning. The community-based program provides parent education, comprehensive health and mental health services, and home visits.

Home Instruction Program for Preschool Youngsters (HIPPY) is an educational enrichment program that builds on the natural bond between a parent and child. The home visitation model helps parents prepare their preschool-aged children for successful, early school experiences and strengthens the bond between schools, families, and communities.

Parent Child Home Program (PCHP) is a home visitation program serving families challenged by the many obstacles to educational success, including poverty, low levels of education, and language difficulties. In play sessions with parents and children, the home visitor demonstrates various parenting techniques. An emphasis is placed on parent-child interaction and the development of verbal and language skills necessary to succeed in school.

Hawaii's Healthy Start Program is a multisite program in Hawaii that screens, identifies, and provides services to families at risk for child abuse and neglect. Most participants are enrolled after the birth of a child; however, approximately 10 percent of participants enroll during the prenatal period.

Project 12-Ways takes a comprehensive approach to prevention that uses an ecobehavioral model to teach parents new skills and knowledge regarding basic parenting, child development, and safety, while providing support to address some of the underlying problems affecting families. At intake, each family's individual needs are assessed and goals identified. Project counselors recommend services and meet with each family once or twice per week, monitoring the family's progress. Started in 1979 in Illinois, the model has since been replicated in California and is now a statewide model in Oklahoma.

Respite and Crisis Care Programs

Respite care services provide short-term care to children who have disabilities or chronic or terminal illnesses, who are in danger of abuse or neglect, or who have experienced abuse or neglect. For caregivers in stressful situations (they may be parents, foster or adoptive parents, or other relatives or guardians), respite care services provide temporary relief from the ongoing responsibilities of caring for children in the home. Crisis care is a unique form of respite. It is provided to children, with or without a disability, when the family is in crisis. Crisis care services may be referred to as crisis respite, emergency respite, crisis nursery, crisis stabilization, or shelter care.

When family caregivers are not able to take a break from constantly providing care and supervision for their children, stress builds. This elevated stress can lead to increased incidences of abuse, divorce, and out-of-home placement of the dependent family member. Respite services are provided in a variety of settings, within or outside of the family home. Services are generally short term (ranging from a few hours to a few weeks), and are provided on either a planned or an emergency basis. Both respite and crisis care services can be provided by other family members, friends, neighbors, community recreation programs, child or dependent care providers or centers, home health aides, family resource centers, community human service providers and respite or crisis care agencies. In addition to care and supervision, many respite and crisis care providers also offer a variety of support services to families, including referrals to other programs, counseling, case management, meals, transportation, social activities, lodging, medications, personal care, and assistance with activities of daily living.

Family Resource Center

Family resource centers are sometimes called family support centers, family centers, parent-child resource centers, family resource schools, or parent education centers. Each family resource center works with community members to develop specific services that meet the needs of the people who use the center and the community that surrounds it. This is accomplished by involving community members in design, implementation, and evaluation. Many centers require that advisory boards oversee the day-to-day operation of the centers, and that more than one-half of the board members be parents.

Family resource centers are located in a variety of community settings and serve diverse populations. Depending upon the resources available in the community, family resource centers may be located in churches, school buildings, hospitals, housing projects, restored buildings, or new structures. Based in the places where families naturally congregate, family resource centers serve as a central support within the community around which families can build their lives, regardless of the challenges they face.

Family resource centers promote both the strengthening of families through formal and informal sources of support and the restoration of a strong sense of community. Services may include parent skill training, drop-in centers, home visiting, job training, substance abuse prevention, violence prevention, services for children with special needs, mental health or family counseling, child care, literacy, respite and crisis care services, assistance with basic economic needs, and housing.

What Do We Know about the Effectiveness of Prevention?

Home Visitation Programs

Research on the impact of home visitation programs is one area in which there is a relative abundance of evidence, and that evidence, while not universally positive across all evaluations, suggests that home visiting can be an effective approach. David Olds, at the University of Colorado Health Sciences Center, has pioneered high quality, experimental research in the area of home visitation. Through the course of several replications and long-term follow-up studies over a period of 20 years, Dr. Olds has found positive, short-term and long-term outcomes for young, first-time mothers and their children in several areas, including decreased rates of child maltreatment, juvenile delinquency, and maternal criminality; increased economic self sufficiency; and increased social-emotional development.

The 1999 Future of Children report on home visiting programs also noted that despite some positive findings, many of the programs still struggled in numerous areas. Challenges were raised concerning enrolling, engaging, and retaining families. Similar issues were raised about the use of paraprofessionals versus nurses, staff retention, and the training needed by home visitors. When program benefits were demonstrated, this often only impacted a subset of families, and benefits were rarely seen for all program goals. The following are findings on home visitation from other recent work.

An evaluation of Family TIES, a program of services for first-time teen mothers during pregnancy, found that teen mothers who received weekly home visits made significantly higher gains in creating a safe and healthy home environment compared with participants who received traditional family support services at a health center. The program had no significant effect on the childbearing philosophies or psychological well-being of participating mothers.

An evaluation of the Healthy Start program, part of the Hampton Family Resource Project that provides home-based, parent education and support services to high-risk mothers, found several positive outcomes for families, including reductions in pregnancy risk status, birth complications, and subsequent pregnancies, and increases in childhood immunization rates and the number of adequate/safer home environments. The study also reported a reduced number of confirmed reports of child abuse and neglect.

An evaluation of STEEP (Steps Toward Effective, Enjoyable Parenting), an intensive intervention program of home visits and group sessions for high-risk women and their first-born children, found that compared to a control group, program participants demonstrated better understanding of child development, better life management skills, fewer depressive symptoms, and more organized and appropriately stimulating home-environments. The STEEP program also served as a buffer against stress, enabling parents to remain more sensitive to their children's needs even in the face of stressful life circumstances.

Leventhal suggests 9 factors that are necessary for successful home-based services. They include: early intervention, intensive services over a sustained period, development of a therapeutic relationship between the home visitor and parent, careful observation of the home situation, focus on parenting skills, child-centered services focusing on the needs of the child, provision of "concrete" services (e.g., shelter, health care), inclusion of fathers in services, and ongoing review of family needs to determine frequency and intensity of services.

Parent Education

Some research also has concentrated on the impact of programs that provide education for parents that can reduce risks to children. The record is neither rich nor, on the whole, particularly compelling. However, a few studies have demonstrated positive findings. Many of the existing studies in this area rely on outcomes that do not include actual child maltreatment reports, but focus on short-term gains in knowledge, skills, or abilities. Thus, taken as a whole, little is known about the impact of these programs on child maltreatment in the long term.

From the late 1980s to the early 1990s, the William Penn Foundation funded 14 child abuse prevention demonstration programs in Philadelphia and surrounding suburban areas, and sponsored one of the most comprehensive evaluations of parent education services in the early 1990s. The National Committee for Prevention of Child Abuse conducted the evaluation of this initiative, integrating outcomes from all 14 programs. Data were gathered from 1,078 parents who received services between March 1990 and July 1991 across the 14 sites.

Researchers found that parents' potential for physical child abuse decreased significantly as measured by the Child Abuse Potential Inventory (CAP). Participants exhibiting the highest risk at pretest (i.e., the highest CAP scores) showed the greatest gains at post-test (i.e., the greatest decrease in CAP scores). Total CAP scores, as well as three subscales (distress, rigidity, and unhappiness), decreased significantly. In addition to an observed reduction in child abuse potential, there were observed reductions in the use of corporal punishment and inadequate supervision of their children, while participants demonstrated greater responsiveness to the emotional needs of their children.

More recent evaluations of programs also have focused on families considered to be at risk for child maltreatment. The Bavolek Nurturing Program is a parenting education program that specifically focuses on four parenting constructs, including inappropriate parental expectations, lack of empathy toward the child, belief in corporal punishment, and parent-child role reversal. A secondary analysis using a convenience sample of at-risk rural families found significant improvements from pre- to post-test in each of these four areas, as measured by the Adult-Adolescent Parenting Inventory, with the post-test results consistent with nurturing parenting attitudes. While the results of the study were positive, the researchers acknowledge critical limitations, including the lack of a control group.

Another such program offered 12-week parent education services to teen mothers in an effort to promote healthy, nurturing families. In an analysis of mothers participating in this program, researchers found positive, though not statistically significant, increases in knowledge of child development and attitudes toward parenting and discipline. Furthermore, families who participated in the parent education program had significantly fewer substantiated reports of child maltreatment than families who did not participate in the program.

An earlier study focused on a group of high-risk mothers receiving services through an intensive parent education program administered by the National Institute of Mental Health. Mothers with at least one child and who were considered very high risk for child maltreatment were recruited for the program during pregnancy (prior to 26 weeks gestation). The intensive program offered concrete services (e.g., assistance with transportation, assistance returning to school, arranging care for children, reducing bad habits such as smoking and overeating, and financial management), as well as abstract services (e.g., assisting the participant in better understanding others and themselves, and providing someone with whom to talk).

Following participation in the study, mothers reported high rates of satisfaction with the program and improvements in their parenting and life skills. Both staff and participants reported that positive growth had occurred in 13 areas of the mothers' lives between onset of pregnancy (or entry into the program) and the interview (conducted at least one year after the intervention had begun).

School-Based Programs for Prevention of Child Sexual Abuse

Programs for children and parents that are designed to raise awareness about child sexual abuse is another area where there has been a recent and relatively concentrated research focus. Available research suggests that such programs can be successful at imparting information, but there is little evidence to conclude that these programs actually prevent child sexual abuse. A recent study published in 2000 utilized meta-analysis techniques to evaluate existing school-based, child sexual abuse prevention programs. Based on 27 control group studies, the study reported that children who participated in prevention programs performed significantly higher than control group children on outcome measures used in the studies, indicating improvements in knowledge and skills concerning sexual abuse. In the process of developing the sample of studies to include in the analysis, the researchers indicated that they identified no studies that had analyzed the effect of prevention programs on actual rates of abuse.

Few studies have attempted to establish a relationship between acquisition of knowledge about child sexual abuse and subsequent behavior change in children. In perhaps the only study of its kind, Finkelhor et al. conducted a national telephone survey of 2,000 children ages 10–16. The researchers found that children who had participated in school-based sexual abuse prevention programs not only demonstrated greater knowledge about sexual abuse, but also reported that these children were more likely to exhibit protective behaviors and utilize protective strategies when threatened or victimized.

In a follow-up study conducted the next year, during which a considerable proportion of the original 2,000-child sample was recontacted, the researchers again found that children who had participated in school-based sexual abuse prevention programs were more likely to use protective strategies (e.g., yelling, running, telling an authority). However, there was no evidence that these children, when threatened with abuse, were any more likely to stop the victimization than children who had not participated in school-based sexual abuse prevention programs.

Since then, two recent studies have explored the correlation between knowledge gains and behavior change, and actual victimization. In an important recent study of 825 female undergraduates, for example, researchers found that young women who had not participated in a school-based prevention program were nearly twice as likely to have experienced child sexual abuse as young women who had participated in a program. Also within the last few years, results of a survey of high school students found that students who had participated in a general abuse prevention program were significantly less likely to have reported an incident of physical abuse. There appeared to be no difference between the two groups of students in terms of the incidence of sexual abuse. Both of these studies, however, utilized small, local samples and relied considerably on self-report data of past experiences. Thus, there are important concerns with the generalizability of the results, as well as the vulnerability of the data to the hazards of memory.

Chapter 41

What Does the Child Protection Process Look Like?

This chapter traces the child protection process beginning with the identification and reporting of suspected child maltreatment. Every State has enacted reporting laws. These laws provide guidance to individuals required to identify and report suspected maltreatment, require investigations by specified agencies to determine if a child was abused, and provide for the delivery of protective services and treatment to maltreated children and their families. Reports of maltreatment required under such laws activate the child protection process, which includes:

- Intake
- Initial assessment and investigation
- Family assessment
- Case planning
- Service provision
- Evaluation of family progress
- Case closure

Identification

The first step in any child protection response system is the identification of possible incidents of child maltreatment. Medical personnel,

---

Excerpted from *A Coordinated Response to Child Abuse and Neglect: The Foundation for Practice,* 2003. National Clearinghouse on Child Abuse and Neglect Information. Available online at http://nccanch.acf.hhs.gov/pubs/usermanuals/foundation/chapnine.cfm.

educators, child care providers, mental health professionals, law enforcement personnel, the clergy, and other professionals are often in a position to observe families and children on an ongoing basis and identify abuse or neglect when they occur. Private citizens, such as family members, friends, and neighbors, also may identify suspected incidents of child maltreatment.

To ensure that community professionals working with children and families recognize possible indicators of child maltreatment, preservice and inservice training must be provided on an ongoing basis. In addition, public awareness campaigns should be planned and implemented to promote understanding of the problem in the community.

Reporting

The next step in responding to child maltreatment is to report the suspected incident. Although there is tremendous variation in the requirements described in State reporting laws, they typically:

- Specify selected individuals mandated to report suspected child maltreatment;
- Define reportable conditions;
- Explain how, when, and to whom reports are to be filed and the information to be contained in the report;
- Describe the agencies designated to receive and investigate reports;
- Describe the abrogation of certain privileged communication rights (e.g., doctor-patient);
- Provide immunity from legal liability for reporters;
- Provide penalties for failure to report and false reporting.

Key aspects of reporting laws are described in the sections that follow.

State Statutes

To review a summary of reporting laws, visit the State Statutes section of the National Clearinghouse on Child Abuse and Neglect Web site at www.calib.com/nccanch/statutes.

Mandatory Reporters

Every State has statutes identifying mandatory reporters of child maltreatment and the circumstances under which they are required to report. This designation creates a legal responsibility to report, which can result in criminal and civil liability for failure to report as required. In approximately 18 States, any person who suspects child abuse or neglect is required to report. Most States, however, limit mandatory reporting to professionals working with children. Individuals typically designated as mandatory reporters include:

- Physicians, nurses, hospital personnel, and dentists
- Medical examiners
- Coroners
- Mental health professionals
- Social workers
- School personnel
- Child care providers
- Law enforcement officers

In addition, any person in any State may report incidents of suspected abuse or neglect. The legal standards used to determine when a mandatory reporter is required to notify authorities of abuse or neglect also vary slightly from State to State. Typically, a report must be made when a reporter has reasonable cause to know, suspect, or believe that a child has been abused or neglected.

Reporting Procedures

Every State has reporting laws specifying procedures that a mandatory reporter must follow when making a report of suspected child abuse and neglect. Generally, these procedures specify how, where, when, and what to report.

How and When to Report

The majority of States require that reports of child maltreatment be made orally—either by telephone or in person—to the specified authorities. Some States require that a written report follow the oral report, while in other States written reports are filed only upon request, and still other States require written reports only from mandated reporters.

Reports of suspected maltreatment are required by statute to be made immediately to protect children from potentially serious consequences that may be caused by a delay in reporting. While an individual may want to collect additional information before reporting, waiting for proof may place the child in danger.

Who Receives the Reports

Each State designates specific agencies to receive reports of child abuse and neglect. In most States, child protective services (CPS) has the primary responsibility for receiving reports. Other States allow reports to be made to either CPS or law enforcement. Some State laws require that certain forms of maltreatment—such as sexual abuse, child pornography, or severe physical abuse—be reported to law enforcement in addition to CPS. The nature of the relationship of the alleged perpetrator may also affect where reports are made. Most alleged cases of child maltreatment within the family are reportable to CPS. Depending on the State, reports of allegations of abuse or neglect by other caregivers, such as foster parents, daycare providers, teachers or residential care providers, may need to be filed with a law enforcement office. Additionally, in some States, allegations of abuse in out-of-home care are reported to a centralized investigative body within CPS at the State or regional level.

In most States, statutes also include requirements for cross-system reporting procedures or information sharing among professional entities. Typically, reports are shared among social services agencies, law enforcement, and prosecutors' offices.

Contents of the Report

Reporting laws also describe the information that must be contained in the report. Typically, reports contain the following information:

- The name, age, sex, and address of the child;
- The nature and extent of the child's injuries or condition;
- The name and address of the parent or other person(s) responsible for the child's care;
- Any other information relevant to the investigation.

It is essential that reporters provide as much detailed information as possible about:

- The child, the child's condition, and the child's whereabouts;
- The parents and their whereabouts;
- The person alleged to have caused the child's condition and his or her current location;
- The family, including other children in the home;
- The type and nature of the maltreatment, such as the length of time it has been occurring, whether the maltreatment has increased in severity or frequency, and whether objects or weapons were used.

If the alleged maltreatment occurred in an out-of-home care setting, reporters should provide information about the setting, such as hours of operation; number of other children in the facility, if known; and identification of any others in the facility who may have information about the alleged maltreatment. The more comprehensive the information provided by the reporter, the better able CPS staff will be to evaluate the appropriateness of the report for CPS intervention, determine the urgency of the response needed, and prepare for an initial assessment and investigation, if warranted.

While most States allow anonymous reporting, it is preferred that reporters provide their name and contact information. This information will enable a caseworker to ask follow-up questions or obtain clarification. At intake, caseworkers should discuss immunity for reporters, issues of confidentiality, and the extent and nature of follow up with the reporter upon completion of the initial assessment or investigation.

Special Issues, Exceptions, and Penalties Related to Reporting

To encourage reporting of child maltreatment and provide protection for reporters, State statutes include provisions related to privileged communications, immunity for reporters, and penalties for failure to report. The laws also discourage intentionally false reporting through specified penalties.

Privileged Communications

The law provides special protection to communications in certain relationships. For example, the content of communications between an attorney and client, physician and patient, and clergy and congregant often is protected by a privilege. This means that professionals in such relationships are prohibited from disclosing confidential information communicated to them by their client, patient, or penitent to any unauthorized person. Mandatory child abuse reporting statutes specify when communications are confidential. The attorney-client privilege is most frequently maintained by States. The privilege pertaining to clergy-congregant also is frequently recognized by States. Most States, however, void the physician-patient, mental health professional-patient, and husband-wife privileges in instances of child maltreatment. When a privileged communication is voided, a mandated reporter must report instances of child maltreatment and cooperate in the ensuing investigation.

Immunity to Reporters

Every State provides immunity from civil or criminal liability for individuals making reports of suspected or known instances of child abuse or neglect. Immunity provisions typically apply both to mandatory reporters and permissive reporters (i.e., individuals not required under law to report). These provisions may not prevent the filing of civil lawsuits, but they help prevent, within limitations, an outcome unfavorable to the reporter. Immunity provisions, like other aspects of reporting statutes, vary from State to State. The majority of jurisdictions require that reports be made in good faith. A number of States include a presumption in their statutes that the reporter is acting in good faith. Immunity, therefore, does not extend to reports made maliciously or in bad faith.

Penalties for Failure to Report

To encourage reporting, the majority of States now provide in their reporting statutes a specific penalty for failure to report suspected cases of abuse. Most of these jurisdictions impose penalties on mandatory reporters who knowingly or willfully fail to report suspected abuse. Failure to report is typically classified as a misdemeanor. Sanctions specified in the statutes are generally in the form of a fine or imprisonment.

Penalties for False Reporting

In order to prevent malicious or intentional false reporting, the majority of States impose penalties for false reporting of abuse. Most of these jurisdictions impose penalties on mandatory reporters who knowingly or willfully file a false report of abuse or neglect. False reporting is typically classified as a misdemeanor. Sanctions specified in the statutes are generally in the form of a fine or imprisonment.

Problems in Reporting

Paradoxically, both underreporting and over-reporting have been cited as problems in the identification of child abuse and neglect.

Underreporting

Numerous professionals admit that during their careers, they have failed to report suspected maltreatment to the appropriate agencies. One possible reason is that professionals still lack training and knowledge about legal obligations and procedures for reporting. The issue of subjectivity also may account for some of the underreporting of abuse. Many laws defining child maltreatment are broadly written with ambiguous requirements, which may result in professionals lacking guidance and clarity regarding when intervention is required.

One of the biggest obstacles to reporting is personal feelings. Some people do not want to get involved. Others have difficulty reporting a person they suspect is an abuser, especially if they know that person well. Still others may think they can help the family more by working with the child or family themselves. Mandated reporters may believe that their professional relationship with the child will be strained if they report their suspicions of abuse. When a professional has established a relationship with a parent or family prior to recognizing maltreatment, reporting becomes a delicate issue.

Some reporters also may be reluctant to report because they have had negative experiences with CPS or they view social services agencies as overburdened, understaffed, or incompetent. At times, professionals become concerned that nothing will be done if they report or that the investigation and service provision will do more harm than good. Consequently, they choose not to report. This reluctance to report, which can have serious consequences for a child in an unsafe situation, underscores the critical need for ongoing communication and feedback between CPS and mandated reporters. It also underscores the need for CPS to function sensitively and competently in the best interests of the child while creating as little disruption as possible.

Professionals must report regardless of their concerns or previous experiences. The law requires it, and no exemptions are granted to those who have had a bad experience. In addition, while reporting does not guarantee that the situation will improve, not reporting guarantees that, if abuse and neglect exists, the child will continue to be at risk of further and perhaps more serious harm.

Over-Reporting

Only a portion of reports received and investigated by CPS reflect children who are found to be victims of, or at risk for, maltreatment. While the children and families in these reports may be in need of help or services, they frequently do not meet the legal definition of maltreatment in that family's jurisdiction. This apparent pattern of over-reporting raises several concerns. First, children and families who will not receive child welfare services may be subjected to an intrusive public agency investigation. Second, these reports may divert CPS resources from higher risk cases. Over-reporting may occur in a community following a serious case of child maltreatment that receives a lot of media attention. There is often a significant increase in the number of reports of suspected child maltreatment made during such times, in part because the community's awareness has been heightened.

Intake

Intake is the point at which reports of suspected child maltreatment are received by the agency designated by the State (typically the CPS agency and sometimes the police department). The agency receiving the report must make two primary decisions at intake:

- Does the reported information meet the statutory and agency guidelines for child maltreatment?
- How urgent is the required response?

The first decision consists of three essential steps:

1. Gathering sufficient information from the reporter to allow accurate decision-making;
2. Evaluating the information to determine if it meets the statutory and agency guidelines for child maltreatment;
3. Assessing the credibility of the reporter based on the relationship of the alleged victim and family, knowledge of the family and circumstances, and apparent motives for reporting.

There will be a check of agency records and State central registries to determine if the family is currently involved in an open case or has a history of involvement in a maltreatment case. (A central registry is a database containing information on all previously substantiated reports of child maltreatment.)

When the agency determines that an initial assessment or investigation is warranted, the report is "screened in"; cases closed without further investigation are referred to as "screened out." While screening rates vary substantially across States, CPS agencies screened in and investigated approximately 62 percent of the nearly 3 million report referrals received nationwide in 2000. In some instances, screened out cases will receive referrals to other community services (e.g., substance abuse treatment, mental health services, child care, domestic violence shelters, or income support agencies).

Once the CPS agency determines that an initial assessment is warranted, the immediacy of the response is evaluated. The decision regarding the urgency of the response is based on an analysis of the information gathered to determine if the child is at imminent risk of serious harm. This decision will be based upon a number of factors including:

- The nature of the act or omission;
- The severity of harm to the child;
- The relationship of the child to the person responsible for the maltreatment;
- The access of the perpetrator to the child;
- The child's vulnerability (e.g., due to age, illness, or disability);
- The other known cases of maltreatment by the parent or caregiver;
- The availability of persons who can protect the child.

Some CPS agencies provide guidelines for initial assessment response times, although it is difficult to generalize. Caseworkers are required to respond to reports within a specified time, typically ranging from 24 to 72 hours on more serious cases. If it is determined that the child in a report may not be safe, caseworkers must respond immediately.

Initial Assessment or Investigation

The initial assessment or investigation follows the intake process for those reports that are screened in.

Primary Initial Assessment or Investigation Decisions

The purpose of the initial assessment or investigation of cases of child abuse and neglect is to determine the following:

- Is child maltreatment substantiated as defined by State statute?
- Is the child at risk of maltreatment and what is the level of risk?
- Is the child safe, and if not, what type of agency or community response will ensure the child's safety in the least intrusive manner?
- If the child's safety cannot be assured within the family, what type and level of care does the child need?
- Does the family have emergency needs that must be met?
- Should ongoing agency services be offered to the family to reduce the risk or address the treatment needs of the child?

CPS agencies and law enforcement are each responsible for conducting initial assessments or investigations in cases of child abuse and neglect. Table 41.1 presents the primary decisions or issues considered at this stage according to the agency that typically considers the decision.

Major Types of Investigation Dispositions

Substantiated is an investigation disposition that concludes that the allegation of maltreatment or risk of maltreatment was supported or founded by State law or State policy. This is the highest level of finding by a State Agency.

Indicated or Reason to Suspect is an investigation disposition that concludes that maltreatment cannot be substantiated under State law or policy, but there is reason to suspect that the child may have been maltreated or was at risk of maltreatment. This is applicable only to States that distinguish between substantiated and indicated dispositions.

Not Substantiated is an investigation disposition that determines that there is not sufficient evidence under State law or policy to conclude that the child has been maltreated or is at risk of being maltreated.

Involvement of Other Professionals

In addition to CPS and law enforcement, other disciplines have a role to play in the initial assessment process:

Medical personnel may be involved in assessing and responding to the medical needs of a child or parent and perhaps in documenting the nature and extent of maltreatment. It is helpful to have

Table 41.1. Primary Decisions Considered during Initial Assessment or Investigation

CPS

- Is the child safe? If not, what measures are necessary to ensure the child's safety?
- Did the child suffer maltreatment or is he or she threatened by harm as defined by the State reporting law?
- Is maltreatment likely to occur in the future? If so, what is the level of risk of maltreatment?
- Are there emergency needs in the family that must be met?
- Are continuing agency services necessary to protect the child and reduce the risk of maltreatment occurring in the future?

Law Enforcement

- Did a crime occur?
- Who is the alleged offender?
- Is there evidence to arrest the alleged offender?
- Has all physical evidence been obtained, preserved, and/or photographed?
- Have all witnesses been interviewed?

CPS and Law Enforcement

- Do sources of corroboration or witnesses exist?
- Has all physical evidence been obtained or preserved?
- Are there any other victims (e.g., siblings)?
- Should the child be taken into protective custody?

medical practitioners in each community who have had specific training in child maltreatment because they will provide a more complete and accurate evaluation than will an examiner without specific training.

Mental health personnel may be involved in assessing the effects of any alleged maltreatment and in determining the validity of specific allegations. At this stage of the CPS process, referrals to mental health providers are primarily for help in determining whether abuse occurred, whether there is sufficient information to file charges related to child maltreatment, and whether the child is capable of providing valid and reliable information. In addition, referrals to mental health practitioners may be made for assistance in assessing the safety of the child. For example, parents or caregivers may be referred for an evaluation of their mental status, the presence of psychiatric problems, personality disorders, or substance abuse.

Teachers and child care providers may be involved in providing direct information about the effects of maltreatment and in describing information pertinent to risk assessment. In addition, during the investigative stage, educators provide support for the efforts of CPS and law enforcement. For example, if the CPS caseworker or law enforcement needs to interview the child in the school, the school should provide a private place for the interview.

Foster care, residential, or child care licensing personnel may participate in the initial assessment if abuse is allegedly committed by an out-of-home caregiver. Each State differs with respect to who is responsible for initially assessing or investigating allegations of child abuse and neglect in out-of-home care. In some States, local CPS staffs have responsibility for investigating certain types of allegations, for example, those in foster care and daycare. Frequently, the investigation of alleged maltreatment in institutional settings is handled by central or regional CPS or licensing staff, rather than by local CPS agencies. Depending on the nature of the allegations, law enforcement agencies also will assume a primary role in investigating these types of cases.

Other community service providers also may have past experience with the child or family and may be used as a resource in addressing any emergency needs that the child or family may have.

Differential Response Systems

Over the past decade, States have begun to enhance CPS practice and build community partnerships in responding to cases of child maltreatment. One area of CPS reform emphasizes greater flexibility in responding to allegations of abuse and neglect. A dual track or multiple track response permits CPS agencies to respond differentially according to the children's safety, the degree of risk present, and the family's needs for support services. Implementation models vary across States piloting differential response systems. Typically, in cases where abuse and neglect are severe or serious criminal offenses against children have occurred, an investigation will commence. The investigation focuses on evidence gathering and may include a referral to law enforcement. In less serious cases of child maltreatment, where the family may benefit from community services, an assessment will be conducted. In these cases the facts regarding what happened will be obtained, but the intervention will emphasize the comprehensive assessment of family strengths and needs and an appropriate match with community services.

The assessment is designed to be a process where parents or caregivers are partners with CPS, and that partnership begins with the very first contact. In addition, the family's support network is frequently brought into the process. States that have implemented the differential response strategy have shown that a majority of cases now coming to CPS can be handled safely through an approach that emphasizes service delivery and voluntary family participation as well as the fact finding of traditional CPS investigations.

Investigation in Out-of-Home Care Settings

In cases of child maltreatment in out-of-home care (e.g., residential facilities, foster homes), an investigation must be completed by an independent authority designated by the State. For cases involving out-of-home care abuse, there are other decisions and issues to consider:

- Did the reported event occur?
- Are personnel actions indicated and, if so, are they being initiated appropriately by the child care facility?
- What responsibility do others in the facility have for any incident of maltreatment, and is a corrective action plan needed to prevent the likelihood of future incidents?

- Can the problem, if validated, be addressed administratively?
- Is the administrative authority responsible and, if so, in what manner?
- Should the facility's or foster care or other child care provider's license be revoked?

These decisions are made by thoroughly gathering and analyzing information from and about the child, family, or in some cases, the out-of-home provider. Typically, a protocol is employed for interviewing the child victim, family members, the person alleged to have maltreated the child, and others possessing information about the child and the family.

Family Assessment

The family assessment is a comprehensive process for identifying, considering, and weighing factors that affect the child's safety, permanency, and well-being. The family assessment is a process designed to gain a greater understanding about the strengths, needs, and resources of the family so that children can be safe and the risk of maltreatment can be reduced. The family assessment is initiated immediately after the decision is made that ongoing services are needed. The following are the key decisions made as a result of the family assessment:

- What are the risks and needs of this family that affect safety, permanency, or well-being?
- What are the effects of maltreatment that affect safety, permanency, and well-being?
- What are the individual and family strengths?
- How do the family members perceive their conditions, problems, and strengths?
- What must change in order for the effects of maltreatment to be addressed and for the risk of maltreatment to be reduced or eliminated?
- What is the parent's or caregiver's level of readiness for change? What is their motivation and capacity to assure safety, permanency, and well-being?

Family assessment should be strengths-based, culturally sensitive, and developed with the family. In addition to gathering information regarding problems, risks, and needs, strengths should be identified that may mitigate the identified concern(s) and the family's stated goals as they relate to each problem. The strengths identified will provide the foundation upon which the family can change.

Assessments should be conducted in a partnership with the family to help parents or caregivers recognize and remedy conditions so children can safely remain in their own home. Family assessments must be individualized and tailored to the unique strengths and needs of each family. When possible, this assessment also should be undertaken in conjunction with the extended family and support network through family decision-making meetings and other processes designed to involve this network in the process.

Planning

The comprehensive assessment of the family's circumstances and conditions is the foundation on which the case plan is built. Armed with this knowledge, CPS caseworkers, other service providers or community professionals, and the family and its support network will determine the best possible strategies for reducing or eliminating the behaviors and conditions contributing to the risk of maltreatment of the child. The purposes of case planning are to identify the strategies with clients that will help address the effects of maltreatment and lessen the risk of further abuse and neglect; to provide a clear and specific guide for the professional and the family for changing the behaviors and conditions that impact risk; to provide a benchmark for measuring client progress toward achieving outcomes; and to provide a framework for case decision-making.

The key decisions made at the case planning stage are:

- What are the client outcomes that, when achieved, will indicate that risk has been reduced and the effects of maltreatment have been successfully addressed?
- What goals must be accomplished to achieve the outcomes?
- What intervention approaches or services will facilitate the successful goal achievement and the accomplishment of outcomes?
- How and when will progress toward achievement of these outcomes and goals be evaluated?

In order to achieve the client outcomes, the case plan must be developed with, not for, the family. Involving the family in planning serves several purposes. It facilitates the family's investment in and commitment to the plan, it empowers parents or caregivers to take the necessary action to change behavior, and ensures that the agency and the family are working toward the same end. Some CPS agencies use models that optimize family strengths in the planning process. These models bring together the family, the extended family, and others important in the family's life—for example, friends, clergy, neighbors—to make decisions regarding how best to ensure the safety of the family members.

Concurrent Planning

The passage of the Adoption and Safe Families Act (ASFA) in 1997 has resulted in time limits for permanency for children and termination of parental rights so that children are provided safe, stable, and permanent placements more quickly. Concurrent planning works toward reunification of children in care with their birth families while at the same time establishing a back-up permanency plan that will be implemented if the children cannot be reunified with their birth family. The concurrent plan provides a safeguard to assure secure childhood attachments by developing a stronger bond to the birth families and simultaneously supporting ties between the child and other possible permanent families, for example, kin or foster parents. Concurrent permanency plans provide a structured approach to move children quickly from temporary foster care to the stability of a safe and continuous family home.

Service Provision

Once the case plan has been developed, the CPS caseworker must provide or arrange for services identified in the plan to help family members achieve the outcomes, goals, and tasks outlined in the case plan. Selecting and matching interventions that will support the family in achieving outcomes and goals is a major responsibility in child protection.

The needs of families are often complex. Child abuse and neglect is caused by multiple and interacting intrapersonal, interpersonal, and environmental factors. Interventions need to address as many of these contributing issues as possible. Research on the effectiveness of child abuse and neglect treatment suggests that successful intervention with maltreating families requires addressing both the interpersonal and concrete needs (e.g., housing, child care) of all family members. Evaluation projects found that programs that rely solely upon professional therapy, without augmenting the service strategies with other supportive or remedial services to children and families, will offer less opportunity for maximizing client gains.

Therefore, each community must provide a broad range of services to meet the multidimensional needs of abused and neglected children and their families. These may include:

- Services provided to the entire family (e.g., family preservation services, multisystemic therapy for children and families, or family strengthening programs);
- Services provided specifically to parents or caregivers (e.g., sex offender treatment, parent education, substance abuse treatment, or mutual support programs);
- Services provided to children (e.g., counseling, therapeutic preschool, peer-based training, or mentoring programs).

Depending on the assessed needs, strengths, and safety issues, services may be provided either in or out of the family's home. When a child is unsafe because the risk of imminent harm is great or when the child's behavioral and emotional needs cannot be addressed at home, out-of-home placement services, such as foster care, should be considered.

Selection of services in a particular case is based on:

- Assessing factors that contribute to the risk of maltreatment;
- Identifying family strengths;
- Targeting outcomes for change;
- Identifying treatment approaches best suited to the desired outcome, based on any available research evidence;
- Listing resources available and accessible in the community.

The CPS caseworker serves as the case manager, articulating the needs of the family, coordinating services provided to them, and advocating on their behalf. The case management functions include: collecting and analyzing information, reaching decisions at all stages of the case process, coordinating services provided by others, and directly providing supportive services. This critical case-management function requires open and continuous communication among CPS, the family, and other service providers; developing a teamwork relationship;

clarifying roles and responsibilities in delivering and monitoring services; and reaching consensus on goals and methods for monitoring progress toward goal achievement.

Evaluation of Family Progress

Evaluating whether risk behaviors and conditions have changed is central to case decisions. Monitoring change should begin as soon as an intervention is implemented and should continue throughout the life of a case until appropriate outcomes have been achieved.

The importance of evaluating family progress is to help answer the following questions:

- Is the child safe? Have the protective factors, strengths, or the safety factors changed, warranting a change or elimination of the safety plan or the development of a safety plan?
- What changes, if any, have occurred with respect to the conditions and behaviors contributing to the risk of maltreatment?
- What outcomes have been accomplished and how does the caseworker know that they have been accomplished?
- What progress has been made toward achieving case goals?
- Have the services been effective in helping clients achieve outcomes and goals and, if not, what adjustments need to be made to improve outcomes?
- What is the current level of risk in the family?
- Have the risk factors been reduced sufficiently so that parents or caregivers can protect their children and meet their developmental needs so the case can be closed?
- Has it been determined that reunification is not likely in the ASFA-required time frames and there is no significant progress toward outcomes? If so, is an alternative permanent plan goal needed?

Since intervention and service provision to families at risk of maltreatment is a collaborative effort between CPS and other agencies or individual providers, the evaluation of family progress must be a collaborative venture. It is the CPS caseworker's responsibility to manage the comparison of client progress based on information reported from all service providers. In some cases, it may be appropriate to convene a team meeting to review the progress in relation to the family assessment and the case plan.

The process of evaluating family progress is a continual case management function. Once the case plan is established, each client contact will be focused on assessing the progress being made to achieve established outcomes, goals, and tasks, and to reassess safety. Formal case evaluations should occur at regular intervals. Good practice suggests evaluation of progress at least every 3 months.

Case Closure

Closure is the point at which the agency no longer maintains an active relationship with the family. The decision to end the agency's involvement must be based on the monitoring and evaluation of the case. ASFA requires decisions regarding case closure to be made in conjunction with the family and individuals important to the family. The preeminent concerns that inform case closure decisions are based on safety and permanency outcomes. The agency should support the family's right to self-determination by ending services when the risks to child safety have been reduced significantly and the family believes they no longer need services.

Chapter 42

Government Programs Related to the Welfare of Children

Approximately 879,000 children were found to be victims of child maltreatment in 2000. Maltreatment categories typically include neglect, medical neglect, physical abuse, sexual abuse, and psychological maltreatment. Almost two-thirds of child victims (63%) suffered neglect (including medical neglect); 19 percent were physically abused; 10 percent were sexually abused; and 8 percent were psychologically maltreated. Child fatalities are the most tragic consequence of maltreatment. Approximately 1,200 children died of abuse or neglect in the year 2000—a rate of 1.71 children per 100,000 children in the population. The increase in the rate of fatalities compared to earlier years is hypothesized to be largely attributable to improved reporting. Youngest children were the most vulnerable. Children younger than one year old accounted for 44 percent of child fatalities and 85 percent of child fatalities were younger than 6 years of age.

Children in foster care numbered 556,000 in September 2000. Most of these children will return to their homes, but more than 70,000 cannot return safely. Many of these children are considered to have special needs because they are older, members of minority or sibling groups, or physically, mentally or emotionally disabled. They often need special assistance in finding adoptive homes. During fiscal year (FY) 2001, over 250,000 children received Title IV-E adoption

---

"Child Welfare: Protecting the Well-Being of Children," from the Administration on Children, Youth and Families, Department of Health and Human Services, 2002. Available online at http://www.acf.dhhs.gov/news/facts/chilwelf.html.

assistance, which is a subsidy to families who adopt special needs children.

Foster Care/Adoption Assistance/Independent Living

For those children who cannot remain safely in their homes, foster care provides a stable environment that assures a child's safety and well-being while their parents attempt to resolve the problems that led to the out of home placement. When the family cannot be reunified, foster care provides a stable environment until the child can be placed permanently with an adoptive family. Authorized under title IV-E of the Social Security Act, Foster Care and Adoption Assistance programs provide Federal matching funds of 50 to 80 percent, depending on the state's per capita income, to states which directly administer the programs. Under Foster Care, funds are available for monthly payments to foster care providers on behalf of foster children. These payments vary from state to state.

Under Adoption Assistance, funds are available for a one-time payment for the costs of adopting a child as well as for monthly subsidies to adoptive families for care of the child (who is eligible for welfare under the former Aid For Dependent Children (AFDC) program or for Supplemental Security Income). Similar to Foster Care, the amounts vary from state to state.

Additionally, funds received under Foster Care and Adoption Assistance are used by states to assist costs related to child placement and case management activities; training for staff, foster parents, and adoptive parents; foster and adoptive parent recruitment; and other relevant expenses. Assistance is also available to current or former foster care youth age 16 and older to help in the transition to independent living. The Independent Living program provides grants to states for education and employment assistance, training in daily living skills, and individual and group counseling.

In December 1999, The Foster Care Independence Act of 1999 was signed into law. This legislation helps ensure that young people who leave foster care get the tools they need to make the most of their lives. It empowers them by providing better educational opportunities, access to health care, training, housing assistance, counseling and other services.

The Act increased the annual funding for the Independent Living program and expanded the services and supports available to help prepare foster care youth for the transition to adulthood. These programs are funded jointly by the federal and state governments.

Monthly payments to families and institutions vary from state to state. Under the new legislation, states are now required to serve youth up to 21years old, enabling more young people to obtain a college education. It also enables states to provide time-limited financial assistance to help these youth with living expenses as they develop the skills and education needed to move successfully into the workforce. In addition, the new law gives states the option to let these young people remain eligible for Medicaid up to age 21.

In FY 2002, funding for Foster Care is $5.05 billion, $1.4 billion for Adoption Assistance and $140 million for Independent Living.

Promoting Safe and Stable Families

The primary goals of Promoting Safe and Stable Families (PSSF) are to prevent the unnecessary separation of children from their families, improve the quality of care and services to children and their families, and ensure permanency for children by reuniting them with their parents, by adoption or by another permanent living arrangement. The programs include: family support, family preservation, time-limited family reunification and adoption promotion and support services.

The services are designed to help State child welfare agencies and eligible Indian tribes establish and operate integrated, preventive family preservation services and community-based family support services for families at risk or in crisis. Funds go directly to child welfare agencies and eligible Indian tribes to bc used in accordance with their 5-year plans. Other grant funds are set aside for nationally funded evaluation, research, and training and technical assistance projects. In addition, funds are set-aside for court improvement programs.

PSSF services are based on several key principles. The welfare and safety of children and of all family members should be maintained while strengthening and preserving the family. It is advantageous for the family as a whole to receive services which identify and enhance its strengths while meeting individual and family needs. Services should be easily accessible, often delivered in the home or in community-based settings, and they should respect cultural and community differences. In addition, they should be flexible, responsive to real family needs, and linked to other supports and services outside the child welfare system. Services should involve community organizations and residents, including parents, in their design and delivery. They should be intensive enough to keep children safe and meet family needs, varying between preventive and crisis services. Funding for Promoting Safe and Stable Families was $305 million in 2002.

Child Abuse and Neglect Prevention and Treatment

The Child Abuse Prevention and Treatment Act (CAPTA) funds States and grantees in several different ways: by providing funds and technical assistance for prevention and intervention; supporting research, service improvement programs, and demonstration projects; collecting data about the problem, its consequences, and the effectiveness of prevention and treatment services; facilitating information dissemination and exchange; and supporting policy development and professional education.

Community-based Family Resource and Support Grants fund statewide networks of local child abuse and neglect prevention and family resource programs. To receive these funds, states must have in place a trust fund or other funding mechanism that pools Federal, state, and private funds and makes them available for child abuse and neglect prevention and family resource programs. Funding was $33.4 million in FY 2002.

Basic State Grants provide assistance in developing, strengthening, and implementing child abuse and neglect prevention and treatment programs. Funding was $22 million in FY 2002. Federal funds also support research on the causes, prevention, and treatment of child abuse and neglect. These demonstration programs identify the best means of preventing maltreatment and treating troubled families. Funding was $26 million in FY 2002.

Child Welfare Services

The Child Welfare Services program provides grants to states and Indian tribes under title IV-B of the Social Security Act. Services are available to children and their families without regard to income. Publicly funded Child Welfare Services are directed toward the goal of keeping families together. They include preventive intervention so that, if possible, children will not have to be removed from their homes. If this is not possible, placements and permanent homes through foster care or adoption can be made. In addition, reunification services are available to encourage the return home, when appropriate, of children who have been removed from their families.

Each state receives a base amount of $70,000. Additional funds are distributed in proportion to the state's population of children under age 21 multiplied by the complement of the state's average per capita income. The state match requirement is 25 percent. Funding was approximately $292 million in FY 2002.

The Department of Health and Human Services, Administration on Children and Families (HHS/ACF) has other programs that address the welfare of children at risk. The Adoption Opportunities program eliminates barriers to adoption and helps to find permanent homes for children, particularly those with special needs, who would benefit by adoption. In FY 2002, funding for Adoption Opportunities was $27.3 million.

The Abandoned Infants Assistance program provides grants to help identify ways to prevent the abandonment of children in hospitals and to identify and address the needs of infants and young children, particularly those with acquired immune deficiency syndrome (AIDS) and prenatal drug or alcohol exposure. In FY 2002, $12.2 million was available for Abandoned Infants Assistance. The Infant Adoption Awareness Training program has funded grantees to develop curricula and implement training programs to train designated staff of eligible health centers in providing adoption information and referrals to pregnant women on an equal basis with all other courses of action included in non-directive counseling to pregnant women. In FY 2001, $8.6 million was awarded to four grantees to implement this new program, which was enacted in October 2000. In FY 2002, $9.9 million was available.

Special Initiatives

Better Outcomes for Children

The 1994 Amendments to the Social Security Act (SSA) authorize the U.S. Department of Health and Human Services (DHHS) to review State child and family service programs to ensure conformance with the requirements in titles IV-B and IV-E of the SSA. Traditionally, reviews have focused primarily on assessing State agencies' compliance with procedural requirements, as evidenced by case file documentation, rather than on the results of services and States' capacity to create positive outcomes for children and families. In addition, reviews have not provided States with opportunities for making improvements before penalties have been imposed.

On January 25, 2000, the DHHS published a final rule in the Federal Register to establish a new approach to monitoring State child welfare programs. Under the rule, which became effective March 25,

2000, States will be assessed for substantial conformity with certain Federal requirements for child protective, foster care, adoption, family preservation and family support, and independent living services. The Children's is administering the new review system. The system comprises two review components: (1) child and family services and (2) title IV-E foster care eligibility reviews.

The new child and family services reviews are an important tool that will enable the Children's Bureau to accomplish the following: (1) ensure conformity with Federal child welfare requirements; (2) determine what is actually happening to children and families as they are engaged in child welfare services; and (3) assist States to enhance their capacity to help children and families achieve positive outcomes.

Ultimately, the goal of the reviews is to help States to improve child welfare services and achieve the following outcomes for families and children who receive services:

Safety: Children are, first and foremost, protected from abuse and neglect. Children are safely maintained in their homes whenever possible and appropriate.

Permanency: Children have permanency and stability in their living situations. The continuity of family relationships and connections is preserved for families.

Family and Child Well-Being: Families have enhanced capacity to provide for their children's needs. Children receive appropriate services to meet their educational needs. Children receive adequate services to meet their physical and mental health needs.

The Federal government conducts the reviews in partnership with State child welfare agency staff; peer consultants round out the review teams. The reviews are structured to help States identify strengths and areas for improvement within their agencies and programs. Technical assistance is provided to the States to help them make improvements in identified areas.

State Child Welfare Waiver Demonstrations

Under authority from Congress, HHS could approve Child Welfare Demonstration Projects for up to 10 states a year in each of the five Fiscal Years 1998–2002. Under this initiative, HHS could waive certain provisions of the titles IV-B and IV-E of the Social Security Act (while maintaining all protections for children in foster care) and states could carry out demonstration projects to test innovations in service delivery and financing in order to strengthen outcomes for children and families involved with the child welfare system. All demonstrations are required to have a rigorous, independent evaluation and must be cost-neutral. Currently, there are 21 demonstration projects being implemented in 18 States (several States have more than one project). States with currently approved projects are: California, Colorado, Connecticut, Delaware, Illinois, Indiana, Maine, Maryland, Michigan, Mississippi, Montana, New Hampshire, New Mexico, North Carolina, Ohio, Oregon, Texas, Washington). The states will be expanding the array and improving the quality of child welfare services currently available. Among the innovations being tested are assisted guardianship/kinship permanence, managed care/ capitated payment systems, the flexible use of Federal funds at the community level, intensive service options, substance abuse services, and tribal administration of title IV-E foster care funds.

National Adoption Internet Photolisting Service— AdoptUSKids

The Children's Bureau is implementing a project to operate and maintain the National Adoption Internet Photolisting Web site, AdoptUSKids, and a National Adoption Information Exchange System. The purpose of this initiative is to eliminate barriers to adoption and to provide permanent homes for children who would benefit from adoption, particularly children with special needs, including infants with life-threatening conditions. The website and information exchange are designed to link eligible children with qualified prospective adoptive parents and to promote national recruitment efforts to reach prospective parents for children awaiting adoption. The initiative will implement a national public education campaign about the adoption of children with special needs. It will also provide training and technical assistance to State and Tribal child welfare and adoption agencies on recruitment planning to develop an adequate pool of adoptive families that represent the ethnic and racial diversity of children in the State for whom adoptive families are needed. Recruitment efforts will also target foster families since 64% of the children adopted from the foster care system in FY 1999 were adopted by foster parents. The project will provide assistance to support groups for adoptive parents, adopted children and siblings of adopted children. Studies will be conducted to identify the barriers to completing adoptions and pinpoint the factors that lead to favorable long-term outcomes for families that adopt children with special needs.

Chapter 43

The Adoption and Safe Families Act (ASFA)

What is the Adoption and Safe Families Act?

The Adoption and Safe Families Act (ASFA), Public Law 105-89, was enacted in November 1997 with bipartisan support. ASFA amends the 1980 Adoption Assistance and Child Welfare Act by taking further steps to promote safety and permanence for children who have been alleged or determined to be abused and/or neglected. Congress and the Administration were especially concerned about reports that children were being left in, or returned from foster care to, unsafe family situations and that an estimated 100,000 children were in foster care waiting for adoptive families. ASFA includes a number of specific provisions that require or provide incentives for states to change policies and practices to better promote children's safety and adoption or other permanency options. ASFA also requires the Department of Health and Human Services (HHS) and the U.S. General Accounting Office (GAO) to prepare several reports to assist Congress in making future decisions on behalf of children in the child welfare system. ASFA provides a unique opportunity to begin to move children who have been lingering in foster care without permanent plans into permanent homes. By clearing the system of these cases, the child welfare system should better be able to respond to children just entering care so they and their families can get the help they need and prompt permanency decisions can be made.

Children's Defense Fund, "Adoption and Safe Families Act Basics," Washington, DC. 2000.

What does ASFA do to help keep children safe?

ASFA enhances children's safety by:

Specifying that a child's health and safety must be paramount when decisions are made about the initial removal of a child from his or her home, the return home, and the care a child receives while in foster care or in an adoptive family.

Clarifying that there is nothing in federal law requiring that a child remain in or be returned to an unsafe home. Federal law requires that state child welfare agencies make reasonable efforts to prevent the unnecessary placement of children in foster care and to reunify children in foster care with their families. ASFA includes specific examples where it would not be reasonable to require services to reunify children with their families and invites states to establish others in state law, if they have not already. The situations specified in ASFA where reasonable efforts are not required include where a court determines that a parent has committed murder or voluntary manslaughter of another of his/her children or a felony assault that results in serious bodily injury to his/her child; a parent has subjected the child to aggravated circumstances as defined in state law; or the parental rights to a sibling of the child have been involuntarily terminated.

What are the primary ways that ASFA promotes adoption and other permanency options for children?

ASFA intends to promote adoption and other permanency options by:

Establishing expedited timelines for determining whether children who enter foster care can be moved into permanent homes promptly—their own homes, adoptive homes or other planned permanent living arrangements. Two new timelines are imposed. First, permanency hearings must be held for children no later than 12 months after they enter foster care (6 months earlier than under prior law). Second, state agencies must review their existing caseloads and track new children entering care so that termination of parental rights (TPR) proceedings will be initiated for children who have been under the responsibility of the state for 15 out of the most recent 22 months, unless, in individual cases, certain exceptions apply.

Requiring that termination of parental rights proceedings be initiated in additional circumstances—when a child is an abandoned infant, or in cases where a parent has committed murder, voluntary manslaughter, or felony assault of another of his/her children. Again, in individual cases, certain exceptions might be applied even in these situations.

Offering adoption incentive payments for states that increase their adoptions of foster children over a base year. States that increase the number of adoptions of foster children in a given fiscal year over a base year will receive a bonus for each child adopted above the base year number.

Does the new TPR provision mean that parents' rights automatically will be terminated after a child is in care for a defined period of time?

No. ASFA requires that termination of parental rights proceedings be initiated when a child is in foster care for 15 out of the most recent 22 months. Once the TPR petition is filed and the proceedings are initiated, a court must determine first whether there are grounds for termination of the parents' rights (eventually both parents rights must be terminated for a child to be free for adoption), and second whether it would be in the child's best interest to do so.

What exceptions does ASFA provide to the requirement that a TPR petition be filed?

ASFA clearly associates termination of parental rights with adoption. It requires that the state agency, concurrently with its filing of a TPR petition, must identify, recruit, process, and approve a qualified family for adoption. It then specifies several circumstances that may make termination inappropriate at a particular time. ASFA includes three circumstances in which a decision could be made in an individual case that a TPR petition should not be filed, even though the child has been in care for 15 out of 22 months or one of the serious offenses by a parent against a child has been committed.

The exceptions are:

1. The child is in the care of a relative;
2. The state agency documents a compelling reason why filing is not in the best interest of the child; or

3. The state agency has not provided to the child's family, consistent with the time period in the case plan, the services deemed necessary to return the child to a safe home.

The recently issued ASFA regulations emphasize the importance of these exceptions being applied on a case-by-case basis. Decisions about the appropriateness of pursuing termination of parental rights, just like decisions about reasonable efforts and permanency plans, should be based on the individual needs of each child and family. It also is important to remember that ASFA requires that permanency plans for the child continue to be scrutinized after the first permanency hearing until a child is in a permanent placement. The court must continue to make a determination that reasonable efforts to move a child toward permanence are being made, there must be reviews at least every six months of the child's status, and a subsequent permanency hearing must be held at least every twelve months.

In making decisions about the appropriateness of initiating termination of parental rights proceedings, efforts should be made not to overburden the courts with cases in which termination is neither necessary nor appropriate. Clearly if adoption is the plan, termination is both necessary and appropriate. However, if the permanency plan is something else, such as permanent placement with a legal guardian for whom adoption has been ruled out, the steps to move toward that goal will be different.

Which children in care do the new ASFA permanency timelines apply to?

The new timelines in ASFA apply to all children entering foster care after November 19, 1997 (the effective date of ASFA), as well as those children already in care on that date.

- The timing of permanency hearings for all children will be moved up to within 12 months of the date the child enters foster care, or in the case of children already in care, 12 months from the last permanency hearing (referred to previously as a "dispositional" hearing).
- The 15 out of the most recent 22 months clock for filing a TPR petition begins running when a child enters foster care, for those entering after November 19, 1997. For children already in care on November 19, 1997, states are required to phase in the filing of TPR petitions beginning with children for whom the

permanency plan is adoption or who have been in care the longest. Generally, a state agency has 18 months from the end of its state's first legislative session that began after November 19, 1997, to review its caseload and to file TPRs for the children for whom they are appropriate.

Is it true that a state will get a bonus for every foster child who is adopted?

No. ASFA provides for a bonus to a state only for adoptions that represent an increase over the number of adoptions achieved in an established base period in that state. For example, if 250 adoptions is the base level, and 253 children are adopted in a specific fiscal year, the state will receive bonus payments for only three children. The bonuses are $4,000 for each foster child adopted above the base and an additional $2,000 ($6,000 total) if the child has special needs and is eligible for the federal Adoption Assistance program. (A capped amount of $20 million was originally set aside for these bonuses, and that amount has been increased to $43 million for at least fiscal year (FY) 2000). It is also important that ASFA requires states to use their bonus funds for child welfare services, including post adoption services.

What other provisions in ASFA will help promote permanence for children?

The following provisions in ASFA all were intended by Congress to help promote prompt permanence for children in foster care:

Reasonable efforts toward permanence. ASFA explicitly requires that when a child in foster care cannot be reunified with family members, state agencies must make reasonable efforts to place the child in a timely manner in accordance with the child's permanency plan and to complete whatever steps are necessary to finalize the plan. These steps, including specific recruitment efforts to find adoptive families, must be documented in the child's case plan. Consistent with this, ASFA clarifies that reasonable efforts to place a child for adoption or with a legal guardian may be made concurrently with reasonable efforts to reunify a child.

Continuation of the Family Preservation and Support Services Program. ASFA changes the name of this program to the Promoting Safe and Stable Families program and continues funding for three years, increasing it $20 million each year. It also expands the uses of the program funds to explicitly require that significant portions of the funds be used for family reunification and adoption promotion activities, as well as for family support and family preservation activities. These were the only new resources in ASFA, other than the adoption bonuses.

Attention to geographic barriers to adoption. ASFA requires state agencies to develop plans for the effective use of cross-jurisdictional resources to facilitate timely adoptive or permanent placements for waiting children. States also are prohibited from denying or delaying a child's adoptive placement when an approved family is available outside of the jurisdiction.

Expanded health coverage for adopted children with special needs. States not already providing health coverage to adopted children with special needs for whom there is an adoption assistance agreement through Medicaid or their own state funds are required to do so.

Notice and right to be heard for certain caregivers. ASFA requires that foster parents and any pre-adoptive parents or relatives caring for a child in foster care must be given notice of, and an opportunity to be heard in, any reviews or hearings involving the child. Although some states already do this, others do not. ASFA specifically states that it is not requiring party status for all of these caregivers.

Continuing eligibility for federal adoption assistance. Children who were previously adopted and eligible for the federal Adoption Assistance program under Title IV-E of the Social Security Act, but whose earlier adoption was dissolved (because the parent died or the parents' rights were terminated) will continue to be eligible for Title IV-E Adoption Assistance payments if adopted again after October 1, 1997.

Use of Federal Parent Locator Service. State child welfare agencies are authorized to use the Federal Parent Locator Services to assist in locating absent parents for the purpose of making or enforcing child custody or visitation orders, including termination of parental rights proceedings.

Congressional encouragement of standby guardianship laws. ASFA includes a Sense of the Congress that states should have laws and procedures that would permit a parent who is chronically ill or near death to designate a standby guardian for their children without surrendering their own rights. This standby guardian could step in temporarily when the parent is incapacitated, and permanently if the parent should die.

Does ASFA provide any increased flexibility to states to protect children and to ensure them permanence?

Yes. ASFA specifically expands the ability of states to obtain federal waivers to demonstrate new approaches to child welfare reform. ASFA provides for HHS to grant such waivers to up to ten states a year. To date, 30 waivers have been awarded in 21 states and the District of Columbia. States have chosen to use their federal foster care funds more flexibly to establish subsidized legal guardianship programs for relatives caring for children in foster care; offer wrap-around services to young people in foster care with special needs; coordinate substance abuse treatment and child protection services; and to offer preventive in-home services, reunification services, or enhanced services for other children in foster care.

What reports to Congress are required by ASFA?

The Secretary of HHS was required to prepare the following reports and submit them to the House Ways and Means and Senate Finance Committees in Congress. Those that are completed are accessible online at www.acf.dhhs.gov/programs/cb:

- *Blending Perspectives and Building Common Ground: A Report to Congress on Substance Abuse and Child Protection* (Released April 1999).
- *Progress Report to the Congress on Conducting A Study of Performance-Based Financial Incentives in Child Welfare* (Released 1999).
- "Notice of the Final List of Child Welfare Outcomes and Measures" (Published in the *Federal Register* on August 20, 1999, Volume 64, Number 161).
- Secretary's Report on Kinship Care (Forthcoming) This report is to discuss the extent of the placement of children in foster care with relatives and recommendations for appropriate strategies to support these caregivers. It is to be prepared by the Secretary

of HHS after consultation with the Kinship Care Advisory panel established by ASFA.

- General Accounting Office Report on Inter-jurisdictional Adoptions. (Forthcoming) GAO must conduct a study to consider how to improve procedures and policies to facilitate timely and permanent adoptions of children across state and county jurisdictions. It must forward the study and any recommendations to improve procedures to Congress.

When did these new ASFA requirements take effect in the states?

The ASFA requirements were effective immediately unless a state indicated that it needed new legislation to comply with the new ASFA provisions, which most did. In that case, the changes became effective in the state at the beginning of the first quarter that begins after the end of the first state legislative session after ASFA was enacted. This means that in a state where the 1998 legislative session ended in April 1998, ASFA provisions became effective on July 1, 1998. But in a state that just passed its ASFA legislation on February 1,1999, it went into effect on April l, 1999.

How many states have passed legislation to comply with ASFA?

All 50 states and the District of Columbia have passed legislation in response to ASFA. The nature of the legislation varies significantly. In some states, like Illinois, California, and Virginia, the changes made were relatively minor because major changes had been made earlier in response to other reform efforts in the states in anticipation of ASFA. Many states confined their changes to those required by ASFA.

What is known about state activities undertaken in response to ASFA?

The National Conference of State Legislatures (NCSL) has prepared useful summaries of the ASFA legislation passed by each state, as well as an analysis of selected provisions. These materials can be accessed through NCSL's website at www.ncsl.org. A State Legislative Report, 1998 State Legislative Responses to the Adoption and Safe Families Act of 1997, is also available on their website, or from NCSL at (303) 830-2200.

The General Accounting Office also issued a report, *Foster Care: States' Early Experiences Implementing the Adoption and Safe Families Act* (December 1999), which can be obtained online at www.gao .gov.

What has been done on the federal level to implement ASFA?

HHS's Administration for Children and Families (ACF) has conducted numerous briefings and training sessions for states, localities, and others. On January 25, 2000 it also issued final regulations implementing the foster care provisions of ASFA. These regulations also established procedures for Federal review of State Child and Family Services Plans, review of state eligibility for federal Title IV-E funds, and implementation of the Multi-Ethnic Placement Act (MEPA).

For a summary of the final ASFA regulations, consult the CDF publication, "Implementing the Adoption and Safe Families Act: An Overview of the Federal Regulations." To request a copy, call Cynthia Kirkland at (202) 662-3568. The complete text of the final regulations can be accessed online at www.access.gpo.gov. On February 17, 2000, the House Ways and Means Subcommittee on Human Resources held a hearing on the new child and family service review system. Testimony from that hearing is available at www.house.gov/ways_means. For a more detailed side-by-side comparison of the final regulations, public comments and federal child welfare law, contact Georgetown University Law Center Federal Legislation Clinic at (202) 662-9595 or access its website online at www.law.georgetown.edu/clinics/ flc.index.html.

Special looks at ASFA

In addition to CDF and NCSL, a variety of other organizations and agencies are publishing special looks at the new law. Other resources include:

- *P.L. 105-89, Adoption and Safe Families Act of 1997, Issues for Tribes and States Serving Indian Children* is a November 1999 publication by the National Indian Child Welfare Association and the National Resource Center for Organizational Improvement and can be obtained by calling (207) 780-5810.
- *The Adoption and Safe Families Act: Exploring the Opportunity for Collaboration Between Child Mental Health and Child Welfare*

Service Systems is a 1999 publication by the National Technical Assistance Center for Children's Mental Health at Georgetown University's Child Development Center. To order a copy, call (202) 687-8803.

Chapter 44

Becoming a Foster Parent

A Foster Parent? Who? Me?!

One profession of child care that gets very little recognition is foster care. Foster care is a product of adults who cannot or will not perform the parental duties for their own children. Foster children are the innocent victims of circumstances they have no control over. A child alone is unable to protect his or herself from physical and sexual abuse. A foster child often suffers from neglect. Basic human needs that are denied a child can mean malnutrition, illness and even death if someone does not intervene to help this child. They are children in desperate need of safety and security.

Sadly, the demand for foster care is great. Incredibly, most people are not even aware of this great call to serve. Many children end up in foster care because, as George, a foster dad for over twenty years puts it, "The stork left her in the wrong place the first time." Providing foster care is an admirable duty and a privilege. It can be a very difficult job. The reward is the personal satisfaction from doing the

---

Text in this chapter is excerpted from "A Foster Parent? Who? Me?!" and "Self Evaluation Quiz for Prospective Foster Parents," both by Patti Swoboda are reprinted with permission from Answers4Families, a partnership of the Nebraska Health & Human Services System and the Center on Children, Families, and the Law at the University of Nebraska in Lincoln. For additional information, visit www.answers4families.org.

job well, meeting the challenges successfully and making an important difference in another person's life. Foster care is another field in child care that, when well done, makes a valuable contribution to society and the future of our nation.

Foster parent? Who? Me? Before you can answer this question, a prospective foster parent has much to consider.

Consider the commitment. To agree to provide foster care is to agree to welcome a stranger into your home. This type of a commitment must have support by all members of the foster family. You must be willing to give a large chunk of your time to drive the child to appointments and activities. You will invest time in making phone calls to therapists, doctors and the caseworker. A foster child may need more time and attention from you than your other children because of this child's exposure to rejection, instability and emotional upheaval. The child may suffer from the abuse and neglect already mentioned and so it will take time for the child to build up trust. The child may act out feelings of rage, confusion, frustration and abandonment through bizarre behavior. A foster child may imitate some of the gross behavior s/he has experienced and it may be shocking to the unprepared foster family. No one can correct inappropriate behavior over night. Helping a child to progress and overcome past horror is very time consuming.

Consider the impact this child might have on you and your family. You will have one more person to pick up after, do laundry for and to cook for. Will your children resent the time and attention you must give to the foster child? What kind of an influence will the foster child be on your children? Maybe your children will mimic behaviors of the foster child that you object to. Your children may become aware of the existence of cruelty in this world. Your children might also learn what it is to truly care about another human being. They may learn more about compassion and understanding. Your children may even come to appreciate their own lives and circumstances a little bit better.

Consider the invasion of privacy. Many people will become involved in your life. A foster child is not the only one who will enter your life. Child Protective Services, biological parents, case worker, family support worker, therapist, respite providers and the Foster Care Review Board will all play a role in the care of your foster child. Inconveniences and frustrations do occur. For example, you arrange your schedule to accommodate a foster child's appointment with a therapist or a visitation with the biological parent only to have that appointment canceled at late notice. If you are unlucky, you may encounter nonprofessionalism: forgotten phone calls, disruptive, unannounced visits without regard to your personal schedule and informational neglect and mistakes.

Consider the risks to you and your family. A bitter foster child may make a false allegation against you or one of your family members. A child may be destructive and cause damage to your property. Severe cases may pose emotional and physical danger to your family. These are all reasons why it is important to get complete information and ask as many questions about the history of your potential foster child. Things don't always work out.

Lina, an experienced foster mother of more than twenty years has found sexual perpetration cases to be the hardest. "All children bring happiness, some by arriving, some by leaving."

Consider your feelings. A heart that is big enough to let a foster child in, risk's attachment to that child. That big heart may break when your foster child leaves. You may set yourself up to experience feelings of failure or anger if things do not work out. Resa Mallet, a family therapist with the Omaha Psychiatric Association believes it is important for a foster parent to maintain a professional attitude towards providing foster care. She believes it is important to acknowledge the difference between parent and foster parent. Foster parents follow a different set of realistic expectations than that of biological natural parents.

Consider broken promises. People may disappoint you. Offers to help during the time you are considering foster care may dissipate once the child is in your home. Promises easily made can easily break. Be prepared to stand alone with your family in providing foster care. Something else to consider is the benefits of foster care. The privilege of helping to develop a young person's life has priceless rewards. Some of these rewards are helping an abused child to adjust and function better. Witnessing the change from an angry child to a happier child and to be part of that change is rewarding to the heart and soul. The awesome accomplishment of restoring hope for that child's future is better than any trophy or gold medal. All are possible rewards of a successful foster care relationship.

Other benefits include an education, a network of financial support and meeting some terrific people involved in foster care. The education comes from learning about the foster care system, learning from the experiences of the foster child and discovering things about yourself. One anonymous foster parent reports her discovery of nearly unlimited patience, a vital ingredient to the success of foster care. "Before taking in my foster child, I knew I had patience but I was amazed to learn just how much patience I have. My patience seems endless! I can handle things I never imagined I would need to handle and it doesn't stress me out. Sometimes it wears me down, but I remain patient. I have never before done anything that has made me so proud as taking in my foster child."

The network of financial support includes compensation from the state and child care payment coverage to a licensed provider. It includes Medicaid to pay for all medical expenses for your foster child. There are grants and scholarships that your foster child is eligible for. This financial support helps to enable you to provide opportunities to your foster child. An example is to enroll a foster child into a fun summer camp because she qualifies for a special scholarship that covers expenses.

Another example is signing him up in that baseball league because a grant will cover the cost of his uniform and ball fees. These are some of the ways foster parents and supportive organizations make dreams come true!

Foster parent? Who? Me? No, foster care is not for you if :

1. You are impatient. It takes a great deal of patience to be a foster parent.
2. You are a perfectionist. A person who is inflexible will not make a good foster parent. A foster child brings his or her own perceptions of family life and values. The child needs to feel accepted for who s/he is. Boundaries need to be clear and established. However, a foster parent must understand the child's resistance to rules and family ways is the likely result of his or her non-chosen situation and not a result of stubbornness.
3. You want a second income. State compensation is small in comparison to the demands of this job.
4. You are looking for religious converts.
5. You are bored and just want something to do.
6. You are looking to compensate for your feelings of inadequacy or you crave a distraction to an unhappy, unstable life.

7. You regard all foster children as dysfunctional and untrustworthy.

Foster parents and therapists surveyed for this information make the following recommendations for people considering the job of foster parenting:

1. Know why you want to provide foster care.
2. Evaluate the skills you have that qualifies you to provide foster care: patience, time, and abilities to cope with the complications and problems the foster child is suffering.
3. Maintain an attitude that is more professional than maternal. View foster care as a job to establish safe boundaries. Create a secure environment that allows the child to progress as a person and enjoy a period of peace and happiness.
4. Allow the child plenty of transition time. A newcomer to a strange home does not adapt over night.
5. Make certain your expectations for the foster child are realistic and reasonable.
6. Believe a trainer or caseworker when you are told some kids are extremely hard to handle.
7. Ask questions! Get the clearest idea possible as to where this case is going. Determine the length of time this child will be in your care.
8. Investigate and explore all of your options. Find out about subsidized adoption, legal guardianship and other care options available to you. Investigate the opportunities available to your foster child.
9. Take advantage of the support available to you. Ask your caseworker for help and advice.
10. If you find your foster child is impossible to work with, then admit defeat and move on. Arrange for the removal of the child from your home. It is better for the child and it is better for you. Personality clashes do happen. Fostering can only be effective between people who can work together.
11. You must have patience and compassion.

12. Foster care is a very important job. It is not an easy job.
13. Happy endings do not always happen. The reward is in the 'doing' of this job.
14. Check your motives. Are you doing this for the child or for yourself?
15. Be realistic about the time you can give to foster care and about the skills you do or do not have.

If you are a preschool teacher or child care provider who accepts foster children into your care, here are a few tips:

- Treat foster children the same as the others in your care.
- If you have a nursing background, consider taking in a special needs child with a disability. Children learn from each other. A foster child may realize s/he is not the only one with problems. A disability may be a worse problem than being in foster care.
- Some foster families do communicate with the biological parents. Communicating a foster child's progress and concerns to a foster parent is as important as communication is to the other parents.
- Establish clear rules between yourself and the foster parent regarding dismissal and release of the foster child to an adult. Get names and phone numbers to call if verification is needed for releasing the child to an adult unknown to you.
- Contact the Department of Social Services and ask how you can provide help for these children.
- Terri Jackson, Therapist with OPTIONS Counseling Center would like everyone to know, "That no matter what has happened to a child, if they can experience nurturing, safety and acceptance for even a brief period of time in their life, it can make a difference in their formation as an adult."

Foster parent? Yes! You!

Self-Evaluation Quiz for Prospective Foster Parents

"As we do to our children, so will they do to society."

—*Karl Menninger*

Partners in foster care are many. However, a foster parent is the primary caregiver. A foster parent is responsible for the foster child 24 hours a day. This quiz is designed to help evaluate your skills that are necessary for this special field of child care. Answer yes, no or maybe to the following questions:

1. Can you and your family adapt to the changes a foster child will make in your lives?
2. Is the rest of the family as committed as you are in serving the needs of the foster child?
3. Can you accept and deal with the many people and agencies a foster parent must work with?
4. Are you patient and understanding of the child's needs?
5. Can you deal with the emotional baggage that comes with a foster child: anger, stress, confusion, masturbation, depression, fear, etc.?
6. Can you handle behavior that you and your family are not used to?
7. Can you accept and work with the child's individuality and the different values and set of rules this child is accustomed to?
8. Can you handle your feelings and those of your family when the time comes to let go?
9. Are you prepared to take your place in the rejection line of this foster child? (A foster child may feel rejected by the biological parents and past foster families.)
10. Are you comfortable asking questions about the child's background and taking advantage of the support that is available to foster parents?

All people in the profession of child care should answer "yes" to number 4. If you answer "no" to any of these questions, you might not be a candidate for becoming a foster parent. If you answered "yes" to all or if your answers were all "yes" and a few "maybe" than you may want to consider becoming a foster parent. There is much to consider. Get in touch with Child Protective Services and check it out.

Chapter 45

What You Should Know about Adopting or Fostering a Sexually Abused Child

As a prospective adoptive parent, you may have some valid concerns about sexual abuse. You may wonder what the special needs are of children who have been sexually abused and whether you will be able to meet those needs. By acquiring more knowledge, you will feel more confident in taking on the challenges and rewards of adopting a child with special needs.

Many parents who have already adopted sexually abused children feel that their greatest obstacle was lack of information about sexual abuse in general; about their particular child's history; and about helpful resources such as support groups, skilled therapists and sensitive reading materials. This article will provide you with some basic information about child sexual abuse as well as some special considerations for parents who adopt these children.

What do parents need to know when adopting a child who has experienced sexual abuse?

Parents who adopt children who have experienced sexual abuse need the wisdom of Solomon, the strength of Hercules and the patience of Mother Theresa. If you fall short in any of these areas, do not despair. You are in good company. Perhaps, more important is your

---

National Adoption Information Clearinghouse, 1990. Available online at http://naic.acf.hhs.gov/pubs/f_abused.cfm. Despite the older date of this document, is still provides the necessary background information for people who are parenting sexually abused children.

desire to help a young person grow into a healthy, trusting adult. This is a privilege and one which brings real satisfaction to those who have adopted.

What do parents need to be aware of about themselves?

It is very important for you as prospective adoptive parents to be honest with yourselves and with your adoption worker about a number of things.

Is there a history of sexual abuse in either the mother or father's past? If there is, how were those experiences resolved? Did you decide to just forget about it and chalk it up as one of those things that just happened? Or did you get help, from your parents, a teacher, a minister, a therapist or someone who could help you work through your feelings about having been abused? Parents with unresolved abuse experiences in their history may be at greater risk for either abusing the child again, or for keeping too much physical and emotional distance, for fear of abusing the child. Parent/Survivors in local support groups regularly address these phenomena.

How comfortable are you as prospective parents, with your own sexuality and with your sexual relationship(s)? Can you talk comfortably about sex? Do you give yourselves permission to acknowledge your own sexual feelings, thoughts, fantasies, and fears? Do you have a well-established relationship, which allows for direct and open communication? A child who has been sexually abused may need to talk about what happened to him or her. The child's behavior may be seductive or blatantly sexual at times. A parent must be able to deal with this.

In addition, there are some other issues that are important for adoptive parents to consider. They are:

A willingness to be different, or experience embarrassing situations, at least for a while. Children who have been sexually abused may behave toward their adoptive parents in ways which are different than non-abused children. For example, Lisa, age 8, began shouting loudly, in public places like the supermarket, that her father had abused her. In fact, it was her biological father and not her adoptive father who had abused her, but the strangers in the supermarket obviously did not make the distinction.

An ability to wait for the child's commitment while not putting off making your own. An abused child is often untrusting and tied to the past. A child may repeatedly test your commitment to him or her. She or he may feel that if you really and truly saw her or him as they are, with all the scars, that you would not really want him or her.

Many parents have the hope that their love will immediately ease the mistrust their child has of the world and all its adults. What one adoptive parent learned was "love has a different meaning for my daughter. To her, it's simply a deal: You do this for me and I'll do that for you. What a shock to discover that love is not enough." A true, trusting love based on more than just bargaining can come to pass with a sexually abused child, but it will take time, consistency and patience.

A sense of humor. As with most situations in life, a good hearty laugh helps.

What do parents need to be aware of about their child who has been sexually abused?

Children who have experienced sexual abuse will probably need help in learning new behaviors and ways of relating. Some of the behaviors and emotions you may see expressed by your child are:

Withdrawal: Overwhelmed by the feelings she or he has experienced, the child may retreat physically or emotionally. As a parent, you may feel confused or resentful. It can be very isolating to have someone close to you tune you out. Unless you think there is danger of physical harm to the child or others, the best course of action is to reassure the child that you care and that you will provide the limits and boundaries that your child needs.

Mood Swings: A moment's tenderness can quickly explode into anger. The child may be full of confidence one day, only to sink into despair the next. It is difficult to see someone you care about in pain, but you cannot control the feelings of someone else. Point out that these mood swings are occurring. Do not allow yourself to be unfairly blamed. Try to stay calm and accepting that sometimes the child does not even know when or why his/her mood swings are occurring. Crying jags can be part of these mood swings. Accept that it is beyond your power to make it all better. Sometimes when a parent tries to rescue a child from his or her pain, he or she ends up feeling guilty, resentful and frustrated when it does not work. When a caterpillar is emerging from the cocoon, it must have a period of time to build strength in its wings. If the butterfly is released from its cocoon before its time, its strength will be diminished and it will not be able to survive on its own.

Anger: The first target for the child's angry feelings may be the person he or she has come to feel the safest with—you. When a person's angry feelings are completely out of proportion to what is going on, it probably has nothing to do with the present situation. Something in the present is triggering and re-stimulating old memories and feelings. The safety of the current situation allows these feelings to be expressed. Recognize that this is actually a sign of health, but do not accept unacceptable behavior; and never expose yourself to physical violence.

You can assure your child that you are willing to work out the problem at hand, but in a safe and supportive manner. For example, a child may be offered a pillow to beat on in order to vent his or her anger.

Unreasonable Demands: Some children learn the survival skills of manipulation and control. They may feel entitled to make unreasonable demands for time, money or material goods. It is important not to play into or get trapped by these demands. You need to maintain a healthy relationship with your child. This will help the child reduce these demands.

Sexual Behaviors: Since the abuse was acted out sexually, the child needs help in sorting out the meaning of abuse, sex, love, caring and intimacy. Some children may try to demand sexual activity, while others may lose interest in any form of closeness. Think of all the needs that are met through sex: intimacy, touch, validation, companionship, affection, love, release, nurturance. Children need to be re-taught ways that these needs can be met that are not sexual.

A child who has been sexually abused may feel:

- I am worthless and bad
- No person could care for me without a sexual relationship
- I am damaged goods (no one will want me again)
- I must have been responsible for the sexual abuse because
    - It sometimes felt good physically
    - It went on so long

    - I never said "no"
    - I really wasn't forced into it
    - I never told anyone
- I hate my body
- I am uncomfortable with being touched because it reminds me of the abuse
- I think I was abused but sometimes I think I must have imagined it
- I blame my (biological) mother or father for not protecting me but I can't talk about it; I don't want to hurt him/her

A child who has been sexually abused will benefit from clear guidelines that set the rules both in the home and outside. These kinds of rules will help provide the structure, comfort and security which all children need to grow into healthy adults. Experts in the field of adoption and child sexual abuse believe these guidelines are particularly important during the first year after placement, when the child is working hard to establish new relationships with his/her adoptive family and to build trust.

The following guidelines address topics with specific reference to children who have been sexually abused.

Privacy: Everyone has a right to privacy. Children should be taught to knock when a door is closed and adults need to role model the same behavior.

Bedrooms and Bathrooms: These two locations are often prime stimuli for children who have been sexually abused, since abuse commonly occurs in these rooms.

By the time children enter first grade, caution should be used about children of the opposite sex sharing bedrooms or bath times. It is not advisable to bring a child who has been sexually abused into your bed. Cuddling may be over-stimulating and misinterpreted. A safer place to cuddle may be the living room couch.

Touching: No one should touch another person without permission. A person's private parts (the area covered by a bathing suit) should not be touched except during a medical examination or, in the case of young children, if they need help with bathing or toileting.

Clothing: It is a good idea for family members to be conscious of what they wear outside of the bedroom. Seeing others in their underclothes or pajamas may be over-stimulating to a child who has been sexually abused.

Saying "No": Children need to learn that it is their right to assertively say "no" when someone touches them in a way they do not like. Help them to practice this.

Sex Education: All children, including the child who has been sexually abused, need basic information about how they develop sexually. They also will benefit from an atmosphere in which it is OK to talk about sex. Appropriate words for body parts, such as penis, vagina, breasts and buttocks, will give the child the words to describe what happened to him or her. Suggestive or obscene language is sometimes a trigger for old feelings for a child who was sexually abused, and should not be allowed.

No Secrets: Make it clear that no secret games, particularly with adults, are allowed. Tell children if an adult suggests such a game, they should tell you immediately.

Being Alone with One Other Person: If your child is behaving seductively, aggressively or in a sexually acting out manner, these are high risk situations. During those times, it is advisable not to put yourself in the vulnerable position of being accused of abuse. In addition, other children may be in jeopardy of being abused. Therefore, whenever possible during these high risk situations, try not to be alone with your child or allow him/her to be alone with only one other child.

Wrestling and Tickling: As common and normal as these childhood behaviors are, they are often tinged with sexual overtones. They can put the weaker child in an overpowered and uncomfortable or humiliating position. Keep tickling and wrestling to a minimum.

Behaviors and Feelings: Help children differentiate between feelings and behaviors. It is normal to have all kinds of feelings, including sexual feelings. However, everyone does not always act on all the feelings he or she has. Everyone has choices about which feelings he or she acts on, and everyone (except very young children) must take responsibility for his or her own behavior.

Will our child and family need professional help?

It is very likely that at some time or other parents of a child who was sexually abused will need professional help and support for themselves and their child. The type of therapy that will be the most helpful, that is, individual, couple or family therapy, will depend on a family's particular situation. When a child is being seen in individual therapy, it is important that the parents, who have the primary responsibility for the child, be in close contact with the therapist, or included in the therapy. Try to choose a therapist who is knowledgeable about both sexual abuse and adoption issues and with whom you feel comfortable. If parents are not familiar with the therapy resources in their area, they may want to ask their adoption agency or local mental health center for a referral.

Support groups for adoptive parents or sexually abused children and support groups for victims/survivors are another helpful resource. Adoptive parents who have had a chance to talk with others who understand the experience of parenting a sexually abused child say that this kind of sharing is very useful. Dr. Nicholas Groth, a leading psychologist in the field of sexual abuse, along with many children and adult victims/survivors, say that groups for children can be most effective in the healing process. The opportunity to talk and share with other children who have also experienced sexual abuse reduces a child's sense of isolation and belief that he/she is the only one to whom this has ever happened.

Is the healing ever completed?

Recovery from child sexual abuse is an on-going process. As this process unfolds, the child will ideally move from victim to survivor to thriver. Developmental stages, particularly adolescence and young adulthood, may trigger old feelings about the abuse. For example, the time when an adolescent's body begins to develop physically, or when he or she marries, or becomes a parent may restimulate old feelings and memories.

As discussed earlier, so many factors can influence the extent of the damage to the abused child. While adoptive parents cannot erase what happened to their child earlier in his/her life, you have a wonderful opportunity to provide your child with new, healthier experiences. Those who have made the commitment to parenting a sexually abused child say that the rewards of helping a child grow into a healthy, vibrant adult are very satisfying indeed.

What behaviors or signs might you see in a child who has been sexually abused?

While no one sign or behavior can be considered absolute proof that sexual abuse has occurred, you should consider the possibility of sexual abuse when one or several of these signs or behaviors are present.

Physical signs:

- Scratches, bruises, itching, rashes, cuts or injuries, especially in the genital area
- Venereal disease
- Pregnancy in (young) adolescents
- Blood or discharge in bedding or clothes, especially underwear

Behavioral signs:

- Aggressive behavior towards younger children
- advanced sexual knowledge for the child's age
- Seductive or sexy behavior towards adults or peers
- Pseudo-mature behavior (for instance, a girl who is eight and dresses like a 16 year-old, wears makeup and generally acts too old for her age, or a young boy who attempts to be his mother's man in every sense of the word)
- Regressed behavior (for example, the child who has been toilet trained starts wetting the bed)
- Excessive masturbation, masturbation in public places, difficulty with being re-focused to another behavior
- Poor relationships with peers
- Fear of a particular person, place or thing (for example, if the abuse occurred in the bathroom, the child may show fear in that room)
- Sudden or extreme changes in behavior (for instance, a previously good student starts having trouble with school work, a child who was not sad before starts crying frequently or acting sad, or a formerly cooperative child acts defiantly or is uncooperative or unusually overly cooperative)
- Eating disorders (overeats, under-eats)

Additional behavioral signs in pre-teens and adolescents:

- Self-mutilation (the child may repeatedly pick at scabs, cut him/herself with a razor blade, bite his/her finger or arm, burn him/herself with a cigarette)
- Threatening or attempting suicide
- Using drugs or alcohol
- Becoming promiscuous (a child is sexually active without discrimination, or just has that reputation)
- Being prudish (the child avoids any sexuality, does not see him/herself as a sexual being in any way)
- Prostitution
- Fire-setting
- Lying, stealing
- Running away
- Isolating self or dropping friends
- Pre-occupation with death (the child may write poems about death, may ask a lot of questions about death, such as "What does it feel like and where do people go?")

Some additional behavioral signs in children who have been ritualistically/satanically abused:

- Bizarre nightmares
- Sadistic play (for example, mutilation of dolls or small animals)
- Self-mutilation
- Pre-occupation with death
- Increased agitation on certain dates which represent satanic high holy days
- A constant fear of harm and extreme fear of being alone

Are all children affected equally by child sexual abuse?

There is a myth that all children who have been sexually abused are damaged goods and that the damage is for life. In fact, with guidance and support a child who has experienced sexual abuse can certainly recover and go on to live a happy, successful life with loving and trusting relationships. However, there are many factors which influence the extent of the child's trauma and subsequent healing process. Some of these are:

The age of the child when the abuse began. Children abused very early in life may carry body or sensory memories of the abuse but will not have the words to express their rage. One adult survivor of sexual abuse figured out, with the help of therapy, that the reason she became sexually stimulated when she heard and felt a room fan was because a fan had always been on when she was molested as a child. Children who are abused pre-pubescently, during the time when their sexuality is emerging, may carry greater effects of the abuse.

The relationship of the primary perpetrator to the child. A child's trust of his/her primary caretaker is central to their relationship. Therefore, when abuse occurs in this context, the betrayal is intensified.

How long the abuse occurred. The longer the abuse occurred, the more likely the victim is to feel that he/she should have been able to stop it and thus he or she feels more guilty.

Whether there was violence involved. In most cases where the abuse included violence or potential violence (that is, the victim was made to understand that without cooperation there would be violence) the child will have experienced additional trauma and therefore damage to his/her development.

The social system available to the child at the time of abuse. The child who had someone to tell about the abuse will suffer less than the child who had no one to tell. And even in some cases where the support system is available, the child may choose not to tell for fear of the consequences. For example, the child may think, "If I tell my father that my brother is abusing me and he believes me, then my father may do something drastic like hurt my brother or send me to jail."

When children reveal their secrets, the response of adults will vary. It is important to stay as calm as possible so as not to further traumatize the child. The rage you may feel is natural, but the child may perceive that it is directed at him or her. The child needs a safe, supportive atmosphere in which to talk. Children also benefit enormously from hearing that this has happened to other children, male and female.

Ego development of the child at the time of the abuse. If the child has a firmly established concept of his or her sexual identity, the abuse will have less impact. Children who are abused by a same sex perpetrator often have deeply felt fears about whether this means they are homosexual. One way in which parents can help allay this fear is to explain that our bodies have many nerve endings. If these nerve endings are stimulated, they will react. For example, if a bright light hits your eyes, your first response will be to blink or to shade them from the light. A simple concept to use with children is that of tickling. If a child is ticklish, he or she will laugh when tickled. It does not matter whether the person tickling is male or female; the child is reacting to the experience.

If the perpetrator is of the opposite sex, questions of identity may also come into play. For example a boy who is abused by a woman and is not aroused, may doubt his masculinity. If he is aroused physically, but not emotionally, he may equally doubt his masculinity. The same identity issues for girls may hold true.

If the child has a positive self-concept, that is, if he or she feels valued at the time the abuse occurred, there will be fewer repercussions. In fact, children with good self-esteem are more likely to feel they can say no and/or tell someone about the abuse.

Do boys who are abused have special issues?

Boys who are sexually abused face some additional problems because of persistent myths in our society. Males are rarely viewed as fitting the victim role. When boys get hurt, they are often told act like a man, don't be a sissy, control your emotions. The message to boys is to stand on their own two feet and to take care of themselves. Under these circumstances, a male victim is less likely to tell and therefore cannot begin a healing process. This increases the chances that he may take on the role of the victimizer in an attempt to master his own experience.

A further complication for boys is that the media portray boys who have sexual experiences with older women as going through a rite of passage rather than as victims of sexual exploitation. Movies such as "Summer of '42" and "Get Out Your Handkerchiefs" are prime examples of this.

What about juvenile sex offenders?

Some children who have been sexually abused go on to abuse other children. While this is a serious problem, the exact percentage of sexual abuse victims who become abusers is not known. It is important to realize that these children are victims as well as offenders and need to receive counseling from qualified therapists who understand both aspects of the problem. The therapist must be able to be empathic and understanding of the victim but confrontational with the victimizer.

Victimizers have triggers that precede their behavior. For example, a child may abuse another child when he or she finds him or herself in a vulnerable or stressful situation. Sometimes this is because he or she lacks control or power. This may be when the child gets called a name at school or believes he or she is being punished unfairly. The therapist must help the child to not only recognize his/her own individual triggers but also, to understand the consequences of acting out these impulses.

In other instances, past experiences have left the child overly sexually stimulated. The child needs education and suggestions of alternative positive behaviors to replace the sexually victimizing behavior.

Chapter 46

When Domestic Violence Cases Threaten Children's Well-Being

Police and prosecutors say they sometimes feel like they are walking a tightrope when they intervene in domestic violence cases. Each step into a heated domestic situation requires careful balance. On the one hand, the justice system must hold batterers accountable for their violent behavior; on the other hand, a woman needs to control her life and find safety and security for herself and her children as best she can.

As research reveals more about the effects of domestic violence on children, prosecutors are finding that both thc law and public opinion have raised expectations for what criminal justice professionals should do and actually can do.

Some States have enacted legislation to better protect children exposed to violence, but the new laws are raising concern about the impact on mothers. Critics hypothesize that battered women will be increasingly charged with criminal child abuse or failure to protect their children if they do not take action against their batterer and could eventually lose custody. Others fear that children who are exposed to domestic violence will increasingly be forced to testify and therefore to "choose sides" in the cases against their mother or father.

This chapter describes some of the issues prosecutors should be aware of when they handle domestic violence cases involving children, especially in light of recent legislation aimed to protect children. It is

---

Excerpted from "Prosecutors, Kids, and Domestic Violence Cases." by Debra Whitcomb. From *National Institute of Justice Journal,* Number 248, 2002. U.S. Department of Justice, Office of Justice Program, National Institute of Justice.

the product of an NIJ-funded exploratory study that relied on two sources of data: a national telephone survey of prosecutors and field research in five jurisdictions.

The exploratory study sought answers to the following questions:

- How are new laws, now in effect in a small number of States, affecting practice?
- What challenges do prosecutors face when children are exposed to domestic violence?
- What can prosecutors do to help battered women and their children?

Why the New Laws?

Children who witness domestic violence often manifest behavioral and emotional problems, poor academic performance, and delinquency.[1] Sadly, violence against women and violence against children often coexist in families—the frequency of child abuse doubles in families experiencing intimate partner violence, compared to families with nonviolent partners, and the rate of child abuse escalates with the severity and frequency of the abuse against the mother.[2]

Domestic violence is also a known risk factor for recurring child abuse reports[3] and for child fatalities.[4] In addition, domestic violence frequently coexists with substance abuse, so that children are exposed to the effects of dangerous substances and the parental neglect that usually comes with addiction.[5]

One large study involving 9,500 HMO members revealed that the 1,010 people who reported that their mothers had been treated violently also reported being exposed to other adverse childhood experiences, such as substance abuse (59 percent reported exposure), mental illness (38 percent), sexual abuse (41 percent), psychological abuse (34 percent), and physical abuse (31 percent).[6]

It is generally recognized that the well-being of children who witness domestic violence is tied closely to that of their mothers,[7] but the mother's interests and the child's may not always be identical or even compatible. A mother may face serious concerns about her financial and physical well-being if she separates from her violent partner. She may lack resources or social networks to extricate herself from dangerous relationships, and the community's support system may be inadequate. Her efforts to seek help may be thwarted by waiting lists, lack of insurance, or high fees for services. She may believe that she and her children are better off staying with the violent partner despite the consequences.[8]

Meanwhile, the children remain in perilous environments. Child protection agencies may feel compelled to intervene to forestall the escalating risk of harm to children. Unfortunately, in many jurisdictions, a referral to the child protection agency is perceived as a mixed blessing. Many child protection agencies do not have adequate resources to respond to the volume of domestic violence reports they receive when exposure to violence is defined as a form of child maltreatment by law or policy. Elsewhere, critics charge, protective services workers are too quick to remove children from violent homes, inappropriately blaming women for the actions of their abusive partners.

How Are New Laws Affecting Practice?

The words of San Diego City Attorney Casey Gwinn capture the climate of growing concerns related to children and violence in the home:

> "...children must be a central focus of all we do in the civil and criminal justice system...from the initial police investigation through the probationary period, we must prioritize children's issues."[9]

Police officers are being encouraged to note the presence of children when they respond to domestic violence incidents and to collaborate with mental health professionals to address the children's trauma and anxiety.[10] Battered women's shelters are hiring staff to work with children and developing policy for alerting child protection agencies when needed.[11] Juvenile and family courts are sponsoring programs to meet the needs of battered women whose children are at risk for maltreatment.[12] Child protection agencies are instituting training and protocols to better identify domestic violence; some are hiring domestic violence specialists to help develop appropriate case plans.[13] Legislators, too, are taking action by enhancing penalties when domestic violence occurs in front of children and creating new criminal child abuse offenses for cases involving children who are exposed to domestic violence.

The new laws are affecting prosecutors in different ways. For example, district attorneys in Multnomah County, Oregon, where a new law recently upgraded domestic violence offenses to felonies when children are present,[14] issued nearly 150 percent more felony domestic violence cases in the year that the new law was passed.

In both Salt Lake County, Utah, and Houston County, Georgia, where committing domestic violence in the presence of a child is a new crime of child abuse,[15] prosecutors tend to use these charges as bargaining chips to exert leverage toward guilty pleas on domestic violence charges.

In these jurisdictions, the new State laws remind law enforcement investigators to document children as witnesses and to take statements from them whenever possible, which may strengthen prosecutors' domestic violence cases even if the children cannot testify.

To understand how prosecutors are responding to the changing attitudes, researchers asked them to explain how they would respond to three different scenarios involving children and domestic violence:

1. An abused mother is alleged to have abused her children.
2. Both mother and children are abused by the same male perpetrator.
3. Children are exposed to domestic violence, but not abused themselves.

For each scenario, respondents answered these questions:

- Would your office report the mother to the child protection agency?
- Would your office prosecute the mother in the first scenario for the abuse of her children?
- Would your office report or prosecute the mother in scenarios 2 and 3 for failure to protect her children from abuse or exposure to domestic violence?

Many respondents noted the lack of statutory authority in their States to prosecute mothers for failure to protect their children, especially from exposure to domestic violence. Some explained that they consider mothers' experience of victimization in their decisions to report or prosecute battered mothers for their children's exposure to abuse or domestic violence.

Factors in these decisions commonly include the severity of injury to the child, chronicity of the domestic violence, the degree to which the mother actively participated in the abuse of her child, and prior history of failure to comply with services or treatment plans.

Prosecutors in States with laws either creating or enhancing penalties for domestic violence in the presence of children were significantly more likely to report battered mothers for failure to protect their children from abuse or from exposure to domestic violence, but there was no significant difference in the likelihood of prosecution. (See Table 46.1.)

The more tangible benefits of the new laws—particularly those in Utah and Georgia—may accrue to the children. By identifying children as victims, these statutes:

- Allow children access to crime victims compensation funds to address health or mental health needs resulting from their exposure to domestic violence.
- Enable the courts to issue protective orders on the children's behalf (potentially affording prosecutors another tool for monitoring offenders' behavior).
- Signal a need to file a report with the child protection agency, even in the absence of laws naming domestic violence as a condition of mandatory reporting.

What Can Prosecutors Do?

Research suggests a number of steps prosecutors can take to help children who are exposed to domestic violence:

- Employ every available avenue to enforce the terms of no-contact orders and probationary sentences. Field research suggests that these measures may offer the most powerful means of holding domestic violence offenders accountable for their behavior.

Table 46.1. Prosecutors' Responses to Scenarios Involving Children and Abuse

Scenario	Would *Report* At Least Sometimes	Would *Prosecute* At Least Sometimes
Mom Abuses Children	94%	100%
Mom Fails to Protect from Abuse	63%	77.5%
Mom Fails to Protect from Exposure	40%	25%

- Establish protocols within prosecutors' offices to encourage information sharing among prosecutors with responsibility for domestic violence and child abuse caseloads.
- Identify avenues for early intervention (e.g., by placing greater emphasis on misdemeanor prosecution).
- Train law enforcement investigators to note the presence of children in domestic violence incidents and to take statements from them whenever appropriate to do so.
- Encourage law enforcement agencies to adopt a model of law enforcement-mental health partnership that was pioneered in New Haven, Connecticut, as a means of ensuring that children who are exposed to violence receive timely and appropriate therapeutic intervention.[16] Be prepared, however, to develop policies or protocols to guide law enforcement officers' decisions to report these incidents to the child protection agency.
- Wherever possible, prosecute domestic violence offenders on concurrent charges of child endangerment, emotional abuse, or other available charges reflecting the danger to children who witness violence. These additional charges can be used to argue for stricter conditions of pretrial release or probation, or perhaps for upward deviation from sentencing guidelines.
- Provide training on domestic violence, child abuse, and the impact of domestic violence on children for all prosecutors, victim advocates, and other court personnel whose job responsibilities include responding to allegations of family violence.
- Promote increased attention to services for battered women. Women cannot reasonably be expected to extricate themselves from dangerous relationships if the financial and social supports are not available in their communities. Particular attention should be paid to substance abuse treatment; one recent study suggests that substance abuse predicts non-cooperation with prosecution among battered women.[17]
- Ensure that social service agencies will connect with families that have been reported for domestic violence, both to offer referrals for needed services and to monitor future incidents. Some avenues need to be available for offering needed services to children in troubled families before they suffer serious harm.

No other institution in the community has the capacity and power to force offenders to confront and change their behavior. As political leaders in their communities, prosecutors have the status and opportunity to advocate for needed change, whether legislative, fiscal, or programmatic in nature. Prosecutors can bring together people with disparate views and hammer out ways to overcome distrust and conflict toward a common goal: protection of battered women and their children.

The Survey and Its Findings

The study involved a telephone survey of prosecutors and in-depth site visits to five jurisdictions to collect information about current practice and to identify promising practices in response to cases involving domestic violence and child victims or witnesses.

The final report, *Children and Domestic Violence: Challenges for Prosecutors,* (NCJ 185355; grant 99-WT-VX-0001) is available from NCJRS. To order a copy, call 1-800-851-3420.

Findings from the Telephone Survey

The 128 prosecutors who completed the telephone survey worked in 93 offices in 49 States. The offices had jurisdiction over both felony and misdemeanor cases at either the county or district level. Nearly half (48 percent) of the jurisdictions had units or prosecutors responsible for all family violence cases, 38 percent had separate domestic violence and child abuse prosecutors or units. The other respondents represented the singular perspectives of domestic violence (10 percent) or child abuse (4 percent). Specific findings include the following:

Most respondents (78 percent) agreed that the presence of children provides added incentive to prosecute domestic violence cases. A few individuals pointed to the children's capacity to testify as an important factor in their decisions.

A majority of prosecutors' offices (59 percent) are aggressively pursuing enhanced sanctions for domestic violence offenders when incidents involve children as victims or witnesses. Most commonly, prosecutors argue for harsher sentencing or file separate charges of child endangerment. Responding offices in which prosecutors had received at least some training on the co-occurrence of domestic violence and child maltreatment (65 percent) were significantly more likely to report employing these avenues in applicable cases.

Most jurisdictions lack a policy for prosecutors and investigators to identify co-occurring cases of domestic violence and child maltreatment. None of the 35 responding offices with separate domestic violence and child abuse units had protocols directing prosecutors in these units to inquire about co-occurrence or to communicate with one another when relevant cases arise. About half were aware of protocols directing law enforcement officers to ask about child victims or witnesses when investigating domestic violence reports. About one-fourth knew of protocols directing investigators to inquire about domestic violence when responding to child abuse reports.

Findings from the In-Depth Site Visits

Dallas, Texas. Prosecutors in Dallas pursue a fairly strict no-drop policy for domestic violence cases, and the presence of children only strengthens their resolve to move cases forward. However, with reluctant women, the officials can offer the option of filing an affidavit of non-prosecution. This document helps women who fear retribution from their abusive partners because it allows the women to demonstrate their efforts to terminate law enforcement's intervention. However, it has no effect on the prosecutor's decision making or the court's proceedings.

Where there are concurrent charges of domestic violence and child abuse, prosecutors try to coordinate the cases to optimize the sanctions against the offender and the safety of the mother and children. For example, the family violence prosecutor can use child abuse cases to support the domestic violence charge. Even if the child abuse is a felony and the domestic violence is a misdemeanor, prosecutors may accept a plea to jail time on the domestic violence charge and a 10-year deferred adjudication on the child abuse charge, which typically carries with it numerous conditions (e.g., no contact, participation in substance abuse treatment, and so on). This avenue ensures a domestic violence conviction while imposing strict court oversight on the child abuse charge.

Respondents observed that deferred adjudication or a probation sentence is, in some ways, more severe and more effective than jail time, precisely because of the conditions that can be imposed, the length of time that the offender can remain under the court's supervision, and the threat of revocation and incarceration.

San Diego, California. Prosecutors in San Diego are both aggressive and creative in finding ways to enhance sanctions for perpetrators of domestic violence and child abuse. For example, domestic violence offenders can be charged with child endangerment when a child:

- Calls 911 to report domestic violence.
- Appears fearful, upset, or hysterical at the scene.
- Is an eyewitness to the incident.
- Is present in a room where objects are being thrown.
- Is in a car during a domestic violence incident.
- Is in the arms of the victim or suspect during an incident.[a]

Anyone convicted of child endangerment and sentenced to probation will be required to complete a yearlong child abuser's treatment program.

Several programs support the prosecutors. For example, the Child Advocacy Project (CAP) provides services to children and families in reported incidents of abuse, neglect, exploitation, or domestic violence that are not investigated for criminal justice system intervention. Through a collaboration with the San Diego Police Department and Children's Hospital Center for Child Protection, the San Diego City Attorney's Office reviews these reports with an eye toward any angle that might support a misdemeanor prosecution with the goal of creating an avenue for service delivery. Most defendants plead guilty and receive informal probation with referrals to parenting and counseling programs.

Salt Lake County, Utah. In May 1997, Utah became the first State to enact legislation specifically addressing the issue of children who witness domestic violence. Notable elements of this statute include the following:

- It creates a crime of child abuse, not domestic violence.
- It does not require the child to be physically present during the incident of domestic violence. The perpetrator simply must be aware that a child may see or hear it.
- Unless the precipitating domestic violence incident is quite severe, it requires at least one previous violation or act of domestic violence in the presence of a child. A police incident report

documenting an earlier act in the presence of a child will suffice for this purpose.

Although criminal justice agencies in Salt Lake County were not able to provide statistical data, anecdotal evidence suggests that:

- The law is infrequently applied to mothers. But it could be applied if the women were arrested in the underlying incident of domestic violence.
- The law is largely symbolic. It adds minimal time to the offender's sentence—perhaps 6 months if the sentences for the domestic violence and child abuse charges run consecutively.
- The crime is relatively easy to prove, requiring either (a) testimony from the responding officer, (b) testimony or excited utterances from the victim parent, or (c) a 911 tape that records children's voices.

Concurrent with the enactment of the new criminal statute, Utah's Department of Child and Family Services created a new category of child abuse and neglect: "Domestic Violence-Related Child Abuse," or DVRCA, defined as "violent physical or verbal interaction between cohabitants in a household in the presence of a child."

In adopting the new category, the department hired domestic violence advocates and developed a protocol to guide child protection workers in their determinations.

Houston County, Georgia. Prosecutors in Houston County, Georgia, actively use new provisions of Georgia's "cruelty to children" statute that pertain to domestic violence committed in the presence of children. Because cruelty to children is almost always a misdemeanor offense, it makes little difference in the penalties imposed on a batterer; indeed, the sentence typically runs by concurrently with the underlying domestic violence charge. However, the law does give prosecutors a stronger argument for no contact as a condition of bond. Violations of no-contact orders are charged as aggravated stalking, a felony offense in Georgia.

Prosecutors perceive the severe consequences of violating no-contact orders as perhaps the most effective response to domestic violence among the sanctions available to them.

Also, by identifying children as victims of the family violence battery, the new law accomplishes at least three things:

- It helps to counter batterers' threats to gain custody of a child.
- It makes the children eligible for crime victims compensation.
- It enables the court to impose no-contact orders on the children's behalf.

Multnomah County, Oregon. The study team selected Multnomah County (Portland), Oregon, because Oregon enacted legislation upgrading certain assault offenses from misdemeanors to felonies when a child witnesses the crime. The felony upgrade applies only to assault in the fourth degree, a misdemeanor offense that applies to many incidents of domestic violence. Assaults in the first, second, or third degree are felonies that require more serious injuries or the use of weapons.

Even though the felony upgrade applies to defendants with prior convictions (either one against the same victim or three against any victims) regardless of the presence of children, prosecutors observe that the large majority of elevated cases are those involving child witnesses.

The felony upgrade law has had a noteworthy impact on the District Attorney's Office: The number of felonies reviewed more than tripled in 1998 (the year in which the law became effective), while the number of misdemeanors reviewed remained nearly constant. Also, the number of felonies issued exceeded the number of misdemeanors for the first time.

In that same year, the proportion of issued domestic violence cases declined. This pattern held true for misdemeanors as well as felonies. Prosecutors may have imposed higher standards as they began to interpret and apply the new law.

Notes

1. For a comprehensive review, see Edleson, J., "Children's Witnessing of Adult Domestic Violence," *Journal of Interpersonal Violence,* 14(1999): 839-870.

2. Strauss, M., R.J. Gelles, and S. Steinmetz, *Behind Closed Doors: Violence in the American Family,* New York: Doubleday/ Anchor, 1980.

3. English, D.J., D.B. Marshall, S. Brummel, and M. Orme, "Characteristics of Repeated Referrals to Child Protective Services in Washington State," *Child Maltreatment,* 4(1999): 297-307.

4. U.S. Advisory Board on Child Abuse and Neglect, *A Nation's Shame: Fatal Child Abuse and Neglect in the United States*, Washington, DC: U.S. Department of Health and Human Services, Administration for Children and Families, 1995.

5. U.S. Department of Health and Human Services, *Blending Perspectives and Building Common Ground: A Report to Congress on Substance Abuse and Child Protection*, Washington, DC: Administration for Children and Families, Substance Abuse and Mental Health Services Administration, Assistant Secretary for Planning and Evaluation, 1999.

6. Felitti,V.J., R.F. Anda, D. Nordenberg, et al., "Relationship of Childhood Abuse and Household Dysfunction to Many of the Leading Causes of Death in Adults," *American Journal of Preventive Medicine,* 14 (1998): 250.

7. Osofsky, J.D., "The Impact of Violence on Children," *The Future of Children: Domestic Violence and Children,* 9(1999): 33-49.

8. Hilton, N.Z., "Battered Women's Concerns About Their Children Witnessing Wife Assault," *Journal of Interpersonal Violence,* 7(1992): 77-86.

9. Personal communication, January 2000.

10. Marans, S., S.J. Berkowitz, and D.J. Cohen, "Police and Mental Health Professionals: Collaborative Responses to the Impact of Violence on Children and Families," *Child and Adolescent Psychiatric Clinics of North America,* 7(1998): 635-651.

11. Saathoff, A.J., and E.A. Stoffel, "Community-Based Domestic Violence Services," *The Future of Children: Domestic Violence and Children,* 9(1999): 97-110.

12. See, e.g., Lecklitner, G.L., N.M. Malik, S.M. Aaron, and C.S. Lederman, "Promoting Safety for Abused Children and Battered Mothers:Miami-Dade County's Model Dependency Court Intervention Program," *Child Maltreatment,* 4(1999): 175-182.

13. Whitney, P., and L. Davis, "Child Abuse and Domestic Violence in Massachusetts: Can Practice Be Integrated in a Public Child Welfare Setting?" *Child Maltreatment,* 4(1999): 158-166.

14. Oregon's legislation can be found at ORS 163.160(3)(b).

15. Utah: U.C.A. Section 76-5-109.1; Georgia: O.C.G.A. Section 16-5-70.

16. Marans, Berkowitz, and Cohen, "Police and Mental Health Professionals," see note 10.

17. Goodman, L., L. Bennett, and M.A. Bennett, "Obstacles to Victims' Cooperation with the Criminal Prosecution of Their Abusers: The Role of Social Support," *Violence and Victims,* 14(1999): 427-444.

Additional Note Regarding Survey Findings

a. Gwinn, C., "Domestic Violence and Children: Difficult Issues," Presentation for the National College of District Attorneys, 1998.

Part Six

Parenting Challenges

Chapter 47

Positive Ways a Parent Can Change a Child's Behavior

Child Behavior: What Parents Can Do to Change Their Child's Behavior

What is normal behavior for a child?

Normal behavior in children depends on the child's age, personality, and physical and emotional development. A child's behavior may be a problem if it doesn't match the expectations of the family or if it is disruptive. Knowing what to expect from your child at each age will help you decide what is normal behavior.

What can I do to change my child's behavior?

Children tend to continue a behavior when it is rewarded and stop a behavior when it is ignored. Consistency in your reaction to a behavior is important because rewarding and punishing the same behavior at different times confuses your child. When your child's behavior is a problem, you have 3 choices:

- Decide the behavior is not a problem because it's appropriate to the child's age and stage of development.

This chapter begins with text reproduced with permission from http://familydoctor.org/handouts/201.html. Excerpts from books by Elizabeth Pantley are individually cited within the chapter.

- Attempt to stop the behavior, either by ignoring it or by punishing it.
- Introduce a new behavior that you prefer.

How do I stop misbehavior?

The best way to stop unwanted behavior is to ignore it. This way works best when you're able to wait for results. When you want the behavior to stop immediately, you can use the time-out method. Physical punishment is less effective.

Why shouldn't I use physical punishment?

Many parents use physical punishment (such as spanking) to stop undesirable behavior. The biggest drawback to this method is that although the punishment stops the bad behavior for a while, it doesn't give the child an alternative. If the child doesn't know a good behavior, he or she is likely to return to the bad behavior. Physical punishment becomes less effective with time and can cause the child to behave aggressively. It can also be carried too far—into child abuse. Other methods of punishment are preferred and should be used whenever possible.

How do I use the time-out method?

Decide ahead of time the behaviors that will result in a time out—usually tantrums, or aggressive or dangerous behavior. Choose a time-out place that is uninteresting for the child and not frightening—usually a chair, a corner, or a playpen. When you're away from home, consider using a car or a restroom as a time-out place.

When the unacceptable behavior occurs, tell the child the behavior is unacceptable and give 1 warning that you will put the child in time out if the behavior doesn't stop. Remain calm and don't look angry. If the child goes on misbehaving, take him or her to the time-out area.

Set a timer so the child will know when time out is over. Time out should be brief—generally 1 minute for each year of age—and should begin immediately after reaching the time-out place or after the child calms down. You should stay within sight or earshot of the child but don't talk to him or her. If the child leaves the time-out area, gently return him or her to the area and consider resetting the timer. When the time out is over, let the child leave the time-out place. Don't discuss the bad behavior but look for ways to praise good behavior later on.

How do I encourage a new, desired behavior?

One way to encourage good behavior is to use a reward system. This way works best in children over 2 years of age. It can take up to 2 months to work. Keeping a diary of behavior can be helpful to parents, to show gradual changes in their child.

Choose 1 to 2 behaviors you would like to change (such as bedtime behavior, toothbrushing or picking up toys). Choose a reward your child would enjoy. Examples of good rewards are an extra bedtime story, delaying bedtime by a half hour, a preferred snack or, for older children, earning points toward a special toy, a privilege or a small amount of money.

Explain the desired behavior and the reward to the child. For example, "If you get into your pajamas and brush your teeth before this TV show is over, you can stay up a half hour later." Request the behavior only 1 time. If the child does what you ask, give the reward. You can help the child if necessary but don't get too involved. Because any attention from parents, even negative attention, is so rewarding to children, they may prefer to have parental attention instead of a reward at first. Transition statements, such as, "In 5 minutes, play time will be over," are helpful when you are teaching your child new behaviors.

This system helps you avoid power struggles with your child. However, you must live with your child's choice. If your child chooses not to behave as you ask, the child is not punished; he or she simply does not get the reward.

What are some examples of this method?

Beat the Clock (best method for a dawdling child): Ask the child to do a task. Set a timer. If the task is done before the timer rings, the child gets a reward. To decide the amount of time to give the child, figure out the child's "best time" to do that task and add 5 minutes.

The Good Behavior Game (good when you're trying to teach a new behavior): Write a short list of good behaviors on a chart and mark the chart with a star each time you see the good behavior. After the child has earned a small number of stars (depending on the child's age), give him or her a reward.

Good Marks/Bad Marks (best method for difficult, highly active children): In a short time (about an hour) put a mark on a chart or on the child's hand each time you see him or her performing a good behavior. For example, if you see your child playing quietly, solving a problem without fighting, picking up toys or reading a book, you would mark the chart. After a certain number of marks, give the child a reward. You can also make negative marks each time a bad behavior occurs. If you do this, you only give the child a reward if there are more positive marks than negative marks.

Developing Quiet Time (often useful when you're making supper): Ask the child to play quietly alone or with a sibling for a short time (maybe 30 minutes). Check on the child frequently (every 2 to 5 minutes, depending on the child's age) and give a reward or a token for each few minutes the child was quiet or playing well. Gradually increase the intervals (go from checking the child's behavior every 2 to 5 minutes to checking every 30 minutes), but continue to give rewards for each time period the child was quiet or played well.

What else can I do to help my child behave well?

Make a short list of important rules. Avoid power struggles and "no win" situations. Try not to go to extremes. When you think you've overreacted, it's better to use your common sense to solve the problem, even if you have to be inconsistent just this once.

Accept your child's basic personality, whether it's shy, social, talkative or active. Basic personality can be changed a little, but not very much. Try to avoid situations that can make your child cranky, such as becoming overly stimulated, tired or bored. Don't criticize your child in front of other people. Describe the child's behavior as bad, but don't label the child as bad. Praise your child often when he or she deserves it. Touch your child affectionately and often.

Develop little routines and rituals, especially at bedtimes and meal times. Provide transition remarks (such as, "In 5 minutes, we'll be eating dinner."). Allow your child choices whenever possible. You can ask, "Do you want to wear your red pajamas or your blue pajamas to bed tonight?"

As children get older, they enjoy becoming involved in household rule making. Don't debate the rules at the time of misbehavior but invite the child to participate in rule making at another time.

Children who learn that bad behavior is not tolerated and that good behavior is rewarded are learning skills that will last them a lifetime.

Time Out

By Elizabeth Pantley, author of Kid Cooperation and Perfect Parenting. *© 2002. Elizabeth Pantley, www.pantley.com/elizabeth.*

It's been around since dunce caps and corners. With a modern twist, Time Out can be a valuable discipline tool.

As we go about the business of teaching our children proper behavior, there are times when emotions threaten to get out of control. When this happens, it's wise to separate yourself from your child so that you can both cool off. Time Out can be used as an effective, positive tool. There are three different ways to use Time Out, each having a different purpose.

To give the child time and space to cool off and calm down. The key here is in the attitude of the parent. In advance, let your child know that when her behavior is out of control she'll be asked to go to her room. Tell her that when she is calm and under control she may join the family. How she chooses to use the time is her business, as long as it's respectful of people and property. Screaming or pounding the door is not acceptable, reading a book or other activities is fine. This is a valuable life skill that will prevent your child from flying off the handle and saying and doing things she might regret later.

Never drag a child to his Time Out. This robs you of the upper hand and makes you look foolish. Let him know in advance that when asked to remove himself he needs to do so immediately. If he does not, he'll be choosing to give up a privilege (one you have specified in advance), in addition to Time Out.

To give the parent time and space to cool off and calm down. There are times when we get so angry at our children that we want to scream, hit, or ground them for life! This is the time to use a four-letter-word: E X I T. Make a brief statement, "I'm so angry, I need a minute to think." Then go to your room or send the child to his room so that you can calm down and regroup. This will help you get yourself under control, and it provides good modeling for your children.

As a method for stopping a specific misbehavior. This can be an excellent way to put an immediate stop to a child's action. It brings a strong message, "This behavior is unacceptable and it will stop now." There are several keys: Be quick. Catch your child in the act. Delayed reactions dilute the effect. Use selectively. Use for hitting, talking back, and whining or other specific problems. Don't over-use. Keep calm. Your anger only adds fuel to the fire and changes the focus from the behavior of the child to your anger. This prevents you from being in control. Stick with it. Once you say, "Time Out," don't back down or be talked out of it. If you decide to use Time Out to control hitting, for example, use it every time your child hits, even if he spends most of the day in Time Out! Eventually, he'll decide that it's more fun to play without hitting than to sit alone in his room.

Time Out is one more effective discipline tool for parents. When used with other positive parenting methods it helps you feel good about the job you are doing with your kids.

The Power of Choice

Excerpted with permission by New Harbinger Publications, Inc. (www.newharbinger.com) from Kid Cooperation, How to Stop Yelling, Nagging and Pleading and Get Kids to Cooperate *by Elizabeth Pantley (www.pantley.com/elizabeth, copyright 1996).*

Would you like to get your kids to willingly cooperate? Stop the daily battles? Teach your kids valuable life skills? If your answer is "Yes! Yes! Yes!" then read on.

There are so many things we must get our children to do and so many things me must stop them from doing! Get up. Get dressed. Don't dawdle. Do your homework. Eat. It goes on and on. We can get our kids to cooperate and at the same time allow them to learn self-discipline and develop good decision-making skills. How? By offering choices.

Giving a choice is a very powerful tool that can be used with toddlers through teenagers. This is one skill that every parent should have tattooed on the back of his or her hand as a constant reminder. Parents should use this skill every day, many times a day. Giving children choices is a very effective way to enlist their cooperation because children love having the privilege of choice. It takes the pressure out of your request and allows a child to feel in control. This makes a child more willing to comply.

Using choice is an effective way to achieve results, and when you get in the habit of offering choices you are doing your children a big favor. As children learn to make simple choices—Milk or juice?—they get the practice required to make bigger choices—Buy two class T-shirts or one sweatshirt?—which gives them the ability as they grow to make more important decisions—Save or spend? Drink beer or soda? Study or fail? Giving children choices allows them to learn to listen to their inner voice. It is a valuable skill that they will carry with them to adulthood.

You should offer choices based on your child's age and your intent. A toddler can handle two choices, a grade-school child three or four. A teenager can be given general guidelines. Offer choices such that you would be happy with whatever option your child chooses. Otherwise, you are not being fair. For example, a parent might say, "Either eat your peas or go to your room," but when the child gets up off his chair, the parent yells, "Sit down and eat your dinner, young man!" (So that wasn't really a choice, was it?) Here are some ways in which you can use choice:

- Do you want to wear your Big Bird pajamas or your Mickey Mouse pajamas?
- Do you want to do your homework at the kitchen table or the desk?
- Do you want to wear your coat, carry it, or put on a sweatshirt?
- Would you prefer to let the dog out in the yard or take him for a walk?
- Do you want to run up to bed or hop like a bunny?
- What do you want to do first, take out the trash or dry the dishes?
- Do you want to watch 5 more minutes of TV or 10?

A typical problem with choices is the child who makes up his own choice! For example, "Taylor, do you want to put on your pajamas first, or brush your teeth?" To which little Taylor answers, "I want to watch TV." What to do? Just smile sweetly and say, "That wasn't one of the choices. What do you want to do first, put on your pajamas or brush your teeth?" If your child is still reluctant to choose from the options that you offer, then simply ask, "Would you like to choose or shall I choose for you?" If an appropriate answer is not forthcoming then you can say, "I see that you want me to choose for you." Then follow through. Make your choice and help your child—by leading or carrying him—so that he can cooperate.

Winning the Chore War

By Elizabeth Pantley, author of Kid Cooperation and Perfect Parenting
© 2002. Elizabeth Pantley, www.pantley.com/elizabeth.

"How many times do I have to remind you to take out the trash?" Sound familiar? Household jobs are a part of every family's daily life, yet they tend to create ongoing conflict. Give yourself a pat on the back if you assign your kids chores. It's an important way kids learn responsibility. Even children as young as two years old can help out around the house. Here are a few pointers for making the process easier on everybody.

Have a plan. Kids thrive on routine. It's best if they have routine chores that they do at regular times. For instance, clearing the table is done right after eating. Trash is taken out immediately after the kitchen is cleaned up. Bed is made right after dressing. The more you develop these routines, the less reminding you will have to do. When you do have to remind your child it can be a brief statement, such as "Trash Time." With more than one child you can rotate chores, but keep in mind it will take extra effort to develop new routines. Visual reminders help kids stay on track. A poster, chart, or job board can help kids stay focused.

Train and encourage. Use a four-step process when introducing a new job. First, you do the job, narrating as you work, while the child

Table 47.1. Who Does What?

Following is a list of ideas to get you thinking about what your kids are capable of doing. Don't underestimate your children! The same child who runs a complicated computer game can certainly manage the washer and dryer!

Ages 2–3
- Put away toys
- Help set table

Ages 4–5
- Get the mail
- Help with yard work
- Feed pets

Ages 6–7
- Clear table after meals
- Pour own drinks and get snacks
- Empty wastebaskets

Ages 8–9
- Sweep or mop floor
- Load and run dishwasher
- Run/take own bath

Ages 10–11
- Help prepare dinner
- Mow lawn
- Clean kitchen

Ages 12–14
- Grocery shop (small list)
- Prepare a dinner meal
- Clean bathrooms

watches. Next, do the job together. Third, the child does the job while you watch, coach, and encourage. Fourth, the child is ready to go it alone. If you eliminate training then you open the door for battles since you will both be operating under different expectations.

Follow through. Once you decide on a plan, do your best to stick to it every day. If you allow excuses and delays then you'll find yourself fighting with your child. If you have a kid who fights the routine, establish a consequence for failure to complete chores and follow through without anger or threats.

Sibling Rivalry

By Elizabeth Pantley, author of Kid Cooperation and Perfect Parenting *© 2002. Elizabeth Pantley, www.pantley.com/elizabeth.*

The word "sibling" refers to brothers and sisters, and "sibling rivalry" means the competitive feelings and actions that often occur among children in a family. There are things that you can do to try to reduce sibling rivalry.

- Treat each child as an individual. Help children understand that they are treated differently by you and have different privileges and responsibilities because they are different individuals.
- Respect each child's space, toys, and time when he wants to be alone, away from his sibling.
- Avoid labeling or comparing one child to the other. This feeds into their competitiveness.
- When a new child comes into the family, adequately prepare the older sibling for her new important role. Make her feel like it's her baby, too.
- Play detective. Watch and note when siblings are not getting along (before dinner, in the car, before bed) and plan separate quiet activities for those times.
- Watch how you treat each child to see if you are contributing to the rivalry. Make sure you are not playing favorites.
- Have realistic expectations of how they should get along, cooperate, share, and like each other.

- Positively reinforce them when they are getting along or when they solve their own conflicts.
- Make each child feel special and important. Try to spend one-on-one time with each child every day.
- Take time out for yourself to re-energize. Remember, sibling rivalry is a normal and expected part of family life.

Setting Rules and Consequences with Teens

By Elizabeth Pantley, author of Kid Cooperation and Perfect Parenting *© 2002. Elizabeth Pantley, www.pantley.com/elizabeth.*

Rules and consequences are critical to negotiating your way through the teen years. Both the rules and the consequences may change as your teen's needs (and desires) develop. It helps to ask yourself some questions about your rules periodically. General questions to ask about rules:

- Are they reasonable?
- Have the reasons for the rules been explained thoroughly?
- Are there too many?
- Are they enforceable?
- Has my teen been involved in making any of the rules?
- Are they consistent with other parents' (those whom you respect) rules?
- Whose needs are the rules designed to meet?

Depending on the answers to these questions and what you've decided is your bottom line, you may be able to negotiate a relaxation of these rules, as your teen is more able to make mature decisions. Or you may find that the rules are entirely unenforceable, meaning either that you need to make changes in your life in order to enforce them or you need to give them up. For example, you may decide that you should arrange your schedule to allow being home more of the time, or simply that you need to be more aware when you are at home.

Remember, no matter how reasonable the rules are, your teen's job is to challenge them. This means that you need to be prepared to impose consequences. Consequences need to meet certain conditions in order to be effective. They should:

Be related to the behavior so they make sense. Being grounded for every infraction doesn't allow connection to a specific behavior, but if your teen damages someone else's property, part of the consequence might be to help pay for the damage.

Teach your teen how to express feelings and desires in acceptable ways. You don't damage other people's property just because you're angry; anger can be expressed with words.

Not be so severe or unenforceable that there is no hope of compliance. Being grounded for 6 months will contribute to noncompliance.

Be useful in changing behavior. They need to be unpleasant enough that your teen doesn't want to repeat the consequence. They should not include things that you want your child to learn to enjoy, like going to Grandma's for a weekend.

Teach self-control. Help your teen see the benefits of more freedom, less control, or something tangible like driving.

What kinds of consequences might be useful with your teen?

The answer to this varies, depending on your values and the personality, intensity, and interests of your teen. Sometimes he or she can help you find workable consequences. However, be careful because children will sometimes be harsher on themselves than you might think necessary. The goal is to prevent unacceptable behavior and teach your teen to make mature decisions. Think through consequences in advance and take time to manage your own anger or frustration before talking to your teen.

Chapter 48

Nine Steps to More Effective Parenting

Raising children is one of the toughest and most fulfilling jobs in the world—and the one for which you may feel the least prepared. Here are some ways to tackle your child-rearing responsibilities that will help you feel more fulfilled as a parent, and enjoy your children more, too.

1. Nurture Your Child's Self-Esteem.

Children start developing their sense of self as babies when they see themselves through your eyes. Your tone of voice, your body language, and your every expression are absorbed by your child. Your words and actions as parents affect your child's developing self-image more than anything else in his world. Consequently, praising your child for his accomplishments, however small, will make him feel proud; letting him do things for himself will make him feel capable and independent. By contrast, belittling your child or comparing him unfavorably to another child will make him feel worthless.

Avoid making loaded statements or using words as weapons: "What a stupid thing to do!" or "You act more like a baby than your little brother!" Comments like these bruise the inside of a child as much

---

This information was provided by KidsHealth, one of the largest resources online for medically reviewed health information written for parents, kids, and teens. For more articles like this one, visit www.KidsHealth.org, or www.TeensHealth.org.

as blows would the outside. Choose your words carefully and be compassionate. Let your child know that everyone makes mistakes and that you still love him, even when you don't love his behavior.

2. Catch Your Child Being Good.

Have you ever stopped to think about how many times you react negatively to your child in a given day? You may find that you are criticizing far more than you are complimenting. How would you feel about a boss who treated you with that much negative guidance, even if well-intentioned?

The more effective approach is to catch your child doing something right: "You made your bed without being asked—that's terrific!" or "I was watching you play with your sister and you were very patient." These statements will do more to encourage good behavior over the long run than repeated scoldings. Make a point of finding something to praise every day. Be generous with rewards—your love, hugs, and compliments can work wonders and are often reward enough. Soon you will find you are "growing" more of the behavior you would like to see.

3. Set Limits and Be Consistent with Your Discipline.

Discipline is necessary in every household. The goal of discipline is to help children choose acceptable behaviors and learn self-control. Children may test the limits you establish for them, but they need those limits to grow into responsible adults. Establishing house rules will help children understand your expectations and develop self-control. Some house rules might include: no TV until homework is done, and no hitting, name-calling, or hurtful teasing is allowed.

You may want to have a system in place: one warning, followed by consequences such as a time-out or loss of privileges. A common mistake parents make is failure to follow through with consequences when rules are broken. You can't discipline a child for talking back one day, and ignore it the next. Being consistent teaches your child what you expect.

4. Make Time for Your Children.

With so many demands on your time, it's often difficult for parents and children to get together for a family meal, let alone spend some quality time together. But there is probably nothing your child would like more. Get up 10 minutes earlier in the morning so you can eat breakfast with your child, or leave the dishes in the sink and take a walk after dinner. Children who are not getting the attention they want from their parents often act out or misbehave because they are assured of being noticed that way.

Many parents find it mutually rewarding to have prescheduled time with their child on a regular basis. For instance, tell your child that Tuesday is his special night with Mommy, and let him help decide how you will spend your time together. Look for other ways to connect with your child—put a note or something special in his lunchbox.

Adolescents seem to need less undivided attention from their parents than younger children. Because there are fewer windows of opportunity for parents and teens to get together, parents should do their best to be available when their teen does express a desire to talk or participate in family activities. Attending concerts, games, and other events with him communicates caring and lets you get to know about him and his friends in important ways.

Don't feel guilty if you're a working parent. It is the many little things you do with your child—making popcorn, playing cards, window shopping—that he will remember.

5. Be a Good Role Model.

Young children learn a great deal about how to act by watching you. The younger they are, the more cues they take from you. Before you lash out or blow your top in front of your child, think about this: is that how you want him to behave when he's angry? Be constantly aware that you are being observed by your children. Studies have shown that children who hit usually have a role model for aggression at home.

Model the traits you wish to cultivate in your child: respect, friendliness, honesty, kindness, tolerance. Exhibit unselfish behavior. Do things for other people without expecting a reward. Express thanks and offer compliments. Above all, treat your children the way you expect other people to treat you.

6. Make Communication a Priority.

You can't expect children to do everything simply because you, as parent, "say so." Children want and deserve explanations as much as adults do. If we don't take time to explain, children will begin to wonder about our values and motives and whether they have any basis. Parents who reason with their children allow them to understand and learn in a nonjudgmental way.

Make your expectations clear. If there is a problem, describe it to your older child, express your feelings about it, and invite your child to work on a solution with you. Be sure to include consequences. Make suggestions and offer choices. Be open to your child's suggestions as well. Negotiate with him. Children who participate in decisions are more motivated to carry them out.

7. Be Flexible and Willing to Adjust Your Parenting Style.

If you frequently feel "let down" by your child's behavior, it may be because you have unrealistic expectations for him. Parents who think in "shoulds" (for example, "He should be potty-trained by now") may find it helpful to do more reading on the matter or talk to other parents or child development specialists.

Your child's environment has an impact on his behavior, and you may be able to modify his behavior by changing his environment. If you find yourself constantly saying "No" to your 2-year-old, look for ways to restructure his surroundings so that fewer things are off-limits. This will cause less frustration for both of you.

As your child changes, you will gradually have to change your parenting style. Chances are, what works with your child now won't work as well in a year or two.

Teenagers tend to look less to their parents and more to their peers for role models. Continue to provide guidance, encouragement, and appropriate discipline while allowing your child to earn more independence. And seize every available moment to make a connection!

8. Show That Your Love Is Unconditional.

As a parent, you are responsible for correcting and guiding your child. But how you express your corrective guidance makes all the difference in how your child receives it. When you have to confront your child, avoid blaming, criticizing, or fault-finding, which undermine self-esteem and can lead to resentment. Instead, strive to nurture and encourage even when you are disciplining your child. Make sure he knows that although you want and expect him to do better next time, you love him no matter what.

9. Be Aware of Your Own Needs and Limitations As a Parent.

Face it—you are an imperfect parent. You have strengths and weaknesses as a family leader. Recognize your abilities—"I am loving and dedicated." Vow to work on your weaknesses—"I need to be more consistent with discipline." Try to have realistic expectations for yourself, your spouse, and your children. You don't have to have all the answers—be forgiving of yourself. And try to make parenting a manageable job. Focus on the areas that need the most attention rather than trying to address everything all at once. Admit it when you're burned out. Take time out from parenting to do things that will make you happy as a person (or as a couple). Focusing on your needs does not make you selfish. It simply means you care about your own well-being, which is another important value to model for your children.

Chapter 49

Information for Step Parents

Stepfamily Myths

Myths are beliefs that strongly influence the way people in stepfamilies adjust to their new family and react to one another. The following myths about stepfamilies can be stumbling blocks on the stepfamily journey.

Myth #1: Love occurs instantly between the child and the stepparent.

This is the expectation that because you love your new partner you will automatically love his or her children; or that the children will automatically love us because we are such nice people. Of course, if we think about it, we recognize that establishing relationships takes time; that it does not happen overnight or by magic.

Even if we recognize the time factor involved, it is hard to accept that sometimes we are willing to have a relationship with someone who is not willing to have a relationship with us. That hurts, and when people hurt, they may become resentful and angry.

Stepfamily adjustment will be helped if we come to the relationships with our stepchildren with minimal, and, therefore, more realistic, expectations about how the relationships will develop. We may

---

"Stepfamily Myths" and "Frequently Asked Questions (FAQs)." Reprinted with permission from the Stepfamily Association of America, http://saafamilies.org.

then be pleased when respect and friendship blossom and less disappointed if it takes more time than we anticipated.

Myth #2: Children of divorce and remarriage are forever damaged.

Children go through a painful period of adjustment after a divorce or remarriage. Adults often respond to their children's pain with guilt. Somehow they feel they can make it up to them. This leads to difficulties in responding appropriately to our children's hurt and setting appropriate limits—an important part of parenting.

Researchers have hopeful news about children of divorce and remarriage. Although it takes some time, most children do recover their emotional equilibrium. Five and 10 years later most are found to be no different, in many important ways, from kids in first marriage families.

Myth #3: Stepmothers are wicked.

This myth is based on the fairy stories we all hear as children. Because these stories tell about stepmothers who are not kind, nice, or fair, we may be confused about our roles when we become stepmothers. We are nice people, wanting to do a good job, but the world seems to have another idea about stepmothers.

This negative concept of the stepmother role impacts us in a very personal way and we may be very self-conscious about our stepparenting. Research tells us that stepmothers have the most difficult role in the stepfamily. (But, if you are a stepmother, you knew that already.)

Myth #4: Adjustment to stepfamily life occurs quickly.

People are optimistic and hopeful when they remarry. They want life to settle down and to get on with being happy. If your hope or expectation is that once the wedding vows are spoken life will return to normal (whatever that is), you are going to be disappointed.

Because stepfamilies are such complicated families, the time it takes for people to get to know each other, to create positive relationships, and to develop some family history is significant, usually at least four years.

Myth #5: Children adjust to divorce and remarriage more easily if biological fathers (or mothers) withdraw.

Children will always have two biological parents, and will adjust better if they can access both. This means they need to be able to see their nonresidential parent and to think well of him or her. Sometimes visitation is painful for the nonresidential parent, but it is very important to the child's adjustment and emotional health, except in those rare instances of parental abuse or neglect.

It helps if the residential parent and stepparent can work toward a parenting partnership with all the adults involved. Sometimes this can't happen right away, but it can be something to work toward.

Myth #6: Stepfamilies formed after a parent dies are easier.

People need time to grieve the loss of a loved one, and a remarriage may reactivate unfinished grieving. These emotional issues may get played out in the new relationship with detrimental effects.

Another problem is that it can be difficult to think realistically about the person who has died. He or she exists in memory, not in reality, and sometimes gets elevated to sainthood.

When people remarry after the death of a spouse, they may want a relationship similar to the one before. When people remarry after a divorce, they are usually looking for something very different. New partners may find themselves competing with a ghost.

Myth #7: Part-time stepfamilies are easier.

Relationships take time. Stepfamilies where the children only visit occasionally are hampered by the lack of time to work on relationships.

If your stepchildren come every other weekend, there is less time for one-on-one time between the stepchild and stepparent, and less time for family activities. Since stepfamilies follow an adjustment process (stages of development), it may take the part-time stepfamily longer to move through the process.

Myth #8: There is only one kind of family.

This is the myth that says you will be just like a first marriage (or biological) family. Today there are lots of different kinds of families; first marriage, single parent, foster, and stepfamilies to name a few. Each is valuable and has different characteristics. Just because there are two adults in the stepfamily doesn't mean that it recreates a biological family. If this is what you are hoping for, you will be frustrated when it doesn't happen.

Frequently Asked Questions

What is a stepfamily?

A stepfamily is a family in which one or both of the adult partners bring children from a previous relationship. Children in stepfamilies are referred to as:

- Siblings—biologically related; from the same parents.
- Stepsiblings—not biologically related; parents are married to each other.
- Half-siblings—partially related biologically (i.e., share one parent).
- Mutual child—a child born to the remarried couple.
- Residential stepchildren—live in the household with the remarried couple the majority of the time.
- Nonresidential stepchildren—live in the household less than half of the time.

A stepfamily household: A stepfamily is formed when a parent marries a person who is not their child's other biological parent. People can be members of a stepfamily and not live all of the time in the stepfamily household. For instance, when both of a child's parents remarry, the child becomes a member of two stepfamilies—a stepfamily in the mother's new household and a stepfamily in the father's new household.

Unfortunately, the Census Bureau does not recognize that the child can be a member of two stepfamilies. The Census Bureau only counts the household where the child lives most of the time. Since divorce courts still typically decide that mom will become the primary custodial parent, you can see that our stepfamily statistics usually only count biological mom and stepdad households (also known as Stepfather Households). Our statistics do not include the biological father and stepmother household even when the child spends a lot of time with them.

Of course, the reverse is true if a divorced custodial dad marries again. In this case, the children primarily live with dad and stepmom so the statistics will include their household (also known as Stepmother Households) and the child's mother and stepfather's household would not be counted in the stepfamily statistics.

This Census Bureau's method of counting stepfamilies doesn't make much sense at a time when our country is putting so much emphasis on the continued involvement (emotionally, financially, and day-to-day activities) of both biological parents in a child's life.

What can stepfamilies do to be successful?

Nurture and enrich the couple relationship:

- Affirm each other frequently. Demonstrate affection.
- Spend alone time together.
- Be honest and open.
- Practice positive communication.
- Fight fairly.
- Remember that little things mean a lot.

Reveal and understand emotions. Deal with and resolve the loss/pain from previous relationship so that it does not continue to interfere with the present one. Rid yourself of the bitterness which often exists after a divorce.

Encourage the children to express and process their feelings. Because emotions are often more intense in a stepfamily and there are more complicating factors, it is important that emotions be expressed in productive ways.

Have realistic expectations. All members of the stepfamily need to get to know each other well before a remarriage takes place. The myths of instant love and its antithesis of never-ending, unsolvable problems need to be dispelled.

Develop new roles. Understand that a new family is being created and that all members will be developing some new roles and changing others. Former spouses must learn to co-parent, which is often very difficult. Children should not be used as messengers between households or as pawns in a power struggle. The non-custodial parent needs to develop a new role and continue to demonstrate love and concern.

Stepparents, obviously, have to develop a new role with the children. Depending upon custodial arrangements, different roles are possible. The role of friend is a positive one and can be assumed if the children do not spend much time in the household of the stepparent. Generally, it is recommended to begin the relationship as a friend. Custodial stepparents need to develop a type of parenting role.

Neither authoritarian nor permissive discipline seems to work as well in a stepfamily as democratic discipline. Shared roles and responsibilities have benefits in the stepfamily.

Grandparents are often neglected in stepfamily research. They, too, assume new roles and can play an instrumental role in stepfamily success. Educating grandparents, as well as other stepfamily members, is highly recommended.

Clear, open, honest communication is vital. The couple relationship needs to remain strong. Struggles in which the biological parent feels in the middle or the stepparent feels alone can be very detrimental.

Whichever roles are finally assumed, the goal is family integration. It is important that stepfamilies begin to develop a sense of unity, while keeping in mind that this is not a biological family.

Seek support, and see the positive. Learn about stepfamily dynamics by reading stepfamily books.

Positive affirmation is important. Hopefully, support is evident from family, friends, and the community in general. Attend an Stepfamily Association of America (SAA) support group. Join the Stepfamily Association to learn more about stepfamily living, and support SAA's efforts to make every stepfamily a success. Emphasize the positive. Stepfamilies have many strengths.

Chapter 50

Talking to Your Child about Sexual Abuse

Childhood should be about sweetness and light, not gloom and doom. So why broach the subject of something as awful as sexual abuse with your child? Why bring it up if it may never happen? Is it really necessary to make such a big deal about it? You bet it is, for these reasons and more:

- Without prior knowledge of what it is and how to recognize it, young children may not recognize their victimization as sexual abuse.
- Kids often keep quiet about the abuse because they think disclosure will bring consequences even worse than being victimized again.
- Children often get the feeling that something they did caused the abuse, and therefore think that something must be wrong with them or that it's their fault.

An estimated one out of five women and one out of 10 men report having been sexually abused in childhood, according to the American Academy of Pediatrics (AAP). So if you think your child's safe or immune,

---

This information was provided by KidsHealth, one of the largest resources online for medically reviewed health information written for parents, kids, and teens. For more articles like this one, visit www.KidsHealth.org, or www.TeensHealth.org.

think again. In fact, you owe it to your child—whether toddler or teen—to talk about the subject and make sure she's informed.

What Is Sexual Abuse?

When a child is sexually abused, she can be assaulted (or physically harmed) or exploited, which involves verbal or emotional abuse. The abuser, usually an adult or older child whom the child knows, will force, trick, bribe, threaten, or pressure her into sexual activity. Such forms of child abuse include:

- sexual touching and fondling of a child
- having the child touch the abuser's genitals or perform oral sexual acts on the abuser
- forced or unforced vaginal or anal sexual intercourse with a child
- exposure to adult sexual activity or pornographic movies or photos
- having a child pose, undress, or perform in a sexual manner
- spying on a child while she's in a bathroom or bedroom

Because most children are trusting and because they usually know the abuser, physical force is rarely needed. And children are often taught to obey their elders, a lesson that perpetrators can use to their advantage.

Effects of Sexual Abuse on Children

Because physical evidence of sexual abuse is often absent or difficult to detect, concerned adults should be aware of unusual changes in behavior. A normally talkative child may become quiet and withdrawn, or a reticent child may suddenly exhibit promiscuous or sexually inappropriate behavior. A well-adjusted child may suddenly withdraw from those closest to her or become fearful of being with a particular person (who may be the abuser). A child who is being abused may even begin to abuse other children. Children who have been sexually abused may also:

- copy adult sexual behavior
- insist on sexual play with other children, toys, pets, or themselves

- display sexual knowledge beyond what's normal for their age or maturity level
- have unexplained pain, swelling, or bleeding around the genitals or mouth
- have urinary tract infections or sexually transmitted diseases (STDs)

Sexual abuse has been termed the "silent problem" because children often are either afraid to tell, having been threatened by the abuser to keep quiet, or are too young or too ashamed to put what has happened into words. They may be confused by the feelings that accompany the abuse, and they may blame themselves for it. Abuse also may betray their sense of trust, because it often involves telling on a loved one. If they can't tell their secret to those they trust, they may begin to think that they can't trust anyone and learn to repress their feelings. If they close themselves off, they may begin to feel helpless, which can have long-lasting effects on their future relationships, emotional health, and attainment of educational and career goals.

Another problem is that at first, particularly if the abuser is a loved one, some children may like the extra attention shown to them because it makes them feel special. And some children may feel guilty that they didn't initially resist. When they do want out, they may feel unable to act because they didn't say no at first. The child may also fear getting the abuser into trouble, or damaging or severing her relationship with an abusing loved one if she tells or resists—concerns that perpetrators often play upon to continue their control of the situation.

How Can I Talk to My Child?

As frightening as it may be, the reality is that you can never completely protect your child from sexual abuse. However, you can teach her about it so that she'll be aware of what it is and how to protect herself against it.

In a calm and caring manner, you'll want to give your child age-appropriate information to ensure her safety and well-being. Before you get to specifics, though, tell your child that she's loved, valued, and deserves to be safe. Also, never tell her to "do anything an adult tells you to do." When you're sure she understands, follow these guidelines with your child's level of understanding and maturity in mind.

When Talking to a Preschooler

- teach the proper names for body parts
- tell her that her body belongs to her and that no one has the right to touch her private parts or to hurt her in any way
- tell her that this applies to everyone she knows and not just strangers
- make sure she knows it's OK to say no to anything that makes her feel uncomfortable, even if the request is from a relative or friend
- tell her to tell to you if any adult asks her to keep a secret

When Talking to a Grade-Schooler

- explain that some adults have problems, and if something feels wrong to her, it probably is
- explain that some adults are confused about sex and sometimes they try to kiss, touch, or hug children in a way that makes kids feel uncomfortable
- tell her to come to you even if she's afraid of what may happen, if it seems easier to try to forget about it, or if someone has threatened her not to tell
- tell her you will believe her and protect her if she tells you about abuse and that you will never blame or be angry with her for doing so
- give straightforward answers if they ask about sex
- stress personal safety and encourage your child to get away from the abuser as quickly and safely as possible

When Talking to a Teenager

- explain that sexual violence is any sexual act that breaks a person's trust or threatens her safety
- explain that sexual assault may feel good at first, but later on she may feel bad inside
- discuss rape, date/acquaintance rape, sexually transmitted diseases, and unintended pregnancy

- tell her nobody has the right to force her to do any act that she considers sexual (kissing, hugging, any contact with the breasts or genitals, sexual intercourse, etc.)
- reiterate the importance of saying no, telling an adult if something wrong or something that felt wrong has happened, and keeping her body safe

Experts caution against using the "good touch-bad touch" explanation because young children tend to think of a "bad touch" as one that causes physical pain or involves hitting. Many types of sexual contact are not painful, do not cause injury, and may even "feel good" to the child. So instead, tell your child exactly what an "OK" touch might be—a pat on the back, a rub on the head, a high five, and so on. Ask your child to name some touches and let her know whether they're OK.

Here's something else to consider. When grandparents and other relatives come for a visit, hugs and kisses are expected. But many children don't want to get close right away—or at any point during the visit—and they shouldn't be forced to. This is another kind of violation of a child's private space. Tell your child she doesn't have to hug or kiss anyone, even relatives, if she doesn't want to. Explain it to loved ones, too, and suggest that they break the ice by playing with your child first. That way, a hug may happen on its own, and the spontaneity can make it that much more special.

I Think My Child Is Being Abused—What Should I Do?

Keeping calm is key. If you overreact, your child may think you're angry at her instead of at what's happened to her.

Realize that talking about the abuse can be extremely difficult if your child has been sworn to secrecy. You may get an inkling from some vague statements in which she hints about the abuse, or she may confide in a friend first.

If you find out that your child has been abused, here's what you can do to help her immediately:

- Believe her. In most cases, children do not lie about sexual abuse.
- Tell her you're proud of her for telling and that she's not to blame.
- Protect her privacy. Don't tell people who don't need to know.

- Report the abuse to the police or your local child protection service agency, no matter who the abuser is. If the suspected abuser is a member of your family, your state's department of protective services will be involved.
- Never confront the offender in your child's presence. Let the police handle all contact with him or her.
- Call your child's doctor. A medical exam may be needed to collect evidence and can determine whether your child may have any physical injuries that need care.

Some parents may find it difficult to accept that a family member or friend has abused their child in this way, especially if the abuser is a spouse or even a grandparent. Some parents may deny the truth—or perhaps even become angry with their child—because it is too painful for them to accept (perhaps because of their own history of abuse). But such a denial may do even more emotional harm to a child who has been sexually abused. It is the ability of the child and parent to communicate that is protective overall.

Getting Help

Sexual abuse must be reported to the police or your local child protective services agency, even if the offender is a close friend or relative. As quickly as possible, call your child's doctor and get a medical exam for evidence and assurance that there is no physical damage. In some cases, the doctor may refer your child to a specialist or a hospital-based sexual abuse diagnostic and management team for the examination. Ask your child's doctor or the sexual abuse specialists involved in the care of your child to recommend a mental health professional to whom you and/or your child can talk, or contact the agencies listed in Additional Resources for support groups and community service organizations.

Unfortunately, many sexually abused children never get the chance to tell. They live with shame and guilt for many years, and some become offenders as adults. With help, however, children who have been sexually abused can regain self-esteem, cope with guilt, and begin to heal.

Chapter 51

Physical Discipline: Is It Okay to Spank a Child?

The Spanking Debate

Some parents think that using physical force to discipline children is unwise at best and leads to child abuse at worst. Others, including many policy makers, regard an occasional smack on the behind or stinging slap on the wrist as a normal and necessary part of child rearing. A meta-analysis of 88 studies—including more than 36,000 participants—published this year in the journal *Psychological Bulletin* suggests that people who favor corporal punishment should have second thoughts. The author, Elizabeth Thompson Gershoff of Columbia University, argues that although cause-and-effect relationships may be difficult to prove, spanking has so many unfortunate associations that anyone who recommends it as a policy carries a heavy burden of proof.

Gershoff defines corporal punishment as physical force used with the intention of causing pain, but not injury, in order to correct or control a child's behavior. She distinguishes it from physical abuse, as defined by the National Clearinghouse on Child Abuse and Neglect: the infliction of physical injury, intentionally or not, by punching, beating, kicking, biting, burning, or shaking. To that list she adds yanking hair, twisting ears, and making a child stand in the same place for a long time, even if no injury results. Simple spanking may also

---

Excerpted from the November 2002 issue of the *Harvard Mental Health Letter*. www.health.Harvard.edu.

amount to abuse if it's done too often, too hard, or for too long, or if the child is less than a year or more than 12 years old.

In most studies, corporal punishment is found to have one desirable effect—getting a child (especially one with behavior problems and a tendency to resist authority) to comply immediately with a parent's legitimate demands. Apart from that, the data are anything but reassuring. Studies show that children who are spanked have a less trusting and affectionate relationship with their parents and feel less guilt about misbehavior, as opposed to concern about being caught. They are also more likely to be physically abused by their parents (statistically, this is the strongest association of all) and, when they grow up, more likely to abuse their own spouses and children.

In both childhood and adulthood, they're more aggressive and have poorer mental health and a higher rate of criminal and other antisocial behavior. The more often and the longer and harder they are spanked, the worse the outcome. These associations are consistently strongest for boys and for older children, ages 10–12 (spanking is most common at ages 2–8 and rare after puberty).

Gershoff explains that children whose parents hit them may feel pain, anger, and fear that lead them to ignore the disciplinary message and to resent the parent instead. Some lose their incentive to internalize social values and develop self-control. They concentrate on their own grievance instead of thinking about the act for which they were punished and the harm it caused or might have caused. Physical aggression seems to be an acceptable and effective way to solve problems. They learn to interpret other people's behavior as hostile and requiring a hostile response. For other children, corporal punishment may evoke feelings of helplessness that make them vulnerable to depression and anxiety. Parents who abuse their children report that more than two-thirds of abuse incidents begin with corporal punishment. Spanking may work on an abuser like the first drink on a confirmed alcoholic.

Gershoff notes some reservations and critics offer further objections. These involve two main issues: the influence of surrounding circumstances, including other actions and attitudes of parents, and the difficulty telling cause from effect.

As Gershoff admits, studies rarely provide much information about the circumstances. They almost never record whether the punishment was deliberate or impulsive, a first resort or a last resort. They don't indicate whether it was imposed by an affectionate or a rejecting parent, or whether the parent gave reasons and explanations.

Gershoff's critics question whether the meta-analysis shows that corporal punishment harms children between the ages of 2 and 6, when it's most common. They also point out that many studies don't distinguish between ordinary spanking and more severe punishments, including pushing, grabbing, throwing things, and slapping the face. In some studies, most children who were spanked were also physically abused. In other studies, no one asked about physical abuse. According to this view, parents who move from spanking to abuse are different from most—less likely to use other forms of discipline and concerned more about their own feelings than about the child's needs.

Gershoff admits that the quality of family life and the motives of parents make a difference. Adults who strike children impulsively, in anger, probably do more harm because they seem frightening and unpredictable. Corporal punishment makes more sense if the parent tries other methods of discipline first and, when spanking or slapping seems necessary, explains the reasons for it. It's less risky if used not merely for disobedience, or even to correct bad manners or punish aggression, but to prevent actions that could cause immediate harm to the child or others—stopping a child from running into a busy street or sticking a finger into an electrical socket. (Critics say those are exactly the situations in which spanking is most likely.) Although the issue is controversial, some believe corporal punishment has different and more beneficial effects if it's fully accepted within a culture. Ethnic, class, religious, and geographical differences may also affect the outcome of spanking. On all these questions, there's little evidence.

Still, Gershoff insists that the meaning and value of corporal punishment should not be judged merely on evidence about moderate and occasional spanking by loving parents who give reasons for their actions. The descent from spanking or slapping to physical abuse is too easy, and the connection can't be denied. She also points out that more severe forms of corporal punishment are common. Nearly a third of parents of 2- to 8-year-olds admit to paddling a child—a practice also authorized by schools in many parts of the country.

She adds that studies relying on interviews—as do most of those in the meta-analysis—are more likely to underreport punishment that borders on physical abuse.

Another critical issue is when being hit is the cause of a child's misbehavior and when it is the result. Many studies record the behavior and the punishment during the same period of time, which makes it impossible to tell. Even if more aggressive or antisocial behavior is shown to occur after spanking than before, spanking isn't necessarily one of the causes. Heredity and temperament matter, too. Parents are more likely to spank an irritable or aggressive child. Aggressive parents may transmit their aggressiveness genetically and may also spank the child more. Besides, studies on the long-term effects of corporal punishment have had to rely on the recollections of parents and older or adult children. It's easy to see how memories could be distorted by the outcome.

The best answer to cause-and-effect questions is an experiment—obviously an impossible one to do. Effective programs for the prevention of physical abuse discourage spanking, but that's not necessarily one of the reasons for their effectiveness; they have other components, including anger management and training in problem-solving. One possibility for a sort of thought experiment is to have children view videos of various forms of punishment and say what they think and feel.

Even without experimental proof, though, Gershoff thinks it's clear that the relationship between spanking and aggressive behavior goes both ways. She points out that if studies showed that corporal punishment was followed by more desirable behavior in children, few would deny that it was a cause of the improvement.

Gershoff recommends defining the limits of corporal punishment more clearly for both legal and research purposes. How long must spanking have to continue before we call it physical abuse? Is taking a belt to a child's bottom or washing a child's mouth out with soap corporal punishment or abuse? Existing laws are hard for family court judges and child protective services to interpret.

Gershoff concludes that unless new evidence to the contrary appears, parents and schools should avoid using force to discipline children, mainly because it is too easily abused. She notes that several European countries and Israel have banned corporal punishment, and a United Nations committee has declared it incompatible with the United Nations Convention on the Rights of the Child (which Congress has refused to ratify). Laws against corporal punishment are unlikely in the United States because of our deference to parents' rights. In any case, Gershoff thinks that what we need most is not new laws but better education about the consequences of current practices.

References

Baumrind, D. et al. "Ordinary Physical Punishment: Is It Harmful? Comment on Gershoff (2002)," *Psychological Bulletin* (July 2002): Vol. 128, No. 4, pp. 580-89.

Holden, G.W. "Perspectives on the Effects of Corporal Punishment: Comment on Gershoff (2002)," *Psychological Bulletin* (July 2002): Vol. 128, No. 4, pp. 590-95.

Gershoff, E.T. "Corporal Punishment by Parents and Associated Child Behaviors and Experiences: A Meta-Analytic and Theoretical Review," *Psychological Bulletin* (July 2002): Vol. 128, No. 4, pp. 539-79.

Gershoff, E.T. "Corporal Punishment, Physical Abuse, and the Burden of Proof: Reply to Baumrind, Larzelere, and Cowan (2002), Holden (2002), and Parke (2002)," *Psychological Bulletin* (July 2002): Vol. 128, No. 4, pp. 602-11.

Parke, R.D. "Punishment Revisited—Science, Values, and the Right Question: Comment on Gershoff (2002)," *Psychological Bulletin* (July 2002): Vol. 128, No. 4, pp. 596-601.

Chapter 52

Is the Withholding of Medical Treatment for Religious Reasons a Form of Child Abuse?

Physician Studies Fate of Ill Children "Treated" by Faith Healing

Many cases of religiously motivated medical neglect never become public due to cover-ups, lack of investigations and poor record keeping, according to postdoctoral fellow's research.

Most pediatric research takes place in a medical or scientific setting such as a clinic or lab. But one postdoctoral fellow in forensic pediatrics is more likely to conduct his work in a cemetery. Seth Asser, M.D., studies the deaths of children due to medical neglect on religious grounds.

In the past 15 years, more than 200 children have died in the United States because their parents relied exclusively on faith to heal them. The children died of treatable ailments such as diabetes or dehydration.

"Typical parents cannot relate to this topic because it is so unbelievable," said Asser. "But freedom of belief doesn't allow you to throw away a young life." Last year Asser became a fellow at the Medical

---

Reprinted with permission from, "Physician Studies Fate of Ill Children 'Treated' by Faith Healing," by Scott J. Turner, *George Street Journal,* Volume 26, April 12, 2002. © Brown University; And "Religious Exemptions from Health Care for Children," reprinted with permission from Children's Healthcare is a Legal Duty (CHILD, Inc.). © 2001. All rights reserved. For additional information about religion-based medical neglect, visit www.childrens healthcare.org.

School and at Hasbro Children's Hospital after working close to 20 years as an intensive-care pediatrician, primarily in San Diego and San Antonio. He is also a former medical director for the county-administered California Children Services in San Diego.

In 1998, Asser published a paper in the journal *Pediatrics* that evaluated the deaths of 172 children between 1975 and 1995 from families of 23 religious groups whose rituals dictated that healing must occur through prayer. The article was the largest study ever conducted of such deaths. The study found that 140 fatalities "were from conditions for which survival rates with medical care would have exceeded 90 percent," and that overall only three children would likely not have benefited from medical care. "Not only did they die needlessly, but many of the deaths were slow and painful," Asser said.

Public officials, said Asser's co-author, Rita Swan, have long ignored these deaths. Swan is president of Children's Healthcare Is a Legal Duty (CHILD). This Iowa-based nonprofit organization works to protect children from abusive religious and cultural practices, especially religion-based medical neglect. There are "many laws that allow parents to deprive their children of various kinds of health care on religious grounds," said Swan. "The religious exemption laws are a rare example of discrimination de jure: laws that deprive one group of children of protections afforded to others."

Many cases of religiously motivated medical neglect never become public due to cover-ups, lack of investigations and poor record keeping, Asser said. His most recent findings provide bone-chilling evidence that some individuals and groups look outside of medicine for healing illness and disease.

Asser studied the deaths of youngsters in an obscure religious congregation. In 1998, 78 graves of children buried since 1955 were discovered in a cemetery of the Followers of Christ Church in the suburbs of Oregon City. The finding sparked widespread publicity about poor record keeping and inadequate investigations. Last fall Asser flew to Oregon to examine public records for information about cause of death. He tramped through mud to record data on the children buried in the Followers of Christ cemetery. Asser combed through the group's telephone directory and counted the people coming to a service at the Followers church, as he stood on the sidewalk receiving their hostile glares.

These methods allowed Asser to compare the proportion of child deaths for the group with statewide numbers. Children born into the Followers of Christ Church were 4.5 times more likely to die compared to peers in the surrounding population, he found. "Once again many of the deaths were from conditions easily prevented or treatable," Asser said. After the deaths were publicized, Oregon repealed laws giving religious exemptions to charges of child abuse, neglect, manslaughter, criminal mistreatment, and criminal nonsupport.

In fact, no children in the Oregon Followers of Christ Church have died of medical neglect since the repeal, Asser said, and members were witnessed taking children to doctors. Concluded Asser, "To stop these preventable deaths, other states should promptly repeal similar exemption laws."

"Children don't have the option of saying 'yes' or 'no' to care if their parents decide to deny them that care," said Carole Jenny, M.D., professor of pediatrics and director of the Child Protection Program at Hasbro Children's Hospital. "In addition, children are not competent to understand the long-term consequences of foregoing medical care in life-threatening situations," she said. "Society needs to make sure they are protected until they are able to make those decisions on their own."

Jenny is "proud" of Asser's work. Religiously-motivated medical neglect is "not a popular topic to study—people are often afraid to stand up for these kids," she said. "Many powerful institutions are on the 'other side' of the issue." Swan thinks that few physicians would have the patience to gather the information that Asser does. "It's quite a tedious project to track down data on these kids," she said, adding that "a coroner who has not reported a child's death to law enforcement may not be happy to have a researcher inquire about a case and implicitly expose the coroner's indifference."

Asser has followed the events in Attleboro, Mass., closely. There, two religious sect members have been charged with murder in the starvation death of their year-old son. Two other religious sect members were jailed for refusing to provide information on the whereabouts of their child or its remains. "Despite the local tradition of independence in New England," Asser said, "we don't tolerate people who dispose of children as if they were used tissues."

Asser said he would continue to collect data on religion-motivated medical neglect to "push legislators to change laws." He advocates for medical care for a simple reason: It saves lives. "Witnesses to some of these deaths tell how the babies died," Asser said. "Each story is worse than the last. They died in pain. They died horribly. They died within easy access to top-notch medical facilities. These are examples of how hard-headed some parents can be in the face of what is reasonable and logical and good—protecting and saving the lives of their own children."

Religious Exemptions from Health Care For Children

Exemptions from Preventive and Diagnostic Measures

- 48 states have religious exemptions from immunizations. Mississippi and West Virginia are the only states that require all children to be immunized without exception for religious belief.
- The majority of states have religious exemptions from metabolic testing of newborns. Such tests detect disorders that will cause mental retardation and other handicaps unless they are treated. Sometimes the treatment is simply dietary control until the child's body is able to metabolize protein.
- Colorado, Delaware, Florida, Idaho, Iowa, Maine, Michigan, Minnesota, Nevada, and Pennsylvania have religious exemptions from prophylactic eyedrops for newborns. The eyedrops prevent blindness of infants who have been infected with venereal diseases carried by their mothers.
- Delaware, Illinois, Kansas, Maine, Massachusetts, New Jersey, and Rhode Island have religious exemptions from screening children for lead poisoning.
- California has a religious exemption from tuberculosis testing of public school teachers. In Van Nuys, California, in 1954, schoolteacher Cora Sutherland died of tuberculosis after having exposed hundreds of children to the disease. She had submitted an affidavit swearing to be free of infectious disease in lieu of a required chest x-ray. A Christian Science practitioner had charged $65.00 a month to treat her for "living congestion and over activity."
- California, Colorado, Michigan, Minnesota, and Ohio statutes offer religious exemptions from physical examinations of school children.
- Connecticut, New Jersey, Oregon, and West Virginia have religious exemptions from hearing tests for newborns.
- Oregon and Pennsylvania have religious exemptions from bicycle helmets.
- Oregon has a religious exemption from Vitamin K that is given to newborns to prevent spontaneous hemorrhage.

- California, Colorado, Massachusetts, Michigan, Minnesota, and Ohio have statutes excusing students with religious objections from studying about disease in school.

Exemptions from Providing Medical Care for Sick Children

Thirty-nine states have religious exemptions from child abuse or neglect charges in the civil code. Thirty-one states have a religious defense to a criminal charge. States with a religious defense to the most serious crimes against children include:

- Iowa and Ohio with religious defenses to manslaughter
- Delaware and West Virginia with religious defenses to murder of a child
- Arkansas with a religious defense to capital murder
- Oregon with a religious defense to homicide by abuse.

States with a religious defense to child endangerment, criminal abuse or neglect, and/or cruelty to children include Alabama, Delaware, Georgia, Idaho, Indiana, Iowa, Kansas, Louisiana, Maine, Minnesota, Missouri, Nevada, New Hampshire, New Jersey, New York, Ohio, Oklahoma, South Carolina, Tennessee, Texas, Utah, Virginia, West Virginia, and Wisconsin.

Florida's religious exemption appears only in the juvenile code, but has been ruled a defense to felony abuse charges.

States with a religious exemption to nonsupport include Alaska, California, Colorado, Idaho, Missouri, and South Dakota.

Several exemption statutes, both in the civil and criminal codes, have ambiguities that may make them merely a statement of one's right to pray rather than a right to withhold necessary medical care from a child. Some prosecutors have filed criminal charges and won convictions under chapters of the code that do not have religious exemptions. Nevertheless, some church officials have continued to advise members that the exemption laws confer the right to withhold medical care no matter how sick the child is and even that the laws were passed because legislators understood prayer to be as effective as medicine.

Federal Policy

In response to Christian Science church lobbying, the federal government began requiring states to enact religious exemptions from child abuse and neglect charges in 1974. CHILD founders Rita and Douglas Swan lobbied for several years against this regulation. The federal government rescinded it in 1983.

In 1996, however, Congress enacted a law stating that the federal Child Abuse Prevention and Treatment Act (CAPTA) did not include "a Federal requirement that a parent or guardian provide a child any medical service or treatment against the religious beliefs of the parent or guardian." Furthermore, Sen. Dan Coats, R-Indiana, and Congressman Bill Goodling, R-Pennsylvania, claimed during floor discussion that parents have a First Amendment right to withhold medical care from children.

CHILD Inc. believes the present law is a glaring and potentially lethal discrimination against a class of children. CAPTA mandates that states in the grant program have laws requiring parents to provide needed medical care for their children, but simultaneously allows those states to give parents in faith-healing sects the right to withhold all medical treatment from children.

In January, 1997, within a month after the religious exemption was added to CAPTA, the Christian Science church got HB1104 introduced in Maryland that exempted believers in spiritual healing from all civil and criminal charges regardless of the harm to the child, using language taken verbatim from the new federal law. HB1104 was defeated.

CAPTA was up for reauthorization in the 2001–2002 session and several organizations have called upon Congress to remove the exemption, including the United Methodist Church, National Association of Medical Examiners, Justice for Children, and the National Child Abuse Coalition, which consists of about thirty national organizations working to prevent child abuse.

Data on Injuries to Children Because of Religion-Based Medical Neglect

Two studies indicate that Christian Science adults have higher mortality rates than the general population. See William Simpson, "Comparative longevity in a college cohort of Christian Scientists," *Journal of the American Medical Association (JAMA)* 262 (Sept. 22-29, 1989): 1657-8, and William Simpson, "Comparative mortality in two college groups, 1945-83," *Mortality and Morbidity Weekly Report* 40(August 23, 1991):579-82.

Pediatrician Seth Asser and CHILD president Rita Swan have published a study of 172 deaths of children when medical care was withheld on religious grounds. They found that 140 of the children would have had at least a 90% likelihood of survival with medical care. See Seth Asser and Rita Swan, "Child fatalities from religion-motivated medical neglect," *Pediatrics* 101(April 1998):625-9.

Deaths of Christian Science children between 1974 and 1994 from the following causes are in CHILD's files: 5 of meningitis, 3 of pneumonia, 2 of appendicitis, 5 of diabetes, 2 of diphtheria, 1 of measles, 8 of cancer, 1 of septicemia, 1 of a kidney infection, 1 of a bowel obstruction, and 1 of heart disease.

Between 1973 and 1990, 65 Faith Assembly children are known to have died of treatable illnesses without medical care. In 1983 the Centers for Disease Control and the Indiana Board of Health conducted a study of Faith Assembly members, who shun all medical care including obstetrics. Pregnant women in Faith Assembly were 86 times more likely to die than other expectant mothers in Indiana. The mortality rate for Faith Assembly infants up to 28 days old was 270% higher. See Andrew Kaunitz, Craig Spence, et al., "Perinatal and maternal mortality in a religious group avoiding obstetrical care," *American Journal of Obstetrics and Gynecology* 150 (Dec. 1, 1984):826-31.

The Oregonian reports that 78 children have died since 1955 in the Followers of Christ Church in Oregon City, a church opposed to medical care. Twelve children have died in an Idaho affiliate of the Followers of Christ. See Mark Larabee and Peter Sleeth, "Faith healing raises questions of the law's duty-belief or life?" *The Oregonian* (June 7, 1998):1.

Sects claiming a religious exemption from immunizations have had outbreaks of polio, measles, whooping cough, and diphtheria. In 1991 there were 492 measles cases in Philadelphia among children associated with Faith Tabernacle and First Century Gospel Church, which refuse immunizations. Six children died.

Christian Science schools in the St. Louis area have had four major measles outbreaks between 1985 and 1994. The first included three deaths of young people. The 1994 outbreak had 247 cases. It spread to children in public schools and cost St. Louis County more than $100,000 to manage. Two recent studies indicate that religious and philosophical exemptions to immunizations increase cases of disease. Daniel Feikin et al. in "Individual and community risks of measles and pertussis associated with personal exemptions to immunization," *JAMA* 284 (December 27, 2000):3145-50, studied all reported confirmed measles cases among Colorado children aged 3 to 18 years during 1987-1998 and all reported confirmed and probable pertussis cases among the same population for 1996-98. The authors found that exemptors were 22 times more likely to acquire measles and 6 times more likely to acquire pertussis than vaccinated children. Furthermore, the authors found that at least 11% of vaccinated children who contracted measles acquired the infection through contact with an exemptor.

Daniel Salmon, et al., "Health consequences of religious and philosophical exemptions from immunization laws: individual and societal risk of measles," *JAMA* 282 (July 7, 1999):47-53, found children with religious or philosophical exemptions from immunizations were 35 times more likely to contract measles than vaccinated children.

Chapter 53

Important Information for Parents of Children with Osteogenesis Imperfecta (OI)

OI Issues: Child Abuse

Osteogenesis imperfecta (OI) is characterized by bones that break easily. A minor accident may result in a fracture; some fractures may occur while a child is being diapered, lifted, or dressed. It is possible for a person with OI to break a bone without being aware of it. Children who are not diagnosed at birth often suffer a series of painful fractures before health care professionals are able to diagnose the condition.

Child abuse is also characterized by broken bones. In recent years, Americans have become increasingly aware of this problem and major efforts have been undertaken to protect children. Child abuse is a pattern of behavior that often is passed down from one generation to the next. Many abusive parents were themselves abused as children. Open, honest discussion of the issue not only can ensure the safety of countless children but can also encourage parents who wish to break the cycle of abusive behavior to seek the help they need.

This chapter contains information from "OI Issues: Child Abuse," revised April, 2002, and "Is This an Abused Child? Or Does He Have Osteogenesis Imperfecta?" revised may 2003. Provided by the National Institutes of Health Osteoporosis and Related Bone Diseases—National Resource Center (www.osteo.org) and the Osteogenesis Imperfecta Foundation (www.oif.org). Reprinted with permission. For additional information, visit the Osteogenesis Imperfecta Foundation website or call them toll free at 800-981-2663.

Diagnosis: OI or child abuse?

False accusations of child abuse may occur in families with children who have milder forms of OI and/or in whom OI has not previously been diagnosed. Types of fractures that are typically observed in both child abuse and OI include:

- fractures in multiple stages of healing
- rib fractures
- spiral fractures
- fractures for which there is no adequate explanation of trauma

When the fracture seems incompatible with the reported cause of the injury, child abuse is often suspected. And, unfortunately, when false accusations of child abuse occur, families become victimized.

The following practical advice, together with competent legal advice from a family law attorney, is intended to help parents who have been accused of child abuse.

1. Each state has its own policy for dealing with child abuse cases. We strongly suggest that you secure the advice and, if possible, the services of a family law attorney as soon as charges of child abuse are brought. Attorney referral services are generally offered by each state's Bar Association. If you are not satisfied with the services that your attorney is providing, don't be afraid to find another attorney to handle your case.

2. Remember, physicians and social services case workers are doing their jobs; whoever reported the suspected child abuse to the social services authorities may be bound by law to do so. Everyone involved is concerned about what is best for the child.

3. Seek the best medical diagnosis available. It is of utmost importance that the health care professional (including, but not limited to, an orthopedist familiar with OI) conducting the evaluation have considerable experience in both diagnosing and treating OI.

4. A consultation with a geneticist familiar with OI may reveal a family history of mild OI if symptoms such as blue-tinted sclera (the white part of the eye), presenile hearing loss, rickets,

dental problems, short stature, and/or a history of broken bones are identified.

5. Most often, child abuse is suspected when the explanation given by the child or parent does not appear to match the injury found by the treating physicians and other medical personnel. The decisions of the social services agency are based heavily on the medical information given to the agency by the physician.

6. Unless you advise the case worker, do not change the hospital or physicians who are providing medical services to your child. Changes made without the knowledge of the case worker may be interpreted as an attempt to hide the child abuse.

7. Keep the case worker up to date on what is happening. Attempt to confirm with the case worker that he/she understands what you have told them. Demonstrate that you truly want to work together for what is best for your child. Resistance toward the case worker may be interpreted as guilt.

8. If your child is being taken from your home, you may request that he or she be taken to the home of a grandparent or other relative.

9. When the problem is resolved, insist that the charges be taken off all records, including computerized records. If this is not done, you may be registered as an abusive parent until your youngest child is 18 years of age.

Is This an Abused Child? Or Does He Have Osteogenesis Imperfecta?

A child is brought into the emergency room with a fractured leg. The parents are unable to explain how the leg fractured. X-rays reveal several other fractures in various stages of healing. The parents say they did not know about these fractures, and cannot explain what might have caused them. Hospital personnel call child welfare services to report a suspected case of child abuse. The child is taken away from the parents and placed in foster care.

Scenes like this occur in emergency rooms every day. But in this case, the cause of the fractures is not child abuse. It is osteogenesis imperfecta, or OI. OI is a genetic disorder characterized by bones that break easily—often from little or no apparent cause. A person with

OI may sustain just a few or as many as several hundred fractures in a lifetime.

What is osteogenesis imperfecta?

Osteogenesis imperfecta is a genetic disorder. Most cases involve a defect in type 1 collagen—the protein scaffolding of bone and other connective tissues. People with OI have a faulty gene that instructs their bodies to make either too little type 1 collagen or poor quality type 1 collagen. The result is bones that break easily plus other connective tissue symptoms.

Most cases of OI are caused by a dominant genetic defect. Most children with OI inherit the disorder from a parent who has OI. Some adults with very mild OI may not have been diagnosed as children. Approximately 25% of children with OI are born into a family with no history of the disorder. In these cases, the genetic defect occurred as a spontaneous mutation. Because the genetic defect is usually dominant—whether inherited from a parent or due to a spontaneous mutation—an affected person has a 50% chance of passing on the disorder to each of his or her children.

Several forms of OI have been described, representing wide variations in appearance and severity from one individual to another. Types of OI range from lethal in the newborn period to very mild. Recent research has identified two new moderately severe types that do not appear to have a type 1 collagen defect. It is estimated that 50,000 people have OI in the United States. It occurs in approximately 1:10,000 births.

Following are the clinical features of the major types of OI. Clinical features vary widely not only between types, but within types, and even within the same family. Children with milder OI, in particular, may have few obvious clinical features of OI.

Is it OI or child abuse?

When health care professionals, child welfare workers, and law enforcement officials see an unexplained fracture in a child who appears normal and whose bones appear otherwise normal on x-ray, they often suspect child abuse. Tragically, however, OI is often mistaken for child abuse. When a child has osteogenesis imperfecta:

- Fractures may occur during ordinary activities, such as changing a diaper or burping the baby, or when an infant tries to crawl or pull to a stand. There may be no obvious indication that a fracture has occurred, other than the child crying or refusing to put weight on a limb.

- All types of fractures may occur, including rib fractures and spiral fractures, with little or no apparent trauma.
- The child may bruise easily, again with little or no apparent cause.
- There may be no history of OI in the family, as some cases of OI occur due to a spontaneous genetic mutation. In other cases, a parent's case of mild OI may have gone undiagnosed.
- X-rays may reveal old fractures in various stages of healing that went undetected.
- The OI child may not exhibit the hallmark clinical features of OI, such as blue sclera, bone deformity, or brittle teeth.
- Infants and children with mild or moderate OI may have bones that appear normal on x-rays.

Fortunately, there are several steps that professionals can take to help determine whether fractures are due to undiagnosed osteogenesis imperfecta.

Obtain a family history. Was either parent ever diagnosed with OI or any brittle bone disorder? Do either parent, siblings, or extended family members have a history of childhood fractures, spinal curvature, brittle teeth, hearing loss, or other clinical features that might indicate that they have a mild case of OI that was never diagnosed? It is not uncommon for the severity of OI to vary even within the same family.

Look for clinical features of OI in the child—blue sclera; translucent, opalescent, or discolored teeth (even in unerupted teeth in babies); a triangular shaped face; barrel-shaped rib cage; easy bruising; thin skin; excessive sweating; and other features. However, it is possible for children with OI to exhibit none or few of the outward clinical features. Some signs such as dentinogenesis imperfecta, hearing loss, bone deformity and short stature are age-dependent and may not be evident in an infant. In its mildest form, OI may exhibit only as unexplained bone fractures in childhood.

Consult a health care professional who has experience diagnosing or treating children with OI. OI remains primarily a clinical diagnosis.

Table 53.1. Clinical Features of Osteogenesis Imperfecta (*continued on next page*)

Type I (Mild)

Most common and mildest type of OI.

Bones predisposed to fracture. Most fractures occur before puberty.

Normal or near-normal stature.

Loose joins and muscle weakness.

Sclera (whites of the eyes) usually have a blue, purple, or gray tint.

Triangular face.

Tendency toward spinal curvature.

Bone deformity absent or minimal.

Brittle teeth possible.

Hearing loss possible, often beginning in early teens.

Collagen structure is normal, but the amount of collagen is less than normal.

Type II (Perinatal Lethal)

Most severe form.

Frequently lethal at or shortly after birth, often due to respiratory problems.

Numerous fractures and severe bone deformity evident at birth.

Small stature with underdeveloped lungs.

Collagen is improperly formed.

Type III (Progressive)

Progressive bone deformity, often severe.

Bones fracture easily. Fractures are often present at birth, and x-rays may reveal healed fractures that occurred before birth.

Short stature.

Sclera have a blue, purple, or gray tint.

Loose joints and poor muscle development in arms and legs.

Barrel-shaped rib cage.

Triangular face.

Spinal curvature.

Respiratory problems possible.

Brittle teeth possible.

Hearing loss possible.

Collagen is improperly formed.

Table 53.1. Clinical Features of Osteogenesis Imperfecta (*continued from previous page*)

Type IV (Moderate Severe)

Between Type I and Type III in severity.

Bones fracture easily, most before puberty.

Shorter than average stature.

Sclera are white or near-white (i.e. normal in color)

Mild to moderate bone deformity.

Spinal curvature.

Barrel-shaped rib cage.

Triangular face.

Brittle teeth possible.

Hearing loss possible.

Collagen is improperly formed.

Type V and VI (Novel Forms)

Recently identified types of OI.

At this time no collagen defect has been found.

Characteristics are similar to Type IV OI.

Additional Type V characteristics include:

- Dense band adjacent to the growth plate of long bones.
- Development of hypertrophic calluses from fracture or surgery.
- Calcification of the membrane between the radius and the ulna.

Type VI bones have a "fish scale" appearance when viewed under a microscope.

Other clinical features that may occur in people with all types of OI are thin, smooth skin; loose joints; low muscle strength; and excessive sweating. People with OI may also bruise easily; however, because fractures often occur with very little trauma and during normal activities, it is common for a child to have no bruising around the fracture site.

Generally, clinical geneticists are familiar with OI diagnosis. They have available to them biochemical (collagen) and molecular (DNA) tests that can help confirm a diagnosis of OI in some situations. A skin biopsy can be analyzed to determine if the quantity or quality of type 1 collagen is abnormal. This approach identifies almost 90% of persons known to have OI. A DNA test can be done on a blood sample to try to locate the mutations that cause OI. Several hundred mutations have been identified. This test identifies about 90% of people with OI. A few individuals test positive for OI on one test and not the other. Approximately 10% of individuals with mild or moderate OI test negative for OI through collagen or DNA testing, despite having the disorder.

It has been estimated that 7% of children who have signs suggesting abuse have an underlying medical condition that explains the injuries (Wardinsky). Besides OI, other conditions that feature fragile bones and bruising include Ehlers-Danlos syndrome, glutaric acidaemia type 1, hypophosphatasia, disorders of vitamin D metabolism, disorders of copper metabolism such as Menkes syndrome, and premature birth (Marlowe).

OI is *not* normally associated with calcium or phosphate deficiency, so it cannot be diagnosed by measuring the levels of these substances in the blood.

The national Osteogenesis Imperfecta Foundation maintains a list of orthopedists and geneticists who are reputed to have experience with all types of OI. Foundation staff can suggest appropriate professionals as needed.

Resources

Marlowe A, Pepin MG, Byers PH. Testing for osteogenesis imperfecta in cases of suspected non-accidental injury. *J Med Genet* 2002; 39:382-6.

Wardinsky TD, Vizacarrondo FE, Cruz BK. The mistaken diagnosis of child abuse: a three-year USAF Medical Center analysis and literature review. *Mil Med* 1995;160:15-20.

Part Seven

Additional Help and Information

Chapter 54

Glossary of Terms Related to Child Abuse

Adoptive Parent: A person with the legal relation of parent to a child not related by birth, with the same mutual rights and obligations that exist between children and their birth parents.

Age: Age calculated in years at the time of the report of abuse or neglect, or as of December 31 of the reporting year.

Alcohol Abuse: Compulsive use of alcohol that is not of a temporary nature. Applies to infants addicted at birth, or who are victims of fetal alcohol syndrome, or who may suffer other disabilities due to the use of alcohol during pregnancy.

Alleged Perpetrator Report Source: An individual who reports an alleged incident of child abuse or neglect in which he/she caused or knowingly allowed the maltreatment of a child.

Alleged Victim: Child about whom a report regarding maltreatment has been made to a Child Protective Services (CPS) agency.

Alleged Victim Report Source: A child who alleges to have been a victim of child maltreatment and who makes a report of the allegation.

Excerpted from *Child Maltreatment 2001*, U.S. Department of Health and Human Services, Administration on Children, Youth and Families. Available online at http://www.acf.hhs.gov/programs/cb/publications/cm01/appendb.htm.

American Indian/Alaskan Native: A person having racial origins in any of the original peoples of North and South America (including Central America), and who maintains tribal or community affiliation.

Anonymous or Unknown Report Source: An individual who reports a suspected incident of child maltreatment without identifying himself or herself; or the type of reporter is unknown.

Asian: A person having racial origins in any of the original peoples of the far east, southeast Asia, or the Indian sub-continent, including, for example, Cambodia, China, Guam, India, Japan, Korea, Malaysia, Pakistan, the Philippine Islands, Thailand, and Vietnam.

Assessment: A process by which the CPS agency determines whether the child and/or other persons involved in the report of alleged maltreatment is in need of services.

Behavior Problem: Behavior of the child in the school and/or community that adversely affects socialization, learning, growth, and moral development. May include adjudicated or non-adjudicated behavior problems. Includes running away from home or a placement.

Biological Parent: The birth mother or father of the child rather than the adoptive or foster parent or the stepparent.

Black/African-American: A person whose ancestry is any of the black racial groups of Africa.

Caretaker: A person responsible for the care and supervision of the child who was reported.

Case Management Services: Activities for the arrangement, coordination, and monitoring of services to meet the needs of children and their families.

Child: A person less than 18 years of age or considered to be a minor under state law.

Child Date of Birth: The month, day and year of the child's birth. If the child is abandoned or the date of birth is otherwise unknown, approximate date of birth.

Child Day Care Provider: A person with a temporary caretaker responsibility for the child who is not related to the child, such as a day care center staff member, a family day care provider, or a babysitter. Does not include persons with legal custody or guardianship of the child.

Child ID: A unique identification assigned to each child. This identification is not the state child identification but is an encrypted identification assigned by the state for the purposes of the NCANDS data collection.

Child Victim: A child for whom an incident of abuse or neglect has been substantiated or indicated by an investigation or assessment. A state may include some children with other dispositions as victims.

Children/Families in Need of Services: Disposition by a child welfare agency after an assessment; children or families with this assessment are generally not considered to be victims of maltreatment.

Closed without a Finding: Disposition that does not conclude with a specific finding because the investigation could not be completed for such reasons as: the family moved out of the jurisdiction; the family could not be located; or necessary diagnostic or other reports were not received within required time limits.

Counseling Services: Beneficial activities that apply the therapeutic processes to personal, family, situational or occupational problems in order to bring about a positive resolution of the problem or improved individual or family functioning or circumstances.

Court Action: Legal action initiated by a representative of the cps agency on behalf of the child. This includes, for instance, authorization to place the child, filing for temporary custody, dependency, or termination of parental rights. It does not include criminal proceedings against a perpetrator.

Court-Appointed Representative: A person required to be appointed by the court to represent a child in a neglect or abuse proceeding. May be an attorney or a court-appointed special advocate (or both) and is often referred to as a guardian ad litem. Makes recommendations to the court concerning the best interests of the child.

County of Report: The geopolitical substate jurisdiction from which the report of child maltreatment originated. The unique identification number assigned to the county under the federal information processing standards (FIPS) guidelines is preferred.

County of Residence: The geopolitical substate jurisdiction in which the child subject of a report was residing at the time of the report. The unique identification number assigned to the county under the federal information processing standards (FIPS) guidelines is preferred.

Day Care Services: Beneficial activities provided to a child or children in a setting that meets applicable standards of state and local law, in a center or in a home, for a portion of a 24-hour day.

Domestic Violence: Incidents of inter-spousal physical or emotional abuse perpetrated by one of the spouses or parent figures upon the other spouse or parent figure in the child victim's home environment.

Drug Abuse: Compulsive use of drugs that is not of a temporary nature. Applies to infants addicted at birth.

Education and Training Services: Beneficial activities provided to improve knowledge or daily living skills and to enhance cultural opportunities.

Education Personnel: An employee of a public or private educational institution or program; includes teachers, teacher assistants, administrators and others directly associated with the delivery of educational services.

Emotionally Disturbed: A condition, which must be clinically diagnosed, exhibiting one or more of the following characteristics over a long period of time and to a marked degree: an inability to build or maintain satisfactory interpersonal relationships; inappropriate types of behavior or feelings under normal circumstances; a general pervasive mood of unhappiness or depression; or a tendency to develop physical symptoms or fears associated with personal problems. Includes persons who are schizophrenic or autistic.

Employment Services: Beneficial activities provided to assist individuals in securing employment or acquiring learning skills that promote opportunities for employment.

Family: A group of two or more persons related by birth, marriage, adoption, or emotional ties.

Family Planning Services: Educational, comprehensive medical or social activities which enable individuals, including minors, to determine freely the number and spacing of their children and to select the means by which this may be achieved.

Family Preservation Services: Activities designed to protect children from harm and to assist families at risk or in crisis, including services to prevent placement, to support the reunification of children with their families, or to support the continued placement of children in adoptive homes or other permanent living arrangements.

Family Support Services: Community-based preventative activities designed to alleviate stress and promote parental competencies and behaviors that will increase the ability of families to successfully nurture their children, enable families to use other resources and opportunities available in the community, and create supportive networks to enhance child-rearing abilities of parents.

Financial Problem: A risk factor related to the family's inability to provide sufficient financial resources to meet minimum needs.

Foster Care: Twenty-four-hour substitute care for children placed away from their parents or guardians and for whom the state agency has placement and care responsibility. This includes, but is not limited to, family foster homes, foster homes of relatives, group homes, emergency shelters, residential facilities, child care institutions, and pre-adoptive homes regardless of whether the facility is licensed and whether payments are made by the state or local agency for the care of the child, or whether there is federal matching of any payments made.

Foster Care Services: Beneficial activities associated with 24-hour substitute care for children placed away from their parents or guardians and for whom the state agency has placement and care responsibility.

Foster Parent: Individual licensed to provide a home for orphaned, abused, neglected, delinquent or disabled children, usually with the approval of the government or a social service agency. May be a relative or a non-relative.

Friend: A non-relative acquainted with the child, the parent, or caretaker including: landlords, clergy, or youth group workers (e.g., scouts, Little League coaches), etc.

Health-Related and Home Health Services: Activities provided to attain and maintain a favorable condition of health.

Hispanic or Latino: A Mexican, Puerto Rican, Cuban, Central or South American person, or person of other Spanish cultural origin, regardless of race. Whether a person is Hispanic is determined by how others define him or by how he defines himself.

Home-Based Services: In-home activities provided to individuals or families to assist with household or personal care and improve or maintain adequate family well-being. Includes homemaker, chore, home maintenance, and household management services.

Housing Services: Beneficial activities designed to assist individuals or families in locating, obtaining or retaining suitable housing.

Inadequate Housing: A risk factor related to substandard, overcrowded, or unsafe housing conditions, including homelessness.

Independent and Transitional Living Services: Beneficial activities designed to help older youth in foster care or homeless youth make the transition to independent living.

Indicated or Reason to Suspect: An investigation disposition that concludes that maltreatment cannot be substantiated under state law or policy, but there is reason to suspect that the child may have been maltreated or was at risk of maltreatment. This is applicable only to states that distinguish between substantiated and indicated dispositions.

Information and Referral Services: Resources or activities designed to provide facts about services made available by public and private providers, after a brief assessment of client needs (but not a diagnosis and evaluation) to facilitate appropriate referral to these community resources.

Initial Investigation: Face-to-face contact with the alleged victim, when this is appropriate, or contact with another person who can provide information essential to the disposition of the investigation or assessment.

Intentionally False: Unsubstantiated investigation disposition about which it has been concluded that the person reporting the alleged incident of maltreatment knew that the allegation was false.

Investigation: The gathering and assessment of objective information to determine if a child has been or is at risk of being maltreated. Generally includes face-to-face contact with the victim and results in a disposition as to whether the alleged report is substantiated or not.

Investigation Disposition: A determination made by a social service agency that evidence is or is not sufficient under state law to conclude that maltreatment occurred.

Juvenile Court Petition: A legal document filed with the court of original jurisdiction overseeing matters affecting children requesting that the court take action regarding the child's status as a result of an investigation; usually a petition requesting the child be declared a dependent or delinquent child, or that the child be placed in an out-of-home setting.

Learning Disability: A disorder in basic psychological processes involved in understanding or using language, spoken or written, that may manifest itself in an imperfect ability to listen, think, speak, read, write, spell or use mathematical calculations. The term includes conditions such as perceptual disability, brain injury, minimal brain dysfunction, dyslexia, and developmental aphasia.

Legal, Law Enforcement, or Criminal Justice Personnel: A person employed by a local, state, tribal, or federal justice agency including law enforcement, courts, district attorney's office, probation or other community corrections agency, and correctional facilities.

Legal Services: Beneficial activities provided by a lawyer, or other person(s) under the supervision of a lawyer, to assist individuals in seeking or obtaining legal help in civil matters such as housing, divorce, child support, guardianship, paternity and legal separation.

Living Arrangement: The environment, e.g., family or foster care, in which a child was residing at the time of a report.

Maltreatment: An act or failure to act by a parent, caretaker, or other person as defined under state law which results in physical abuse, neglect, medical neglect, sexual abuse, emotional abuse, or an act or failure to act which presents an imminent risk of serious harm to a child.

Maltreatment Death: Death of a child as a result of abuse or neglect, because either: (a) an injury resulting from the abuse or neglect was the cause of death; or (b) abuse and/or neglect were contributing factors to the cause of death.

Maltreatment Disposition Level: The disposition of an alleged maltreatment. The disposition level may be substantiated, indicated (reason to suspect), unsubstantiated, closed (no finding), other, or unknown.

Maltreatment Type: A particular form of child maltreatment determined by investigation to be substantiated or indicated under state law. Types include physical abuse, neglect or deprivation of necessities, sexual abuse, psychological or emotional maltreatment, and other forms included in state law.

Medical Neglect: A type of maltreatment caused by failure by the caretaker to provide for the appropriate health care of the child although financially able to do so, or offered financial or other means to do so.

Medical Personnel: A person employed by a medical facility or practice, including physicians, physician assistants, nurses, emergency medical technicians, dentists, dental assistants and technicians, chiropractors and coroners.

Mental Health Personnel: A person employed by a mental health facility or practice, including psychologists, psychiatrists, therapists, etc.

Mental Health Services: Beneficial activities which aim to overcome issues involving emotional disturbance or maladaptive behavior adversely affecting socialization, learning, or development. Usually provided by public or private mental health agencies and includes both residential and non-residential activities.

Mental Retardation: Significantly subaverage general cognitive and motor functioning existing concurrently with deficits in adaptive behavior that adversely affect socialization and learning; must be clinically diagnosed.

Military Family Member: A person who is the legal dependent of an individual on active duty in the armed services of the united states.

Military Member: A person on active duty in the armed services of the United States, including army, navy, air force, or marine corps; excludes inactive reserve, national guard, and retired.

Native Hawaiian or Other Pacific Islander: A person having racial origins in any of the original peoples of Hawaii, Guam, Samoa, or other Pacific Islands.

Neglect or Deprivation of Necessities: A type of maltreatment that refers to the failure by the caretaker to provide needed, age-appropriate care although financially able to do so, or offered financial or other means to do so.

Neighbor: A person living in close geographical proximity to the child or family.

Non-Caretaker: A person who is not responsible for the care and supervision of the child, including school personnel, friends, neighbors, etc.

Not Substantiated: Investigation disposition that determines that there is not sufficient evidence under state law or policy to conclude that the child has been maltreated or is at risk of being maltreated.

Notifications: Mandated or courtesy contacting of other agencies with overlapping or potentially overlapping jurisdiction concerning a report of child maltreatment.

Other: The state coding for this field is something other than the codes in the NCANDS record layout.

Out-of-Court Contact: Contact, which is not part of the actual judicial hearing, between the court-appointed representative and the child victim. Such contacts enable the court-appointed representative to obtain a first-hand understanding of the situation and needs of the child victim, and to make recommendations to the court concerning the best interests of the child.

Parent: The birth mother/father, adoptive mother/father, or step mother/father of the child.

Perpetrator: The person who has been determined to have caused or knowingly allowed the maltreatment of the child.

Perpetrator Age at Report: Age of an individual determined to have caused or knowingly allowed the maltreatment of a child. Age is calculated in years at the time of the report of child maltreatment.

Perpetrator ID: A unique identification assigned to each perpetrator. This identification is not the actual state perpetrator identification but is an encrypted identification assigned by the state for purposes of the NCANDS data collection.

Perpetrator Maltreatment: Type of substantiated maltreatment a specific perpetrator was involved in the on the record for a specific child.

Perpetrator Prior Abuser: Perpetrator with previous substantiated or indicated incidents of child maltreatment.

Perpetrator Relationship: Primary role of the perpetrator with a child victim of maltreatment.

Petition Date: The month, day, and year that a juvenile court petition was filed.

Physical Abuse: Type of maltreatment that refers to physical acts that caused or could have caused physical injury to the child.

Physically Disabled: Having a physical condition that adversely affects the day-to-day motor functioning, such as cerebral palsy, spina bifida, multiple sclerosis, orthopedic impairments, and other physical disabilities.

Post-Investigation Services: Beneficial activities provided or arranged by the child protective services agency, social services agency, and/or the child welfare agency for the child/family as a result of needs discovered during the course of the investigation. Include such services as family preservation, family support, and foster care provided as a result of the report of alleged child maltreatment, or offered prior to the report and continued after the disposition of the investigation. Post-investigation services are delivered within the first 90 days after the disposition of the report.

Pregnancy and Parenting Services for Young Parents: Beneficial activities for married or unmarried adolescent parents and their families to assist them in coping with social, emotional, and economic problems related to pregnancy and to plan for the future.

Preventive Services: Beneficial activities aimed at preventing child abuse and neglect. Such activities may be directed at specific populations identified as being at increased risk of becoming abusive and may be designed to increase the strength and stability of families, to increase parents' confidence and competence in their parenting abilities, and to afford children a stable and supportive environment. They include child abuse and neglect preventive services provided through federal funds such as the child abuse and neglect state grant, the community-based family resource and support grant, the promoting safe and stable families program (Title IV-B, subpart 2), maternal and child health block grant, social services block grant (Title XX), and state and local funds. Such activities do not include public awareness campaigns.

Prior Victim: A child victim with previous substantiated or indicated incidents of maltreatment.

Psychological or Emotional Maltreatment: Type of maltreatment that refers to acts or omissions, other than physical abuse or sexual abuse, that caused, or could have caused, conduct, cognitive, affective, or other mental disorders. Includes emotional neglect, psychological abuse, mental injury, etc. Frequently occurs as verbal abuse or excessive demands on a child's performance and may cause the child to have a negative self-image and disturbed behavior.

Public Assistance: Any one or combination of the following welfare or social services programs: AFDC, general assistance, Medicaid, SSI, food stamps, etc.

Race: The primary taxonomic category of which the individual identifies himself or herself as a member, or of which the parent identifies the child as a member.

Receipt of Report: The log-in of a call to the agency from a reporter alleging child maltreatment.

Removal Date: The month, day, and year that the child was removed from the care and supervision of his parents or parental substitutes, during or as a result of an investigation by the child protective services or social services agency. If a child has been removed more than once, the removal date is the first removal in concert with the investigation.

Removed from the Home: The removal of the child from his/her normal place of residence to a substitute care setting by a cps or social services agency.

Report: Notification to the CPS agency of suspected child maltreatment; can include one or more children.

Report Date: The month, day, and year that the responsible agency was notified of the suspected child maltreatment.

Report Disposition: The conclusion reached by the responsible agency regarding the report of maltreatment pertaining to the child.

Report Disposition Date: The month, day, and year that a decision was made by the child protective services agency or court regarding the disposition of a report or investigation of alleged child maltreatment.

Report ID: A unique identification assigned to each report of child maltreatment. This identification is not the actual state report identification but is an encrypted identification assigned by the state for the purposes of the NCANDS data collection.

Report Source: The category or role of the person who makes a report of alleged maltreatment.

Reporting Period: The 12-month period for which data are submitted to the NCANDS; generally refers to the calendar year.

Residential Facility Staff: An employee of a public or private group residential facility, including emergency shelters, group homes, and institutions.

Respite Care Services: Beneficial activities involving temporary care of the child(ren) to provide relief to the caretaker. May involve care of the children outside of the caretaker's own home for a brief period of time, such as overnight or for a weekend. Not considered by the state to be foster care or other placement.

Response Time with Respect to the Initial Investigation: The time from the log-in of a call to the agency from a reporter alleging child maltreatment to the face-to-face contact with the alleged victim, where this is appropriate, or to contact with another person who can provide information.

Response Time with Respect to the Provision of Services: The time from the log-in of a call to the agency from a reporter alleging child maltreatment to the opening of a case for ongoing services.

Service Date: Date of the report disposition or a date decided by the state to be more appropriate. The service date for cases for which services were continued (or changed) as a result of the investigation disposition is the date of the most recent case opening prior to the receipt of the report.

Services: Non-investigative public or private beneficial activities provided or continued as a result of an investigation or assessment. In general, such activities occur within 90 days of the report.

Sex: The gender of a person at the time of the report.

Sexual Abuse: A type of maltreatment that refers to the involvement of the child in sexual activity to provide sexual gratification or financial benefit to the perpetrator, including contacts for sexual purposes, molestation, statutory rape, prostitution, pornography, exposure, incest, or other sexually exploitative activities.

Social Services Personnel: An employee of a public or private social services or social welfare agency, or other social worker or counselor who provides similar services.

Source of Report: Person who makes a report to the CPS agency alleging child maltreatment.

Special Services-Disabled: Beneficial activities for persons with developmental or physical disabilities, or visual or auditory impairments, to maximize their potential, help alleviate the effects of physical, mental or emotional disabilities, and enable them to live in the least restrictive environment possible.

Special Services-Juvenile Delinquent: Beneficial activities for youth (and their families) who are, or who may become, involved with the juvenile justice system.

State/Territory: The U.S. Postal service two-character abbreviation used to indicate the state/territory.

Stepparent: The husband or wife, by a subsequent marriage, of the child victim's mother or father.

Substance Abuse Services: Beneficial activities designed to deter, reduce, or eliminate substance abuse or chemical dependency.

Substantiated: A type of investigation disposition that concludes that the allegation of maltreatment or risk of maltreatment was supported or founded by state law or state policy. This is the highest level of finding by a state agency.

Substitute Care Provider: A person providing out-of-home care to children, such as a foster parent or residential facility staff.

Transportation Services: Beneficial provision of or arrangement for travel, including travel costs of individuals, in order to access social services, or obtain medical care or employment.

Unknown: The state collects data for this field, but the data for this particular report (or child) were not captured or are missing.

Visually or Hearing Impaired: A clinically diagnosed handicapping condition related to a visual impairment or permanent or fluctuating hearing or speech impairment that may significantly affect functioning or development.

White: A person of European, North African, or Middle Eastern origin.

Chapter 55

Child Abuse and Neglect Prevention Resources

The following organizations are among many that provide information on resources for preventing child abuse and neglect. Inclusion on this list is for information purposes and does not constitute an endorsement by the Clearinghouse or the Children's Bureau.

AVANCE, Inc. (AVANCE)
National Headquarters
301 South Frio St.
Suite 380
San Antonio, TX 78207
Phone: 210-270-4630
Fax: 210-270-4612
Website: http://www.avance.org

AVANCE's mission is to provide support and education services which will strengthen low-income families. AVANCE's focus is on community-based intervention that is family-centered, preventive, comprehensive, and continuous through the integration and collaboration of services. The AVANCE Family Support and Education Program is an example of one of AVANCE's programs: Targeted primarily at Hispanic at-risk parents with young children, the program aims to strengthen parent-child relationships and the parental role of advocate for the child.

"Child Abuse and Neglect Prevention Resource Listing," National Clearinghouse on Child Abuse and Neglect Information, 2004. Available online at http://nccanch.acf.hhs.gov/pubs/reslist/rl_dsp.cfm?subjID=78.

American Humane Association (AHA)
Child Welfare Division
63 Inverness Dr. East
Englewood, CO 80112-5117
Phone: 303-792-9900
Fax: 303-792-5333
Toll-Free: 866-242-1877
Website: http://www.americanhumane.org
E-Mail: children@americanhumane.org

The American Humane Association's mission is preventing cruelty, abuse, neglect, and exploitation of children and animals. AHA's Child Welfare Division has worked for many years to improve the public and private child welfare systems so they can respond more effectively to the needs of abused and neglected children. AHA is a national association of child protection programs, agencies, and individuals, and its membership includes State and local social service agencies, child advocates, courts, hospitals, schools, mental health professionals, and concerned citizens in every State. AHA information assists professionals and citizens in making informed decisions about how to help children and families in crisis. The association also develops resources and programs which help communities and citizens prevent child abuse.

American Professional Society on the Abuse of Children (APSAC)
National Office
P.O. Box 26901
CHO 3B-3406
Oklahoma City, OK 73190
Phone: 405-271-8202
Fax: 405-271-2931
Website: http://www.apsac.org

The American Professional Society on the Abuse of Children addresses all facets of the professional response to child maltreatment: prevention, assessment, intervention, and treatment. APSAC membership reflects all of the major disciplines which respond to child maltreatment, including mental health, medicine, child protective services, and law enforcement. APSAC publications and training cover all aspects of child maltreatment, including emotional and other types of neglect and physical and sexual abuse.

Association of Junior Leagues International Inc. (AJLI)
132 West 31st Street, 11th Floor
New York, NY 10001-3406
Phone: 212-951-8300
Fax: 212-481-7196
Website: http://www.ajli.org
E-Mail: info@ajli.org

The Association of Junior Leagues International is an organization of women committed to promoting voluntarism, developing the potential of women, and improving communities through effective action and leadership of trained volunteers. The AJLI offers programs in many areas including youth services, family support services, and child welfare (adoption, child abuse and neglect, foster care, domestic violence, and permanency planning).

Boys and Girls Clubs of America
National Headquarters
1230 West Peachtree Street, NW
Atlanta, GA 30309
Phone: 404-487-5700
Website: http://www.bgca.org

The Boys and Girls Clubs of America seeks to inspire and enable young people, especially those from disadvantaged circumstances, to realize their full potential as productive, responsible and caring citizens. Clubs provide specialized services and programs focusing on social issues such as family support, gang prevention, and personal safety as well as prevention programs aimed at substance abuse and premature sexual activity.

Center for Effective Discipline (CED)
155 West Main Street, Suite 1603
Columbus, OH 43215
Phone: 614-221-8829
Fax: 614-221-2110
Website: http://www.stophitting.org
E-Mail: info@StopHitting.org

The Center for Effective Discipline provides educational information to the public on the effects of corporal punishment of children and alternatives to its use. CED is the headquarters for and the coordinator of both the National Coalition to Abolish Corporal Punishment in Schools (NCACPS) and End Physical Punishment of Children (EPOCH-U.S.A.).

Center for the Prevention of Sexual and Domestic Violence (CPSDV)
2400 North 45th Street, No. 10
Seattle, WA 98103
Phone: 206-634-1903
Fax: 206-634-0115
Website: http://cpsdv.org
E-Mail: cpsdv@cpsdv.org

The Center for the Prevention of Sexual and Domestic Violence is an inter-religious educational resource that addresses issues of sexual and domestic violence. CPSDV's goal is to engage religious leaders in the task of ending abuse, and to serve as a bridge between the religious and secular communities.

Chadwick Center for Children and Families
3020 Children's Way
MC 5016
San Diego, CA 92123
Phone: 858-966-5814
Fax: 858-966-8535
Website: http://www.charityadvantage.com/chadwickcenter
E-Mail: chadwickcenter@chsd.org

The Chadwick Center's mission is to protect children and strengthen families through prevention, treatment, education, public policy, advocacy, and research in the areas of child maltreatment and family violence. The Center uses a multidisciplinary, family-centered approach.

Child Abuse Prevention Network
Website: http://child-abuse.com/capn.shtml

The Child Abuse Prevention Network, originally launched as an outreach effort of the Family Life Development Center at Cornell University, is sponsored by LifeNET, Inc. Through the World Wide Web, the Network provides professionals with online tools and support for the identification, investigation, treatment, adjudication, and prevention of child abuse and neglect.

Childhelp U.S.A.
15757 North 78th Street
Scottsdale, AZ 85260
Toll-Free: 800-4-A-CHILD
Phone: 480-922-8212

Fax: 480-922-7061
TDD: 800-2-A-CHILD
Website: http://www.childhelpusa.org

Childhelp U.S.A. is dedicated to meeting the physical, emotional, educational, and spiritual needs of abused and neglected children by focusing its efforts and resources in the areas of treatment, prevention, and research. Its programs and services include the operation of the Childhelp U.S.A. National Child Abuse Hotline, residential treatment facilities for severely abused children, child advocacy centers that reduce the trauma of child abuse victims during the interview and examination process, group homes, foster family selection, training and certification, Head Start programs for at-risk children, child abuse prevention programs, and community outreach.

Children's Bureau (CB)
330 C Street, SW
Washington, DC 20447
Website: http://www.acf.hhs.gov/programs/cb

The Children's Bureau, the oldest Federal agency for children and families, is located within the Department of Health and Human Services' Administration for Children and Families, Administration on Children, Youth and Families. The Bureau is responsible for assisting States in the delivery of child welfare services designed to protect children and to strengthen families. The Bureau provides grants to States, Tribes, and communities to operate a range of child welfare services including child protective services, family preservation and support, foster care, adoption, and independent living.

Children's Defense Fund (CDF)
National Headquarters
25 E Street, NW
Washington, DC 20001
Phone: 202-628-8787
Website: http://www.childrensdefense.org
E-Mail: cdinfo@childrensdefense.org

The Children's Defense Fund focuses on key issues affecting the well-being of children by helping develop, implement, and monitor State and Federal policies. CDF gathers and disseminates data on children, promotes public education, provides technical assistance to State and local child advocates, and pursues an annual Federal legislative agenda.

Family Life Development Center (FLDC)
Cornell University
Martha Van Rennelaer Hall
Ithaca, NY 14853-4401
Phone: 607-255-7794
Fax: 607-255-8562
Website: http://www.human.cornell.edu/centers/fldc

The mission of the Family Life Development Center is to improve professional and public efforts to understand and act upon risk and protective factors in the lives of children, youth, families, and communities that affect family strengths, child well-being, and youth development. The FLDC accomplishes its mission through research, training, outreach, education, and program development and implementation. Current areas of special interest include childhood violence prevention and evaluation of programs designed to prevent abuse and neglect. The FLDC operates the National Data Archive on Child Abuse and Neglect (NDACAN) which promotes scholarly exchange among researchers and makes original data available for secondary analysis.

Freddie Mac Foundation
8250 Jones Branch Drive
Mailstop A40
McLean, VA 22102
Phone: 703-918-8888
Fax: 703-918-8895
Website: http://www.freddiemacfoundation.org
E-Mail: freddiemac_foundation@freddiemac.com

The Freddie Mac Foundation provides funds for various nonprofit organizations that work on behalf of children, youth and families. The Foundation focuses on children and prevention-oriented programs. Typically, grants are awarded to programs which build strong families, prevent child abuse and neglect, and recruit foster and adoptive parents. Among the Foundation's major programs are Healthy Families America and Wednesday's Child U.S.A., a campaign to promote adoptions.

General Federation of Women's Clubs (GFWC)
1734 N Street, NW
Washington, DC 20036-2990
Toll-Free: 800-443-4392
Phone: 202-347-3168
Fax: 202-835-0246

Website: http://www.gfwc.org
E-Mail: gfwc@gfwc.org

The General Federation of Women's Clubs is the world's largest and oldest women's volunteer organization. GFWC's members include business owners, teachers, elected officials, homemakers, corporate executives, college students, and retirees. The organization's members are united by dedication to community improvement through volunteer service. GFWC advocates for conservation, quality education, health, civic awareness, safety, and crime prevention. The Federation's Advocates for Children Program is a referral and networking resource for Club members interested in assisting children. The program focuses on advocacy on behalf of children, prevention, and on improving public awareness of the importance of early intervention.

Institute for Family Development
Main Office and Training Division
34004 16th Avenue South, Suite 200
Federal Way, WA 98003-8903
Phone: 253-874-3630
Fax: 253-838-1670
Website: http://www.institutefamily.org

The Institute for Family Development (formerly the Behavioral Sciences Institute) is a private, nonprofit agency founded to develop innovative and cost-effective solutions to the growing problems of child abuse and neglect, juvenile delinquency, and family conflict. The Institute's mission is to improve the lives of children, youth, and families through community-based services and supports. Families are served in their own homes and neighborhoods, 24 hours a day. The HOMEBUILDERS program, an intensive, in-home family counseling and skill-building program, is the oldest and best-documented family preservation program in the United States.

International Society for the Prevention of Child Abuse and Neglect (ISPCAN)
25 West 560 Geneva Road, Suite L2C
Carol Stream, IL 60188
Phone: 630-221-1311
Fax: 630-221-1313
Website: http://ispcan.org
E-Mail: ISPCAN@ispcan.org

The International Society for Prevention of Child Abuse and Neglect, founded in 1977, is the only multidisciplinary international organization that brings together a global cross-section of committed professionals to work towards the prevention and treatment of child abuse, neglect and exploitation. ISPCAN's mission is to prevent cruelty to children in every nation, in every form: physical abuse, sexual abuse, neglect, street children, child fatalities, child prostitution, children of war, emotional abuse, and child labor. ISPCAN is committed to increasing public awareness of all forms of violence against children, developing activities to prevent such violence, and promoting the rights of children in all regions of the world.

Military Family Resource Center (MFRC)
1745 Jefferson Davis Hwy.
CS4, Suite 302
Room 309
Arlington, VA 22202-3424
Phone: 703-602-4964
Fax: 703-602-0189
Website: http://mfrc.calib.com
E-Mail: mfrcrequest@calib.com

The Military Family Resource Center is a resource for military members and their families, professionals, and policy makers. MRFC offers publications and resource referrals for information on the military lifestyle and quality of life issues for single and married service members and their families. MFRC also provides information on quality of life policies, the latest research initiatives, and model programs.

National Alliance of Children's Trust and Prevention Funds (ACT)
Department of Psychology
Michigan State University
East Lansing, MI 48824-1117
Phone: 517-432-5096
Fax: 517-432-2476
Website: http://www.msu.edu/user/millsda
E-Mail: alliance@psy.msu.edu

The mission of the National Alliance of Children's Trust and Prevention Funds is to build and maintain a system of services, laws, practices, and attitudes that prevents child abuse and neglect. The Alliance assists Children's Trust and Prevention Funds at the State and national levels.

National Center for Missing and Exploited Children (NCMEC)
Charles B. Wang International Children's Building
699 Prince Street
Alexandria, VA 22314-3175
Toll-Free: 800-THE-LOST
Phone: 703-274-3900
Website: http://www.missingkids.com

The National Center for Missing and Exploited Children provides assistance to parents, children, law enforcement, schools, and the community in recovering missing children and raising public awareness about ways to help prevent child abduction, molestation, and sexual exploitation. The Center sponsors the CyberTipLine for online reporting of the sexual exploitation or molesting of children. One special program offered by the Center is the NetSmartz Workshops, for teaching Internet safety.

National Children's Advocacy Center (NCAC)
Administrative Offices
200 Westside Square, Suite 700
Huntsville, AL 35801-4546
Phone: 256-533-0531
Fax: 256-534-6883
Website: http://www.ncac-hsv.org
E-Mail: webmaster@ncac-hsv.org

The National Children's Advocacy Center provides prevention, intervention, and treatment services to physically and sexually abused children and their families with a child-focused team approach. NCAC also operates the Southern Regional Children's Advocacy Center which provides education and training to support the development of Children's Advocacy Centers nationwide.

National Children's Alliance (NCA)
1612 K Street NW, Suite 500
Washington, DC 20006
Phone: 202-452-6001
Toll-Free: 800-239-9950
Website: http://www.nca-online.org
E-Mail: info@nca-online.org

The National Children's Alliance is a nonprofit membership organization that provides training, technical assistance, and networking opportunities to communities seeking to plan, establish, and improve Children's Advocacy Centers. These Centers further the goal of serving abused children through a comprehensive approach to services for victims and their families.

National Clearinghouse on Child Abuse and Neglect Information
330 C Street, SW
Washington, DC 20447
Phone: 703-385-7565
Fax: 703-385-3206
Toll-Free: 800-FYI-3366
Website: http://www.calib.com/nccanch
E-Mail: nccanch@calib.com

The National Clearinghouse on Child Abuse and Neglect Information, a service of the Children's Bureau, helps professionals locate information on child abuse and neglect and related child welfare issues. Among its resources, the Clearinghouse offers a bibliographic database of child maltreatment and related child welfare materials, summaries of State laws concerned with child abuse and neglect and child welfare, fact sheets, resource lists, bulletins, and other publications. Jointly with the National Adoption Information Clearinghouse (NAIC), the National Clearinghouse on Child Abuse and Neglect Information publishes the Children's Bureau Express an online digest of news and resources for professionals concerned with child maltreatment, child welfare, and adoption.

National Council on Child Abuse and Family Violence (NCCAFV)
1025 Connecticut Avenue NW
Suite 1012
Washington, DC 20036
Toll-Free: 800-799-7233
Phone: 202-429-6695
Fax: 831-655-3930
TTY: 800-787-3244
Website: http://www.nccafv.org
E-Mail: info@nccafv.org

The National Council on Child Abuse and Family Violence is a non-profit organization serving as a private sector response to the problems of child, spousal, and elderly abuse. The Council's primary purpose is to strengthen, professionally and practically, community child abuse and family violence prevention and treatment programs nationwide. A broad range of activities is included in the Council's three major program areas: public awareness and education, professional development, and organizational development.

National Exchange Club Foundation for the Prevention of Child Abuse
3050 Central Avenue
Toledo, OH 43606
Toll-Free: 800-924-2643
Phone: 419-535-3232
Fax: 419-535-1989
Website: http://www.preventchildabuse.com
E-Mail: info@preventchildabuse.com

The National Exchange Club Foundation focuses on improving the lives of children and families through the prevention of child abuse. The Foundation works to counter abuse by working directly with parents through the parent aide program. The Foundation also coordinates a nationwide network of nearly 100 Exchange Club Child Abuse Prevention Centers which use the parent aide program and provide support to families at risk for abuse.

National Resource Center for Community-Based Family Resource and Support Programs (FRIENDS)
20 North Wacker Drive, Suite 1100
Chicago, IL 60606
Phone: 312-338-0900
Fax: 312-338-1522
Website: http://www.friendsnrc.org

FRIENDS is the National Resource Center for the Community-Based Family Resource Services program (CBFRS). FRIENDS supports State efforts to create a statewide network of community-based, family-centered, prevention-focused, family resource and support programs. The goal is to strengthen families and lessen the occurrences of child abuse and neglect. FRIENDS (it stands for Family Resource Information, Education, and Network Development Services) offers a range of services to assist States, Tribal organizations, and local programs in developing community-based family resource programs and networks. FRIENDS is part of the Children's Bureau Training and Technical Assistance Network.

Parents Anonymous, Inc.
675 West Foothill Boulevard, Suite 220
Claremont, CA 91711-3475
Phone: 909-621-6184
Fax: 909-625-6304
Website: http://www.parentsanonymous.org
E-Mail: parentsanonymous@parentsanonymous.org

Parents Anonymous helps parents provide nurturing environments for their families. The organization is dedicated to strengthening families through strategies that promote mutual support and parental leadership. For State and local contacts, visit the Parents Anonymous website.

Prevent Child Abuse America
200 South Michigan Avenue, 17th Floor
Chicago, IL 60604-2404
Phone: 312-663-3520
Fax: 312-939-8962
Website: http://www.preventchildabuse.org
E-Mail: mailbox@preventchildabuse.org

Prevent Child Abuse America is committed to promoting legislation, policies, and programs that help prevent child abuse and neglect, support healthy childhood development, and strengthen families. Working with chapters in 37 States and the District of Columbia, Prevent Child Abuse America provides leadership to promote and implement prevention efforts at the national and local levels.

Prevent Child Abuse and Neglect Through Dental Awareness (PANDA)
Missouri Dental Association
P.O. Box 104900
230 West McCarty
Jefferson City, MO 65110-4900
Phone: 573-634-3436
Fax: 573-635-0764
Website: http://www.modental.org/programs/3panda.html

The Missouri coalition known as P.A.N.D.A (Prevent Child Abuse and Neglect Through Dental Awareness) was created to address a lack of reporting by dental professionals of suspected child abuse and neglect. P.A.N.D.A's educational programs include a history of family violence in our society, clinical examples of confirmed child abuse and neglect, and discussions of legal liability issues involved in reporting child maltreatment. Programs now extend beyond dental audiences to include physicians, nurses, teachers, child care workers, and anyone interested in preventing family violence.

STOP IT NOW!
P.O. Box 495
Haydenville, MA 01039
Phone: 413-268-3096
Website: http://www.stopitnow.com
E-Mail: info@stopitnow.org

STOP IT NOW! calls on all abusers and potential abusers to seek immediate help. The organization's goal is to educate adults about how to stop sexual abuse and to increase public awareness of the trauma of child sexual abuse.

Safer Society Foundation, Inc.
P.O. Box 340
Brandon, VT 05733-0340
Phone: 802-247-3132
Fax: 802-247-4233
Website: http://www.safersociety.org

The Safer Society Foundation, Inc., a nonprofit agency, is a national research, advocacy, and referral center on the prevention and treatment of sexual abuse. The Foundation provides training and consultation, research, sex offender treatment referrals, a computerized program network, and a resource library. It also publishes materials for the prevention and treatment of sexual abuse.

Shaken Baby Syndrome Prevention Plus (SBS Prevention Plus)
649 Main Street, Suite B
Groveport, OH 43125
Toll-Free: 800-858-5222
Phone: 614-836-8360
Fax: 614-836-8359
Website: http://www.sbsplus.com
E-Mail: sbspp@aol.com

Shaken Baby Syndrome Prevention Plus develops, studies, and distributes informational materials which discourage Shaken Baby Syndrome and other physical child abuse and promote positive parenting and child care.

Chapter 56

Family Violence Resources

The following organizations are among many that provide information on family violence. If you are in crisis, call 911, your local domestic violence program, or the 24-hour National Domestic Violence Hotline at 800-799-7233. Inclusion on this list is for information purposes and does not constitute an endorsement by the Clearinghouse or the Children's Bureau.

ABA Center on Children and the Law
740 15th St. NW
Washington, DC 20005-1022
Phone: 202-662-1720
Fax: 202-662-1755
Website: http://www.abanet.org/child
E-Mail: ctrchildlaw@abanet.org

The ABA Center on Children and the Law seeks to improve the laws, policies, and judicial procedures affecting children by supporting legal representation for youth, facilitating coordination between attorneys and caseworkers, reducing court delays, and providing training to court professionals involved in child welfare.

"Family/Domestic Violence Resource Listing," National Clearinghouse on Child Abuse and Neglect Information, 2004. Available online at http://nccanch.acf.hhs.gov/pubs/reslist/rl_dsp.cfm?subjID=28.

Alliance for Children and Families
11700 West Lake Park Drive
Milwaukee, WI 53224-3099
Phone: 414-359-1040
Fax: 414 359-1074
E-Mail: info@alliance1.org
Website: http://www.alliance1.org

The Alliance is an association representing private, nonprofit child and family service organizations. Its members provide an array of services ranging from residential care to domestic abuse prevention and intervention. The mission of the Alliance is to strengthen the ability of its members to serve and advocate for children, families, and communities. The Alliance was formed by a merger between Family Service America and the National Association of Homes and Services for Children in 1998.

Association of Junior Leagues International Inc. (AJLI)
132 West 31st Street
11th Floor
New York, NY 10001-3406
Phone: 212-951-8300
Fax: 212-481-7196
Website: http://www.ajli.org
E-Mail: info@ajli.org

The Association of Junior Leagues International is an organization of women committed to promoting voluntarism, developing the potential of women, and improving communities through effective action and leadership of trained volunteers. The AJLI offers programs in many areas including youth services, family support services, and child welfare (adoption, child abuse and neglect, foster care, domestic violence, and permanency planning).

Center for the Prevention of Sexual and Domestic Violence (CPSDV)
2400 North 45th Street
No. 10
Seattle, WA 98103
Phone: 206-634-1903
Fax: 206-634-0115
Website: http://www.cpsdv.org
E-Mail: cpsdv@cpsdv.org

The Center for the Prevention of Sexual and Domestic Violence is an inter-religious educational resource that addresses issues of sexual and domestic violence. CPSDV's goal is to engage religious leaders in the task of ending abuse, and to serve as a bridge between the religious and secular communities.

Chadwick Center for Children and Families

3020 Children's Way
MC 5016
San Diego, CA 92123
Phone: 858-966-5814
Fax: 858-966-8535
Website: http://www.charityadvantage.com/chadwickcenter
E-Mail: chadwickcenter@chsd.org

The Chadwick Center's mission is to protect children and strengthen families through prevention, treatment, education, public policy, advocacy, and research in the areas of child maltreatment and family violence. The Center uses a multidisciplinary, family-centered approach.

Family Life Development Center (FLDC)

Cornell University
Martha Van Rennelaer Hall
Ithaca, NY 14853-4401
Phone: 607-255-7794
Fax: 607-255-8562
Website: http://www.human.cornell.edu/centers/fldc

The mission of the Family Life Development Center is to improve professional and public efforts to understand and act upon risk and protective factors in the lives of children, youth, families, and communities that affect family strengths, child well-being, and youth development. The FLDC accomplishes its mission through research, training, outreach, education, and program development and implementation. Current areas of special interest include childhood violence prevention and evaluation of programs designed to prevent abuse and neglect. The FLDC operates the National Data Archive on Child Abuse and Neglect (NDACAN) which promotes scholarly exchange among researchers and makes original data available for secondary analysis.

Family Research Laboratory (FRL)
126 Horton Social Science Center
University of New Hampshire
Durham, NH 03824-3586
Phone: 603-862-1888
Website: http://www.unh.edu/frl

The Family Research Laboratory devotes its attention to understanding family violence and the effect of violence on families through comprehensive literature reviews and research-based studies. Research topics in all aspects of family violence and abuse include physical abuse of children, corporal punishment of children, child sexual abuse, pornography, violence between siblings, parental abductions, and missing and abducted children.

Family Violence Prevention Fund (FVPF)
383 Rhode Island Street, Suite 304
San Francisco, CA 94103-5133
Phone: 415-252-8900
Fax: 415-252-8991
TTY: 800-595-4889
Website: http://endabuse.org
E-Mail: fund@endabuse.org

The Family Violence Prevention Fund is dedicated to preventing and reducing domestic violence. The Fund creates public awareness campaigns and develops public policy initiatives in the areas of public health, child welfare, the law, public education, immigration, international settings, and the workplace. The specialized Children's Programs stress the need for new prevention strategies, community collaboration, and outreach to offer support and intervention to children affected by witnessing abuse and violence in their homes and lives.

Family Violence Sexual Assault Institute (FVSAI)
6160 Cornerstone Court East
San Diego, CA 92121
Phone: 858-623-2777, Ext. 416
Fax: 858-646-0761
Website: http://www.fvsai.org
E-Mail: fvsai@alliant.edu

The Family Violence Sexual Assault Institute is a resource center that maintains a clearinghouse of references and unpublished papers concerning all aspects of family violence and sexual assault. The FVSAI's mission is to share and disseminate information, provide networking opportunities among professionals, and assist with program evaluation, consultation, and training that promotes violence-free living.

National Center for Victims of Crime (NCVC)
2000 M Street NW
Suite 480
Washington, DC 20036
Toll-Free: 800-FYI-CALL
Phone: 202-467-8700
Fax: 202-467-8701
TDD: 800-211-7996
Website: http://www.ncvc.org

The National Center for Victims of Crime provides direct services and resources, advocates for passage of laws and public policies, and delivers training and technical assistance to organizations, counselors, and attorneys who assist victims of crime.

National Clearinghouse on Child Abuse and Neglect Information
330 C Street SW
Washington, DC 20447
Phone: 703-385-7565
Fax: 703-385-3206
Toll-Free: 800-FYI-3366
Website: http://www.calib.com/nccanch
E-Mail: nccanch@calib.com

The National Clearinghouse on Child Abuse and Neglect Information, a service of the Children's Bureau, helps professionals locate information on child abuse and neglect and related child welfare issues. Among its resources, the Clearinghouse offers a bibliographic database of child maltreatment and related child welfare materials, summaries of State laws concerned with child abuse and neglect and child welfare, fact sheets, resource lists, bulletins, and other publications. Jointly with the National Adoption Information Clearinghouse (NAIC), the National Clearinghouse on Child Abuse and Neglect Information publishes the Children's Bureau Express an online digest of news and resources for professionals concerned with child maltreatment, child welfare, and adoption.

National Coalition Against Domestic Violence (NCADV)

P.O. Box 18749
Denver, CO 80218
Phone: 303-839-1852
Fax: 303-831-9251
Website: http://www.ncadv.org

The National Coalition Against Domestic Violence is a tax-exempt membership organization which works to stop violence in the lives of women and children by representing a network of more than 2,000 shelters, safe homes, and counseling programs. The Coalition's efforts include helping to set priorities for Federal funding, producing various publications, sponsoring national conferences, developing and promoting model programs, operating a clearinghouse for information and technical assistance, fostering public policy, promoting public awareness, and providing direct services.

National Council of Juvenile and Family Court Judges (NCJFCJ)

P.O. Box 8970
Reno, NV 89507
Phone: 775-784-6012
Fax: 775-784-6628
Website: http://ncjfcj.unr.edu
E-Mail: admin@ncjfcj.unr.edu

The National Council of Juvenile and Family Court Judges is dedicated to improving the court system's handling of juvenile and family matters through applied research, technical assistance, and continuing education of judges and juvenile justice professionals on family violence, child abuse and neglect, and child protection and custody.

National Council on Child Abuse and Family Violence (NCCAFV)

1025 Connecticut Avenue NW
Suite 1012
Washington, DC 20036
Toll-Free: 800-799-7233
Phone: 202-429-6695
Fax: 831-655-3930
TTY: 800-787-3244
Website: http://www.nccafv.org
E-Mail: info@nccafv.org

The National Council on Child Abuse and Family Violence is a nonprofit organization serving as a private sector response to the problems of child, spousal, and elderly abuse. The Council's primary purpose is to strengthen, professionally and practically, community child abuse and family violence prevention and treatment programs nationwide. A broad range of activities is included in the Council's three major program areas: public awareness and education, professional development, and organizational development.

National Criminal Justice Reference Service (NCJRS)
P.O. Box 6000
1600 Research Boulevard
Rockville, MD 20849-6000
Toll-Free: 800-851-3420
Phone: 301-519-5500
Fax: 301-519-5212
TTY: 301-947-8374
Website: http://www.ncjrs.org
E-Mail: askncjrs@ncjrs.org

The National Criminal Justice Reference Service is one of the world's most extensive resources for information on criminal and juvenile justice; it provides services to an international community of policy makers and professionals. NCJRS is a collection of clearinghouses supporting all the bureaus of the U.S. Department of Justice's Office of Justice Programs: the National Institute of Justice, the Office of Juvenile Justice and Delinquency Prevention, the Bureau of Justice Statistics, the Bureau of Justice Assistance, the Office for Victims of Crime, and the OJP Program Offices. It also supports the Office of National Drug Control Policy. NCJRS answers inquiries, conducts computerized database searches, distributes publications, and makes referrals. The Service's database of nearly 125,000 documents includes studies on police arrest policy in spouse abuse incidents and recidivism rates for sexual abuse offenders.

Office for Victims of Crime (OVC)
810 7th Street NW
Washington, DC 20531
Toll-Free: 800-627-6872
Phone: 866-OVC-TTAC
TTY: 877-712-9279
Website: http://www.ojp.usdoj.gov/ovc
E-Mail: askovc@ojp.usdoj.gov

The Office for Victims of Crime was established by the 1984 Victims of Crime Act (VOCA) to oversee diverse programs that benefit victims of crime. OVC provides substantial funding to State victim assistance and compensation programs, the lifeline services that help victims to heal. The agency also supports training designed to educate criminal justice and allied professionals on the rights and needs of crime victims. OVC is one of five bureaus and four offices with grant-making authority within the Office of Justice Programs of the U.S. Department of Justice.

Office on Violence Against Women (OVW)
810 7th Street NW
Washington, DC 20531
Toll-Free: 800-799-SAFE (7233)
Phone: 202-307-6026
Fax: 202-307-3911
TDD: 800-787-3224
TTY: 202-307-2277
Website: http://www.ojp.usdoj.gov/vawo
E-Mail: askvawo@ojp.usdoj.gov

The Violence Against Women Office is part of the U.S. Justice Department's Office of Justice Programs (OJP). The VAWO handles the Department's legal and policy issues regarding violence against women, coordinates Departmental efforts, provides national and international leadership, and responds to requests for information regarding violence against women. The Violence Against Women Office works closely with other components of OJP (the Office of Legal Policy, the Office of Legislative Affairs, the Office of Intergovernmental Affairs, the Immigration and Naturalization Office, the Executive Office for United States Attorneys, U.S. Attorneys' Offices, and State, Tribal and local jurisdictions) to implement the mandates of the Violence Against Women Act and subsequent legislation.

Packard (David and Lucille) Foundation Children, Families and Communities Program
The Future of Children
300 Second Street, Suite 200
Los Altos, CA 94022
Phone: 650-917-7110
Fax: 650-941-2273
Website: http://www.packard.org

One of the major program areas of the Foundation is the Children, Families, and Communities Program. The Program focuses on children's access to high-quality health care, the development of children and youth, the economic security of families, and the reduction of violence in homes. The *Future of Children* is a publication of this Program. The primary purpose of this journal is to promote effective policies and programs for children by providing policymakers and service provide with objective information based on the best available research.

Chapter 57

Resources for Child Welfare and Other Legal Information

Child Welfare and the Law Resource Listing

The following organizations are among many that provide information on child welfare legal issues for legal, court, and agency professionals serving children and families. Inclusion on this list is for information purposes and does not constitute an endorsement by the Clearinghouse or the Children's Bureau.

ABA Center on Children and the Law
740 15th St. NW
Washington, DC 20005-1022
Phone: 202-662-1720
Fax: 202-662-1755
Website: http://www.abanet.org/child
E-Mail: ctrchildlaw@abanet.org

The ABA Center on Children and the Law seeks to improve the laws, policies, and judicial procedures affecting children by supporting legal representation for youth, facilitating coordination between attorneys and caseworkers, reducing court delays, and providing training to court professionals involved in child welfare.

"Child Welfare and the Law Resource Listing," available online at http://nccanch.acf.hhs.gov/pubs/reslist/rl_dsp.cfm?subjID=25, and "Foster Care Resource Listing," available online at http://nccanch.acf.hhs.gov/pubs/reslist/rl_dsp.cfm?subjID=29. Both from National Clearinghouse on Child Abuse and Neglect Information, 2004.

American Bar Association (ABA)
740 15th Street NW
Washington, DC 20005-1019
Phone: 202-662-1000
Toll-Free: 800-285-2221
Website: http://www.abanet.org
E-Mail: askaba@abanet.org

The ABA provides law school accreditation, continuing legal education, information about the law, programs to assist lawyers and judges in their work, and initiatives to improve the legal system for the public. ABA publications include a "Consumer's Guide to Legal Help," with lawyer and pro bono attorney locator services.

American Bar Association Family Law Section
Family Law Section
750 North Lake Shore Drive
Chicago, IL 60611
Phone: 202-662-1000
Website: http://www.abanet.org/family/home.html
E-Mail: familylaw@abanet.org

The American Bar Association Family Law Section was organized to improve the administration of justice in the field of family law. Areas such as divorce, custody, adoption, alimony, and support are within the scope of the Family Law Section, as are emerging issues such as third party parental rights, marital torts, federal and interstate legislation, mediation, and the complicated questions of paternity, perinatal drug addiction, bankruptcy to deprive divorcing spouses of property, and genetic engineering. The Web site has a special section devoted to "General Public Resources," including frequently asked questions and "how to find an attorney."

American Prosecutors Research Institute (APRI)
99 Canal Center Plaza, Suite 510
Alexandria, VA 22314
Phone: 703-549-9222
Fax: 703-836-3195
Website: http://www.ndaa-apri.org

APRI is the research, training and technical assistance affiliate of the National District Attorneys Association (NDAA). The institute, a nonprofit research and program development resource for prosecutors at all levels of government, is committed to providing interdisciplinary responses to complex problems of criminal justice. Child abuse, abduction, and exploitation are among APRI's major focuses, as is juvenile justice. An APRI program, the National Center for Prosecution of Child Abuse (NCPCA), is a leading resource for expert legal assistance, training, court reform, and up-to-date information on criminal child abuse investigations and prosecutions.

Association of Administrators of the Interstate Compact for the Placement of Children (ICPC)
American Public Human Services Association
810 First Street NE, Suite 500
Washington, DC 20002-4267
Phone: 202-682-0100
Fax: 202-289-6555
Website: http://icpc.aphsa.org
E-Mail: icpcinbox@APHSA.org

The Interstate Compact for the Placement of Children is a uniform State law establishing a contract among party States to ensure that children placed across state lines receive adequate protection and services. The primary function of the ICPC is to protect the interests of both the children and the States by requiring that certain procedures be followed in the interstate placement of children who are being adopted, placed with relatives, or going into residential care or foster family homes.

Association of Administrators of the Interstate Compact on Adoption and Medical Assistance (AAICAMA)
American Public Human Services Association
810 First Street NE, Suite 500
Washington, DC 20002-4267
Phone: 202-682-0100
Fax: 202-289-6555
Website: http://aaicama.aphsa.org
E-Mail: loppenheim@aphsa.org

The Association of Administrators of the Interstate Compact on Adoption and Medical Assistance facilitates the administration of the ICAMA. The Compact is the legal mechanism by which member States regulate and coordinate the interstate delivery of services to children with special needs who are adopted pursuant to adoption assistance agreements. Along with advocating State participation in the ICAMA, the Association provides technical and legal assistance, education and training, and materials on practice and policy issues.

Juvenile Justice Clearinghouse (JJ)
P.O. Box 6000
Rockville, MD 20849-6000
Toll-Free: 800-638-8736
Fax: 301-519-5212
Website: http://www.ojjdp.ncjrs.org/about/clearh.html
E-Mail: askjj@ncjrs.org

The Juvenile Justice Clearinghouse was established by the Federal Government's Office of Juvenile Justice and Delinquency Prevention (OJJDP) as a resource for people interested in juvenile justice, delinquency issues, and the OJJDP. JJ provides assistance with information on specific juvenile justice and delinquency prevention issues and help with ordering publications, requesting materials and information on conferences, and obtaining information on grants and funding opportunities.

National Adoption Information Clearinghouse (NAIC)
330 C Street SW
Washington, DC 20447
Toll-Free: 888-251-0078
Phone: 703-352-3488
Fax: 703-385-3206
Website: http://www.calib.com/naic
E-Mail: naic@calib.com

NAIC offers information on all aspects of adoption for professionals, policy makers, and the general public. The Clearinghouse develops and maintains a computerized database of books, journal articles, and other materials on adoption and related topics, conducts database searches, publishes materials on adoption, and gives referrals to related services and experts in the field. NAIC also maintains a database of experts knowledgeable in various areas of adoption practice. NAIC's primary audiences are adoption professionals and adoptive parents and children.

National Association of Counsel for Children (NACC)
1825 Marion Street
Suite 340
Denver, CO 80218
Toll-Free: 888-828-NACC
Website: http://www.naccchildlaw.org
E-Mail: advocate@NACCchildlaw.org

The National Association of Counsel for Children works to improve the legal protection and representation of children by training and educating child advocates and by effecting policy and legal systems change. The NACC sponsors conferences and seminars on important issues confronting child advocates and files amicus curiae briefs in selected court cases affecting children. The Association also has a legislative agenda, a national child advocate awards program, and a speakers bureau.

National Center for State Courts (NCSC)
300 Newport Avenue
Williamsburg, VA 23185
Toll-Free: 800-616-6164
Phone: 415-543-3307
Fax: 415-956-9024
Website: http://www.ncsconline.org
E-Mail: knowledge@ncsc.dni.us

The National Center for State Courts is an independent, nonprofit organization dedicated to the improvement of the justice system. NCSC accomplishes its mission by providing leadership and service to State courts, helping them improve the administration of justice and better serve the public. Leadership activities include developing policies to enhance State courts, advancing the interests of State courts within the Federal Government, fostering State court adaptation to future changes, securing sufficient resources for State courts, strengthening State court leadership, facilitating State court collaboration, and providing a model for organizational administration.

National Child Welfare Resource Center on Legal and Judicial Issues
740 15th Street NW, 9th Floor
Washington, DC 20005-1009
Phone: 202-662-1736
Fax: 202-662-1755
Website: http://www.abanet.org/child/rclji/home.html

The National Child Welfare Resource Center on Legal and Judicial Issues, a service of the Children's Bureau, is dedicated to achieving safety, permanence, and well-being for abused and neglected children through improved laws and judicial decision-making. The Center provides training, technical assistance, and consultation to agencies and courts on all legal and judicial aspects of the child welfare system, including court improvement, reasonable-efforts requirements, legal representation of children and their families, guardianship, and other emerging child welfare issues. The Center also works to broaden the knowledge of agencies, courts, and other professionals on issues involving foster care, permanency planning, and adoption.

National Clearinghouse on Child Abuse and Neglect Information
330 C Street SW
Washington, DC 20447
Toll-Free: 800-FYI-3366
Phone: 703-385-7565
Fax: 703-385-3206
Website: http://www.calib.com/nccanch
E-Mail: nccanch@calib.com

The National Clearinghouse on Child Abuse and Neglect Information, a service of the Children's Bureau, helps professionals locate information on child abuse and neglect and related child welfare issues. Among its resources, the Clearinghouse offers a bibliographic database of child maltreatment and related child welfare materials, summaries of State laws concerned with child abuse and neglect and child welfare, fact sheets, resource lists, bulletins, and other publications. Jointly with the National Adoption Information Clearinghouse (NAIC), the National Clearinghouse on Child Abuse and Neglect Information publishes the Children's Bureau Express an online digest of news and resources for professionals concerned with child maltreatment, child welfare, and adoption.

National Conference of State Legislatures (NCSL)
1560 Broadway, Suite 700
Denver, CO 80202
Phone: 202-624-5400
Fax: 202-737-1069
Website: http://www.ncsl.org
E-Mail: info@ncsl.org

The National Conference of State Legislatures promotes information sharing by tracking legislation and policy issues in State legislatures and the effect of Federal initiatives on the States. The NCSL offers information, publications, conferences, consulting services, and professional development seminars. The NCSL also advocates for the States by lobbying, testifying, and collaborating on Capitol Hill.

National Council of Juvenile and Family Court Judges (NCJFCJ)

P.O. Box 8970
Reno, NV 89507
Phone: 775-784-6012
Fax: 775-784-6628
Website: http://ncjfcj.unr.edu
E-Mail: admin@ncjfcj.unr.edu

The National Council of Juvenile and Family Court Judges is dedicated to improving the court system's handling of juvenile and family matters through applied research, technical assistance, and continuing education of judges and juvenile justice professionals on family violence, child abuse and neglect, and child protection and custody.

National Court Appointed Special Advocate Association

100 West Harrison Street
North Tower, Suite 500
Seattle, WA 98119
Toll-Free: 800-628-3233
Fax: 206-270-0078
Website: http://www.nationalcasa.org
E-Mail: inquiry@nationalcasa.org

The National Court Appointed Special Advocate Association is a non-profit organization created to support the development, growth, and continuation of court appointed special advocate (CASA) programs. CASA volunteers advise courts on the best interests of children who may be victims of abuse or neglect. The Association provides support in training, legal research, fundraising, public awareness, and government relations services to local CASA groups.

National Institute of Justice (NIJ)

810 7th Street NW
Washington, DC 20531
Phone: 202-307-2942
Website: http://www.ojp.usdoj.gov/nij

The National Institute of Justice is the research, development, and evaluation agency of the U.S. Department of Justice. The Institute researches crime control and justice issues, and provides evidence-based knowledge and tools to meet the challenges of crime and justice, mostly at the State and local levels.

National Legal Aid and Defender Association
1625 K Street NW, Suite 800
Washington, DC 20006-1604
Phone: 202-452-0620
Fax: 202-872-1031
Website: http://www.nlada.org
E-Mail: info@nlada.org

The National Legal Aid & Defender Association provides support, technical assistance, services, and advocacy for public and pro bono justice system professionals who serve primarily low-income clients, families, and communities.

Office for Victims of Crime (OVC)
810 7th Street NW
Washington, DC 20531
Toll-Free: 800-627-6872
Phone: 866-OVC-TTAC
TTY: 877-712-9279
Website: http://www.ojp.usdoj.gov/ovc
E-Mail: askovc@ojp.usdoj.gov

The Office for Victims of Crime was established by the 1984 Victims of Crime Act (VOCA) to oversee diverse programs that benefit victims of crime. OVC provides substantial funding to State victim assistance and compensation programs, the lifeline services that help victims to heal. The agency also supports training designed to educate criminal justice and allied professionals on the rights and needs of crime victims. OVC is one of five bureaus and four offices with grant-making authority within the Office of Justice Programs of the U.S. Department of Justice.

Foster Care Resource Listing

The following organizations are among many that provide information on foster care. Inclusion on this list is for information purposes and does not constitute an endorsement by the Clearinghouse or the Children's Bureau.

American Foster Care Resources, Inc. (AFCR)
P.O. Box 271
King George, VA 22485
Phone: 540-775-7410

Fax: 540-775-3271
Website: http://www.afcr.com
E-Mail: afcr@afcr.com

AFCR is a publisher of resource materials for foster care providers, the children in care and their families, and the placing agency's staff and administration. AFCR's publications cover such topics as ADHD, discipline, sexual abuse, independent living, recruitment, and support groups.

American Humane Association (AHA)
Child Welfare Division
63 Inverness Dr. East
Englewood, CO 80112-5117
Toll-Free: 866-242-1877
Phone: 303-792-9900
Fax: 303-792-5333
Website: http://www.americanhumane.org
E-Mail: children@americanhumane.org

The American Humane Association's mission is preventing cruelty, abuse, neglect, and exploitation of children and animals. AHA's Child Welfare Division has worked for many years to improve the public and private child welfare systems so they can respond more effectively to the needs of abused and neglected children. AHA is a national association of child protection programs, agencies, and individuals, and its membership includes State and local social service agencies, child advocates, courts, hospitals, schools, mental health professionals, and concerned citizens in every State. AHA information assists professionals and citizens in making informed decisions about how to help children and families in crisis. The association also develops resources and programs which help communities and citizens prevent child abuse.

Annie E. Casey Foundation (AECF)
701 St. Paul Street
Baltimore, MD 21202
Phone: 410-547-6600
Fax: 410-547-6624
Website: http://www.aecf.org

The Annie E. Casey Foundation works to build better futures for disadvantaged children and their families. The primary mission of the

AECF is to foster public policies, human service reforms, and community supports that meet the needs of today's vulnerable children and families.

Association of Administrators of the Interstate Compact for the Placement of Children (ICPC)
American Public Human Services Association
810 First Street NE, Suite 500
Washington, DC 20002-4267
Phone: 202-682-0100
Fax: 202-289-6555
Website: http://icpc.aphsa.org
E-Mail: icpcinbox@APHSA.org

The Interstate Compact for the Placement of Children is a uniform State law establishing a contract among party States to ensure that children placed across state lines receive adequate protection and services. The primary function of the ICPC is to protect the interests of both the children and the States by requiring that certain procedures be followed in the interstate placement of children who are being adopted, placed with relatives, or going into residential care or foster family homes.

Casey Family Programs
1300 Dexter Avenue North, Third Floor
Seattle, WA 98109-3542
Toll-Free: 800-228-3559
Phone: 206-282-7300
Fax: 206-282-3555
Website: http://www.casey.org
E-Mail: info@casey.org

Casey Family Programs provides an array of services for children and youth, with foster care as it core. Casey services include adoption, guardianship, kinship care, and family reunification. Casey is also committed to helping youth in foster care make a successful transition to adulthood.

Casey National Center for Resource Family Support (CNC)
1808 Eye Street NW, Fifth Floor
Washington, DC 20006-5427
Toll-Free: 888-295-6727
Phone: 202-467-4441

Fax: 202-467-4499
Website: http://www.casey.org/cnc
E-Mail: cncinfo@casey.org

The CNC is a source for information, technical assistance, written materials, and referrals to both resource families (foster, adoptive, and kinship care families) and child welfare professionals who work with and on behalf of them.

Chapin Hall Center for Children
1313 East 60th Street
Chicago, IL 60637
Phone: 773-753-5900
Fax: 773-753-5940
Website: http://www.chapin.uchicago.edu

Chapin Hall is a research and development center focusing on policies, practices, and programs affecting children and the families and communities in which they live. The Center devotes special attention to children facing significant problems such as abuse or neglect, poverty, and mental or physical illnesses, and to the service systems designed to address these problems.

Children's Bureau (CB)
330 C Street SW
Washington, DC 20447
Website: http://www.acf.hhs.gov/programs/cb

The Children's Bureau, the oldest Federal agency for children and families, is located within the Department of Health and Human Services' Administration for Children and Families, Administration on Children, Youth and Families. The Bureau is responsible for assisting States in the delivery of child welfare services designed to protect children and to strengthen families. The Bureau provides grants to States, Tribes, and communities to operate a range of child welfare services including child protective services, family preservation and support, foster care, adoption, and independent living.

Foster Family-Based Treatment Association (FFTA)
1415 Queen Anne Road
Teaneck, NJ 07666
Toll-Free: 800-414-FFTA
Website: http://www.ffta.org
E-Mail: ffta@ffta.org

The Foster Family-Based Treatment Association is a membership organization committed to enhancing the lives of children and their families by strengthening family-based organizations. Treatment foster care is a model of care that provides children with a combination of traditional foster care and residential treatment centers, with the treatment occurring within the foster family home.

Freddie Mac Foundation
8250 Jones Branch Drive
Mailstop A40
McLean, VA 22102
Phone: 703-918-8888
Fax: 703-918-8895
Website: http://www.freddiemacfoundation.org
E-Mail: freddiemac_foundation@freddiemac.com

The Freddie Mac Foundation provides funds for various nonprofit organizations that work on behalf of children, youth and families. The Foundation focuses on children and prevention-oriented programs. Typically, grants are awarded to programs which build strong families, prevent child abuse and neglect, and recruit foster and adoptive parents. Among the Foundation's major programs are Healthy Families America and Wednesday's Child USA, a campaign to promote adoptions.

Girls and Boys Town
14100 Crawford Street
Boys Town, NE 68010
Toll-Free: 800-448-3000
Phone: 402-498-1300
Fax: 402-498-1348
TDD: 800-448-1833
Website: http://www.girlsandboystown.org
E-Mail: publicrelations@girlsandboystown.org

Girls and Boys Town, the original Father Flanagan's Boys' Home, is an organization that cares for troubled children—both boys and girls—and for families in crisis. The mission is to change the way America cares for at-risk children. Girls and Boys Town provides treatment and care of troubled boys and girls and conducts research and development of programs to meet the ever-changing needs of these children and their families.

National Adoption Information Clearinghouse (NAIC)
330 C Street SW
Washington, DC 20447
Toll-Free: 888-251-0078
Phone: 703-352-3488
Fax: 703-385-3206
Website: http://www.calib.com/naic
E-Mail: naic@calib.com

NAIC offers information on all aspects of adoption for professionals, policy makers, and the general public. The Clearinghouse develops and maintains a computerized database of books, journal articles, and other materials on adoption and related topics, conducts database searches, publishes materials on adoption, and gives referrals to related services and experts in the field. NAIC also maintains a database of experts knowledgeable in various areas of adoption practice. NAIC's primary audiences are adoption professionals and adoptive parents and children.

National Association of Foster Care Reviewers (NAFCR)
4665 Lower Roswell Road, Suite 156
Marietta, GA 30068
Phone: 770-977-5892
Fax: 770-565-6652
Website: http://www.nafcr.org
E-Mail: info@nafcr.org

The National Association of Foster Care Reviewers is a membership organization devoted to the development and expansion of foster care review systems and citizen review programs. NAFCR works to promote permanent families for children by assuring that every child in foster care receives independent, timely, quality case reviews, and to advocate on behalf of abused and neglected children nationwide by using the information gathered during the review process.

National Clearinghouse on Child Abuse and Neglect Information
330 C Street SW
Washington, DC 20447
Toll-Free: 800-FYI-3366
Phone: 703-385-7565
Fax: 703-385-3206
Website: http://www.calib.com/nccanch
E-Mail: nccanch@calib.com

The National Clearinghouse on Child Abuse and Neglect Information, a service of the Children's Bureau, helps professionals locate information on child abuse and neglect and related child welfare issues. Among its resources, the Clearinghouse offers a bibliographic database of child maltreatment and related child welfare materials, summaries of State laws concerned with child abuse and neglect and child welfare, fact sheets, resource lists, bulletins, and other publications. Jointly with the National Adoption Information Clearinghouse (NAIC), the National Clearinghouse on Child Abuse and Neglect Information publishes the Children's Bureau Express an online digest of news and resources for professionals concerned with child maltreatment, child welfare, and adoption.

National Foster Parent Association (NFPA)
7512 Stanich Avenue, No. 6
Gig Harbor, WA 98335
Toll-Free: 800-557-5238
Phone: 253-853-4000
Fax: 253-853-4001
Website: http://www.nfpainc.org
E-Mail: info@NFPAinc.org

The National Foster Parent Association is a nonprofit volunteer organization established in 1972. The Association's purpose is to bring together foster parents, agency representatives, and people in the community to improve the foster care system. NFPA promotes mutual coordination, cooperation, and communication among foster parents, foster parent associations, child care agencies, and other child advocates in an effort to encourage the recruitment and retention of foster parents and to inform the Association's membership and the general public of particular children needing foster care placement.

National Governors Association and NGA Center on Best Practices (NGA)
Hall of States
444 North Capitol Street
Washington, DC 20001-1512
Phone: 202-624-5300
Website: http://www.nga.org

The mission of the National Governors Association and the NGA Center for Best Practices is to encourage the exchange of ideas and information in the States; identify and share the States' best practices and innovations; provide expert customized technical assistance to Governors; identify emerging issues and assist Governors in producing creative and effective responses; assist Governors in developing strategies for evaluating current state programs; explore and develop approaches to transfer responsibility from the federal government to the States and to establish new partnerships among federal, State, and local governments; and to help Governors explore and develop public and private partnerships. The NGA has a long history of focusing on the needs of young children and the actions both the private and public sectors can take to help families meet those needs. Focus areas include child welfare, children and families, welfare reform, fatherhood, foster care and adoption, and youth development.

National Resource Center for Foster Care and Permanency Planning (NRCFCPP)

Hunter College School of Social Work
129 East 79th Street
New York, NY 10021
Phone: 212-452-7053
Fax: 212-452-7051
Website: http://www.hunter.cuny.edu/socwork/nrcfcpp
E-Mail: nrcfcpp@shiva.hunter.cuny.edu

The National Resource Center for Foster Care and Permanency Planning is funded by the Children's Bureau of the U.S. Department of Health and Human Services. Its mission is to provide information, training, and technical assistance on permanency planning for children in foster care. The Center addresses permanency planning issues through policy analysis, research, and information dissemination.

National Resource Center for Youth Development (NRCYD)

University of Oklahoma, College of Continuing Education
4502 East 41st Street, Building 4W
Tulsa, OK 74135
Phone: 918-660-3700
Fax: 918-660-3737
Website: http://www.nrcys.ou.edu/nrcyd
E-Mail: hlock@ou.edu

The National Resource Center for Youth Development was created to help States, tribes and agencies implement the Adoption and Safe Families Act (1997) and the Foster Care Independence Act (1999).

Funded by the Children's Bureau of the U.S. Department of Health and Human Services, the Center provides training and technical assistance in developing policies that incorporate the legislation. The Center also assists the States and agencies in building capacity to deliver culturally competent, competency-based services; incorporate youth development/involvement approaches into all areas of programs and services; prepare for the statewide assessment portion of the CFSR initiative; develop and implement program improvements based on the CFSR review; and assist in permanency planning for adolescents.

Orphan Foundation of America (OFA)
Tall Oaks Village Center
12020-D North Shore Drive
Reston, VA 20190-4977
Phone: 571-203-0270
Fax: 571-203-0273
Website: http://www.orphan.org
E-Mail: help@orphan.org

The Orphan Foundation of America's mission is to provide opportunities for America's foster youth to continue their education, to increase awareness of the number and plight of older teens leaving the bureaucratic maze of foster care, to highlight the potential of America's foster youth and the importance of supporting their dreams, and to offer direct opportunities for citizens, business, and civic organizations to assist older foster youth.

Chapter 58

State Toll-Free Child Abuse Reporting Numbers

Each State designates specific agencies to receive and investigate reports of suspected child abuse and neglect. Typically, this responsibility is carried out by child protective services (CPS) within a Department of Social Services, Department of Human Resources, or Division of Family and Children Services. In some States, police departments also may receive reports of child abuse or neglect.

Many States have an in-State toll-free number for reporting suspected abuse. The reporting party must be calling from the same State where the child is allegedly being abused for the following numbers to be valid. Following is a list of these numbers.

For States not listed, or when the reporting party resides in a different State than the child, please call Childhelp, 800-4-A-Child (800-422-4453), or your local CPS agency.

Alaska (AK)
800-478-4444

Arizona (AZ)
888-SOS-CHILD
(888-767-2445)

Arkansas (AR)
800-482-5964

Connecticut (CT)
800-842-2288
800-624-5518 (TDD/hearing impaired)

"State Toll-Free Child Abuse Reporting Numbers Resource Listing," National Clearinghouse on Child Abuse and Neglect Information, 2003. Available online at http://nccanch.acf.hhs.gov/pubs/organizations/tollfree.cfm. Resources verified February 2004.

Delaware (DE)
800-292-9582

District of Columbia (DC)
202-671-SAFE (7233)

Florida (FL)
800-96-ABUSE
(800-962-2873)

Illinois (IL)
800-252-2873
(From out of state, call
217-524-2606)

Indiana (IN)
800-800-5556

Iowa (IA)
800-362-2178

Kansas (KS)
800-922-5330

Kentucky (KY)
800-752-6200

Maine (ME)
800-452-1999

Maryland (MD)
800-332-6347

Massachusetts (MA)
800-792-5200

Michigan (MI)
800-942-4357

Mississippi (MS)
800-222-8000

Missouri (MO)
800-392-3738

Montana (MT)
866-820-KIDS (5437)

Nebraska (NE)
800-652-1999

Nevada (NV)
800-992-5757

New Hampshire (NH)
800-894-5533

New Jersey (NJ)
800-792-8610
800-835-5510 (TDD/hearing impaired)

New Mexico (NM)
800-797-3260

New York (NY)
800-342-3720

North Carolina (NC)
Contact the appropriate County Department of Social Services for the number for Child Protective Services.

North Dakota (ND)
800-245-3736

Oklahoma (OK)
800-522-3511

Oregon (OR)
800-854-3508, ext. 2402

Pennsylvania (PA)
800-932-0313

Rhode Island (RI)
800-RI-CHILD
(800-742-4453)

Texas (TX)
800-252-5400

Utah (UT)
800-678-9399

Virginia (VA)
800-552-7096

Washington (WA)
866-END-HARM
(866-363-4276)

West Virginia (WV)
800-352-6513

Wyoming (WY)
800-457-3659

Chapter 59

How to Report Child Pornography

Citizen Reporting

Report the site address for child pornography found on the Internet to your Internet Service Provider and your local or state Federal Bureau of Investigation (FBI) or Customs office listed in your telephone directory. Also, you can easily report child pornography online by forwarding the site address to the National Center for Missing and Exploited Children (NCMEC) at http://www.cybertipline.com. NCMEC will forward your report to the appropriate investigative agency for follow-up.

Reporting Child Pornography Found in the U.S. Mail

If you have information regarding the use of the U.S. Mail to send child pornography, contact the U.S. Postal Inspection Service listed in the white pages of your local telephone directory. Or visit their website at http://www.usps.com/postalinspectors.

Reporting by Electronic Service Providers

The Protection of Children from Sexual Predators Act amends the Victims of Child Abuse Act of 1990 by requiring online service providers

---

U.S. Department of Justice, Criminal Division, Child Exploitation and Obscenity Section, 2002. Available online at http://www.usdoj.gov/crominal/ceos/report.htm.

to report evidence of child pornography offenses to law enforcement agencies.

The Act also amends 18 U.S.C. Section 2702(b) of the Electronic Communications Privacy Act of 1986 to create an exception to the general statutory bar against a public provider's voluntary disclosure of customer communications to third parties. The online industry is encouraged to familiarize itself with the Electronic Communications Privacy Act of 1996, 18 U.S.C. Section 2701, et.seq.

The reporting section, 42 U.S.C. Section 13032, which is similar to 42 U.S.C. Section 13031, Child Abuse Reporting, requires anyone who is engaged in providing an electronic communication service to the public, and obtains knowledge of a violation of the child exploitation statutes, to report such violation to a law enforcement agency or agencies. The Attorney General is in the process of designating a federal law enforcement agency which will be responsible for receiving such reports by electronic service providers. A failure to report is subject to a civil fine of up to $50,000 in the first instance and $100,000 for any subsequent failure. No service provider may be held civilly liable for any action taken in good faith to comply with the reporting requirement.

The online industry is also encouraged to familiarize itself with 47 U.S.C. Section 230. This "Good Samaritan" blocking and screening statute states that:

> "no provider ... shall be held liable on account of any action voluntarily taken in good faith to restrict access to or availability of material that the provider ... considers to be obscene, lewd, lascivious, filthy, excessively violent, harassing, or otherwise objectionable, whether or not such material is constitutionally protected...."

Index

Index

Page numbers followed by 'n' indicate a footnote. Page numbers in *italics* indicate a table or illustration.

A

D

E

O

P

S

T

X

Z

Health Reference Series

COMPLETE CATALOG

Adolescent Health Sourcebook

Basic Consumer Health Information about Common Medical, Mental, and Emotional Concerns in Adolescents, Including Facts about Acne, Body Piercing, Mononucleosis, Nutrition, Eating Disorders, Stress, Depression, Behavior Problems, Peer Pressure, Violence, Gangs, Drug Use, Puberty, Sexuality, Pregnancy, Learning Disabilities, and More

Along with a Glossary of Terms and Other Resources for Further Help and Information

Edited by Chad T. Kimball. 658 pages. 2002. 0-7808-0248-9. $78.

"It is written in clear, nontechnical language aimed at general readers. . . . Recommended for public libraries, community colleges, and other agencies serving health care consumers."
—*American Reference Books Annual, 2003*

"Recommended for school and public libraries. Parents and professionals dealing with teens will appreciate the easy-to-follow format and the clearly written text. This could become a 'must have' for every high school teacher." —*E-Streams, Jan '03*

"A good starting point for information related to common medical, mental, and emotional concerns of adolescents." —*School Library Journal, Nov '02*

"This book provides accurate information in an easy to access format. It addresses topics that parents and caregivers might not be aware of and provides practical, useable information." —*Doody's Health Sciences Book Review Journal, Sep-Oct '02*

"Recommended reference source."
—*Booklist, American Library Association, Sep '02*

AIDS Sourcebook, 3rd Edition

Basic Consumer Health Information about Acquired Immune Deficiency Syndrome (AIDS) and Human Immunodeficiency Virus (HIV) Infection, Including Facts about Transmission, Prevention, Diagnosis, Treatment, Opportunistic Infections, and Other Complications, with a Section for Women and Children, Including Details about Associated Gynecological Concerns, Pregnancy, and Pediatric Care

Along with Updated Statistical Information, Reports on Current Research Initiatives, a Glossary, and Directories of Internet, Hotline, and Other Resources

Edited by Dawn D. Matthews. 664 pages. 2003. 0-7808-0631-X. $78.

ALSO AVAILABLE: *AIDS Sourcebook, 1st Edition.* Edited by Karen Bellenir and Peter D. Dresser. 831 pages. 1995. 0-7808-0031-1. $78.

AIDS Sourcebook, 2nd Edition. Edited by Karen Bellenir. 751 pages. 1999. 0-7808-0225-X. $78.

"Highly recommended."
—*American Reference Books Annual, 2000*

"Excellent sourcebook. This continues to be a highly recommended book. There is no other book that provides as much information as this book provides."
—*AIDS Book Review Journal, Dec-Jan 2000*

"Recommended reference source."
—*Booklist, American Library Association, Dec '99*

"A solid text for college-level health libraries."
—*The Bookwatch, Aug '99*

Cited in *Reference Sources for Small and Medium-Sized Libraries, American Library Association, 1999*

Alcoholism Sourcebook

Basic Consumer Health Information about the Physical and Mental Consequences of Alcohol Abuse, Including Liver Disease, Pancreatitis, Wernicke-Korsakoff Syndrome (Alcoholic Dementia), Fetal Alcohol Syndrome, Heart Disease, Kidney Disorders, Gastrointestinal Problems, and Immune System Compromise and Featuring Facts about Addiction, Detoxification, Alcohol Withdrawal, Recovery, and the Maintenance of Sobriety

Along with a Glossary and Directories of Resources for Further Help and Information

Edited by Karen Bellenir. 613 pages. 2000. 0-7808-0325-6. $78.

"This title is one of the few reference works on alcoholism for general readers. For some readers this will be a welcome complement to the many self-help books on the market. Recommended for collections serving general readers and consumer health collections."
—*E-Streams, Mar '01*

"This book is an excellent choice for public and academic libraries."
—*American Reference Books Annual, 2001*

"Recommended reference source."
—*Booklist, American Library Association, Dec '00*

"Presents a wealth of information on alcohol use and abuse and its effects on the body and mind, treatment, and prevention." —*SciTech Book News, Dec '00*

"Important new health guide which packs in the latest consumer information about the problems of alcoholism." —*Reviewer's Bookwatch, Nov '00*

SEE ALSO *Drug Abuse Sourcebook, Substance Abuse Sourcebook*

Allergies Sourcebook, 2nd Edition

Basic Consumer Health Information about Allergic Disorders, Triggers, Reactions, and Related Symptoms, Including Anaphylaxis, Rhinitis, Sinusitis, Asthma, Dermatitis, Conjunctivitis, and Multiple Chemical Sensitivity

Along with Tips on Diagnosis, Prevention, and Treatment, Statistical Data, a Glossary, and a Directory of Sources for Further Help and Information

Edited by Annemarie S. Muth. 598 pages. 2002. 0-7808-0376-0. $78.

ALSO AVAILABLE: *Allergies Sourcebook, 1st Edition.* Edited by Allan R. Cook. 611 pages. 1997. 0-7808-0036-2. $78.

"This book brings a great deal of useful material together. . . . This is an excellent addition to public and consumer health library collections."
—*American Reference Books Annual, 2003*

"This second edition would be useful to laypersons with little or advanced knowledge of the subject matter. This book would also serve as a resource for nursing and other health care professions students. It would be useful in public, academic, and hospital libraries with consumer health collections." —*E-Streams, Jul '02*

Alternative Medicine Sourcebook, 2nd Edition

Basic Consumer Health Information about Alternative and Complementary Medical Practices, Including Acupuncture, Chiropractic, Herbal Medicine, Homeopathy, Naturopathic Medicine, Mind-Body Interventions, Ayurveda, and Other Non-Western Medical Traditions

Along with Facts about such Specific Therapies as Massage Therapy, Aromatherapy, Qigong, Hypnosis, Prayer, Dance, and Art Therapies, a Glossary, and Resources for Further Information

Edited by Dawn D. Matthews. 618 pages. 2002. 0-7808-0605-0. $78.

ALSO AVAILABLE: *Alternative Medicine Sourcebook, 1st Edition.* Edited by Allan R. Cook. 737 pages. 1999. 0-7808-0200-4. $78.

"Recommended for public, high school, and academic libraries that have consumer health collections. Hospital libraries that also serve the public will find this to be a useful resource." —*E-Streams, Feb '03*

"Recommended reference source."
—*Booklist, American Library Association, Jan '03*

"An important alternate health reference."
—*MBR Bookwatch, Oct '02*

"A great addition to the reference collection of every type of library." —*American Reference Books Annual, 2000*

Alzheimer's Disease Sourcebook, 3rd Edition

Basic Consumer Health Information about Alzheimer's Disease, Other Dementias, and Related Disorders, Including Multi-Infarct Dementia, AIDS Dementia Complex, Dementia with Lewy Bodies, Huntington's Disease, Wernicke-Korsakoff Syndrome (Alcohol-Reated Dementia), Delirium, and Confusional States

Along with Information for People Newly Diagnosed with Alzheimer's Disease and Caregivers, Reports Detailing Current Research Efforts in Prevention, Diagnosis, and Treatment, Facts about Long-Term Care Issues, and Listings of Sources for Additional Information

Edited by Karen Bellenir. 645 pages. 2003. 0-7808-0666-2. $78.

ALSO AVAILABLE: *Alzheimer's, Stroke & 29 Other Neurological Disorders Sourcebook, 1st Edition.* Edited by Frank E. Bair. 579 pages. 1993. 1-55888-748-2. $78.

ALSO AVAILABLE: *Alzheimer's Disease Sourcebook, 2nd Edition.* Edited by Karen Bellenir. 524 pages. 1999. 0-7808-0223-3. $78.

"Provides a wealth of useful information not otherwise available in one place. This resource is recommended for all types of libraries."
—*American Reference Books Annual, 2000*

"Recommended reference source."
—*Booklist, American Library Association, Oct '99*

SEE ALSO *Brain Disorders Sourcebook*

Arthritis Sourcebook, 2nd Edition

Basic Consumer Health Information about Osteoarthritis, Rheumatoid Arthritis, Other Rheumatic Disorders, Infectious Forms of Arthritis, and Diseases with Symptoms Linked to Arthritis, Featuring Facts about Diagnosis, Pain Management, and Surgical Therapies

Along with Coping Strategies, Research Updates, a Glossary, and Resources for Additional Help and Information

Edited by Amy L. Sutton. 600 pages. 2004. 0-7808-0667-0. $78.

ALSO AVAILABLE: *Arthritis Sourcebook, 1st Edition.* Edited by Allan R. Cook. 550 pages. 1998. 0-7808-0201-2. $78.

". . . accessible to the layperson."
—*Reference and Research Book News, Feb '99*

Asthma Sourcebook

Basic Consumer Health Information about Asthma, Including Symptoms, Traditional and Nontraditional Remedies, Treatment Advances, Quality-of-Life Aids, Medical Research Updates, and the Role of Allergies, Exercise, Age, the Environment, and Genetics in the Development of Asthma

Along with Statistical Data, a Glossary, and Directories of Support Groups, and Other Resources for Further Information

Edited by Annemarie S. Muth. 628 pages. 2000. 0-7808-0381-7. $78.

"A worthwhile reference acquisition for public libraries and academic medical libraries whose readers desire a quick introduction to the wide range of asthma information." —*Choice, Association of College & Research Libraries, Jun '01*

"Recommended reference source."
—*Booklist, American Library Association, Feb '01*

"Highly recommended." —*The Bookwatch, Jan '01*

"There is much good information for patients and their families who deal with asthma daily."
—*American Medical Writers Association Journal, Winter '01*

"This informative text is recommended for consumer health collections in public, secondary school, and community college libraries and the libraries of universities with a large undergraduate population."
—*American Reference Books Annual, 2001*

■

Attention Deficit Disorder Sourcebook

Basic Consumer Health Information about Attention Deficit/Hyperactivity Disorder in Children and Adults, Including Facts about Causes, Symptoms, Diagnostic Criteria, and Treatment Options Such as Medications, Behavior Therapy, Coaching, and Homeopathy

Along with Reports on Current Research Initiatives, Legal Issues, and Government Regulations, and Featuring a Glossary of Related Terms, Internet Resources, and a List of Additional Reading Material

Edited by Dawn D. Matthews. 470 pages. 2002. 0-7808-0624-7. $78.

"Recommended reference source."
—*Booklist, American Library Association, Jan '03*

"This book is recommended for all school libraries and the reference or consumer health sections of public libraries." —*American Reference Books Annual, 2003*

■

Back & Neck Disorders Sourcebook

Basic Information about Disorders and Injuries of the Spinal Cord and Vertebrae, Including Facts on Chiropractic Treatment, Surgical Interventions, Paralysis, and Rehabilitation

Along with Advice for Preventing Back Trouble

Edited by Karen Bellenir. 548 pages. 1997. 0-7808-0202-0. $78.

"The strength of this work is its basic, easy-to-read format. Recommended."
—*Reference and User Services Quarterly, American Library Association, Winter '97*

Blood & Circulatory Disorders Sourcebook

Basic Information about Blood and Its Components, Anemias, Leukemias, Bleeding Disorders, and Circulatory Disorders, Including Aplastic Anemia, Thalassemia, Sickle-Cell Disease, Hemochromatosis, Hemophilia, Von Willebrand Disease, and Vascular Diseases

Along with a Special Section on Blood Transfusions and Blood Supply Safety, a Glossary, and Source Listings for Further Help and Information

Edited by Karen Bellenir and Linda M. Shin. 554 pages. 1998. 0-7808-0203-9. $78.

"Recommended reference source."
—*Booklist, American Library Association, Feb '99*

"An important reference sourcebook written in simple language for everyday, non-technical users. "
—*Reviewer's Bookwatch, Jan '99*

■

Brain Disorders Sourcebook

Basic Consumer Health Information about Strokes, Epilepsy, Amyotrophic Lateral Sclerosis (ALS/Lou Gehrig's Disease), Parkinson's Disease, Brain Tumors, Cerebral Palsy, Headache, Tourette Syndrome, and More

Along with Statistical Data, Treatment and Rehabilitation Options, Coping Strategies, Reports on Current Research Initiatives, a Glossary, and Resource Listings for Additional Help and Information

Edited by Karen Bellenir. 481 pages. 1999. 0-7808-0229-2. $78.

"Belongs on the shelves of any library with a consumer health collection." —*E-Streams, Mar '00*

"Recommended reference source."
—*Booklist, American Library Association, Oct '99*

SEE ALSO *Alzheimer's Disease Sourcebook*

■

Breast Cancer Sourcebook

Basic Consumer Health Information about Breast Cancer, Including Diagnostic Methods, Treatment Options, Alternative Therapies, Self-Help Information, Related Health Concerns, Statistical and Demographic Data, and Facts for Men with Breast Cancer

Along with Reports on Current Research Initiatives, a Glossary of Related Medical Terms, and a Directory of Sources for Further Help and Information

Edited by Edward J. Prucha and Karen Bellenir. 580 pages. 2001. 0-7808-0244-6. $78.

"It would be a useful reference book in a library or on loan to women in a support group."
—*Cancer Forum, Mar '03*

"Recommended reference source."
—*Booklist, American Library Association, Jan '02*

"This reference source is highly recommended. It is quite informative, comprehensive and detailed in nature, and yet it offers practical advice in easy-to-read language. It could be thought of as the 'bible' of breast cancer for the consumer." —*E-Streams, Jan '02*

"The broad range of topics covered in lay language make the *Breast Cancer Sourcebook* an excellent addition to public and consumer health library collections."
—*American Reference Books Annual 2002*

"From the pros and cons of different screening methods and results to treatment options, *Breast Cancer Sourcebook* provides the latest information on the subject."
—*Library Bookwatch, Dec '01*

"This thoroughgoing, very readable reference covers all aspects of breast health and cancer. . . . Readers will find much to consider here. Recommended for all public and patient health collections."
—*Library Journal, Sep '01*

SEE ALSO *Cancer Sourcebook for Women, Women's Health Concerns Sourcebook*

Breastfeeding Sourcebook

Basic Consumer Health Information about the Benefits of Breastmilk, Preparing to Breastfeed, Breastfeeding as a Baby Grows, Nutrition, and More, Including Information on Special Situations and Concerns Such as Mastitis, Illness, Medications, Allergies, Multiple Births, Prematurity, Special Needs, and Adoption

Along with a Glossary and Resources for Additional Help and Information

Edited by Jenni Lynn Colson. 388 pages. 2002. 0-7808-0332-9. $78.

SEE ALSO *Pregnancy & Birth Sourcebook*

"Particularly useful is the information about professional lactation services and chapters on breastfeeding when returning to work. . . . *Breastfeeding Sourcebook* will be useful for public libraries, consumer health libraries, and technical schools offering nurse assistant training, especially in areas where Internet access is problematic."
—*American Reference Books Annual, 2003*

Burns Sourcebook

Basic Consumer Health Information about Various Types of Burns and Scalds, Including Flame, Heat, Cold, Electrical, Chemical, and Sun Burns

Along with Information on Short-Term and Long-Term Treatments, Tissue Reconstruction, Plastic Surgery, Prevention Suggestions, and First Aid

Edited by Allan R. Cook. 604 pages. 1999. 0-7808-0204-7. $78.

"This is an exceptional addition to the series and is highly recommended for all consumer health collections, hospital libraries, and academic medical centers."
—*E-Streams, Mar '00*

"This key reference guide is an invaluable addition to all health care and public libraries in confronting this ongoing health issue."
—*American Reference Books Annual, 2000*

"Recommended reference source."
—*Booklist, American Library Association, Dec '99*

SEE ALSO *Skin Disorders Sourcebook*

Cancer Sourcebook, 4th Edition

Basic Consumer Health Information about Major Forms and Stages of Cancer, Featuring Facts about Head and Neck Cancers, Lung Cancers, Gastrointestinal Cancers, Genitourinary Cancers, Lymphomas, Blood Cell Cancers, Endocrine Cancers, Skin Cancers, Bone Cancers, Sarcomas, and Others, and Including Information about Cancer Treatments and Therapies, Identifying and Reducing Cancer Risks, and Strategies for Coping with Cancer and the Side Effects of Treatment

Along with a Cancer Glossary, Statistical and Demographic Data, and a Directory of Sources for Additional Help and Information

Edited by Karen Bellenir. 1,119 pages. 2003. 0-7808-0633-6. $78.

ALSO AVAILABLE: *Cancer Sourcebook, 1st Edition.* Edited by Frank E. Bair. 932 pages. 1990. 1-55888-888-8. $78.

New Cancer Sourcebook, 2nd Edition. Edited by Allan R. Cook. 1,313 pages. 1996. 0-7808-0041-9. $78.

Cancer Sourcebook, 3rd Edition. Edited by Edward J. Prucha. 1,069 pages. 2000. 0-7808-0227-6. $78.

"This title is recommended for health sciences and public libraries with consumer health collections."
—*E-Streams, Feb '01*

". . . can be effectively used by cancer patients and their families who are looking for answers in a language they can understand. Public and hospital libraries should have it on their shelves."
—*American Reference Books Annual, 2001*

"Recommended reference source."
—*Booklist, American Library Association, Dec '00*

Cited in *Reference Sources for Small and Medium-Sized Libraries, American Library Association, 1999*

"The amount of factual and useful information is extensive. The writing is very clear, geared to general readers. Recommended for all levels." —*Choice, Association of College & Research Libraries, Jan '97*

SEE ALSO *Breast Cancer Sourcebook, Cancer Sourcebook for Women, Pediatric Cancer Sourcebook, Prostate Cancer Sourcebook*

Cancer Sourcebook for Women, 2nd Edition

Basic Consumer Health Information about Gynecologic Cancers and Related Concerns, Including Cervical Cancer, Endometrial Cancer, Gestational Trophoblastic Tumor, Ovarian Cancer, Uterine Cancer, Vaginal Cancer, Vulvar Cancer, Breast Cancer, and Common Non-Cancerous Uterine Conditions, with Facts about Cancer Risk Factors, Screening and Prevention, Treatment Options, and Reports on Current Research Initiatives

Along with a Glossary of Cancer Terms and a Directory of Resources for Additional Help and Information

Edited by Karen Bellenir. 604 pages. 2002. 0-7808-0226-8. $78.

ALSO AVAILABLE: *Cancer Sourcebook for Women, 1st Edition.* Edited by Allan R. Cook and Peter D. Dresser. 524 pages. 1996. 0-7808-0076-1. $78.

"An excellent addition to collections in public, consumer health, and women's health libraries."
—*American Reference Books Annual, 2003*

"Overall, the information is excellent, and complex topics are clearly explained. As a reference book for the consumer it is a valuable resource to assist them to make informed decisions about cancer and its treatments." —*Cancer Forum, Nov '02*

"Highly recommended for academic and medical reference collections." —*Library Bookwatch, Sep '02*

"This is a highly recommended book for any public or consumer library, being reader friendly and containing accurate and helpful information."
—*E-Streams, Aug '02*

"Recommended reference source."
—*Booklist, American Library Association, Jul '02*

SEE ALSO *Breast Cancer Sourcebook, Women's Health Concerns Sourcebook*

■

Cardiovascular Diseases & Disorders Sourcebook, 1st Edition

SEE *Heart Diseases & Disorders Sourcebook, 2nd Edition*

■

Caregiving Sourcebook

Basic Consumer Health Information for Caregivers, Including a Profile of Caregivers, Caregiving Responsibilities and Concerns, Tips for Specific Conditions, Care Environments, and the Effects of Caregiving

Along with Facts about Legal Issues, Financial Information, and Future Planning, a Glossary, and a Listing of Additional Resources

Edited by Joyce Brennfleck Shannon. 600 pages. 2001. 0-7808-0331-0. $78.

"Essential for most collections."
—*Library Journal, Apr 1, 2002*

"An ideal addition to the reference collection of any public library. Health sciences information professionals may also want to acquire the *Caregiving Sourcebook* for their hospital or academic library for use as a ready reference tool by health care workers interested in aging and caregiving." —*E-Streams, Jan '02*

"Recommended reference source."
—*Booklist, American Library Association, Oct '01*

■

Child Abuse Sourcebook

Basic Consumer Health Information about the Physical, Sexual, and Emotional Abuse of Children, with Additional Facts about Neglect, Munchausen Syndrome by Proxy (MSBP), Shaken Baby Syndrome, and Controversial Issues Related to Child Abuse, Such as Withholding Medical Care, Corporal Punishment, and Child Maltreatment in Youth Sports, and Featuring Facts about Child Protective Services, Foster Care, Adoption, Parenting Challenges, and Other Abuse Prevention Efforts

Along with a Glossary of Related Terms and Resources for Additional Help and Information

Edited by Dawn D. Matthews. 620 pages. 2004. 0-7808-0705-7. $78.

■

Childhood Diseases & Disorders Sourcebook

Basic Consumer Health Information about Medical Problems Often Encountered in Pre-Adolescent Children, Including Respiratory Tract Ailments, Ear Infections, Sore Throats, Disorders of the Skin and Scalp, Digestive and Genitourinary Diseases, Infectious Diseases, Inflammatory Disorders, Chronic Physical and Developmental Disorders, Allergies, and More

Along with Information about Diagnostic Tests, Common Childhood Surgeries, and Frequently Used Medications, with a Glossary of Important Terms and Resource Directory

Edited by Chad T. Kimball. 662 pages. 2003. 0-7808-0458-9. $78.

■

Colds, Flu & Other Common Ailments Sourcebook

Basic Consumer Health Information about Common Ailments and Injuries, Including Colds, Coughs, the Flu, Sinus Problems, Headaches, Fever, Nausea and Vomiting, Menstrual Cramps, Diarrhea, Constipation, Hemorrhoids, Back Pain, Dandruff, Dry and Itchy Skin, Cuts, Scrapes, Sprains, Bruises, and More

Along with Information about Prevention, Self-Care, Choosing a Doctor, Over-the-Counter Medications, Folk Remedies, and Alternative Therapies, and Including a Glossary of Important Terms and a Directory of Resources for Further Help and Information

Edited by Chad T. Kimball. 638 pages. 2001. 0-7808-0435-X. $78.

"A good starting point for research on common illnesses. It will be a useful addition to public and consumer health library collections."

—*American Reference Books Annual 2002*

"Will prove valuable to any library seeking to maintain a current, comprehensive reference collection of health resources. . . . Excellent reference."

—*The Bookwatch, Aug '01*

"Recommended reference source."

—*Booklist, American Library Association, July '01*

Communication Disorders Sourcebook

Basic Information about Deafness and Hearing Loss, Speech and Language Disorders, Voice Disorders, Balance and Vestibular Disorders, and Disorders of Smell, Taste, and Touch

Edited by Linda M. Ross. 533 pages. 1996. 0-7808-0077-X. $78.

"This is skillfully edited and is a welcome resource for the layperson. It should be found in every public and medical library." —*Booklist Health Sciences Supplement, American Library Association, Oct '97*

Congenital Disorders Sourcebook

Basic Information about Disorders Acquired during Gestation, Including Spina Bifida, Hydrocephalus, Cerebral Palsy, Heart Defects, Craniofacial Abnormalities, Fetal Alcohol Syndrome, and More

Along with Current Treatment Options and Statistical Data

Edited by Karen Bellenir. 607 pages. 1997. 0-7808-0205-5. $78.

"Recommended reference source."

—*Booklist, American Library Association, Oct '97*

SEE ALSO *Pregnancy & Birth Sourcebook*

Consumer Issues in Health Care Sourcebook

Basic Information about Health Care Fundamentals and Related Consumer Issues, Including Exams and Screening Tests, Physician Specialties, Choosing a Doctor, Using Prescription and Over-the-Counter Medications Safely, Avoiding Health Scams, Managing Common Health Risks in the Home, Care Options for Chronically or Terminally Ill Patients, and a List of Resources for Obtaining Help and Further Information

Edited by Karen Bellenir. 618 pages. 1998. 0-7808-0221-7. $78.

"Both public and academic libraries will want to have a copy in their collection for readers who are interested in self-education on health issues."

—*American Reference Books Annual, 2000*

"The editor has researched the literature from government agencies and others, saving readers the time and effort of having to do the research themselves. Recommended for public libraries."

—*Reference and User Services Quarterly, American Library Association, Spring '99*

"Recommended reference source."

—*Booklist, American Library Association, Dec '98*

Contagious Diseases Sourcebook

Basic Consumer Health Information about Infectious Diseases Spread by Person-to-Person Contact through Direct Touch, Airborne Transmission, Sexual Contact, or Contact with Blood or Other Body Fluids, Including Hepatitis, Herpes, Influenza, Lice, Measles, Mumps, Pinworm, Ringworm, Severe Acute Respiratory Syndrome (SARS), Streptococcal Infections, Tuberculosis, and Others

Along with Facts about Disease Transmission, Antimicrobial Resistance, and Vaccines, with a Glossary and Directories of Resources for More Information

Edited by Karen Bellenir. 625 pages. 2004. 0-7808-0736-7. $78.

Contagious & Non-Contagious Infectious Diseases Sourcebook

Basic Information about Contagious Diseases like Measles, Polio, Hepatitis B, and Infectious Mononucleosis, and Non-Contagious Infectious Diseases like Tetanus and Toxic Shock Syndrome, and Diseases Occurring as Secondary Infections Such as Shingles and Reye Syndrome

Along with Vaccination, Prevention, and Treatment Information, and a Section Describing Emerging Infectious Disease Threats

Edited by Karen Bellenir and Peter D. Dresser. 566 pages. 1996. 0-7808-0075-3. $78.

Death & Dying Sourcebook

Basic Consumer Health Information for the Layperson about End-of-Life Care and Related Ethical and Legal Issues, Including Chief Causes of Death, Autopsies, Pain Management for the Terminally Ill, Life Support Systems, Insurance, Euthanasia, Assisted Suicide, Hospice Programs, Living Wills, Funeral Planning, Counseling, Mourning, Organ Donation, and Physician Training

Along with Statistical Data, a Glossary, and Listings of Sources for Further Help and Information

Edited by Annemarie S. Muth. 641 pages. 1999. 0-7808-0230-6. $78.

"Public libraries, medical libraries, and academic libraries will all find this sourcebook a useful addition to their collections."

—*American Reference Books Annual, 2001*

"An extremely useful resource for those concerned with death and dying in the United States."
—*Respiratory Care, Nov '00*

"Recommended reference source."
—*Booklist, American Library Association, Aug '00*

"This book is a definite must for all those involved in end-of-life care." —*Doody's Review Service, 2000*

Dental Care & Oral Health Sourcebook, 2nd Edition

Basic Consumer Health Information about Dental Care, Including Oral Hygiene, Dental Visits, Pain Management, Cavities, Crowns, Bridges, Dental Implants, and Fillings, and Other Oral Health Concerns, Such as Gum Disease, Bad Breath, Dry Mouth, Genetic and Developmental Abnormalities, Oral Cancers, Orthodontics, and Temporomandibular Disorders

Along with Updates on Current Research in Oral Health, a Glossary, a Directory of Dental and Oral Health Organizations, and Resources for People with Dental and Oral Health Disorders

Edited by Amy L. Sutton. 609 pages. 2003. 0-7808-0634-4. $78.

ALSO AVAILABLE: *Oral Health Sourcebook, 1st Edition.* Edited by Allan R. Cook. 558 pages. 1997. 0-7808-0082-6. $78.

"Unique source which will fill a gap in dental sources for patients and the lay public. A valuable reference tool even in a library with thousands of books on dentistry. Comprehensive, clear, inexpensive, and easy to read and use. It fills an enormous gap in the health care literature." —*Reference and User Services Quarterly, American Library Association, Summer '98*

"Recommended reference source."
—*Booklist, American Library Association, Dec '97*

Depression Sourcebook

Basic Consumer Health Information about Unipolar Depression, Bipolar Disorder, Postpartum Depression, Seasonal Affective Disorder, and Other Types of Depression in Children, Adolescents, Women, Men, the Elderly, and Other Selected Populations

Along with Facts about Causes, Risk Factors, Diagnostic Criteria, Treatment Options, Coping Strategies, Suicide Prevention, a Glossary, and a Directory of Sources for Additional Help and Information

Edited by Karen Belleni. 602 pages. 2002. 0-7808-0611-5. $78.

"Invaluable reference for public and school library collections alike." —*Library Bookwatch, Apr '03*

"Recommended for purchase."
—*American Reference Books Annual, 2003*

Diabetes Sourcebook, 3rd Edition

Basic Consumer Health Information about Type 1 Diabetes (Insulin-Dependent or Juvenile-Onset Diabetes), Type 2 Diabetes (Noninsulin-Dependent or Adult-Onset Diabetes), Gestational Diabetes, Impaired Glucose Tolerance (IGT), and Related Complications, Such as Amputation, Eye Disease, Gum Disease, Nerve Damage, and End-Stage Renal Disease, Including Facts about Insulin, Oral Diabetes Medications, Blood Sugar Testing, and the Role of Exercise and Nutrition in the Control of Diabetes

Along with a Glossary and Resources for Further Help and Information

Edited by Dawn D. Matthews. 622 pages. 2003. 0-7808-0629-8. $78.

ALSO AVAILABLE: *Diabetes Sourcebook, 1st Edition.* Edited by Karen Bellenir and Peter D. Dresser. 827 pages. 1994. 1-55888-751-2. $78.

Diabetes Sourcebook, 2nd Edition. Edited by Karen Bellenir. 688 pages. 1998. 0-7808-0224-1. $78.

"An invaluable reference." —*Library Journal, May '00*

Selected as one of the 250 "Best Health Sciences Books of 1999." —*Doody's Rating Service, Mar-Apr 2000*

"This comprehensive book is an excellent addition for high school, academic, medical, and public libraries. This volume is highly recommended."
—*American Reference Books Annual, 2000*

"Provides useful information for the general public."
—*Healthlines, University of Michigan Health Management Research Center, Sep/Oct '99*

". . . provides reliable mainstream medical information . . . belongs on the shelves of any library with a consumer health collection." —*E-Streams, Sep '99*

"Recommended reference source."
—*Booklist, American Library Association, Feb '99*

Diet & Nutrition Sourcebook, 2nd Edition

Basic Consumer Health Information about Dietary Guidelines, Recommended Daily Intake Values, Vitamins, Minerals, Fiber, Fat, Weight Control, Dietary Supplements, and Food Additives

Along with Special Sections on Nutrition Needs throughout Life and Nutrition for People with Such Specific Medical Concerns as Allergies, High Blood Cholesterol, Hypertension, Diabetes, Celiac Disease, Seizure Disorders, Phenylketonuria (PKU), Cancer, and Eating Disorders, and Including Reports on Current Nutrition Research and Source Listings for Additional Help and Information

Edited by Karen Bellenir. 650 pages. 1999. 0-7808-0228-4. $78.

ALSO AVAILABLE: *Diet & Nutrition Sourcebook, 1st Edition.* Edited by Dan R. Harris. 662 pages. 1996. 0-7808-0084-2. $78.

"This book is an excellent source of basic diet and nutrition information." —*Booklist Health Sciences Supplement, American Library Association, Dec '00*

"This reference document should be in any public library, but it would be a very good guide for beginning students in the health sciences. If the other books in this publisher's series are as good as this, they should all be in the health sciences collections."

—*American Reference Books Annual, 2000*

"This book is an excellent general nutrition reference for consumers who desire to take an active role in their health care for prevention. Consumers of all ages who select this book can feel confident they are receiving current and accurate information." —*Journal of Nutrition for the Elderly, Vol. 19, No. 4, '00*

"Recommended reference source."

—*Booklist, American Library Association, Dec '99*

SEE ALSO *Digestive Diseases & Disorders Sourcebook, Eating Disorders Sourcebook, Gastrointestinal Diseases & Disorders Sourcebook, Vegetarian Sourcebook*

Digestive Diseases & Disorders Sourcebook

Basic Consumer Health Information about Diseases and Disorders that Impact the Upper and Lower Digestive System, Including Celiac Disease, Constipation, Crohn's Disease, Cyclic Vomiting Syndrome, Diarrhea, Diverticulosis and Diverticulitis, Gallstones, Heartburn, Hemorrhoids, Hernias, Indigestion (Dyspepsia), Irritable Bowel Syndrome, Lactose Intolerance, Ulcers, and More

Along with Information about Medications and Other Treatments, Tips for Maintaining a Healthy Digestive Tract, a Glossary, and Directory of Digestive Diseases Organizations

Edited by Karen Bellenir. 335 pages. 2000. 0-7808-0327-2. $78.

"This title would be an excellent addition to all public or patient-research libraries."

—*American Reference Books Annual, 2001*

"This title is recommended for public, hospital, and health sciences libraries with consumer health collections." —*E-Streams, Jul-Aug '00*

"Recommended reference source."

—*Booklist, American Library Association, May '00*

SEE ALSO *Diet & Nutrition Sourcebook, Eating Disorders Sourcebook, Gastrointestinal Diseases & Disorders Sourcebook*

Disabilities Sourcebook

Basic Consumer Health Information about Physical and Psychiatric Disabilities, Including Descriptions of Major Causes of Disability, Assistive and Adaptive Aids, Workplace Issues, and Accessibility Concerns

Along with Information about the Americans with Disabilities Act, a Glossary, and Resources for Additional Help and Information

Edited by Dawn D. Matthews. 616 pages. 2000. 0-7808-0389-2. $78.

"It is a must for libraries with a consumer health section." —*American Reference Books Annual 2002*

"A much needed addition to the Omnigraphics ***Health Reference Series***. A current reference work to provide people with disabilities, their families, caregivers or those who work with them, a broad range of information in one volume, has not been available until now. . . . It is recommended for all public and academic library reference collections." —*E-Streams, May '01*

"An excellent source book in easy-to-read format covering many current topics; highly recommended for all libraries." —*Choice, Association of College and Research Libraries, Jan '01*

"Recommended reference source."

—*Booklist, American Library Association, Jul '00*

Domestic Violence Sourcebook, 2nd Edition

Basic Consumer Health Information about the Causes and Consequences of Abusive Relationships, Including Physical Violence, Sexual Assault, Battery, Stalking, and Emotional Abuse, and Facts about the Effects of Violence on Women, Men, Young Adults, and the Elderly, with Reports about Domestic Violence in Selected Populations, and Featuring Facts about Medical Care, Victim Assistance and Protection, Prevention Strategies, Mental Health Services, and Legal Issues

Along with a Glossary of Related Terms and Resources for Additional Help and Information

Edited by Dawn D. Matthews. 628 pages. 2004. 0-7808-0669-7. $78.

ALSO AVAILABLE: *Domestic Violence & Child Abuse Sourcebook, 1st Edition.* Edited by Helene Henderson. 1,064 pages. 2001. 0-7808-0235-7. $78.

"Interested lay persons should find the book extremely beneficial. . . . A copy of ***Domestic Violence and Child Abuse Sourcebook*** should be in every public library in the United States."

—*Social Science & Medicine, No. 56, 2003*

"This is important information. The Web has many resources but this sourcebook fills an important societal need. I am not aware of any other resources of this type." —*Doody's Review Service, Sep '01*

"Recommended for all libraries, scholars, and practitioners." —*Choice, Association of College & Research Libraries, Jul '01*

"Recommended reference source."

—*Booklist, American Library Association, Apr '01*

"Important pick for college-level health reference libraries." —*The Bookwatch, Mar '01*

"Because this problem is so widespread and because this book includes a lot of issues within one volume, this work is recommended for all public libraries."

—*American Reference Books Annual, 2001*

Drug Abuse Sourcebook

Basic Consumer Health Information about Illicit Substances of Abuse and the Diversion of Prescription Medications, Including Depressants, Hallucinogens, Inhalants, Marijuana, Narcotics, Stimulants, and Anabolic Steroids

Along with Facts about Related Health Risks, Treatment Issues, and Substance Abuse Prevention Programs, a Glossary of Terms, Statistical Data, and Directories of Hotline Services, Self-Help Groups, and Organizations Able to Provide Further Information

Edited by Karen Bellenir. 629 pages. 2000. 0-7808-0242-X. $78.

"Containing a wealth of information . . . . This resource belongs in libraries that serve a lower-division undergraduate or community college clientele as well as the general public." *—Choice, Association of College and Research Libraries, Jun '01*

"Recommended reference source." *—Booklist, American Library Association, Feb '01*

"Highly recommended." *—The Bookwatch, Jan '01*

"Even though there is a plethora of books on drug abuse, this volume is recommended for school, public, and college libraries." *—American Reference Books Annual, 2001*

SEE ALSO *Alcoholism Sourcebook, Substance Abuse Sourcebook*

■

Ear, Nose & Throat Disorders Sourcebook

Basic Information about Disorders of the Ears, Nose, Sinus Cavities, Pharynx, and Larynx, Including Ear Infections, Tinnitus, Vestibular Disorders, Allergic and Non-Allergic Rhinitis, Sore Throats, Tonsillitis, and Cancers That Affect the Ears, Nose, Sinuses, and Throat

Along with Reports on Current Research Initiatives, a Glossary of Related Medical Terms, and a Directory of Sources for Further Help and Information

Edited by Karen Bellenir and Linda M. Shin. 576 pages. 1998. 0-7808-0206-3. $78.

"Overall, this sourcebook is helpful for the consumer seeking information on ENT issues. It is recommended for public libraries." *—American Reference Books Annual, 1999*

"Recommended reference source." *—Booklist, American Library Association, Dec '98*

■

Eating Disorders Sourcebook

Basic Consumer Health Information about Eating Disorders, Including Information about Anorexia Nervosa, Bulimia Nervosa, Binge Eating, Body Dysmorphic Disorder, Pica, Laxative Abuse, and Night Eating Syndrome

Along with Information about Causes, Adverse Effects, and Treatment and Prevention Issues, and Featuring a Section on Concerns Specific to Children and Adolescents, a Glossary, and Resources for Further Help and Information

Edited by Dawn D. Matthews. 322 pages. 2001. 0-7808-0335-3. $78.

"Recommended for health science libraries that are open to the public, as well as hospital libraries. This book is a good resource for the consumer who is concerned about eating disorders." *—E-Streams, Mar '02*

"This volume is another convenient collection of excerpted articles. Recommended for school and public library patrons; lower-division undergraduates; and two-year technical program students." *—Choice, Association of College & Research Libraries, Jan '02*

"Recommended reference source." *—Booklist, American Library Association, Oct '01*

SEE ALSO *Diet & Nutrition Sourcebook, Digestive Diseases & Disorders Sourcebook, Gastrointestinal Diseases & Disorders Sourcebook*

■

Emergency Medical Services Sourcebook

Basic Consumer Health Information about Preventing, Preparing for, and Managing Emergency Situations, When and Who to Call for Help, What to Expect in the Emergency Room, the Emergency Medical Team, Patient Issues, and Current Topics in Emergency Medicine

Along with Statistical Data, a Glossary, and Sources of Additional Help and Information

Edited by Jenni Lynn Colson. 494 pages. 2002. 0-7808-0420-1. $78.

"Handy and convenient for home, public, school, and college libraries. Recommended." *—Choice, Association of College and Research Libraries, Apr '03*

"This reference can provide the consumer with answers to most questions about emergency care in the United States, or it will direct them to a resource where the answer can be found." *—American Reference Books Annual, 2003*

"Recommended reference source." *—Booklist, American Library Association, Feb '03*

■

Endocrine & Metabolic Disorders Sourcebook

Basic Information for the Layperson about Pancreatic and Insulin-Related Disorders Such as Pancreatitis, Diabetes, and Hypoglycemia; Adrenal Gland Disorders Such as Cushing's Syndrome, Addison's Disease, and Congenital Adrenal Hyperplasia; Pituitary Gland Disorders Such as Growth Hormone Deficiency, Acromegaly, and Pituitary Tumors; Thyroid Disorders Such as Hypothyroidism, Graves' Disease, Hashimoto's Disease, and Goiter; Hyperparathyroidism; and Other Diseases and Syndromes of Hormone Imbalance or Metabolic Dysfunction

Along with Reports on Current Research Initiatives

Edited by Linda M. Shin. 574 pages. 1998. 0-7808-0207-1. $78.

"Omnigraphics has produced another needed resource for health information consumers."

—American Reference Books Annual, 2000

"Recommended reference source."

—Booklist, American Library Association, Dec '98

Environmental Health Sourcebook, 2nd Edition

Basic Consumer Health Information about the Environment and Its Effect on Human Health, Including the Effects of Air Pollution, Water Pollution, Hazardous Chemicals, Food Hazards, Radiation Hazards, Biological Agents, Household Hazards, Such as Radon, Asbestos, Carbon Monoxide, and Mold, and Information about Associated Diseases and Disorders, Including Cancer, Allergies, Respiratory Problems, and Skin Disorders

Along with Information about Environmental Concerns for Specific Populations, a Glossary of Related Terms, and Resources for Further Help and Information

Edited by Dawn D. Matthews. 673 pages. 2003. 0-7808-0632-8. $78.

ALSO AVAILABLE: *Environmentally Induced Disorders Sourcebook, 1st Edition.* Edited by Allan R. Cook. 620 pages. 1997. 0-7808-0083-4. $78.

"Recommended reference source."

—Booklist, American Library Association, Sep '98

"This book will be a useful addition to anyone's library." *—Choice Health Sciences Supplement, Association of College and Research Libraries, May '98*

". . . a good survey of numerous environmentally induced physical disorders . . . a useful addition to anyone's library."

—Doody's Health Sciences Book Reviews, Jan '98

". . . provide[s] introductory information from the best authorities around. Since this volume covers topics that potentially affect everyone, it will surely be one of the most frequently consulted volumes in the *Health Reference Series.*" *—Rettig on Reference, Nov '97*

Environmentally Induced Disorders Sourcebook, 1st Edition

SEE *Environmental Health Sourcebook, 2nd Edition*

Ethnic Diseases Sourcebook

Basic Consumer Health Information for Ethnic and Racial Minority Groups in the United States, Including General Health Indicators and Behaviors, Ethnic Diseases, Genetic Testing, the Impact of Chronic Diseases, Women's Health, Mental Health Issues, and Preventive Health Care Services

Along with a Glossary and a Listing of Additional Resources

Edited by Joyce Brennfleck Shannon. 664 pages. 2001. 0-7808-0336-1. $78.

"Recommended for health sciences libraries where public health programs are a priority."

—E-Streams, Jan '02

"Not many books have been written on this topic to date, and the *Ethnic Diseases Sourcebook* is a strong addition to the list. It will be an important introductory resource for health consumers, students, health care personnel, and social scientists. It is recommended for public, academic, and large hospital libraries."

—American Reference Books Annual 2002

"Recommended reference source."

—Booklist, American Library Association, Oct '01

"Will prove valuable to any library seeking to maintain a current, comprehensive reference collection of health resources. . . . An excellent source of health information about genetic disorders which affect particular ethnic and racial minorities in the U.S."

—The Bookwatch, Aug '01

Eye Care Sourcebook, 2nd Edition

Basic Consumer Health Information about Eye Care and Eye Disorders, Including Facts about the Diagnosis, Prevention, and Treatment of Common Refractive Problems Such as Myopia, Hyperopia, Astigmatism, and Presbyopia, and Eye Diseases, Including Glaucoma, Cataract, Age-Related Macular Degeneration, and Diabetic Retinopathy

Along with a Section on Vision Correction and Refractive Surgeries, Including LASIK and LASEK, a Glossary, and Directories of Resources for Additional Help and Information

Edited by Amy L. Sutton. 543 pages. 2003. 0-7808-0635-2. $78.

ALSO AVAILABLE: *Ophthalmic Disorders Sourcebook, 1st Edition.* Edited by Linda M. Ross. 631 pages. 1996. 0-7808-0081-8. $78.

Family Planning Sourcebook

Basic Consumer Health Information about Planning for Pregnancy and Contraception, Including Traditional Methods, Barrier Methods, Hormonal Methods, Permanent Methods, Future Methods, Emergency Contraception, and Birth Control Choices for Women at Each Stage of Life

Along with Statistics, a Glossary, and Sources of Additional Information

Edited by Amy Marcaccio Keyzer. 520 pages. 2001. 0-7808-0379-5. $78.

"Recommended for public, health, and undergraduate libraries as part of the circulating collection."

—E-Streams, Mar '02

"Information is presented in an unbiased, readable manner, and the sourcebook will certainly be a necessary addition to those public and high school libraries

where Internet access is restricted or otherwise problematic." —*American Reference Books Annual 2002*

"Recommended reference source."
—*Booklist, American Library Association, Oct '01*

"Will prove valuable to any library seeking to maintain a current, comprehensive reference collection of health resources. . . . Excellent reference."
—*The Bookwatch, Aug '01*

SEE ALSO *Pregnancy & Birth Sourcebook*

Fitness & Exercise Sourcebook, 2nd Edition

Basic Consumer Health Information about the Fundamentals of Fitness and Exercise, Including How to Begin and Maintain a Fitness Program, Fitness as a Lifestyle, the Link between Fitness and Diet, Advice for Specific Groups of People, Exercise as It Relates to Specific Medical Conditions, and Recent Research in Fitness and Exercise

Along with a Glossary of Important Terms and Resources for Additional Help and Information

Edited by Kristen M. Gledhill. 646 pages. 2001. 0-7808-0334-5. $78.

ALSO AVAILABLE: *Fitness & Exercise Sourcebook, 1st Edition.* Edited by Dan R. Harris. 663 pages. 1996. 0-7808-0186-5. $78.

"This work is recommended for all general reference collections."
—*American Reference Books Annual 2002*

"Highly recommended for public, consumer, and school grades fourth through college."
—*E-Streams, Nov '01*

"Recommended reference source." —*Booklist, American Library Association, Oct '01*

"The information appears quite comprehensive and is considered reliable. . . . This second edition is a welcomed addition to the series."
—*Doody's Review Service, Sep '01*

"This reference is a valuable choice for those who desire a broad source of information on exercise, fitness, and chronic-disease prevention through a healthy lifestyle." —*American Medical Writers Association Journal, Fall '01*

"Will prove valuable to any library seeking to maintain a current, comprehensive reference collection of health resources. . . . Excellent reference."
—*The Bookwatch, Aug '01*

Food & Animal Borne Diseases Sourcebook

Basic Information about Diseases That Can Be Spread to Humans through the Ingestion of Contaminated Food or Water or by Contact with Infected Animals and Insects, Such as Botulism, E. Coli, Hepatitis A, Trichinosis, Lyme Disease, and Rabies

Along with Information Regarding Prevention and Treatment Methods, and Including a Special Section for International Travelers Describing Diseases Such as Cholera, Malaria, Travelers' Diarrhea, and Yellow Fever, and Offering Recommendations for Avoiding Illness

Edited by Karen Bellenir and Peter D. Dresser. 535 pages. 1995. 0-7808-0033-8. $78.

"Targeting general readers and providing them with a single, comprehensive source of information on selected topics, this book continues, with the excellent caliber of its predecessors, to catalog topical information on health matters of general interest. Readable and thorough, this valuable resource is highly recommended for all libraries."
—*Academic Library Book Review, Summer '96*

"A comprehensive collection of authoritative information." —*Emergency Medical Services, Oct '95*

Food Safety Sourcebook

Basic Consumer Health Information about the Safe Handling of Meat, Poultry, Seafood, Eggs, Fruit Juices, and Other Food Items, and Facts about Pesticides, Drinking Water, Food Safety Overseas, and the Onset, Duration, and Symptoms of Foodborne Illnesses, Including Types of Pathogenic Bacteria, Parasitic Protozoa, Worms, Viruses, and Natural Toxins

Along with the Role of the Consumer, the Food Handler, and the Government in Food Safety; a Glossary, and Resources for Additional Help and Information

Edited by Dawn D. Matthews. 339 pages. 1999. 0-7808-0326-4. $78.

"This book is recommended for public libraries and universities with home economic and food science programs." —*E-Streams, Nov '00*

"Recommended reference source."
—*Booklist, American Library Association, May '00*

"This book takes the complex issues of food safety and foodborne pathogens and presents them in an easily understood manner. [It does] an excellent job of covering a large and often confusing topic."
—*American Reference Books Annual, 2000*

Forensic Medicine Sourcebook

Basic Consumer Information for the Layperson about Forensic Medicine, Including Crime Scene Investigation, Evidence Collection and Analysis, Expert Testimony, Computer-Aided Criminal Identification, Digital Imaging in the Courtroom, DNA Profiling, Accident Reconstruction, Autopsies, Ballistics, Drugs and Explosives Detection, Latent Fingerprints, Product Tampering, and Questioned Document Examination

Along with Statistical Data, a Glossary of Forensics Terminology, and Listings of Sources for Further Help and Information

Edited by Annemarie S. Muth. 574 pages. 1999. 0-7808-0232-2. $78.

"Given the expected widespread interest in its content and its easy to read style, this book is recommended for most public and all college and university libraries."
—*E-Streams, Feb '01*

"Recommended for public libraries."
—*Reference & User Services Quarterly, American Library Association, Spring 2000*

"Recommended reference source."
—*Booklist, American Library Association, Feb '00*

"A wealth of information, useful statistics, references are up-to-date and extremely complete. This wonderful collection of data will help students who are interested in a career in any type of forensic field. It is a great resource for attorneys who need information about types of expert witnesses needed in a particular case. It also offers useful information for fiction and nonfiction writers whose work involves a crime. A fascinating compilation. All levels." —*Choice, Association of College and Research Libraries, Jan 2000*

"There are several items that make this book attractive to consumers who are seeking certain forensic data. . . . This is a useful current source for those seeking general forensic medical answers."
—*American Reference Books Annual, 2000*

Gastrointestinal Diseases & Disorders Sourcebook

Basic Information about Gastroesophageal Reflux Disease (Heartburn), Ulcers, Diverticulosis, Irritable Bowel Syndrome, Crohn's Disease, Ulcerative Colitis, Diarrhea, Constipation, Lactose Intolerance, Hemorrhoids, Hepatitis, Cirrhosis, and Other Digestive Problems, Featuring Statistics, Descriptions of Symptoms, and Current Treatment Methods of Interest for Persons Living with Upper and Lower Gastrointestinal Maladies

Edited by Linda M. Ross. 413 pages. 1996. 0-7808-0078-8. $78.

"... very readable form. The successful editorial work that brought this material together into a useful and understandable reference makes accessible to all readers information that can help them more effectively understand and obtain help for digestive tract problems."
—*Choice, Association of College & Research Libraries, Feb '97*

SEE ALSO *Diet & Nutrition Sourcebook, Digestive Diseases & Disorders, Eating Disorders Sourcebook*

Genetic Disorders Sourcebook, 2nd Edition

Basic Consumer Health Information about Hereditary Diseases and Disorders, Including Cystic Fibrosis, Down Syndrome, Hemophilia, Huntington's Disease, Sickle Cell Anemia, and More; Facts about Genes, Gene Research and Therapy, Genetic Screening, Ethics of Gene Testing, Genetic Counseling, and Advice on Coping and Caring

Along with a Glossary of Genetic Terminology and a Resource List for Help, Support, and Further Information

Edited by Kathy Massimini. 768 pages. 2001. 0-7808-0241-1. $78.

ALSO AVAILABLE: *Genetic Disorders Sourcebook, 1st Edition.* Edited by Karen Bellenir. 642 pages. 1996. 0-7808-0034-6. $78.

"Recommended for public libraries and medical and hospital libraries with consumer health collections."
—*E-Streams, May '01*

"Recommended reference source."
—*Booklist, American Library Association, Apr '01*

"Important pick for college-level health reference libraries." —*The Bookwatch, Mar '01*

"Provides essential medical information to both the general public and those diagnosed with a serious or fatal genetic disease or disorder." —*Choice, Association of College and Research Libraries, Jan '97*

Head Trauma Sourcebook

Basic Information for the Layperson about Open-Head and Closed-Head Injuries, Treatment Advances, Recovery, and Rehabilitation

Along with Reports on Current Research Initiatives

Edited by Karen Bellenir. 414 pages. 1997. 0-7808-0208-X. $78.

Headache Sourcebook

Basic Consumer Health Information about Migraine, Tension, Cluster, Rebound and Other Types of Headaches, with Facts about the Cause and Prevention of Headaches, the Effects of Stress and the Environment, Headaches during Pregnancy and Menopause, and Childhood Headaches

Along with a Glossary and Other Resources for Additional Help and Information

Edited by Dawn D. Matthews. 362 pages. 2002. 0-7808-0337-X. $78.

"Highly recommended for academic and medical reference collections." —*Library Bookwatch, Sep '02*

Health Insurance Sourcebook

Basic Information about Managed Care Organizations, Traditional Fee-for-Service Insurance, Insurance Portability and Pre-Existing Conditions Clauses, Medicare, Medicaid, Social Security, and Military Health Care

Along with Information about Insurance Fraud

Edited by Wendy Wilcox. 530 pages. 1997. 0-7808-0222-5. $78.

"Particularly useful because it brings much of this information together in one volume. This book will be a handy reference source in the health sciences library, hospital library, college and university library, and medium to large public library."
—*Medical Reference Services Quarterly, Fall '98*

Awarded "Books of the Year Award"
—*American Journal of Nursing, 1997*

"The layout of the book is particularly helpful as it provides easy access to reference material. A most useful addition to the vast amount of information about health insurance. The use of data from U.S. government agencies is most commendable. Useful in a library or learning center for healthcare professional students."
—*Doody's Health Sciences Book Reviews, Nov '97*

■

Health Reference Series Cumulative Index 1999

A Comprehensive Index to the Individual Volumes of the Health Reference Series, Including a Subject Index, Name Index, Organization Index, and Publication Index

Along with a Master List of Acronyms and Abbreviations

Edited by Edward J. Prucha, Anne Holmes, and Robert Rudnick. 990 pages. 2000. 0-7808-0382-5. $78.

"This volume will be most helpful in libraries that have a relatively complete collection of the Health Reference Series." —*American Reference Books Annual, 2001*

"Essential for collections that hold any of the numerous *Health Reference Series* titles."
—*Choice, Association of College and Research Libraries, Nov '00*

■

Healthy Aging Sourcebook

Basic Consumer Health Information about Maintaining Health through the Aging Process, Including Advice on Nutrition, Exercise, and Sleep, Help in Making Decisions about Midlife Issues and Retirement, and Guidance Concerning Practical and Informed Choices in Health Consumerism

Along with Data Concerning the Theories of Aging, Different Experiences in Aging by Minority Groups, and Facts about Aging Now and Aging in the Future; and Featuring a Glossary, a Guide to Consumer Help, Additional Suggested Reading, and Practical Resource Directory

Edited by Jenifer Swanson. 536 pages. 1999. 0-7808-0390-6. $78.

"Recommended reference source."
—*Booklist, American Library Association, Feb '00*

SEE ALSO *Physical & Mental Issues in Aging Sourcebook*

■

Healthy Children Sourcebook

Basic Consumer Health Information about the Physical and Mental Development of Children between the Ages of 3 and 12, Including Routine Health Care, Preventative Health Services, Safety and First Aid, Healthy Sleep, Dental Care, Nutrition, and Fitness, and Featuring Parenting Tips on Such Topics as Bedwetting, Choosing Day Care, Monitoring TV and Other Media, and Establishing a Foundation for Substance Abuse Prevention

Along with a Glossary of Commonly Used Pediatric Terms and Resources for Additional Help and Information.

Edited by Chad T. Kimball. 647 pages. 2003. 0-7808-0247-0. $78.

■

Healthy Heart Sourcebook for Women

Basic Consumer Health Information about Cardiac Issues Specific to Women, Including Facts about Major Risk Factors and Prevention, Treatment and Control Strategies, and Important Dietary Issues

Along with a Special Section Regarding the Pros and Cons of Hormone Replacement Therapy and Its Impact on Heart Health, and Additional Help, Including Recipes, a Glossary, and a Directory of Resources

Edited by Dawn D. Matthews. 336 pages. 2000. 0-7808-0329-9. $78.

"A good reference source and recommended for all public, academic, medical, and hospital libraries."
—*Medical Reference Services Quarterly, Summer '01*

"Because of the lack of information specific to women on this topic, this book is recommended for public libraries and consumer libraries."
—*American Reference Books Annual, 2001*

"Contains very important information about coronary artery disease that all women should know. The information is current and presented in an easy-to-read format. The book will make a good addition to any library." —*American Medical Writers Association Journal, Summer '00*

"Important, basic reference."
—*Reviewer's Bookwatch, Jul '00*

SEE ALSO *Heart Diseases & Disorders Sourcebook, Women's Health Concerns Sourcebook*

■

Heart Diseases & Disorders Sourcebook, 2nd Edition

Basic Consumer Health Information about Heart Attacks, Angina, Rhythm Disorders, Heart Failure, Valve Disease, Congenital Heart Disorders, and More, Including Descriptions of Surgical Procedures and Other Interventions, Medications, Cardiac Rehabilitation, Risk Identification, and Prevention Tips

Along with Statistical Data, Reports on Current Research Initiatives, a Glossary of Cardiovascular Terms, and Resource Directory

Edited by Karen Bellenir. 612 pages. 2000. 0-7808-0238-1. $78.

ALSO AVAILABLE: *Cardiovascular Diseases & Disorders Sourcebook, 1st Edition.* Edited by Karen Bellenir and Peter D. Dresser. 683 pages. 1995. 0-7808-0032-X. $78.

"This work stands out as an imminently accessible resource for the general public. It is recommended for

the reference and circulating shelves of school, public, and academic libraries."

—*American Reference Books Annual, 2001*

"Recommended reference source."

—*Booklist, American Library Association, Dec '00*

"Provides comprehensive coverage of matters related to the heart. This title is recommended for health sciences and public libraries with consumer health collections."

—*E-Streams, Oct '00*

SEE ALSO *Healthy Heart Sourcebook for Women*

Household Safety Sourcebook

Basic Consumer Health Information about Household Safety, Including Information about Poisons, Chemicals, Fire, and Water Hazards in the Home

Along with Advice about the Safe Use of Home Maintenance Equipment, Choosing Toys and Nursery Furniture, Holiday and Recreation Safety, a Glossary, and Resources for Further Help and Information

Edited by Dawn D. Matthews. 606 pages. 2002. 0-7808-0338-8. $78.

"This work will be useful in public libraries with large consumer health and wellness departments."

—*American Reference Books Annual, 2003*

"As a sourcebook on household safety this book meets its mark. It is encyclopedic in scope and covers a wide range of safety issues that are commonly seen in the home." —*E-Streams, Jul '02*

Hypertension Sourcebook

Basic Consumer Health Information about the Causes, Diagnosis, and Treatment of High Blood Pressure, with Facts about Consequences, Complications, and Co-Occurring Disorders, Such as Coronary Heart Disease, Diabetes, Stroke, Kidney Disease, and Hypertensive Retinopathy, and Issues in Blood Pressure Control, Including Dietary Choices, Stress Management, and Medications

Along with Reports on Current Research Initiatives and Clinical Trials, a Glossary, and Resources for Additional Help and Information

Edited by Dawn D. Matthews and Karen Bellenir. 600 pages. 2004. 0-7808-0674-3. $78.

Immune System Disorders Sourcebook

Basic Information about Lupus, Multiple Sclerosis, Guillain-Barré Syndrome, Chronic Granulomatous Disease, and More

Along with Statistical and Demographic Data and Reports on Current Research Initiatives

Edited by Allan R. Cook. 608 pages. 1997. 0-7808-0209-8. $78.

Infant & Toddler Health Sourcebook

Basic Consumer Health Information about the Physical and Mental Development of Newborns, Infants, and Toddlers, Including Neonatal Concerns, Nutrition Recommendations, Immunization Schedules, Common Pediatric Disorders, Assessments and Milestones, Safety Tips, and Advice for Parents and Other Caregivers

Along with a Glossary of Terms and Resource Listings for Additional Help

Edited by Jenifer Swanson. 585 pages. 2000. 0-7808-0246-2. $78.

"As a reference for the general public, this would be useful in any library." —*E-Streams, May '01*

"Recommended reference source."

—*Booklist, American Library Association, Feb '01*

"This is a good source for general use."

—*American Reference Books Annual, 2001*

Infectious Diseases Sourcebook

Basic Consumer Health Information about Non-Contagious Bacterial, Viral, Prion, Fungal, and Parasitic Diseases Spread by Food and Water, Insects and Animals, or Environmental Contact, Including Botulism, E. Coli, Encephalitis, Legionnaires' Disease, Lyme Disease, Malaria, Plague, Rabies, Salmonella, Tetanus, and Others, and Facts about Newly Emerging Diseases, Such as Hantavirus, Mad Cow Disease, Monkeypox, and West Nile Virus

Along with Information about Preventing Disease Transmission, the Threat of Bioterrorism, and Current Research Initiatives, with a Glossary and Directory of Resources for More Information

Edited by Karen Bellenir. 634 pages. 2004. 0-7808-0675-1. $78.

Injury & Trauma Sourcebook

Basic Consumer Health Information about the Impact of Injury, the Diagnosis and Treatment of Common and Traumatic Injuries, Emergency Care, and Specific Injuries Related to Home, Community, Workplace, Transportation, and Recreation

Along with Guidelines for Injury Prevention, a Glossary, and a Directory of Additional Resources

Edited by Joyce Brennfleck Shannon. 696 pages. 2002. 0-7808-0421-X. $78.

"This publication is the most comprehensive work of its kind about injury and trauma."

—*American Reference Books Annual, 2003*

"This sourcebook provides concise, easily readable, basic health information about injuries. . . . This book is well organized and an easy to use reference resource suitable for hospital, health sciences and public libraries with consumer health collections."

—*E-Streams, Nov '02*

"Practitioners should be aware of guides such as this in order to facilitate their use by patients and their families." —*Doody's Health Sciences Book Review Journal, Sep-Oct '02*

"Recommended reference source." —*Booklist, American Library Association, Sep '02*

"Highly recommended for academic and medical reference collections." —*Library Bookwatch, Sep '02*

Kidney & Urinary Tract Diseases & Disorders Sourcebook

Basic Information about Kidney Stones, Urinary Incontinence, Bladder Disease, End Stage Renal Disease, Dialysis, and More

Along with Statistical and Demographic Data and Reports on Current Research Initiatives

Edited by Linda M. Ross. 602 pages. 1997. 0-7808-0079-6. $78.

Learning Disabilities Sourcebook, 2nd Edition

Basic Consumer Health Information about Learning Disabilities, Including Dyslexia, Developmental Speech and Language Disabilities, Non-Verbal Learning Disorders, Developmental Arithmetic Disorder, Developmental Writing Disorder, and Other Conditions That Impede Learning Such as Attention Deficit/ Hyperactivity Disorder, Brain Injury, Hearing Impairment, Klinefelter Syndrome, Dyspraxia, and Tourette Syndrome

Along with Facts about Educational Issues and Assistive Technology, Coping Strategies, a Glossary of Related Terms, and Resources for Further Help and Information

Edited by Dawn D. Matthews. 621 pages. 2003. 0-7808-0626-3. $78.

ALSO AVAILABLE: *Learning Disabilities Sourcebook, 1st Edition.* Edited by Linda M. Shin. 579 pages. 1998. 0-7808-0210-1. $78.

"Teachers as well as consumers will find this an essential guide to understanding various syndromes and their latest treatments. [An] invaluable reference for public and school library collections alike." —*Library Bookwatch, Apr '03*

Named "Outstanding Reference Book of 1999." —*New York Public Library, Feb 2000*

"An excellent candidate for inclusion in a public library reference section. It's a great source of information. Teachers will also find the book useful. Definitely worth reading." —*Journal of Adolescent & Adult Literacy, Feb 2000*

"Readable . . . provides a solid base of information regarding successful techniques used with individuals who have learning disabilities, as well as practical suggestions for educators and family members. Clear language, concise descriptions, and pertinent information for contacting multiple resources add to the strength of this book as a useful tool." —*Choice, Association of College and Research Libraries, Feb '99*

"Recommended reference source." —*Booklist, American Library Association, Sep '98*

"A useful resource for libraries and for those who don't have the time to identify and locate the individual publications." —*Disability Resources Monthly, Sep '98*

Leukemia Sourcebook

Basic Consumer Health Information about Adult and Childhood Leukemias, Including Acute Lymphocytic Leukemia (ALL), Chronic Lymphocytic Leukemia (CLL), Acute Myelogenous Leukemia (AML), Chronic Myelogenous Leukemia (CML), and Hairy Cell Leukemia, and Treatments Such as Chemotherapy, Radiation Therapy, Peripheral Blood Stem Cell and Marrow Transplantation, and Immunotherapy

Along with Tips for Life During and After Treatment, a Glossary, and Directories of Additional Resources

Edited by Joyce Brennfleck Shannon. 587 pages. 2003. 0-7808-0627-1. $78.

Liver Disorders Sourcebook

Basic Consumer Health Information about the Liver and How It Works; Liver Diseases, Including Cancer, Cirrhosis, Hepatitis, and Toxic and Drug Related Diseases; Tips for Maintaining a Healthy Liver; Laboratory Tests, Radiology Tests, and Facts about Liver Transplantation

Along with a Section on Support Groups, a Glossary, and Resource Listings

Edited by Joyce Brennfleck Shannon. 591 pages. 2000. 0-7808-0383-3. $78.

"A valuable resource." —*American Reference Books Annual, 2001*

"This title is recommended for health sciences and public libraries with consumer health collections." —*E-Streams, Oct '00*

"Recommended reference source." —*Booklist, American Library Association, Jun '00*

Lung Disorders Sourcebook

Basic Consumer Health Information about Emphysema, Pneumonia, Tuberculosis, Asthma, Cystic Fibrosis, and Other Lung Disorders, Including Facts about Diagnostic Procedures, Treatment Strategies, Disease Prevention Efforts, and Such Risk Factors as Smoking, Air Pollution, and Exposure to Asbestos, Radon, and Other Agents

Along with a Glossary and Resources for Additional Help and Information

Edited by Dawn D. Matthews. 678 pages. 2002. 0-7808-0339-6. $78.

"This title is a great addition for public and school libraries because it provides concise health information on the lungs."

—*American Reference Books Annual, 2003*

"Highly recommended for academic and medical reference collections." —*Library Bookwatch, Sep '02*

Medical Tests Sourcebook, 2nd Edition

Basic Consumer Health Information about Medical Tests, Including Age-Specific Health Tests, Important Health Screenings and Exams, Home-Use Tests, Blood and Specimen Tests, Electrical Tests, Scope Tests, Genetic Testing, and Imaging Tests, Such as X-Rays, Ultrasound, Computed Tomography, Magnetic Resonance Imaging, Angiography, and Nuclear Medicine

Along with a Glossary and Directory of Additional Resources

Edited by Joyce Brennfleck Shannon. 654 pages. 2004. 0-7808-0670-0. $78.

ALSO AVAILABLE: *Medical Tests, 1st Edition.* Edited by Joyce Brennfleck Shannon. 691 pages. 1999. 0-7808-0243-8. $78.

"Recommended for hospital and health sciences libraries with consumer health collections."

—*E-Streams, Mar '00*

"This is an overall excellent reference with a wealth of general knowledge that may aid those who are reluctant to get vital tests performed."

—*Today's Librarian, Jan 2000*

"A valuable reference guide."

—*American Reference Books Annual, 2000*

Men's Health Concerns Sourcebook, 2nd Edition

Basic Consumer Health Information about the Medical and Mental Concerns of Men, Including Theories about the Shorter Male Lifespan, the Leading Causes of Death and Disability, Physical Concerns of Special Significance to Men, Reproductive and Sexual Concerns, Sexually Transmitted Diseases, Men's Mental and Emotional Health, and Lifestyle Choices That Affect Wellness, Such as Nutrition, Fitness, and Substance Use

Along with a Glossary of Related Terms and a Directory of Organizational Resources in Men's Health

Edited by Robert Aquinas McNally. 644 pages. 2004. 0-7808-0671-9. $78.

ALSO AVAILABLE: *Men's Health Concerns Sourcebook, 1st Edition.* Edited by Allan R. Cook. 738 pages. 1998. 0-7808-0212-8. $78.

"This comprehensive resource and the series are highly recommended."

—*American Reference Books Annual, 2000*

"Recommended reference source."

—*Booklist, American Library Association, Dec '98*

Mental Health Disorders Sourcebook, 2nd Edition

Basic Consumer Health Information about Anxiety Disorders, Depression and Other Mood Disorders, Eating Disorders, Personality Disorders, Schizophrenia, and More, Including Disease Descriptions, Treatment Options, and Reports on Current Research Initiatives

Along with Statistical Data, Tips for Maintaining Mental Health, a Glossary, and Directory of Sources for Additional Help and Information

Edited by Karen Bellenir. 605 pages. 2000. 0-7808-0240-3. $78.

ALSO AVAILABLE: *Mental Health Disorders Sourcebook, 1st Edition.* Edited by Karen Bellenir. 548 pages. 1995. 0-7808-0040-0. $78.

"Well organized and well written."

—*American Reference Books Annual, 2001*

"Recommended reference source."

—*Booklist, American Library Association, Jun '00*

Mental Retardation Sourcebook

Basic Consumer Health Information about Mental Retardation and Its Causes, Including Down Syndrome, Fetal Alcohol Syndrome, Fragile X Syndrome, Genetic Conditions, Injury, and Environmental Sources

Along with Preventive Strategies, Parenting Issues, Educational Implications, Health Care Needs, Employment and Economic Matters, Legal Issues, a Glossary, and a Resource Listing for Additional Help and Information

Edited by Joyce Brennfleck Shannon. 642 pages. 2000. 0-7808-0377-9. $78.

"Public libraries will find the book useful for reference and as a beginning research point for students, parents, and caregivers."

—*American Reference Books Annual, 2001*

"The strength of this work is that it compiles many basic fact sheets and addresses for further information in one volume. It is intended and suitable for the general public. This sourcebook is relevant to any collection providing health information to the general public."

—*E-Streams, Nov '00*

"From preventing retardation to parenting and family challenges, this covers health, social and legal issues and will prove an invaluable overview."

—*Reviewer's Bookwatch, Jul '00*

Movement Disorders Sourcebook

Basic Consumer Health Information about Neurological Movement Disorders, Including Essential Tremor, Parkinson's Disease, Dystonia, Cerebral Palsy, Huntington's Disease, Myasthenia Gravis, Multiple Sclerosis, and Other Early-Onset and Adult-Onset Movement Disorders, Their Symptoms and Causes, Diagnostic Tests, and Treatments

Along with Mobility and Assistive Technology Information, a Glossary, and a Directory of Additional Resources

Edited by Joyce Brennfleck Shannon. 655 pages. 2003. 0-7808-0628-X. $78.

■

Muscular Dystrophy Sourcebook

Basic Consumer Health Information about Congenital, Childhood-Onset, and Adult-Onset Forms of Muscular Dystrophy, Such as Duchenne, Becker, Emery-Dreifuss, Distal, Limb-Girdle, Facioscapulohumeral (FSHD), Myotonic, and Ophthalmoplegic Muscular Dystrophies, Including Facts about Diagnostic Tests, Medical and Physical Therapies, Management of Co-Occurring Conditions, and Parenting Guidelines

Along with Practical Tips for Home Care, a Glossary, and Directories of Additional Resources

Edited by Joyce Brennfleck Shannon. 600 pages. 2004. 0-7808-0676-X. $78.

■

Obesity Sourcebook

Basic Consumer Health Information about Diseases and Other Problems Associated with Obesity, and Including Facts about Risk Factors, Prevention Issues, and Management Approaches

Along with Statistical and Demographic Data, Information about Special Populations, Research Updates, a Glossary, and Source Listings for Further Help and Information

Edited by Wilma Caldwell and Chad T. Kimball. 376 pages. 2001. 0-7808-0333-7. $78.

"The book synthesizes the reliable medical literature on obesity into one easy-to-read and useful resource for the general public."
—*American Reference Books Annual 2002*

"This is a very useful resource book for the lay public."
—*Doody's Review Service, Nov '01*

"Well suited for the health reference collection of a public library or an academic health science library that serves the general population." —*E-Streams, Sep '01*

"Recommended reference source."
—*Booklist, American Library Association, Apr '01*

" Recommended pick both for specialty health library collections and any general consumer health reference collection." — *The Bookwatch, Apr '01*

■

Ophthalmic Disorders Sourcebook, 1st Edition

SEE *Eye Care Sourcebook, 2nd Edition*

■

Oral Health Sourcebook

SEE *Dental Care & Oral Health Sourcebook, 2nd Ed.*

Osteoporosis Sourcebook

Basic Consumer Health Information about Primary and Secondary Osteoporosis and Juvenile Osteoporosis and Related Conditions, Including Fibrous Dysplasia, Gaucher Disease, Hyperthyroidism, Hypophosphatasia, Myeloma, Osteopetrosis, Osteogenesis Imperfecta, and Paget's Disease

Along with Information about Risk Factors, Treatments, Traditional and Non-Traditional Pain Management, a Glossary of Related Terms, and a Directory of Resources

Edited by Allan R. Cook. 584 pages. 2001. 0-7808-0239-X. $78.

"This would be a book to be kept in a staff or patient library. The targeted audience is the layperson, but the therapist who needs a quick bit of information on a particular topic will also find the book useful."
—*Physical Therapy, Jan '02*

"This resource is recommended as a great reference source for public, health, and academic libraries, and is another triumph for the editors of Omnigraphics."
—*American Reference Books Annual 2002*

"Recommended for all public libraries and general health collections, especially those supporting patient education or consumer health programs."
—*E-Streams, Nov '01*

"Will prove valuable to any library seeking to maintain a current, comprehensive reference collection of health resources. . . . From prevention to treatment and associated conditions, this provides an excellent survey."
—*The Bookwatch, Aug '01*

"Recommended reference source."
—*Booklist, American Library Association, July '01*

SEE ALSO *Women's Health Concerns Sourcebook*

■

Pain Sourcebook, 2nd Edition

Basic Consumer Health Information about Specific Forms of Acute and Chronic Pain, Including Muscle and Skeletal Pain, Nerve Pain, Cancer Pain, and Disorders Characterized by Pain, Such as Fibromyalgia, Shingles, Angina, Arthritis, and Headaches

Along with Information about Pain Medications and Management Techniques, Complementary and Alternative Pain Relief Options, Tips for People Living with Chronic Pain, a Glossary, and a Directory of Sources for Further Information

Edited by Karen Bellenir. 670 pages. 2002. 0-7808-0612-3. $78.

ALSO AVAILABLE: *Pain Sourcebook, 1st Edition.* Edited by Allan R. Cook. 667 pages. 1997. 0-7808-0213-6. $78.

"A source of valuable information. . . . This book offers help to nonmedical people who need information about pain and pain management. It is also an excellent reference for those who participate in patient education."
—*Doody's Review Service, Sep '02*

"The text is readable, easily understood, and well indexed. This excellent volume belongs in all patient education libraries, consumer health sections of public libraries, and many personal collections."

—*American Reference Books Annual, 1999*

"A beneficial reference." —*Booklist Health Sciences Supplement, American Library Association, Oct '98*

"The information is basic in terms of scholarship and is appropriate for general readers. Written in journalistic style . . . intended for non-professionals. Quite thorough in its coverage of different pain conditions and summarizes the latest clinical information regarding pain treatment." —*Choice, Association of College and Research Libraries, Jun '98*

"Recommended reference source."

—*Booklist, American Library Association, Mar '98*

Pediatric Cancer Sourcebook

Basic Consumer Health Information about Leukemias, Brain Tumors, Sarcomas, Lymphomas, and Other Cancers in Infants, Children, and Adolescents, Including Descriptions of Cancers, Treatments, and Coping Strategies

Along with Suggestions for Parents, Caregivers, and Concerned Relatives, a Glossary of Cancer Terms, and Resource Listings

Edited by Edward J. Prucha. 587 pages. 1999. 0-7808-0245-4. $78.

"An excellent source of information. Recommended for public, hospital, and health science libraries with consumer health collections." —*E-Streams, Jun '00*

"Recommended reference source."

—*Booklist, American Library Association, Feb '00*

"A valuable addition to all libraries specializing in health services and many public libraries."

—*American Reference Books Annual, 2000*

Physical & Mental Issues in Aging Sourcebook

Basic Consumer Health Information on Physical and Mental Disorders Associated with the Aging Process, Including Concerns about Cardiovascular Disease, Pulmonary Disease, Oral Health, Digestive Disorders, Musculoskeletal and Skin Disorders, Metabolic Changes, Sexual and Reproductive Issues, and Changes in Vision, Hearing, and Other Senses

Along with Data about Longevity and Causes of Death, Information on Acute and Chronic Pain, Descriptions of Mental Concerns, a Glossary of Terms, and Resource Listings for Additional Help

Edited by Jenifer Swanson. 660 pages. 1999. 0-7808-0233-0. $78.

"This is a treasure of health information for the layperson." — *Choice Health Sciences Supplement, Association of College & Research Libraries, May 2000*

"Recommended for public libraries."

—*American Reference Books Annual, 2000*

"Recommended reference source."

—*Booklist, American Library Association, Oct '99*

SEE ALSO *Healthy Aging Sourcebook*

Podiatry Sourcebook

Basic Consumer Health Information about Foot Conditions, Diseases, and Injuries, Including Bunions, Corns, Calluses, Athlete's Foot, Plantar Warts, Hammertoes and Clawtoes, Clubfoot, Heel Pain, Gout, and More

Along with Facts about Foot Care, Disease Prevention, Foot Safety, Choosing a Foot Care Specialist, a Glossary of Terms, and Resource Listings for Additional Information

Edited by M. Lisa Weatherford. 380 pages. 2001. 0-7808-0215-2. $78.

"Recommended reference source."

—*Booklist, American Library Association, Feb '02*

"There is a lot of information presented here on a topic that is usually only covered sparingly in most larger comprehensive medical encyclopedias."

—*American Reference Books Annual 2002*

Pregnancy & Birth Sourcebook, 2nd Edition

Basic Consumer Health Information about Conception and Pregnancy, Including Facts about Fertility, Infertility, Pregnancy Symptoms and Complications, Fetal Growth and Development, Labor, Delivery, and the Postpartum Period, as Well as Information about Maintaining Health and Wellness during Pregnancy and Caring for a Newborn

Along with Information about Public Health Assistance for Low-Income Pregnant Women, a Glossary, and Directories of Agencies and Organizations Providing Help and Support

Edited by Amy L. Sutton. 626 pages. 2004. 0-7808-0672-7. $78.

ALSO AVAILABLE: *Pregnancy & Birth Sourcebook, 1st Edition.* Edited by Heather E. Aldred. 737 pages. 1997. 0-7808-0216-0. $78.

"A well-organized handbook. Recommended."

—*Choice, Association of College and Research Libraries, Apr '98*

"Recommended reference source."

—*Booklist, American Library Association, Mar '98*

"Recommended for public libraries."

—*American Reference Books Annual, 1998*

SEE ALSO *Congenital Disorders Sourcebook, Family Planning Sourcebook*

Prostate Cancer Sourcebook

Basic Consumer Health Information about Prostate Cancer, Including Information about the Associated Risk Factors, Detection, Diagnosis, and Treatment of Prostate Cancer

Along with Information on Non-Malignant Prostate Conditions, and Featuring a Section Listing Support and Treatment Centers and a Glossary of Related Terms

Edited by Dawn D. Matthews. 358 pages. 2001. 0-7808-0324-8. $78.

"Recommended reference source."

—*Booklist, American Library Association, Jan '02*

"A valuable resource for health care consumers seeking information on the subject. . . .All text is written in a clear, easy-to-understand language that avoids technical jargon. Any library that collects consumer health resources would strengthen their collection with the addition of the *Prostate Cancer Sourcebook*."

—*American Reference Books Annual 2002*

■

Public Health Sourcebook

Basic Information about Government Health Agencies, Including National Health Statistics and Trends, Healthy People 2000 Program Goals and Objectives, the Centers for Disease Control and Prevention, the Food and Drug Administration, and the National Institutes of Health

Along with Full Contact Information for Each Agency

Edited by Wendy Wilcox. 698 pages. 1998. 0-7808-0220-9. $78.

"Recommended reference source."

—*Booklist, American Library Association, Sep '98*

"This consumer guide provides welcome assistance in navigating the maze of federal health agencies and their data on public health concerns."

—*SciTech Book News, Sep '98*

■

Reconstructive & Cosmetic Surgery Sourcebook

Basic Consumer Health Information on Cosmetic and Reconstructive Plastic Surgery, Including Statistical Information about Different Surgical Procedures, Things to Consider Prior to Surgery, Plastic Surgery Techniques and Tools, Emotional and Psychological Considerations, and Procedure-Specific Information

Along with a Glossary of Terms and a Listing of Resources for Additional Help and Information

Edited by M. Lisa Weatherford. 374 pages. 2001. 0-7808-0214-4. $78.

"An excellent reference that addresses cosmetic and medically necessary reconstructive surgeries. . . . The style of the prose is calm and reassuring, discussing the many positive outcomes now available due to advances in surgical techniques."

—*American Reference Books Annual 2002*

"Recommended for health science libraries that are open to the public, as well as hospital libraries that are open to the patients. This book is a good resource for the consumer interested in plastic surgery."

—*E-Streams, Dec '01*

"Recommended reference source."

—*Booklist, American Library Association, July '01*

■

Rehabilitation Sourcebook

Basic Consumer Health Information about Rehabilitation for People Recovering from Heart Surgery, Spinal Cord Injury, Stroke, Orthopedic Impairments, Amputation, Pulmonary Impairments, Traumatic Injury, and More, Including Physical Therapy, Occupational Therapy, Speech/ Language Therapy, Massage Therapy, Dance Therapy, Art Therapy, and Recreational Therapy

Along with Information on Assistive and Adaptive Devices, a Glossary, and Resources for Additional Help and Information

Edited by Dawn D. Matthews. 531 pages. 1999. 0-7808-0236-5. $78.

"This is an excellent resource for public library reference and health collections."

—*American Reference Books Annual, 2001*

"Recommended reference source."

—*Booklist, American Library Association, May '00*

■

Respiratory Diseases & Disorders Sourcebook

Basic Information about Respiratory Diseases and Disorders, Including Asthma, Cystic Fibrosis, Pneumonia, the Common Cold, Influenza, and Others, Featuring Facts about the Respiratory System, Statistical and Demographic Data, Treatments, Self-Help Management Suggestions, and Current Research Initiatives

Edited by Allan R. Cook and Peter D. Dresser. 771 pages. 1995. 0-7808-0037-0. $78.

"Designed for the layperson and for patients and their families coping with respiratory illness. . . . an extensive array of information on diagnosis, treatment, management, and prevention of respiratory illnesses for the general reader."

—*Choice, Association of College and Research Libraries, Jun '96*

"A highly recommended text for all collections. It is a comforting reminder of the power of knowledge that good books carry between their covers."

—*Academic Library Book Review, Spring '96*

"A comprehensive collection of authoritative information presented in a nontechnical, humanitarian style for patients, families, and caregivers."

—*Association of Operating Room Nurses, Sep/Oct '95*

SEE ALSO *Lung Disorders Sourcebook*

Sexually Transmitted Diseases Sourcebook, 2nd Edition

Basic Consumer Health Information about Sexually Transmitted Diseases, Including Information on the Diagnosis and Treatment of Chlamydia, Gonorrhea, Hepatitis, Herpes, HIV, Mononucleosis, Syphilis, and Others

Along with Information on Prevention, Such as Condom Use, Vaccines, and STD Education; And Featuring a Section on Issues Related to Youth and Adolescents, a Glossary, and Resources for Additional Help and Information

Edited by Dawn D. Matthews. 538 pages. 2001. 0-7808-0249-7. $78.

ALSO AVAILABLE: *Sexually Transmitted Diseases Sourcebook, 1st Edition.* Edited by Linda M. Ross. 550 pages. 1997. 0-7808-0217-9. $78.

"Recommended for consumer health collections in public libraries, and secondary school and community college libraries."
—*American Reference Books Annual 2002*

"Every school and public library should have a copy of this comprehensive and user-friendly reference book."
—*Choice, Association of College & Research Libraries, Sep '01*

"This is a highly recommended book. This is an especially important book for all school and public libraries." —*AIDS Book Review Journal, Jul-Aug '01*

"Recommended reference source."
—*Booklist, American Library Association, Apr '01*

"Recommended pick both for specialty health library collections and any general consumer health reference collection." —*The Bookwatch, Apr '01*

■

Skin Disorders Sourcebook

Basic Information about Common Skin and Scalp Conditions Caused by Aging, Allergies, Immune Reactions, Sun Exposure, Infectious Organisms, Parasites, Cosmetics, and Skin Traumas, Including Abrasions, Cuts, and Pressure Sores

Along with Information on Prevention and Treatment

Edited by Allan R. Cook. 647 pages. 1997. 0-7808-0080-X. $78.

". . . comprehensive, easily read reference book."
—*Doody's Health Sciences Book Reviews, Oct '97*

SEE ALSO *Burns Sourcebook*

■

Sleep Disorders Sourcebook

Basic Consumer Health Information about Sleep and Its Disorders, Including Insomnia, Sleepwalking, Sleep Apnea, Restless Leg Syndrome, and Narcolepsy

Along with Data about Shiftwork and Its Effects, Information on the Societal Costs of Sleep Deprivation, Descriptions of Treatment Options, a Glossary of Terms, and Resource Listings for Additional Help

Edited by Jenifer Swanson. 439 pages. 1998. 0-7808-0234-9. $78.

"This text will complement any home or medical library. It is user-friendly and ideal for the adult reader."
—*American Reference Books Annual, 2000*

"A useful resource that provides accurate, relevant, and accessible information on sleep to the general public. Health care providers who deal with sleep disorders patients may also find it helpful in being prepared to answer some of the questions patients ask."
—*Respiratory Care, Jul '99*

"Recommended reference source."
—*Booklist, American Library Association, Feb '99*

■

Sports Injuries Sourcebook, 2nd Edition

Basic Consumer Health Information about the Diagnosis, Treatment, and Rehabilitation of Common Sports-Related Injuries in Children and Adults

Along with Suggestions for Conditioning and Training, Information and Prevention Tips for Injuries Frequently Associated with Specific Sports and Special Populations, a Glossary, and a Directory of Additional Resources

Edited by Joyce Brennfleck Shannon. 614 pages. 2002. 0-7808-0604-2. $78.

ALSO AVAILABLE: *Sports Injuries Sourcebook, 1st Edition.* Edited by Heather E. Aldred. 624 pages. 1999. 0-7808-0218-7. $78.

"This is an excellent reference for consumers and it is recommended for public, community college, and undergraduate libraries."
—*American Reference Books Annual, 2003*

"Recommended reference source."
—*Booklist, American Library Association, Feb '03*

■

Stress-Related Disorders Sourcebook

Basic Consumer Health Information about Stress and Stress-Related Disorders, Including Stress Origins and Signals, Environmental Stress at Work and Home, Mental and Emotional Stress Associated with Depression, Post-Traumatic Stress Disorder, Panic Disorder, Suicide, and the Physical Effects of Stress on the Cardiovascular, Immune, and Nervous Systems

Along with Stress Management Techniques, a Glossary, and a Listing of Additional Resources

Edited by Joyce Brennfleck Shannon. 610 pages. 2002. 0-7808-0560-7. $78.

"Well written for a general readership, the *Stress-Related Disorders Sourcebook* is a useful addition to the health reference literature."
—*American Reference Books Annual, 2003*

"I am impressed by the amount of information. It offers a thorough overview of the causes and consequences of

stress for the layperson. . . . A well-done and thorough reference guide for professionals and nonprofessionals alike." —*Doody's Review Service, Dec '02*

■

Stroke Sourcebook

Basic Consumer Health Information about Stroke, Including Ischemic, Hemorrhagic, Transient Ischemic Attack (TIA), and Pediatric Stroke, Stroke Triggers and Risks, Diagnostic Tests, Treatments, and Rehabilitation Information

Along with Stroke Prevention Guidelines, Legal and Financial Information, a Glossary, and a Directory of Additional Resources

Edited by Joyce Brennfleck Shannon. 606 pages. 2003. 0-7808-0630-1. $78.

■

Substance Abuse Sourcebook

Basic Health-Related Information about the Abuse of Legal and Illegal Substances Such as Alcohol, Tobacco, Prescription Drugs, Marijuana, Cocaine, and Heroin; and Including Facts about Substance Abuse Prevention Strategies, Intervention Methods, Treatment and Recovery Programs, and a Section Addressing the Special Problems Related to Substance Abuse during Pregnancy

Edited by Karen Bellenir. 573 pages. 1996. 0-7808-0038-9. $78.

"A valuable addition to any health reference section. Highly recommended."
—*The Book Report, Mar/Apr '97*

". . . a comprehensive collection of substance abuse information that's both highly readable and compact. Families and caregivers of substance abusers will find the information enlightening and helpful, while teachers, social workers and journalists should benefit from the concise format. Recommended."
—*Drug Abuse Update, Winter '96/'97*

SEE ALSO *Alcoholism Sourcebook, Drug Abuse Sourcebook*

■

Surgery Sourcebook

Basic Consumer Health Information about Inpatient and Outpatient Surgeries, Including Cardiac, Vascular, Orthopedic, Ocular, Reconstructive, Cosmetic, Gynecologic, and Ear, Nose, and Throat Procedures and More

Along with Information about Operating Room Policies and Instruments, Laser Surgery Techniques, Hospital Errors, Statistical Data, a Glossary, and Listings of Sources for Further Help and Information

Edited by Annemarie S. Muth and Karen Bellenir. 596 pages. 2002. 0-7808-0380-9. $78.

"Invaluable reference for public and school library collections alike." —*Library Bookwatch, Apr '03*

Transplantation Sourcebook

Basic Consumer Health Information about Organ and Tissue Transplantation, Including Physical and Financial Preparations, Procedures and Issues Relating to Specific Solid Organ and Tissue Transplants, Rehabilitation, Pediatric Transplant Information, the Future of Transplantation, and Organ and Tissue Donation

Along with a Glossary and Listings of Additional Resources

Edited by Joyce Brennfleck Shannon. 628 pages. 2002. 0-7808-0322-1. $78.

"Along with these advances [in transplantation technology] have come a number of daunting questions for potential transplant patients, their families, and their health care providers. This reference text is the best single tool to address many of these questions. . . . It will be a much-needed addition to the reference collections in health care, academic, and large public libraries."
—*American Reference Books Annual, 2003*

"Recommended for libraries with an interest in offering consumer health information." —*E-Streams, Jul '02*

"This is a unique and valuable resource for patients facing transplantation and their families."
—*Doody's Review Service, Jun '02*

■

Traveler's Health Sourcebook

Basic Consumer Health Information for Travelers, Including Physical and Medical Preparations, Transportation Health and Safety, Essential Information about Food and Water, Sun Exposure, Insect and Snake Bites, Camping and Wilderness Medicine, and Travel with Physical or Medical Disabilities

Along with International Travel Tips, Vaccination Recommendations, Geographical Health Issues, Disease Risks, a Glossary, and a Listing of Additional Resources

Edited by Joyce Brennfleck Shannon. 613 pages. 2000. 0-7808-0384-1. $78.

"Recommended reference source."
—*Booklist, American Library Association, Feb '01*

"This book is recommended for any public library, any travel collection, and especially any collection for the physically disabled."
—*American Reference Books Annual, 2001*

■

Vegetarian Sourcebook

Basic Consumer Health Information about Vegetarian Diets, Lifestyle, and Philosophy, Including Definitions of Vegetarianism and Veganism, Tips about Adopting Vegetarianism, Creating a Vegetarian Pantry, and Meeting Nutritional Needs of Vegetarians, with Facts Regarding Vegetarianism's Effect on Pregnant and Lactating Women, Children, Athletes, and Senior Citizens

Along with a Glossary of Commonly Used Vegetarian Terms and Resources for Additional Help and Information

Edited by Chad T. Kimball. 360 pages. 2002. 0-7808-0439-2. $78.

"Organizes into one concise volume the answers to the most common questions concerning vegetarian diets and lifestyles. This title is recommended for public and secondary school libraries." —*E-Streams, Apr '03*

"Invaluable reference for public and school library collections alike." — *Library Bookwatch, Apr '03*

"The articles in this volume are easy to read and come from authoritative sources. The book does not necessarily support the vegetarian diet but instead provides the pros and cons of this important decision. The *Vegetarian Sourcebook* is recommended for public libraries and consumer health libraries."

—*American Reference Books Annual, 2003*

Women's Health Concerns Sourcebook, 2nd Edition

Basic Consumer Health Information about the Medical and Mental Concerns of Women, Including Maintaining Health and Wellness, Gynecological Concerns, Breast Health, Sexuality and Reproductive Issues, Menopause, Cancer in Women, the Leading Causes of Death and Disability among Women, Physical Concerns of Special Significance to Women, and Women's Mental and Emotional Health

Along with a Glossary of Related Terms and Directories of Resources for Additional Help and Information

Edited by Amy L. Sutton. 748 pages. 2004. 0-7808-0673-5. $78.

ALSO AVAILABLE: *Women's Health Concerns Sourcebook, 1st Edition.* Edited by Heather E. Aldred. 567 pages. 1997. 0-7808-0219-5. $78.

"Handy compilation. There is an impressive range of diseases, devices, disorders, procedures, and other physical and emotional issues covered . . . well organized, illustrated, and indexed." —*Choice, Association of College and Research Libraries, Jan '98*

SEE ALSO *Breast Cancer Sourcebook, Cancer Sourcebook for Women, Healthy Heart Sourcebook for Women, Osteoporosis Sourcebook*

Workplace Health & Safety Sourcebook

Basic Consumer Health Information about Workplace Health and Safety, Including the Effect of Workplace Hazards on the Lungs, Skin, Heart, Ears, Eyes, Brain, Reproductive Organs, Musculoskeletal System, and Other Organs and Body Parts

Along with Information about Occupational Cancer, Personal Protective Equipment, Toxic and Hazardous Chemicals, Child Labor, Stress, and Workplace Violence

Edited by Chad T. Kimball. 626 pages. 2000. 0-7808-0231-4. $78.

"As a reference for the general public, this would be useful in any library." —*E-Streams, Jun '01*

"Provides helpful information for primary care physicians and other caregivers interested in occupational medicine. . . . General readers; professionals."

— *Choice, Association of College & Research Libraries, May '01*

"Recommended reference source."

—*Booklist, American Library Association, Feb '01*

"Highly recommended." —*The Bookwatch, Jan '01*

Worldwide Health Sourcebook

Basic Information about Global Health Issues, Including Malnutrition, Reproductive Health, Disease Dispersion and Prevention, Emerging Diseases, Risky Health Behaviors, and the Leading Causes of Death

Along with Global Health Concerns for Children, Women, and the Elderly, Mental Health Issues, Research and Technology Advancements, and Economic, Environmental, and Political Health Implications, a Glossary, and a Resource Listing for Additional Help and Information

Edited by Joyce Brennfleck Shannon. 614 pages. 2001. 0-7808-0330-2. $78.

"Named an Outstanding Academic Title."

—*Choice, Association of College & Research Libraries, Jan '02*

"Yet another handy but also unique compilation in the extensive Health Reference Series, this is a useful work because many of the international publications reprinted or excerpted are not readily available. Highly recommended." —*Choice, Association of College & Research Libraries, Nov '01*

"Recommended reference source."

—*Booklist, American Library Association, Oct '01*

Teen Health Series

Helping Young Adults Understand, Manage, and Avoid Serious Illness

Cancer Information for Teens

Health Tips about Cancer Awareness, Prevention, Diagnosis, and Treatment

Including Facts about Frequently Occurring Cancers, Cancer Risk Factors, and Coping Strategies for Teens Fighting Cancer or Dealing with Cancer in Friends or Family Members

Edited by Wilma R. Caldwell. 428 pages. 2004. 0-7808-0678-6. $58.

■

Diet Information for Teens

Health Tips about Diet and Nutrition

Including Facts about Nutrients, Dietary Guidelines, Breakfasts, School Lunches, Snacks, Party Food, Weight Control, Eating Disorders, and More

Edited by Karen Bellenir. 399 pages. 2001. 0-7808-0441-4. $58.

"Full of helpful insights and facts throughout the book. . . . An excellent resource to be placed in public libraries or even in personal collections."
—American Reference Books Annual 2002

"Recommended for middle and high school libraries and media centers as well as academic libraries that educate future teachers of teenagers. It is also a suitable addition to health science libraries that serve patrons who are interested in teen health promotion and education." *—E-Streams, Oct '01*

"This comprehensive book would be beneficial to collections that need information about nutrition, dietary guidelines, meal planning, and weight control. . . . This reference is so easy to use that its purchase is recommended." *—The Book Report, Sep-Oct '01*

"This book is written in an easy to understand format describing issues that many teens face every day, and then provides thoughtful explanations so that teens can make informed decisions. This is an interesting book that provides important facts and information for today's teens." *—Doody's Health Sciences Book Review Journal, Jul-Aug '01*

"A comprehensive compendium of diet and nutrition. The information is presented in a straightforward, plain-spoken manner. This title will be useful to those working on reports on a variety of topics, as well as to general readers concerned about their dietary health."
—School Library Journal, Jun '01

Drug Information for Teens

Health Tips about the Physical and Mental Effects of Substance Abuse

Including Facts about Alcohol, Anabolic Steroids, Club Drugs, Cocaine, Depressants, Hallucinogens, Herbal Products, Inhalants, Marijuana, Narcotics, Stimulants, Tobacco, and More

Edited by Karen Bellenir. 452 pages. 2002. 0-7808-0444-9. $58.

"The chapters are quick to make a connection to their teenage reading audience. The prose is straightforward and the book lends itself to spot reading. It should be useful both for practical information and for research, and it is suitable for public and school libraries."
—American Reference Books Annual, 2003

"Recommended reference source."
—Booklist, American Library Association, Feb '03

"This is an excellent resource for teens and their parents. Education about drugs and substances is key to discouraging teen drug abuse and this book provides this much needed information in a way that is interesting and factual." *—Doody's Review Service, Dec '02*

■

Fitness Information for Teens

Health Tips about Exercise, Physical Well-Being, and Health Maintenance

Including Facts about Aerobic and Anaerobic Conditioning, Stretching, Body Shape and Body Image, Sports Training, Nutrition, and Activities for Non-Athletes

Edited by Karen Bellenir. 425 pages. 2004. 0-7808-0679-4. $58.

■

Mental Health Information for Teens

Health Tips about Mental Health and Mental Illness

Including Facts about Anxiety, Depression, Suicide, Eating Disorders, Obsessive-Compulsive Disorders, Panic Attacks, Phobias, Schizophrenia, and More

Edited by Karen Bellenir. 406 pages. 2001. 0-7808-0442-2. $58.

"In both language and approach, this user-friendly entry in the *Teen Health Series* is on target for teens needing information on mental health concerns." *—Booklist, American Library Association, Jan '02*

"Readers will find the material accessible and informative, with the shaded notes, facts, and embedded glossary insets adding appropriately to the already interesting and succinct presentation."

—*School Library Journal, Jan '02*

"This title is highly recommended for any library that serves adolescents and parents/caregivers of adolescents." —*E-Streams, Jan '02*

"Recommended for high school libraries and young adult collections in public libraries. Both health professionals and teenagers will find this book useful."

—*American Reference Books Annual 2002*

"This is a nice book written to enlighten the society, primarily teenagers, about common teen mental health issues. It is highly recommended to teachers and parents as well as adolescents."

—*Doody's Review Service, Dec '01*

Sexual Health Information for Teens

Health Tips about Sexual Development, Human Reproduction, and Sexually Transmitted Diseases

Including Facts about Puberty, Reproductive Health, Chlamydia, Human Papillomavirus, Pelvic Inflammatory Disease, Herpes, AIDS, Contraception, Pregnancy, and More

Edited by Deborah A. Stanley. 391 pages. 2003. 0-7808-0445-7. $58.

Skin Health Information For Teens

Health Tips about Dermatological Concerns and Skin Cancer Risks

Including Facts about Acne, Warts, Hives, and Other Conditions and Lifestyle Choices, Such as Tanning, Tattooing, and Piercing, That Affect the Skin, Nails, Scalp, and Hair

Edited by Robert Aquinas McNally. 430 pages. 2003. 0-7808-0446-5. $58.

Sports Injuries Information For Teens

Health Tips about Sports Injuries and Injury Protection

Including Facts about Specific Injuries, Emergency Treatment, Rehabilitation, Sports Safety, Competition Stress, Fitness, Sports Nutrition, Steroid Risks, and More

Edited by Joyce Brennfleck Shannon. 425 pages. 2003. 0-7808-0447-3. $58.

Health Reference Series

Adolescent Health Sourcebook
AIDS Sourcebook, 3rd Edition
Alcoholism Sourcebook
Allergies Sourcebook, 2nd Edition
Alternative Medicine Sourcebook, 2nd Edition
Alzheimer's Disease Sourcebook, 3rd Edition
Arthritis Sourcebook
Asthma Sourcebook
Attention Deficit Disorder Sourcebook
Back & Neck Disorders Sourcebook
Blood & Circulatory Disorders Sourcebook
Brain Disorders Sourcebook
Breast Cancer Sourcebook
Breastfeeding Sourcebook
Burns Sourcebook
Cancer Sourcebook, 4th Edition
Cancer Sourcebook for Women, 2nd Edition
Caregiving Sourcebook
Child Abuse Sourcebook
Childhood Diseases & Disorders Sourcebook
Colds, Flu & Other Common Ailments Sourcebook
Communication Disorders Sourcebook
Congenital Disorders Sourcebook
Consumer Issues in Health Care Sourcebook
Contagious & Non-Contagious Infectious Diseases Sourcebook
Death & Dying Sourcebook
Dental Care & Oral Health Sourcebook, 2nd Edition
Depression Sourcebook
Diabetes Sourcebook, 3rd Edition
Diet & Nutrition Sourcebook, 2nd Edition
Digestive Diseases & Disorder Sourcebook
Disabilities Sourcebook
Domestic Violence Sourcebook, 2nd Edition
Drug Abuse Sourcebook
Ear, Nose & Throat Disorders Sourcebook
Eating Disorders Sourcebook
Emergency Medical Services Sourcebook
Endocrine & Metabolic Disorders Sourcebook
Environmentally Health Sourcebook, 2nd Edition
Ethnic Diseases Sourcebook
Eye Care Sourcebook, 2nd Edition
Family Planning Sourcebook
Fitness & Exercise Sourcebook, 2nd Edition
Food & Animal Borne Diseases Sourcebook
Food Safety Sourcebook
Forensic Medicine Sourcebook
Gastrointestinal Diseases & Disorders Sourcebook
Genetic Disorders Sourcebook, 2nd Edition
Head Trauma Sourcebook
Headache Sourcebook
Health Insurance Sourcebook
Health Reference Series Cumulative Index 1999
Healthy Aging Sourcebook
Healthy Children Sourcebook